Study New Testament for Lesbians, Gays, Bi, and Transgender.

With Extensive Notes on Greek Word Meaning and Context.

Translated with notes by Dr A. Nyland

Study New Testament for Gay, Lesbian, Bi, and Transgender: With Extensive Notes on Greek Word Meaning and Context ©
Translation and notes by Dr A. Nyland.
© Copyright by Ann Maxwell-Nithsdale Nyland 2007

First edition
Study New Testament for Lesbians, Gays, Bi, and Transgender. First published in 2007 by Smith and Stirling Publishing
Australia.
www.smithandstirling.com
All rights reserved.

National Library of Australia Cataloguing-in-Publication Data

Nyland, Ann.
Study New Testament for gay, lesbian, bi, and transgender :
notes on greek word meaning and context.

1st Ed.
Bibliography.
ISBN 9780980443011 (pbk.).

1. Bible. N.T. - Translating. 2. Bible. N.T. English -
Versions. 3. Homosexuality - Biblical teaching. 4.
Homosexuality - Religious aspects - Christianity. 5.
Ethics in the Bible. 6. Christian ethics - Biblical
teaching. I. Title.

241.66

The Source New Testament (TSNT) is based primarily on the Greek texts of the UBS Fourth Revised Edition.

TABLE OF CONTENTS.

Table of Background Information.

Glossary

Etymological Fallacy. This the wrongful assumption that the etymology of a word is its actual meaning.

Grammatical gender. English is the only language in which masculine and feminine genders denote male and female persons. In other languages, grammatical gender is not related to biological (natural) gender. It is difficult for people who understand only English to grasp this basic point. Other languages assign grammatical gender to persons, inanimate objects, concepts, and in fact to all nouns, adjectives, and pronouns. The grammatical gender can be at odds with biological gender. The Greek word for a descendant (even a male descendant) is feminine gender as in Rom. 5.12, "a descendant of Jesse will come". There are two Greek words for a group of persons eating together, one of which is feminine gender and the other word is neuter, even a group comprised wholly of men.

The Greek word for "fox" (even a male fox) is feminine gender. The Greek word for "eagle" (even a female eagle) is masculine gender. The Greek word for "old woman" is neuter gender. Even the word *patris*, which means one's hometown, one's homeland, commonly rendered in Bibles as "fatherland", is feminine gender. The priestly class of Luke 1:5 (*ephemeria*) is feminine gender. *Hegemonia*, the complete rule, leadership, over another (as in Luke 3:1) is feminine gender.

The Hebrew word for "Holy Spirit" (Old Testament) is feminine gender, and the Greek word for "Holy Spirit" (New Testament) is neuter gender. The pronoun used to refer to the Holy Spirit in the original Hebrew language of Scripture is "she", and the pronoun used to refer to the Holy Spirit in the Greek is "it". In English, people choose to substitute "she" and "it" with the English pronoun "he". Obviously, we do not think of the Holy Spirit as a woman when reading the Old Testament, and as a neuter thing when reading the New Testament. The gender is grammatical, not biological, and there is no necessary relation between the two.

Idiom. The idiomatic expression "pigs might fly" should not be translated into Greek word-for-word, as "pigs" + "might fly" but by an expression to express an impossibility in the target language. The Greek, "You're a bombustard bird!" should be translated by English idiom, "You're taking nonsense!". The Greek, "a Tithonus of a person" should be translated by English idiom, "a senile person." The Greek, "to put on the cap of Hades" should be translated by English idiom, "to become invisible." The Greek, "garlic-primed" should be translated by English idiom, "very angry." The Greek, "to have swallowed garlic" should be translated by English idiom, "to be ready to fight." The Greek, "It's gone to the polecat!" should be translated by English idiom, "It's gone to the dogs!" The Greek, "to have Sisyphean wiles" should be translated by English idiom, "to be very cunning."

In the New Testament, the Greek, "kicking against the goads," should be translated by the English idiom, "you're whipping a dead horse!" In the New Testament, the Greek, "if your eye is evil" should be translated by English idiom, "if you are stingy with money."

That is correct basic translation procedure. Misunderstanding by people who speak only English, or by improperly taught beginner Greek students, arises over the term "literal" translation.

Litotes. An example is "not undistinguished city", typical Greek litotes (an ironic understatement using a negative of its contrary) which means in English "a most distinguished city". "I am not a little tired" is the way a Greek would have said "I am completely exhausted!" For litotes see Rom. 1:16; 10:11; 1 Pet. 2:6; Rev. 3:5.

Metonymy. The substitution of a word describing the nature or significance of an object instead of the object itself.

Semantic Range. The range of meanings possessed by a word. It is important to note that all the English meanings possible for a particular Greek word do not apply at the same time. E.g. the semantic range of the English word "port": a suitcase, a strong wine, a harbor, the left side of the ship. "Port" does not have all these meanings at the same time. Regard the following: *"They were all very drunk in the morning. The police arrested them at the bar and put them in jail for the night. They became drunk after drinking numerous bottles of port."* The meaning of a word in a particular context does not extend to others in its semantic range. In the above passage, the word "port" always means a strong drink, and has nothing to do with ships. In the New Testament, *adelphos* ("fellow believer", "fellow member") when used of church members has nothing to do with membership of a family, just as the English word "port" when used of drinking the strong wine has no nuance of somewhere to put ships. There is no relationship between the two meanings. The English word "bear" can mean a large animal, to put up with something, or carry something. It does not have all meanings at the same time.

Synecdoche. A figure of speech in which the part is named but the whole is understood. The word "faces" in "We noticed new faces at school", is synecdoche for "people".

Transliterate. To "transliterate" (noun, "transliteration") means to put the Greek letters into English letters. Example: ἀνόητος. The transliteration is *anoetos*. The meaning is "loss of senses". In the N.T., the translators traditionally decided to transliterate certain words and not translate them, e.g. "angels" (a transliteration) rather than the translation "messengers".

Translator's Note. It is not the duty of the translator to correct or change the original writer's grammar in any way, to do so would be a gross error. This is certainly not the job of the translator. I have retained the tone of the writer of each book. If the Greek is colloquial, I translate the colloquial tone, if the Greek is formal, I translate the formal tone. If the Greek repeats an adjective, I repeat an adjective. I certainly do not put the Greek into nice correct English if the original Greek is not nice correct Greek. To "correct" the original language is a most grave translation error. Note that much of the New Testament is dialogue, and people often do not follow formal rules of grammar when speaking. I translate such speech accordingly.

"Is there a man, learned or unlearned, who will not, when he takes the volume into his hands, and perceives that what he reads does not suit his traditonal tastes, break out immediately into violent language, and call me a forger, and a profane person for having the nerve to add anything to the ancient books, or to make any changes or corrections to them?
It is useless to play the lyre for a donkey.
So great is the strength of established usage that even acknowledged corruptions please most people, for they prefer to have their copies nice rather than accurate."
Jerome (4th c. AD)

Introduction.

Generally speaking, many Christians are judgmental and do not approve of women as Church leaders, divorced people, or homosexuals. However, these biases are not supported by the Bible itself. Some may appear to be, due to mistranslation, others are not supported even by that. Many Christians, when shown that a word they thought meant one thing in fact means something entirely different, simply do not wish to know. They prefer to disregard the evidence in order to adhere to their own closely held traditions.

In the New Testament, Jesus railed against legalistic religious leaders, and told us to beware of them. He at no point told us to beware of women as Church leaders, of divorced people, or of homosexuals. And of course he would not, as the New Testament in the original Greek does not speak against these three groups in any way whatsoever.

History.

For centuries, parts of the Church have tried to prevent correct Bible translation reaching the hands of the people. The first hand-written English language Bible manuscripts were produced in the 1380s AD by John Wycliffe, an Oxford scholar. Some years after he died, the Pope ordered his bones dug up and destroyed.

The Roman church executed people found with a Bible written in any language other than Latin. One of Wycliffe's followers, Hus, was burned at the stake in 1415, and Wycliffe's Bibles were thrown in the fire. In 1517 seven people were burned at the stake by the Roman Catholic Church for teaching their children to say the Lord's Prayer in English rather than in Latin.

Johann Gutenberg invented the printing press in the 1450s. The first book ever printed was a Latin language Bible. In the 1490s another Oxford professor, and the personal physician to King Henry the 7th and 8th, Thomas Linacre, read the Gospels in Greek, and was horrified at the difference between the original Greek and the Latin Vulgate. He wrote about the shocking Vulgate translation of the original Greek in his diary.

Erasmus was compelled to correct the vastly inaccurate Latin Vulgate. In 1516 he published a Greek-Latin Parallel New Testament. This was the first non-Latin Vulgate text of the scripture to be produced in over 1,000 years. The 1516 Greek-Latin New Testament of Erasmus further focused attention on just how corrupt and inaccurate the Latin Vulgate was.

In the 1530s Martin Luther published the entire Bible in German. Just prior to that Tyndale was forced to flee from England for translating the New Testament into English from the original Greek. In 1525-1526 the *Tyndale New Testament* became the first printed edition of the scripture in the English language. They were burned as fast as the Bishop could confiscate them. The church declared it contained thousands of errors. People found in possession of one of Tyndale's New Testaments were burned to death. Tyndale was imprisoned for 500 days and then strangled and burned at the stake in 1536.

Myles Coverdale and John Rogers (alias Thomas Matthew) were followers of Tyndale. They continued his English Bible project. Coverdale finished translating the Old Testament, and in 1535 printed the first complete Bible in the English language. However, instead of the original Greek, he translated from Luther's German text and the Latin. The first complete English Bible was printed on October 4, 1535, and is known as the *Coverdale Bible.*

In 1537 John Rogers under the pseudonym Thomas Matthews worked with Tyndale on the second complete English Bible. This was the first English Bible translated from the original Biblical languages of Greek and Hebrew. It was a composite made up of Tyndale's Pentateuch and New Testament (1534-1535 edition) and Coverdale's Bible and some of Roger's own translation of the text. John Rogers was burned at the stake on February 4, 1555, for refusing to renounce his translation work.

In 1539, Thomas Cranmer, the Archbishop of Canterbury, hired Myles Coverdale at the bequest of King Henry VIII to publish the "Great Bible". It became the first English Bible authorized for public use, and was distributed to every church and chained to the pulpit. A reader was even provided so that the illiterate could hear the Bible read in English. Cranmer's Bible, published by Coverdale, was known as the Great Bible due to its great size.

King Henry VIII had requested that the Pope permit him to divorce his wife and marry his mistress. The Pope refused so Henry renounced Roman Catholicism and declared that as he was the reigning head of State he was also the new head of the Church. This new branch of the Church became known as the Anglican Church or the Church of England. King Henry took on the role of the Pope. His first act was to annoy Rome by funding the printing of the scriptures in English. This was the first legal English translation of the Bible.

In the 1550s, the Church at Geneva, Switzerland, was sympathetic to the reformer refugees. Among those who met in Geneva were Myles Coverdale and John Foxe (publisher of the Foxe's Book of Martyrs), Thomas Sampson and William Whittingham. With the help of theologians John Knox and John Calvin, the Church of Geneva set out to produce a Bible. The New Testament was completed in 1557, and the complete Bible was first published in 1560. It became known as the *Geneva Bible*. The *Geneva Bible* was the first Bible to add numbered verses to the chapters, for the purpose of finding passages easily. There were extensive marginal notes and references next to every chapter. This was a first. The *Geneva Bible* remained more popular than the *King James Version* for many decades. It was the first Bible taken to America, and was the Bible of the Puritans and Pilgrims. The *Geneva Bible* has been out of print since 1644.

At end of Queen Mary's reign, the reformers were able to return to England. The Anglican Church, now under Queen Elizabeth I, allowed the printing and distribution of Geneva Bibles. However, the notes were strongly against the Church. It was decided to have a new Bible produced which did not have these bothersome notes. In 1568, a revision of the Great Bible known as the *Bishop's Bible* was introduced. It did not become popular.

In 1582, the Roman Catholic Church decided to have an official Roman Catholic English translation. Instead of translating from the original Greek, they used the corrupt Latin Vulgate. This version became known as the *Rheims New Testament.*

Upon the death of Queen Elizabeth I, Prince James VI of Scotland became King James I of England. Clergy approached the new King in 1604 and announced their desire for a new translation to replace the Bishop's Bible. James was none too happy about the notes which disparaged kings. About 50 people made a new translation, heavily using several other translations rather than translating from the original Greek. They relied heavily upon translations: *Tyndale's New Testament, The Coverdale Bible,*

The Matthews Bible, The Great Bible, The Geneva Bible, the Rheims New Testament, and they relied heavily upon the Latin Vulgate. The King James Bible was printed in 1611. It is often called "The Authorised Version" but it was never actually authorized by the king or the church. It was an Anglican version printed to compete with the Protestant Geneva Bible, by the very people who opposed Protestants and in many cases ordered their execution.

The King James Bible produced by the Anglican Church took decades to overcome the Protestant Church's popular Geneva Bible. Both the Roman Catholic Church and the Anglican Church persecuted Protestants throughout the 1600s. John Bunyan who wrote Pilgrim's Progress was imprisoned by the Anglican church for the crime of preaching the Gospel. The Puritans and the Pilgrims who left England for America rejected the King James Version and took with them the Geneva Bible.

In the 1880s the English Revised Version become the first English Bible version to become popular after the KJV times. This was also noteworthy as it was the first time that the 14 Apocryphal books were omitted. Up until the 1880s every Protestant Bible (not just Catholic Bibles) had 80 books rather than 66. The original 1611 King James Version contained the Apocrypha, as did all the earlier Bible versions. The Apocrypha has only been missing from the Bible in the last 120 years.

The Bible in Modern Times.

Many people are not aware that most available Bible translations are backed by denominations or specific ideological groups. Certain members of the USA "Religious Right" have successfully controlled the availability and content of some Bible versions. In 1997, lobbyists applied considerable pressure to the publisher (Zondervan) of the New International Inclusive Language Bible (NIVI) which was published in England, not to release it in the USA. The NIVI's crime? To translate gender language accurately; for example, to translate the Greek word meaning "person" by the English word "person" instead of the traditional "man". The lobbyists alleged that it was "tampering with" God's Word, and "misquoting God".

In 2001 the Religious Right lobbied to prevent the New Testament translation known as Today's New International Version (TNIV) being used by three major denominations. Their own national Christian bookstore chain refused to sell it. The lobbyists have been spawned mainly by the anti-equality for women organization The Council on Biblical Manhood and Womanhood (CBMW) which is allied closely with the Southern Baptists. The Southern Baptist Convention's giant bookstore chain Lifeway Christian Resources is the parent of Broadman and Holman Publishers which publishes the Holman Christian Standard Bible. Lifeway bookstores refused to sell the TNIV. Of the Holman Christian Standard Bible, R. Albert Mohler, president of Southern Baptist Theological Seminary in Louisville, said he was excited "if for no other reason than we will have a major translation we can control."

A number of the same lobbyists were members of the Translation Committee of the English Standard Version (ESV) Bible, a direct market competitor to the TNIV. The ESV had on its board of advisors several people who were signatories against the TNIV immediately upon its release. It is worth noting that the ESV was released only shortly before the TNIV. The ESV was published by Crossway Books, the President of which, Lane T. Dennis, was one of the original CBMW Council members and later on the CBMW Board of Reference. Crossway Books publish many books by CBMW members.

The foremost lobbyists are members of the secretive organization Council for National Policy (CNP) which is hostile to the idea of separation of church and state, and lobbies against the Equal Rights Amendment. The CNP enjoys tax free status, and plans the strategy for the Religious Right. Among its members have been *Christian Coalition* founder and *The Council on Biblical Manhood and Womanhood* founding member Pat (Marion) Robertson; founder of *Focus on the Family* James Dobson; founders of *Concerned Women for America* and members of *The Council on Biblical Manhood and Womanhood* Beverly and Tim LaHaye; John Ashcroft, the Bush administration's former Attorney General; Ed Meese, the Reagan administration's Attorney General; *Christian Coalition* executive director Ralph Reed; the *U.S. Taxpayers Party* founder, Howard Phillips; *Gun Owners of America* head Larry Pratt; *Christian Reconstructionists* (who favor the death penalty for abortionists, homosexuals, uncontrollable teenagers, among others) including Gary North and R.J. Rushdoony.

It is disturbing that the very group which arguably has done more than any other in history to control the availability and content of Bibles is one of the most politically powerful groups. Nevertheless, there are various reasons why errors in word meaning continue to be promulgated in Bibles.

Word meaning.

For centuries, the meanings of numerous New Testament words remained unknown, thus translators were left to guess. In the late 1880s and again in the mid 1970s, large amounts of papyri and inscriptions were discovered. These impacted our knowledge of word meaning in the New Testament to such a degree that scholars labeled the finds "sensational" and "dramatic." The papyri were written at the time of the New Testament, and touched upon all aspects of life, comprising everyday private letters from ordinary people, contracts of marriage and divorce, tax papers, official decrees, birth and death notices, and business documents. Large numbers of previously uncommon words found in the New Testament now appeared commonly in everyday documents as well as on inscriptions, and so mysteries of word meaning were solved. (This has nothing to do with the Dead Sea Scrolls.)

> Yet nearly every New Testament translation of today follows the traditional translations of the earlier versions, which were published centuries before the evidence from the papyri and inscriptions revealed to us the meanings of numerous New Testament words.

In 1895, the celebrated German scholar Deissmann published a large body of papyri, and between 1914 and 1929 Moulton and Milligan published documentary ("documentary" or "non-literary" meaning papyri and inscriptions) vocabulary in eight volumes in their *Vocabulary of the Greek Testament*. Although this was an enormous advance, Moulton and Milligan still had no entry for about 17 percent of New Testament words. Of the words they did include in their lexicon, there were 800 words for which they did not list documentary attestation. Due to ongoing discoveries, the work was out of date before the last volume had been published. Nearly every recent New Testament dictionary and concordance is based on this old work while some are based on work prior even to that of Moulton and Milligan.

Recent discoveries of word meaning have revolutionized our understanding of words which appear in the New Testament, but sadly, this scholarship has been largely ignored by Bible translators. Several thousand Greek inscriptions and papyri were published for the first time, or reissued, in 1976. In that year alone, 15 volumes of recently discovered papyri were published. Light was thrown on a large number of words previously unattested. Finds are ongoing: several thousand new inscriptions come to light each year. In the last two decades, four thousand inscriptions have been found at Ephesos alone. These discoveries have been largely overlooked by Bible translators, despite greatly exciting New Testament scholars and lexicographers. Laypersons and a significant number of Bible translators alike are unaware of the main body of scholarship as it is tucked away in technical academic journals. Thus the dictionary work we see in today's New

Testament translations follows Tyndale's translation of 1534 and the King James Version of 1611 with a disregard for modern evidence for Greek word meaning.

For centuries Matthew 11:12 (for example) caused problems for translators, and left readers wondering why heaven should suffer violence or be forcefully seized by people. Only in recent years was it discovered that the sentence is full of technical legal terminology of the time. The actual translation is, "From the time of John the Baptizer until now, Heaven's Realm is being used or even robbed by people who have no legal right to it. This stops those who do have a legal right to it from enjoying their own property."

The word ἀρσενοκοίτης, *arsenokoites*, in 1 Cor. 6:9 and 1 Tim. 1:10 has been assumed to mean "homosexual". However, the word does not mean "homosexual", and its range of meaning includes one who anally penetrates another (female or male), a rapist, a murderer, or an extortionist. When used in the meaning "anal penetrator", it does not apply exclusively to males as the receptors, as it was also used for women receptors. The word does not appear in any Greek literary source until the poets of the Imperial period. This late occurrence is most significant as the Greeks wrote at length on male-male sexual relationships.

The cognate verb appears in the *Sibylline Oracles* ii.73 μὴ ἀρσενοκοιτεῖν, μὴ συκοφαντεῖν, μήτε φονεύειν, *me arsenokoitein, me sukophantein, mete phoneuein*, where it is in company with committing extortion and committing murder. Pseudo-Macarius Aegyptius, *Homiliae spirituales* IV 4.22, stated that the people of Sodom sinned greatly and did not repent, and "created the ultimate offense in their evil purpose against the angels, wishing to work *arsenokoitia* upon them". Aristides said that the Greek gods commit murders and poisonings, adulteries, thefts and *arsenokoites* in the context of rape. The 6th c. astrologer Rhetorius Aegyptius used the term as women with the receptors: "*arsenokoites* (of women) and rapists of women."

Relevant Knowledge.

E.D. Hirsch stated, "To grasp the words on a page we have to know a lot of that isn't down on the page."[1] The reader's context determines how a certain passage will be understood. Linguist specialist in Bible translation, Ernst-August Gutt, explained contextual implications with this example.[2]

Mother: "What's your new teacher like?"

Daughter: "He rides to school on a motorbike."

If the daughter liked men who rode motorbikes, the mother would know that her daughter liked the teacher.

However, if the daughter did not like men who rode motorbikes, the mother would know that the daughter disliked the teacher.

Yet if the reader read without context the question by the mother and the answer by the daughter, the reader would not know whether or not the daughter liked the teacher, and in fact, the reader could well assume that the daughter was not answering the mother's question. Some context would be necessary for the reader to arrive at the correct conclusion.

As would be expected, the original writers of the Bible did not supply extra information to their readers when such context was well known to their readers. It was simply unnecessary. Gutt states, "Returning to Bible

---

[1] E. D. J. Hirsch, *Cultural literacy: What every American needs to know*, Boston, Houghton Mifflin, 1987, p. 3. Quoted by Gutt, below.

[2] Ernst-August Gutt, "Relevance theory and translation: Toward a new realism in Bible translation." Paper presented at the 2004 International Meeting of the Society of Biblical Literature, 25.-28.7.2004, Groningen, Netherlands, pp. 3ff.

translation, it is obvious that in many cases the cognitive environment of the target language audience shows very little resemblance to that of the original audience."[1] He continues, "One of the most surprising facts about modern Bible translation is that this major barrier to successful comprehension is given very little attention... The fact that differences in background knowledge are likely to cause major comprehension problems for the modern reader are rarely mentioned."[2]

Dr Gutt even suggests warnings should appear in the prefaces of Bible translations. He states, "They are also important, to alert them to the possibility that even seemingly clear texts may actually have quite a different meaning, due to differences in background knowledge. This possibility of misunderstanding is, in some ways, more serious than that of obscurity, since obscurity will be noticed, but misinterpretations often go unrecognised."[3]

Contexts of certain Biblical passages have come to light only in recent times, and the contexts have shown the original interpretation, and thus traditional translation, to be gravely wrong. For example, in Matthew 19 the Rabbis asked Jesus about his interpretation of Deuteronomy 24:1. The context, discovered only in recent years, was that there were two different Forms of Divorce available at the time. The "Any Matter" is a technical term from Jewish divorce law, a Form of Divorce introduced by the Rabbi Hillel. The other Form of Divorce, divorce on the ground of "General Sexual Immorality", was available to both men and women, both of whom were able to divorce the partner on the specific grounds based on Exodus 21:10-11. This traditional type of divorce was becoming rarer by the start of the 1st c., being replaced by the "Any Matter" divorce, which was for men only, and popular as no grounds had to be shown and there was no court case. For an "Any Matter" divorce, the man simply had to write out a certificate of divorce and give it to his wife. By Jesus' time, the "Any Matter" was the more popular form of divorce, but the rabbis were still arguing about the legalities of it. The disciples of Shammai were particularly opposed to it.

Matthew 19:3-8 has been mistranslated giving the impression that Jesus was asked the question, "Is it ever legal to divorce?" and he answered, "No, except on the grounds of sexual immorality." This is not the case. Jesus was asked if it was legal to divorce on the grounds of "Any Matter" and he answered, "No, only on the grounds of 'General Sexual Immorality'". In other words, he was disagreeing with the "Any Matter" form of divorce. Jesus certainly was not saying that at that time, or in the time to come, people were never to divorce except on the ground of sexual immorality.

In another example, Romans 1 and Jude have been said to speak against homosexuality. However, the "flesh of different kind" was referring not to homosexuality but to "The Watchers" (angels) coming to earth and "whoring after" human women. This is well documented in the literature of the time. 2 Enoch speaks of those who "went against nature" and "who boast of their wicked deeds, stealing, lies, calumnies, envy, rancour, fornication, murder, and who, accursed, steal the souls of men, who, seeing the poor take away their goods and themselves wax rich, injuring them for other men's goods; who being able to satisfy the empty, made the hungering to die; being able to clothe, stripped the naked; and who knew not their creator, and bowed to the soulless and lifeless gods, who cannot see nor hear, vain gods, who also built hewn images and bow down to unclean handiwork." (Trans. Lawrence.) In similar language in Romans 1, Paul speaks of those who "exchanged God's truth for the lie, the idol, and worshipped and served the creation other than the Creator.. the females exchanged natural sex for what is other than nature.

---

[1] Ibid., p. 11.
[2] Ibid., p. 13.
[3] Ibid., p. 14.

And the same goes for males too. The males got rid of natural sex with the female and burned with their mutual yearning – males producing indecency with one another, and as a result got what was coming to them for their mistake. They didn't think it fit to acknowledge God, so he gave them an unfit mind, to do things that are not appropriate. They have been filled with every kind of wrongdoing, evil, greedy grasping behavior, malice - full to the utmost with jealousy, murder, quarrels, deceit, nasty dispositions. They are people who give out information, whether true or false, which is detrimental to the character or welfare of others. They are slanderers, God haters, insolent, arrogant, boastful, inventors of bad deeds. They are not obedient to parents, they don't have intelligence, they do not keep covenant, they do not have natural affection, they do not have mercy."

Jude speaks of angels who did not uphold their own office, and that God has held them with eternal ropes down in the gloom. In the next sentence Jude says that "just like these" Sodom and Gomorrah "who went after different flesh" serve as an example of those who undergo punishment in the eternal fire. Jude quotes *1 Enoch* in verses 14-15. *1 Enoch* 6-10 states that 200 angels came to earth, lusted after human women causing "defilement" and producing progeny. The *Book of Jubilees* 5 sets out the punishment by God upon these angels. *2 Enoch* 10 states, "And (they)… showed me there a very terrible place, and there were all manner of tortures in that place: cruel darkness and unilluminated gloom, and there is no light there, but murky fire constantly flaming aloft, and there is a fiery river coming forth, and that whole place is everywhere fire, and everywhere there is frost and ice, thirst and shivering, while the bonds are very cruel... This place is reserved for those who sin against nature." Note the words "sin against nature".

The *Testament of Naphtali* 3.3.4-5 states that the women of Sodom had sex with angels, who "changed the order of their nature, whom also the Lord cursed at the flood, and for their sakes made desolate the earth, that it should be uninhabited and fruitless." Note the term "changed the order of their nature" which is similar to Jude's term, "went after different flesh" and to Paul's statement, "for the females exchanged natural sex for what is other than nature. And the same goes for males too," in Romans 1:26.

The context in Romans 1 and Jude is angels having sex with humans, as well as committing other crimes. In fact, the context cannot be more obvious in Jude 6-7, "**6** And as for the Messengers who did not uphold their own office but deserted their own places, he (the Lord) has held them firmly in eternal ropes down in the gloom, waiting for the Judgment of the Great Day. **7** Just like these, Sodom and Gomorrah as well as the surrounding cities, which in a similar way committed *porneia* and went after different flesh, serve as an example of those who undergo punishment in the eternal fire." *1 Enoch* 10 says the main angel who was responsible for abandoning his office in this way was bound hand and foot and cast into in darkness where he would remain until the Great Day of Judgement.

Note the "just like these" in verse 7. Jude is spelling it out very clearly, Messengers (angels) did not uphold their own office, are held with ropes in darkness/gloom, and just like these, Sodom and Gomorrah went after strange flesh (angels having sex with human women). This is most certainly nothing to do with homosexuality: it is not even anything at all to do with sex between human beings.

Traditions with no basis in fact.

Faulty traditions abound in the Christian community. Some of these have arisen from mistranslation, but some have not. The following traditions demonstrate the ease with which one can be misled by religious tradition alone. The popular belief remains that there were "three" "wise men" and that these people visited Jesus as a baby in a manager. However, the Bible does not mention the number, and in fact states that they visited Jesus in a house.

(History tells us that Jesus was around two years of age at the time.) At no time does the Bible, in any translation, suggest or imply that the "wise men" were present soon after Jesus' birth. Further, not one Bible version states the number "three"; this is purely unfounded tradition based perhaps on the number of different types of gifts, not even number of gifts. In another instance, there is much talk and speculation in some of the Christian community as to who the "Antichrist" could be, despite the fact that there is no mention of a single "Antichrist" figure anywhere in the Bible. The word only appears in the First and Second Letters of John, only briefly, and is identified as those people (plural) who do not agree that Jesus the Anointed One has come in human form. The word is not mentioned in Revelation. These misconceptions are all based on correct translation, so it is not surprising that misconceptions based on mistranslation are perpetrated. Turning to translation matters, in what is surely to be seen as censorship, the word *Magos* is translated widely as "wise man" in the context of the young Jesus, "sorcerer" in Acts, and "astrologer" in Daniel.

Many modern translators have followed the KJV, whether directly or through the lexicons (dictionaries). For example, the word παιδάριον, *paidarion*, in John 6:9 is translated as follows: "lad" (KJV, NKJ, RSV, NAS), "boy" (NIV, PME, Weymouth, TNIV), "small boy" (JB), "little boy" (Amplified). Yet παιδάριον, *paidarion*, can mean "slave", "young (free) man," "young (free) woman", "child," "girl," "manservant," "soldier". All these meanings have been well attested in the *Septuagint* alone. There is no evidence for the exclusive term "lad" or "boy".[1] The lexicon BAGD's (the predecessor of BDAG) entry disregarded the evidence from the *Septuagint*, and ignored *BGU* 2347.3 where παιδάριον, *paidarion*, is clearly shown to be an adult man. *BGU* was published three years earlier than BAGD.

Deliberate Changes.

The *NKJV, NIV, TEV, Phillips Modern English, RSV, Jerusalem Bible, New English Bible* and the *Living Bible* changed the female name Junia to a masculine name. The *KJV, NJKV* and *Living Bible* changed the female name Nympha to a masculine name, and changed "the church that is in her house" to "the church that is in his house". The *NKJV* reversed the order of "mother and brothers". The *NJKV* and *KJV* reversed the order of Priscilla (woman) and Aquila (man) when the couple was presented in a teaching context. The KJV, *NKJV* and *Tyndale Bible* added the words "a man" to a sentence about a woman being in a position of responsibility, and the *Living Bible, New English Bible, Phillips Modern English* changed it to a word to include both genders.

Theological bias has influenced Bible translators to err from the text in other ways. For example, the straightforward and simple Greek sentence of 1 Cor. 11:10 which simply states that a woman ought to show her own authority on her head has been completely altered in most Bible versions to state that a woman must wear a covering (the word "veil" does not appear in the Greek) to show she is under a man's authority. The Greek sentence does not mention a man or husband.

The translations of most New Testament versions are based on a lack of understanding of Greek word meaning and context and display a disregard for published academic research which shows passages in earlier translations to be wrong.

---

[1] For further reading, see commentary in G.M. Simpson, *A Semantic Study of Words for Young Person, Servant and Child in the Septuagint and other early Koine Greek*, Sydney, 1976, pp. 95, 182f.

The Good News of Matthew.[1]

Matthew frequently speaks against the sect of the Sadducees, which was wiped out in the war with the Romans in 66-70 AD. Likewise, the temple tax mentioned in 17:24-27 did not continue after the temple was destroyed. This effectively places Matthew's work prior to this date. The evidence suggests that Luke and Matthew did not know of each other's work, thus dating both works around the same time as each other. Luke is dated c. 62 AD. The consensus of opinion places Matthew's authorship to the mid 60s AD.

Eusebius quotes Irenaeus c. 170 AD as saying, "Matthew published the Good News in writing also, among the Hebrews in their own language, while Peter and Paul in Rome were preaching the Good News and founding the church."[2] Peter and Paul were first in Rome together in the early 60s. Eusebius also quotes Papias as saying, "Matthew compiled the sayings in the Hebrew language, but everyone translated them as they were able".[3] Papias' (c. 130 AD) words appear in a later Latin translation, *Against Heresies*, Ante-Nicene Fathers, 3.1.1.[4] There is doubt as to whether the "sayings" are those we know as the Gospel of Matthew.

Eusebius quotes of Clement of Rome (c. 101 AD) as saying that the first of the four gospels which are unquestionable was Matthew, "who was once a Tax Profiteer but later an apostle." Clement, writing from Rome to Corinth c. 96 AD, refers to Matthew. Matthew is quoted as early as c. 110 AD by Ignatius and by Polycarp's *Letter to the Philippians*. The writer was Matthew, also known as Levi. Matthew was a wealthy Tax Profiteer, and one of the Twelve disciples. The Tax Profiteers of Palestine were wealthy individuals who belonged to the upper (or upper-middle) classes of society. The Tax Profiteer purchased one or more taxes in a specific region at auction. The state tax was sold to the purchaser for a set period. It was usually limited to a village. The right was purchased yearly at the beginning of the New Year. The Tax Profiteer made their profit by collecting more than the sum contracted to the state. The profit generally amounted to 12% per annum.

The common impression today is that Tax Profiteers were given to extortion and oppression, but the evidence is to the contrary: there were very few petitions and edicts against them.

Eusebius and Irenaeus hold that Matthew was a Jewish Christian, writing for an audience of Jewish Christians. Indeed, the evidence suggests that his Good News (gospel) was written from and for the churches of Galilee. Matthew focuses on Galilee, and is familiar with its geography. He focuses particularly on Capernaum. Matthew avoids the Jewish "sacred name" God. Matthew is familiar with Jewish customs and history,[5] and translates Hebrew words for the Greek listeners, while not explaining Jewish culture.[6]

---

[1]   The title, "According to Matthew" is found in *Aleph* B. By the 5th century it was "The Good News According to Matthew", and later, "The Holy Good News According to Matthew".

[2]   Eusebius, *Historia Ecclesiastica* V.8, 2.

[3]   Eusebius, *Historia Ecclesiastica* III.39. 16.

[4]   There is no evidence to suggest that Papias was Irenaeus' source. Later, Origen, Jerome, Augustine all stated that Matthew's gospel was originally written in Hebrew.

[5]   Matthew correctly calls Herod Antipas "Tetrarch" rather than "King".

[6]   Such as tithing and phylacteries, cf. Matt. 23:5, 23.

According to Matthew.

Ch.1. This is the book about the beginning of the Anointed One, who was of David's family, and Abraham's family. *2* Abraham fathered Isaac, Isaac fathered Jacob, Jacob fathered Judah and his brothers. *3* Judah fathered Perez and Zarab by Tamar, Perez fathered Hezron, and Hezron fathered Ram. *4* Ram fathered Amminadab, Amminadab fathered Nahshon, and Nahshon fathered Salmon, *5* Salmon fathered Boaz by Rahab, Boaz fathered Obed by Ruth, Obed fathered Jesse, *6* Jesse fathered David the king. David fathered Solomon by the wife of Uriah. *7* Solomon fathered Rehoboam, Rehoboam fathered Abijah, Abijah fathered Asa. *8* Asa fathered Jehosophat, Jehosophat fathered Joram, Joram fathered Uzzaiah. *9* Uzziah fathered Jotham, Jotham fathered Ahaz, Ahaz fathered Hezekiah. *10* Hezekiah fathered Manasseh, Manasseh fathered Amon, Amon fathered Josiah. *11* Josiah fathered Jeconiah and his brothers at the time they were deported to Babylon. *12* After they were deported to Babylon, Jeconiah fathered Shealtiel, and Shealtiel fathered Zerabbalel. *13* Zerabbabel fathered Abiud, Abiud fathered Eliakim, Eliakim fathered Azor. *14* Azor fathered Zadok, Zadok fathered Achim, Achim fathered Eliud. *15* Eliud fathered Eleazar, Eleazar fathered Mattham, Mattham fathered Jacob. *16* Jacob fathered Joseph, the husband of Mary, from whom was born Jesus who is called the Anointed One. *17* So then there are fourteen generations from Abraham to David, fourteen generations from David to the Babylonian captivity, and fourteen generations from the Babylonian exile to the Anointed One.

18-23 This is how the birth of Jesus the Anointed One happened. His mother Mary was engaged to Joseph. Now before they got together,[1] it turned out that she was pregnant from[2] the Holy Spirit. *19* Joseph, her husband, was a fair person. He didn't want to disgrace her, so he thought he should split up with her privately.[3] *20* While[4] he was considering this, a Messenger [5]of the Lord appeared to him in a dream and said, "Joseph, David's descendant! Don't be afraid to marry Mary! The baby she is having is from the Holy Spirit. *21* She will give birth to a son, and you will name him 'Jesus'. He is going to save his people from their sins!"

---

[1] συνέρχομαι, *sunerchomi*, euphemism for sexual intercourse. It can also mean "get married" or "assemble (used of crowds)".

[2] Genitive of source, not of agent.

[3] There were two forms of breaking off the betrothal. Jospeh had decided to use the "Any Matter" form (see note on Matthew 19:3) which did not require any proof of wrongdoing. If Joseph had used the other form, he would have tried to prove Mary guilty of adultery in court, and thus avoided paying her marriage inheritance. By Joseph's use of the "Any Matter" form, Mary was spared any embarrassment. This is why Matthew describes him as "a fair person".

[4] The attention prompter ἰδού, *idou*, is not translated here. It is often translated "behold" or "look", but is simply a prompter of attention. It can be translated "Listen!", "Pay attention!", "Look!" or even "Hey!" or "Hey you!" In most cases it is jarring in English translation and is better omitted. The other two prompters of attention in the N.T. are ἴδε, *ide*, which occurs far less frequently than ἰδού, *idou*, and ἄγε, *age*, which occurs only twice, in James 4:13 and 5:1.

[5] ἄγγελος, *aggelos*, commonly rendered as its transliteration "angel" but the meaning is "messenger". The word occurs for an ordinary messenger as well as a supernatural messenger. For the pagan supernatural messenger (pagan "angel") context see inscriptions *ZPE* 30 (1978) 257 n. 7, and *EG* IV.210 (2nd c AD); as well as dedication to pagan *TAM* V, 1.185. The word also occurs in *TAM* V, 1.159 but it is not clear whether the messenger was a human or supernatural messenger. There is evidence for the term occurring in contexts where a derivation from Judasim has been ruled out. There is as yet no conclusive evidence as to whether the famous "Thera angels" were in fact Christian, cf. *IG* XII, 3 (1898) 455, 933-74; *IG* XII, Suppl. (1904) 1636, 1637 (2nd – 3rd c. AD).

22 All this was done so that the words spoken by the Lord through the prophet[1] would happen, *23* "The unmarried girl[2] will be pregnant and give birth to a son, and they will call him Immanuel." ("Immanuel" in Hebrew means "God is with us.")

24-25 When Joseph woke up from his sleep he did what the Messenger of the Lord ordered him to do. He married[3] Mary, *25* and did not have sex[4] with her until she had the son. He named him "Jesus".

Ch.2:1-2 After Jesus was born in Bethlehem (in Judea) - this was in the time that Herod[5] was King - Official Spiritual Advisers came to Jerusalem from the east. *2* They enquired, "Where can we find the one who was born King of the Jews? We've seen his star in its rising.[6] We've come to worship[7] him!"

Magoi, "Official Spiritual Advisers".

Magos is a Mede word meaning "Priest". The Magoi were originally involved in spiritism before the Zoroastrian religion found its way to Persia. Magoi had been established over the state religion of Persia by Darius the Great – a secular as well as religious post. They became the priestly caste of the Persian Empire. Throughout the Persian Empire, the Magoi were the Official Spiritual Advisors to the Persian king. Persia had no state religion. The Magoi always led the processions when the army marched out, and sacrificed one horse a month to the spirit of Cyrus. One Magos had the permanent job of looking after (both in a spiritual and physical sense) the tomb of Cyrus of Great. By Jesus' time, the Persian Empire had long been gone, conquered by Alexander the Great. Alexander's successors had taken over the various parts of the Old Persian Empire. The Macedonians left the conquered people their own religion and customs, and merely imposed a superficial administration. By the time of Jesus' birth, the Magoi may have been the Official Spiritual Advisors to the Seleucid state.

Magoi were astronomers, astrologers, dream interpreters and spellcasters. In fact, one of the titles given to Daniel was "Chief of the Magoi".[8] Herodotos

---

[1] προφήτης, *prophetes*, prophet, a common word which occurs frequently throughout the N.T. and is found in many inscriptions such as the Rosetta stone; *OGIS* 56.4 (238 BC); *OGIS* 3.18 (beginning of 1st c BC). It usually referred to a religious official, and always to a priest in Egypt.

[2] παρθένος, *parthenos*, "unmarried woman", "girl of marriageable age" not παρθένιος, *parthenios* "virgin" (of either gender). The actual word παρθένος, *parthenos*, carries no connotation of virginity, cf. G.R. Horsley, *NDIEC* 4.222. In reference to *IG* XIV (1890) 1648 *ll*.1-10, Horsley states, "Theodosia is called *parthenos* at the age of 18, and is about to be married. This example confirms nicely the notion of *parthenos* as a girl of marriageable age (cf. *LSJ*, s.v., 2). The discussion of the word in Spicq, *NLNT* 111.516-25 provides a number of documentary references. While virginity may have been expected, the word does not require that connotation." The word is very widely attested for the above meaning. The correct translation of this word has caused some trouble for certain Bibles which translated the word correctly, as some prefer to substitute the correct meaning with the word "virgin" for theological reasons. At any rate, verse 25 does make it clear that Mary was a virgin when Jesus was born.

[3] παραλαμβάνω, *paralambano*, to get married, to take a wife or mistress, cf. Hdt. 4.155; Xen. Oec. 7.6.

[4] γινώσκω, *ginosko*. Its meaning "to have sex with", is well attested.

[5] Herod died in 4 B.C.

[6] "Star" equally means "shooting star", "flame", "light", "fire".

[7] προσκυνέω, *proskuneo*. General meaning, to worship, to pay homage, to do obeisance to (someone, often a god, sometimes a master).

[8] Daniel 5:11. Daniel is said to have been made "chief of the magicians, enchanters, Chaldeans, and astrologers".

tells us that the Magoi were interpreters of dreams and visions. He names the Magoi as one of the Median tribes. He states that sacrifices could not be performed unless a Magos was present,[1] and speaks of their sorcery and spells.[2] Strabo, XV, also notes that "the Magoi kept upon the altar a quantity of ashes and an immortal fire."

It was customary for the Magoi to travel with oriental luxury and a large entourage, which included cavalry for protection. The myth of the number "three" (which does not appear in any Bible version) is far from the truth – they rarely traveled in such small numbers. Tertullian, *Ante-Nicene Fathers*, Vol. III wrote, "We know the mutual alliance of magic and astrology. The interpreters of the stars, thus were the first....to present him gifts" and "The east commonly held kings versed in magic." Justin and Origen described the Magoi as "astrologers".

3-6 Now when he heard this, Herod the King became quite upset. He wasn't the only one - so did the whole of Jerusalem. *4* He collected all the chief priests and Bible scholars in an attempt to find out where the Anointed One was to be born. *5* This is what he was told: "In Bethlehem of Judea – that's what the prophet wrote: *6* 'And you, Bethlehem, in the land of Judah, you are important among the rulers of Judah! A shepherd will come from you, someone who will be a shepherd for my people Israel.'"

7-10 Then Herod summoned the Official Spiritual Advisers to a secret meeting, and ascertained from them the precise time the star had become visible. *8* He sent them to Bethlehem with the instructions, "Go and execute a thorough search for the young child! When you've found him, send news to me, and I'll come and worship him." *9* As soon as they'd heard what the king had to say, they left. The star, which they'd seen in its rising, moved along in front of them until it hovered over where the child was. *10* When they saw the star they were extremely happy.

11-14 When they arrived at the house[3] they saw the child with his mother Mary. They fell down and worshipped him. Then they opened their treasures

---

[1] Herodotos 1.131-2 states, "As for the Persian customs, I personally know they are these: … The sacrificer cuts up the victim limb to limb in portions, boils the flesh, makes a small heap of the softest grass they can find, preferably clover, and places all the meat on it. When this has been done, a Magos man comes near and chants the song of the birth of the gods over it, as Persian tradition relates it, for no sacrifice can be offered without a Magos." See also 7.43. Herodotos, 1.140, also states that the Magoi do not bury their dead unless the body had first been mangled by a bird or dog. He states that they are unlike any other priests, as they kill animals with their own hands, excepting dogs and people only, that they kill everything, ants, snakes, creeping and flying things, and take great pride in it. See Herodotos 3.63, 65-71, 126 for the Magians winning the kingship after the death of Cambyses.

[2] Herodotos, 7.113-114: "Xerxes.. came to the river Strymon.. By that water the Magoi killed white horses, thus offering sacrifice for good omens. Having used these enchantments and many others as well on the river, they passed over it at the Edonian town of Nine Ways by the bridges which they found over it. There, having learned that Nine Ways was the name of the place, they buried alive that number of boys and girls, children of the people of the country."

[3] The incorrect myths about this incident are 1. There were 3. (The number is not mentioned but they usually traveled in large numbers.) 2. They were wise men. (The usual Bible versions translate the same word as "astrologers" in Daniel" and as "sorcerer" in Acts.) 3. They went to the stable when Jesus was a baby. (They went to the house when Jesus was just under 2 years old.) 4. They were kings. (They were not.) 5. The star they followed was bright. (The N.T. does not say this.) Note the word "house". This was some time, probably just under two years, after Jesus' birth.

and presented him gifts: gold, frankincense, and myrrh.[1] *12* They didn't go back the way they had come, but left in another direction for their own country, because they had been divinely warned in a dream not to return to Herod. *13* After they left, a Messenger of the Lord appeared to Joseph in a dream and said, "Get going! Take the child and his mother with you and flee to Egypt! Stay there until I speak to you! Herod intends to find the child and kill him!"

14 So in the night, Joseph took the child and his mother and left for Egypt. *15* They stayed there until Herod died. In fact, the words spoken by the Lord through the prophet came to pass: "I called my Son out of Egypt."

16-18 Then Herod realized that the Official Spiritual Advisers had made a fool of him, and he got extremely angry. He ordered the death of all the male children up to the age of two years old in Bethlehem and the whole area around it. *17* He'd figured out the age from the information supplied by the Official Spiritual Advisers. *18* Then the words spoken by Jeremiah the prophet were fulfilled: "A cry was heard in Ramah, weeping and much lamenting; Rachel weeping for her children, and not willing to be comforted, because they are all dead."

Herod "the Great".

Herod "the Great", the son of Antipater, was born in 73 BC and died in 4 BC. He was named "the Great" by Josephus to distinguish him from the others of that name. He was an Idumaean, and thus a descendant of the Edomites who were believed to be descended from Esau.

The Senate appointed Herod as ruler of the Jews in 40 BC. He enjoyed the patronage of Mark Antony. After the Battle of Actium in 31 BC, Herod was in a precarious position, but traveled to Rhodes to meet Augustus and subsequently became his friend. Herod murdered people to further his position: Antigonus (his military opponent, 37 BC); the high priest Aristobulus, Antigonus' son (36 BC); the former high priest Hyrcanus II (30 BC); Mariamne, Herod's wife and Hyrcanus' grand-daughter (29 BC); Alexandra, Mariamne's mother (28 BC); his sons from Mariamne: Alexander and Aristobulus (7 BC); Antipater, his son with his first wife Doris (4 BC, only five days before he himself died). Macrobius, who wrote in the 4th c. AD, stated, "When [Augustus] heard that Herod king of the Jews had ordered all the boys of Syria under the age of two years to be put to death and that the king's son was among those killed, he said, 'I'd rather be Herod's pig than Herod's son.'" Josephus also criticized Herod: "[Herod] died on the fourth day after having his son Antipater killed... He was a man who was cruel to everyone alike, and he gave in easily to anger and had contempt for justice."

When Herod was on his deathbed, he arranged for respected citizens from the villages to be seized and held in the Hippodrome to be executed upon his death. Josephus quotes the order as follows: "I know that the Jews will celebrate my death by a festival, yet I myself can obtain a vicarious mourning and a splendid funeral, if you will consent to follow my instructions. Regarding these men here in custody: the moment I expire, have them surrounded by soldiers and massacred, so that all Judea and every household will mourn for me, whether they want to or not!"

---

[1] An extreme amount of wealth. The Magoi weren't likely to have a little box with each of the three types of gift wrapped up! They were extremely wealthy, in today's terms, millionaires. Note that there were 3 types of gifts, not 3 gifts. We are not told the quantities of each. Frankincense and myrrh were highly expensive. Pliny states that the price of the most prized variety of myrrh per pound was up to 50 denarii (around $5,000 in today's terms), and that the highest price for cultivated myrrh was 11 denarii (around $1,100 in today's terms). In Diocletian's edict regulating prices, the price of best quality frankincense was set at 100 denarii per pound (around $10,000 in today's terms).

19-23 When Herod came to the end of his life, a Messenger of the Lord appeared in a dream to Joseph in Egypt and **20** said, "On your way! Take the child and his mother with you and go to the land of Israel! The people who wanted to kill the child are dead."

21 Off Joseph went. He took the child and his mother and headed for Israel. *22* But when he heard that Archelaus[1] was king over Judea in his father Herod's place, he was afraid to go there. As he'd been divinely warned in a dream, he turned away to the region of Galilee, *23* and settled in the city of Nazareth. So the prophet's words, that he would be called a Nazarene, came true.

Nazareth.

There are no references to Nazareth in the Old Testament, the Talmud, or the writings of Josephus. In 1962 an inscription was discovered in Caesarea Maritima and it names Nazareth as one of the towns where members of the priestly classes settled after the destruction of Jerusalem in 135 AD. The tablet is dated to the 1st century AD. Nazareth is between the Sea of Galilee and the Mediterranean Sea. It was a small village, watered only by a small spring. Archeological evidence suggests it was uninhabited from the 8th to 2nd centuries BC. The Via Maris, the merchant route from the Mediterranean coast to Capernaum and further to Damascus, passed within six miles. Another Roman military route between the Sea of Galilee and the Mediterranean Sea passed nearby.

Ch.3:1-4 In those times John the Baptizer turned up. He was preaching in the Judean wilderness, *2* "Change your minds![2] Heaven's Realm[3] is close!"

3 John is the very person spoken of by the prophet Isaiah: "A voice of one calling in the wilderness, 'Prepare the road for the Lord, clear a straight pathway for him.'"

4 John himself was dressed in camel's hair with a leather belt around his waist. He ate locusts and wild honey - this was what he lived on.

5-10 Then people from Jerusalem and all Judea and the whole neighborhood around the Jordan River went to see him. *6* They publicly admitted their sins, and he baptized them in the Jordan River. *7* Then he saw a lot of Pharisees[4] and Sadducees coming to the baptism. "You pack of snakes!" he yelled. "Who advised you to escape from the anger that's coming? *8* Come on then, do something to prove that you've really and truly changed your minds! *9* And don't think you can say to yourselves, 'Abraham's our ancestor!' I'm telling you that God has the power to make Abraham some descendants out of these stones! *10* The ax is already at the root of the trees! Every tree which doesn't produce good fruit is cut down and thrown into the fire!

---

[1] When Herod died in 4 BC, half his kingdom - Judea, Idumaea and Samaria - was given to Archelaus. The remainder was split in half. The territories of Galilee and Perea were given to Herod Antipas, and the Trachonitis and Gaulanitis regions were given to Herod Phillip.

[2] To change one's mind or reverse one's attitude. "Repent" is a coined religious term.

[3] The phrase often translated "Kingdom of God" is correctly the Realm where God's way of doing things happens. It is a present realm, not a future kingdom. Matthew avoids the use of the name "God" as he was writing to the Jews, and they did not permit the use of the sacred name "God".

[4] Synecdoche must be considered with the word "Pharisees" throughout the N.T., thus when the word "Pharisees" appears in the gospels, the reference is not to Pharisees in general, but only certain of their number. After all, in Luke 13:31 Pharisees warn Jesus that Herod Antipas intends to have him executed. In Acts 5:33-42, the Pharisee Gamaliel I supports Peter and John. Pharisees who were members of the Sanhedrin also supported Paul, cf. Acts 22:30-23:10.

11-12 "Yes, it's a fact that I baptize you in water to show that you have changed your minds, but the person who is coming is more powerful than I am! I'm not even good enough to carry his sandals! He will baptize you with the fire of the Holy Spirit! *12* He's got a broom and he is going to sweep everything clean. If you're a pile of rubbish – look out! You'll be swept out the door and thrown into a fire, and no one's going to put the fire out!

13-17 Then Jesus came from Galilee to be baptized by John in the Jordan River. *14* But John tried to stop him. *"I'm* the one who needs to be baptized by you, but *you* are coming to me!" he said.

15 "This is how it's got to be at this point: it's the right thing to do," Jesus told him. So John did it. *16* The second he was baptized, Jesus came up from the water. At once, the skies opened up, and he saw the Spirit of God descend like a dove and land on him. *17* Suddenly out of the skies came a shout: "This is my much loved Son! I am very pleased with him!"

Ch.4:1-4 Then the Spirit led Jesus into the desert to be put through an ordeal[1] by Slanderer-Liar. *2* After he had fasted for forty days and forty nights, he got hungry. *3* Adversary who was putting him through the trial said, "If you really are the Son of God, then order these stones to turn into bread!"

4 Jesus answered, "The Scriptures say, 'Humans[2] won't live just on bread alone. They will live on every word that comes out of God's mouth.'"

5-6 Then Slanderer-Liar took him to the sacred city and put him on the very top of the Temple. *6* "Come on then!" he said. "If you're the Son of God, jump off! The Scriptures say, 'He will assign his Messengers to protect you. They will catch you, so that you won't so much as hit your foot on a stone!'"

7-11 Jesus answered, "The Scriptures say, 'How dare you provoke the Lord your God!'"

8 Next Slanderer-Liar took him along to a very high mountain and showed him all the kingdoms of the world and their splendor. *9* "I'll give you all this – all you have to do is fall down and worship me!"

10 "Get lost, Adversary!" said Jesus. "The Scriptures say 'You will worship the Lord your God! He is the only one you must serve!'"

11 Then Slanderer-Liar left, and Messengers turned up and provided for Jesus.

12-16 When Jesus heard that John had been imprisoned, he went back to Galilee. *13* He moved from Nazareth and went to live in Capernaum by the sea in the area of Zebulun and Naphtali. *14* Then the words spoken by Isaiah the prophet came to pass: *15* "The land of Zebulun and the land of Naphtali, the road to the sea, over the Jordan River, Galilee of the non-Jews. *16* The people sitting in darkness have seen a huge light, and light has risen on those who sat in the shadowy region of death."

17 From then on Jesus preached, "Change your minds! Heaven's Realm is close!"

18-22 While Jesus was walking beside the sea of Galilee he saw two brothers, Simon (later called Peter) and his brother Andrew. They were

---

[1] πειράζω, *peirazo*, means to put through an ordeal, to harass, not to tempt. πειρασμός, *peirasmos*, "tribulation", "oppression", commonly appears in N.T. translations as "temptation". Note however, Rev. 3:10 where both words appear, and both words commonly appear in most N.T. translations as "tribulation" and "trial" respectively, not "temptation" and "tempt". πειράζω, *peirazo*, has no documentary attestation in MM, but does in Spicq. ἡ πεῖρα, *he peira*, is an ordeal, an attempt on or against someone, a means of attacking, cf. Soph. *Aj.* 2, Aesch. *Theb.* 499. To attempt an action at sea, Thuc. 7.71. An attempt, enterprise, Thuc. 3.20, Aesch. *Pers.* 719, Soph. *Aj.* 290: from this comes the word πειρατής, *peirates*, a pirate.

[2] The Greek uses the generic non-gender specific ἄνθρωπος, *anthropos*.

fishermen, and were casting a net into the sea. *19* "Follow me!" he called to them. "I will make you fishers for people!"

20 Immediately they threw away their catching nets and followed him. *21* When he was leaving there, he saw two other brothers, James (Zebedee's son) and his brother John, in the boat with their father Zebedee. They were mending their nets, and he called them. *22* Immediately they left the boat and their father, and followed him.

23-25 Jesus went around all Galilee teaching in the synagogues and announcing the Good News of the Realm and healing[1] all kinds of sicknesses and all kinds of disease. *24* He became famous all over Syria. People brought sick people who were afflicted with various diseases and torments, people who had evil spirits, people who suffered from convulsions, as well as paralytics, and he healed them. *25* He was followed by huge crowds from Galilee, The Ten Cities, Jerusalem, Judea and beyond the Jordan River.

Ch.5:1-11 Upon seeing the huge crowds, Jesus climbed up a hill. He sat down and his disciples went over to him. *2* He taught as follows: *3* "Happy, spiritually, are the financially poor,[2] because theirs is Heaven's Realm. *4* Happy are those who mourn, because they will be encouraged. *5* Happy are those who are not angry or prone to temper, because they will inherit the earth. *6* Happy are those who hunger and thirst to be just, because they will have their fill. *7* Happy are the merciful, because they will obtain mercy. *8* Happy are those with purified minds, because they will see God. *9* Happy are the peacemakers, because they will be called God's children.[3] *10* Happy are those who bear the wounds of persecution for the sake of justice, because theirs is Heaven's Realm. *11* Happy are you whenever they heap insults on you, and persecute you and tell all kinds of evil lies about you because of me.

12-16 "Be very happy! In fact shout happily, because you have a huge reward in the heavenly places! They also persecuted the prophets who lived before your time. *13* You are the salt that flavors the earth, but if the salt becomes tasteless, how will it get its flavor back? It's good for nothing but to be thrown into the garbage and to end up being trampled under people's feet. *14* You are the light to light up the world. A city on the top of a hill can't be hidden! *15* And who puts a bucket over a light? Instead, they put a light somewhere where it will shine light on everything in the house. *16* So see to it that your light

---

[1] θεραπεύω, *therapeuo*, describes the result of treatment which embraces physical and psychological therapies, and usually involves a permanent change of lifestyle. (*IG* IV² 1, no. 126.) Continuity of action is always stressed with this verb. L. Wells, *The Greek language of Healing from Homer to New Testament Times*, (Berlin: Walter de Gruyter, 1998), pp. 35, 39, 83, 510. In Thucydides' graphic account of the plague, either the present participle is used (2.47.4; 2.51.2; 2.51.3), or the cognate form (2.51.4) or the future participle (2.51.5). Xenophon's use of the word (*Cyropaedia* 3.2.12; *Memorabilia* 4.3.9) echoes that of Thucydides. From Isocrates' writing, it is evident that the concept of emotional support is implicit. Isocrates, *Aegineticus* 11, 20-33 describes treatment, and the resultant healing demands a response in the person who needs the healing – this person takes an active part in the healing process. Note that the opposite Greek word means "neglect". θεραπεύω, *therapeuo,* is associated with hearing the Word and is often associated with a preaching context. It is ongoing: recovery may be rapid or slow.

[2] πτωχός, *ptokhos*, "financially destitute", not merely πενιχρός, *penikhros*, "poor". πενιχρός, *penikhros*, occurs in *P.Oxy.* 3273 and tells of the confusion between two men of the same name and same village. One was mistakenly nominated for the other man's office, although he was ἄθετος καὶ πενιχρός, *athetos kai penikhros*, lacking the financial means to be appointed to the office. πτωχός, *ptokhos*, is the word used for beggars.

[3] υἱός, *huios.* See note on Luke 11:11.

shines, that people see the good things you do and they will realize that the reason is God, your Father in the heavenly places.

17-20 "Don't think that I came to destroy the Law or the Prophets – no way! I came to complete them, not to destroy them. *18* Let me make this clear, that while the sky and the earth are still here, not one tiny letter or even part of a letter will disappear from the Law - not until it has all been completed. *19* "A person who breaks even the tiniest little one of these commandments and teaches people to break them, will be insignificant in Heaven's Realm! On the other hand, the person who keeps the commandments and teaches them to others, will be important in Heaven's Realm! *20* I'm telling you that unless you are far more fair-minded[1] than the Bible scholars and the Pharisees, there is no way you will enter Heaven's Realm!

21-26 "You have heard that it was said to those in ancient times, 'You must not murder', and 'Whoever murders, will be in danger of the judgment'. *22* I myself am telling you that someone who is angry with a fellow believer[2] without a reason has to answer to the local court! And someone who says to a fellow believer, 'Stupid idiot!' has to answer to the district court, but whoever calls someone 'You Complete Fool!' will be thrown into the burning Garbage Pit Gehenna![3]

23 "Now if you bring your offering to the altar and then remember that your fellow believer has a grudge against you, *24* you are to leave your offering there in front of the altar. Go and make friends with your fellow believer, and

---

[1] δικαιοσύνης, *dikaiosunes*, fair-mindedness, uprightness, righteous dealing. The sense, "uprightness", "justice", "fair-mindedness" is commonly attested in honorific inscriptions, figuring usually in the context of ἀρετή, *arete*, and εὐσέβεια, *eusebeia*. See also δίκαιον, *dikaion*, in the sense "fair-minded" in *IG* XIV.1976.

[2] ἀδελφός, *adelphos*, singular; ἀδελφοί, *adelphoi*, plural. The Greek word *adelphos* can mean "sibling" (of either gender), a member (male or female) of an association ("fellow believer" in the case of Christians or Jews), a "husband" or "wife" as a term of address between spouses, and in the plural can mean "brothers and sisters" ("siblings"); and "fellow members (of an association)." The Greek word for "sister" is either *adelphos* or, far more commonly, *adelphe*, but for siblings which include females as well as males, the word is *adelphoi*. Thus the plural, *adelphoi*, can mean siblings or members of an association. In English, we say "brothers and sisters", but Greek commonly does not do that. The Greek says *adelphoi*. For example, *P.Oxy* 713 (Oxyrhynchos A.D. 97) states, "My father died leaving me and my *adelphoi* Diodorus and Theis, his heirs, and his property transferred to us." Note that Diodorus is a man's name, and Theis is a woman's name.
The word is commonly used in the meaning "fellow believer/s". See, for example, *P.Iand.* 6, a letter to "fellow believers", and *CE* 13, a letter from John the Deacon to a "fellow believer". Moulton and Milligan (MM), the lexicon of the papyri discovered prior to the early 1900s, state, "For the use of *adelphoi* to denote members of the same religious community cf. *P.Tor* 1 i.20 (ii BC)...and in *P.Par* 42 I etc (ii BC) the same designation is applied to the 'fellows' of a religious corporation established in the Serapeum of Memphis." They also cite *P.Tebt* 1.12 on which one town clerk addresses another as *adelphos*. For *adelphos* as a term of address (to people who are not siblings), they cite *P.Flor* II.228 (3 AD); *P.Tebt* II.314.12 (2 AD); *BGU* IV. 1209.2 (23 BC). For its use as "fellow believer" in the Christian papyri they cite *P.Grenf* II.73.

[3] The words "Gehenna", "Hades" and "Tartarus", three very different places in the Greek, are usually all just called "Hell" in most Bible versions. Gehenna was a real place on earth. It was the Jerusalem rubbish dump, and was just outside the city. Smoke went up from it at all times as the rubbish was burning continually. It was full of maggots, and the bodies of the worst criminals were thrown there. Josiah used it for the burning of offal. It used to be the site of child sacrifice to Molech.

then come back and offer your gift. *25* "If you see a legal trial looming, come to an agreement with your opponent[1] before it lands in the courts. Otherwise your opponent will hand you over to the judge and the judge will hand you over to the officer and you will be thrown into prison! *26* Listen to me - you won't get out of there, until you have paid the very last cent!

27-30 "You have heard the saying, 'You must not commit adultery.' *28* Now I am telling you that anyone who considers sleeping with a married woman[2] has already committed adultery with her in his mind. *29* If your right eye sets a trap for you, rip it out and throw it away! It's better for one of your body parts to perish, than for your whole body to be thrown into the Garbage Pit Gehenna. *30* And if your right hand sets a trap for you, cut it off and throw it away! It's better for one of your body parts to perish, than for your whole body to be thrown into the Garbage Pit Gehenna.

31-32 "It has been said, 'Whoever divorces his wife, must return her dowry and give her a legal divorce.'[3] *32* But now I'm saying that a man who divorces his wife, unless it's on the grounds of 'General Sexual Immorality'[4] makes her commit adultery; and whoever marries such a divorced person commits adultery.[5]

33-37 "You have heard the ancient saying, 'You must not swear an oath that you don't intend to keep. You must keep your oaths to the Lord.' *34* Listen to it! In fact, don't swear an oath at all! Don't swear by heaven, as it is God's throne. *35* Don't swear by the earth, as it is his footstool. Don't swear by Jerusalem, as it is the city of the great King. *36* And what's the point of swearing by your head, because you can't make one hair white or black! *37* But

---

[1] This is technically a defendant opponent-at-law.

[2] The term "adultery" applies to a married woman.

[3] To give a woman a divorce meant to return her dowry. Separation legally equaled divorce. Divorce was instant upon separation: that is, by the very act of someone leaving the relationship, the divorce was legally enacted. There was no other legal requirement like the one we have in contemporary times. There was no document of divorce itself devoid of property matters. Here, in the statement "let him return her dowry" the reference is to the formal document drawn up reflecting both parties' agreement about possession of property, custody of children, and return of dowry. Without this formal document, the woman could be left destitute. When a wife was divorced from her husband, she and any children of whom she had custody had to leave the home of her former husband. She then had to live with her parents, or in her own house if she had one. The divorced wife left her husband's house and received back her dowry. For divorcing a wife without cause the husband paid a 50% (or 100%) penalty of the value of the dowry, unless he paid the dowry's value immediately. If the wife initiated the divorce, the value of the dowry was returned within 10-60 days. The 50% penalty applied if the dowry was returned later. A common form of marriage was by cohabitation, that is, once a couple started living together they were considered to be married. See S.R. Llewelyn, "Paul's Advice on Marriage and the Changing Understanding of Marriage in Antiquity", *NDIEC* 6.2-11; S.R. Llewellyn, "Jewish and Christian Marriage", *NDIEC* 6.12-18; J. Modrzejewski, "La structure juridique du mariage grec," *Scritti in onore di Orsolina Montevechhi*, (Bologna, 1981), pp. 261-264; J.F. Gardner, *Women in Roman Law and Society*, (Beckenham, 1986), pp. 97-116; For return of the dowry upon divorce see G. Hage, *Eheguterrechtliche Verhaltnisse in den griechischen Papyri Agyptens bis Diokletian*, (Koln-Graz, 1968), pp. 89-99. For the nature of the dowry, *ibid.*, pp. 27, 36-62. See note on Matt. 19:3, 9.

[4] That is, someone divorced by the "Any Matter" Method, not the "General Sexual Immorality" Method.

[5] Jesus is declaring the "Any Matter" form of divorce invalid.

when you say 'Yes', mean it! When you say 'No', mean it! Anything more than that is from the Evil One!

38-42 "You have heard the saying, 'An eye for an eye and a tooth for a tooth.' *39* But let me make this clear: don't oppose an evil person at all! Instead, if someone slaps you across your face, let them! *40* If someone wants to sue you in court and take your shirt, give them your coat as well! *41* If someone conscripts[1] you and makes you go with them for one mile, go with them for two miles![2] *42* Give people whatever they ask from you, and don't turn away people who want to borrow from you!

43-48 "You have heard the saying, 'You must love your neighbor and hate your enemy.' *44* But I tell you to love your enemies, and pray for those who put curses[3] on you! *45* Then you really will be the children of your Father in the heavenly places. He makes his sun rise on the evil as well as the good, and sends rain on the just as well as on the unjust. *46* Now then, if you love people who love you, do you expect to get a reward? Even Tax Profiteers do that! *47* And if you just say 'hello' to your fellow believers, what's the big deal about that? Even the people who worship other gods do that! *48* So then if you do all these things you will be a whole person, just as your Father in heaven is whole.

Tax Profiteers.

The Tax Profiteer purchased one or more taxes in a specific region at auction. A state tax was sold at auction to the purchaser for a set period. It was usually limited to a village. The right was purchased yearly at the beginning of the New Year. The Tax Profiteer made their[4] profit by collecting more than the sum contracted to the state. The profit generally amounted to 12% per annum. The *telones*, Tax Profiteer, purchased taxes in cash and could only demand taxes within a set amount. Unlike the Roman *publicanus*, the *telones* was a small businessperson, not a large corporation. The *telones*, Tax Profiteers of Palestine, were wealthy and belonged to the upper-middle or upper classes of society.

The King James Version translates "publicans", following the (Latin) Vulgate's *publicanus*. Tyndale's 1534 translation also had "publican". However, the Latin *publicani* is not the translation of the Greek τελῶναι, *telonai*. A *publicanus* was a Roman *equites* whose *societas publicanorum* had contracted the collection of tributes and taxes in a province. *Publicani* subcontracted the collection of taxes to the cities which were often forced into oppressive agreements. Caesar restored the former Hellenistic system of taxation, reducing direct taxation, and changing the collection to cities. Augustus shifted the tax collection to the local civic authorities.

Ch.6:1-4 "Take care that you don't do the right thing in front of people just so they will notice you! If you do, you sure won't have a reward from your Father who is in the heavenly places! *2* So when you do charitable deeds, don't make a big song and dance about it like the overly critical, hair

---

[1]   Usually a technical term for conscripting into war service. See below note.

[2]   People traveling on official business were given special passes (*diplomata*) which gave them authority to request help from civilians to aid them in their travels. Sometimes the system was abused. Epiktetos, *Discourses* 4, 1, 79, states, "You should, as far as you can and as long as you may, treat your body like a laden donkey. If it is commandeered, and a soldier seizes it, let it go! Do not resist or complain. Otherwise you will be beaten up, and will still lose your donkey." Apuleius' *Metamorphoses*, 9, 39ff tell of a soldier who attempts to requisition a donkey from a gardener, who beats up the soldier. The gardener is arrested. See also Pliny, *Letters*, 10, 45, 46.

[3]   καταράομαι, *kataraomai*. See note on Luke 6:28.

[4]   Female Tax Profiteers were well attested: e.g., *ed. pr.* P.J. Sijpesteijn, "A female tax-collector", *ZPE* 61 [1985] 71-3, [Small Oasis, 8 April, 187A.D].

splitting, pedantic religious people[1] do in the streets, so people will praise them. It's a fact, their reward is paid in full! *3* When you do a charitable deed, keep it to yourself and don't tell anyone. *4* Make sure it's a secret. And your Father who is watching you in secret will reward you.[2]

5-13 "And when you pray, you must not be like the overly critical, hair splitting, pedantic, religious people, because they love to pray standing in the synagogues and on street corners, so people can see them. For a fact, their reward is paid in full! *6* But when you pray, go into your storehouse, shut the door, and pray to your Father in secret. Your Father who sees what is done in secret will reward you.

7 "When you pray, you must not say the same thing over and over again like the people who worship other gods do. They think they will be heard because they speak for such a long time. *8* Don't be like them! Your Father knows what you need before you ask him. *9* So then, pray like this:[3] 'Our Father who is in the heavenly places, May your Name be treated as sacred! *10* May your Realm come! May your purpose be done on earth just like your purpose is done in heaven! *11* Give us our bread that we need for tomorrow, today! *12* Cancel our loans for us, in the same way also that we have canceled the loans of people who owe us money.[4] *13* And do not put us through an ordeal.[5] Rather, rescue us from the Evil One.'

14-15 Now if you don't hold people's mistakes against them,[6] your Father of the heavenly places won't hold your mistakes against you. *15* But if you do

---

[1] ὑποκριτής, *hupokrites*, usually mistranslated as "hypocrite" was actually an overly critical, hair splitting, pedantic, religious (legalistic) type. Indeed, ὑποκριτής, *hupokrites*, has today become our word "hypocrite". However, this modern meaning has as yet only been traced back to the 13th century A.D. ὑποκριτής, *hupokrites*, developed a meaning of one who recited Greek poetry or drama, particularly Homer. These people were not actors in our sense of the word and the word ὑποκριτής, *hupokrites*, also described someone who spoke eloquently and was skilled in speaking out the written word. It did not come to mean "actor" (that is, someone pretending to be someone they are not) until the 2nd c. A.D. At the time the New Testament was written, ὑποκριτής, *hupokrites*, meant "hypercritical", "overcritical", not meaning critical of people, but critical in overly examining matters. It refers a nit-picking, pedantic sort of person, someone who splits hairs and is legalistic. See study by W.F. Albright and C.S. Mann, "Appendix: Hupokrisis, Hupokrites, Hupokrinesthai", The *Anchor Bible: Matthew*, (New York: Doubleday, 1982), pp. cxv-cxxiii. On p.73 Albright and Mann state, "In face of the evidence nothing can justify the continued use of the word 'hypocrite' in our English translations."

[2] The word "openly" does not appear here, nor is there any implication of it in the grammar. It appears in the Textus Receptus, and thereby in the KJV, as it was added by copyists in order to make a parallelism with the preceding phrase "in secret".

[3] "Pray like this", not pray in these words. It is ironic that the very passage of Scripture where we are warned not to pray by repeating words over and over again is the very passage which is more than any other repeated over and over again!

[4] The same words are used in Deut. 15:2 for the cancellation of debts, and lending. The word ἁμαρτία, *hamartia*, "sin" does not occur here.

[5] περιασμός, *periasmos*, ordeal. The cognate verb πειράζω, *peirazo*, means to put through an ordeal, to be harassed, not to be tempted. See note on Matt. 4:1.

[6] ἀφίημι, *aphiemi*, used in a legal sense, "discharge", "remit", cf. Hdt. 6.30; Dem. 540.11; Arist. *Clouds*, 1426, Andoc. 13.19. ἀφίημι, *aphiemi*, is here with the dative of person, accusative of thing and dative of advantage (with a common genitive of possession). ἀφίημι, *aphiemi*, means "forgive" if it has the accusative of person, which is not the case here. Here it has the dative of person, which is used in a legal sense, to cancel a loan (debt) or remit a charge. The word "loans", τὰ ὀφείλματα, *ta opheilemata*, is used for loans or

hold people's mistakes against them, then your Father will hold your mistakes against you.[1]

16-18 "When you fast don't be like the overly critical, hair splitting, pedantic religious people who put on a sad face! They disguise their faces so people will think they're fasting. Let me make this clear; they will get what's coming to them! *17* When you fast, make sure you wash your hair and wash your face, *18* so that people can't tell you're fasting just by looking at you. You'll only appear that way to your Father who is in the secret place, and your Father who is watching you in secret will reward you!

19-24 "Don't put your wealth in a bank for yourselves on earth, where moths and rust can destroy it and where thieves can break in and steal it! *20* Instead, put your wealth in a bank in heaven, where moths and rust don't destroy it, and thieves don't break in and steal it. *21* In fact, your mind will be where your bank is! *22* The body's light is generosity.[2] If you are generous, you will be full of light. *23* But if you are greedy,[3] your whole body will be in darkness! And if the light in you is in fact dark, then the darkness in you is huge! *24* "No one can be the slave servant[4] of two masters; then they would hate one and love the other, or alternatively would be loyal to the one and despise the other. You are not able to serve both God and wealth.[5]

25-34 "This is why I tell you this: don't worry about your life, what you're going to eat or what you're going to drink. Don't worry about your body, about what clothes you will wear. Isn't life more important than food? Isn't the body more important than clothing? *26* Take birds for example - they don't sow seed or harvest crops or gather it into barns, and your Father of heaven feeds them.

---

monetary debts in the Greek language. The quote from the famous historian Thucydides 2.40 shows his use of the word: "it will be more like paying back a loan than giving something spontaneously."

[1] παράπτωμα, *paraptoma*, "blunder", always distinguished from ἁμαρτία, *hamartia*, "sin", in the N.T.

[2] Word for word "The body's light is the eye" but is in fact an idiom. "Eye" was the Greek metaphor for generosity. Here ὀφθαλμός, *ophthalmos*, but note, ὄμμα, *omma*, "eye" is a formally polite term of endearment meaning "treasure", cf. Aristophanes, *Acharnians*, 1184; Aeschylus, *Cho.* 238; Sophocles, *Aj.* 977.

[3] πονηρός, *poneros*, eye being evil is Greek idiom for being greedy and stingy.

[4] δουλεύω, *douleuo*, to be a slave servant, the noun being δουλὸς, *doulos*. The word usually translated "servants" in most N.T. versions is not "servant", but "slave". It most certainly does not mean "bondservant", although some translators have used this as a euphemism for "slave". Slaves of the time were sometimes considered to be on the same level as children, and many were eventually adopted. Sometimes they inherited the master's property. Of course, others were treated as slaves in accordance with our modern perception of the word. Due to the complex nature of the relationship, the term is here rendered "slave servant". See discussion in S.R. Llewelyn, "Slaves and Masters" *NDIEC* 6.48-81; "The Legal Capacity of a Slave", *NDIEC* 7.165f.

[5] μαμωνᾶς, *mamonas*. Mammon was a common Hebrew word in the second temple period. It appears in Ben Sira (Ecclesiastes) 31:11 and in the Mishnaic Hebrew of 1st c. Jewish teachers. Contemporary Jewish commentary interpreted the word as "wealth", as did the Qumran writings. Some commentaries wrongly state that it is an Aramaic word exclusively or that Mammon was the Syrian demon-god of greed or at the least the personification thereof. Such interpretations appear in *The Catholic Encyclopedia*, Vol IX, New York 1910; C. Padjen, "Mammon", Dept. Theology, University of Notre Dame, 1997; A.L. Munroe, "Money, Mammon and Wealth", Paper presented at the Faith-Learning Institute, Cedarville College, (Cedarville, OH, 1995).

Aren't you worth more than birds? *27* Which of you can add any time to your lifespan[1] just by worrying? *28* And why do you worry about clothes? Think about how the lilies of the field grow; they don't work or spin wool! *29* Yet I'm telling you that even Solomon in all his splendor was not dressed like one of these! *30* And since God clothes the grass of the field in this way, which today exists, but tomorrow is thrown into a cooking pan, how much more will he clothe you, you person with little faith?

31 "So don't worry and say, 'What are we going to eat?' or 'What are we going to drink?' or 'What are we going to wear?' *32* The people who worship other gods go running after all these things. Your Father of heaven knows that you need all these things. *33* Make your priority to go running after Heaven's Realm, as well as seek his justice, and all these things will be set in front of you! *34* So don't be preoccupied about the next day, for the next day will be preoccupied about its own things! The day takes cares of[2] its own problems.

Ch.7:1-6 "Do not judge, in case you are judged. *2* You will be judged with the sort of judgment with which you judge! That same measure will be used to judge you! *3* And why is it that you look at the splinter in your fellow believer's eye, but don't give a thought to the plank of wood in your own eye? *4* How can you say to your fellow believer, 'Let me take out the splinter in your eye,' but there's a plank of wood in your own eye! *5* You overly critical, hair splitting, pedantic religious person! First take the plank of wood out of your own eye, and then you'll be able to see clearly to take the splinter out of your fellow believer's eye!

6 "Don't give anything sacred to dogs or throw your pearls in front of pigs, because they'll crush them underfoot and tear you to pieces!

7-12 "Ask and it will be given to you, seek and you will find, knock and the door will be opened for you.[3] *8* Everyone who asks receives, and everyone who seeks finds, and the door will be opened for the person who knocks. *9* Would any one of you, if your child asked for bread, hand them a stone? *10* And what if they asked you for a fish? Would you hand them a snake? *11* So then, if you know how to give good gifts to your children although you are evil, how much more will your Father in the heavenly places give good gifts to people who ask him! *12* Treat others how you would like to be treated! This is the meaning of the Law and the Prophets.

13-20 "Go in through the narrow gateway. The road that leads to Destruction is a very wide road and the gateway to it is open ground. Many people go through it! *14* On the other hand, the road that leads to Life has oppressions along the way and the gateway is narrow, and few people find it!

---

[1]   Equally, "Which of you can add 1 cubit (18 inches/1 metre) to your height?" The semantic range of ἡλικία, *helikia*, includes "lifespan" and "height". The semantic range of πῆχυς, *rekhus*, includes "length", "time" (as in Psalm 39:5), or "cubit".

[2]   ἀρκετός (ἀρκέω), *arketos* (*arkeo*) in its primary meaning "wards off", verbal adjective used in active sense.

[3]   It has been written in many commentaries that this means we are to ask continually, knock continually and seek continually. However the use of the present infinitive in Hellenistic Greek commonly expressed a general command, whether to an individual or group. The aorist imperative is preferred for a command which relates to conduct or attitude in a specific case, and as such commands are less frequent in the New Testament, we find the present imperative to be more common. Thus the present imperative in Matthew 7:7 does not mean "Keep on asking": it means, "Ask" and we are to realize that this is a general command, rather than to ask only in a specific incident. For full discussion see J. Thorley, "Aktionsart in New Testament Greek: Infinitive and Imperative", *NovT* 31 (1989) 290-315; B.M. Fanning, *Verbal Aspect in New Testament Greek*, (Oxford: Clarendon Press, 1990), *passim*.

15 "Beware of false prophets. They will come to you in sheep's clothing, but inwardly they're vicious hungry wolves. *16* You will have no trouble recognizing them by the consequences of their actions. Does anyone pick grapes from thorn bushes, or figs from thistles? *17* Nice fruit grows on good trees, but evil fruit grows on rotten trees. *18* Evil fruit can't grow on a good tree, and nice fruit can't grow on a rotten tree. *19* Every tree that doesn't produce nice fruit is cut down and thrown into the fire. *20* In the same way too you will recognize them by what they produce.

21-23 "Only the person who carries out the purpose of my Father who is in the heavenly places will enter Heaven's Realm. Not everyone who says, 'Lord, Lord', will enter it! *22* On that day many will say to me, 'Lord, Lord, haven't we prophesied in your name? Haven't we thrown out demons in your name and done many wonders in your name?'

23 "Then I will admit to them, 'I never fully knew you! Get away from me, you lawless lot!'

24-27 "Everyone who hears what I have to say and acts on it can be compared to a wise man who built his house on rock. *25* The rain poured down, the floods came, the wind beat on the house, but it didn't fall down because it was built on rock. *26* Everyone who hears what I have to say and doesn't act on it can be compared to a stupid man who built his house on the sand. *27* The rain poured down, the floods came, the wind beat on the house, and it fell down flat!"

28-29 Jesus had finished speaking. The people were deeply impressed by his teaching *29* because he taught with authority, not like the Bible scholars.

Ch.8:1-4 Large crowds followed Jesus down from the mountain. *2* A leper arrived and threw himself to his knees to worship him. He exclaimed, "Lord, if you want to, you can make me clean!"

3 Jesus touched him. He said, "I want to! Be cleansed!" and immediately he was cleansed from his leprosy. *4* Jesus said "See to it that you don't tell anyone. Off you go, show yourself to the priest and make the offering that Moses commanded. This will be proof that you don't have leprosy anymore."

5-13 *5-6* When Jesus entered Capernaum, a Roman officer in charge of 100 men turned up. "Lord, my servant is lying at home paralyzed!" he begged. "He's undergoing terrible torture!"

7 "I will come and heal him!" Jesus replied.

8 The Roman officer in charge of 100 men answered, "Lord, I'm not worthy enough to have you come under my roof! Please just say the word, and my servant will be instantly divinely healed![1] *9* I too am a person under authority, and I have soldiers under me. I tell one soldier, 'Go!' and he goes, I tell another soldier, 'Come here!' and he comes; I tell my slave, 'Do this!' and he does it!"

10 Jesus was amazed. He said to the people who followed, "For a fact, I haven't found such great faith even in Israel! *11* Let me emphasize this, many will come from east and west, and sit down with Abraham, Isaac and Jacob in

---

[1] ἰάομαι, *iaomai*, "instantly divinely healed". ἰάομαι, *iaomai* was used to refer to miraculous healing by the agency of Asklepios and also by doctors. It was associated with divine intervention and used by the Hippokratic medical school in the sense of a quick-fix cure. In Greek literature from Homer to NT times it usually occurs in the aorist stressing its instant aspect. Galen uses it to refer to the miraculous healing of a man who had swelled up so much that he could not move. E.& L. Edelstein, *Asclepius: A Collection and Interpretation of the Testimonies*, 1945, Vol. 1., Baltimore, T 458, *De Morborum Differentiis* Cp. 9, [VI, p. 869 K.] ἰάομαι, *iaomai* is the verb used in the LXX to describe healing by God. See also *IG* 11^2 1.1.772.13 (Athens, 252/1 BC); *PSI* 6.6665.5 (Philadelpheia, 111 BC); *IG* 11^2 3.1.4514.14 (Athens, II AD). Note unusual use in *P.Was.Univ.* 2.106.3 (Oxyrhynchos, 18 BC), letter, "Dionysia to Panchetes her brother, many greetings. ...You heard that the builders have fixed my house..."

Heaven's Realm, *12* but the people of the Realm will be thrown into outer darkness! There will be great sorrow, pain and anguish!"

13 Jesus said to the Roman officer in charge of 100 men, "On your way! You've got what you believed!" And his servant was instantly divinely healed at that very moment.

14-17 When Jesus arrived at Peter's house, he saw his mother-in-law sick in bed with fever. *15* He touched her hand, and the fever left her. She jumped up and made dinner for him. *16* When evening came, many people who had evil spirits to were brought to him. He threw out the spirits by speaking and healed everyone who was sick. *17* This fulfilled Isaiah the prophet's words: "He took our sicknesses and carried away our diseases."

18-22 Jesus saw a crowd gathering, so gave orders to leave for the other side of the lake. *19* A Bible scholar came up said, "Teacher, I'll follow you wherever you go!"

20 "Foxes have dens and birds have nests," Jesus replied, "but the Human Being[1] doesn't have anywhere to stay for the night!"[2]

21 One of the other disciples said, "Lord, please let me go to organize my father's funeral."

22 But Jesus refused. "Follow me! Let the dead bury their own dead!"

23-27 He got into a boat and his disciples followed. *24* Suddenly a storm came up on the sea, so huge that the waves began swamping the boat. Jesus was asleep. *25* His disciples went over to him and exclaimed, "Lord, save us! We're sinking!"

26 Jesus remarked, "Why are you scared, you faithless lot?"

Then he got up and rebuked the winds and the sea, and there was a great calm. *27* The people were amazed! "Who is this guy!" they said incredulously. "Even the winds and the sea listen[3] to him!"

---

[1] ὁ υἱὸς τοῦ ἀνθρώπου, *ho huios tou anthropou*, meaning a person associated with humanity, a translation of *bar nasha*, an Aramaic periphrasis for "person", would be read word for word as "one associated with humanity" (as it is in non-gender specific language and "humanity" is in the singular). However, *bar nasha* means "one associated with people", "a person", "the person", "humanity", "the representative person". *The Anchor Bible* translates "The Man". The title is a direct reference to Daniel 7:13-14. See lengthy discussion in J. Massingberd Ford, "'Son of Man – A Euphemism?" *JBL* 87 (1968), 257-67: Albright, W.F. and Mann, C.S. *Matthew: A New Translation with Introduction and Commentary*, (New York: Doubleday, 1982), pp. CLVI-CLVII, 95; G. Dalman, *The Works of Jesus*, Eng. trans. by D.M. Kay, (Edinburgh, 1902); V. Taylor, *op.cit.*, p. 197.

υἱός, *huios*, with a noun refers to a member of a class of people, and should not be translated as "son/child of". The *Benai Israel*, translated in the KJV as "children/sons of Israel" should be translated as "members of the class of people called Israel" = "Israelites". The expression is also Greek, and found as early as Homer. Note also that ἄνθρωπος, *anthropos*, is the word for human, humanity, person. Grammatically, it is the common gender and not the masculine.

[2] Jesus is traveling. He is not saying he is a homeless person, merely that he is not in his home town and has nowhere to stay the night.

[3] ὑπακούω, *hupakouo*, listen (and act on it), pay attention, cf. Plato *Rep.* 459 C "..and we commonly consider that a comparatively low-grade doctor can treat patients who are prepared to follow a diet and do not need medicine..."; Hdt 3.14, Cleomenes listened to temptation; to listen to, to give ear to, cf. Arist. *Wasps.* 273; 319; *Il.* 8.4 "...Zeus...held an assembly of the gods on...Olumpos. He began to address them, and all the gods gave him their attention."; *Od.* 14.485 "He readily paid attention"; Eur. *Alc.* 400, "Listen, mother, listen to me, I beg of you. Mother, it is me who is calling you..." *Il.* 8. 4. "Listen to me all you gods."; "To listen and answer" cf. *Od* 4.283 "...we heard you calling and were both tempted to jump up and come out or give an instant answer from within." *Od* 10.83

28-34 When Jesus got to the other side, to the Gadarenes district, he was met by two people who had evil spirits. They were coming out of the cemetery. In fact, they were so extremely fierce that it wasn't safe for anyone to take the road past the cemetery. *29* Suddenly they shouted, "What are you meddling with us for, Son of God? Have you come here to torment us? You're not supposed to yet!"

30 There was a large herd of pigs feeding some distance away. *31* The demon-gods[1] kept begging him, "If you're going to throw us out, please send us into that herd of pigs!"

32 So he granted it, "Off you go!"

They came out and went into the pigs. Suddenly the whole herd stampeded over the edge of the cliff into the sea and drowned. *33* The pig keepers ran away. They went into the city and spread the news about the whole incident, including the news about the people who'd had the evil spirits. *34* Then the whole city came out to meet Jesus. They begged him to leave their region.

Ch.9:1-8 Jesus got into a boat and crossed back over to his own city. *2* Some people brought a paralyzed person lying on a stretcher over to him. When Jesus saw their faith he said to the paralyzed person, "Be brave, my child, your sins are canceled!"

3 Immediately some of the Bible scholars exclaimed to each other, "He's blaspheming!"

4 Jesus knew what they were thinking. "Why do you think evil thoughts?" he questioned them. *5* "What's easier to say, 'Your sins are canceled,' or to say, 'Get up and walk'? *6* But so that you know that the Human Being has power on earth to cancel sins…" He broke off and said to the paralyzed person, "Get up, take up your bed and go to your house!" *7* With that, the paralyzed person got up and went home. *8* When the crowds saw this, they were shocked. They praised God for giving people power such as this.

9-13 As Jesus passed on from there, he saw a person by the name of Matthew sitting at the Tax Profiteer's office, and said to him, "Follow me!" Matthew jumped up and followed him. *10* While he was in the house reclining at the dinner table, several Tax Profiteers and sinners arrived and reclined with him and his disciples.

11 When the Pharisees noticed that, they said to his disciples, "How come your teacher sits with Tax Profiteers and sinners?"

12 "Who needs a doctor:[2] healthy people or sick people?" Jesus replied. "Now go and figure out what this means, *13* 'I'm looking for mercy, not religious sacrifice.' I'm not here to invite righteous people, I'm here to invite sinners."

"Herdsman calls to herdsman as one brings in his flocks and the other answers as he drives out his." "To answer an enquiry" cf. Andoc 15.13. "To answer a knock at the door" cf. Plato *Crito* 43A.

[1] δαίμων, *daimon*, "demon-god", not to be confused with, δαιμόνιον, *daimonion*, "demon". It occurs only here and in Rev. 16:14; 18:2. The parallel gospels use δαιμόνιον, *daimonion*, here for Matthew's use of δαίμων, *daimon*.

[2] ἰατρός, *iatros*, a qualified medical practitioner. *I.Stratonikeia* 2.1.1202.6, 11 (Stratonikeia, II) "Epaphroditos, you raised up many sick people. As a doctor you were very friendly to everyone, and good at your profession and diligent in character, for you learnt deeper understanding of your profession. But you could not save yourself from disease, for Fate is more masterful than doctors"; *P.Oxy* 1.40.5, 9 (Oxyrhynchos, II-III), "Psasnis presented himself and said, 'I am a doctor by profession and have treated these very people who have brought the case against me.' Eudaimon said, 'Perhaps you treated them badly. Inform the *strategos* if you are a public service doctor, suitably qualified, for then you will have immunity from the case".

14-17 Then John's disciples asked him, "Why is it that we and the Pharisees fast, but your disciples don't fast at all?"

15 Jesus replied, "Are wedding guests sad while they are celebrating with the bridegroom? Of course not! They are only sad when the bridegroom leaves, and then they will fast. *16* And no one mends clothes with a patch of unshrunk cloth, because the patch will shrink and make an even worse tear. *17* No one puts new wine into old wineskins. That makes the wineskins burst. Then the wine is spilled, and the wineskins are ruined. Instead, they put new wine into new wineskins, and both are safe."

18-22 He was right in the middle of announcing this to them, when a ruler arrived and worshipped him on his knees. "My daughter has just died," he said, "but if you come and lay your hand on her, she will live!" *19* Jesus got up and went with him, and so did his disciples.

20 Suddenly a woman who had been subject to a blood loss for twelve years came from behind and touched the hem of his robe. *21* She had said to herself, "If only I can touch his robe, I will be rescued and preserved."[1]

22 But Jesus turned to her and said, "Cheer up, daughter, your faith has made you well!" At that very instant, the woman was rescued and preserved.

23-26 When Jesus arrived at the ruler's house and saw the flute players and the noisy crowd making a disturbance, *24* he said, "Get out of the way! The young girl's[2] not dead – she's just asleep!" They responded by poking fun at him.

25 His response was to throw the crowd outside. Then he went inside and grabbed the young girl by the hand. *26* This news spread all over the land.

27-34 When Jesus left there, two blind people followed him. They yelled out, "Have pity on us, David's descendant!"

28 When he arrived at the house, the blind people came over to him. Jesus asked them, "Do you believe that I am able to do this?"

"Yes, Lord!" they replied.

29 Then he touched their eyes and said, "It will happen to you because of your faith!" *30* And their eyes were opened! Jesus spoke sternly to them, "See, no one is to know about it."

31 On the contrary, as soon as they left they spread the news about him all over land. *32* While they were leaving, some people brought a mute who had a evil spirit to Jesus. *33* When the demon was thrown out the mute person spoke plainly. The crowds were shocked. "Nothing like this has ever happened in Israel!" they exclaimed.

34 The Pharisees' opinion was, "He's throwing out demons by the power of the demons' ruler!"

35-38 Jesus traveled around all the cities and villages, teaching in their synagogues, proclaiming the Good News of Heaven's Realm, and healing all kinds of disease and all kinds of ailments. *36* But when he saw the crowds he was deeply moved with compassion, because they were stressed and helpless,

---

[1] σώζω, *sozo*, in healing context, "rescue and preserve". It describes deliverance from suffering (and possible death) *IG* II[2], no. 4514 (App. 3:3) *l*.13 and is associated with divine intervention, usually in life-threatening situations/illnesses/injuries. σώζω, *sozo*, was used in the meaning "rescue and preserve" by Homer, *Iliad* 11.828-831, and Athenian authors, for example, Euripides, *Hippolytos*, 497, 501, 705. It was used by Aristides (Publius Aelius), in the meaning "rescue or preserve from danger". E.& L. Edelstein, *Asclepius: A Collection and interpretation of the testimonies*, 1945, Vol. 1., Baltimore, T 282, *Or*. 38.19. Galen uses it to refer to the result of being rescued and preserved from a life-threatening abscess. E.& L. Edelstein, *Asclepius: A Collection and interpretation of the testimonies*, 1945, Vol. 1., Baltimore, T 458, *De Libris Propriis* Cp. 2, [II, p99 M.]

[2] κοράσιον, *korasion*, young girl, used only in familiar language, often as a pet name.

like sheep without a shepherd. *37* Then he said to his disciples, "On the one hand there's a big harvest, but on the other hand there are not enough workers. *38* So then put a request to the Harvest Master so that he will throw workers into his harvest!"

Ch.10:1-8 Jesus called over the Twelve disciples. He gave them power to throw out unclean spirits, and to heal all kinds of sicknesses and all kinds of ailments. *2* Here are the names of the Twelve apostles:[1] Simon (called Peter) and his brother Andrew, and James and John the sons of Zebedee, *3* Philip, Bartholomew, Thomas, Matthew the Tax Profiteer, James (Alphaeus' son), Thaddeus, *4* Simon the Caananite, and Judas Iscariot, the one who later betrayed him. *5* Jesus sent out these twelve people with the orders: "Don't travel to where the non-Jews live, and don't go into a Samaritan city. *6* You are to go to the Israelites – they're like a flock of lost sheep! *7* This is what you are to preach on your travels: 'Heaven's Realm is close!' *8* "Heal the sick, raise the dead, cleanse the lepers, throw out demons! Be generous because you have been treated generously!

9-15 "Don't take a lot of money in your wallets. *10* Don't pack a bag for your trip, and don't take an extra shirt, shoes, or walking stick – a worker deserves board and lodging. *11* When you arrive at a city or village, ask around and find out who the worthy people are and stay with them until it's time to leave. *12* When you go into someone's home, be very nice. If the home is worthy, bless it with peace. *13* But if it isn't worthy, take your peace blessing back. *14* Now if you come across certain people who don't want to hear what you have to say and don't treat you well, this is what you are to do. When you leave that particular house or city, shake the dust from your feet - this will demonstrate that you think they are pagans![2] *15* Let me make this clear, the land of Sodom and Gomorrah will be better off in the Day of Judgment than that city!

16-20 "I'm sending you out like sheep into a pack of wolves! So have the practical wisdom of serpents and be as uncorrupt as doves. *17* But beware of people! They will drag you to the authorities! They will beat you in their synagogues with the Roman whip embedded with metal strips that rip off the flesh. *18* Because of me, you will be dragged off to politicians and kings to give evidence to them as well as to the non-Jews.   *19* Now, when you're hauled before these authorities, don't be preoccupied about what you will say. Words will actually be given to you at the time. *20* You won't be the ones doing the talking. It will be the Spirit of your Father who is speaking through you.

21-25 "People will turn on each other - a sibling[3] will have their sibling executed, and a parent,[4] their child, and children will turn against their parents[5] and have them executed. *22* Lots of people will hate you because of

---

[1]   ἀπόστολος, *apostolos*, a person or thing (such as ship) that is sent out, a messenger, envoy. Occurs in *P.Oxy* II.522 as "ship"; *Syll.* 153 as "fleet"; in *P.Oxy* X.1259 as "message".
[2]   The shaking of the dust is idiom for the act of demonstrating that the people are considered to be pagans.
[3]   ὁ ἀδελφός, *ho adelphos*. See note on Matt. 5:22.
[4]   πατήρ, *pater*, occurs in the papyri and inscriptions as an honorific title. The word could mean "father" but also meant "female parent/mother", or just "parent", non-gender specific. P.J. Sijpesteijn lists two examples in papyri of individual women called *pater*, *Tyche* 2.171-74.
[5]   The use of γονεύς, *goneus*, instead of πατέρες, *pateres*, in verse 4 is interesting. γονεύς, *goneus*, occurs here where the attitude of children to parents is in focus. This is echoed in the papyri of the time and follows an old tradition. The Eleusinian precept was that people were to honor their parents: γονεῖς τιμᾶν, *goneus timan*. A inscription (aretalogy of Iris) from the late second or earliest first century B.C. had the word γονεῖς, *goneis*, when describing children

me. But the person who lasts to the end will be rescued and preserved. *23* If they persecute you in one city, escape to another one! You will still have some options open when the Human Being comes! *24* A student isn't better than the teacher, an employee isn't better than the boss. *25* A student should be pleased to be like the teacher and an employee should be pleased to be like the boss. Since they called me, the boss and teacher, Beelzebub, imagine what they will call my employees and students!

26-28 "Don't be afraid of them! Everything will come out into the open. *27* What I tell you now in the dark, speak in broad daylight! What you hear in private, go public with! *28* Don't be afraid of people who kill the body but can't kill the soul! Instead, fear him who can destroy both soul and body in the Garbage Pit Gehenna!

29-33 "Aren't two sparrows sold for a penny? Your Father is aware of every sparrow that falls out of its tree! *30* In fact he knows how many hairs you have on your head! *31* So then don't be afraid – you're worth more than lots of sparrows.

32 "If someone acknowledges me publicly, I will acknowledge them in front of my Father who is in the heavenly places. *33* If someone denies me publicly, I will deny them in front of my Father in the heavenly places.

34-42.Ch.11:1 "Don't think that I came to bring peace on the earth! No, I have come with a razor blade, *35* to cut between a person and their parent, a daughter and her mother, a daughter-in-law and her mother-in-law! *36* Someone's enemies will be those close to them! *37* Anyone who puts their father or mother first, before me, isn't worthy of me. Anyone who puts their son or daughter first, before me, isn't worthy of me. *38* And anyone who doesn't pick up their cross and follow me isn't worthy of me!

39 "The person who gets a life without my help will lose it. The person who lets it all go and lets me take over will get a life. *40* The person who welcomes you actually welcomes me. *41* The person who welcomes me welcomes the one who sent me. The person who welcomes a prophet simply because they are a prophet, will receive a prophet's reward. The person who welcomes a just person simply because they are a just person, will receive a just person's reward. *42* And whoever gives one of my followers a cup of cold water simply because that person is my follower, will be rewarded for sure – and let me make this very clear!"

1 After Jesus finished instructing his twelve disciples, he left to proclaim his teachings in their cities.

2-6 John was in prison. When he heard about what the Anointed One was doing, he sent his disciples *3* to enquire, "Are you the Coming One, or do we look for someone else?"

4 This was Jesus' response: "Go and tell John what you can hear and see for yourselves: *5* the blind see again, the crippled are walking about, lepers are cleansed and the deaf hear, the dead have risen and the financially poor are having the Good News announced[1] to them. *6* The person who doesn't reject me because of what I do is a happy person!"

---

honoring their parents, and πατέρες, *pateres*, when not in that specific context: "You made parents (γονεῖς, *goneis*) honored by their children, in that you cared for them not only as parents (πατέρων, *pateron*), but also as gods." (Y. Grandjean, *Une nouvelle aretalogie d'Isis a\ Maronée* (Lieden, 1975), pls. 1-3.) Note that the use in the inscription parallels the use here in Ephesians. See also *I.Kyme* 41 for γονεῖς, *goneis,* used of attitude from children to parents.

[1] εὐαγγελίζομαι, *euaggelizomai.* There are several εὐαγγελ-, *euaggel-* words in the N.T. ("announce the Good News"). This is not a "specialist" Christian term at all. Horsley, *NDIEC* 3.12, states, "These parallels with NT vocabulary and usage illustrate how normal is the language employed in the NT." See *P.Oxy.* 3313 (2nd C. A.D.), "You gave us great happiness when you

7-10 After John's disciples left, Jesus started telling the crowds about John. "What did you expect to see when you went out into the wilderness? A skinny plant blowing around in the wind? *8* What did you expect to see? A person wearing fancy clothes? No way! People who wear fancy clothes live in palaces. *9* What did you expect to see? A prophet? That's right, and he's more than a prophet. *10* He is the prophet mentioned here: 'I send my messenger on ahead of you. He will prepare the road for you.'

11-15 "I tell you, no human in history has been more important than John the Baptizer! Yet the most insignificant person in Heaven's Realm is more important than he! *12* From the time of John the Baptizer until now, Heaven's Realm is being used or even robbed by people who have no legal right to it.[1] This stops those who do have a legal right to it from enjoying their own property.[2]

13 "All the Prophets and the Law prophesied what was going to happen up to the time of John. *14* If you're willing to accept what they say, he is the Elijah who was meant to come! *15* If you have ears you had better listen!

---

announced the good news of most noble Sarapion's marriage." For εὐαγγελίζομαι, *euaggelizomai*, and εὐαγγελίζω, *euaggelizo*, see *IGRR* 4; *P.Oxy* 16 ("I again announce the Good News..."); *P.Oxy* 33313; *P.Giss*.27 = *CPJ* 2, in which a slave is coming to announce the good news of a victory. For εὐαγγέλιον, *euaggelion*, see *SB* 1 (soon after 238 AD), "since I have become aware of the good news..."; (this is listed with others in BDAG showing the Christian usage which, however, parallels the ordinary secular usage.) There are many non-N.T. instances of the neuter plural noun of εὐαγγέλιον, *euaggelion*, (εὐαγγέλια, *euaggelia*) in Hellenistic times, used to prefer to good news of victories connected with royalty. The singular only occurs in the N.T. The word dates back to Classical times, e.g. Aristophanes, *Knights*, 656. Horsley, *NDIEC* 2.13, notes that the word is used three times by Cicero in letters to Atticus (60 B.C. to 45 B.C.) εὐαγγελιστής, *euaggelistes*, occurs in the N.T. only in Acts 21:8; Eph. 4:11 and 2 Tim. 4:5. In pagan use, it referred to the proclaimer of oracular messages. In Christian sources (and possibly non-Christian documentary sources; *IG* XII.1 is problematical) it referred to those who announced good news, e.g. *P.Oxy* 8, 1151.45; *P.Lond.* 5; SB 3.1; *CPR* 1. See also Spicq, *NLNT* 3.296-306. Note also that the name Euangelos is well attested with no Christian connection.

[1] *Bia* refers to illegal forcible acquisition. The term is a technical legal term referring to the act of hindering an owner or lawful possessor of his/her enjoyment of immovable property. This was technically known as *bia* in legal terminology. *Bia* was a term used in public, civil and criminal law, and its most prevalent usage was in criminal law. It was used for different wrongs that entail the use of force. It is important to note that the use of property without the lawful consent of the owner was considered to be a *bia*, and the suit prosecuted against the *bia* did not have to depend on actual force used by the accused. The point was that it was contrary to the legal owner's rights, and thus was considered to be a forcible act. See lengthy discussion in S.R. Llewelyn, "Forcible Acquisition and the Meaning of Matt. 11.12", *NDIEC* 7, 1994, pp. 130-162.

[2] ἁρπάζω, *harpazo*, used of immovable property means to plunder. It was associated with *bia* as a legal technical term. O. Betz, "Jesu Heiliger Krieg", *NovT* 2 (1958), pp. 125ff, *idem*, "The Eschatological Interpretation of the Sinai-Tradition in Qumran and in the New Testament", *RQ* 6 (1967), pp. 99ff; Llewelyn, *ibid.*, p. 154 states, "Sufficient evidence has already been cited above to show that both βία (*bia*) and ἁρπάζω (*harpazo*), together with their cognates were used in legal terminology with reference to forcible acquisition." See *P.Oxy.* XLV 3240 (AD 88/9) for the use of ἁρπάζω, *harpazo*, for the illegal seizure of land.

16-19 "To what can I compare this race of people? It's like children who sit in the playgrounds and yell to their friends, *17* 'We played music for you but you didn't dance - we cried and you weren't sad!'

18 "John didn't go around eating or drinking, and they say, 'He's got a demon!' *19* The Human Being went around eating and drinking, and they say, 'He's a greedy pig and a drunkard! He's friends with Tax Profiteers and sinners.' Yet Wisdom[1] is shown to be right, by the people who associate with it!"

20-24 "Then Jesus began to reproach the cities in which he had done powerful things, because they didn't change their minds. *21* "Woe to you, Korazin, woe to you Bethsaida! If the powerful things done in you had been done in Tyre and Sidon,[2] they would have changed their minds long ago! They would have dressed in rags and put ashes on their heads to show they were sorry! *22* Tyre and Sidon will be better off than you in the Day of Judgment! *23* And you, Capernaum, will you be lifted up to heaven? No! You will be brought down to Hades,[3] because if the powerful things done in you had been done in Sodom, Sodom would still be here today! *24* The land of Sodom will be better off than you in the Day of Judgment!

Tyre.

Tyre in Roman Syria is mentioned in both the Old and New Testaments. As an island, it was very successful at defending itself from the Egyptians, Amorites and Babylonians. It fell to Alexander the Great who built a causeway across to it. Today it is in Lebanon, just across from Israel, and has been shelled frequently. In Paul's time it was an important and well defended port with marble streets, mosaic pavements, and huge granite colonnades from Aswan. It had a city of the dead with hundreds of huge marble sarcophagi.

25-30 It was about that time that Jesus said, "I agree with you in full, Father, Lord of heaven and earth, that you have hidden these things from clever people and have revealed them to ordinary people. *26* Yes, Father, this seemed good to you."

27 Jesus said to the people, "My Father has handed everything over to me. No one can really know me unless they know my Father. I am the only one who can understand the Father, but you too can understand him if you will let me reveal him to you. *28* If you are tired and weighed down, come to me and have a rest! *29* Harness up, with me at the reins, and learn from me. I am gentle and kind, and you will have a break from work. *30* I harness you up with kindness and don't weigh you down."

---

[1] σοφία, *sophia*, "wisdom" . Further understanding of the Greek concept of wisdom is to be found in Euripides' tragic play *Bacchae*. In the play Dionysus epitomizes wisdom, and Pentheus represents the wrong type of wisdom, ἄνομον, *anomon*, and ἄδικον, *adikon*. The conflict between the right and wrong types of wisdom is developed throughout the play and is basic to the meaning.

[2] Sidon was a port city like Tyre and prospered, like Tyre, through trade and the production of purple dye.

[3] The Greeks considered Hades to be the underworld, full of ghosts or wraiths of people who had died. The *Odyssey* speaks of Odysseus raising spirits from Hades and notes that these spirits could be strengthened when they drank blood. It also speaks of people continuing their earthly ways – for example, one person was hunting. It was spoken of as a terrifying, eerie place, but not specifically a place of punishment like Tartarus. Hades is commonly translated as "Hell" in most Bible versions, as are "Gehenna" and "Tartarus", yet to the Greeks, they were separate places. Tartarus was the lowest region of the underworld, said to be as far below Hades as the earth is under the sky. Tartarus was the place where the very wicked were punished, and the place where the angels who "went after strange flesh" (i.e. angels who "whored after" human women) were bound.

Ch.12:1-8 About that time Jesus went through the grain fields on the Sabbath. His disciples were hungry, so they started picking heads of grain and eating them. *2* The Pharisees noticed and said to Jesus, "Hey there, your disciples are breaking the Sabbath rules!"

3 Jesus answered, "Haven't you read what David did when he and his friends were hungry – *4* how he entered the House of God and ate the sacred bread?[1] It wasn't legal for him or his friends to eat it - it was only legal for the priests to eat it! *5* Haven't you read in the Law that on the Sabbath the priests in the temple desecrate the Sabbath,[2] but they're not guilty? *6* Listen to what I'm saying - in this place there is something more important than the temple! *7* But if you had understood the meaning of this statement, 'I am looking for mercy and not sacrifice,' you would not have condemned innocent people! *8* The Human Being is the Master of the Sabbath!"

9-15 After he left there, he went into their synagogue. *10* There was a person who had a withered hand! A question was put to Jesus: "Is it legal to heal on the Sabbath?" They asked the question in anticipation of his answer so they could bring charges against him.

11 This was Jesus' response. "Let's say one of you had a sheep that fell into a ditch on the Sabbath – is there any one of you that wouldn't grab it and lift it out? *12* Isn't a person worth more than a sheep? So obviously it's legal to do good things on the Sabbath!" *13* Then he said to the person, "Stretch out your hand." And the person stretched it out, and it was put right, restored to its original undamaged state,[3] just like the other one. *14* So the Pharisees went out and plotted against Jesus. They were making plans as to how they could kill him. *15* When Jesus discovered it, he left. He was followed by large crowds, and he healed them all.

16-21 However, he warned them not to tell anyone who he really was. *17* This was so that the words spoken by the prophet Isaiah would come to pass: *18* "My Son whom I have chosen, I dearly love him, I am pleased with him. I will place my Spirit upon him, and he will announce justice to the non-Jews. *19* He will not cause arguments or shout, and no one will hear his voice in the main streets. *20* He will not break a plant lying crushed. He will not put out a flame barely burning. His victory will bring justice, *21* and the non-Jews will set their hope on his name."

22-28 Then someone with a blind and mute spirit was brought over. Jesus healed him and the mute spoke and saw. *23* All the crowds were beside themselves with amazement! "Could this one be David's descendant?" they exclaimed.

24 When the Pharisees heard about it, they said, "He is driving out demons with the power of Beelzebub, the demon ruler!"

---

[1] This describes the 12 freshly baked loaves of bread placed every Sabbath in 2 rows on a table before God in the tabernacle and later eaten by the priests. (Leviticus 34.5-9)

[2] That is, the priests do work in connection with offering sacrifice on the Sabbath, and this actually breaks the Sabbath.

[3] ὑγίης, *hugies*, restoration to original undamaged state. ὑγίης, *hugies*, is used to describe a broken goblet which was restored to its original condition by the Greek healing god Asklepios. (*IG* IV[2], no. 121, 10.) There are 43 inscriptions of the Asklepios (healing cult of the god Asklepios) at Epidauros, and 29 of these describe the healing as ὑγίης, *hugies*. For example, a man who arrived blind and with only one eyeball departed seeing with both eyes (App. 2:1, 9), a bald man's hair grew again (App. 2:1, 19), and a crippled man walked unaided (App. 2:2, 35). ὑγίης, *hugies* is used to describe the restoration to the original undamaged state the patient enjoyed before the onset of the disorder for which the patient needed healing.

25 But Jesus knew what they were thinking. He said, "Every country that fights against itself ends up a wilderness, and every city or household that fights against itself won't last. *26* If Adversary throws out Adversary, he has thrown himself out! So how can his kingdom last? *27* And if I'm throwing out demons by Beelzebub's power, by whose power do your own people throw them out? This is why they will be your judges! *28* Yet if I throw out demons by the Spirit of God's power, then Heaven's Realm is here for sure!

29-32 "How can someone break into a strong person's house and rob it, unless they tie up[1] the strong person first? Then they can take off with the whole lot! *30* The person who isn't on my side is against me, and the person who doesn't gather people with me scatters them away! *31* This is the reason I tell you that people will be forgiven for every sin and blasphemy, but they will not be forgiven for blasphemy against the Spirit. *32* If you speak against the Human Being, you will be forgiven for it, but if you speak against the Holy Spirit, you will not be forgiven for it, neither in this age nor in the age to come.

33-37 "You know whether a tree is or good or bad by the fruit it produces. If you grow a good tree you will have good fruit, but if you grow a bad tree you will have bad fruit. *34* You pack of snakes! How can you, being evil, speak good things? The mouth speaks those things which overflow from the mind. *35* A good person hurls out good things out of the good stored up in them, and an evil person hurls out evil things out of the evil stored up in them. *36* It's a fact that people will have to give an account of every non-working word on the Day of Judgment – *37* for by your words you will have your rights claimed for you, and by your words you will be condemned!"

38-42 Then some of the Bible scholars and Pharisees said, "Teacher, we want you to give us a sign!"

39 "An evil and adulterous race of people looks for a sign," he replied, "but the only sign it will get is the sign of the prophet Jonah. *40* Jonah was in the belly of the sea-monster for three days and three nights, and the Human Being will be deep in the earth for three days and three nights. *41* The people of Nineveh will join in the judgment against this group of people and condemn them, because they changed their minds when Jonah preached, and indeed something more important than Jonah is here. *42* The queen of the south will join in the judgment against this group of people and condemn them, because she came from the ends of the earth to hear Solomon's wisdom. Truly something greater than Solomon is here!

43-46 "When an unclean spirit goes out of a person, it goes through waterless places, looking for rest, and doesn't find it. *44* Then it says, 'I'll go back to my house.' When it returns, it finds it vacant, swept and put in order. *45* Then it brings along seven other spirits more evil than itself, and they set up home. Then the person is worse off than they were in the first place! This is what will also happen with this evil group of people!"

46-50 While Jesus was still speaking to the crowds, his mother and siblings[2] were standing outside, wanting to speak with him. *47* Someone said to him, "Hey there, your mother and siblings are standing outside. They want to speak with you."

48 Who is my mother and who are my siblings?" Jesus asked. *49* He pointed to his disciples and said, "Here are my mother and my siblings! *50*

---

[1] δέω, *deo*, "bind", "tie up", is a most significant word. The pagans used the same term in their magical practices. The word "bind" occurs in the magical spells (or more specifically, words of power) known as the *Ephesian Grammata*. For example, see magic spell against a competitor in a chariot race: "I conjure you up, holy beings and holy names; join in aiding this spell, and bind, enchant, thwart, strike, overturn etc...".

[2] ἀδελφοί, *adelphoi*. See note on Matt. 5:22. Here Jesus uses the collective term for siblings, and then to be emphatic follows with the separate terms.

Whoever does the purpose of my Father in the heavenly places is indeed my brother, and sister, and mother."

Ch.13:1-9 On the same day Jesus left the house and sat by the sea. *2* Large crowds collected to see him, so he sat on a boat while the whole crowd stood on the shore. *3* He told them many things in examples. "A farmer went out to sow seed. *4* While he was sowing, some seed fell on the roadside, and the birds ate it. *5* Some seed fell on shallow soil over gravel. The plants immediately sprang up *6* but when the sun came up, they got scorched and withered away because they didn't have any roots. *7* Some seed fell among thorns which shot up and choked them. *8* Other seed fell on fertile ground and produced a harvest. The harvest produced thirty, sixty, or even a hundred times more than had been sown. *9* If you have ears you had better listen!"

10-15 The disciples approached to ask Jesus, "Why do you speak to them in examples?"

11 He answered, "You are permitted to know the secret hidden truths of Heaven's Realm, but they are not permitted to know. *12* More will be given to the person who already has something, and that person will have abundance. But those who don't have anything, even what they do have will be taken away. *13* I'm speaking to them in examples, because their eyes are open but they don't see, and they hear so much they still don't listen, nor do they understand. *14* This fulfills Isaiah's prophecy. It says: 'You will hear but will not understand. You will see, but not perceive. *15* The minds of this people have grown dull, their ears are hard of hearing They have shut their eyes. Otherwise they would see with their eyes, hear with their ears, understand with their minds, turn, and I would instantly divinely heal them.'

16-23 "You can be happy because your eyes see and your ears hear! *17* Many prophets and people who were just wished to see and hear what you see and hear. *18* Now listen to the example of the farmer. *19* The seed which fell on the roadside represents people who hear the message about the Realm but don't understand it, and the Evil One snatches away the understanding from their minds.

20 "The seed on stony places represents the people who hear the Word and immediately receive it quite happily. *21* But they don't have any roots, and so it only lasts for a while. When problems or persecution arise because of the Word, they immediately trip up. *22* The seed among the thorns represents the people who hear the Word, and preoccupation for this world and the treachery of wealth choke the Word, and they don't produce a harvest. *23* The seed on the good ground represents the people who hear the Word and understand it. These people really do bear fruit and produce a harvest. Some people produce a harvest a hundred times more than was sown; some produce sixty times more, and others thirty."

24-30 Then Jesus set another example in front of them. "This is a story about Heaven's Realm. A farmer sowed good seed in his field. *25* While everyone was asleep, his enemy planted troublesome weeds in the middle of the wheat then ran away. *26* When the grain had sprouted and produced a crop, then the troublesome weeds appeared too. *27* The owner's workers asked, 'Sir, didn't you sow good seed in your field? So why does it have troublesome weeds?'

28 "'An enemy did this!' he answered.

"The servants asked, 'Do you want us to go and rip out the weeds?'

29 "'No," he replied, "in case while you're in the process of ripping out the weeds you accidentally uproot the wheat at the same time. *30* Let both of them grow together until the harvest. Then at harvest time I'll tell the harvesters to collect the weeds first and tie them in bundles so they can be burned up, but to collect the wheat and put it in my barn."

31-32 He set another example in front of them: "This is a story about Heaven's Realm. Someone planted a mustard seed in their field. *32* A mustard seed is the smallest of all the seeds – that's for sure! But when it grows it's even larger than vegetables. In fact, it grows into a tree, and even birds roost in its branches!"

33-35 He told them another example. "This is a story about Heaven's Realm. A woman took some yeast and baked it in three lumps of dough, and then all the bread rose." *34* Jesus told the crowd all these things by using examples. In fact, he didn't speak to them without using examples. *35* This is so that the words spoken by the prophet would come to pass: "I will speak in examples, I will utter things kept hidden from the foundation of the world."

36-43 Then Jesus sent the crowds away and went into the house. His disciples came up and said, "Would you please explain the example of the weeds in the field to us."

37 "The person who sows the good seed is the Human Being," he answered. *38* "The field is the world, the good seeds are the people associated with the Realm, but the weeds are the people associated with the Evil One. *39* The enemy who sowed them is Slanderer-Liar, the harvest is the end of the age, and the harvesters are the Messengers. *40* The weeds are collected and burned in the fire, and this is what it will be like at the end of this age. *41* The Human Being will send out his Messengers, and they will collect everything that offends and those who practice illegal acts from his Realm. *42* They will throw them into the fiery furnace. There will be great sorrow, pain and anguish in the fiery furnace! *43* Then the people who are just will shine like the sun in their Father's Realm. If you have ears you had better listen!

44-52 "This is a story about Heaven's Realm. A person came across some treasure in a field, and hid it again there. They are so thrilled to find it that they sell everything they own to buy the field. *45* This is a story about Heaven's Realm. It is like a merchant searching for beautiful pearls. *46* When he had found one expensive pearl, he sold everything that he had to buy it. *47* This is a story about Heaven's Realm. It is like a net that was cast into the sea and drew up some of every kind of fish. *48* When it was full, they hauled it to shore and sat down and put the good fish in storage, but threw the bad fish away. *49* This is what it will be like at the end of the age. The Messengers will come out and separate the evil from the just *50* and throw the evil ones into the fiery furnace. There will be great sorrow, pain and anguish. *51* Have you understood all these things?"

They answered, "Yes".

52 He continued, "So then every Bible scholar who is instructed about Heaven's Realm is like a housekeeper, who produces both new and old things from the storeroom."

53-58 When Jesus had finished telling these examples, he left. *54* He arrived in his native land, where he taught them in their synagogues. They were beside themselves with amazement and exclaimed, "Where did this one get this wisdom and these powers? *55* Isn't he the skilled craftsperson's[1] son? Isn't his mother called Mary? And aren't his brothers James, Joseph, Simon

---

[1]   τέκτων, *tekton*, occurs only here and in Mark 6:3 in the N.T. and is properly translated as "skilled craftsperson". The word can mean any skilled craftsperson, metal worker cf. Eur. *Alc.* 5, sculptor cf. Eur. *Alc.* 348; Soph. *Tr.* 768, and even a master in any art, such as a gymnastic master, Pindar, N.5.90, or "master" in general, Aesch. *Ag.* 1406. The translation "carpenter" of the King James followed the limited scholarship of the 1600s. The word does appear as "joiner", "carpenter" in the *Iliad* 6.315, 5.59, 13.390, and in other authors such as Xen., *Mem.* 1.2, 37, yet Homer also uses the word to describe a craftsperson in horn, *Il.* 4.110. The Anchor Bible translates τέκτων, *tekton*, as "builder". Metaphorically, τέκτων, *tekton*, refers to the author, maker, cf. τέκτων γένους, *tekton genous*, the author of a race (of people), Aesch. *Supp.* 594, cf. 283. See also Aesch. *Ag.* 152, Eur. *Med.* 408.

and Judas? *56* Aren't his sisters here with us? So where on earth did he get all these ideas?"

57 They were quite annoyed with him. Jesus exclaimed, "A prophet is without honor only in their own hometown and in their own family!" *58* He was unable to do many powerful works there because of their absence of faith.

Ch.14:1-5 At that time Herod the Tribal Ruler heard the report about Jesus, *2* and said to his servants, "This is John the Baptizer! He's risen from the dead and that's why these powers are at work in him!"

3 Herod had arrested John and imprisoned him,[1] on account of Herodias – Herodias was Herod's brother Philip's wife – *4* because John had said to him, "Your marriage to her is illegal."[2]

5 Herod wanted to have John put to death, but he was afraid of the crowd's reaction, because they considered John to be a prophet.

6-12 During Herod's birthday celebration, the daughter of Herodias danced for the guests who reclined at dinner with him. Herod was so pleased by this *7* that he promised, under oath, to give her whatever she wanted. *8* Having been prompted by her mother, she said, "Give me John the Baptizer's head right here on a plate!"

9 The king was sorry, but he gave the order because of his oaths and his guests. *10* So he had John beheaded in prison. *11* John's head was brought on a plate and given to the young girl, and she took it to her mother. *12* John's disciples came and removed the body and buried it, and reported the deed to Jesus.

13-18 When Jesus heard about it, he left by boat and went to a deserted place by himself. The crowds found out and followed him on foot from the cities. *14* When Jesus went out he saw a big crowd, and he was moved with compassion for them and healed their sick. *15* When evening came, his disciples went to him. "This is a deserted place, and it's well past time for the evening meal! Send the crowds away so they can go off to the villages and buy something to eat," they suggested.

16 Jesus said, "They don't need to go away! *You* give them something to eat!"

17 "We haven't got anything - only five loaves of bread and two fish!" they exclaimed.

18 "Bring them here to me!" Jesus ordered.

19-21 Jesus ordered the crowds to sit down on the grass. He picked up the five loaves of bread and the two fish, and looking up to heaven, he blessed them and broke them into pieces. He gave the loaves of bread to the disciples, and the disciples gave them to the crowds. *20* And everyone ate their fill, and they picked

---

[1]   At Herod's prison fortress Machaerus.

[2]   John the Baptizer's statement would have been seen as political. Herod had sent his wife back home to her father King Aretas of the Nabatean Arabs, and married his sister-in-law Herodias. King Aretas took the act as an insult, invaded Antipas's land, and had a resounding victory over him in battle. The Romans had to intervene to prevent Herod losing his kingdom. Nevertheless, there was much unrest among Herod's Nabatean subjects. Herod would no doubt have been humiliated by John's statement, as it publicly called attention to the political cost of Herod's actions.

Herodias was still married to Herod's brother Philip. Polygamy was still practiced by Jews in Palestine, but was not supposed to happen in Graeco-Roman society. The document *P.Yadin* 10 (Palestine, 126 AD) is a marriage contract between Judah and his second wife Babatha. That is to say, Judah had another wife, and upon his marriage to Babatha, was married to two women at once. *P.Yadin* 10 is an Aramaic contract. Judah chose a Greek marriage contract for his daughter's (monogamous) marriage two years later (*P.Yadin* 18) but for his polygamous marriage, had to choose an Aramaic contract.

up twelve wicker baskets full of leftovers. *21* The number of those who had eaten was about 5,000 men plus women and children.

22-27 Immediately Jesus invited his disciples to get into the boat and go on ahead of him to the other side, while he sent the crowds away. *23* After he'd sent the crowds away, he went up on the mountain by himself to pray. By evening, he was alone there. *24* But by now the boat was far from land, and was tossed by the waves as the wind was against them. *25* About three o'clock in the morning Jesus went out to them, walking on the sea. *26* When the disciples saw him walking on the sea, they screamed in terror, "It's a ghost!"

27 Immediately Jesus said, "Cheer up! I am existence! Don't be scared!"

28-36 Peter said, "Lord, if it's really you, command me to come out to you on the water!"

29 "Come!" Jesus said.

When Peter had got down out of the boat, he walked on the water to go to Jesus. *30* But when he noticed the wind, he got scared, and began to sink. He yelled out, "Lord, save me!"

31 Immediately Jesus reached out and grabbed him. He said, "You small faith person! Why were you uncertain?"

32 When they got into the boat, the wind dropped. *33* The people in the boat worshipped him. "You're truly the Son of God!" they exclaimed. *34* When they'd crossed over, they landed at Gennesaret. *35* When the locals recognized Jesus, they sent word through the surrounding region and brought along all the sick people. *36* They urged him to let them touch the hem of his clothes. In fact, everyone who touched it was brought safely through their sickness.

Ch.15:1-9 Then the Bible scholars and Pharisees who were from Jerusalem went to Jesus and asked, *2* "Why do your disciples overstep the mark when it comes to the elders' tradition? They don't wash their hands in a special ceremonial way when they eat!"

3 "Why do your traditional teachings cause you to overstep the mark as well when it comes to the commandment of God?" Jesus responded. *4* "God says, 'Honor your father and your mother,' and 'The person who physically or verbally abuses[1] their father or mother, must certainly be put to death!'

5 "But you say, 'Whoever says to their father or mother, "What you thought you would get from me, I am keeping for myself – I just have to say it's dedicated to God and then I can keep it,"' *6* then that person does not honor their father or mother! In this way you have made God's Word useless by your traditional teachings! *7* You overly critical, hair splitting, pedantic religious types! Isaiah prophesied about you correctly when he said, *8* 'These people honor me with their lips, but their heart is far from me. *9* And in vain they worship me, their teachings are rules made up by people.'"

10-14 He called the crowd over and said, "Listen to this and understand it. *11* It's not what goes into the mouth that pollutes a person, but it's what comes out of the mouth that pollutes a person."

12 Then his disciples came up and asked, "Did you know that the Pharisees were offended when they heard that saying?"

13 Jesus replied, "Every plant which my Father of heaven hasn't planted will be uprooted! *14* Leave them alone! They are blind guides. If a blind person leads a blind person, both of them will fall into a ditch!"

15-20 Peter asked, "Please explain this example to us!"

---

[1] κακολογέω, *kakologeo*, refers to verbal and/or physical assault. The verb appears in papyrus documents where someone accuses another of verbal and/or physical assault. See *Aeg.* 50.43-45 (= *SB* 11018) (Oxyrhynchos, I/II); *P.Ryl.* 2.150.9 (40 A.D.); *BGU* 6.1247.10 (Syene or Ombros, c. 149/8). In the papyri and in Classical examples it occurs in the context of litigation, unlike the N.T. context. In the N.T. it occurs also in Mark 7:10; 9:39; Acts 19:9.

16 "Don't you have a clue yet!" Jesus exclaimed. *17* "Don't you understand that whatever goes in the mouth, goes into the stomach. Then it comes out and goes into a toilet! *18* The things that come out of the mouth actually come from the mind, and they pollute a person. *19* Out of the mind come evil thoughts, murders, adulteries, *porneia,*[1] thefts, telling lies about people, and blasphemies. *20* These are the things that pollute a person. Eating with unwashed hands cannot pollute a person!"

21-28 Jesus left there and headed for the region of Tyre and Sidon. *22* A Canaanite woman came from that region and shouted to him, "Have pity on me, Lord, David's descendant! My daughter has a evil spirit – and badly!"

23 But he didn't say a thing. His disciples urged him, "Send her away, she's calling out after us!"

24 He answered, "I was only sent to the lost sheep of the house of Israel."

25 She came and fell on the ground in front of him, and said, "Lord, help me!"

26 "It's not good to take the children's bread and throw it to the little dogs!" Jesus answered.

27 "Yes, Lord," she said, "but even the little dogs eat the crumbs which fall from their master's table."

28 Then Jesus answered, "My dear lady, you have great faith! You will get what you want!" And her daughter was instantly divinely healed at that very moment.

29-32 Jesus moved on from there, and went around the Sea of Galilee. He went up on the mountain and sat down. *30* Large crowds went to him, and along with them were lame, blind, mute, crippled people, as well as many others. They put them directly in front of Jesus, and he healed them. *31*

---

[1] πορνεία, *porneia,* a term referring to acts condemned in the Law of Moses, acts encompassing idolatry and/or pornography, vice, certain sexual acts. No equivalent English term. Leviticus 18 lists idolatry and ritually unclean sexual acts against the laws of Moses (and here Paul mentions "ritual uncleanness" in verse 24), and in 18:3 states, "You must not do the deeds of the land of Canaan into which I am about to bring you." These included incest, sex with in-laws, sex with a woman as a rival to her sister, women or men having sex with animals, child offerings to Molech, male homosexual sex, sex with a woman during menstruation. Note also that the polytheistic Canaanites were particularly despised in the Old Testament, and male temple prostitution was part of their worship of their goddess Asherah. Cult prostitution and eunuchs castrating themselves (and thereafter dressing in women's clothing, cf. Deuteronomy 22:5) both figured in the worship of the Canaanite goddess Astarte.

Note that the Hebrew *keleb* in Deuteronomy 23:19 which speaks of temple prostitution ("You shall not bring the cost of a prostitute or the price of a dog (keleb) into the house of YHWH your God for any vow, for both of them are certainly an abomination to YHWH your God") has been demonstrated to be a male homosexual receptive prostitute in Cannaanite temple worship.

Leviticus 18, although referring to Cannaanite worship practices, has been cited by people who oppose homosexuality. However, it should be noted that these very same Biblical passages prohibit a woman having sex when she has her period, and forbid people eating rabbit, bacon, and seafood that does not have scales or fins, forbid wearing mixed fabric, and planting mixed seed. Thus people who believe, despite the evidence to the contrary, that Leviticus is speaking of homosexuality itself rather than Canaanite temple prostitution, should not in good conscience eat bacon, shrimp, wear polyester blend clothes, and so on. Further, Leviticus 18 supports polygamy.

At any rate, speaking of the Old Covenant, Hebrews 9: 10 states, "The gifts and sacrifices were only on the level of eating and drinking and cleansing rites – regulations for things of the natural realm to stay in effect until the time a new way was laid down."

Consequently, the crowd was shocked when they saw the mute speaking, the crippled restored to their original undamaged state, the lame walking, and the blind seeing, and they praised the God of Israel.

32-39 Jesus called his disciples over and said, "I feel compassionate about the crowd. They've stayed with me for three days now and they don't have a thing to eat. I don't want to send them away hungry, in case they get weak as they travel away."

33 His disciples exclaimed, "How on earth are we going to get enough bread right out here in the desert to fill up such a large crowd!"

34 Jesus asked, "How many loaves do you have?"

"Seven, and a few little fish," they said.

35 Jesus ordered the crowd to sit down on the ground. *36* He took the seven loaves and the fish and after expressing thankfulness, broke them into pieces and gave them to his disciples, and the disciples gave them to the crowd. *37* They all ate their fill. Afterwards they picked up seven large person-sized mat baskets full of leftovers. *38* There were 4,000 men who'd eaten as well as women and children. *39* He sent the crowd away, got into the boat, and went to the region of Magadan.

Ch.16:1-4 The Pharisees and Sadducees arrived, and asked Jesus to prove himself by showing them a sign from heaven. *2* He answered, "In the evening you say, 'Red at night, shepherds' delight!' *3* and early in the morning you say, 'Red in the morning, shepherds' warning!' You know how to tell what's going on with the sky, but you can't tell what's going on in these times *4* A wicked and adulterous group of people wants a sign, but the only sign it will get is the sign of Jonah!" At that he promptly left them.

5-12 When his disciples arrived at the other side, they discovered they had forgotten the bread. *6* Jesus said to them, "Watch out for and avoid the yeast of the Pharisees and the Sadducees!"

7 They discussed this amongst themselves and said, "It must be because we didn't bring any bread!"

8 Jesus, aware of it, said to them, "You faithless lot, why are you discussing the fact that you don't have any bread with each other? How come you still don't understand? *9* Don't you remember the five loaves of bread that fed the five thousand and how many baskets of leftovers you picked up? *10* Don't you remember the seven loaves of bread that fed the four thousand and how many large baskets of leftovers you picked up? *11* How come you don't understand that I wasn't talking about bread? Avoid the yeast of the Pharisees and Sadducees!"

12 Then they caught on to the fact that he wasn't telling them to avoid the yeast in bread, but to beware of the teaching of the Pharisees and Sadducees.

13-20 When Jesus arrived in the region of Caesarea Philippi, he asked his disciples, "Who do people say that I, the Human Being, am?"

14 They answered, "Some say John the Baptizer, but others say Elijah, and others say you're Jeremiah or one of the prophets."

15 "But you - who do you say I am?" he asked.

16 Simon Peter answered, "You're the Anointed One, the Son of the living God."

17 "You are a blessed person, Simon Bar-Jonah!" Jesus exclaimed. "This wasn't revealed to you by human beings but by my Father in the heavenly places *18* I certainly say that you are Peter, the stone, and I will build my assembly upon me, the rock,[1] and Hades' gates will not triumph in an

---

[1]   In the Greek, the "this" refers to Jesus, not Peter. He is playing on words. "Peter," ὁ πέτρος, *ho petros*, is the Greek word for "stone" and ἡ πέτρα, *he petra*, is the Greek word for a rock, or shelf or ledge of rock, cliff or boulder, used in "upon this rock (πέτρα, *petra*, not πέτρος, *petros*, Peter) I will build my church". They are different Greek words. See use in Eur. *Medea*, 28-9;

encounter with my assembly! *19* I will give you the keys to Heaven's Realm, and whatever you tie up on earth will have been tied up in the heavenly places, and whatever you release on earth will have been released in the heavenly places." *20* Then he ordered his disciples not to tell anyone that he was the Anointed One.

21-23 From that time on, Jesus started pointing out to his disciples that he must go to Jerusalem, and experience many things at the hands of the elders, chief priests and Bible scholars, and be killed, and be raised on the third day. *22* Peter took him aside and started rebuking him. He said, "No way, Lord! This won't happen to you!"

23 Jesus turned to Peter and said, "Get out of my way, Adversary! You want to trap me - your mind isn't on the things of God, just on human things."

24-28 Then Jesus said to his disciples, "If anyone wishes to follow me, that person will have to utterly deny themselves, and take up their cross and follow me. *25* The person who wants to preserve their life[1] will lose it, but whoever lets go of their life for my sake will find it. *26* What good will it do someone if they gain the whole world and lose their own life? What will a person give in exchange for their very life? *27* The Human Being is to come with the splendor that surrounds his Father, bringing his Messengers, and then he will reward each person for their actions. *28* I tell you, there are some standing here who will not experience[2] death until they see the Human Being coming in his Realm!"

Ch.17:1-8 Six days later Jesus took Peter, James and his brother John up on a high mountain in private. *2* His appearance was changed right in front of them! His face shone like the sun, and his clothes became as white as the light. *3* And Moses and Elijah appeared, talking with him! *4* Peter said to Jesus, "Lord, it's nice that we're here. If you like, let's make shelters here - one for you, one for Moses and one for Elijah." *5* While he was still speaking, a bright cloud cast its shadow over them. Suddenly a voice came out of the cloud. It said, "This is my much loved Son. I'm very pleased with him. Pay attention to him!"

6 When the disciples heard it, they fell on their faces and were very frightened. *7* Jesus went over and touched them. He said, "Get up! There is no need to be frightened!" *8* When they looked up, they didn't see anyone except Jesus.

9-13 As they were traveling down the mountain, Jesus ordered them, "Don't mention the Appearance[3] to anyone until the Human Being has risen from among the dead."[4]

10 His disciples asked, "Why do the Bible scholars say that Elijah must come first?"

11 "Elijah does come to restore things to their original condition," Jesus answered. *12* "Let me make this clear, Elijah has already come! They didn't recognize him but did what they liked to him. They are about to treat the Human Being in the same way."

13 Then the disciples realized that he was talking about John the Baptizer.

14-18 While they were approaching the crowd, a person came up to him, knelt down and said, *15* "Lord, have pity on my son! He has convulsions and

---

Eur. *Andr.* 537; Soph. *OT*, 334ff. However, some (dating to back Tertullian in the 3rd c.) argue that the 2 words here have the same meaning. Much earlier than Tertullian, the *Shepherd of Hermas* states that Jesus is the rock.

[1] The Greek word in verses 25-26 can mean either "life" or "soul".

[2] γεύσωνται, *geusontai* (aorist subjunctive of γεύομαι, *geuomai*), "experience". (Means "taste" when used in the context of foods.)

[3] ὅραμα, *horama*, was used in pagan religion to describe the appearance of gods in their bodily form, cf. Liddell & Scott, *s.v.* The term occurs only here in the N.T. outside Acts, where it appears 11 times.

[4] ἐκ νεκρῶν, *ek nekron*, from among the dead, that is, from the abode of the dead.

he suffers really badly! He often falls into the fire and into the water! *16* I brought him to your disciples, but they couldn't heal him."

17 Jesus answered, "You faithless and perverse group of people, how long will I be with you! How long do I have to put up with you? Bring him here to me!"

18 Jesus rebuked the demon, and it came out of him and the child was healed from that very time.

19-23 Then the disciples went to Jesus privately and said, "Why couldn't we threw it out?"

20 "Because you don't have much faith!" he answered. "Let me make this clear, if you have faith like a mustard seed, you will say to this mountain, 'Move from here to there,' and it will move, and nothing will be impossible for you!'[1]

22 While they were assembling in Galilee, Jesus told them, "The Human Being is about to be betrayed and arrested. *23* He will be executed, and on the third day he will be raised up." And they were all extremely sad.

24-27 When they reached Capernaum, the people who collected the annual temple tax[2] went to Peter and said, "Doesn't your teacher pay the annual temple tax?"

25 "He sure does!" Peter answered.

When he arrived at the house, Jesus anticipated him and said, "What do you think about this, Simon? Who do the kings of the earth take taxes from, from their people or from the others?"

26 "From the others," he replied.

Jesus said to him, "In that case their people are exempt. *27* Nevertheless, so that we don't offend them, go to the sea, cast in a hook, and take the fish that comes up first. When you've opened its mouth, you will find a valuable coin. Take that and give it to them. It's enough for the both of us."

Ch.18:1-7 About that time the disciples asked Jesus, "Who is the most important in Heaven's Realm?"

2 Jesus called a child over, and put the child[3] down in the middle of them. *3* He said, "Let me emphasize this, unless you change and become like children, there is no way you will enter Heaven's Realm! *4* The person who brings themselves down to the level[4] of this child is greater in Heaven's Realm. *5* The person who welcomes one child like this in my name welcomes me. *6* If someone causes one of these little ones who believe me to fall into a trap, they'd be better off if a stone block were hung around their neck, and they were drowned in the ocean depths! *7* How sad for the world because of traps! It's necessary for traps to come, nevertheless how sad for that person who causes the trap!

8-14 "If your hand or foot causes you to fall into a trap, cut it off and throw it away. It's better for you to enter into life disabled and lame, rather than to have two hands or two feet and be thrown into the fire that never goes out.[5] *9* And if your eye causes you to fall into a trap, rip it out and throw it away! It's better for you to enter into life with one eye, rather than to have both your eyes and be thrown into the fire of the Garbage Pit Gehenna. *10* Make sure you don't despise one of these little ones! I'm telling you that their Messengers constantly see the face of my Father in the heavenly places.[6] *12* What do you think? If

---

1   Verse 21 (omitted here) is not original and was added by copyists.

2   The annual temple tax due from everyone over 20 years of age.

3   Bible versions traditionally translate the personal pronoun here as "him", but the personal pronoun in the Greek is "it" following the neuter grammatical gender of "child". The gender of the child is not mentioned, and the Greek provides no clues.

4   ταπεινόω, *tapeinoo*: the noun refers to those who are of a low level in society – they may be poor, brought down in some way, weak, downcast.

5   Equally, "fire for an age".

6   Verse 11 (omitted here) is not original and was added by copyists.

someone has 100 sheep, and one of them wanders off,[1] don't they leave the 99 and go to the mountains to look for the one that's wandered off? *13* And if they happen to find it, they are happier about it than the 99 that didn't wander off! *14* Clearly, it is not the purpose of your Father in the heavenly places that one of these little ones should perish.

15-17 "If your fellow believer sins against you, go and tell them the problem in private. If they listen to you, you have won over your fellow believer. *16* But if they won't listen, take one or two other people with you, so that 'every word can be confirmed by the evidence of two or three witnesses.' *17* If they refuse to listen, tell the assembly, but if they refuse even to listen to the assembly, think of them as you would a pagan or a Tax Profiteer.

18-20 "I'm telling you the truth - whatever you tie up[2] on earth will have been tied up in heaven, and whatever you release on earth will have been released in heaven. *19* Let me make this quite clear, if two of you agree about anything that you ask, my Father in the heavenly places will do it for you. *20* For where two or three people are gathered together in my Name, I am certainly there in their midst."

21-27 Then Peter asked, "Lord, how often should I forgive a fellow believer who has sinned? Up to seven times?"

22 Jesus said to him, "I'm not just going to say up to seven times, but up to seventy times seven! *23* Heaven's Realm can be compared to this situation: there was a certain king who wanted to settle accounts with his slave servants. *24* Just as he began to settle accounts, someone who owed him several million dollars[3] was hauled in front of him. *25* But as he couldn't pay, and payment had to be made, the master ordered that he must be sold along with his wife and children and everything he had. *26* Then the slave servant threw himself down at his feet and said, 'Master, please be patient with me, and I'll pay you everything!' *27* The master was moved with compassion, let him go and canceled the debt.

28-35 "But that very slave servant went out and found one of his fellow slave servants who owed him a few dollars. He grabbed him by the throat and nearly choked him. He demanded, 'Pay me what you owe me!'

29 "So then his fellow slave servant fell down and begged him, 'Be patient with me, and I'll pay you.'

30 "He refused and threw him into prison where he had to stay until the debt was paid. *31* So when his fellow slave servants saw what happened they were very upset, and reported the whole story to their master. *32* Then his master called him over and said, 'You evil slave servant! I canceled all that debt for you because you begged me - *33* shouldn't you too have had compassion on your fellow slave servant? I had pity on you!'

34 "His master was angry and sent him to the torturers, where he had to stay until he could pay the whole debt. *35* This is what my Father in the heavenly places will do to you, if each of you, from your heart, does not cancel any wrongs done to you by your fellow believers!'"

---

[1] πλανάω, *planao*, "to wander off the path", the cognate noun being πλάνη, *plane*. See Rom. 1:27. πλανάω, *planao*, occurs twice in this verse, and once in the next, and elsewhere in Matt. in 22:29; 24:4, 5, 11, 24.

[2] Future perfect periphrastic construction, cf. Matt. 16:19. Most translations say "Whatever you bind on earth will be bound in heaven...and whatever you loose on earth will be loosed in heaven," making the "will be bound" and "will be loosed" future passive tense. However, in the Greek the tense is not future passive. In both cases (both "bind" and "loose") there is a periphrastic construction with the future of the verb "to be" with the perfect passive participle, "will have been bound / loosed". This is an unusual construction.

[3] "10,000 talents" = 60 million denarii. A single talent represented the lifetime wage of a laborer.

Ch.19:1-6 When Jesus had finished these sayings, he left Galilee and headed for the region of Judea beyond the Jordan River. *2* Big crowds followed him, and he healed them. *3* The Pharisees went to put him to the test. They said, "Is it legal for a person to divorce his wife on the grounds of 'Any Matter'?"[1]

4 Jesus answered, "Haven't you read that he who created in the beginning made people male and female, *5* and said, 'for this reason a person will leave his father and mother and be united with his wife and the two will become a single body? *6* Thus they are no longer two[2] but a single body. So then what God has united, no one is to break apart!"

7-12 They asked, "Why then did Moses command[3] that a certificate of divorce is to be given upon divorce?"

8 "Because you are hard-hearted!"[4] Jesus answered. "That's why Moses permitted you to divorce your wives, but it wasn't so from the beginning. *9* In fact, whoever divorces his wife, unless it's on the grounds of 'General Sexual Immorality',[5] and marries someone else, commits adultery."[6]

---

[1] The Rabbis were asking Jesus about his interpretation of Deuteronomy 24:1. The "Any Matter" is a technical term from Jewish divorce law, a form of divorce introduced by the Rabbi Hillel. The other type of divorce, divorce on the ground of "General Sexual Immorality", was available to both men and women, both of whom were able to divorce the partner on the specific grounds based on Exodus 21:10-11. This traditional type of divorce was becoming rarer by the start of the first century, being replaced by the "Any Matter" divorce, which was for men only, and popular as no grounds had to be shown and there was no court case. For an "Any Matter" divorce, the man simply had to write out a certificate of divorce and give it to his wife. By Jesus' time, the "Any Matter" was the more popular form of divorce, but the rabbis were still arguing about the legalities of it. The disciples of Shammai were particularly opposed to it. For the "Any Matter" divorce see Josephus, *AJ* 4.253, "He who desires to be divorced from his wife who is living with him on the grounds of 'Any Matter'…must certify in writing…"; Philo, *Special Laws* 3.30, "…if a woman is parting from her husband on the grounds of 'Any Matter'"; see also the Rabbinic Commentary *Sifré Deuteronomy* 269. For modern scholarship, see D. Instone-Brewer, *Divorce and Remarriage in the Church*, (Cumbria: Paternoster Press, 2003). See also note on Matt. 1:19.

Jesus' answer to the Pharisees' question, "Is it legal for a person to divorce his wife on the grounds of 'Any Matter'?" appears in verse 9: "Whoever divorces from his wife, unless it's on the grounds of 'General Sexual Immorality', and marries someone else, commits adultery". Thus Jesus declares the divorce on the grounds of "Any Matter" invalid.

[2] D. Instone-Brewer (*op.cit.*, p. 51) suggests that here Jesus is stressing the single and the "two" to stress monogamy, as Jewish polygamy was so widespread at the time.

[3] The Pharisees use the word "command" to stress their belief that divorce was compulsory after adultery. Jesus responds by using the word "permitted" – divorce upon adultery of one partner was not a command, rather, it was permitted.

[4] A Jewish term meaning the stubborn continuation of a particular action without wishing to change.

[5] Another technical legal term from Jewish divorce law: the other grounds for divorce, the more traditional divorce prior to Hillel's introduction of the "Any Matter" divorce. Here Jesus is saying he disagrees with the Any Matter form of divorce, saying it is invalid.

[6] Jesus is simply saying that if someone divorces by a form other than the grounds of the "General Sexual Immorality" form of divorce, they are not properly divorced and thus not free to remarry, and further are committing adultery if they do so. He is continuing his statement that he disagrees with the "Any Matter" form of divorce.

10 His disciples said to him, "If this is the situation with husband and wife, it's better not to get married at all!"[1]

11 But Jesus answered, "This doesn't apply to everyone, but only to those to whom it has been given. *12* Now, there are eunuchs who were born that way from their mother's womb, and there are eunuchs who were made that way by human intervention, and there are eunuchs who have made themselves eunuchs for the sake of Heaven's Realm. If it applies to you, then accept it!

13-15 Then little children were brought to him so he could lay hands on them and pray, but the disciples objected. *14* "Leave the little children alone!" Jesus insisted. "Don't stop them coming to me. This, that is to say, the little children coming to me, is a good analogy of Heaven's Realm." *15* He laid hands on them then left.

16-19 Someone asked him, "Teacher, what good thing can I do to get eternal life?"

17 "Why do you ask me about what is good?" Jesus answered. *18* There is One who is good; but if you really want life, keep the commandments!"

"Which ones?" they asked.

Jesus said, "'You must not murder,' 'You must not commit adultery,' 'You must not steal,' 'You must not tell lies about people,' *19* "'Honor your father and mother,' and 'Love your neighbor the same way you love yourself.'"

20-24 "I've kept all these commandments! What's left to do?" the young man exclaimed.

21 Jesus answered, "If you want to be complete, go and sell your belongings and give them to the financially poor, and you will have a money bank in the heavenly places. Then come and follow me!"

22 But when the young man heard that he went away sad, as he had a lot of possessions. *23* Jesus said to his disciples, "For a fact, it is hard for a rich person to enter Heaven's Realm! *24* Let me emphasize this: pigs might fly[2] before a rich person enters Heaven's Realm!"

25-30 When his disciples heard this, they were besides themselves with terrible shock and exclaimed, "Well then - who can be saved?"

26 Jesus looked straight at them and said, "It's impossible with people, but with God everything is possible!"

27 Then Peter said, "Hey, we have left everything and followed you – so what do we get out of it?"

28 "In the new creation, when the Human Being sits on his glorious throne, you, my followers, will also sit on twelve thrones, judging the twelve tribes of Israel!" Jesus answered. *29* "And everyone who has left houses, brothers, sisters, fathers, mothers, children or farms, on account of me, will get back a hundred times more than they gave, and will inherit eternal life. *30* Many prominent people will end up unimportant, and unimportant people will end up prominent.

It is most important to note the significance of the above. The way this passage has been (mis)translated gives the impression that Jesus was asked the question, "Is it ever legal to divorce?" and he answered, "No, except on the grounds of sexual immorality." This is not the case. Jesus was asked if it was legal to divorce on the grounds of "Any Matter" and he answered, "No, only on the grounds of 'General Sexual Immorality'". In other words, he was disagreeing with the "Any Matter" form of divorce (the other form of divorce at the time being on the "General Sexual Immorality" grounds). Jesus certainly was not saying that at that time, or in the time to come, people were never to divorce except on the ground of sexual immorality.

[1] The disciples are shocked at Jesus' rejection of the "Any Matter" form of divorce.

[2] See note on Luke 18:25.

Ch.20:1-7 "This is a story about Heaven's Realm. It is like a landowner who went out early in the morning to hire workers for his vineyard. *2* After he agreed with the workers on the normal day's wage, he sent them into his vineyard. *3* At nine o'clock in the morning he went out and saw other people standing around in the marketplace doing nothing. *4* He said to them, 'You can all go into the vineyard too, and I'll pay you the going rate.'

"And off they went. *5* He went out again at noon and at three in the afternoon, and did the same thing. *6* About five in the afternoon he went out and found other people standing around. He said to them, 'Why have you been standing around here all day doing nothing?'

7 "'Because no one hired us!" they replied.

"'You go into the vineyard too!' he told them.

8-16 "When evening came, the owner of the vineyard said to his manager, 'Call the workers and give them wages, beginning with the last and working your way to the first.' *9* When the people who were hired about five in the afternoon arrived, each of them received a full day's wage. *10* When the people who'd come first arrived, they thought they'd get more, but they received a full day's wage. *11* When they got it they complained about the landowner. *12* 'The people who came last have only worked for an hour,' they complained, 'but you've made them equal to us, and we're the ones who've put up with the whole weight of it as well as the scorching heat!'

13 "The manager turned to one of his workers and explained, 'My friend, I'm not doing you an injustice! Didn't you agree with me on a normal day's wage? *14* Take what's yours and go away. I want to give this last person the same as you. *15* Surely I have a legal right to do whatever I like with my own things? Or are you jealous[1] because I am kind?' *16* So the last will end up first and the first will end up last!'"

17-19 As Jesus was going up to Jerusalem, he took the twelve disciples aside on the road and said, *18* "Hey, we're going up to Jerusalem, and the Human Being will be betrayed to the chief priests and the Bible scholars, and they will condemn him to be executed! *19* They will give him to the non-Jews who will make fun of him and beat him with the Roman whip embedded with metal spurs designed to rip off the flesh, and crucify him. On the third day he will rise again!"

20-23 The mother of Zebedee's sons came to him with her sons. She knelt down and asked something from him.

---

[1] ὀφθαλμός πονηρός, *ophthalmos poneros*, literally, to have the evil eye. According to pagan religion, a person who had the power of the evil eye would exercise this power when they became jealous (or angry). The person who used the evil eye was said to bewitch the victim resulting in either physical problems or mind control of some sort. See Galatians 3:1, where the word βασκαίνω, *baskaino*, to use words to cast a spell on someone by means of the evil eye, is used. Some believed that to see one's reflection made one liable to the effects of the evil eye, and the spell was broken by spitting three times, cf. Theokritos, VI, 35-40. A 3rd century A.D. stone inscription tells of the effects upon one who testifies to having the evil eye put on him, with the result that his wife and children were killed. *ed. CIG* (1877; repr. 1977) 9668, *l.*2. A funerary epigram for Apollodorus, Pfuhl/Mobius 1.1021 (pl. 153; = E. Schwertheim, *Die Inschriften von Kyzikos und Umgebung*, 1 [*IK* 26.1; Bonn, 1980] 493 [pl. 34], describes Hades as casting his evil eye upon honorable things. Note also *IG* VII 581.5 (Megara, early 1 AD), conclusion to a verse epitaph: "Hades puts the evil eye on the good." An amulet described by J. Russell, *JOB* 32.539-548 has the wording "the seal of Solomon holds in check the evil eye." *TAM* 3.1.810.8 (Termessos, 11-111 AD), verse epitaph for silversmith: "Fate put the evil eye on me and took me." *1.Kret* 2.3.44.16 (Aptera, III AD), verse epitaph for wife, "I Neikon wrote this, who was her husband, but now longer, for the evil eye was put on me."

21 "What do you want?" Jesus asked.

She answered, "Give permission for these two sons of mine to have the highest places of honor in your Kingdom, one sitting on your right side and the other on the left!"

22 "You don't know what you're asking!" Jesus responded. "Are you able to experience the suffering I am about to experience?"

"Yes we can!" they insisted.

23 "You will certainly experience the suffering I am about to experience!" Jesus told them. "But it's not up to me to say who will sit in places of honor, at my right side and at my left! My Father has prepared those places for the ones he has chosen."

24-28 When the ten heard, they were annoyed with the two brothers. *25* Jesus called them over. He said, "You know that the rulers of the non-Jews act like big shots over them, and their high officials make sure they use their authority over them. *26* You are not to do this! The person who wants to become important needs to be your servant, *27* and the person who wants to be the most prominent, needs to be your slave. *28* In the same way the Human Being did not come to be served, but to serve, and to exchange his life for those who are held hostage!"

29-34 As they were leaving Jericho, a big crowd followed him. *30* There were two blind people sitting beside the road. When they heard that Jesus was going past, they yelled out, "Have pity on us, Lord, David's descendant!"

31 The crowd told them sharply to be quiet, but they yelled out even louder, "Have pity on us, Lord, David's descendant!"

32 Jesus stood still and called out, "What do you want me to do for you?"

33 "Lord, we want to see!" they replied. *34* Jesus had compassion. He touched their eyes. Immediately they could see, and they followed him.

Ch.21:1-3 As they approached Jerusalem, they arrived at Bethphage on the Mount of Olives. Jesus sent out two disciples *2* with the instructions, "Go into the village across from you. You will immediately find a donkey tied up. Her foal will be with her. Untie them and bring them to me. *3* If anyone says anything to you, you will say, 'The Lord needs them,' and they'll send them immediately."[1]

4-5 This was done so that the words spoken by the prophet would be fulfilled: *5* "Tell the people of Zion, your King is coming to you, gentle, and riding a donkey, on a foal, the progeny of a donkey."

6-9 The disciples went off and carried out Jesus' instructions. *7* They brought the donkey and the foal, put their clothes on them, and Jesus mounted up. *8* A large crowd spread their clothes on the road, and others cut down branches from the trees and spread them on the road. *9* The crowds, those in front and those who followed, called out, "Hosanna to David's descendant; blessed is the one who comes in the Name of the Lord; Hosanna to the Highest Realms!"

10-11 When Jesus arrived at Jerusalem, all the city was stirred up. "Who is this?" some people asked, *11* and the crowds replied, "This is the prophet Jesus from Nazareth of Galilee!"

12-13 Jesus went into the temple and chased out all the buyers and dealers. He overturned the tables of the money changers and the dove sellers' seats. *13* "The Scriptures say," he yelled, 'My house will be known as a house of prayer,' but you have made it a thieves' hangout!"

14-16 Blind and crippled people came to him in the temple, and he healed them. *15* When the chief priests and the Bible scholars saw the wonderful things he did, and the children calling out in the temple, "Hosanna to David's

---

[1]   The official transport system allowed for a legitimate claimant to borrow a donkey, and return it afterwards. Donkeys were part of the public transport service. See S.R. Llewelyn, "Systems of Transport and Roman Administration: The Provision of Transport for Persons," *NDIEC* 7.58-92.

descendant," they were indignant. *16* "Do you hear what they're saying?" they demanded.

"Yes!" Jesus responded. "Have you ever read, 'You have prepared praise to come from the mouths of children and babies'?"

17-22 Jesus left them behind and went out of the city to Bethany, and spent the night there. *18* Early in the morning, when he was heading back to the city, he got hungry. *19* He saw a fig tree by the road, and went up to it but found nothing but leaves on it. He said to it, "No fruit will ever grow on you again!" Immediately the fig tree withered away.

20 When the disciples saw it, they were amazed. "Why did the fig tree die so quickly?" they asked.

21 Jesus answered, "If you have faith and are not undecided, you will do more than I did to the fig tree. If you tell this mountain, 'Be removed! Be thrown into the sea', it will happen! *22* If you ask for something in prayer, and believe, you will get it!"

23-27 Jesus arrived at the temple. The chief priests and the elders of the people confronted him while he was teaching. They demanded, "By what authority are you doing these things? And who gave you this authority?"

24 "I will ask you one thing too," Jesus answered, "and if you tell me, I will tell you by what authority I do these things! *25* The baptism John carried out - where was it from? From heaven or from people?"

They argued among themselves, and said, "If we say, 'From heaven,' he's going to say to us, 'Then how come you don't you believe him?' *26* But if we say, 'From people,' then we'd have to be afraid of the crowd, because they all think that John is a prophet!"

27 So they answered Jesus, "We don't know!"

"Then I'm certainly not going to tell you by what authority I do these things!" he replied.

28-32 Jesus continued, "What do you think about this? A person had two children, and he went to the first and said, 'My child, go and work today in my vineyard!'

29 "'I will not!' he answered, but afterwards regretted it and went.

30 "He went to the second and said the same thing. And he answered, 'Yes sir!' but he didn't go.

31 "Which of the two did what his father wanted?"

"The first one!" they answered.

"Tax Profiteers and prostitutes will enter Heaven's Realm before you do," Jesus pointed out. *32* "John's character was one of justice. You didn't believe him, but Tax Profiteers and prostitutes believed him! Even when you saw that, you didn't regret it afterwards and believe him.

33-41 "Listen to another example. There was a certain person, a landowner, who planted a vineyard and put a hedge around it, dug a wine press in it and built a tower. He leased it out to farmers and set out on a journey. *34* When vintage time got close, he sent his slave servants to the farmers to collect its fruit. *35* The farmers grabbed his slave servants, beat one, killed one and stoned another. *36* Next he sent other slave servants, more than the first, and they did the same to them. *37* Last of all he sent his son to them. 'They will respect my son!' he said to himself. *38* But when the farmers saw the son, they said to each other 'This is the heir! Come on, let's kill him and get the inheritance!'

39 "They grabbed him, threw him out of the vineyard and murdered him. So *40* So then, when the owner of the vineyard comes, what's he going to do to those farmers?"

41 They answered, "He will see to it that those bad people have a horrible death. Then he will lease the vineyard to other farmers who will give him his share of each harvest."

42-43 Jesus said to them, "Haven't you ever read in the Scriptures, 'The stone which the builders rejected, has become the cornerstone; this was done by the Lord, and it is wonderful to see!'"?

43 "This is why I say to you that Heaven's Realm will be taken from you and given to a nation that will benefit from it."[1]

45-46 Upon hearing his examples, the chief priests and Pharisees realized he was talking about them. *45* They fully intended to arrest him, but they weren't able to carry it out. They were afraid of the crowds' reaction, as the crowds took him for a prophet.

Ch.22:1-6 Jesus responded by speaking again in examples. *2* "This is a story about Heaven's Realm. It is like a certain king who arranged a marriage for his son," he explained. *3* "He sent his slave servants to call the invited guests to the wedding but they didn't want to come. *4* Next he sent other slave servants with the instructions, 'Tell the invited guests, "I have prepared the feast – all the meat is ready! Everything is ready! Come to the wedding."'

5 "But they couldn't care less, and they went away. One went to his own farm, another went to his business, *6* but the rest of them grabbed his slave servants and beat them up badly, killing them.

7-14 "The king was furious and sent his armies. They destroyed those murderers and burned down their city. *8* Then the king said to his slave servants, 'The wedding is ready, but the invited guests weren't worthy of the honor. *9* So go out to the highways and invite anyone you find to the wedding.'

10 "The slaves went out to the highways and collected everyone they found, both good and bad, and the wedding hall was filled with guests reclining at the table. *11* But when the king came in to see the guests reclining at the table, he came across a person who wasn't wearing wedding clothes.

12 "'Friend, why did you come without wedding clothes?" the king asked, but the person was muzzled[2] and didn't say a word. *13* "Then the king said to his servants, 'Tie up his hands and feet, throw him right out into the dark - there will be great sorrow, pain and anguish!' *14* Many are invited but few are chosen!"

15-22 Then the Pharisees plotted to trick Jesus by catching him out on something he said. *16* They sent their disciples, along with Herod's followers and supporters to ask, "Teacher, we know that you're sincere and teach God's way accurately, and that you don't care about anyone's opinion, and you don't play favorites. *17* So tell us, what's your opinion? Is it legal to pay the Roman poll-tax to Caesar, or not?"[3]

18 Jesus knew their evil. He said, "Why are you hassling me, you overly critical, hair splitting, pedantic religious types? *19* Show me the tax money!"

They brought him the Roman coin.

20 "Whose portrait is this?" Jesus asked them. "Whose inscription is it?"

21 "Caesar's!" they replied.

---

[1]   Verse 44 is omitted as, although ancient, it is not original.

[2]   φιμόω, *phimoo*, is a technical term from pagan magic. It was used in the papyri and in Egypto Syrian Greek to denote the binding of a person by means of a spell, cf. Rohde, Psyche, ii. 124 . This is the same word used by Jesus when speaking to the sea in Mark 4:39: "Jesus fully woke up and rebuked the wind and the sea, saying, 'Keep still! Be bound!' And the wind dropped and there was a great calm." The verb is, "Be muzzled!" but translated as "bound" in the magical texts. This is one of the two technical terms used for binding in Greek pagan magic.

[3]   κῆνσος, *kensos*, the poll-tax, was paid directly to the Romans. It was especially hated by the Jews as a sign of subjection. The question was cunning: a "Yes" answer would disgust the Jews, and a "No" answer would set the Roman authorities against Jesus.

"Give back to Caesar what belongs to Caesar," Jesus said, "and give back to God what belongs to God!"[1] *22* When they heard this, they were amazed. They left him and took off.

23-28 On the same day the Sadducees, who say there is no resurrection, went to speak to Jesus. This is the question they put, *24* "Teacher, Moses said, 'If someone dies childless, his brother must marry his widow and produce children with her.' *25* Let's say there were seven brothers. The first brother married and died. As he's childless, he leaves his wife to his brother. *26* The second one dies in the same way, so does the third. This keeps happening right up to the seventh brother. *27* In the end the woman dies too. *28* So in the resurrection, whose wife of the seven brothers is she going to be? They all had her!"

29-33 Jesus answered, "You are wandering off the right track because you don't know the Scriptures or the power of God! *30* In the resurrection they don't marry or get married, but they're like Messengers in heaven.

31 "But about the resurrection of the dead, haven't you read what was spoken to you by God, *32* 'I am the God of Abraham, the God of Isaac, and the God of Jacob'? God is not the God of the dead, he is the God of the living!" *33* Upon hearing his teaching the crowds were beside themselves with amazement.

34-40 But when the Pharisees heard that he had silenced the Sadducees, they held a meeting. *35* One of them, a lawyer, asked a question, trying to trap him: *36* "Teacher, which is the most important commandment in the Law?"

37 He answered, "'You must love the Lord your God with all your heart, with all your soul, and with all your understanding.' *38* This is the great first commandment. *39* The second most important is like it: 'You must love your neighbor in the same way you love yourself.' *40* The Law and the prophets depend on these two commandments!"

41-46 While the Pharisees were assembled, Jesus asked them, *42* "What do you think about the Anointed One? Whose descendant is he?"

"David's descendant," they answered.

43 "Well," Jesus began, "how can David call him 'master'? He said by the leading of the Spirit, *44* 'The Lord said to my master, "Sit here in the place of honor at my right side, until I put your enemies under your feet."' *45* So then if David calls him 'master', how can he be David's descendant?"

46 No one could come up with an answer to this, and from that day forward, no one dared question him any more!

Ch.23:1-7 Then Jesus addressed the crowds and his disciples. *2* "The Bible scholars and the Pharisees are teachers of Moses' Law. *3* So practice and follow everything they tell you to do, but don't do what they actually do! They don't practice what they preach! *4* They make up heavy burdensome rules and weigh people down with them, but they themselves won't lift a finger to help! *5* Everything they do is just for the show of it! They put extra large leather prayer boxes with scripture verses under their arms and on their foreheads. They put extra long tassels on the edge of their coats so they can look important. *6* They love having the places of honor at celebrations, the best seats in the synagogues, *7* and they love it when people give them formal greetings in the market places. They love it when people call them by the title, 'Rabbi'.

8-12 "But you, don't you be called 'Rabbi'! You have one Teacher and you are all fellow believers! *9* And you're not to call anyone on earth 'Father'. You have one Father, and he is in the heavenly places. *10* And don't be called 'Leader'! You have one Leader, the Anointed One. *11* The most important

---

[1]   Scholars have noted that this reply certainly does not encourage subservience to the state, merely minimum performance. See D. Daube, "Responsibilities of Masters and Disciples in the Gospels," *NTS* 19 (1972/3) 15; S.R. Llewelyn, "Tax Collection and the τελῶναι of the New Testament," *NDIEC* 8.75.

person among you will be your servant. *12* People who elevate themselves will be brought down, and people who bring themselves down will be elevated.

13-22 "Woe to you, Bible scholars and Pharisees, you overly critical, hair splitting, pedantic religious types, because you shut people out of Heaven's Realm! You don't go in there yourself, and what's more, you stop other people from going in too!¹

15 "Woe to you, Bible scholars and Pharisees, you overly critical, hair splitting, pedantic religious lot! You travel by land and sea to win one convert to Judaism, and when you've won that person, you make them twice as much a part of the Garbage Pit Gehenna as you are! *16* Woe to you, blind guides! You say, 'It doesn't mean anything to swear by the temple, but if you swear by the temple's gold, you are bound by oath.' *17* You blind fools! What's more important, the gold or the temple that made the gold sacred? *18* And you say, 'It doesn't mean anything to swear by the altar, but whoever swears by the offering that's on it, is bound by oath.'

19 "What blindness! What's more important, the offering or the altar that makes the offering sacred? *20* So whoever swears an oath by the altar, swears by it and everything on it. *21* So whoever swears an oath by the temple, swears by it and by God who lives in it. *22* So whoever swears an oath by heaven, swears by God's throne and by God who sits on it!

23-28 "Woe to you, Bible scholars and Pharisees, you overly critical, hair splitting, pedantic religious types! You make sure you pay the tithe on herbs; mint, anise and cumin, but you neglect the more important things of the Law, justice, mercy and faith. You should have practiced these, and not neglected the others! *24* Blind guides! You strain your water to avoid swallowing a gnat, but you gulp down a camel!

25 "Woe to you, Bible scholars and Pharisees, overly critical, hair splitting, pedantic religious types! You clean the outside of the cup and dish, but inside they are full of robbery and lack of control. *26* Blind Pharisee! First clean the inside of the cup and dish! Then it will mean something that the outside is clean.

27 "Woe to you, Bible scholars and Pharisees, overly critical, hair splitting, pedantic religious types, because you are like whitewashed tombs which look beautiful on the outside, but inside they're full of dead bones and filth! *28* In the same way too you outwardly appear righteous to people, but inside you are full of overly critical, hair splitting, pedantic religious behavior² and illegal acts!

29-36 "Woe to you, Bible scholars and overly critical, hair splitting, pedantic religious types, because you build the tombs of the prophets and decorate the monuments of the people who were right with God. *30* You say, 'If we'd lived in the days of our ancestors, we would not have taken part with them in the death of the prophets!' *31* By saying that, you are actually giving evidence against yourselves – evidence that you are descendants of those who murdered the prophets *32* You might as well finish what your ancestors started!

33 "Snakes! Pack of vipers! How can you escape being sentenced to the Garbage Pit Gehenna? *34* "Because of this, I'm sending you prophets, wise people, and Bible scholars. Some of them you will kill and crucify! Some you will beat in the synagogues with the Roman whip of leather straps embedded with metal designed to rip off the flesh! You will chase them from city to city – *35* but as a result all the just blood shed on the earth will come upon you - from the blood of just Abel to the blood of Zechariah, Berechiah's son, whom you murdered between the sanctuary and the altar. *36* I tell you, all this will happen to your race of people!

---

1   Verse 14 is omitted as it is not original and was added by copyists.
2   ὑπόκρισις, *hupokrisis*, behaviour of a ὑποκριτής, *hupokrites*. See note on Matt. 6:2.

37-39 "Jerusalem, Jerusalem, you who murder the prophets and stone the people who are sent to you! How often I wanted to gather your children together, like a hen gathers her chickens under her wings, but you refused! *38* Your temple is a deserted place! *39* Let me make this clear – you won't see me from now on until you say, 'Happy is the one who comes in the Lord's name.'"

Ch.24:1-2 As Jesus was leaving the temple, his disciples came up to point out the structure of the temple buildings. *2* "You see all this?" he remarked. "Every single stone will be pulled down – there won't be one stone left on top of another!"

3-14 As Jesus sat on the Mount of Olives, the disciples came to him privately. "Tell us! When will this happen? What's going to be the sign of your Coming,[1] and of the completion of the age?" they asked.

4 "Watch out that no one makes you wander off the right track!" Jesus answered. *5* "Many people will come claiming my authority! They will say, 'I am the Anointed One'. They will make lots of people wander off the right track!

6 "You will hear wars nearby and you will hear reports of wars. Don't be alarmed: these things must happen, but the end is not at this time. *7* Nation will rise against nation, and kingdom will rise against kingdom. There will be famines and earthquakes in various places. *8* All these things are the beginning of birthing labor. *9* Then they will hand you over to the authorities to be oppressed and killed. All nations will hate you because of my name. *10* Many people will fall into traps, and betray and hate one another. *11* Many false prophets will turn up and make lots of people wander off the right track. *12* And because illegality is rampant, many people's love will chill. *13* But the one who endures to the end will be rescued and preserved. *14* This Good News of the Realm will be proclaimed in the whole inhabited world as a witness to all nations, and then the end will come!"

15-22 "So then when you see the detestable thing[2] that causes devastation, spoken of by Daniel the prophet, standing in the sacred place - (*note from Matthew*: The one who reads this aloud is to take note!) – *16* then those in Judea must flee to the mountains! *17* The person on the roof must not go down to get anything from the house! *18* The person in the field must not go back to get any clothes! *19* But alas for those who are pregnant and for those who are breastfeeding babies in those days! *20* Pray that your escape won't be in winter or on the Sabbath. *21* Then there will be great oppression – and oppression like it has never been seen from the beginning of the world right up until this time - no, and never will be again! *22* Unless those days are cut short, no living thing would be saved, but because of the chosen people those days will be cut short.

---

[1] παρουσία, *parousia*, means "coming", "arrival", "visit", (sometimes referred to as the "Advent" in N.T.), often of the coming of an official, the presence of an official after their arrival, cf. *P.Oxy* 47 (1980) 3357 (late 1), a business letter; *SIG*³ 741.111, 1V; *SEG* 821.10. See the verb in an edict and speech of Nero (which states that as many people as possible were to be present in Corinth on November 28, *l*.4) in *AGI* 9 (Akraipia in Boitia, 28 November, 67 AD), repeated as no. 64 in E.M. Smallwood, *Documents Illustrating the Principates of Gaius, Claudius and Nero*, Cambridge, 1967 and in *SIG*³ 814. See L. Robert, *Hellenica* 13 (1965) 129-131 for a discussion of the cognate verb πάρειμι, *pareimi*, used for gods from the time of Homer. The cognate verb appears in the future in a letter stating that the correspondent will be present at a court case, *P.XV Cng.* 8.8 (Philadelphia, III BC, pl. 7a). See also *BGU* 2211, pp. 1-2 (pl.1) (Alexandria, c. 192) *l*.5, a letter about an official's coming, "..who is now intending to be present…in the land". For further reading, see A Deissmann, *Light from the Ancient Near East*, Grand Rapids, 1980, pp.368-73; L. Robert, *Hellenica*, 13 (1965) 129-31.

[2] βδέλυγμα, *bdelugma*, is used in the Old Covenant (Old Testament) for an idol or an offering to idols.

23-27 "Then if anyone says to you, 'Here is the Anointed One,' or 'There he is!' don't believe it! *24* False anointed ones and false prophets will turn up and show great miraculous signs that would, if it were possible, lead the chosen ones off the right track.

25 "See, I have told you beforehand! *26* So if they say to you, 'He's in the desert' don't go out, or 'He's in the bank,' don't go out! *27* The Coming of the Human Being will be like the lightning that comes out of the east and flashes across the sky to the west! *28* Where you find the corpse, there you find the eagles!

29-31 "Immediately after the oppression of those days the sun will be darkened, and the moon will not give its light, the stars will fall from the sky, and the powers of the heavenly places will be shaken. *30* At that time the Human Being's sign will appear in the sky. Then all the earth's races of people will mourn when they see the Human Being coming with power and great splendor on the clouds of the sky. *31* He will send his Messengers with a loud signal call of the trumpet. They will collect his chosen ones from the four corners of the earth, from one end of the skies to the other.

32-35 "Learn this example from the fig tree! When its branches sprout and grow leaves you realize that summer is near! *33* So too, when you see all these things, realize that it is near, at the doors! *34* Let me emphasize that this nation will by no means pass away until all these things have happened. *35* The sky and the earth will pass away, but my words will by no means pass away.

36-39 "No one knows when that day and hour will be, not even the Messengers of the heavenly places or the Son. Only my Father knows. *37* The Coming of the Human Being will be just like it was in the time of Noah. *38* In the days before the flood, they were eating and drinking, marrying and being married, until the day that Noah went into the ark. *39* They didn't realize what was going on until the flood took them all away. The Coming of the Human Being will be like this.

40-44 "At that time two men will be in the field, one will be taken and the other left. *41* Two women will be grinding at the mill, one will be taken and the other one left. *42* So keep your wits about you - you don't know which day your Lord will come! *43* Realize this, that if the owner of the household had known the time of the night the thief would come, they would have kept their wits about them and not allowed their house to be broken into. *44* So be ready! The Human Being is coming at a time you don't expect.

45-51.Ch.25:1-5 "Who then is a trustworthy and wise slave servant - someone the master has made ruler over the household staff, someone who gives them food at mealtimes? *46* That slave servant is in a happy state if the master arrives and finds him doing what he is supposed to do. *47* He will put him in charge of all his possessions. *48* But if the bad slave servant says to himself, 'My master's away a long time', *49* and starts beating up on his fellow slaves, and eating and drinking with the drunkards, *50* then his master will come when he's least expecting it. *51* He will chop him in half and his fate will be with the overly critical, hair splitting, pedantic religious types. There will be great sorrow, pain and anguish.

1 "This is also a story about Heaven's Realm. Ten unmarried girls[1] took their lamps and went out to meet the bridegroom. *2* There were five silly ones and five sensible ones. *3* The silly ones didn't take any oil with their lamps. *4* On the other hand, the wise ones took oil containers with their lamps. *5* The bridegroom was away a long time, so they all got tired and went to sleep.

6-13 "At midnight there was a shout, 'Here's the bridegroom! Go out and meet him!'

7 "Then all the girls got up and got their lamps ready. *8* The silly ones said to the wise ones, 'Give us some of your oil! Our lamps are going out!'

---

[1] παρθένος, *parthenos*. See note on Matt. 1:23.

9 "But the wise ones answered, 'No, if we do that, we might not have enough! Go away and buy your own!'

10 "The bridegroom came while they were away buying it. Everyone who was ready went with him to the wedding and the door was shut. *11* Afterwards the other girls came too, and said, 'Sir, sir, open the door!'

12 "But he answered, 'I tell you I don't know you!'

13 "So then keep your wits about you, because you don't know the day nor the hour.

14-20 "It's like a person going away from home, who calls his own slave servants and entrusts his possessions to them. *15* He gives one of them five bags of money, another two bags of money, another one bag of money, depending on their ability. He immediately sets off on his travels. *16* The person who had the five bags of money traded with them, and made another five bags of money. *17* The person who had the two bags of money did the same thing and made another two. *18* The person who had one bag of money dug a hole in the ground and buried it. *19* After a long time the slave servants' boss came back to settle accounts with them. *20* The person who had the five bags of money brought along five extra bags of money. He said, 'Boss, you gave me five bags of money, and I've made five extra bags of money!"

21-23 "Well done, you good trustworthy slave servant!" the boss said. "You've been trustworthy with a few things, now I'm putting you in charge of lots of things! Let's go and celebrate!'

22 "The person who had the two bags of money said, 'Boss, you gave me two bags of money to me, and I've made two extra bags of money!"

23 "'Well done, you good trustworthy slave servant!' the boss said. 'You've been trustworthy over a few things, now I'm putting you in charge of lots of things! Let's go and celebrate!'

24-30 "The person who had been given the one bag of money spoke up. 'Boss, I know you're a severe person! You can make money from practically nothing! *25* The person who had been given the one bag of money spoke up. 'Boss, I know you're a severe person! You can make money from practically nothing!

26 "'You evil, lazy slave servant!' the boss reprimanded him. 'You knew that I can make money from practically nothing! *27* Well then, you should have deposited my money with the public bankers, and then I could have had the interest when I came back! *28* Take this bag of money from him! Give it to the person who has ten bags of money! *29* Even more – to overflowing! - will be given to a person who has! But a person who doesn't have – even what they do have will be taken away! *30* Throw that unprofitable slave out into the dark! There will be great sorrow, pain and anguish!'

31-36 "When the Human Being comes in his splendor along with all his Messengers, he will sit on his glorious throne. *32* All the nations will be assembled in front of him. He will separate them from each another, just like a shepherd separates sheep from goats. *33* He will put the sheep on his right side and the goats on the left. *34* Then the King will say to those on his right side, 'Come on, people blessed by my Father, inherit the Realm which has been prepared for you since the foundation of the world! *35* You gave me food when I was hungry, you gave me a drink when I was thirsty, you took me in when I was a stranger, *36* you gave me clothes when I didn't have any, you visited me when I was sick, you visited me when I was in prison.

37-40 "Then the people who are right with God will answer him, 'Lord, when did we feed you when you were hungry? When did we give you a drink when you were thirsty? *38* When did we take you in when you were a stranger? When did we give you clothes when you didn't have any? *39* When did we visit you when you were sick or in prison?' *40* And the King will answer, 'If you did it for the least important of my brothers and sisters,[1] you did it for me!'

---

[1] See note on Matt. 5:22.

41-46 "Then he will say to those on the left side, 'Get out of my sight, you doubly cursed[1] ones! Off you go, into the permanent fire prepared for Slanderer-Liar and his messengers! *42* I was hungry and you didn't give me any food, I was thirsty and you didn't give me a drink, *43* I was a stranger and you didn't take me in, I didn't have any clothes and you didn't give me any, I was sick and in prison and you didn't visit me!'

44 "This will be their response: 'Lord, when did we see you hungry, thirsty, a stranger, without clothes, sick or in prison, and didn't give you what you needed?' *45* He will answer, 'If you didn't do it for the least important of my brothers and sisters, you didn't do it for me!' *46* These people will go off to rehabilitation for a set period of time,[2] but the people who are right with God will go off into eternal life."

Ch.26:1-5 After Jesus finished all these sayings, he said to his disciples, *2* "You know that the Passover is in another two days, and the Human Being is to be handed over to be crucified."

3 The chief priests and the elders of the people assembled at the chief priest's palace - his name was Caiaphas. *4* They plotted to arrest Jesus by some deception and then kill him. *5* However, they figured, "We'd better not do it during the feast, in case it causes a riot!"

6-13 When Jesus was in Bethany at Simon the leper's house, *7* a woman turned up carrying an alabaster flask of very expensive perfumed oil.[3] She

---

[1]   καταράομαι, *kataraomai*. See note on Luke 6:28.
[2]   αἰώνιος, *aionios*, "for a set period of time" (e.g. TAM 2 (1944) 910) or "forever" often the later use (e.g. SEG 853, typical acclamation for an Emperor).(ἐκ τοῦ αἰῶνος, *ek tou aionos*, "since the world began", see P.Oxy. 42.) (Note also its meaning "life", e.g. *P.Oxy*.1.33, "led off to death (i.e. from life)". In the Old Covenant it was used, for example, to describe the term of Israel's possession of Canaan (Gen. 17:8; 48:4) and the term of Aaron's priesthood (Num. 25:13). The word κόλασις, *kolasis*, "correction", "rehabilitation", (usually rendered in Bibles as "punishment" which more properly is τιμωρία, *timoria*) was originally a gardening term, used for pruning trees. The Greek writers used κόλασις, *kolasis*, to refer to rehabilitation, to the correction of wrongdoers so that they would not do wrong again. Generally τιμωρία, *timoria,* refers to retributive punishment and κόλασις, *kolasis*, to remedial discipline. Clement of Alexandria (*Stromateis* 4.25; 7.16) defines κόλασις, *kolasis*, as discipline, and τιμωρία, *timoria,* as the return of evil for evil. Aulus Gellius (*The Attic Nights* 7.14) states that κόλασις, *kolasis*, is given so that a person may be corrected, while τιμωρία is given so that dignity and authority may be vindicated. Aristotle (*Rhetoric* 1.10) states that κόλασις, *kolasis*, is for the sake of the one who experiences it, while τιμωρία, *timoria,* is for the sake of the one who inflicts it. Plato uses κόλασις, *kolasis*, in the sense that one punishes (κόλασις, *kolasis*) a wrongdoer so that the wrongdoer will not commit wrong again (*Protagoras* 323B). See discussion on the definition of κόλασις, *kolasis*, as rehabilitation and τιμωρία, *timoria,* as punishment in W. Barclay, *The Plain Man looks at the Apostles' Creed*, (London: George Allen & Unwin, 1987), pp. 225-7, and in C. Walsh, *The Problem of Hell: Is the existence of hell compossible with the existence of God?* Thesis, Honours in Philosophy, (Adelaide, Australia: University of Adelaide, 1996), pp. 1-4, 31-33. Both κόλασις, *kolasis*, and τιμωρία, *timoria,* appear in *P.Coll.Youtie* 1 30 (198/9): τιμωρία, *timoria,* as "punishment" (with ἐσχατος, *eskhatos*, capital punishment), and κόλασις, *kolasis*, in a more general sense. The threat of τιμωρία, *timoria,* was associated with prefectural διάγνωσις, *diagnosis*, the equivalent to *cognito*, the full judicial trial which included the admission of evidence and the handing down of judgment. See discussion in *NDIEC* 1.47-49.
[3]   μύρον, *muron*, perfumed ointment. See *IGUR* 1245.17-19. It was used in burial for the dead as well as a luxury item. The word also occurs in both

poured the perfumed oil on Jesus' head while he was reclining at the dinner table. *8* When his disciples saw it, they were indignant. "What a waste!" they muttered. *9* "This perfumed oil could have been sold for such-and-such an amount and given to the beggars!"

10 But when Jesus realized what was going on, he said, "Why upset this lady? She's done me a good turn. *11* You always have beggars around, but you don't always have me with you! *12* This lady was pouring this perfumed oil on my body for my burial! *13* Indeed, what she has done will be talked about in her memory throughout the entire world where the Good News is proclaimed!"

14-16 Then one of the Twelve by the name of Judas Iscariot went to the chief priests. *15* "What are you willing to give me if I hand Jesus over to you?" he enquired.

They agreed to pay him thirty pieces of silver. *16* So from that moment on Judas kept an eye open for an opportunity to betray Jesus.

17-25 On the first day of the feast of Unleavened Bread, the disciples asked Jesus, "Where would you like us to prepare the Passover meal for you?"

18 He replied, "Go into the city to so-and-so and tell him, 'The teacher says, "My time is near, I am to keep the Passover at your house with my disciples.'"'

19 So the disciples did as Jesus had directed them and they prepared the Passover meal. *20* When evening came Jesus reclined at the table with the Twelve. *21* While they were eating, he said, "One of you is going to betray me!"

22 They became very upset. Each and every one of them kept saying to him, "I'm not the one, am I?"

23 "One of you who has shared the meal with me will betray me!" he answered. *24* "What's been written about the Human Being will happen to him for sure, but woe betides that person who betrays the Human Being! That person would have been better off if he'd never been born!"

25 Judas, the one who was going to betray him, said, "Rabbi, it's not me, is it?"

"You said it!" Jesus said.

26-30 While they were eating, Jesus picked up some bread, and after blessing it broke it into pieces. He gave it to the disciples and said, "Take it, eat it, this is my body!"

27 He picked up the wine cup, and expressed thankfulness. He gave it to them and said, "Drink from it, all of you. *28* This is my blood which seals the covenant, my blood shed to cancel[1] the sins of many people. *29* I will not drink this produce of the vine from now on until the day I drink it new with you in my Father's Kingdom." *30* After they had sung a festive praise song,[2] they went out to the Mount of Olives.

---

meanings in Mark 14:3-8, John 12:1-7, Luke 7:36-56. In Mark and John, the μύρον, *muron,* is identified as νάρδου, *nardou,* spikenard. See note on Mark 14:3.

[1] ἄφεσις, *aphesis,* "cancellation" (not "forgiveness"), a setting free, a quittance or discharge, a dismissal, e.g., ἄφεσις φόνου, *aphesis phonou,* a discharge from murder, Id. *Legg.* 869D; *PSI* 8.972, a dismissal of the matter (referring to an assault).

[2] ὑμνέω, *humneo,* to sing an ὕμνος, *humnos.* ὕμνος, *humnos,* (usually translated as "hymn") was a festive song sung in worship, not necessarily a song sung to stringed instruments. There were 2 types of ὕμνος, *humnos*: 1. In lyric meter and this was actually sung to the *kithara,* a type of lute or lyre. 2. In epic meter, *viz,* dactylic hexameter. When a ὕμνος, *humnos,* was sung in lyric meter it was either chanted, or sung in a way which sounded like chanting. This type of ὕμνος, *humnos,* was not sung to stringed instruments. The Greeks often used castanets and maracas to sing this type of ὕμνος, *humnos.* In the epic meter, the chanting or singing was often improvised. It consisted of 6 feet a line. The first 5 could be dactyls but last had to be a spondee. (A spondee was rare in the 5th). The only substitute for the dactyl was the spondee. In fact, the whole beat could

31-35 Then Jesus said, "All of you will reject me because of what I do tonight, as the Scriptures say, 'I will strike the Shepherd and all the sheep will be scattered!' *32* But after I have been raised, I will go ahead of you to Galilee."

33 Peter insisted, "Even if we all reject you because of what you do, I will never reject you!"

34 "Let me tell you that tonight, before the rooster crows, you will deny that you know me three times!" Jesus responded.

35 "No way!" Peter exclaimed. "Even if I have to die with you, I will not deny you!" All the disciples said the same thing.

36-41 Then Jesus went with them to a place called Gethsemane. He said to the disciples, "Sit down here while I go off and pray over there."

37 He took Peter and the two sons of Zebedee along with him, and he started to get sad and very distressed. *38* Then he said to them, "My soul is extremely, deathly sad. Please stay and keep watch[1] with me." *39* Then he went a little further on and fell on his face, and prayed, "Father, if it's possible, let this suffering be taken away from me – but it's not what I want that counts, but what you want."

40 Then he went to the disciples and found they were asleep. He said to Peter, "What! You couldn't even keep watch with me for one hour! *41* Keep watch and pray, so that you may be spared trying times. The spirit is eager but human nature is weak."

42-44 Again, the second time, he went away and prayed, "Father, if there's no other way for this to happen without me suffering, then let your purpose be done!" *43* He came and found them asleep again, as their eyelids were heavy. *44* He left them and went away again and prayed the third time, saying the same words.

45-50 Then he went over to his disciples and said, "Are you going to sleep and rest indefinitely? This is now the time that the Human Being is betrayed into sinners' hands. *46* Get up! Let's go! My betrayer is near!"

47 While he was still speaking, Judas, one of the Twelve, arrived with a large crowd from the chief priests and elders of the people carrying swords and clubs. *48* His betrayer had arranged this sign: "Whoever I kiss, he's the One, arrest him!"

49 He went straight up to Jesus and said, "Hello, Rabbi!" and kissed him warmly.

50 Jesus said, "Friend, what are you here for?"

Then they grabbed Jesus and arrested him.

51-56 One of the people with Jesus drew his sword, struck the slave servant of the chief priest and cut off his ear.

52 "Put away your sword!" Jesus exclaimed. "People who take up the sword are killed by the sword! *53* Hasn't it occurred to you that I can pray right now to my Father, and he will provide me with more than 12 army divisions

---

be all spondees. For further reading see Raven, D.S., *Greek Metre*, (London: Faber, 1962), particularly pages 44-55, 56ff, 64, 114, 130. *Humnos* occurs in Eph. 5:19 and Col. 3:16, and *humneo* (apart from here) in Mark 14:26; Acts 16:25, and Heb. 2:12.

[1] γρηγορέω, *gregoreo*, is a rare word which occurs 22 times in N.T. John AL Lee & GHR Horsley, "A Lexicon of the NT with Documentary Parallels: Some Interim Entries, 2" *FilNT* 10 (1997) p. 71 translate the example from *PSI* 14.1413.9 (Egypt, II-III AD, letter) as "Keep your wits about you!": "Make it your business to buy the wood also for the doors. It's very urgent. Note that Dosas son of Ma..kos has some at Herennios' place. Don't pay more than a moderate price. I believe that Alexandros son of Theb... will come. Keep your wits about you!" Equally possible here: "keep watch", "stay awake", "be alert".

each of 600 Messengers? *54* But then how would the Scriptures be fulfilled? It has to happen like this!"

55 Then Jesus said to the crowds, "You've come to arrest me with swords and clubs as if I'm a robber! I was sitting with you day after day, teaching in the temple, and you didn't arrest me! *56* But this whole thing was done to fulfill the prophetic writings!" At that point all the disciples left him and ran away.

57-61 Then the people who'd arrested Jesus took him off to Caiaphas the chief priest, to an assembly of the Bible scholars and the elders. *58* Peter was following Jesus at a distance to the chief priest's courtyard. He went inside and sat with the attendants to see how it would all turn out. *59* The chief priests and the whole council tried to find some false evidence against Jesus so they could put him to death. *60* They couldn't find any, even though many false witnesses came forward. At last two came forward *61* and said, "This man said, 'I am able to destroy the temple of God and build it in three days.'"

62-68 The chief priest got up and asked Jesus, "Aren't you going to answer these allegations?"

63 Jesus kept silent. The chief priest said to him, "I put you under oath by the living God to tell us whether you are the Anointed One, the Son of God."

64 "You said it!" Jesus replied. "And what's more, after this you will see the Human Being sitting at the right hand of the Power[1] and coming in the clouds of the sky."

65 Then the chief priest ripped his shirt as a formal act of judgment[2] and exclaimed, "He has blasphemed! We don't need any more witnesses! Now you've heard his blasphemy! *66* What do you think?"

"He deserves the death penalty!" they answered.

67 Then they spat in his face and beat him up and others slapped him around. *68* "Prophesy to us, Anointed One! Who's the one who hit you?" they taunted.

69-75 Peter sat outside in the courtyard. A servant girl went over to him and remarked, "You were with Jesus of Galilee!"

70 But he denied it in front of everyone. "I haven't got a clue what you're talking about!" he said.

71 When he'd gone out the gateway, another girl saw him and said to the bystanders, "He was with Jesus of Nazareth."

72 But he denied it again with an oath, "I don't know the person!"

73 A little later the people who were standing around came up and said to Peter, "Surely you're one of them! Come on, your dialect gives you away!"

74 So Peter started calling down curses and swearing oaths: "I don't know the person!" And at that very point a rooster crowed. *75* Then Peter remembered Jesus' words, "Before the rooster crows, you will deny that you know me three times." He went away and cried bitterly.

Ch.27:1-4 And dawn arrived, and all the chief priests and elders of the people formed a plan to have Jesus put to death. *2* Then they tied him up and took him off to Pilate the governor. *3* When Judas his betrayer saw that Jesus had been condemned, he had a change of heart. He tried to return the thirty pieces of silver to the chief priests and the elders. *4* "I have sinned by betraying innocent blood!" he told them.

"Could we care less?" they replied. "That's your business!"

5-10 Judas threw down the pieces of silver in the temple and went away and hanged himself. *6* The chief priests took the silver pieces and said, "It isn't legal to put them in the treasury – it's blood money!"

7 They consulted with each other, and bought the potter's field as a burial ground for foreigners with the silver pieces. *8* This is the reason it was given the

---

[1]   That is, God: the Jewish avoidance of the Sacred Name.

[2]   The ripping of the clothes by the chief priest was a formal judicial act regulated in the Talmud.

name "The Field of Blood" which it has to this very day. *9* Thus the words spoken by Jeremiah the prophet were fulfilled: "And they took the thirty pieces of silver, the price they set on him (the amount the Israelites had agreed to pay) *10* and used the money for the potter's field, as the Lord instructed me."

11-18 Jesus stood in front of the governor. The governor asked, "Are you the King of the Jews?"

"You said it!" Jesus answered.

12 The whole time he was being accused by the chief priests and elders, he made no reply. *13* Then Pilate said, "Aren't you listening to all the evidence they're bringing against you?" *14* But Jesus didn't say a thing in response, and the governor was amazed.

15 At the time of the feast the governor was accustomed to releasing to the crowd their choice of prisoner. *16* At that time they had a notorious prisoner called Barabbas. *17* So when they'd assembled, Pilate said to them, "Which one do you want me to release to you, Barabbas, or Jesus who is called the Anointed One?

18 He realized that they had handed Jesus over because they were jealous of him.

19-26 While Pilate was sitting in court, his wife sent this message to him: "Don't have anything to do with that righteous person! I've experienced a lot in a dream today about him."

20 The chief priests and the elders persuaded the crowds to ask for Barabbas as this would result in Jesus being executed. *21* "Which of the two do you want me to release?" the governor asked.

"Barabbas!" they exclaimed.

22 Pilate asked, "Then what should I do with Jesus who is called the Anointed One?"

"Crucify him!" the crowd answered.

23 "Why, what's he done wrong?" Pilate asked.

They all called out again, even louder, "Crucify him!"

24 When Pilate saw that it was no use and a riot was about to start,[1] he got some water and washed his hands in front of the crowd. "I am innocent of the blood of this person!" he said. "That's your business!"

25 All the people answered, "We'll take the blame – so will our children!" *26* Then he released Barabbas, and after he had Jesus beaten with a Roman whip of leather straps embedded with metal designed to rip off the flesh, he sent him off to be crucified.

---

[1]   John 19:4-12 explains the whole matter more fully, whereas Matthew glosses over it. In John 19:12 the Jews say to Pilate. "If you let this person go, you're no Friend of Caesar's! Anyone who claims to be a king opposes Caesar!" These two sentences constitute blackmail, or at the very least, a most significant implied threat. "Friend of Caesar" was a technical term describing a group which included senators, *equites* (a wealthy class known as the Knights or the Equestrian order) and others who had access to the emperor. Pilate's very political being was dependent on this relationship. Every person in the Empire was committed by the terms of the oath of loyalty to the Caesarian family to report disloyal behavior by others. The Jews were pressuring Pilate by the fact that he was a "Friend of Caesar". In reference to this, P. Barnett states, "One false move and his appointment would be canceled and his career finished." *Jesus and the Rise of Early Christianity: A History of New Testament Times*, (Illinois: InterVarsity, 1999), p. 147. Furthermore, Pilate's patron had been Sejanus, who had recently fallen from power in AD 31 as he was plotting against the Emperor. This placed Pilate in a precarious position. For further reading, see P.L. Maier, "Sejanus, Pilate and the Date of the Crucifixion," *Church History* 37 (1968) 1-11.

27-31 Then the governor's soldiers took Jesus into the governor's residence and gathered the whole company of 600 soldiers around him. *28* They stripped him and put a scarlet[1] robe on him. *29* After they had woven a crown out of thorns, they put it on his head, and put a stick in his right hand. They knelt down in front of him and made fun of him, saying, "Greetings, King of the Jews!"

30 They spat on him and kept hitting him over the head with the stick. *31* After they made fun of him, they took the robe off, put his clothes back on, and took him away to be crucified.

32-38 On their way out they found a person from Cyrene, called Simon. They conscripted him to carry Jesus' cross. *33* When they arrived at a place by the name of Golgotha, which means "Place of a Skull", *34* they gave Jesus a drink of wine mixed with a painkiller.[2] After he tasted it, he wouldn't drink it.

35 When they had crucified him they divided his clothes among them by casting lots. *36* Then they sat down and kept watch. *37* Above his head they placed the charge which read, "This is Jesus, the King of the Jews."

38 Then two robbers[3] were crucified with him, the one on his right side and the other on his left.

39-44 The people who went past abused him, shaking their heads. *40* They said, "Hey you! You're supposed to destroy the temple and build it in three days, so save yourself! If you're the Son of God, get down from the cross!"

41 In the same way the chief priests along with the Bible scholars and elders also mocked, *42* "He saved others, but he can't save himself! If he's the King of Israel, he can come down from the cross right now and then we'll believe him! *43* He trusted God, so God can rescue him now if he really wants to! After all, he did say, 'I am the Son of God!'"

44 Even the robbers who were crucified with him taunted him in the same way.

45-53 From midday until 3 p.m. darkness covered all the land.[4] *46* About 3 p.m. Jesus called out loudly, "Eli, Eli, lama sabachthani?" which means, "My God, My God, why have you abandoned me?"

---

[1] κόκκινος, *kokkinos*, "scarlet", "crimson", a color of the purple (πορφυροῦς, *porphurous*) trade. Note the parallel account in Mark 15:17, 20 uses πορφυροῦς, *porphurous* instead of κόκκικος, *kokkikos*. Purple was a status color, as can be seen from other N.T. references, Mark 15:17, 20; Luke 16:19; Rev. 17:3, 4; 18:12, 16. The use of purple was not restricted to the wealthy as purple dyes were available in a variety of dyes and qualities, but color-fast purple derived from murex was highly expensive. The purple industry is most associated with Tyre (see *I.Tyre* 1), but was also important in Philippi, Thessalonike, Phrygia, Lydia, and Egypt. The Church Fathers, the Stoics and Cynics all produced moralizing sermons against purple and its accompanying status. However, Apollonia of Tyana had made known his disapproval much earlier, in the 1st c.

[2] Spice with myrrh added in sufficient quantity to turn the wine into the drug. The intention was to ease the pain, and was in accordance with Jewish custom, based on Prov. 24.74.

[3] ληστής, *lestes*. LSJ *s.v.* have "robber, pirate", "especially by sea, a buccaneer". Louw and Nida *s.v.* "one who robs by force and violence – 'robber, highwayman.'" The word as "robber" is well attested in the papyri and inscriptions, e.g. *P.Oxy* I.139.23; *P.Petr* III.28; *P.Lips* I.37.29. For the adjective (which occurs commonly), see *P.Tebt* I.53.11.

[4] In AD 52 Thallus wrote a history of the eastern Mediterranean world dating from the late Bronze Age, and wrote about the darkness which came at this time. In AD 221 Julius Africanus quoted Thallus' work. Soon after AD 137, Phlegon, a Greek author in Caria, wrote that in the 4th year of the 202nd Olympiad (c. AD 33), there was a great darkness and it became night at the 6th hour of the day. There was a major earthquake in Bithynia as well as

47 When some of the bystanders heard this, they exclaimed, "He's calling for Elijah!" *48* Immediately one of them ran and got a sponge, filled it with the soldier's issue of wine vinegar and put it on a stick, and offered it to him to drink. *49* The rest said, "Leave him alone - let's see if Elijah will save him!"

50 Jesus cried again with a loud voice and gave up the Spirit.

51 And the veil of the temple that separated the Holy of Holies from the Holy Place was torn in two from top to bottom, and the earth quaked and the rocks split. *52* The graves were opened and many of the bodies of the people devoted to God who had died were raised up. *53* They came out of the graves after Jesus' resurrection, and went into the sacred city and appeared to many.

54-61 Now when the Roman officer in charge of 100 men and those with him who were guarding Jesus saw the earthquake and everything that happened, they were extremely frightened. "This person truly was the Son of God!" they exclaimed.

55 Many women were watching from a distance. They were the women who had followed Jesus from Galilee and had been materially providing[1] for him. *56* Among them were Mary Magdalene, Mary the mother of James and Joseph, and the mother of Zebedee's sons. *57* When early evening came, a rich person from Arimathea named Joseph arrived. He too had become a disciple of Jesus. *58* Joseph went to Pilate to request Jesus' body. As a result, Pilate ordered the body to be handed over to him. *59* When Joseph had taken the body, he wrapped it in a clean piece of fine linen *60* and put it in his new tomb which he had hewn out of the rock. He rolled a large stone against the door of the tomb, and left.

61 And Mary Magdalene was there, and the other Mary, sitting in front of the tomb.

62-66 On the next day, the day after the Day of Preparation, the chief priests and Pharisees went as a group to Pilate. *63* They said, "Sir, we remembered that when he was still alive, that imposter said, 'I am to rise after three days.' *64* So please order that the tomb be secured until the third day, in case his disciples come and steal him, and tell the people, 'He has risen from among the dead.' Then this case of fraud will be worse than the first!"

65 "You may have guards," Pilate replied. "Off you go, make it as secure as you can." *66* They went away and sealed the stone, and secured the tomb by posting guards.

Ch.28:1-4 After the Sabbath, as the first day of the week began to dawn, Mary Magdalene and the other Mary came to see the tomb. *2* There was a major earthquake! A Messenger of the Lord came down from heaven. He rolled back the stone and sat on it. *3* His face was like lightening, and his clothing as white as snow. *4* The guards shook in fear of him, and lay like corpses.

5-10 The Messenger said to the women, "There's no need to be afraid! I know that you're looking for Jesus who was crucified. *6* He's not here. He has risen, as he said he would. See for yourselves the place where the Lord lay! *7* Go off quickly and tell his disciples that he has risen from among the dead. In fact he is going on ahead of you to Galilee. You'll see him there. Take note! I have told you!"

8 They left the tomb quickly, fearful yet very happy, and ran to report to his disciples. *9* Jesus met them, and said, "Hello!" They went to him and held his feet and worshipped him. *10* Then Jesus said to them, "Don't be afraid! Go and tell the fellow believers to go to Galilee, and they'll see me there."

---

disruption in Nicaea. For further reading, see P.L. Maier, *Pontius Pilate*, (Wheaton: Tyndale House, 1968).

[1] διακονέω τινί, *diakoneo tini*, "provide materially (for someone)", cf. P. Barnett, *Is the New Testament History?*, (Sydney: Hodder & Stoughton, 1989), p. 75. Note this use in *P. Oxy.* 3313. The subject is the sending of money, 1,000 roses and 4,000 flowers to a wedding, and the senders are very wealthy people.

11-15 While they were on their way, some of the guards went into the city and reported to the chief priests everything that had happened. *12* After they had a meeting with the elders and consulted with each other, they gave a large sum of money to the soldiers with the instructions, *13* "Tell them, 'His disciples stole him in the night while we were asleep.' *14* And if the governor gets to hear about it, we'll persuade him, and we'll cover for you!"

15 So they took the money and did as they were told. And this story is spread among the Jews to this very day.

16-20 The eleven disciples went away to Galilee, to the mountain Jesus had directed them. *17* When they saw him they worshipped him – however, some doubted. *18* Jesus said to them, "All authority has been given to me in heaven and upon the earth. *19* So then, off you go – make disciples of all the nations. Baptize them in the Name of the Father and the Son and the Holy Spirit, *20* and teach them to hold fast to everything that I have commanded you. I am always with you, until the completion of the age."

The Good News according to Mark.

Mark was attested as the author of the gospel from the first half of the second century. Irenaeus, Papias, Tertullian, Origen, Jerome Clement of Alexandria, all ascribe the authorship to Mark. Acts covers the period from c. AD 33-63, and was written after Luke. The general academic opinion is that Mark was written before Luke (late 50s to 60s AD) and Romans (c. AD 57) and was used as source material for the other gospels. This has been variously disputed. L. Wells[1] makes a further case for the priority of Mark based on his healing language and accounts of healing.

Mark, a cousin of Barnabas, was wealthy, educated and bilingual, with Greek as his second language. His mother's house was a major meeting place for the Jerusalem church. Clearly it was a large house as Acts 12:12 tells us that many people were gathered praying and Acts 12:13 speaks of a maid. His two names were John (Hebrew) and Mark (Greek or Latin).

Some suggest that Mark wrote his Good News in Palestine by the late 40s, while others suggest that Mark wrote the Good News in Rome in the early to mid 50s. Papias and Clement of Alexandria state (although Irenaeus does not) that Mark wrote his Good News in connection with Peter while the latter was still living. Note that Mark was closely associated with Peter (who, according to Eusebius, died in 64 AD) in Jerusalem in the 40s (Acts 12:12) and the 60s (1 Pet. 5:13). However, there is a possibility that the young man in 14:51-52 was Mark himself. A literary device of the times was for the author to identify themselves by means of a token. The author would identify themselves by allusion.

Mark's Good News is breathless, vivid and excited - it's a thrill a minute! Mark uses "immediately" frequently, and is fond of present tenses. For example, he will say, "And they're getting on the boat!" (instead of "They got on the boat.")

The Good News according to Mark.

Ch.1:1-3 The Starting Point of the Good News about Jesus the Anointed One, Son of God.

2 The Scriptures say in Isaiah the Prophet: "I'm going to send my messenger ahead of you! He will prepare the road for you. *3* It's the voice of one who shouts in the desert, 'Prepare the road for the Lord, clear a straight pathway for him!'"

4-8 John the baptizer and preacher turned up in the desert. He preached that people should be baptized as a symbol that they had changed their minds, and this resulted in their sins being cancelled. *5* The whole district of Judea and all the people of Jerusalem kept coming out to him. They confessed their sins and were baptized by him in the Jordan River.

6 John dressed in camel's hair. He wore a leather belt around his waist, and he ate locustsand wild honey. *7* "There's someone coming after me and he's stronger than I am!" he preached. "I'm not even fit to bend over and untie his sandals! *8* I baptize you with water, that's for sure, but he will baptize you with the Holy Spirit!"

9-11 And it turned out that at that time Jesus came from Nazareth in Galilee and let himself be baptized by John in the Jordan River. *10* The moment Jesus came out of the water, he saw the skies split open and the Spirit descending upon him like[2] a dove. *11* A voice came out of heaven: "You are my dear Son. You're the one I favored!"

---

[1] Louise Wells, *op.cit.*, p. 130.
[2] Luke 3:22 says the dove was in actual bodily appearance, but Mark merely states that the Spirit descended like a dove (in the way in which a dove descends).

12-13 Immediately the Spirit threw him into the desert. *13* He was in the desert for forty days being put through an ordeal[1] by Adversary. He was with the small wild animals, and the Messengers were providing for him.

14-15 Now after John was arrested, Jesus went to Galilee, and proclaimed the Good News about God. *15* He said, "The appointed time is here, and God's Realm[2] is close! Change your minds, and believe the Good News!"

16-20 As Jesus went past the Sea of Galilee he saw Simon and his brother Andrew casting nets into the lake – they were fishermen. *17* Jesus said, "Come here and follow me, and I will make you fishers of human beings!" *18* Immediately they released their nets and followed him. *19* When he had gone a bit further on, he saw James, Zebedee's son, and his brother John in a ship, preparing their nets. *20* Immediately he called out to them. They left their father Zebedee in the ship with the hired hands[3] and followed him.

21-28 Off they went to Capernaum, and it turned out that on the Sabbath Jesus went into the synagogue and started teaching. *22* They were shocked at his teaching, because he was teaching them like someone who had authority and not just like the Bible scholars. *23* Now there was a person in their synagogue who had an unclean spirit. He screamed out forcefully, *24* "Hey! What are you meddling with us[4] for, Jesus of Nazareth? You've come to destroy us![5] I know who you are – the Holy One of God!"

25 And Jesus reprimanded it sharply[6] and said, "Be bound,[7] and come out of him!"

26 The unclean spirit caused him to spasm[8] and came out of him with a very loud shout. *27* They were all shocked, so much so that they discussed it with each other, and exclaimed, "What on earth's this! A new teaching that has authority! He even orders around the unclean spirits, and they pay attention[9] to him!"

---

[1] πειράζω, *peirazo*. See note on Matt. 4:1.

[2] βασιλεία τοῦ θεοῦ, *basileia tou theou*. This encompasses the idea of the Reign of God, corresponding with the Aramaic *malkuth*, "kingship", "kingly rule", "reign". Throughout his narrative, Mark emphasizes that God's Realm is the place in which God's purpose is done. The Realm is present, not solely future. It does not refer to heaven. Jesus spoke of the realm as present in himself and his ministry, cf. Luke 7:18-23, 10:23f, 11:20, 31f. Note that βασιλεία, *basilea*, refers to the realm of a king, to everything under the king's influence, whereas βασίλειον (τό), *basileion (to)*, refers to the dwelling of the king, the seat of the empire, capital, royal city. See LSJ, *s.v.*

[3] Luke 5:10 states that James and John were partners with Simon in the fishing corporation. Commercial fishermen were usually wealthy, and the high price of fish was a common source of material in Greek comedy, and is noted, for example, in *IG* II[2] (1913; *repr.* 1974) 1103. Fishing guilds wielded much political power, and even where the fishing industry was not large enough to warrant such a guild, fishing co-operatives were formed. See G.H.R. Horsley, "A Fishing Cartel in First-Century Ephesos," *NDIEC* 5.95-114.

[4] The "us" in all likelihood refers to the type of spirit.

[5] This phrase is usually taken as a question. Rather, it is a defiant assertion. See A.E.J. Rawlinson, *The Gospel According to St. Mark*, 7th ed., (London: J.M. Dent & Sons, 1949), p. 16; M. Lagrange, *Évangile selon Saint Marc*, 5th ed., (Paris: La collection scientifique de l'École Biblique, 1929), p. 22; Taylor, *op.cit.*, p. 174.

[6] ἐπιτιμάω, *epitimao*, is a technical term used in Greek pagan religion for gaining control over a spirit.

[7] φιμόω, *phimoo*. See note on Matt. 22:12.

[8] σπαράσσω, *sparasso*, to tear, pull to pieces, to attack, to provoke sickness, to be convulsed, retch with desire to vomit.

[9] ὑπακούω, *hupakouo*. See note on Matt. 8:27.

28 Immediately Jesus' fame spread throughout the whole region around Galilee.

29-31 As soon as they left the synagogue, they went straight to Simon and Andrew's house with James and John. *30* Simon's mother-in-law was lying sick in bed as she was feverish, and they immediately told Jesus about her. *31* Jesus went over to her and helped her up, grabbing her by the hand. The fever left her, and she started providing for them.

32-34 But that evening after sunset, people kept bringing everyone who was unwell and those who had bad spirits in them to Jesus. *33* The whole city gathered at the door! *34* Jesus healed[1] many sick people who were inflicted with various types of diseases. He also threw out lots of evil spirits, but he didn't allow the evil spirits to speak, because they knew who he was.

35-39 At a very early hour, while it was still night, Jesus got up and went out to a solitary area. He stayed there in prayer. *36* And Simon and his companions hunted him down. *37* When they found him, they said, "Everyone's looking for you!"

38 Jesus said to them, "Let's go somewhere else - to the neighboring villages, so that I can preach there too, because this is the reason I've come here." *39* Off he went and preached in their synagogues over the whole of Galilee, and threw out evil spirits.

40-45 A leper came to him calling for help. He said, "If you want to, you can make me clean!"

41 And Jesus, moved with compassion,[2] touched him, and said, "I want to! Be clean!"

42 Immediately the leprosy left him, and he was cleansed. *43* Jesus was deeply moved[3] and sent him off immediately, after instructing him, *44* "Off you go – and see that you don't say a thing to anyone! Show yourself to the priest, and offer the things that Moses ordered for your cleansing, as evidence that you are healed."

45 But he went out and started publicizing it everywhere, and spreading the story around, so that Jesus couldn't go into the city openly any more, but stayed outside in solitary locations. The people came to him from everywhere.

Ch.2:1-7 Jesus went back to Capernaum after a few days, and people heard that he was at home. *2* Such a large crowd gathered that there was no longer enough room to put them, not even near the door. Jesus preached to them. *3* They came[4] to him, bringing a paralyzed person who was carried by four people. *4* As they couldn't get near him because of the crowd, they uncovered the roof above where Jesus was. They made a hole in it[5] and lowered the stretcher with the paralyzed person lying on it. *5* When Jesus saw the paralyzed person's faith, he said, "My child, your sins are forgiven at this very moment!"

6 Now some of the Bible scholars were sitting there and thoroughly considering to themselves, *7* "Why is this guy talking like this? He's blaspheming! Who can forgive sins – only God can do that!

---

[1] θεραπεύω, *therapeuo*. See note on Matt. 4:23.

[2] The textual evidence is inconclusive as to whether Jesus was angry with the leprosy or moved with compassion for the man, although is weighted in favor of the latter.

[3] ἐμβριμάομαι, *embrimaomai*. See John 11:33. Some translations have "strictly warned" which is not in the Greek. The word indicates a strong feeling within oneself.

[4] Mark puts this in the "historic present" tense, a Greek literary device to show urgency. It is also very colloquial. Traditionally, the Greek historic present is not translated by an English present. There are numerous historic presents in Mark.

[5] A roof common to that area would have been made with beams and rafters under a layer of branches and matting covered with trodden-down packed earth. Alternatively, the roof may have been tiled.

8-12 Immediately Jesus discerned in his spirit what they were thinking, and he said, "Why are you thinking these things? *9* What's easier to say, 'Your sins are cancelled right at this moment,' or, 'Get up, pick up your stretcher and walk around?' *10* But so that you will know that the Human Being[1] has the authority to cancel sins on the earth..." At this point he said to the paralyzed person, *11* "I tell you, Get up, pick up your stretcher and go home!"

12 And he got up. Immediately he picked up his stretcher and left right in front of everyone. As a result everyone was beside themselves in shock, and they praised God, and exclaimed, "We've never seen anything like it!"

13-17 Jesus went out again beside the sea. A large crowd went to him, and he started teaching them. *14* As he walked along, he saw Levi, Alphaeus' son, sitting at the Tax Profiteer's office. He said to him, "Follow me," and Levi got up and followed him. *15* While Jesus was reclining for dinner at Levi's house, many Tax Profiteers and sinners were eating with him and his disciples - this was due to the fact that he was followed by so many people. *16* When the Bible scholars who were Pharisees saw him reclining for dinner with sinners and Tax Profiteers they asked his disciples, "Why is he eating with Tax Profiteers and sinners?"

17 Jesus heard them and said, "People who are well don't need a doctor, only people who are sick. I haven't come to invite people who are right with God: instead, I've come to invite sinners."

18-22 John's disciples and Pharisees were fasting. People asked Jesus, "Why do John's disciples and the Pharisees' disciples fast, but your disciples don't?"

19 "Can the wedding guests fast while the bridegroom is with them?" Jesus asked in turn. "No, they can't fast while the bridegroom is with them! *20* But the time will come when the bridegroom will be taken away from them, and that is when they will fast. *21* No one sews a patch of unshrunk cloth on an old coat. If they do, the added piece will tear away from the old one and make the tear worse. *22* And no one pours new wine into old wineskins. If they do, the wine will burst the skins, and then both the wine and the wineskins will be ruined. No, they pour new wine into fresh[2] wineskins."

23-28 On a Sabbath day Jesus was passing by the grain fields. While his disciples were going along, they started picking some heads of grain. *24* The Pharisees kept saying to Jesus, "Hey! Why are they doing this! It's not legal on the Sabbath day!"

25 "Haven't you read what David did when he and his companions felt hungry and found themselves in need?" Jesus answered. *26* "In the time of Abiathar the chief priest, David went into the house of God and ate the sacred bread.[3] Now it was only legal for the priests to eat the sacred bread. Yet David gave some to his companions, too." *27* Jesus added, "The Sabbath was made for the sake of the person – the person wasn't made for the sake of the Sabbath! *28* And so the Human Being is also Master of the Sabbath."

Ch.3:1-6 On another occasion Jesus went to the synagogue, and there was a person who had a withered hand. *2* The Pharisees kept a close eye on Jesus to see if he would heal on a Sabbath, as that would provide them with an opportunity to accuse him. *3* Jesus said to the person who had the withered hand, "Step forward!"

4 Then Jesus asked them, "On the Sabbath day is it legal to do good or to do bad, to save life or to destroy it?" But they kept quiet. *5* Jesus looked around angrily. He was very upset by the insensitivity of their minds. "Stretch out your hand," Jesus said to the person.

---

[1] ὁ υἱὸς τοῦ ἀνθρώπου, *ho huios tou anthropou.* See note on Matt. 8:20.

[2] Mark makes the distinction between νέος, *neos,* "new" (of time), and καινός, *kainos,* "fresh" (of quality).

[3] This describes the 12 freshly baked loaves of bread placed every Sabbath in 2 rows on a table before God in the tabernacle and later eaten by the priests. (Lev. 34.5-9)

The person stretched it out, and his hand was restored to its proper condition.[1] *6* At this the Pharisees left and immediately started plotting with the friends and supporters of Herod Antipas against Jesus, plotting how they were going kill him.

7-12 Jesus withdrew with his disciples to the sea. A large crowd from Galilee followed him, and from Judea, *8* from Jerusalem, Idumaea,[2] and the area beyond the Jordan River and around Tyre and Sidon. They followed him because they'd heard about everything that he was doing. *9* He told his disciples to keep a small boat on hand so that the crowd wouldn't crush him. *10* In fact, he'd healed lots of people. As a result, all those people who had anything wrong with them were falling all over him so they could touch him. *11* When the unclean spirits saw him, they would fall down in front of him and shout, "You are the Son of God!" *12* He strongly warned them against revealing who he was to anyone.

13-19 Jesus went up the mountain and called over the ones he wanted. *14* He appointed twelve whom he also named apostles so that they would be with him and so that he could send them out to preach *15* and have authority to throw out evil spirits. *16* These are the twelve he appointed – Simon (Jesus gave him the name Peter), *17* James (Zebedee's son) and his brother John - (Jesus gave them the name Boanerges, which means "People with thunderous natures") – *18* Andrew, Philip, Bartholemew, Matthew, Thomas, James son of Alphaeus, Thaddeus, Simon the Zealot, *19* as well as Judas Iscariot, who in fact later betrayed him.

20-30 Jesus went to a house, and such a crowd gathered, that they couldn't even sit down to eat a meal! *21* When Jesus' family heard, they went out to grab him. "He's completely out of his mind!" they figured.

22 The Bible scholars who came down from Jerusalem were saying, "He's got the demon god Beelzebub[3] in him!" and "He's throwing out evil spirits by the chief evil spirit's power!"

23 Jesus called them over and spoke to them in examples. "How can someone working for Adversary throw out someone who is working for Adversary?" he asked. *24* "If a kingdom's people fight against themselves, the kingdom can't last. *25* If a household is divided against itself, it can't last. *26* If really, as you say, Adversary is in opposition to himself and his kingdom is divided, it can't last and it will come to an end. *27* But it isn't possible for someone to go into a strong person's house and plunder their possessions, unless they tie up the strong person first. Then they can make off with the property. *28* All people groups will be forgiven for all their sins and any blasphemies they speak, *29* but the person who blasphemes against the Holy Spirit will never be forgiven, but is guilty of an eternal sin." *30* Jesus said this because they were saying, "He has an unclean spirit."

31-35 Jesus' mother and siblings[4] arrived. They stood outside and sent someone in to call him. *32* There was a crowd sitting around him, and they told him, "Your mother, brothers, and sisters are outside looking for you."

---

1   ὑγίης, *hugies*. See note on Matt. 12:13.
2   The area of Idumaea raised olives, grain, sheep and goats, and manufactured glass and pottery. Its major city was Marisa. Antipater, Herod's father, became governor of Idumaea.
3   Some have identified Beelzubub with Adversary (Satan), but there is no evidence to support this. Mark's editorial comment in 3:30 identifies Beelzubub as an unclean spirit. Nowhere in Jewish literature is Adversary called Beelzubub, although other names are applied to him. The early Christian papyri name a large number of evil spirits. The name Beelzubub is not the correct form for the suggested meanings, "Lord of manure", "Lord of the dwelling".
4   The KJV deliberately reverses the order of "mother and brothers", putting "brothers" first. Tyndale's 1534 translation correctly puts "mothers" first.

33 "Who are my mother and siblings?"[1] he asked. *34* He looked around at those sitting in a circle around him, and said, "These are my mother and siblings! *35* Whoever does God's purpose is my brother, sister, and mother."

Ch.4:1-9 Again Jesus began to teach by the sea. The crowd that gathered around him was so large that he got into a ship and sat in it out at sea, with the crowd on the seashore. *2* Jesus said many things to them by examples. *3* "Listen!" he instructed. "A farmer went to sow seed. *4* In the process of sowing the seed, some seed fell along the path, and the birds came and ate it up. *5* Some seed fell on stony ground, the sort of place where there wasn't much soil. It shot straight up, but because the soil didn't have depth, *6* it got scorched when the sun came up, and withered away because there were no roots. *7* Other seed fell around the thorny plants. They grew and choked the seeds, so they didn't produce any grain. *8* Still other individual seeds fell on favorable soil. They grew and ripened and produced a crop – some individual seed multiplied 30 times, some 60 times, and some 100 times!" *9* He added, "If you have ears you had better listen!"

10-20 When Jesus was alone, the disciples[2] and the Twelve asked him about the examples. *11* "The hidden secret of God's Realm has been given to you," he answered. "but everything is said in examples to those on the outside *12* with the result that, 'They look but they do not see. They hear but don't put two and two together. Otherwise they would turn to God and be forgiven.'"

13 "Don't you know the meaning of this example?" he continued. "If not, how will you understand all the examples? *14* The farmer sows the Word. *15* The seed sown along the footpath refers to these people - as soon as they hear the Word, Adversary comes and takes away the Word that was sown in them. *16* The seed sown on stony ground refers to these people – when they hear the Word, they welcome it happily, *17* but it isn't rooted deeply in them so it only lasts for a short time. When oppression or persecution come along because of the Word, they immediately fall into a trap. *18* The seed sown around the thorny bushes refers to these people – they hear the Word, *19* but the concerns of this life, the deceitfulness of wealth and the desire for other things come in and choke the Word, making it unproductive. *20* The seed sown on favorable ground refers to these people – those who hear the Word, welcome it, and have a good harvest – some 30 times, some 60 times, some 100 times more than was sown."

21-23 He said to them, "Surely you don't put a lamp under a bucket or under a bed? Shouldn't it be put on a lamp stand? *22* Everything that is completely covered will be revealed, and everything that is secret will come out into the open. *23* If you have ears you had better listen!"

24-25 "Watch what you hear!" Jesus warned his listeners. "With the same sized measure that you measure out, it will be measured back to you, plus you'll get extra! *25* Even more, to overflowing! - will be given to a person who has! But a person who doesn't have, even what they do have will be taken away from them!"

26-32 "This is a story about God's Realm," Jesus said. "A person throws seed on the ground, *27* sleeps at night and gets up in the day, and the seed sprouts and grows, yet the person doesn't know how. *28* The earth of its own accord grows fruit, first the blade, then the ear of grain, then the full grain. *29* But when the grain ripens, the person immediately sends out the harvesting equipment, because the harvest has arrived."

30 Jesus continued, "What can we say God's Realm is like, or how will we describe it? *31* It is like a mustard seed, which is the smallest seed that you sow

---

[1] ἀδελφοί, *adelphoi*. See note on Matt. 5:22.
[2] "The disciples" as distinguished from the Twelve. Not "those who were around him".

in the ground. *32* And when it is sown, it grows and becomes the biggest of all garden-herbs. It shoots out such large branches that birds can perch in its shade."

33-34 And with this sort of example Jesus spoke the Word to them, as much as they were able to hear. *34* In fact, he didn't say anything to them without using an example. But when he was alone with his own disciples, he explained everything to them.

35-41 On the evening of that day, Jesus said to his disciples, "Let's go over to the other side." *36* So they left the crowd behind, and took him along, just as he was, in the ship. The other ships were with him. *37* Suddenly a violent squall with high winds arose and the waves were breaking over the ship, so that it was quickly filling up with water. *38* Jesus was in the stern,[1] sleeping on a cushion.[2] They all woke him up and said, "Teacher, don't you care that we're sinking?"

39 Jesus woke up[3] and rebuked the wind and the sea. "Be silent!" he ordered. "Be bound!"[4] The wind dropped and there was a great calm.

40 "Why are you so cowardly?" Jesus asked. "How come you don't have any faith?"

41 They were extremely frightened and kept saying to each other, "Who is this one? Even the wind and the sea pay attention to him!"[5]

Ch.5:1-14 They went to the other side of the sea, to the region of the Gerasenes. *2* The very moment that Jesus got out of the ship, a person with an unclean spirit[6] from the tombs went out to meet him. *3* He lived among the tombs, and no one was able to tie him up any more, not even with chains. *4* The reason for this was that he'd often been tied up and he'd burst the chains frequently and had torn them into pieces and no one had the strength to subdue[7] him. *5* Night and day he was hanging around the tombs and in the mountains shrieking and banging[8] himself with stones. *6* When he saw Jesus from a long way off, he ran out and threw himself flat on the ground in front of him. *7* He shouted out loudly, "What are you meddling with me for, Jesus the Son of the Most High God? Swear by God that you won't torture me!"

8 This was in response to Jesus saying, "Come out of the person, you unclean spirit!"

9 "What is your name?" Jesus inquired of him.

He answered, "My name is 'Army division of 6,000 men' because there are lots of us!"

10 He kept urgently begging Jesus not to send them out of the region. *11* There was a large herd of pigs nearby, grazing on the mountainside. *12* The unclean spirits begged Jesus, saying, "Please send us to the pigs, let us go into them!"

---

[1] The place of honor in the ship was the little bench at the back.

[2] A rower's wooden or leather seat.

[3] Jesus woke up fully – the Greek does not say that he got up.

[4] "Peace, be still" is an incorrect translation. The word "peace" does not appear here in any Greek manuscript.

[5] Literally, "pay attention to him (and act on it)."

[6] Unclean spirit, ἀκάθαρτος πνεῦμα, *akathartos pneuma*, not to be confused with δαιμόνιον, *daimonion*, "demon" or δαίμων, *daimon*, "demon-god". Mark mentions unclean spirits and demons but does not mention demon-gods. There are only 4 references to bad spirit-gods in the N.T: Matt: 8:31 (describing this scene, and it seems a strange use of the term on the basis of its infrequent use in the N.T. and that the other accounts avoid the term); Rev. 16:14; 18:2.

[7] δαμάζω, *damazo*, overpower and make subject to one's control. See *I.Prusa.Olymp* 60.3 (Prousa in Bithynia, II), epitaph for a gladiator, "I, Akhilleus, who was victorious in the stadiums of Ares, and overpowered many with slaughtering hands, now lie here fulfilling the bitter decrees of the fates". Occurs elsewhere in NT only in James: 3:7 (twice), 8.

[8] κατακόπτω, *katakopto*, "hitting" or "bruising", not "cutting".

13 Jesus allowed them to. The unclean spirits went off and went into the pigs, and the herd rushed over a cliff into the sea, about 2,000 of them, and drowned. *14* The pig herders ran away and announced the news in the city and the countryside. People came to see what had happened.

15-20 They went to Jesus and saw the man who'd had the 6,000 bad spirits in him, sitting, wearing clothes, and in his right mind,[1] and they were shocked. *16* The witnesses to the event described to the people what had happened to the person who had evil spirits in him, and also about the pigs. *17* They kept asking Jesus to leave their district. *18* While Jesus was getting into the ship, the person who'd had the evil spirits begged him to let him go with him. *19* Jesus wouldn't let him, but said, "Go home to your family and friends and tell them the wonderful things the Lord has done for you, and how he's had compassion on you."

20 And he left and started announcing everything that Jesus had done for him in The Ten Cities,[2] and everyone was amazed.

21-24 When Jesus had crossed back over again to the other side in the ship, a large crowd gathered around him while he was beside the sea. *22* One of the synagogue leaders[3] by the name of Jairus arrived. When he saw Jesus, he fell down in front of him *23* and earnestly begged, "My daughter is at death's door.[4] Please come and lay your hands on her so that she will be rescued and preserved and will live!" *24* Jesus went with him.

24-34 A large crowd followed and crowded in on him. *25* There was a woman who had been subject to a blood loss for twelve years. *26* She had suffered a lot at the hands of many doctors and had spent all the money that she had on them, but instead of getting better, she got worse. *27* When she heard about Jesus, she came up behind him in the crowd and touched his coat, *28* because she had been saying to herself, "If only I can touch his clothes, I will be rescued and preserved!"

29 Immediately the blood flow dried up and her bleeding stopped. She recognized in her body that she had been instantly divinely healed[5] from the disorder. *30* Immediately Jesus discerned that the power that keeps going out from

---

[1]   σωφρονέω, *sophroneo*, has two principal meanings: 1. to be sensible, to be sound-minded, and 2. to come to one's senses. From these meanings, the secondary meanings "to be discreet", "to be moderate", have been derived. In the 1980s, further evidence on this word came to light, showing that the word also denotes "cooperation". See discussion in *NDIEC* 4.151. The word was found on epitaphs, and was used of the father of the emperor Theodosis. *IGM* 2 (Phigalia); *I. Eph.* IV. 1311.

[2]   "The Ten Cities" a Proper Name for a loosely defined group of ten cities west of the lake of Galilee.

[3]   ἀρχισυνάγωγος, *archisunagogos*, the person who presides over the synagogue service, synagogue leader. *I.Smyrna* 1.295.1 (Smyrna, III), "Rufina the Jew, *archisunagogos*, built the tomb for her freedpersons and domestic slaves" (note that Rufina was a woman); *IGRR* 1.782.7 (Perinthos, I); *P.Petsas, AD* 24 (1969) Chron. 300 *l*.4 (Thessalonike, 160); *Donateurs* 7.2,2,3 (Jerusalem, 1), "Theodotos, son of Vettenus, priest and *archisunagogos*, son of *archisunagogos*, grandson of a *archisunagogos*, built the synagogue for the reading of the law and the teaching of the commandments"; *Donateurs* 33.3,4 (Akmonia in Phrygia, I).

[4]   ἐσχάτως, *eschatos*, to be at death's door, to be near to the end of a process or state. See *PHarr* 2.192.15, 22 (Egypt, 167). This is a rare word. Occurs only here in the N.T.

[5]   ἰάομαι, *iaomai*, "instantly divinely healed", occurs only here in Mark. See note on Matt. 8:8.

him had gone out of him,[1] and he turned around in the crowd and said, "Who touched my clothes?"

31 The disciples exclaimed, "You see the crowd crowding in on you, and you ask, 'Who touched my clothes!'"

32 Jesus kept looking around to see who had done it. *33* But the woman, who was afraid and shaking, realizing what had happened to her, came and fell down in front of him and told him the whole truth. *34* "Daughter," he said, "your faith has rescued and preserved you – go in peace. You are healed of your disorder!"

35-43 While he was still speaking, people came from the synagogue leader's house and said, "Your daughter is dead. Why trouble the teacher any more?"

36 But Jesus refused to listen to the report they were giving and said to the synagogue leader, "Don't be afraid, just believe!"

37 He wouldn't let anyone follow him except Peter, James, and John, James' brother. *38* When he arrived at the synagogue ruler's house, he saw an uproar, and people crying and weeping loudly. *39* He went in and said, "What's all this fuss and crying? The little girl's not dead, she's just asleep!"

40 And they poked fun at him, but he threw them all outside.[2] Then he took the little girl's father and mother as well as his companions, and went into the place where the little girl was lying. *41* He grabbed the child's hand and said to her, "Talitha koum", which translated means, "Young girl, I tell you, get up!" *42* Immediately the young girl got up and walked around. She was 12 years old. Immediately they were beside themselves in complete shock. *43* Jesus gave them instructions that no one could find out about it, and also that they must give her something to eat.

Ch.6:1-6 Jesus left there and went to his homeland. His disciples followed him. *2* When the Sabbath came, he started teaching in the synagogue. Many people who heard him were overwhelmed, and said, "Where does this guy get all this from? What's this wisdom that he has? These powerful things that are done by his hands!! *3* Isn't this the skilled craftsperson,[3] Mary's son – James, Joseph, Judas and Simon's brother? And aren't his sisters with us?" They were offended by him.

4 Jesus said to them, "No prophet has honor in their own homeland, among their own relatives, and in their own house."*5* He wasn't able to do any powerful works there, except that he laid his hands on a few chronically ill people and healed them. *6* He was shocked at their lack of faith.

6-13 And Jesus went around the villages teaching. *7* He summoned the Twelve, and started sending them out in pairs. He gave them authority over unclean spirits. *8* He ordered them not to take anything for the trip except a walking stick – no bread, no bag, no wallet. *9* They could wear sandals, but they couldn't wear two shirts.[4]

10 "Whenever you go into a house," he instructed them, "stay at that house until you leave town. *11* And if you come across a place that doesn't welcome you or listen to you, shake the dust off your feet when you leave to show that you consider them to be pagans." *12* So they left and proclaimed that people should change their minds. *13* And they threw out many evil spirits, and anointed lots of chronically-ill people with olive oil and healed[5] them.

---

[1] This is an awkward phrase in the Greek. It means there is personal power which lives in Jesus and emanates from him at all times, and on this occasion some of this went out from him to another.

[2] Some use of force is implied in the Greek.

[3] τέκτων, *tekton*. See note on Matthew 13:55.

[4] The wearing of two shirts (at once) was unsuitable for traveling.

[5] θεραπεύω, *therapeuo*. See note on Matt. 4:23.

14-16 King Herod[1] heard about this, as Jesus' name had become well known. People were saying, "John the Baptizer has been raised from the dead, and that's the reason why powers are at work in him." *15* Others said, "He's Elijah!" Still others said, "He's a prophet, like one of the prophets of long ago!" *16* But when Herod heard this, he said, "Oh no! John, the person I beheaded, has been raised from the dead!"

17-20 For Herod himself had John arrested, and had him tied up and thrown in prison. He did this because of Herodias, his brother Philip's wife, whom he had married. *18* For John had said to Herod, "It isn't legal that you have your brother's wife!"[2]

19 So Herodias had it in for John and wanted to kill him, but she wasn't able to. *20* For Herod was in awe of John, knowing that he was a righteous and holy man, and he protected him. When he listened to John, he was quite puzzled, but he still liked to listen to him.

21-29 Then an opportune time came. It was Herod's birthday, and he was giving a party for his high officials, senior army officers, and the leading citizens of Galilee. *22* Herodias' daughter herself came in and danced, and she flattered Herod and the guests reclining with him for dinner. Then the king said to the young girl, "Ask me whatever you want, and I'll give it to you." *23* He took a strong oath and said, "Whatever you ask me, I'll give you – as much as half my kingdom!"

24 So she went out and asked her mother, "What should I ask for?"

"The head of John the Baptizer!" her mother answered.

25 Immediately she ran in a hurry and asked the king, "I want you to give me the head of John the Baptizer in a bowl and I want it right now!"

26 The king was extremely upset, but he didn't want to refuse her because of his oaths and his guests reclining for dinner. *27* So he immediately sent an executioner with orders to bring John's head. The executioner went out and beheaded John in prison, *28* and brought back his head in a bowl. He gave it to the young girl and she gave it to her mother. *29* John's disciples heard about it, and went off and took his body away and put it in a tomb.

30-44 The apostles gathered around Jesus and told him everything they had done and taught. *31* There were so many people coming and going that they didn't even have a chance to eat, so Jesus said to them, "Come with me! You need to go off by yourselves for a while and rest up."

32 So they went off by themselves in the ship to a deserted spot. *33* Many people saw them leaving and realized where they were headed, so they ran there on foot from all the cities and got there before them. *34* Upon landing, Jesus saw a large crowd. He had compassion for them, because they were sheep without a shepherd. He started teaching them lots of things. *35* By now it was late in the day, and his disciples went to him with the suggestion, "This is a deserted place, and it's already getting late. *36* Dismiss them, so they can go to the neighboring farm districts and villages and buy themselves something to eat."

37 But Jesus answered, "*You*[3] give them something to eat!"

"What! Us!" they exclaimed. "Are we supposed to go and buy close to a year's worth[1] of bread and give it to them!"

---

[1]   Herod (Antipas) was the son of Herod the Great and Malthace. He was the tribal ruler of Galilee and Peraea. The title "king" reflects local custom as in fact he was not a king. After Herod ("the Great") died in 4 BC, half his kingdom - Judea, Idumaea and Samaria - was given to Archelaus. The remainder was split in half. The territories of Galilee and Peraea were given to Herod Antipas (Archelaus's full brother), and the Trachonitis and Gaulanitis regions were given to Herod Phillip. Herod ruled Galilee until his exile in 39 AD.

[2]   See note on Matt. 14:4.

[3]   ὑμεῖς, *humeis*, emphatic.

38 But Jesus said to them in a decisive tone,[2] "How many loaves do you have? Go and see!"

When they had found out they said, "Five, plus two fish." *39* He ordered them to sit down for dinner in orderly groups, all set out like vegetable plots on the green grass. *40* And they took their place for dinner in ranks like flower beds in groups of 100s and 50s. *41* Jesus picked up the five loaves and the two fish, and looked up to heaven.[3] He blessed the loaves then broke them up into pieces and gave them to his disciples to serve the people. He divided up the fish among all of them. *42* They all ate their fill. *43* And the disciples picked up twelve wicker baskets[4] full of leftovers: broken pieces of bread and fish. *44* The number of the men who had eaten was 5,000.

45-52 Immediately Jesus made the disciples get into the ship and go on ahead of him in the direction of Bethsaida, while he dismissed the crowd. *46* After he sent them away, he went off to the mountain to pray. *47* When evening came, the ship was out in the sea, and he was alone on land. *48* He saw them straining at the oars, as there was a headwind. Just after 3 a.m. in the night, he went out in their direction, walking on the sea. He intended to go past them, *49* but they saw him walking on the sea, and thought he was a ghost. They screamed! *50* They all saw him and they were scared! Immediately Jesus spoke to them and said, "Be brave! I am existence! Don't be scared!" *51* He climbed up into the ship with them, and the wind dropped. They were really truly very, very scared, and were beside themselves with absolute shock, *52* as they still hadn't grasped what had happened with the loaves – on the contrary, they were a bit thick in the head.

53-56 When they had crossed over, they landed at Gennesaret and anchored there. *54* The very second they got out of the boat, people recognized Jesus. *55* They ran around through the whole neighboring district and wherever they heard that Jesus was, they carried unwell people on stretchers to him. *56* Wherever he went – villages, cities or the countryside – they put the sick people in the market places[5] there. They begged him to let them touch the edge of his coat, and everyone who touched him was rescued and preserved.

Ch.7:1-7 The Pharisees and some of the Bible scholars who had come from Jerusalem gathered around Jesus *2* and saw some of his disciples eating food with polluted hands - which means they hadn't washed their hands first – *3* as the Pharisees and all the Jews don't eat unless they wash their hands in a special ceremonial way, keeping to the tradition of the elders. *4* When they return from the market place they always wash in a ceremonial way before eating. They also observe many other traditions, such as washing wine cups, jugs, copper utensils and beds in a special way. *5* And so the Pharisees and Bible scholars asked him, "Why don't your disciples keep to the tradition of the elders, instead of eating their food with polluted hands?"

6 Jesus said, "Isaiah prophesied well about you about overly critical, hair-splitting pedantic, religious types,[6] as the Scriptures say, 'The people honor me with their mouths but their hearts are far from me. *7* They worship me uselessly, and their teachings are instructions invented by people.'

8-13 "You have dismissed the commands of God and are keeping to the traditions of people! *9* Well and truly," he added, "you disregard the commands of God in order to keep to your traditional teachings! *10* In fact Moses said, 'Honor your father and mother,' and, 'Anyone who physically or

---

1   200 denarii, worth a year's wages.
2   The two imperatives have a very decisive tone, translated thus.
3   Equally, "the sky".
4   A wicker basket in which the Jews carried food.
5   The common meeting-place.
6   ὑποκριτής, *hupokrites*. See note on Matt. 6:2.

verbally abuses[1] his father or mother will certainly be put to death!' *11* But you let a person say to their father or mother, 'Whatever money you would have got from me, I'm saying is dedicated to God instead so I can keep it', *12* then by your tradition they don't have to do a thing for their father and mother! *13* You make God's Word ineffective by your traditional teachings that you've handed down! And you do many things like that!"

14-15 Jesus called the crowd over again and said, "Listen to me, everyone, and understand this! *15* Nothing outside a person can make a person polluted by going into them! Instead, it's what comes out of a person that makes a person polluted!"[2]

17-23 When Jesus had left the crowd and gone indoors, his disciples asked him about the wise saying. *18* "So, are you dim-witted as well?" he responded. "Don't you understand that nothing that goes into a person from outside can make the person polluted? *19* Because it doesn't go into the mind but into the stomach, and then it goes into the toilet." (In saying this, Jesus declared that all foods were clean.) *20* "It's what comes out of a person that pollutes the person," he added. *21* "Out of people's minds come bad schemes,[3] pornographies, thefts, murders, *22* adulteries, greedy grasping types of behavior, malice, deceit, indecencies, the evil eye, slanders, arrogance,[4] stupidity. *23* All these evils come from within and make a person polluted."

24-30 Jesus left there and went to the district of Tyre. He went into a house and didn't want anyone to find out about it, but he wasn't able to hide it. *25* The very second she heard about him, a woman whose daughter had an unclean spirit fell down in front of him. *26* She was a pagan woman, a Syrio-Phoenician by birth. She begged Jesus to throw the evil spirit out of her daughter. *27* He said to her, "First let the children eat their fill. It's not fitting to take the children's bread and throw it to the little dogs!"[5]

28 "Sir," she answered, "even the little dogs under the table eat the little children's little crumbs."[6]

29 "What a great reply!" Jesus exclaimed. "You may go, the evil spirit has left your daughter!"

30 She went home and found her child lying on the bed, and the evil spirit had left her.

31-37 Then Jesus left the region of Tyre and Sidon and went through the area of The Ten Cities to the Galilee Sea. *32* Some people brought to Jesus someone who was deaf and had trouble speaking. They insisted that Jesus lay hands on the person. *33* Jesus took the person away in private and put his fingers into the person's ears. Then he spit and touched the person's tongue. *34* He looked up to heaven and sighed deeply and said, "Ephphatha!" (which means, "Be completely opened!")

35 Immediately the person's ears were opened and the tongue's binding was removed and the person spoke properly. *36* Jesus ordered everyone not to tell anyone, but the more he told them not to, they more they spread it around. *37*

---

[1] κακολογέω, *kakologeo*. See note on Matt. 15:4.
[2] Verse 16 is omitted as it appears to be a scribal gloss.
[3] διαλογισμός, *dialogismos*. Not simply thoughts but devisings, schemings.
[4] ὑπερηφανία, *huperephania*. The only example of this word in the N.T. In Classical Greek it means "arrogance". For the verb see *P.Flor.* III.
[5] κυνάριον, *kunarion*, not "dogs" but "little dogs" or "puppies", a softer expression than "dogs", being the diminutive of κυvwν, *kuon*. Jews frequently referred to the non-Jews as "dogs".
[6] The woman does not reject Jesus' statement, but agrees and continues the theme in her witty reply. J.D.M. Derrett, *NovT* 15 (1973) 69, pp. 169-170, sees the reply as an allusion to Ps. 17:14 (LXX 16:14), equating infants (νήπιος, *nepios*) with "puppies".

People were completely, utterly beside themselves with extreme shock.[1] They were saying, "He's done everything well! He even makes the deaf hear and the mute speak!"

Ch.8:1-10 Another time a very large crowd gathered. They didn't have anything to eat, so Jesus summoned his disciples and said, *2* "I have compassion for these people – they've been with me for three days now and they don't have anything to eat. *3* If I send them home hungry, they'll get weak on the way. Some of them have come from a long way off."

4 "Where on earth is anyone going to get enough bread to feed them right out here in the wilderness!" his disciples exclaimed.

5 "How many loaves do you have?" Jesus asked.

"Seven," they answered.

6 Jesus told the crowd to sit down on the ground. He picked up the seven loaves and expressed thankfulness. Then he broke them up into pieces and kept giving them to his disciples to keep serving the people, which they did. *7* They had a few small fish as well, so he blessed these too and told the disciples to pass them out. *8* They people ate until they were full. Afterwards the disciples picked up seven large person-sized mat baskets[2] full of broken pieces that were left over in abundance. *9* There were about 4,000 people. Jesus sent them away. *10* He immediately got into the ship with his disciples and went off to the region of Dalmanutha.

11-13 The Pharisees went to Jesus and started asking him questions. To test[3] him, they asked him for a miraculous sign from heaven. *12* He sighed deeply in his spirit and said, "Why does this people group[4] ask for a miraculous sign? There is absolutely no way that a miraculous sign will be given to this people group!" *13* Having said that, he left them, got back in the ship, and crossed over to the other side.

14-21 The disciples had forgotten to bring bread, except for one loaf which was in the boat with them. *15* Jesus gave them the instructions: "See to it that you avoid the yeast of the Pharisees and avoid the yeast of Herod!"

16 They were discussing with other as to why they didn't have any bread. *17* Jesus realized what they were talking about and said to them, "Why are you talking about not having any bread? Don't you catch on yet? Don't you understand? Are your minds still insensitive? *18* You have eyes but you don't observe, and you have ears but you don't pay attention! *19* When I broke up the five loaves for the 5,000, do you remember how many wicker-baskets of pieces you picked up?"

"Twelve," they answered.

20 "And when I broke up the seven loaves for the 4,000, how many large person-sized mat baskets full of pieces did you pick up?"

"Seven," they said.

21 "Then why is it that you don't understand?" Jesus said.

22-26 They arrived in Bethsaida. Some people brought a blind person to Jesus. They insisted that he touch him. *23* Jesus took the blind person by the hand and took him outside the village. He spat on him and laid hands on him, and asked, "Do you see anything?"

24 He looked up and said, "I can make out people that look like trees walking around."

25 And Jesus laid hands on his eyes again. Then the person saw clearly. His eyes were back to normal, and he could see perfectly well.

---

[1]   Nowhere in the N.T., not even in Mark, is such extreme astonishment displayed.

[2]   Not the wicker baskets of Mark 6:43, but a large mat basket capable of carrying a person (see Acts 4.25).

[3]   The same word rendered as "tempt" throughout most Bible versions.

[4]   Tribe, or clan, nation, people. "Generation" in the sense of time.

26 Jesus sent him home and said, "Don't go into town."

27-30 Jesus and his disciples went off to the villages of Caesarea Philippi. Along the road he asked them, "Who do people think I am?"

28 They answered, "Some say John the Baptizer, but others say Elijah, still others say one of the Prophets."

29 "But what about you – who do you think I am?" Jesus asked.

"You're the Anointed One," Peter answered.

30 Jesus forbade them to tell anyone about him.

31-33 Then Jesus started teaching them that the Human Being must experience lots of things and be rejected by the elders, chief priests and Bible scholars, and that he must be killed and rise again after three days. *32* He spoke the Word freely, boldly and openly.[1] Then Peter took him aside and started rebuking him. *33* But after Jesus turned around and looked at his disciples, he rebuked Peter, saying, "Get out of my sight, Adversary! You haven't got your mind on the things of God, just on human things!"

34-38.Ch 9.v.1. Then Jesus summoned the crowd as well as his disciples and said, "Whoever wishes to follow me, must leave self behind, pick up their cross, and follow me. *35* Because the person who wishes to preserve their own life will lose it, but the person who lets their life go for my sake and the Good News will get a life. *36* What good will it do someone if they gain the whole world but lose their own life?[2] *37* What price does a person put on their own life? *38* If anyone is ashamed of me and my words in this adulterous and sinful group of people, then the Human Being will be ashamed of this person when he comes with his Father's splendor with the sacred Messengers."

1 He added, "Let me tell you that some of the people standing here will not experience death until they see God's Realm come with power!"

2-8 Six days later Jesus took Peter, James and John up a high mountain by themselves, and his appearance was changed right in front of them. *3* His clothes became shimmering, intensely white, whiter than any launderer in the whole world could bleach them. *4* Right in front of them appeared Elijah and Moses talking to Jesus! *5* Peter said to Jesus, "Rabbi, it's nice that we're here. Let's make three shelters[3] – one for you, one for Moses and one for Elijah." *6* (He didn't have a clue what he should say because they were so terrified.)

7 A cloud turned up and cast its shadow over them, and a voice came out of the cloud. It said, "This is my dear Son! Listen to him!" *8* Suddenly, as they looked around, they didn't see anyone except Jesus any more.

9-13 As they were coming down the mountain, Jesus ordered them not to tell anyone what they'd seen, until the Human Being had risen from among the dead. *10* So they kept the matter among themselves, speculating as to what "to rise from the dead" could mean. *11* "Why do the Bible scholars say that Elijah must come first?" they asked.

12 "Elijah indeed does come first and restores everything to its original condition," Jesus answered. "So why then do the Scriptures say that that the Human Being must experience a lot and be treated with contempt? *13* But I'm also telling you that Elijah has already come, and they did to him whatever they wanted to, just as was written about him."

14-29 When they reached the disciples, they saw a large crowd around them and the Bible scholars debating with them. *15* The very second that the crowd saw Jesus, they were all utterly amazed and ran up to meet him. *16* Jesus asked, "What are you discussing with them?

17 Some guy in the crowd said, "Teacher, I've brought you my son. *18* He's got a spirit which causes loss of speech. When it gets hold of him, it

---

[1] That is, with *parresia*. See background notes on *parresia* in Acts.

[2] In the Greek there is the one word for "life" and "soul".

[3] The word is used frequently in the Greek of the dwelling place of a pagan god, and of the tabernacle in the wilderness.

throws him down to the ground. He foams at the mouth, gnashes his teeth, and becomes rigid. I asked your disciples to throw it out, but they couldn't."

19 Jesus exclaimed, "You faithless group of people, how long am I going to be with you? How long do I have to put up with you for? Bring the boy over to me!"

20 They brought him over. Immediately the spirit caused him to spasm. He fell on the ground, rolling around and foaming at the mouth.

21 "How long has this been happening to him?" Jesus asked the boy's father.

"From childhood," he answered. *22* It's often thrown him into the fire and into water to kill him! But if you can do anything about it, please have compassion on us and help us!"

23 But Jesus said, "'*If*'[1] you can!' Everything is possible to someone who believes!"

24 Immediately the child's father shouted, "I believe! Help my unbelief!"

25 Jesus saw the crowd running over all together, and he rebuked the unclean spirit and said, "Deaf and mute spirit, I command you, come out of him and don't go back into him any more!"

26 And it screamed, and came out of him with violent spasms. The boy became just like a dead body, with the result that they all said that he must be dead. *27* But Jesus grabbed his hand and raised him up, and he stood up. *28* When Jesus arrived at the house, his disciples asked him in private, "Why couldn't we throw it out?"

29 Jesus answered, "There's absolutely no way that this class of spirit will come out except by prayer."[2]

30-32 They left there and passed through Galilee, but Jesus didn't want anyone to find out about it, *31* as he was teaching his disciples. "The Human Being is to be handed over to people," he told them, "and they will kill him, and after he's killed he will rise again after three days."

32 But they didn't have a clue what he was talking about and were afraid to ask what he meant.

33-37 They arrived in Capernaum. When they were indoors, Jesus asked them, "What were you arguing about on the way?"

34 But they kept quiet, because on the way they had argued about which one was the most important. *35* Jesus sat down, called over the Twelve, and said, "If anyone wants to be first, that person will be the last of all and everyone's servant." *36* He picked up a little child and stood the child in front of them. He hugged the child and said, *37* "The person who welcomes one of these little children in my name welcomes me, and the person who welcomes me doesn't actually welcome me, but actually welcomes the One who sent me."

38-50 John said, "Teacher, we saw someone throwing out evil spirits in your name, and we tried to stop them because they don't follow us."

39 "Don't stop them!" Jesus exclaimed. "No one who does a powerful work in my Name can physically or verbally abuse me soon afterwards! *40* In fact, the person who isn't against us, is for us! *41* There is absolutely no way that a person who gives you a drink of water because you belong to the Anointed One will lose their reward. *42* And whoever sets a trap for the little ones who believe me, would be better off if they'd been thrown into the sea with a large stone tied around their neck!

43-50 "If your hand sets a trap for you, then cut it off!" he continued. "It's better for you to go into life disabled than to have two hands and to be thrown

---

[1] τὸ εἰ δύνῃ, *to ei dune*, most emphatic, thus the italics here.

[2] Some minor manuscripts add "and fasting", but there is no evidence to support its inclusion.

into the fire of the Garbage Pit Gehenna[1] that can't be put out.[2] *45* If your foot sets a trap for you, cut it off! It's better for you to go into life crippled than to have two feet and be thrown into the Garbage Pit Gehenna.[3] *47* If your eye sets a trap for you, throw it away! It's better for you to enter God's Realm with one eye than to be thrown into the Garbage Pit Gehenna, *48* 'where the maggots don't die and the fire can't be put out.' *49* Everyone will be supplied with salt by fire. Salt is fine, but if salt loses its flavor, how can you make it salty again? *50* Keep salt in yourselves and live in peace with each other."[4]

Ch.10:1-9 Jesus left there and went across the Jordan River into the district of Judea. Crowds of people came to see him. He taught them – this was what he usually did. *2* Some Pharisees came and put Jesus to the test[5] by asking him, "Is it permitted for a man to divorce his wife?"[6]

3 "What did Moses command you?" Jesus asked in response.

4 "Moses permitted him to write her a certificate of dissolution and divorce her," they said.

5 Jesus replied, "Moses wrote you this order because of your hard-heartedness. *6* But from the beginning of creation 'He made them male and female. *7* For this reason a person would leave their father and mother and join himself to his wife, *8* and the two would become a single body, so that they're no longer two, but one single body. *9* So then people must not split apart what God has joined together."[7]

---

[1]   Gehenna represented the rubbish dump outside Jerusalem. It was used for burning the bodies of the worst criminals. It was full of maggots and smoke. It was literally the Valley of Hinnon, *Ge Hinnom* in Hebrew.

[2]   Verse 44 was added by copyists.

[3]   The rest of verse 45 and all of verse 46 were added by copyists.

[4]   Verses 44, 46 and most of verse 45 are omitted, as they are not original and were added by copyists.

[5]   Often mistranslated in Bible versions as "tempt" or "tempt to sin".

[6]   This is the parallel passage to Matthew 19:3, except Mark has omitted the words "on the grounds of 'Any Matter'", words which would have been unnecessary to the 1st century hearer/reader. The Rabbis were asking Jesus about his interpretation of Deuteronomy 24:1. The "Any Matter" is a technical term from Jewish divorce law, a form of divorce which was introduced by the Rabbi Hillel. The other type of divorce was available to both men and women who were able to divorce the partner on specific grounds based on Exodus 21:10-11. This type of divorce was becoming rarer by the start of the first century, being replaced by the "Any Matter" divorce, which was for men only, and popular as no grounds had to be shown and there was no court case. For an "Any Matter" divorce, the man simply had to write out a certificate of divorce and give it to his wife. By Jesus' time, the "Any Matter" was the more popular form of divorce, but the rabbis were still arguing about the legalities of it. The disciples of Shammai were particularly opposed to it. See Josephus, *AJ* 4.253, "He who desires to be divorced from his wife who is living with him on the grounds of 'Any Matter…must certify in writing…"; Philo, *Special Laws* 3.30, "if a woman is parting from her husband on the grounds of 'Any Matter'"; see also the Rabbinic Commentary *Sifrev Deuteronomy* 269. For modern scholarship, see D. Instone-Brewer, Divorce and Remarriage in the Church, Cumbria, 2003.

[7]   This whole passage is abbreviated. A fuller account occurs in Matthew 19:3-12. Jesus is saying he disagrees with the "Any Matter" form of divorce. Jesus is simply saying that if someone divorces by a form other than the grounds of the "General Sexual Immorality" form of divorce, they are not properly divorced and so not free to remarry, and thus are committing adultery if they do. He is continuing his statement that he disagrees with the "Any Matter" form of

10-12 When they were back in the house, the disciples kept asking Jesus about this matter. *11* He said, "If someone divorces wife and marries someone else, he commits adultery against her,[1] *12* and if a woman divorces her husband and marries someone else, she has committed adultery."

13-16 People kept bringing little children to Jesus so that he could touch them, but the disciples rebuked these people. *14* When Jesus saw this, he was annoyed. "Let the little children come to me!" he exclaimed. "Don't stop them! God's Realm is like them! *15* There is absolutely no way that someone who doesn't accept God's Realm like a little child will ever enter it."

16 He hugged the little children, laid hands on them and blessed them.

17-31 As Jesus was setting out, someone ran up to him and fell on his knees in front of him. He asked, "Good Teacher, what do I have to do to inherit eternal life?"

18 "Why do you call me good?" Jesus asked. "No one's good, except God. *19* You know the commandments – 'Do not murder, do not commit adultery, do not steal, do not give false evidence, do not commit fraud, honor your father and mother.'"

20 He said, "Teacher, I have kept all these since I was a young man!"

21 Jesus looked hard at him and his heart warmed to him. He said, "There's one thing you come up short in – go away, sell all your riches and give it to the poor, and you will have a money bank in heaven! Then come and follow me."

22 But at this his face fell. He went away sad, as he had a lot of property.

23 Jesus looked around and said to his disciples, "It's so hard for rich people to enter God's Realm!"

24 The disciples were shocked at what he said. But Jesus said again, "Students, it's so hard to enter God's Realm! *25* Pigs might fly before a rich person enters God's Realm!"

26 The disciples were even more amazed and said to each other, "So who can get saved?"

27 Jesus looked at them and said, "With people it's impossible, but not with God –everything's possible with God!"

28 Peter started saying to him, "We've left everything and followed you!"

29 "Let me tell you," Jesus said, "there's no one who's left their home, brothers, sisters, mothers, father,[2] children or properties for me and the Good News *30* who will fail to receive 100 times as much in this present life –

---

divorce. The Mark account is abbreviated which makes understanding more difficult for 21st c. readers.

It is most important to note the significance of the above. The way this passage and the parallel passage in Matthew 19 has been (mis)translated gives the impression that Jesus was asked the question, "Is it ever legal to divorce?" and he answered, "No, except on the grounds of sexual immorality." This is not the case. Jesus was asked if it was legal to divorce on the grounds of "Any Matter" and he answered, "No, only on the grounds of 'General Sexual Immorality'". In other words, he was disagreeing with the form of "Any Matter" form of divorce. He certainly was not saying that at that time, or in the time to come, people were never to divorce except on the ground of sexual immorality.

[1] In Jewish law, a man could commit adultery against another married man but not against his wife. The statement in verse 12 is contrary to the "Any Matter" of Jewish law – only a husband could divorce under "Any Matter". Jesus here is rejecting the "Any Matter" form of divorce, saying that if someone divorces someone under the "Any Matter" form of divorce they are not legally divorced. This is not apparent to the 21st c. reader, as obvious as it was to the readers/hearers of the 1st c.

[2] Tyndale's 1534 translation and the KJV reverse the correct order "mothers and fathers", putting "fathers" first.

homes, brothers, sisters, mothers, children and properties. They'll get persecutions along with it in this life, but they'll also get eternal life in the time to come. *31* But many people who are the most important will be the least important, and the least important will be the most important."

32-34 They were on their way up to Jerusalem. Jesus was leading the way. The disciples were shocked, but those who followed were afraid. Jesus took the Twelve aside again and told them what was going to happen to him. *33* "We are going up to Jerusalem, and the Human Being will be betrayed to the chief priests and Bible scholars. They will condemn him to death and they will hand him over to the non-Jews. *34* The non-Jews will make fun of him and spit on him, violently beat him with a Roman whip of leather straps embedded with metal designed to rip off the flesh, and kill him. Three days later he will rise."

35-40 James and John, Zebedee's sons, went to him and said, "Teacher, we want you to do something for us – whatever we want!"

36 "Well, what do you want me to do for you?" Jesus asked.

37 They answered, "Let one of us sit on your right side, and the other on your left, in your splendor!"

38 You don't know what you're asking!" Jesus said. "Can you suffer the suffering that I'm undergoing or be baptized with the baptism that I'm being baptized with?"

39 "We sure can!" they said.

But Jesus said, "You will indeed suffer the suffering that I'm undergoing, and you will indeed be baptized with the baptism that I'm being baptized with, *40* but to sit at my right or left side – it's not up to me to grant that. These places belong to the ones they've been prepared for."

41-45 When the ten heard about this, they got annoyed with James and John. *42* Jesus called them over and said, "You know that the so-called rulers of the non-Jews act like big shots over them and their high officials wield authority over them. *43* Not so with you – those of you who want to be important must be your servants, *44* and whoever wants to be important must be everyone's servant. *45* The Human Being did not come to be served – he came to serve, and to give his life as the ransom price[1] in the place of many people."

46-52 Jesus and his disciples arrived in Jericho. As they were leaving the city along with a considerable crowd, a blind person called Bartimaeus (Timaeus's son) was sitting beside the road begging. *47* When he heard that it was Jesus of Nazareth, he started shouting, "Jesus, David's descendant, have mercy on me!"

48 Many people sharply told him to shut up, but that only made him shout even more, "David's descendant, have mercy on me!"

49 Jesus stopped and said, "Call him!"

They called to the blind person, "Cheer up! Get up! He's calling you!" *50* He threw his coat away and sprang up and went over to Jesus.

51 "What do you want me to do for you?" Jesus asked.

"My Lord, let me see again!" exclaimed the blind person.

52 Jesus said to him, "Go home, your faith has rescued and preserved you!" Immediately he got his sight back, and followed Jesus along the road.

Ch.11:1-11 As they approached Jerusalem and arrived at Bethphage and Bethany at the foot of the Mount of Olives, Jesus sent out two of his disciples *2* with the instructions, "Go into the village opposite you, and just as you're going in, you'll find a colt that's never been ridden tied up. Untie it and bring it here. *3* If anyone says to you, 'What are you doing there?' tell them, 'The Master needs it and he'll send it back immediately.'"[2]

---

[1] The price of buying back a captive, the purchase price for manumitting slaves. It is associated with the idea of deliverance by purchase.

[2] Donkeys were part of the public transport service. See note on Matt. 21:3.

4 They went away and found a colt outside in the street, tied up by a door. *5* While they were untying it, some bystanders said, "Hey, what are you doing, untying that colt!"

6 They answered just as the Lord told them to, and the people let them go. *7* And they brought the colt to Jesus and threw their coats on it, and he sat on it. *8* Lots of people threw their coats on the road, while others spread out brushwood that they'd cut in the fields. *9* The people who went ahead as well as the people that followed shouted, "Hosanna!", "Blessed[1] is the one who comes in the name of the Lord!" *10* "Blessed is the coming Realm of our ancestor David!", "Hosanna to the Highest Realms!"

11 Jesus entered Jerusalem and went into the temple. He looked around at everything, but since it was getting late he went out to Bethany with the Twelve.

12-14 The next day as they were leaving Bethany, Jesus got hungry. *13* He saw a fig tree that was in leaf in the distance, and went to see if it happened to have any fruit. When he reached it, he found nothing but leaves as it wasn't the season for figs. *14* And in response he said, "No one will ever eat fruit from you again!" His disciples heard what he said.

15-25 They arrived in Jerusalem. Jesus went into the temple and started throwing out the people who were buying and selling there. He overturned the money changers' tables as well as the benches of anyone who was selling doves. *16* He wouldn't let anyone carry merchandise through the temple. *17* He lectured them, "Hasn't it been written that, 'My house will be known as a house of prayer for all nations'? But you have made it a hangout for thieves!"

18 The chief priests and the Bible scholars heard about it and started looking for a way to kill him. This was because they were afraid of him, as the whole crowd was amazed at his teaching. *19* When evening came, they left the city. *20* In the morning, as they went past, they saw the fig tree withered away from the roots. *21* Peter remembered and said to Jesus, "Rabbi, look! The fig tree you cursed[2] has withered!"

22 "Have faith in God!" Jesus answered. *23* "Whoever says to this mountain, 'Be snatched up[3] and thrown into the sea,' and is not undecided,[4] but believes that what they say is happening, will have what they want. *24* It's for this reason that I tell you, when you pray and ask for all the things you want, believe that you have already taken hold of them, and they're yours."[5] *25* He continued, "Whenever you're in a state of praying, if you've got anything against anyone, forgive them, so that your Father in heaven can forgive your mistakes."[6]

27-33 They arrived again in Jerusalem. The chief priests, Bible scholars and the elders came up to Jesus while he was walking in the temple. *28* "By what authority are you doing these things?" they demanded. "Who gave you the authority to do these things?"

29 But Jesus said to them, "I will ask you a single point. Answer me, and then I'll tell you by what authority I do these things! *30* The baptizing carried out by John – was it from heaven or from people? Answer me!"

---

[1] There is the 1 Greek word for the 2 English words "blessed" and "happy".

[2] καταράομαι, *kataraomai*. See note on Luke 6:28.

[3] ἄρθητι, *artheti*, is the aorist imperative passive of αἴρω, *airo*, "be seized", "be snatched up", not "be removed".

[4] διακρίνομαι, *diakrinomai*, the middle voice, to decide, not "doubt" or "hesitate". It also occurs in James 1:6.

[5] Not "believe that you receive them". It is the aorist tense. You are to believe that you have already taken hold of them (in the past). The rest of the sentence is not "and you will receive them". Instead, the Greek says, "and they're yours" or "you've got 'em!" The tense is the present, not the future.

[6] παράπτωμα, *paraptoma*, mistake, blunder, not sin.

Verse 26 is omitted as it is not original and was added by copyists.

31 They talked it over amongst themselves and said, "If we say, 'From heaven,' then he'll say 'So why didn't you believe him?' *32* On the other hand, are we to say, 'From people...'"' (They were afraid of the people, as everyone considered that John really was a prophet.) *33* So they answered Jesus, "We don't know."

So Jesus said to them, "Well then, I'm not going to tell you by whose authority I'm doing these things!"

Ch.12:1-12 Jesus began speaking to them in examples: "A person planted a vineyard, put a fence[1] around it, dug a pit for the wine vat and built a tower.[2] Then he leased it to some farmers and went to a far away country. *2* At vintage time he sent a slave servant to the farmers to collect some of the vineyard produce from the farmers. *3* They grabbed him, tanned his hide and sent him packing[3] empty handed. *4* So the vineyard owner sent another slave servant. They banged him on the head,[4] insulted him and sent him packing. *5* Again he sent another slave servant, and they killed him. He sent many more slave servants, and they killed some and beat the others up. *6* Now he still had one son who he loved. He sent him to them last of all, thinking, 'They will respect my son!' *7* But these farmers said to each other, 'This is the heir – come on, let's kill him, and then we'll get the inheritance!' *8* So they grabbed him, killed him and hurled him out of the vineyard. *9* So what will the vineyard owner do? He will have the farmers put to death, and give the vineyard to other people. *10* Haven't you read the Scripture, 'The stone which the builders rejected has become the cornerstone. *11* This was done by the Lord, and it is wonderful to see!'"

12 They looked for a way to overpower Jesus, as they realized that he had addressed this example to them, but they were afraid of the crowd's reaction. So they gave up and left.

13-17 They sent some Pharisees and some friends and supporters of Herod Antipas to Jesus, to bait a hook[5] for him on what he said. *14* When they arrived, they said to him, "Teacher, we know that you're sincere and don't concern yourself about anyone's opinion, as you don't go by outward appearances, but teach the way of God with all sincerity. So is it legal to pay the Roman poll-tax[6] to Caesar or not? *15* Are we to pay, or not to pay?"

But Jesus, knowing they were overly critical, hair-splitting, pedantic religious[7] types, asked, "Why are you putting me to the test? Bring a Roman coin for me to look at!"

16 So they brought it, and Jesus asked, "Whose portrait is this? Whose inscription is it?"

"Caesar's!" they said.

17 "Give back[1] to Caesar what belongs to Caesar," Jesus remarked, "and give back to God what belongs to God." And they were completely shocked by him.

---

[1] The fence was protection from wild animals.

[2] The tower had two purposes, as a watchtower and as a shelter for the farmers.

[3] Needs to be translated by a colloquial expression.

[4] Meaning of κεφαλιόω, *kephalioo*, unknown in this context. Elsewhere in Greek means "to sum up". There is no verb with the meaning "to wound in the head" in extant Greek literature. See discussion in Taylor, *op.cit.*, p. 474; *NDIEC* 3.70; 4.107.

[5] ἀγρεύω, *agreuo*, "to hook" or "to catch out", a Greek term used in fishing.

[6] The poll-tax was paid directly into the Imperial *fiscus* and was especially hated by the Jews as a sign of subjection, and also because the coin bore the image and inscription of Caesar. The question was carefully posed to Jesus: an affirmative would disgust the people (Jews), and a negative reply would set the Roman authorities against him. Note that Jesus' reply was ambiguous. Daube states, "(This) is by no means a counsel of subservience to the state, rather one of minimum performance." D. Daube, "Responsibilities of Masters and Disciples in the Gospels", *NTS* 19 (1972/3) 15.

[7] ὑπόκρισις, *hupokrisis*, behavior of ὑποκριτής, *hupokrites*. See note on Matt. 6:2.

18-27 The Sadducees, who say there is no resurrection, went to Jesus. They posed the question, *19* "Teacher, Moses wrote for us that if someone's brother dies and leaves a wife but no children, that brother must marry the widow and have children for his brother. *20* Now say there are seven brothers. The first gets married and dies with no children. *21* The second one marries the widow, but he dies too without having any children. The same happens with the third. *22* In fact none of the seven had any children. Finally the woman dies too. *23* At the resurrection, whose wife will she be, since the seven were married to her?"

24 Jesus said to them, "Aren't you mistaken² on account of the fact that you don't know the Scriptures or God's power? *25* When the dead bodies rise they don't marry, but they are like the Messengers in heaven. *26* Now about the dead bodies being raised – haven't you read the passage about the burning bush in the Book of Moses, where God said, 'I am the God of Abraham and the God of Isaac and the God of Jacob'? *27* God is not the God of the dead but the living! You are badly mistaken!"

28-34 One of the Bible scholars who had come and been listening to their dispute, saw that Jesus had answered them well. "Which is the most important of all the commandments?" he asked.

29 Jesus answered, "The most important one is this, 'Listen, Israel, the Lord our God, is the only Lord. *30* You are to love the Lord your God with all your heart, all your soul, all your understanding and all your strength'. *31* This is the second most important: 'You will love your neighbor like you love yourself.' There are no commandments more important than these."

32 "Well said, teacher!" the Bible scholar exclaimed. "You are right in saying that God is the only Lord and there is no other but him! *33* To love him with all your heart, with all your understanding and with all your strength, and to love your neighbor the way you love yourself is far more far-reaching than all the burnt offerings and sacrifices."

34 When Jesus saw that he had answered intelligently, he said, "You are in reach³ of God's Realm." And no one dared ask him questions any more.

35-37 While Jesus was teaching in the temple, he asked, "Why do the Bible scholars say that the Anointed One is David's descendant? *36* David himself, speaking by the Holy Spirit, said, 'The Lord said to my master, 'Sit at my right hand until I put your enemies under your feet.'' *37* "David himself calls him 'master', so how then can he be David's son?"

37-40 The bulk of the people were listening to Jesus with delight. *38* Jesus said in his teaching, "Beware of the Bible scholars, who like to walk around in long cloaks! They like to be greeted in the market places *39* and have the places of honor⁴ in the synagogues and the best seats at dinners. *40* They gobble up widows' property and say long prayers just for the show of it. These people will bring excessive judgment on themselves!"⁵

41-44 Jesus sat down opposite the place where the offerings were put and watched the crowd putting their money into the temple offering box. Many rich people threw in quite a lot. *42* A poor widow came and threw in two very small copper coins⁶ which together were only worth a Roman cent.¹ *43* Jesus called

---

¹ ἀποδίδωμι, *apodidomi*, "give back". The verb implies either that the poll-tax is a debt, or that Caesar should get what's coming to him.

² πλανάω, *planao*, "to wander off the path", the cognate noun being πλάνη, *plane*. See note on Rom. 1:27.

³ God's Realm is taken as present, not future. The imagery is spatial, not temporal.

⁴ The bench facing the people in front of the ark containing the sacred rolls of the Law and the Prophets, a place of honor in the synagogues.

⁵ κρίμα, *krima*, "judgment", not "condemnation".

⁶ A very small copper coin, the smallest in circulation.

his disciples over and said, "This poor widow has put in more into the treasury than all the others. *44* They gave out of their surplus, but she gave out of her lack and put in everything she had – everything she had to live on."

Ch.13:1-2 As Jesus went out of the temple, one of his disciples remarked, "Look, teacher! The size of the stones! The magnificent buildings!"

2 "See these great buildings!" Jesus gestured. "Not even one of these stones will be left on top of the other – every last one of them will be thrown down."

3-8 As Jesus sat on the Mount of Olives opposite the temple, Peter, James, John and Andrew asked him privately, *4* "Tell us, when will all this happen? What is the sign that will indicate that they are about to happen?"

5 Jesus started by saying to them, "Watch out that no one deceives you. *6* Many people will come in my name and say, 'I am he!' and will deceive many people. *7* But when you hear wars nearby as well as reports of wars, don't be alarmed – these things must happen, but the end won't come at that point. *8* Nation will rise against nation and kingdom against kingdom. There will be earthquakes in various places, and famines – these are a beginning of birth pains.

9-13 "Be on your guard! You will be handed over to councils and beaten up in the places of worship. On account of me you will stand before rulers and politicians as witnesses to them. *10* And the Good News must be preached in all the nations. *11* Whenever you are arrested and brought to trial, don't worry beforehand about what you're going to say. Just say whatever is given to you at the time, because it's not you speaking, but the Holy Spirit. *12* Siblings will betray each other and hand each other over to be executed, and the same goes for parents and their children. Children will rise up against parents and have them put to death. *13* Everyone will hate you on account of my name, but the person who endures to the end will be rescued and preserved.

14-18 "But when you see the detestable thing[2] that causes devastation standing where it must not stand," – (*note from Mark*: The one who reads this aloud is to take note!) – "then those who are in Judea must escape to the mountains. *15* A person who is on the roof[3] must not go down into the house, nor go inside to take anything out of the house. *16* The farm laborer must not go back to get a coat. *17* But alas for those who are pregnant and those who are breastfeeding babies in those times! *18* And pray that it won't happen in winter!

19-27 "There will be oppression in such times– oppression such as has never been seen right from the beginning of God's creation, right up until this time – and will never be again. *20* Unless the Lord cuts short that time, no living thing would be saved – but because of the chosen he will cut short those days. *21* Then if anyone says to you, 'It is the Anointed One!' or 'He is here!' don't believe it! *22* False Anointed Ones and false prophets will arise and show miracles and signs in order to cause the chosen to wander off the right track,[4] if it were possible. *23* But you beware! I have told you everything beforehand. *24* But in those times, after that oppression, 'the sun will be darkened, and the moon will not give its light, *25* the stars will fall from the sky, and the powers which are in the heavenly places will be shaken.' *26* Then they will see the Human Being coming in the clouds with great power and splendor. *27* Then he will send the Messengers and gather his chosen from the four winds, from the furthest part of earth to the furthest part of the sky."

---

[1] The quadrans, a Roman coin worth 1/64 of a denarius, daily wage for a laborer.

[2] βδέλυγμα, *bdelugma.* See note on Matt. 24:15.

[3] The flat roof on which men often slept.

[4] ἀποπλανάω, *apoplanao*, occurs only here and in 1 Tim. 6:10. No parallel has been found for the meaning "lead astray" which appears in some translations. See *SB* 4.7464.6 (Arsinoite nome, 248 AD): "A female piglet of my daughter's wandered off in the village."

28-37 "Learn this lesson from the fig-tree! When its branches sprout and grow leaves, you realize that summer is near. *29* In the same way too, when you see these things happening, realize that it's near, right at the door! *30* This people group will definitely not have passed away until these things happen. *31* Sky[1] and earth will pass away, but my words will definitely not pass away. *32* But no one knows the day or the hour, not even the Messengers in heaven or the Son, only the Father knows. *33* Beware! Be alert! You don't know when the time[2] will come! *34* It's like a person going away from home – they leave their house and put their servants in charge. Each one has their assigned task. They tell the person at the door to keep watch. *35* So keep watch! You don't know when the owner of the house will come back – whether it's evening, or at midnight, or when the rooster crows, or at dawn. *36* If he comes suddenly, don't let him find you asleep! *37* But what I am saying to you, I am saying to everyone: keep watch!

Ch.14:1-2 The Passover and the Feast of Unleavened Bread were two days away. The chief priests and Bible scholars were looking for a cunning way to arrest Jesus and kill him. *2* They said, "It can't be during the feast, as the people might riot."

3-9 Jesus was in Bethany at Simon the leper's house, reclining at the dinner table. A woman came with an alabaster jar of very expensive perfumed ointment, made from pure spikenard.[3] She broke the jar and poured some perfumed ointment on his head. *4* But some of them were indignant and said to each other, "Why was this perfumed ointment wasted? *5* It could've been sold for a whole year's wages and given to the poor!" They started threatening her.

6 "Leave her alone!" Jesus ordered. "What are you bothering her for? She's done me a favor! *7* You always have the poor around! You can do them a good turn whenever you want to, but you won't always have me around! *8* She has done what she could – she has anticipated the anointing of my body for burial preparation. *9* Let me tell you, that wherever the Good News is declared throughout the whole world, what she has done will be told in honor of her memory!"

10-11 Judas Iscariot, one of the Twelve, went to the chief priests to betray Jesus to them. *11* When they heard, they were pleased and promised to give him some money. So he started looking for an opportunity to betray him.

12-21 On the first day of the Feast of Unleavened Bread, when it was customary to sacrifice the Passover lamb, Jesus' disciples asked him, "Where would you like us to go to make the preparations for you to eat the Passover Feast?"

13 Jesus sent out two of his disciples[4] with the instructions, "Go into the city, and a person who is carrying a ceramic jar of water will meet you. Follow that person! *14* Say to the owner of the house the person goes into,

---

[1]   Equally, "Heaven".
[2]   καιρός, *kairos*, time in the sense of "you don't know when it will be", not time as in a particular hour.
[3]   νάρδος, *nardos*, spikenard, a type of μύρον, *muron*, perfumed ointment. See *IGUR* 1245.17-19. A luxury item, also was used in burial of the dead. See the accounts in Matt. 26:6-12 = John 12:1-7, and Luke 7:36-56. John also identifies the μύρον, *muron* as νάρδος, *nardos*, spikenard. Spikenard is the name for several plants. Dr Judyth McLeod, a plant ecologist, states that the Biblical *nardos* was in fact lavender, cf. *Lavender, Sweet Lavender*, Sydney, 1989, pp. 12, 73. She notes that oil of spike (spikenard) was used in Egyptian cleansing ritual magic (p. 12). Pliny, *HN* 12.42-46 states that the cost of spikenard perfume is 100 denarii for the Roman pound, whereas the account here in Mark (and John 12:3) places the value at 300 denarii a pound. Nevertheless, the price of luxury items did fluctuate wildly at the time.
[4]   Luke names the two disciples as Peter and John. (Luke 22:8.)

'The teacher says, "Where is the guest room where I can eat the Passover Feast with my disciples?"' *15* The house's owner will show you a large upstairs room, furnished and ready. Make the preparations for us there!"

16 The disciples went away into the city, and found it happened just like Jesus said, and they made the preparations for the Passover. *17* When evening came, Jesus arrived with the Twelve. *18* While they were reclining at the table over dinner, Jesus said, "One of you eating with me will betray me!"

19 They were distressed, and one by one asked him, "Surely it's not me?"

20 Jesus said, "It's one of the Twelve, one who dips in the sauce bowl[1] with me! *21* On the one hand the Human Being is going away just as the Scriptures say about him, but on the other hand, alas for the person who betrays the Human Being! That person would have been better off if they'd never been born!"

22-31 While they were eating, Jesus picked up some bread, pronounced a blessing on it, broke it up into pieces and gave it to them, saying, "Take it, this is my body." *23* He picked up a wine cup and after he expressed thankfulness, he gave it to them, and they all had a drink of it. *24* He said to them, "This is my blood of the Covenant, which is poured out for everyone. *25* I will no longer drink the fruit of the vine until the day when I drink it fresh in God's Realm."

26 After they had sung a festive praise song, they went to the Mount of Olives. *27* Jesus said to them, "All of you will fall into a trap, because the Scriptures say, 'I will strike the Shepherd, and the sheep will be scattered.' *28* But after I have been raised up I will go ahead of you to Galilee."

29 But Peter said, "Even if everyone else falls into a trap, I won't!"

30 "In fact," Jesus responded, "this very day – actually tonight, before the rooster crows twice, you will deny having anything to do with me three times!"

31 But Peter kept on insisting emphatically, "Even if I have to die with you, there's no way I will ever deny you!"

32-38 They went to a place called Gethsemane. Jesus said to his disciples, "Sit here while I pray." *33* He took Peter, James and John along with him, and he began to be extremely troubled and in the depths of extreme heartfelt anguish. *34* "My soul is very sad," he said, "deathly sad. Stay here and keep watch."[2] *35* He went a little further on, and fell on the ground and prayed that, if possible, the Hour might be diverted from him. *36* "Dad! Father! Everything is possible for you! Turn this suffering away from me! However it's not what I want that counts, but what you want!" *37* He came and found them asleep, and said to Peter, "Simon, are you asleep? Didn't you have the strength to stay awake for one hour? *38* Stay awake and pray so that you don't go into an ordeal[3] – the spirit indeed is willing but the natural self is weak."

39-42 Jesus went away again and prayed the same thing. *40* When he came back, he found them asleep again, as their eyes were heavy. They didn't know what to say to him. *41* Then he came back the third time and said to them, "Do you intend to sleep on and on indefinitely and have a rest? Paid in full![4] The time has come! The Human Being is being betrayed into the hands of sinners! *42* Get up! Let's go! My betrayer is here!"

43-50 Immediately, while he was still speaking, Judas, one of the Twelve appeared! He had a large crowd with him armed with large knives and clubs. They had been sent by the chief priests, Bible scholars and elders. *44* His

---

[1]   The common bowl. On the occasion of the Passover Meal it contained Haroseth, a sauce of dates, raisins and vinegar.

[2]   Equally possible in the Greek: stay awake / keep watch/ keep your wits about you. See note on Matthew 26:38.

[3]   περιασμός, *periasmos*. See note on Matt. 6:13.

[4]   A well-known formula of receipt, not "it is enough". Used in the commercial sense in the papyri and ostraca as the technical expression in a receipt, "Paid in full".

betrayer had pre-arranged a signal with them – "The one that I kiss – He's the one! Grab him and take him away without fail!"

45 The second he arrived, he went up to Jesus and said, "Rabbi! Rabbi!" and kissed him. *46* Then they grabbed Jesus and took him away. *47* One of the bystanders drew his sword and struck the chief priest's servant, cutting off his ear.

48 Jesus responded, "What's this – do you think I'm leading a rebellion, coming out to arrest me with large knives and clubs! *49* I was with you day after day in the temple teaching and you didn't arrest me! Well! Let the Scriptures be fulfilled!" *50* Then everyone deserted him and ran away!

51-52 There was a certain young man[1] who was following Jesus. He was wearing fine linen sleeping clothes[2] over his underwear. They started to overpower him, *52* but he abandoned his sleeping clothes and escaped in his underwear.

53-65 They took Jesus away to the chief priest. All the chief priests, the elders and the Bible scholars were assembling. *54* Peter followed him at a distance, right into the courtyard of the chief priest. He was sitting with the servants and warming himself in front of the fire. *55* Now the chief priests and the whole council were looking for evidence against Jesus so they could have him put to death, but they couldn't find any. *56* Lots of people gave false evidence against him, but their stories didn't agree. *57* Then some of them got up and gave false evidence against him. They said, *58* "We heard him say, 'I will destroy this human-built temple and will build another one in three days, one that hasn't been made by people.'"

59 But even then their stories didn't agree. *60* Then the chief priest stood up before the assembly and asked Jesus, "Aren't you going to answer any of the charges these people are bringing against you?"

61 But Jesus kept quiet and didn't answer at all. The chief priest again questioned him, "So[3] you're the Anointed One, the Son of the Blessed One?"[4]

62 "Yes, I am!" Jesus answered. "And you will see the Human Being sitting at the right side of the Power[5] and coming with the clouds of the sky."

63 But the chief priest ripped his shirt as a formal act of judgment[6] and said, "Who needs more witnesses! *64* You've heard the blasphemy! What do you think?" They all condemned Jesus as liable to the death penalty.[7] *65* Then some of them started spitting at him. They blindfolded him and kept beating him up. They were saying, "Prophesy!" The temple police took him and slapped him around.

66-72 While Peter was below in the courtyard, one of the servant girls of the chief priest arrived. *67* When she saw Peter warming himself, she looked at him closely and said, "Hey, you! You were with that Nazarene, Jesus!"

---

[1] There is a possibility that Mark was the young man. A literary device of the times was for the author to identify themselves by means of a token, by allusion. However, Eusebius, *HE* 3.39.12-16, quotes Papias (stating Papias received his information from John the Elder): "Mark became Peter's interpreter and wrote accurately everything that he remembered... For he had not heard the Lord, nor had he followed him." Note that Irenaeus, *Against Heresies*, 5.33.4 states that Papias was "a hearer of John" (the apostle).

[2] Typical clothing for someone newly woken from sleep. Today's equivalent would be pajamas. The fine linen suggests that the young man came from a wealthy family.

[3] Emphatic and contemptuous.

[4] Jewish avoidance of the Sacred Name. εὐλογητός, *eulogetos*, rare word.

[5] The Jewish avoidance of the Sacred Name.

[6] The ripping of the clothes by the chief priest was a formal judicial act regulated in the Talmud.

[7] The judgment reflects a judicial verdict rather than a sentence. The High Council is not able legally to carry out the death sentence.

68 But Peter denied it. "I don't have a clue what you're talking about!" he exclaimed. He went outside on the porch and a rooster crowed.

69 The servant girl looked at him again, and kept saying to the bystanders, "This guy is one of them!"

70 But he denied it again. Soon after, some of the ones standing nearby said to Peter, "Surely you're one of them! You're a Galilean!"

71 Then Peter stared cursing. He swore, "I really don't know this guy you're talking about!" *72* Immediately the rooster crowed the second time. Then Peter remembered that Jesus had said to him, "You will deny you know me three times before the rooster crows twice!" While he was thinking about it he burst out crying.

Ch.15:1-2 Immediately, early in the morning, the chief priests held a council with the elders and Bible scholars and the whole High Council. They put Jesus in chains, took him away and handed him over to Pilate.[1] *2* And Pilate asked him, "Are you the king of the Jews?"

"You said it!" Jesus answered.

3-5 The chief priests accused him of all sorts of things, but he didn't answer at all. *4* But Pilate asked him again and said, "Aren't you going to answer? Look at everything they're accusing you of!"

5 But Jesus didn't answer any more, and Pilate was amazed at this.

6-15 Now it was the custom at the Feast to release one prisoner to the people, whichever one they asked for. *7* There was a particular one named Barabbas who was in prison with the other rebels who had committed murder in the revolt. *8* The crowd went up to Pilate and started asking him to do what he usually did. *9* Pilate asked them, "Do you want me to release the king of the Jews?"

10 He said this because he realized the chief priests had handed Jesus over to him because they were jealous of him. *11* But the chief priests stirred up the crowd to ask Pilate to release Barabbas instead. *12* So Pilate asked them again, "Well, what do you want me to do with the one you call the king of the Jews?"

13 "Crucify him!" they yelled.

14 "Why? What's he done wrong?" Pilate asked.

But that just made them shout even louder, "Crucify him!"

15 Pilate wanted to make the crowd happy[2] so he released Barabbas. He handed Jesus over to be crucified after he had him beaten with the Roman whip of leather straps embedded with metal designed to rip of the flesh.

16-20 The soldiers took Jesus away into the palace, that is, the Roman Governor's headquarters, and they summoned the whole company of 600

---

[1] An inscription of Pontius Pilate (A.D. 26-36) was found in the ruins of the theater at Caesarea and is now in the Israel Museum. It is the only surviving inscription that bears his name.

[2] The reference in John 19:4-12 explains why Pilate wanted to satisfy the crowd. In v. 12 the Jews say to Pilate. "If you let this person go, you're no Friend of Caesar's! Anyone who claims to be a king opposes Caesar!" This was blackmail or a significant implied threat. "Friend of Caesar" was a technical term describing a group which included senators, *equites* (a wealthy class known as the Knights or the Equestrian order) and others who had access to the emperor. Pilate's very political being was dependent on this relationship. The Jews were pressuring Pilate by the fact that he was a "Friend of Caesar". P. Barnett states, "One false move and his appointment would be canceled and his career finished." *Jesus and the Rise of Early Christianity: A History of New Testament Times* (Illinois: InterVarsity, 1999) p. 147. Furthermore, Pilate's patron had been Sejanus, who had fallen from power in AD 31 due to plotting against the Emperor. This placed Pilate in a precarious position. See P.L. Maier, "Sejanus, Pilate and the Date of the Crucifixion," *Church History* 37 (1968) 1-11.

soldiers. *17* They dressed him in purple[1] and plaited a crown out of thorns and put it on him. *18* They saluted him, and mocked, "Greetings, King of the Jews!"

19 Again and again they kept hitting him over the head with a stick and spat on him. Then they got on their knees and pretended to worship him. *20* After they made fun of him, they took off the purple clothes and put his own ones back on him, and then took him out to be crucified.

21-27 There was a certain person passing by on his way in from the country. He was from Cyrene, and his name was Simon. He was the father of Alexander and Rufus. They conscripted[2] him to carry Jesus' cross. *22* They brought Jesus to a place called Golgotha, which means 'The Skull Place'. *23* They tried to give him a painkiller of drugged wine,[3] but he didn't accept it. *24* And they crucified him. They divided his clothes among themselves, casting lots to see who would get what. *25* It was about nine o'clock in the morning when they crucified him.[4] *26* The inscription of the charge against him was, "The King of the Jews." *27* And they crucified two robbers with him – one on his right side and one on his left.

29-32 People who passed by abused him. They shook their heads and taunted, "Well, well! So you're going to destroy the temple and build it again in three days! *30* Come down from the cross and save yourself!"

31 In the same way too the chief priests and the Bible scholars ridiculed him to each other. They said, "He saved other people, but he can't save himself! *32* If he's the Anointed One, Israel's King, let him get off the cross right now! We'll believe it when we see it!"

33-39 At midday darkness covered the whole land until 3 p.m. *34* At 3 p.m. Jesus cried out with a loud voice, "Eloi, Eloi, lama sabachthani?" which means, "My God, my God, why did you desert me?"

35 When some of the bystanders heard that, they said, "He's calling Elijah!"

36 Then someone ran and filled a sponge with the soldiers' issue of wine-vinegar, put it on a stick, and offered it to Jesus to drink. "Leave him alone!" the bystanders exclaimed. "Let's see if Elijah comes to take him down!"

37 But Jesus released a loud sound and breathed his last.[5] *38* The veil of the temple that separated the Holy of Holies from the Holy Place was split in half from top to bottom. *39* When the Roman officer in charge of 100 men, who was standing there in front of Jesus, saw how he died, he said, "This one really was the Son of God!"

40-41 The women were watching on from afar. Among them were Mary Magdalene, Mary (Joses and James' mother – that is, the short[6] James), and Salome. *41* In Galilee these women had followed Jesus and had materially provided for him. Lots of other women who had come up with Jesus to Jerusalem were there too.

42-47 It was the Preparation Day (which is the day before the Sabbath). That evening, *43* Joseph of Arimathea, an influential Council member, who himself was waiting for God's Realm, got up the courage and went to Pilate to ask for Jesus' body. *44* But Pilate was shocked that Jesus was already dead so soon.[7] He

---

[1] πορφυροῦς, *porphurous*, purple, here purple clothing. See note on κόκκικος, *kokkikos*, on Matt. 27:28. See Pliny, *HN* 21.45f.
[2] ἀγγαρεύω, *aggareuo*, 'officialese', a common official term, to press one into military service.
[3] Spice with myrrh added in sufficient quantity to turn the wine into the drug to ease the pain, and was in accordance with Jewish custom, cf. Prov. 24.74.
[4] Crucifixion was of Eastern origin and used by the Romans as a punishment for slaves from the time of the Punic Wars.
[5] Matthew, Luke and John as well as Mark all avoid the words for dying.
[6] Either, "James the younger" or "James the short one".
[7] Crucified people usually lived for two to three days.

summoned the Roman officer in charge of 100 men and asked if Jesus had been dead for some time. *45* When he found out the facts from the Roman officer in charge of 100 men, he presented the corpse to Joseph. *46* Joseph brought a piece of fine new linen. He took him down and wrapped him in the piece of fine new linen. Then he put him in a tomb that had been quarried out of rock. He rolled a stone closely up against the entrance of the tomb. *47* Mary Magdalene and Mary (Joses' mother) took careful note of the location he was put.

Ch.16:1-8 When the Sabbath was over, Mary Magdalene, Mary, James' mother, and Salome purchased spices so that they could go and anoint Jesus' body. *2* Very early on the first day of the week, just after sunrise, they went off to the tomb. *3* They were questioning each other, "Who's going to roll the stone away from the tomb door?"

4 But when they looked up, they saw that the stone had been rolled away! (It was a very large stone!) *5* They went into the tomb and saw a young man dressed in a long white robe sitting on the right side. They were terrified! *6* "Don't be shocked!" he said. "You are looking for Jesus of Nazareth, who was crucified. He has risen! He isn't here! Have a look - there's the place where they put him! *7* Off you go – go and tell his disciples and Peter, 'He's going ahead of you into Galilee. You will see him there, just as he told you.'"

8 They ran out of the tomb, trembling and unable to get their thoughts together. They didn't say a word to anyone, because they were afraid.

The longer ending of Mark.

The evidence suggests that verses 9-19 of Mark 16 were in fact not written by Mark. The author is unknown. The verses are from another document dated to the 1st c., perhaps the second half. The passage is absent from the oldest 2 Greek manuscripts, the Old Latin codex Bobiensis, the Sinaitic Syriac manuscript, about 100 Armenian manuscripts, and the 2 oldest Georgian manuscripts. It is present in the vast number of witnesses including several major witnesses. There appears to have been a prejudice against the passage in early times. It is known that the church of the time did not like the criticism of the disciples in verse 14, and so wrote an expanded version to suit themselves. This expanded version does not appear in any available translations as it is known not to be original, and is dated to the 2nd or 3rd century. A shorter version was circulated but the evidence is strongly against it being genuine. The evidence suggests that the last leaf of Mark was somehow lost, and that verses 9-19 were original, but not written by Mark.

9-13 After Jesus rose early on the first day of the week, he first appeared to Mary Magdalene, from whom he had thrown out seven evil spirits. *10* She went away and told the ones who had been with him while they were mourning and crying. *11* When they heard that he was alive and that she had seen him, they didn't believe her. *12* Afterwards, Jesus appeared to two of them while they were walking to the countryside. He had a different appearance. *13* They went away and told the others, but they didn't believe them either.

14-18 Later on, he appeared to the Eleven while they were reclining at the dinner table. He rebuked them for their unbelief and stubbornness, because they didn't believe the people who'd seen him after he'd risen. *15* "Go into the whole world and proclaim the Good News to the whole creation," he told them. *16* The person who believes and is baptized will be saved, but the person who doesn't believe will be accused. *17* Miraculous signs will follow those who believe. In my Name they will throw out evil spirits, they will speak in new supernaturally given languages. *18* They will shake off snakes, and if they drink anything deadly it won't hurt them. They will lay hands on the sick, and they will recover."

19-20 So then, after the Lord had spoken to them, he was taken up to heaven and sat down at God's right side. *20* And they went out and proclaimed everywhere. The Lord worked with them and guaranteed the Word as valid by the signs that followed them.

The Good News According to Luke.

Luke was recognized as the author of this Good News from the early 2nd c. Eusebius, Irenaeus, Tertullian, Clement of Alexandria, Origen, Jerome, the Muratorian Canon, and the anti-Marcionite Prologue to Luke all attest to authorship by Luke both of the Good News and of Acts. The date is not known precisely: it was after the late 50s, and before the end of the 60s. The book of Acts ends before Paul's trial was over, suggesting that it was written prior to 62/3 AD. It is clear that Luke-Acts is a two volume work[1] and that Luke was written prior to Acts. Matthew and Luke have independently used Mark. The evidence suggests that Matthew and Luke were unaware of each other's work, and thus should be dated around the same time as each other. Matthew was written prior to the war with the Romans in 66-70 AD, and Acts covers events up to 63 AD. 62 AD seems to be the most likely date for the writing of Luke's Good News.

The evidence suggests that Luke was a medical doctor, cf. Colossians 4:14, "Luke, the beloved doctor." The gospels of Luke and Matthew each include 25 healing stories, while Mark includes 19 healing stories. Matthew does not record healing activity by the disciples, while both Luke and Mark do. Mark's account is more detailed than that of Luke, and Mark gives a more detailed account of both miracles of healing and healing practices. Luke and Mark both give precise information about diseases. However, Mark is precise in his use of tense for the healing terms θεραπεύω, *therapeuo*, and ἰάομαι, *iaomai*. θεραπεύω, *therapeuo*, was used for ongoing healing (see note at Luke 4:23), and ἰάομαι, *iaomai*, for instant healing (see note at Matt. 8:8). Luke shows more precise interest in the identity of the sick, and stresses the instantaneous and miraculous healings.

Luke was a non-Jew, writing for an educated non-Jewish audience. Greek was his native language. He was highly educated, and wrote in the "high style" displaying a knowledge of rhetorical forms and literary conventions, as well as a familiarity with the *topoi* of Graeco-Roman culture, and this is highly significant. Luke knows the Torah, but his stylistic and story-telling ability in Greek shows facility in the use of rhetorical conventions, and this does reveal the nature of his audience. Much has been written on Luke's audience. As for Luke's devices in Acts as well as Luke, he does entertain the listener/reader by inserting variety, using direct discourse, letters, and makes much use of the shipwreck *topos* (typical of the Graeco-Roman to suggest the preservation at sea is proof of innocence, cf. Antiphon, *On the Murder of Herodes*, 82-3; Andocides, *On the Mysteries*, 137-38) and of dramatic episodes. These along with his rhetorical skills suggest a wide general audience. His historical notations are few and generally mentioned in passing, while his literary allusions are more obvious.

According to Luke.

Ch.1:1-4 Many people have undertaken to set out a written account[2] of the things that were accomplished among us, *2* precisely as they were handed down to us by those who were eye witnesses and assistants of the Word from the beginning. *3* Because of this it seems good to me too, Honorable[3] Theophilos,[1]

---

[1] See the two prefaces: Luke 1:1-4 and Acts 1:1-2. Acts 1:1-5 recapitulates the conclusion of Luke 24:36-53. Some have compared this to Thucydides' second preface in his *History of the Peloponnesian War*, 5:26ff.
[2] ἀνατάσσω, *anatasso*, "set out (information) in writing", occurs only here in the NT. See *LSCG* 174.14 (Halasarna on Kos, 21 BC); *P.Fam.Tebt* 21.36 (Tebtunis, 122).
[3] κράτιστος, *kratistos*, "honorable", usually of an official. See E.L. Hicks, *The Collection of Ancient Greek Inscriptions in the British Museum*, III.2 (Oxford, 1890) 482 (and addendum on p. 294), A *l.6*, "I learned...that the

as I have closely followed all the events right from the beginning, to write this account and do it accurately and in a systematic manner. *4* I have done this so you can be fully assured that those matters which you have been orally taught are absolutely certain.

5-7 In the time of Herod, the king of Judea, there was a certain priest named Zacharias. He was a member of the priestly order of Abijah. His wife was one of the descendants of Aaron, and her name was Elizabeth. *6* They were both right before God, and they acted blamelessly as to all the commandments and regulations of the Lord. *7* But they didn't have any children, as Elizabeth was barren and they were both getting on in years.

8-11 Now it turned out that while Zacharias was serving God with his priestly duties when his priestly division was on duty, he was chosen by lot – *9* this was in line with the priestly custom - to burn incense when he went into the temple of the Lord. *10* At the time of the incense offering, the whole crowd of people was praying outside. *11* A Messenger of the Lord appeared in front of him, standing on the right side of the incense altar.[2]

12-17 When Zacharias saw him, he got all mixed up and he became quite scared. *13* But the Messenger reassured him, "Zacharias, don't be afraid! Your earnest request has been heard. Your wife Elizabeth will bear you a son, and you must give him the name 'John'. *14* He will be a joy and a delight to you, and lots of people will shout joyfully because of him. *15* He will be important in the Lord's sight! He'll never take wine or sweet fermented liquor and he will be filled with the Holy Spirit even from birth. *16* He will bring back many Israelites[3] to the Lord their God. *17* He will go on ahead of the Lord to prepare people for the Lord. He will be equipped with the same spirit and power that Elijah had, to correct the attitudes of parents to their children. He will correct disobedient people so that they will have the common sense of the people who are right with God, and make ready for the Lord people who are well prepared for him."

18-20 "What's going to make me believe that this is the case! Zacharias asked the Messenger. "Me - I'm an old man, that's for sure, and my wife's well and truly getting on years!"

19 The Messenger answered, "I am Gabriel, who stands in the presence of God, and who was sent to announce this Good News to you! *20* Well then! You will be silent! As you didn't believe my words, which will in fact turn out just as I said, you won't be able to speak a word until the very day it actually happens!"

21-23 The people waited for Zacharias. They were surprised that he was spending such a long time in the temple. *22* When he came out, he couldn't speak to them. They realized that he had seen a vision, because he kept on

---

honorable proconsuls before me regarded the days of the festival of Artemis as sacred." κράτιστος, *kratistos*, as an epithet attached to personal names designates the person as one of status. See *P.Oxy.* 33313 (Oxyrhynchos, II) *ll*.4, 23; *I.Eph.* 1.24. Elsewhere in N.T. only in Acts (1:1 23:26; 24:3; 26:25).

[1] For the name Theophilos, see note on Acts 1:1. Nothing is known of the Theophilos mentioned by Luke.

[2] The place of honor (the south side). The Messenger was standing between the altar and the golden candlestick. The left side (north side) of the altar was the table with the sacred bread.

[3] υἱός, *huios*, with a noun refers to a member of a class of people, and should not be translated as "son/child of…" With a place name, it indicates inhabitants of that place. The *Benai Israel*, translated in the KJV as "children/sons of Israel" actually means "members of the class of people called Israel" and should be translated as "Israelites". The expression is also Greek, and found as early as Homer.

making signs and stayed firmly speechless the whole time. *23* And it turned out that as soon as his time of priestly ministry was completed, he went back home.

24-25 After these events his wife Elizabeth became pregnant and lived in seclusion for five months. *25* "The Lord has done this for me!" she exclaimed. "He was watching over me to take away my inability to have children which the people considered to be a disgrace."

26-29 When Elizabeth was six months pregnant, God sent the Messenger Gabriel to Nazareth, a city in Galilee, *27* to an unmarried girl[1] who was engaged to a man named Joseph, a descendant of David. The unmarried girl's name was Mary. *28* The Messenger greeted her, "Hello there, you highly favored person! The Lord is with you!" *29* But she was deeply disturbed and wondered what sort of greeting this was!

30-38 The Messenger continued, "Don't be afraid, Mary! You've found favor with God! *31* You will become pregnant and give birth to a son, and you are to name him Jesus. *32* He will be very important, and will be called the Son of the Most High, and the Lord God will give him the throne of his ancestor David. *33* He will reign over the house of Jacob forever, and his Realm will never end."

34 "How can this be?" Mary asked the Messenger. "I'm a virgin: I haven't been with a man!"

35 The Messenger answered, "The Holy Spirit will come upon you and the power of the Most High will spread his shadow over you. The one to be born will be sacred and will be called the Son of God. *36* Your relative Elizabeth has also become pregnant with a son in her old age. They said she was unable to have children but now she is six months pregnant! *37* Every spoken word from God has power!"

38 "Fantastic!" Mary exclaimed. "I am the Lord's slave servant! May everything you've said come true!" And then the Messenger left her.

39-41 At that time Mary set out and traveled in a great hurry to the highlands to a city in Judea. *40* She arrived at Zacharias' house and greeted Elizabeth. *41* And when Elizabeth heard Mary's greeting, the baby happily jumped in her womb, and Elizabeth was filled with the Holy Spirit.

42-45 "Happy are you among women, and happy is the child you will give birth to!" Elizabeth called out loudly. *43* "What an honor this is – the Lord's mother visiting me! *44* As soon as I heard your greeting, the baby in my womb jumped for joy! *45* You are in a happy state, because you believed that the things the Lord told you would happen!"

46-55 And Mary said,[2] *47* "My soul greatly praises the Lord, and my spirit rejoices about God my Deliverer. *48* With favor he has looked upon my humble state. From now on all people groups will call me happy *49* because the Almighty One has done great things for me. And sacred is his Name. *50* His mercy is on those who respect[3] him from tribe to tribe. *51* He has performed mighty deeds with his power, those who are arrogant in their thinking he has scattered. *52* He has brought down sovereigns from their thrones, and lifted on high the oppressed poor. *53* He has filled the hungry with good things and the wealthy he has sent away empty-handed. *54* He has helped his servant Israel, remembering to be merciful *55* to Abraham and his descendants forever, just as he promised our ancestors!"

---

[1] παρθένος, *parthenos* (occurs twice in this verse). See note on Matt. 1:23.

[2] Equally, "And she (Elizabeth) said, 'Mary, my soul greatly praises the Lord.'" The Greek is ambiguous as to whether the words were by Mary or Elizabeth.

[3] φοβέομαι, *phobeomai*, usually means to fear, but the Greeks used it in the meaning "respect" when used in the case of gods or things sacred. See, for example, *P.Tebt* I.59, where someone writes to the priests of Tebtunis assuring them of his good will "because from old I revere and worship the temple". The use was consistent from Classical times.

56 Mary stayed with Elizabeth for about three months and then went back home.

57-66 When the time came for Elizabeth to give birth, she had a son. *58* When her neighbors and relatives heard that the Lord had shown her great mercy, they were happy with her. *59* On the eighth day they came to circumcise[1] the little boy. They were trying to name him after his father Zacharias.

60 "No!" his mother insisted. "He is to be called John!"

61 "There's no one among your relatives with that name!" they objected.

62 So they made signs to his father to ascertain what he would perhaps like to call the child. *63* And he asked for a writing tablet, and wrote, "His name is John."

Everyone was amazed. *64* Instantly his mouth was opened and his tongue could work, and he started speaking, praising God. *65* All their neighbors were shocked, and the whole story was passed around right through the hill country of Judea. *66* It was impressed on the minds of everyone who heard it. "What on earth is this child going to turn out to be?" they exclaimed. Clearly, he was in the Lord's hands.

67-79 His father Zacharias was filled with the Holy Spirit and prophesied: *68* "Worthy of all praise is the Lord, the God of Israel, he has visited, he has paid the ransom price for his people. *69* He has raised up a Power to bring deliverance to us in the family of his servant David, *70* as he said through his sacred prophets, through the ages. *71* Deliverance from our enemies, from the power of all who hate us, *72* to show mercy to our ancestors and to remember his sacred covenant, *73* the oath that he swore to our ancestor Abraham. *74* To grant that we would be rescued from the power of our enemies and serve him without fear, *75* and be sacred and right with God in his presence all the days of our life. *79* And you, my child, you will be called 'Prophet of the Most High'. You, my child, will go on in front of the Lord to prepare his way, *77* to show his people how to find salvation by means of the cancellation of their sins, *78* through the compassion of our God. The sun[2] rising from on high will visit, *79* to appear to those who are sitting in darkness and the shadow of death, to guide our feet into the way of peace."

80 The child grew and became spiritually strong. He lived in the wilderness until the time he publicly entered his ministry to Israel.

Ch.2:1-7 In those times Caesar Augustus issued a decree that a census was to be taken of the whole Roman empire. *2* (This was the first census that took place while Quirinius was governor of Syria.)[3] *3* Each person traveled to their

---

[1] περιτέμνω, *peritemno*, here "circumcise", but in general to make an incision around something. *IG* IV².1, 123, 134-7 (Epidauros, IV² BC) details a mouth operation. C.A. Behr, Homm.Vermaseren 1.13-24 discusses the text of Ailios Aristeides, 49, 47, in which the word appears as "an incision around my face". It is well attested as "circumcision" and commonly used in Egypt, as circumcision was expected of Egyptian priests in Roman times. A report of proceedings in which a man presents his sons to the high priest for circumcision was published in 1976: *BGU* 13.2216 (Soknopaiu Nesos, 156). *PSI* 9.1039 (Oxyrhynchos, III) is a list given to the high priest of boys who are candidates for circumcision.

[2] Sun or star.

[3] Equally possible (perhaps slightly less attractive grammatically in the Greek), "This was an earlier enrolment, before Quirinius was governor of Syria." Matthew (2:1) and Luke (1:5-28) place the birth of Jesus in the time of Herod the Great, who died in 4 B.C. Josephus (*A.J.* 18:1-2) tells us that Quirinius conducted the census in Judea in 6 A.D. Augustus instituted a series of censuses. Luke mentions the second one (6 AD) in Acts 5:37. William Ramsay demonstrated that a periodical fourteen-year census in Egypt is given in dated papyri. He noted that several inscriptions indicated that Quirinius was governor of Syria on two occasions, the first prior to A.D. 6 and that a census was recorded between 10 and 5 B.C. Periodic

own city to be enrolled. *4* Joseph also went up from the city of Nazareth in Galilee to Judea, to Bethlehem the city of David, because he belonged to the house and tribe of David, to get himself enrolled. *5* He went with Mary, because she was engaged to be married to him and was expecting a child. *6* It turned out that while they were there, the time came for the baby to be born, *7* and she gave birth to her firstborn, a son. She wrapped him up in baby clothes of strips of cloth[1] and placed him in a manger, because there was no room for them in the guest house.[2]

8-14 There were shepherds in the same district passing the night out in the open, keeping watch over their flocks. *9* A Messenger of the Lord appeared and stood in front of them, and the Lord's splendor shone around them. They were terrified! *10* "Don't be afraid!" the Messenger exclaimed. "I'm here to announce to you very joyful Good News for all the people, *11* namely that today in the city of David a Savior has been born to you: he is the Anointed Lord. *12* This is the sign for you:[3] you will find a baby wrapped up in baby clothes of strips of cloth, lying in a manger."

13 Suddenly the whole population[4] of the heavenly army appeared with the Messenger, praising God, *14* "Honor to God in the Highest Realms, on earth peace to people with whom he is very pleased."

15-20 When the Messengers had left them and gone into heaven, the shepherds said to each other, "Let's go off to Bethlehem! Let's see about this matter that the Lord has told us!" *16* Off they hurried and they discovered Mary and Joseph and the baby, who was lying in the manger. *17* When they had seen him, they spread the news around about what they had been told about this little boy. *18* Everyone who heard it was amazed at what the shepherds said. *19* But Mary kept up all these things to herself and reflected on them in her heart. *20* The shepherds went back, praising God and honoring him for everything they had heard and seen: it had all turned out exactly as they'd been told.

21-24 On the eighth day, when it was time to circumcise him, he was named Jesus, the name the Messenger had given him before he was even conceived. *22* When it was the time for the purification offering required by the Law of Moses, Joseph and Mary took him up to Jerusalem to present him to the Lord. *23* (The Scriptures say in the Lord's Law, "A sacred offering is to be made to the Lord for every firstborn male.") *24* They offered a sacrifice in keeping with the requirements of the Lord's Law, "a pair of doves or two young pigeons."[5]

25-32 There was a person in Jerusalem by the name of Simon, and this person was a just person and godly too. He was waiting for the Encourager[6] of Israel, and the Holy Spirit was upon him. *26* The Holy Spirit had revealed to him that he would not die until he had seen the Lord's Anointed One. *27* The Holy Spirit prompted him to go into the temple courts. The parents had brought in

---

registrations took place every fourteen years and such action was regarded as Augustus' general policy of Augustus, even if instigated by a local governor. Luke tightly attributes the census to a decree of Augustus. See William Ramsey, *The Bearing of Recent Discovery On The Trustworthiness of The New Testament*, (Grand Rapids: Baker Books, 1979) pp. 275 ff.

[1]   The standard baby clothes of the culture.
[2]   This had a wide meaning: guest house, inn, place where burdens were unloosened, general's quarters, reception rooms for messengers.
[3]   The sign is to prove that what is announced is true, not a sign by which to find the baby.
[4]   Equally, "a great number".
[5]   The sacrifice is the type specified for the poor, cf. Lev. 12:8. Note that the Magoi had not yet visited Jesus and given him the expensive presents. Jesus was just under two years of age and living in a house when the Magoi visited.
[6]   An expression for the Messiah, the Anointed One.

the little boy Jesus to carry out the requirements of the custom of the Law. *28* Simon picked up Jesus and praised God. He said, *29* "Right now, Master, discharge your slave peacefully, just as you said. *30* My eyes have seen your Salvation,¹ *31* which was prepared in full view of all the peoples, *32* a Light revealed to the non-Jews a glorious Light revealed to your people Israel."

33-35 Simon's words surprised Jesus' father and mother. *34-35* Simon spoke blessings on them and said to Mary, Jesus' mother, "This child is destined to cause the rise and fall of many Israelites, and to be a miraculous sign which will be disputed. And a large broadsword will pierce through your own soul! - The thoughts of many hearts will be revealed."

36-38 Now there was also a prophet, Anna, the daughter of Phanuel, of the tribe of Asher. She was very old, and had lived as a married woman for seven years after her marriage, *37* and then as a widow until she was 84. She never left the temple but worshipped day and night, fasting and putting earnest requests to God. *38* At that very moment she came in and thanked God. She kept speaking about the little boy to all the people looking forward to the liberation of Jerusalem.

39-40 When Joseph and Mary had done everything required by the Lord's Law, they went back to their own town of Nazareth in Galilee. *40* The little boy grew and became strong. He was filled with wisdom, and had God's favor.

41-45 Every year, Jesus' parents went to Jerusalem for the Passover Feast. *42* When Jesus was twelve years old, they went up to the feast as they usually did. *43* After the Feast was over, the boy Jesus stayed behind in Jerusalem, but his parents were unaware of it. *44* They set off without him, assuming he was with their traveling group, and traveled on for a day. Then they began looking everywhere for him, searching among their relatives and close friends. *45* When they didn't find him, they went back to Jerusalem to search for him.

46-50 After three days they found him in the temple, sitting among the teachers, listening to them and asking them questions. *47* Everyone who heard him amazed at the intelligence shown by his answers. *48* When his parents saw him, they were beside themselves. "Son, why have you treated us like this?" his mother asked. "Hey, your father and I have been searching for you! We've been very distressed!"

49 "Why were you searching for me?" Jesus asked. "Didn't you know I had to be about my Father's business?"

50 But they didn't have a clue what he was talking about.

51-52 Then he went down to Nazareth and paid attention to them. His mother kept all these things to herself. *52* As Jesus grew, so did his wisdom, and both God and people showed him favor.

Ch.3:1-3 In the fifteenth year of the reign of Tiberius Caesar - when Pontius Pilate was governor of Judea, Herod tribal ruler of Galilee,² his brother Philip tribal ruler of Iturea and Traconitis, and Lysanias tribal ruler of Abilenne – *2* in the period of the chief priesthood of Annas and Caiaphas, the word of God came to John, Zechariah's son, in the wilderness. *3* He traveled

---

¹   There are two closely related words for salvation in the N.T., ἡ σωτηρία, *he soteria*, and τὸ σωτήριον, *to soterion*. The latter, which occurs here, is the least common and only occurs in 3 other instances in the N.T.: Luke 3:6; Acts 28:28; Eph. 6:17. It implies a recovery. Otherwise, it is difficult to distinguish between the meanings of the two.

²   This Herod is Herod Antipas. After Herod died in 4 BC, half his kingdom - Judea, Idumaea and Samaria - was given to Archelaus. The remainder was split in half. The territories of Galilee and Peraea were given to Herod Antipas, and the Trachonitis and Gaulanitis regions were given to Herod Phillip. Archelaus and Antipas were full brothers, their mother being Malthace, a Samaritan. Herod ruled Galilee until his exile in 39 AD.

all around the surrounding country of the Jordan River, preaching the baptism of changing minds with a view to the cancellationof sins.

4-6 As the Scriptures say in the book of Isaiah the Prophet's words: "A voice of one calling in the wilderness, prepare the road for the Lord, clear a straight pathway for him. *5* Every ravine will be filled in, every mountain and hill made level. The bends will become straight, the rough roads smooth. *6* And all humankind will see the deliverance brought by God."

7-9 John used to say to the crowds who came to be baptized by him, "You pack of snakes! Who advised you to escape from the anger that's coming? *8* Show some proof that you've really changed your minds! And don't think you can say to yourselves, 'Abraham's our ancestor!' I'm telling you that God has the power to make some Abraham descendents out of these stones! *9* The ax is already at the root of the trees! Every tree which doesn't produce good fruit is cut down and thrown into the fire!

10-14 "So what should we do?" the crowd kept asking.

11 "The person who has two shirts should share with the person who doesn't have a shirt at all," John answered, "and the person who has food should do the same."

12 Tax Profiteers also came to be baptized, and asked, "Teacher, what should we do?"

13 "From now on don't collect any more than you are required to do," John replied.

14 Some soldiers asked, "And we, what should we do?"

"Don't intimidate people to extort money from them," he answered, "and don't inform against anyone for money - be satisfied with your salary."

15-17 All the people were expectant. They were debating among themselves whether perhaps John might be the Anointed One. *16* John declared, "I baptize you with water, that's for sure, but someone more powerful than I am will come. I'm not even good enough to untie his sandals! He will baptize you with the fire of the Holy Spirit! *17* He's got a broom and he is going to sweep everything clean. If you're a pile of rubbish – look out! You'll be swept out the door and thrown into a fire, and no one's going to put the fire out!

18-20 So with many other words of this kind John encouraged the people and announced the Good News to them. *19* But when he rebuked Herod the tribal ruler over Herodias, Herod's brother's wife,[1] and for all the other evil things he had done, *20* Herod also added this to them: he locked up John in prison.

21-22 It turned out that after all the people had been baptized, Jesus was baptized too. While he was praying, heaven[2] was opened, *22* and the Holy Spirit came down in the bodily appearance of a dove. A voice came from heaven, "You are my Son. I am very pleased with you."

23-38 Jesus himself was about thirty years old when he began his ministry. He was the son, so it was thought, of Joseph, the son of Heli, *24* the son of Matthat, the son of Levi, the son of Melki, the son of Jannai, the son of Joseph, *25* the son of Mattathias, the son of Amos, the son of Nahum, the son of Esli, the son of Naggai, *26* the son of Maath, the son of Mattathias, the son of Semein, the son of Josech, the son of Joda, *27* the son of Joanan, the son of Rhesa, the son of Zerabbabel, the son of Shealtiel, the son of Neri, *28* the son of Melki, the son of Addi, the son of Cosam, the son of Elmadam, the son of Er, *29* the son of Joshua, the son of Eliezer, the son of Jorim, the son of Matthat, the son of Levi, *30* the son of Simeon, the son of Judah, the son of Joseph, the son of Jonam, the son of Eliakim, *31* the son of Melea, the son of Menna, the son of Mattatha, the son of Nathan, the son of David, *32* the son of Jesse, the son of Obed, the son of Boaz, the son of Sala, the son of Nahshon, *33* the son of Amminadab, the son of Admin, the son of Hezron, the son of Perez, the son of Judah, *34* the son of Jacob, the son of Isaac, the son of Abraham, the son of Terah, the son of Nahor, *35* the son of Serug, the son of Reu, the son of Peleg, the son of Eber, the son of Sala, *36* the son of Caninan, the son of Arphaxad, the son of Shem, the son

---

[1]   See note on Matt. 14:4.

[2]   Equally, "the sky". Likewise in following verse.

of Noah, the son of Lamech, *37* the son of Methusaleh, the son of Enoch, the son of Jared, the son of Mahalalel, the son of Kenan, *38* the son of Enosh, the son of Seth, the son of Adam, the son of God.

Ch.4:1-4 Jesus, full of the power of the Holy Spirit, returned from the Jordan River and was led around in the desert by the Spirit. *2* There he was put through an ordeal[1] by Slanderer-Liar for forty days. He ate nothing during those days, and at the end of that time he got hungry. *3* Slanderer-Liar said to him, "If you're the Son of God, order this stone to turn into bread!"

4 Jesus answered, "The scriptures say, 'Humans won't live just on bread alone!'"

5-8 Slanderer-Liar took Jesus up on a high mountain, and showed him all the kingdoms of the world in an instant of time. *6* Slanderer-Liar said, "I will give you all this authority and the fame that goes with it, because it's been handed over to me, and I can give it to anyone I want! *7* So there, if you worship me, it will all be yours!"

8 Jesus answered, "The Scriptures say, 'Worship the Lord your God and serve him alone!'"

9-13 Slanderer-Liar took Jesus to Jerusalem and put him on the highest point of the Temple. "Come on then!" he urged, "If you're the Son of God, jump off! *10* The Scriptures say, 'He will assign his Messengers to protect you,' *11* and, 'They will catch you, so that you won't so much as hit your foot on a stone!'"

12 "How dare you provoke[2] the Lord your God!" Jesus exclaimed.

13 When Slanderer-Liar had finished harassing[3] Jesus in every way, he withdrew from him until he could find a suitable opportunity.

14-19 Jesus returned to Galilee by the Spirit's power. News about him spread throughout the whole countryside. *15* He taught in their synagogues and everyone praised him. *16* He went to Nazareth, where he had been brought up, and on the Sabbath Day[4] went into the synagogue, as he customarily did. He stood up to read. *17* The scroll of the prophet Isaiah was handed to him. Unrolling it, he found the passage where it is written: *18* "The Spirit of the Lord is upon me, vecause he has anointed me[5] to announce the Good News to the financially poor.[6] He has sent me out to proclaim freedom for the prisoners of war and recovery of sight for the blind, to set the oppressed free, *19* and to preach the time of acceptance by the Lord."[7]

---

[1] A. Plummer, *A Critical and Exegetical Commentary on the Gospel According to S. Luke: The International Critical Commentary on the Holy Scriptures of the Old and New Testaments*, 4th edition, 1910, p. 107, states, "πειραζόμενος (*peirazomenos*). The word is used here in its commonest sense or 'try' or 'test' with a *sinister* motive." (His emphasis). The word does not mean "tempt".

[2] ἐκπειράζω, *ekpeirazo*, "provoke". See note on Matt. 4:7.

[3] περιασμός, *periasmos*. See note on Matt. 6:13.

[4] The use of the noun ἡμέρα, *hemera*, to refer to sacred days is paralleled in an inscription from Ephesos, c. 162-164, "the honorable proconsuls before me regarded the days of the festival of Artemisia as holy and have made this clear by edict." E.L. Hicks, *The Collection of Ancient Greek Inscriptions in the British Museum*, III.2 (Oxford: O.U.P. 1890) *l.*7.

[5] The KJV follows the scribe's addition "to heal the broken hearted", clearly added to bring the passage into line with the LXX of Is. 61:1.

[6] πτωχός, *ptokhos*, "totally and completely broke", "financially destitute", not πένης, *penes*, "poor".

[7] A quote from the LXX. ἐνιαυτός, *eniautos*, is usually rendered as "year" in the Bible versions and "year" in fact is ἔτος, *etos*. ἐνιαυτός, *eniautos*, means any long period of time, a period of time, a cycle of time. It can mean "years" (plural) as a cycle of time, or "during / in / for a year" with a preposition. ἐνιαυτός, *eniautos*, is also used of the end of labor, the completion of

20-21 Then he closed the scroll, gave it back to an attendant and sat down. The eyes of everyone in the synagogue were fixed on him. *21* He started by saying[1] to them, "Today this scripture is fulfilled in your hearing."

22-27 People were impressed. They were amazed at the gracious words he spoke. But they said, "surely this isn't Joseph's son!"

23 Jesus responded, "I am sure you will quote this proverb to me, 'Doctor, heal yourself!' Do the things in your own hometown that we've heard that you did in Capernaum!"

24 "It's a fact that no prophet is accepted in their own hometown," he continued. *25* "And it sure is a fact there were many widows in Israel in Elijah's time, when the sky was shut for three and a half years and there was a severe famine all through the land. *26* Yet in spite of all that, Elijah was not sent to any of them! He was sent only to a widow in Zarephath in the district of Sidon. *27* And there were many lepers in Israel in the time of Elisha the prophet, yet only one of them was cleansed from leprosy - only Naaman the Syrian!"

28-30 Everyone in the synagogue was infuriated when they heard this. *29* They jumped up and threw him out of town! They were going to throw him off the cliff, and took him right up to the edge of the hill on which the city was built. *30* But he passed through the middle[2] of them and went on his way!

31-32 Then Jesus went down to Capernaum, a city in Galilee, and taught the people on the Sabbath days. *32* They were beside themselves with amazement at his teaching, because his Message had authority.

33-37 In the synagogue was a person who had a spirit, an unclean demon, and it shouted out loudly, *34* "Leave us alone![3] What are you meddling with us[4] for,

---

pregnancy, referring to the time a woman gives birth, which is most relevant here. δεκτός, *dektos*, is a verbal adjective (from the verb δέχομαι, *dekhomai*) referring to ἐνιαυτός, *eniautos*. It refers to taking or receiving something. It can mean to accept something, but to accept in the sense of to take or to receive. In English the word "accept" has two meanings. The first meaning is that we can accept something which is handed to us. The second meaning is that we can say that a child's homework is acceptable, that is, is makes the grade. δεκτός, *dektos*, does carry the latter sense. On the papyrus "Epigram for Apollonios of Tyana", *Belleten* 42 (1978) 402-05, no. 33 (pl. 6) Bowie restores the verb δέχομαι, *dekhomai*, at *1.4* of a person being taken (received) into Heaven. See E. Bowie, *ANRW* II.16.2 (1978) 1687-88); *SEG* 1251; *BE* (1979) 592. This is supported by Horsley, *NDIEC* 3.50. Note also the use of the verb in Acts 3:21, "the Anointed One Jesus ... whom it is necessary for heaven to take (receive) until the time of the return, about which God has spoken by the mouths of all his sacred prophets since the beginning." The verb is also used in Acts 7:59 of Stephen's words, "Lord Jesus, take (receive) my spirit." The genitive of δεκτός, *dektos*, is subjective, "the time that the Lord will take people". It also borders on a possessive genitive, "the time of taking which belongs to the Lord". Moule has commented on this combining of the subjective and possessive genitive in his work, *An Idiom Book of New Testament Greek*, (Cambridge: C.U.P., 1986), 2nd ed., p. 40. Moule translates, "the year when the Lord will accept man".

[1] "Started by saying", inceptive aorist. This is a literary device of Luke's to avoid retelling the whole speech.

[2] "Through the middle": διὰ μέσου, *dia mesou*, is emphatic, implying supernatural event.

[3] ἔα, *ea*, the imperative of ἐανω, *eano*, occurs only here in the N.T. It is equally possible grammatically to be an interjection of anger or dismay, which although common in Attic poetry (cf. Eur. *Hecuba* 501; Plato, *Prot.* 314 D; Aeschylus. *P.V.* 298, 688), was rare in prose.

[4] The "us" in all likelihood refers to the type of spirit.

Jesus of Nazareth? You've come to destroy us![1] I know who you are – the Holy One of God!"

35 Jesus rebuked it, "Be quiet! Come out of him!"

Right in front of everyone, the demon threw the person down and came out without causing any harm in any way. *36* Everyone was awed with amazement and said to each other, "What's going on with his words! His words have authority and power! He gives orders to unclean spirits and they come out!"[2] *37* The news about him spread all over the countryside.

38-39 Jesus left the synagogue and went to Simon's house. Simon's mother-in-law was gripped with a high fever, and they asked Jesus to help her. *39* He bent over above her and rebuked[3] the fever and it let her go. Immediately she got up and began to provide for them.

40-41 When the sun was setting, the people brought everyone who was sick with various kinds of diseases to Jesus. He laid his hands on each one, and healed[4] them. *41* Furthermore, demons also[5] came out of many people as well. They shouted, "You are the Son of God!" But Jesus rebuked them and wouldn't allow them to speak, because they knew that he was the Anointed One.

42-44 At daybreak, Jesus left and went to a deserted place. The crowds kept looking for him, and when they found him they tried to stop him leaving. *43* He said "I must announce the Good News about God's Realm to the other cities as well - this is the very reason I was sent!" *44* He continued preaching in the synagogues of Judea.

Ch.5:1-5 One day Jesus was standing beside Lake Gennesaret, and the crowds were pressing around him to hear God's Word. *2* He saw two boats lying by the lake, but the fishermen had left them and were washing their nets. *3* He got into one of the boats, the one belonging to Simon,[6] and asked him to put out from the shore a little. Then he sat down and taught the crowds from the boat. *4* When he finished speaking, he said to Simon, "Put out to sea, into deep water, and let down the nets for a catch."

5 Simon answered, "Master, we've worked hard all night and haven't caught a thing! But I'll let down the nets because you say so."

6-10 When they let down the nets, they caught such an enormous number of fish that their nets were almost at breaking point. *7* So they signaled their business partners[7] in the other boat to come and assist[1] them, and they came and filled both

---

[1]   This phrase is usually wrongly taken as a question. Rather, it is a defiant assertion.

[2]   The Greek is ambiguous. The alternative is, "What's this Word! For/because with authority and power he gives orders to unclean spirits and they come out!"

[3]   ἐπιτιμάω, *epitimao*. There is no precise English equivalent for this word. Howard Clark Kee, "The Terminology of Mark's Exorcism Stories", *NTS* 14 (1968) 232-246 (followed by Louise Wells, *op.cit.,*, pp. 145-60) has demonstrated that it was a word of command for the bringing of hostile powers under control.

[4]   θεραπεύω, *therapeuo*. See note on Matt. 4:23.

[5]   That is, as well as diseases.

[6]   Simon is Peter.

[7]   μέτοχοι, *metokhoi*, "business partners", cf. *NDIEC* 1.84-5. This word is well attested in the papyri. For example, in 1976 alone, around 40 texts were published which contained the word μέτοχοι, *metokhoi*. The word differs from κοινωνοί, *koinonoi*, "partners", as κοινωνοί, *koinonoi*, refers to partners who in some way share or contribute finances in the same business, whereas μέτοχοι, *metokhoi*, refers to business partners, usually not from the business of the one ownership, who cooperate. For example, two small fishing businesses might cooperate with each other on a regular or occasional basis. During these acts of cooperation, they are referred to as μέτοχοι, *metokhoi*. On the other hand, several people involved in the one fishing

boats so full that they were almost sinking! *8* When Simon Peter saw this, he fell down at Jesus' knees and said, "Keep away from me: I am a sinful man, Lord."

9 He and all his companions were in awed amazement at the catch of fish they had taken! *10* So too were James and John, the sons of Zebedee, Simon's partners.[2] Jesus said to Simon, "Don't be afraid, from now on you will catch people!" *11* After they brought their boats to land they left everything and followed him.

12-16 While Jesus was in one of the towns, a man full of leprosy turned up. When he saw Jesus, he fell on his face and begged, "Lord, if you want to, you can make me clean!"

13 Jesus touched him and said, "I want to! Be cleaned!"

The leprosy left him immediately. *14* Jesus commanded him not to tell anyone about it. "Show yourself to the priest and make an offering for your cleansing exactly as Moses commanded, as proof that you are cleansed," he told him. *15* But rather, the news about Jesus spread even more, and large crowds collected to hear him, and to be healed of their sicknesses. *16* Jesus often withdrew to deserted places so he could pray.

17-20 On one particular day, as Jesus was teaching, the Pharisees and experts in the Law, who had come from every village of Galilee and from Judea and Jerusalem,[3] were sitting there. The power of the Lord was there for Jesus to instantly divinely heal.

18 Some gentlemen[4] carried in a paralyzed person on a stretcher. They wanted to bring him and put him in front of Jesus. *19* They couldn't find a way to do this as they couldn't get past the crowd. Instead, they went up on the roof and lowered him on his stretcher through the tiles into the middle of the crowd, right in front of Jesus. *20* When Jesus saw their faith, he exclaimed, "My friend, your sins are canceled!"

21-26 This set the Bible scholars and the Pharisees debating. "Who's this person who speaks blasphemies!" they complained. "Who can cancel sins! Only God can!"

22 Jesus discerned their debating. "Why are you having this debate?" he asked. *23* Which is easier - to say, 'Your sins are forgiven,' or to say, 'Get up and walk?' *24* But so that you will know that the Human Being[5] has power on earth to cancel sins..." He turned to the paralyzed person and said, "Get up, pick up your stretcher and go home!"

25 Immediately he got up right in front of them, picked up what he had been lying on, and went to his own house, praising God. *26* Everyone was besides themselves in utter amazement and praised God. They were filled with shock! "We have seen incredible things today!" they exclaimed.

---

business are referred to as κοινωνοί, *koinonoi*. See also W.H. Wuellner, *The Meaning of 'Fishers of men'*, Philadelphia, 1967, 26-63.

[1] συλλαμβάνομαι, *sullambanomai*, with dative, "assist" (in a significant, usually work matter) not merely "help". See *P.Oxy* 7.1064; *P.Giss* I.11. In Philippians 4:3, Paul asks the man Synzugos to assist the women Euodia and Syntyche. In *P.Oxy.Hels.* 47a it is used in a request to assist someone until they get the grain measured. See also Hdt. 6.125 and Jos. *Ant.* 12.240.

[2] κοινονός, *koinonos*, "partner". See above note on μέτοχοι, *metokhoi*.

[3] Common Greek hyperbole: they had not literally come from every village in Galilee, Judea and Jerusalem.

[4] ἄνδρες, *andres,* is a formal term of respect used to refer to "ladies and gentlemen". This use is widespread through all Greek literature. In a smaller group, the word is likely to apply to men only and thus the referent is "gentlemen" rather than "fellows" or "guys".

[5] ὁ υἱὸς τοῦ ἀνθρώπου, *ho huios tou anthropou*. See note on Matt. 8:20.

27-31 After this, Jesus went out and noticed a Tax Profiteer by the name of Levi (Matthew),[1] sitting at the Tax Profiteer's office. He said, "Follow me!"

28 He left everything, got up, and followed him. *29* Levi threw a huge party for Jesus at his house, and a large crowd of Tax Profiteers and others were reclining for dinner with them. *30* The Pharisees and their Bible scholars who belonged to their sect complained to his disciples, "Why are you eating and drinking with Tax Profiteers and sinners?"

31 "It's not the completely healthy people who need a doctor – it's the sick people who do!" Jesus answered. *32* I haven't come to invite the righteous, but rather, I've come to invite the sinners to change their minds."

33-39 The group continued to complain, "John's disciples often fast and put earnest requests to God, and so do the Pharisees' disciples, but yours keep on eating and drinking!"

34 "You can't make the wedding guests of the bridegroom fast while they are in the house celebrating the wedding, can you!" Jesus responded. *35* "But the time will come when the bridegroom will be taken away from them – that's the time that they'll fast."

36 He also told them this example: "No one tears a piece from a new coat and puts it on an old one. Otherwise, not only will the new coat be torn, but the patch from the new won't match the old. *37* No one puts new wine into old wineskins. That makes the wineskins burst. Then the wine is spilled, and the wineskins are ruined. *38* Instead, they put new wine into new wineskins. *39* And no one who has drunk old wine wants new wine. They say, 'Old wine's good!'"

Ch.6:1-5 One Sabbath day Jesus was going through the grain fields. His disciples began to pick some heads of grain, rubbing them in their hands and eating them. *2* Some of the Pharisees demanded, "Why are you doing this illegal thing on the Sabbath?"

3 Jesus answered, "Haven't you ever read what David did when he and his companions were hungry? *4* He went into the House of God and took and ate the sacred bread.[2] Yet it was only legal for the priests to eat it! And he gave some of it to his friends, too!" *5* He added, "The Human Being is the Master of the Sabbath!" and continued speaking[3] to them.

6-11 Now on another Sabbath Jesus went into a synagogue and was teaching, and there was a person there whose right hand was withered. *7* The Bible scholars and the Pharisees were keeping an eye on Jesus, as they were looking for a reason to accuse him. They wanted to see if he would heal someone on a Sabbath. *8* But Jesus knew what they were thinking. He said to the man who had the withered hand, "Get up and stand there in front of everyone." So he got up and stood there.

9 Jesus demanded of them, "I ask you, which is legal on the Sabbath, to do good or to do bad, to save life or destroy it?"

10 He looked around at each one of them, and then said to the person, "Stretch out your hand." He did so, and his hand was put right. *11* But the Bible scholars and the Pharisees completely lost their senses, and discussed with each other what they'd like to do to Jesus!

12-16 Now it happened in those days that Jesus went out to the mountain to pray, and spent the whole night in prayer to God. *13* When morning came, he summoned his disciples. He chose twelve of them whom he also named "Apostles" ("sent-out ones"): *14* Simon (whom he named Peter), Andrew (Peter's brother), James, John, Philip, Bartholomew, *15* Matthew, Thomas, James (Alphaeus' son), Simon (who was called the Zealot), *16* Judas (James' son), and Judas Iscariot, who became a traitor.

---

[1]   Levi is Matthew.
[2]   This describes the 12 freshly baked loaves of bread placed every Sabbath in 2 rows on a table before God in the tabernacle and later eaten by the priests. (Lev. 34.5-9)
[3]   "He started to speak…". Literary device implying continuance, to avoid retelling the whole account.

17-19 Jesus came down the mountain with them and stood on a low-lying place. A large crowd of his disciples was there with a large crowd from all over Judea, from Jerusalem, and from the coast of Tyre and Sidon.[1] They had come to hear him and to be instantly divinely healed of their diseases. *18* Those who were troubled by unclean spirits began being healed. *19* The whole crowd tried to touch him, because power was radiating out of him and he was instantly divinely healing them all.

20-23 Jesus looked at his disciples and said, "Happy are the financially poor, because yours is God's Realm. *21* Happy are you who are hungry now, for you will be have your fill. Happy are you who cry now, for you will laugh. *22* Happy are you when people hate you, when they banish you and insult you and reject your name with contempt as if it's evil, because of the Human Being. *23* Rejoice in that day and jump for joy, as you have a great reward in heaven. That is how your ancestors treated the prophets!

24-26 But how sad for you who are rich, you have already received your comfort. *25* How sad for you who are well fed now, you will be hungry. How sad for you who laugh now, you will mourn and weep. *26* How sad for you when all people speak well of you, their ancestors also spoke well of the false prophets.

27-31 "This is what I have to say to those who listen, 'Love your enemies, be good to people who hate you, *28* bless people who put curses on you,[2] and pray for those who talk about you spitefully. *29* If someone punches you on one side of the jaw, offer the other side too. If someone takes your coat, do not stop them taking your shirt! *30* Give people whatever they ask from you, and if anyone takes your possessions, do not demand them back. *31* "To sum up, do to others as you would have them do to you.

32-38 "If you love those who love you, what's the big deal about that? It's a fact that sinners do that. *33* And if you are good to those who are good to you, is that a big deal? Sinners do that too. *34* If you lend to those people

---

[1]   Sidon was a port city like Tyre and prospered, like Tyre, through trade and the production of purple dye.

[2]   καταράομαι, *kataraomai*. This is literally "put curses on one". The reference is not to someone being rude. καταράομαι, *kataraomai*, is a compound of ἀρά, *ara*: ἀρά, or ἀραοῖς, *araois*, "laden with a curse or curses", "cursed", "cursing". καταράομαι, *kataraomai*, was a popular Greek word for "curse". It occurs, for example, in the LXX of Zech. 5.2-4, "He shall be answerable to the Most High God and may the curse's (τὸ ἀράς, *to aras*) sickle enter his house and leave no one behind." Another tomb warning, *MAMA* 6 (1939) 335. 14-20 is, "Such a person shall be doubly cursed (ἐπικατάρατος, *epikararatos*) and may whatever curses (ἀραί, *arai*) stand written in Deuteronomy come upon him and his children and his descendants and his entire family." The same word, ἐπικατάρατος, *epikararatos*, is used in Gal. 3:10, "Doubly cursed is everyone..." and 3:13, "Doubly cursed is everyone who hangs on a tree."

   Two other words for "curse" are ἀνάθεμα, *anathema*, and κατάθεμα, *katathema*, which occurs only once in the N.T. in Rev. 22:3. Both are used on a tomb warning in a 5th century marble stele found in a church: *ed. pr.* M. Hatzidakis, *AD* 29 (1973/4 [1979]) *Chron.* 194 (pl.). The stele states that if anyone attempts to lie another dead body there, that they will be liable κε τὸ ἀνάθεμα κε τὸ κατάθεμα, *ke to anathema ke to katathema*. A post-Constantine Greek sepulchral inscription, *BCH* 101.224-228, contains a warning about opening a grave to the effect that anyone exhuming the grave, apart from the heirs, will bring on themselves "the curse of Judas". Additional tomb warnings with the curse ἀνάθεμα, *anathema*, are, for example, *SEG* 434; *BE* (1977); *IG* IV.628; *IG* III, 2.1428; 193. This was a popular curse, and inscriptions naming it have been found at Argos, Delphi, Naxos, Nicea, Bithynia, Rome and Ravenna. It is clear that ἀνάθεμα, *anathema*, was a curse, although a curse which differed in some way from κατάθεμα, *katathema*, and from the κατάθεμα, *katathema*, of Rev. 22:3.

whom you expect to repay you, is that a big deal? Even sinners lend to sinners, and expect to be repaid the whole amount! *35* Instead, love your enemies, be good to people and lend. Don't expect anything in return, and you will have a big reward, and you will be children of the Most High. He is kind to the ungrateful and evil.

36 "Your Father is compassionate – so you be compassionate too! *37* If you don't judge, you won't be judged! If you don't condemn, you won't be condemned! If you forgive, you will be forgiven! *38* "Give, and it will be given to you; a good sized measuring container, pressed down, shaken up, and poured out to excess so that it runs over, will be put into your wallet. The measuring container you use to measure out to other people, will be used to measure back to you."

39-42 He also told them this example: "Can a blind person lead another blind person! Won't they both fall into a ditch! *40* A student isn't more important than the teacher; but everyone who is fully trained will be like their teacher. *41* "Why is it that you look at the splinter in your fellow believer's[1] eye, but don't give a thought to the plank of wood in your own eye? *42* Why is it that you can say your fellow believer, 'Fellow believer, let me remove that splinter in your eye,' when you don't even take any notice of the plank of wood in your own eye!

"You overly critical, hair splitting, pedantic religious person![2] First take the plank of wood out of your own eye, and then you'll be able to see clearly to take the splinter out of your fellow believer's eye!

43-45 "A good tree doesn't grow bad fruit, and a bad tree doesn't grow good fruit. *44* Every tree is known by its own fruit! People do not pick figs from thorn bushes, or bunches of grapes from bramble bushes. *45* "A good person produces good things out of the good stored up in them, and an evil person produces evil things out of the evil stored up in them. The mouth speaks from the overflow of what is stored up in someone.

46-49.Ch.7:1 "Why do you say, "Yes sir, Yes sir,' but don't do what I say? *47* I will show you what a person who comes to me is like, a person who hears my words and puts them into practice. *48* That person is like a house builder who dug down deep and set the foundations on rock. When a flood came, the torrents of water dashed against that house, but didn't have the strength to shake it because it was well built. *49* But the person who hears my words and does not put them into practice is like a person who built a house on the ground without any foundation. The torrents of water dashed against it, and immediately it collapsed in a heap. This house broke up in a catastrophic way!"

1 When Jesus had finished speaking to the people, he went to Capernaum. **2-5** There was a certain Roman officer in charge of 100 men who had a slave servant. He valued this slave servant considerably. The slave servant was sick, and in fact was at death's door. *3* The Roman officer in charge of 100 men heard about Jesus and sent out Jewish elders to ask him to bring his servant safely through the illness. *4* When they reached Jesus, they pleaded strongly with him, "This person deserves this. *5* He loves our people. In fact, he was the one who built our synagogue."

6-10 So Jesus went with them. He wasn't far from the house when the Roman officer in charge of 100 men sent friends with the message, "Lord, don't trouble yourself, I don't deserve to have you come under my roof! *7* For this reason I didn't even think myself good enough to come to you. But say the word, and my servant will be instantly divinely healed![3] *8* In fact I myself am a person put under authority, with soldiers under me. I tell this soldier, 'Go' and he goes, and I tell that soldier, 'Come' and he comes. I say to my slave servant, 'Do this' and they do it!"

---

[1] ἀδελφοί, *adelphoi*. See note on Matt. 5:22.
[2] ὑποκριτῆς, *hupokrites*. See note on Matt. 6:2.
[3] ἰάομαι, *iaomai*. See note on Matt. 8:8.

9 On hearing this, Jesus was amazed at him. He turned to the crowd that followed him, and said, "I can certainly say that I haven't come across such great faith, even in Israel!" *10* The slave servants who had been sent out returned to the house and found the servant completely healthy.

11-17 Soon afterwards Jesus traveled to a city called Nain. His disciples and a large crowd went too. *12* He was approaching the city gate, and a dead person was being buried - the only son of his mother, and she was a widow. Quite a large crowd was in attendance. *13* When the Lord saw her, he was moved with compassion for her and said, "Don't cry."

14 He went up and touched the coffin, and the bearers stood still. He said, "Young man, I say to you, 'Get up!'"

15 The corpse sat up and began to talk, and Jesus gave him to his mother. *16* The people were all gripped with fear, and praised God, exclaiming, "A great prophet has risen up among us!" and, "God has visited his people!" *17* The news about him spread all through Judea and all around the countryside.

18-23 John's disciples told him about all these things, *19* so he summoned two of his disciples and sent them to Jesus to ask, "Are you the One who was to come, or are we to wait for another?"

20 When the men came to Jesus, they asked, "John the Baptizer has sent us to you to ask, 'Are you the One to was to come, or are we to expect another?'"

21 At that very moment Jesus healed many who had diseases and torments and evil spirits, and granted sight to many blind people. *22* Jesus answered, "Go and tell John what you can hear and see for yourselves: the blind see again, the crippled are walking about, lepers are cleansed and the deaf hear, the dead have risen and the financially poor are having the Good News announced to them. *23* The person who doesn't reject me because of what I do is a happy person!"

24-30 After John's messengers left, Jesus began to speak to the crowd about John: "What did you expect to see when you went out into the wilderness? A skinny plant blowing around in the wind? *25* What did you expect to see? A person wearing fancy clothes? No way! People who wear fancy clothes live in palaces. *26* What did you expect to see? A prophet? That's right, and he's more than a prophet. *27* He is the prophet mentioned here: 'I send my messenger ahead of you. He will prepare the road for you' *28* I tell you, no human in history has been more important than John the Baptizer! Yet the most insignificant person in God's Realm is more important than he!"

29 When they heard this, all the people, even the Tax Profiteers, did the right thing with God by being baptized with the baptism carried out by John. *30* But the Pharisees and experts in the Law refused to be baptized by John, and thus invalidated God's purpose for them.

31-35 Jesus continued, "To what can I compare this people group? *32* It's like children who sit in the playgrounds and yell to their friends, 'We played music for you but you didn't dance - we cried and you weren't sad!' *33* John didn't go around eating nor drinking, and they say, 'He's got a demon!' *34* The Human Being went around eating and drinking, and they say, 'He's a greedy pig and a drunkard! He's friends with Tax Profiteers and sinners.' *35* Yet Wisdom is shown to be right by the actions of people who follow it!"

36-38 Then one of the Pharisees invited Jesus over for dinner. Jesus went to the Pharisee's house and sat down to eat. *37* When a woman in the city who was a sinner learnt that Jesus was reclining for dinner at the Pharisee's house, she brought along an alabaster flask of very expensive perfumed oil.[1] *38* She

---

[1] μύρον, *muron*, perfumed ointment. See *IGUR* 1245.17-19. It was used in burial for the dead as well as a luxury item. The word also occurs in both meanings in Matt. 26:6-12 = Mark 14:3-8 = John 12:1-7. In Mark and John, the μύρον, *muron* is identified as νάρδου, *nardou*, spikenard. See note on Mark 14:3.

was crying, and sat behind him at his feet. She started crying all over his feet. Then she wiped them with her hair, and covered his feet with kisses, and poured the perfumed oil on his feet.

39-43 When the Pharisee who had invited him saw this, he said to himself, "If he were really a prophet, he would know who is touching him and what sort of woman she is - that she's a sinner!"

40 "Simon," Jesus responded, "I've got something to say to you!"

"What is it, teacher?" he asked.

41 "Two people owed money to a certain moneylender," Jesus said. "One owed him five hundred silver coins, and the other owed him fifty. *42* Neither of them were in a position to pay him back, so he let both of them off their debts. So tell me - which of them will love him more?"

43 Simon answered, "I suppose the one who had the bigger debt canceled."

"Yes, you're right," Jesus said.

44-50 Then Jesus motioned to the woman and said to Simon, "Do you see this woman? I came into your house, but you didn't give me any water for my feet, but she cried all over my feet and wiped it off with her hair. *45* You didn't give me a kiss, but from the time I arrived, this woman hasn't stopped kissing my feet. *46* You didn't put olive oil my head, but this woman has put perfumed oil on my head. *47* This is the reason I tell you that her sins, which were many, have been canceled. I can tell you that she loved much. The person who does not understand what it's like to receive forgiveness has little capacity to give love."

48 Jesus said to her, "Your sins are canceled."

49 The people who were reclining for dinner with him started saying to each other, "Who is this guy who even forgives sins!"

50 Then Jesus said to the woman, "Your faith has rescued and preserved you: go in peace!"

Ch.8:1-3 Shortly after this, Jesus made his way from city to city and town to town, announcing the Good News about God's Realm. The Twelve were with him, *2* and so were certain women who had been healed from evil spirits and sicknesses: Mary (known as Mary from Magdalene) - seven demons had gone out of her – *3* and Joanna the wife of Cuza, the manager of Herod's household; Susanna, and many others. These women materially provided[1] for Jesus and the Twelve out of their own funds.

4-8 After a large crowd had gathered from every city, Jesus told them this example. *5* "The farmer went out to plant his seed. As the farmer was planting the seed, some fell along the road - it was trampled on, and the birds ate it up. *6* But some other seed fell on rocky ground, and when it grew, it withered because it didn't have any moisture. *7* But some other seed fell among thorns, and the thorns grew up with it and choked it. *8* Still other seed fell on good soil. It grew and produced a crop a hundred times more than was planted." After Jesus said this, he shouted, "If you have ears you had better listen!"

9-10 His disciples asked him what the example meant. *10* He explained, "You are permitted to know the secret hidden truths of God's Realm, but to others I speak in examples, so that, 'Although they see, they do not observe. Although they hear, they do not understand.'

11-15 "This is the meaning of the example: the seed represents God's Word. *12* Those seeds along the road represent the people who hear the Word, but then Slanderer-Liar comes along and takes Word out of their minds, so that they won't believe it and be saved. *13* Those seeds on the rocky ground represent the people who receive the Word with delight when they hear it, but they don't have any roots. They believe for a while, but they defect when the

---

[1] διακονέω τινί, *diakoneo tini*. See note on Matt. 27:55.

enemy harasses[1] them. *14* The seeds that fell among the thorns represent the people who hear, but as they go through life they are choked by life's preoccupations, wealth and pleasures, and they do not mature. *15* But the seeds on good soil represent the people who have honest and good hearts. They hear the Word and hold onto it. They produce a good harvest by using their steadfast endurance.

16-18 "No one lights a portable lamp and covers it with a bucket or puts it under a bed. Instead, they put it somewhere where it will shine light on everything, so people who come in can see the light. *17* All hidden things will be plainly shown, all secret things will come out into the open. *18* So take care the way you hear this! Even more – to overflowing! - will be given to a person who has! But a person who doesn't have – even what they do have will be taken away!

19-21 Jesus' mother and brothers came to see him, but they couldn't get near him because of the crowd. *20* Someone told him, "Your mother and brothers are standing outside, and they want to see you."

21 He answered, "My mother and my brothers are those who hear God's Word and do it."

22-25 On one particular day Jesus said to his disciples, "Let's go over to the other side of the lake."

So they got into a boat and set sail. *23* As they sailed he fell asleep. A squall came down on the lake and they were beginning to fill up with water and were in danger of sinking. *24* They woke Jesus up and said,, "Master, master! We're doomed!"

He got up and rebuked the wind and the high waves - it stopped and everything was calm. *25* "Where is your faith?" he chastised them.

They were shocked and amazed and said to each other, "Who is this guy? He even gives orders to the wind and the water, and they pay attention[2] to him!"

26-33 They sailed down to the land of the Gerasenes, which is on the shore opposite Galilee. *27* When Jesus had disembarked, a man met him. Now this man was from the city and had demons. For quite some time he hadn't worn clothes or lived in a house, but instead had lived in the cemetery. *28* When he saw Jesus, he shouted out and fell down in front of him, yelling at the top of his voice, "What are you meddling with me for, Jesus, Son of the Most High God? I beg you, don't torture me!"

29 You see, Jesus had ordered the unclean spirit to come out of the person. For a long time ago the unclean spirit had obtained and now held complete mastery of him. Although the man was guarded securely and bound by handcuffs and chains, he kept breaking his bonds, and the demon kept driving him out into the desert. *30* Jesus asked him, "What's your name?"

"Army division of 6,000 men," he replied, because lots of demons had gone into him. *31* The demons kept begging Jesus not to order them to go to the abyss. *32* There was quite a large herd of pigs grazing on the hillside. The demons begged Jesus to let them go into the pigs, and he gave them permission to do so. *33* The demons went out of the person into the pigs, and then the herd rushed over the cliff into the lake and drowned.

34-39 When the pig herders saw what had happened, they ran away and told everyone in the city and the farms, *35* and the people came out to see what had happened. They came up to Jesus and found the person from whom the demons had come out, sitting at Jesus' feet. He was wearing clothes and in his right mind. They were shocked.

36 Those who had seen it told the people how the person who had the bad spirits had been rescued and preserved. *37* The whole crowd of people from the Gerasenes regions asked Jesus to leave them, because they started to be

---

[1] περιασμός, *periasmos*. See note on Matt. 6:13.
[2] ὑπακουω, *hupakouo*. See note on Matt. 8:27.

completely gripped with fear. So he embarked on the ship and left. *38* The man from whom the demons had gone out begged to go with him, but Jesus sent him away with the instructions, *39* "Go back home and tell people how much God has done for you." The man left and told people all over town how much Jesus had done for him.

40-42 On Jesus' return, a crowd welcomed him, as they were all expecting him. *41* A man named Jairus who was a ruler in the synagogue, came and fell down at Jesus' feet, and begged him to come to his house. *42* His only daughter, a girl of about twelve, was dying.

42-48 As Jesus was being led off, the crowds almost crushed him. *43* There was a woman who had suffered a blood loss for the past twelve years. She hadn't found anyone who was able to heal her.[1] *44* She came up behind him and touched the edge of his coat, and immediately the blood loss stopped.

45 Jesus said, "Who touched me?"

When they all denied it, Peter said, "Master, the crowds are crowding and pressing against you!"

46 But Jesus said, "Someone touched me! I know for sure that power has gone out of me."

47 Then the woman, seeing that she couldn't go unnoticed, came up to him shaking and fell in front of him. In front of all the people, she told the reason why she'd touched him and how as soon as she did, she'd been instantly divinely healed.

48 Jesus said, "Daughter, your faith has rescued and preserved you; go in peace!"

49-56 While Jesus was still speaking, someone arrived from the house of Jairus, the synagogue ruler. He said, "Your daughter's dead! Don't disturb the teacher any more!"

50 When Jesus heard this, he said to Jairus, "Don't be afraid. Just believe, and she will be rescued and preserved!"

51 When Jesus arrived at the house, he didn't let anyone go in with him except Peter, John and James, and the young girl's father and mother. *52* They were all crying and mourning for her. "Don't cry," Jesus said, "she's not dead, just asleep!"

53 They made fun of him, knowing that she was in fact dead. *54* He took her by the hand, and called out, "My child, get up!"

55 And her spirit returned and she got up. Jesus told them to give her something to eat. *56* Her parents were astounded. He ordered them not to tell anyone what had happened.

Ch.9:1-6 Jesus called the Twelve together, and gave them the power and authority to heal all demons and diseases, *2* and he sent them out to proclaim God's Realm and to instantly divinely heal the sick. *3* He told them, "Don't take anything for your trip – don't take a walking stick, suitcase, food, money, change of clothes. *4* Choose a house, and stay there until it's time to leave that town. *5* Now if you come across certain people who don't treat you well, when you leave their town shake the dust off your feet to demonstrate that you think they are pagans!"

6 So they set off and passed from one village to another, announcing the Good News and healing people everywhere.

7-9 Herod the tribal ruler heard about everything that was going on. He was completely confused, because some were saying that John had been raised from the dead, *8* and others were saying that Elijah had appeared. Still others were saying that one of the prophets of ancient times had come back to life! *9* "But I myself had John beheaded!" Herod exclaimed. "So who's this I'm hearing all this about?" And he tried to see him.

---

[1] Notice that Luke, said to be a medical doctor, does not mention (as does Mark) that the woman had spent her life savings on doctors!

10-11 When the apostles returned, they told Jesus what they had done. He took them with him and they went off by themselves to a city called Bethsaida. *11* The crowds got to hear of it and followed. He welcomed them and spoke to them about God's Realm, and instantly divinely healed the ones who needed healing.

12-17 Late in the afternoon the Twelve went to him and said, "Send the crowd away! They can go off to the surrounding villages and farms and find food and somewhere to stay for the night – we're in a remote area!"

13 Jesus said, "*You* give them something to eat!"

"But we've only got five loaves of bread and two fish - unless we're to buy some food!" they protested. *14* (There were actually about 5,000 men there.)

Then Jesus said to the disciples, "Get them to recline for dinner and divide them into groups of about fifty each." *15* They did this and everyone sat down for dinner. *16* Jesus picked up the five loaves of bread and the two fish. He looked up to heaven, thanked God and broke them into pieces, then handed them to the disciples to serve the people. *17* They all ate until they had had enough to eat, and then the disciples picked up 12 wicker baskets full of leftovers.

18-27 On one occasion Jesus was praying in private, and his disciples were with him. He put the question to them, "Who do the crowds think I am?"

19 They answered, "Some say you're John the Baptizer, others say Elijah, and different ones say that you're one of the prophets from ancient times who's come back to life."

20 Jesus said to them, "Well, you - who do you say I am?"

"The Anointed One of God," Peter said.

21 Jesus gave them strict warning not to tell anyone. *22* He added, "The Human Being has to experience a lot of things and be rejected by the elders, chief priests and Bible scholars, and he must be killed, and raised back to life on the third day." *23* Then he said to all of them, "If anyone wishes to follow me, they must leave self behind and pick up their cross each day and follow me! *24* The person who lets it all go and lets me take over will get a life. *25* What's the point if a person gains the whole world, but loses their own soul? *26* If anyone is ashamed of me, the Human Being will be ashamed of them when he comes in his splendor and in the splendor of the Father and the sacred Messengers. *27* I'm telling you the truth, some of you who are standing here will definitely not experience death before they see God's Realm."

28-36 About eight days after Jesus said this, he took Peter, John and James with him up to the hill country to pray. *29* While he was praying, the appearance of his face changed, and his clothes turned as bright as a flash of lightning. *30* Suddenly, two men, Moses and Elijah, appeared and talked with Jesus. *31* They discussed his death, which was about to happen at Jerusalem. *32* Peter and his companions became overcome with sleep, but when they were wide awake again they saw his splendor and the two men standing with him. *33* As the men were leaving, Peter said to him, "Master, it's good that we're here. How about we put up three shelters - one for you, one for Moses and one for Elijah." (He didn't know what he was saying!)

34 While he was speaking, a cloud appeared and completely cast its shadow over them, and they were scared as they went into it. *35* A voice came out of the cloud, and said, "This is my Son! I have chosen him - listen to him!" *36* When the voice stopped, they realized that Jesus was alone. The disciples kept this to themselves and didn't tell anyone at that time what they had seen.

37-43 The next day they came down the mountain and a large crowd met Jesus. A gentleman in the crowd yelled out, "Teacher, please take a look at my son – he's my only child. *39* A spirit gets hold of him and he suddenly screams and has convulsions so bad that he foams at the mouth. When it leaves him it gives him a lot of trouble and bruises him. *40* I begged your disciples to drive it out, but they couldn't!"

41 Jesus said, "You unbelieving and distorted people group! How long do I have to put up with you for! Bring your son here." *42* Even while the boy was approaching, the demon threw him down and made him have convulsions. Jesus rebuked the unclean spirit and instantly divinely healed the boy, and gave him back to his father. *43* They were all thunderstruck at God's greatness.

43-45 While they were all being surprised at what Jesus did, he said to his disciples, *44* "Listen carefully to what I'm about to tell you. The Human Being is about to be betrayed into the hands of people."

45 But the disciples didn't have a clue what he meant. It was hidden from them. They didn't understand, and they were afraid to ask him about it.

46-48 Then the disciples began to have an argument about which one of them was likely to be the most important. *47* As Jesus knew what they were thinking, he took a little child and put the little child beside him. *48* Then he said to them, "Whoever welcomes this little child in my Name welcomes me, and whoever welcomes me welcomes the One who sent me. The person who is inferior among you is actually important."

49-50 John said, "Master, we saw someone driving out demons in your Name and we tried to stop him, because he isn't one of us."

50 "Don't try to stop him!" Jesus said, "Because the person who isn't against you, is for you!"

51-56 As the time was getting closer for Jesus to be taken up to heaven, he firmly made up his mind and headed for Jerusalem, *52* and sent messengers on ahead. They went into a Samaritan village to get things ready for him, *53* but the locals didn't welcome him, because he was heading for Jerusalem. *54* When the disciples James and John noticed this, they asked, "Lord, do you want us to call down fire from heaven to destroy them?" *55* But Jesus turned around and rebuked them, *56* and they went to another village.

57-62 As they were traveling along the road, someone said to Jesus, "I will follow you wherever you go."

58 "Foxes have holes and birds of the air have nests," Jesus replied, "but the Human Being has nowhere to stay tonight."[1]

59 Then he said to someone else, "Follow me."

But that person said, "Please let me go and organize my father's funeral first!"

60 Jesus said, "Let the dead bury their own dead, but you go and spread the news of God's Realm."

61 Another person said, "I'll follow you, Lord! Just let me go back and say goodbye to my family first."

62 Jesus replied, "Anyone who has started plowing and keeps looking back is not fit for service in God's Realm."

Ch.10:1-7 After this the Lord appointed seventy[2] others and sent them ahead in groups of two to every city and place he intended to visit. *2* He said to them, "On the one hand there's a big harvest, but on the other hand there are not enough workers. Put some effort into it! Ask the Harvest Master to throw workers into his harvest!"

3 "Off you go!" he continued. "I'm sending you out like sheep into a pack of wolves! *4* Don't take a wallet or shoes, and don't say hello to anyone on the road. *5* When you go into someone's home, be sure to say, 'Peace on this house!' *6* If the home is worthy, bless it with peace. But if it isn't worthy, take your peace blessing back. *7* Stay in that house and eat and drink what they offer you, because the worker deserves their pay. Don't make a habit of moving around from house to house.

---

1   Jesus certainly was not poor and homeless. He was traveling at the time and was merely stating that he had nowhere to stay for the night.

2   Equally, "seventy-two". The textual evidence is divided.

8-12 "When you go into a city and they welcome you, eat what they put in front of you. *9* Heal the sick there and tell them, 'God's Realm is close to you.' *10* But when you go to a city and they don't welcome you, go into the streets and say, *11* 'The very dust of your city which sticks to our feet we wipe off against you! Only realize this - God's Realm is nearby!' *12* I tell you - Sodom will be better off on that day than that city!

13-16 "Woe to you, Korazin! Woe to you, Bethsaida! If the powerful things done in you had been done in Tyre and Sidon, they would have changed their minds long ago! They would have dressed in rags and put ashes on their heads![1] *14* Tyre and Sidon will be better off than you in the Day of Judgment! *15* And you, Capernaum, will you be lifted up to heaven? No, you will go down to Hades! *16* The person who listens to you listens to me, the person who rejects you rejects me, but the person who rejects me rejects the One who sent me."

17-20 The seventy[2] came back and were very happy. They said, "Lord, even the demons yield to us in your Name!"

18 "Yes, I know," Jesus replied. "I was watching Adversary fall like a flash of lightning from the sky. *19* I have given you the authority to trample on snakes and scorpions, and authority over all the enemy's power, and nothing will harm you. *20* But all that aside, don't be happy just because the spirits yield to you, but instead be happy that your names have been written down in the heavenly places."[3]

21-24 At that Jesus was filled with the happiness that comes from the Holy Spirit. He said, "I fully agree with you, Father, Lord of Heaven and earth, because you have hidden these things away from the wise people and the academics, and have revealed them to little children. Yes, Father, that pleased you. *22* My Father entrusted everything to me. No one knows who the Son is except the Father, and no one knows who the Father is except the Son, and anyone to whom the Son chooses to reveal him."

23 Then Jesus turned to his disciples and said privately, "You are really blessed to see what you see. *24* Many prophets and kings wanted to see what you see, but didn't see it, and to hear what you hear but didn't hear it."

25-29 Now, an expert in the Law of Moses stood up to provoke Jesus with a question. He asked, "Teacher, what would I have to do to inherit eternal life?"

26 "What is written in the Scriptures?" Jesus asked in turn. "What do you understand it to say?"

27 He answered, "'Love the Lord your God with all your heart, soul, strength and mind,' and, 'Love your neighbors as much as you love yourself.'"

28 "Yes, that's right," said Jesus. "If you do this, you will live."

29 But he wanted to show that he was the one who was right, so he asked Jesus, "And who is my neighbor!"

30-37 Jesus' comeback was as follows: "A certain person was going down from Jerusalem to Jericho, when robbers attacked him. They ripped off all his clothes, beat him up and ran off, leaving him half dead. *31* A priest happened to be going along the same road, but when he saw him, he went past him on the other side of the road. *32* The same thing happened when a member of the tribe of Levi came on the scene - he crossed the road too and went past on the other side. *33* But there was a certain Samaritan who was traveling on that road. When he saw him, he was moved with compassion for him, and went

---

[1]   A sign of mourning.
[2]   Equally, "seventy-two". See note on Luke 10:1.
[3]   Idiomatic Greek expression meaning, "although you may well be happy that the spirits yield to you, continue to be happy..." It is the same idiom as "I will have mercy and not sacrifice" (Hosea 6:6) which means that mercy is greater than sacrifice, not that sacrifice is forbidden.

over to him. *34* He poured oil and wine[1] on his wounds, and bound them up. Then he put him on his own pack animal, and took him to an inn where he looked after him. *35* The next day he paid the innkeeper two silver coins,[2] and said, 'Please look after him until I get back. If there's any extra cost, I'll certainly reimburse you then.'

36 "So which of these three do you think was a neighbor to the man who was attacked by the robbers?"

37 The expert in the Law of Moses said, "The one who did the act of mercy on him."

Jesus said, "Off you go and do the same!"

38-42 Jesus and his disciples went on their way. He arrived at a village where a woman named Martha welcomed him into her home. *39* She had a sister called Mary, who sat at the Lord's feet and was listening to what he said. *40* Martha was distracted by all the preparations for the meal. She went over to Jesus. "Lord, don't you care that my sister has left me to provide all by myself?" she complained. "Please tell her to take an interest in my work and get stuck right in to the work and do her share!"[3]

41 "Martha, Martha!" the Lord replied, "You're preoccupied and hassled about a lot of things, *42* but only one thing is necessary. Mary has chosen what is better, and it won't be taken away from her."

Ch.11:1-4 At one point Jesus was praying in a certain place. When he finished, one of his disciples said to him, "Lord, please teach us how to pray, just like John taught his disciples to pray too."

2 Jesus said, "When you pray, say, 'Father, may your Name be treated as sacred! May your Realm come! *3* Keep giving us tomorrow's bread today and do so on a daily basis, *4* and cancel our sins, for we also discharge[4] all those in debt to us. And do not bring us to a ordeal.[5]'"

5-8 He said to them, "Let's say one of you has a friend, and you call on him in the middle of the night and say, 'Come on friend, lend me three loaves of bread. *6* A friend of mine who's traveling through has just dropped in, and I don't have anything to give him to eat.' *7* Then the one inside says, 'Stop bothering me! The door's already locked, and the kids are in bed with me. I can't get up and give you anything!' *8* I tell you, although he won't get up and give

---

[1] ἐπιχέω, *epikheo*, "pour over". Occurs only here in N.T. The treatment here, pouring a mixture of wine and olive oil on the wounds, is prescribed by Hippokrates, *Morb. Mul.* 656. W. K. Hobart, *The Medical Language of St. Luke*, Dublin, 1882, p. 28, cites Hippokrates, Dioscorides and Galen, and states, "ἐπιχέων, (*epikheon*) peculiar to St. Luke, is of frequent occurrence in the medical writers and often, too, used in conjunction with ἔλαιον <*elion*, oil> or δἰνος <*oinos*, wine>, or both together."

[2] The silver coin was the denarius, said in Matthew 20:2 to be a laborer's daily wage.

[3] συναντιλαμβάνω, *sunantilambano*. It does not mean "help". It does indeed encompass the meaning "help" but means far much more. It occurs only here and in Rom.6:26 in the N.T. Here Martha asks Jesus to tell Mary to take hold together with her in her work. The verb also encompasses the sense of not only taking hold together with someone, but taking a real interest in what they are doing. This sense is brought out in *I.Lampsakos* 7 (Thasos, I¹B.C.) It further encompasses the sense of achieving a result. From the papyrus evidence, we can see that this verb did not change in meaning from 200 B.C. to the time of Paul's writing.

[4] ἀφίημι, *aphiemi*, with the dative of person is used in a legal sense, to remit a charge or debt. Not "to set free from" which is ἀφίημι, *aphiemi*, with the accusative of person.

[5] περιασμός, *periasmos*. See note on Matt. 6:13.

him the bread because he's his friend, he will get up and give him whatever he needs – and this is because he is shamelessly audacious!"[1]

9-13 "Ask[2] and it will be given to you, seek and you will find, knock and the door will be opened for you. *10* Everyone who asks receives, and everyone who seeks finds, and the door will be opened for the person who knocks. *11* Would any one of you, if your child[3] asked for a fish, hand them a snake? *12* And what if your child asked you for an egg? Would you hand over a scorpion? *13* So then, if you know how to give good gifts to your children although you are evil, how much more will your Father in heaven give the Holy Spirit to those who ask him!"

14-20 Jesus was driving out a lack-of-speech demon. When the demon had gone out, the person who previously couldn't speak was now able to, and the crowd was shocked. *15* But some of them said, "He's driving out the demons by the power of Beelzebub, the ruler of the demons!"

16 Others tried to harass him by asking him for a sign from heaven. *17* But Jesus knew what they were thinking. He said, "Every kingdom that fights against itself ends up a wasteland, and every household that fights against itself won't last. *18* If Adversary throws out Adversary, he has thrown himself out! How could Adversary's kingdom last if it's divided against itself! I'm saying this because you claim that I'm driving out demons by the power of Beelzebub. *19* And if I'm throwing out demons by the demon Beelzebub's power, by whose power do your own people throw them out? This is why they will be your judges! *20* Yet if I throw out demons by God's power, then God's Realm is here for sure!

21-23 "As long as a strong person, fully armed, guards their own house, their possessions are safe. *22* But as soon as someone stronger comes along, attacks and overpowers the strong person, the stronger one takes away the protection on which the strong person relied, and shares out the weapons stripped from the enemy. *23* If you're not on my side you're against me, and if you don't gather with me, you scatter away!

24-26 "When an unclean spirit goes out of a person, it goes through waterless places, looking for rest, and doesn't find it. Then it says, 'I'll go back to my house that I came from!' *25* When it arrives, it finds the house

---

[1]   The word commonly mistranslated in most Bible translations as "persistent" is ἀναίδεα, *anaidea*, which means "shamelessly audacious", "overly bold". It appears in the sense "shamelessly audacious" in *P.Ryl* II.141.19; *OGIS* 665.16 (48-49 A.D.)

[2]   As "ask", "search" and "knock" are present imperatives, there has been much written that the sense is iterative and must be translated "keep on asking", "keep on searching", "keep on knocking". While this can be correct, it is also correct to state that the present imperative was used in general precepts (whether or not to an individual) concerning attitudes and conduct, and the aorist was preferred in commands related to conduct for specific cases. R.W. Funk in his revision of Blass and Debrunner's *A Greek Grammar of the New Testament and Other Early Christian Literature*, (Chicago: C.U.P., 1961), notes that the aorist imperative was much less frequent than the present imperative in the New Testament, for the above context. He notes that the same thing holds true for the Cretan inscriptions, p. 172.

[3]   υἱός, *huios*. The semantic range of *huios* is "child (of either gender)", "inhabitant of a place", "member of a class of people," and *huios* is also used with a noun to express a similarity to the noun. The standard Greek Liddell-Scott-Jones lexicon lists the meanings for *huios* as 1. son, 2. with a place name simply to mean inhabitants of the place name, 3. child, 4. used with numbers of years to indicate age, 5. in some dialects replaced by another Greek word for "child" *pais*, 6. as a general term of affection, 7. as a title of honor, 8. with the word *anthropos* to mean people, 9. with the word "God" to mean "inheritors of the nature of God".

swept out, clean and tidy. *26* Then it goes off and brings along seven other spirits more evil than itself, and they go in and settle down there. So the person ends up in a worse state than they were in to start with."

27-28 As Jesus was saying this, a woman called out from the crowd, "Happy is the woman who was pregnant with you and breast-fed you."

28 Jesus said, "That may be true, but happy are those who hear God's Word and guard it."

29-32 As more and more people came crowding around, Jesus said, "This people group[1] is an evil group! You search for a sign, but the only sign you will get is the sign of Jonah! *30* In the same way that Jonah was a sign to the Ninevites, so will the Human Being be to this people group. *31* The Queen of the South will rise at the Judgment with this group of people and condemn them - she came from the ends of the earth to listen to Solomon's wisdom, and now someone more important than Solomon is here. *32* The Ninevites[2] will stand up with at the Judgment with this people group and condemn them - they changed their minds when Jonah preached, and now someone more important than Jonah is here.

33-36 "No one lights a portable lamp and hides it somewhere, or puts it under a bucket! Instead they put it on a lamp stand, so it shines light on everyone. *34* Your eye is the lamp of your whole body. When your eyes are generous then your whole body is full of light too. But when they're stingy,[3] your body is full of darkness. *35* So be careful that the light in you is not dark. *36* If your whole body is full of light, and none of it is dark, then it will be completely lit up like when a beam of light shines on you!"

37-41 When Jesus had finished speaking, a Pharisee invited him to lunch. He went along and sat down for lunch. *38* But the Pharisee was surprised when he noticed that Jesus didn't wash in the ritual way before dinner. *39* The Lord said to him, "As a matter of fact you Pharisees clean the outside of the cup and dish, but inside you are full of greed and wickedness. *40* You silly twits! Didn't God make both the outside and the inside! *41* However, as for what is inside, if you would give charitable gifts you would be clean all over!"[4]

42-44 "Woe to you, Pharisees, because you give God a tenth of your mint, rue and all other kinds of herbs, but you forget about justice and you forget to love God. You should have done this, without forgetting the rest of it. *43* Woe to you Pharisees! You love the best seats in the synagogues and you like to be greeted with honor in the marketplaces. *44* Woe to you! You are like unmarked graves[5] that people walk over without noticing."

45-52 One of the experts in the Law of Moses complained, "Teacher, when you say all this, you're insulting us, too."

---

[1] "Group" meaning "race/kind/class/tribe" (can also mean "generation"). So too for the rest of the passage.

[2] ἄνδρες Νινευῖται, *andres Nineuitai*, "Ninevites" not "men of Nineveh". The Greeks very commonly put the word ἄνδρες, *andres*, with a place name to indicate the inhabitants of that place. It had nothing to do with the male gender, and the word ἄνδρες, *andres*, should not be translated in the expression.

[3] πονηρός, *poneros*: eye being evil is Greek idiom for being stingy or greedy.

[4] This very simple Greek sentence has caused huge problems for translators and commentators simply because they could not see how giving charitable gifts could benefit the giver. Moule, *op.cit.*, p. 34 states that the verse is "a desperately problematic passage". Some have suggested that the verse was based on an outright mistake, for example, on an Aramaic confusion of words, a view given as a possibility by Zerwick and Grosvenor, *op.cit.*, p. 226. See also Moule, *op.cit.*, p. 186. Yet the Greek is straightforward.

[5] A Jew who stepped on an unmarked grave was considered unclean, so such graves were considered to be quite a nuisance. For this reason tombs were often whitewashed to enhance their visibility.

46 Jesus replied, "And all you experts in the Law of Moses, woe to you, because you impose burdens on people. They can't carry them, and you yourselves don't even lift a finger to help them! *47* Woe to you, because you build tombs for the prophets, and it was your ancestors who killed them! *48* So this means that you approve of what your ancestors did - you built tombs for the prophets that your ancestors killed! *49* This is why God in his wisdom said, 'I will send prophets and apostles to them - they will kill some of them, and persecute some others!'

50 "So this people group will be held responsible for the blood of all the prophets that has been shed since the beginning of the world *51* from the blood of Abel to the blood of Zechariah, who was killed between the altar and the sanctuary. Yes, I tell you, this people group will be held responsible for all of it.

52 "Woe to you experts in the Law because you have taken away the key to the door of knowledge. You yourselves didn't go in, and you have stopped people who were trying to enter!"

53-54 After Jesus left the house, the Bible scholars and the Pharisees held a terrible grudge and questioned him about lots of things, *54* trying to catch him out on something he said.

Ch.12:1-3 Meanwhile, such a vast number of people had gathered that they were all trampling over each other. Jesus started to turn his attention to his disciples, and first of all said, "Avoid the yeast of the Pharisees - by this I mean their overly critical, hair splitting, pedantic religious behavior. *2* Everything that is completely covered will be revealed, and everything that is hidden will come out into the open. *3* What you have said in the dark will be heard in broad daylight, and what you have whispered in someone's ear in a storeroom will be shouted from the rooftops.

4-7 "My friends, don't be afraid of those who kill the body but after that can't do any more. *5* I'll show you who you should be afraid of - be afraid of him, who, after he can kill your body, has the power to throw you into the Garbage Pit Gehenna! Yes, I'm telling you, be afraid of him!

6 "Aren't five sparrows sold for two coins? But God doesn't even forget one of them. *7* In fact, he knows how many hairs you have on your head! So don't be afraid – you're worth more than lots of sparrows.

8-10 "Everyone who publicly declares that they are on my side, the Human Being will also declare he's on their side in front of God's Messengers! *9* But any person who publicly disowns me in front of people, will be disowned in front of God's Messengers. *10* Anyone who says anything against the Human Being will be forgiven, but someone who blasphemes against the Holy Spirit will not be forgiven.

11-12 "When you're hauled before the synagogues, rulers and authorities, don't worry about how to make your defense[1] or what to say. *12* The Holy Spirit will teach you what to say at the time."

13-15 Then someone in the crowd asked, "Teacher, please tell my brother to divide the inheritance with me."

14 Jesus said, "Hey, who appointed me the judge over the two of you or the executor of the will!" *15* Then he said to them, "Watch out! Beware of all types of greedy grasping behavior - your life is not made up by a lot of possessions!"

16-21 He told them the following example. "A certain rich person's farm produced a good crop. *17* He thought to himself, 'What am I to do? I don't have anywhere to store my crops!' *18* Then he said, 'I know what I'll do. I'll pull down my barns and build bigger ones, and I'll store all my grain and other possessions there. *19* Then I can say to myself, "You have enough good things stored up to last for ages. Take it easy - eat, drink, and party on."' *20* But God said to him, 'You silly fool! Tonight you're going to die. And then who's going

---

[1] ἀπολογέομαι, *apologeomai*, "defend", a technical legal term.

to get everything that you've stored up!' *21* And this will be the case with anyone who stores up things for their own use but is not wealthy in God's way."

22-26 Then Jesus said to his disciples, "This is why I tell you – don't worry about your life - what you're going to eat - or about your body - what you're going to wear. *23* Life is more important than food, and the body is more important than clothes. *24* Think about the ravens. They don't plant or harvest crops, and they don't have a bank or a barn, and God feeds them. And look how much more valuable you are than birds! *25* Which of you can add any time to your lifespan just by worrying? *26* So since you can't even do this little thing, why do you worry about the rest?

27-34 "Think about how the wild lilies grow. They don't work hard or make clothes. But I tell you, not even Solomon in all his wealth was dressed as well as one of these! *28* As this is how God clothes the grass of the fields, which is here today and burnt up tomorrow, how much more will he clothe you, you people with little faith? *29* And don't worry about what you're going to eat or drink and don't be unsettled. *30* The people who worship other gods run around worrying about this sort of thing, but your Father knows that you need them. *31* Instead, seek out God's Realm as a priority, and all these things will be given to you! *32* "Don't be afraid, my little group, because your Father is pleased to give you the Realm. *33* Sell your possessions and give charitable gifts. Make for yourselves money bags that never wear out, a bank in the heavenly places that never fails, where there's no thieves to steal it nor clothes-moths to eat it. *34* In fact, your thoughts will be where your bank is!

35-40 "Be dressed ready to go and keep your lamps burning, *36* just like people who were waiting for their boss to return from a wedding reception. The minute he comes and knocks, they can open the door for him. *37* Those slave servants are well off if the boss finds them on duty when he arrives. He will dress up in servant's clothes and will invite them to sit down to dinner and he will serve them. *38* Those slave servants are well off if the boss finds them ready - even if he comes in the middle of the night or the early hours of the morning. *39* But understand this - if the owner of the house had known what time the thief was coming, he wouldn't have let his house be broken in to. *40* You too must be ready, because the Human Being will come at the time you least expect."

41-48 Peter asked him, "Lord, do you mean this example specifically for us, or for everyone?"

42 "Then who is the trustworthy and wise manager," Jesus answered, "who the boss puts in charge of his servants to give them their meals at the correct time? *43* That slave servant will be well off if the boss finds him doing the right thing when he returns. *44* In fact, he will put him in charge of everything he owns. *45* But what if the slave servant thinks, 'The boss is taking a long time getting back,' and then beats up the male and female servants and gobbles up his food and gets drunk! *46* The boss will turn up unexpectedly, on a day he doesn't expect, and at a time he's not aware of. He'll chop him in half and send him to the same fate as the unbelievers! *47* A slave servant who knows what the boss wants and doesn't get ready, or doesn't do what the boss wants, will be well and truly beaten up. *48* But someone who doesn't know and does some wrong things will be beaten less severely. Much will be demanded from those who have been given much. Much more will be asked from those who have been entrusted with much.

49-53 "I have come to bring fire on the earth, and how I wish it had already started! *50* But I have a baptism I must go to, and how distressed I am until it has been done! *51* Do you think I came to bring peace on earth? Not at all, I tell you - not peace, but division. *52* From now on there will be five in one family divided against each other, three against two and two against three. *53* They will be divided - father against son and son against father, mother against daughter and daughter against mother, mother-in-law against daughter-in-law and daughter-in-law against mother-in-law.

54-56 He said to the crowd, "When you see a cloud coming up in the west, you immediately say, 'It's going to rain'- and it does! *55* When the south wind comes up, you say, 'It's going to be hot' - and it is! *56* You overly critical, hair splitting, pedantic, religious types! You know how to interpret the appearance of the earth and the sky. So why is it that you don't know how to interpret the times you're in?

57-59 "Why don't you judge for yourselves what is right? *58* As you and your opponent are going to the magistrate, try hard to settle your dispute on the way, otherwise your opponent might drag you off to the judge. Then the judge might turn you over to the police, and the police might throw you in prison! *59* I tell you, you won't be released until you have repaid every last bit of the fine."

Ch.13:1-5 At that time there were a few people present who told Jesus about the Galileans whose blood Pilate mixed with their sacrifices, by killing them while they were sacrificing![1]

2 Jesus asked, "So do you think that these Galileans were worse sinners than all the other Galileans because this happened to them? *3* No way! But if you don't change your minds, you will all die as well. *4* What about the eighteen people who died when the tower in Siloam fell on them - do you think they were more guilty than everyone else living in Jerusalem? *5* No way! But if you don't change your minds, you will die too."

6-9 Then he told them this example: "A certain person had a fig tree planted in the vineyard, and went to find fruit on it but there wasn't any. *7* So the person said to the gardener, 'For the last three years I've been looking for fruit on this fig tree and I still haven't found any! Cut it down! It's just a waste of space!'

8 "Sir, leave it alone for one more year, and I'll dig around it and fertilize it," the gardener answered. *9* "Then perhaps it will have figs on it next year. If it doesn't, you can cut it down.'"

10-13 One Sabbath day Jesus was teaching in one of the synagogues. *11* There was a woman present who'd had a spirit of sickness for eighteen years. She was bent over double and there was no way she could straighten up. *12* When Jesus saw her, he called her over and said, "Lady, you are freed from your sickness." *13* Then he laid hands on her. Immediately she straightened up and kept praising God.

14-16 The ruler of the synagogue was irritated because Jesus had healed on the Sabbath day. He addressed the crowd, "There are six days on which work should be done! So come and be healed on those days, not on the Sabbath!"[2]

15 "You overly critical, hair splitting, pedantic religious types!" the Lord exclaimed. "You can't tell me that each of you doesn't untie your ox on donkey from the stable on the Sabbath day and lead it out for water! *16* Then shouldn't this descendant of Abraham, whom Adversary well and truly has kept bound for eighteen long years, be set free from what bound her on the Sabbath day?"

17 When he said this, all his opponents[3] were humiliated, but the people were thrilled with all the incredible things he was doing.

18-21 Then Jesus asked, "What is God's Realm like? What can I compare it with? *19* It is like a mustard seed which a person took and planted in the garden.

---

[1] The Galileans who were killed by Pilate while they were sacrificing.

[2] L. Wells, *op.cit.*, p. 151 states, "He (the ruler of the synagogue) obviously understands healing treatment to be work. That a Jewish ruler understands the meaning of *therapeuo* in this way is entirely consistent with the use of the term by all other New Testament authors."

[3] ἀντικείμαι, *antikeimai*, "opponent", "opposing counterpart", one who sets themselves against one, to be opposite or opposed. See *P.Par.* 45.6. Used by the rhetoricians in the meaning "antithetical".

It grew and turned into a tree, and the birds came and perched in its branches." *20* Again he asked, "To what can I compare God's Realm? *21* It is like yeast that a woman took and hid into three batches of flour until all the bread rose."

22-30 Jesus went through the cities and villages, teaching while he made his way to Jerusalem. *23* Someone asked, "Lord, are only a few people going to be saved?"

24 He answered, "Keep up the contest to go in through the narrow door, because many will try to get in and they won't be able to. *25* Once the owner of the house has got up and locked the door, you will be left outside knocking and pleading, saying, 'Sir, please open the door for us!' But he will answer, 'I don't know you and I don't know where you came from.' *26* Then you will start to say, 'We ate and drank with you and you taught in our main streets!' *27* But he will answer, 'I haven't got a clue who you are or where you came from! Get lost, you pack of crooks!' *28* Then you will be in great sorrow, pain and anguish when you see Abraham, Isaac and Jacob and all the prophets in God's Realm - but you yourselves are kicked out. *29* People will come from the east, west, north and south, and will take their seats at the feast in God's Realm. *30* And I can tell you this: some of the ones who now are last will be first and some of the ones who now are first will be last."

31-35 At that time some Pharisees came up to Jesus and said, "You'd better get away from here and go somewhere else - Herod wants to kill you!"

32 He answered, "Go and tell that fox,[1] 'I am to drive out demons and perform instant divine healings today and tomorrow, and on the third day I am to be completed.' *33* In any case, I must keep going today and tomorrow and the next day – Jerusalem's the place where all the prophets die! *34* Jerusalem, Jerusalem! You've killed the prophets and stoned the ones I sent to you! I've often wanted to gather up your people, just like a hen gathers up her chicks under her wings - but you wouldn't let me! *35* Your temple will be deserted! You won't see me again until you say, 'Happy is the one who is coming in the Name of the Lord.'"

Ch.14:1-6 One Sabbath, Jesus went to have lunch at the house of one of the leading Pharisees, and he was being watched closely. *2* There right in front of him was a person who was suffering from excess swelling in the body. *3* Jesus asked the experts in the Law, and the Pharisees, "Is it legal to heal someone on the Sabbath or not?"

4 But they didn't say a word. So Jesus grabbed the person, instantly divinely healed him, and let him go. *5* Then he asked, "If your child[2] or ox falls into a well on a Sabbath day, wouldn't you pull it out at once?" *6* They weren't able to respond.

7-11 Then Jesus noticed that the guests had picked the best seats at the table, so he told them this example: *8* "When someone invites you to a wedding reception, don't recline on the couch in the place of honor, because a person who is more important than you may have been invited. *9* Then the host who invited both of you will have to tell you, 'You'll have to give up your seat to this person.' Then you'll be embarrassed and you'll have to sit in the worst seat. *10* Instead, when you're invited, go and sit in the worst seat. Then when the host comes up, the host will say to you, 'My friend, move up to this place of honor!' Then you'll be honored in front of all the other guests. *11* People who big-note themselves will be put down, and people who humble themselves will be honored."

---

[1]   While the Greeks considered foxes to be sly, the word was used in the Hebrew language to describe someone of low rank, an inept person.

[2]   There is textual possibility that this word is "pig" or perhaps even "sheep" or "son, pig, or ox", cf. John Mill, *Novum Testamentum Graecum*, 2nd. ed., Leipzig, 1723, p. 44, #423; Metzger, *op.cit.*, pp. 138-9.

12-14 Then Jesus also said to his host, "When you have lunch or dinner, don't invite your friends, associates, relatives, or your rich neighbors. If you do, they'll invite you back and you'll be repaid. *13* But when you give a party, invite the poor, the disabled, the crippled, and the blind, *14* and you will be blessed! Although they can't repay you, you will be repaid at the resurrection of the just."

15-24 One of the guests reclining with them for dinner heard this and turned to Jesus. "The person who eats at the feast in God's Realm is certainly blessed!" the guest exclaimed.

16 But Jesus answered, "A certain person was organizing a big party and invited a lot of guests. *17* When the party was ready a slave servant was sent to tell the guests, 'Come on, everything's ready now.'[1] *18* But every one of them began to make excuses. The first one said, 'I've just bought some land, and I have to go and see it. Please accept my apologies.' *19* Another one said, 'I've just bought five pair of oxen, and I'm on my way to try them out. Please accept my apologies.' *20* Still another one said, 'I just got married, so I really can't come.'

21 "The servant came back and reported all this to the boss. Then the owner of the house became angry and ordered the slave servant, 'Hurry out into the streets and alleys of the city and bring in the financially poor, the disabled, the blind and the crippled.' *22* After that happened, the servant said, 'Master, I've done what you said, but there's still some room.' *23* Then the master told the servant, 'Go out into the roads and country lanes and make them come in - I want my house to be full.' *24* I tell you, not one of those invited guests will get so much as a taste of the feast!"

25-33 Large crowds were traveling with Jesus, and he turned to them and said, *26* "No one can be my disciple if they put their father, mother, wife or children - even their own life – before me.[2] *27* And no one can be my disciple unless they carry their own cross and follow me. *28* Suppose one of you wants to build a tower. Surely you'll sit down first and calculate the cost to see if you have enough money to finish it? *29* If you lay the foundation and run out of money, everyone who sees it will poke fun at you, *30* and say, 'This silly fool started building and can't even finish it!' *31* Or suppose a king is about to go to war against another king. Surely he'll sit down first and consider whether he is able to win, if he's only got 10,000 men and the other king has 20,000 men! *32* If he thinks he can't win, he'll send out a delegation while the other one is still a long way off and will negotiate peace terms. *33* In the same way, any one of you who does not give up everything you have cannot be my disciple.

34-35 "Salt is good, but if it loses its flavor, how can it be made salty again? *35* It's not even fit to put on soil or a pile of manure! People throw it out. If you have ears you had better listen!"

Ch.15:1-7 All the Tax Profiteers and sinners were coming close to hear him. *2* But the Pharisees and the Bible scholars were grumbling to each other, "This guy welcomes sinners and eats with them!"

3 But Jesus told them this example. *4* "Suppose one of you has 100 sheep and you lose one of them. Surely you leave the other 99 in the open country and keep looking for the lost sheep until you find it! *5* And when you find it, you're happy! You put it on your shoulders and go back home. *6* Then you call your friends and neighbors and say, 'Come and celebrate - I've found that lost sheep!' *7* "In the same way there will be more celebrating in heaven over one sinner who changes

---

[1]   The sending of the messenger was according to Jewish custom.

[2]   μισέω, *miseo*, "hate" is not always as strong as, and has a wider meaning than, the English word "hate". For example, Homer uses it in the sense "Zeus hated (did not allow) that he should become a prey to the enemy dogs of Troy", *Iliad* 17.272, and Aristophanes uses it in the sense "passion", "grudging" cf. *Birds* 36.

their mind than over the other 99 people who are right with God who don't need to change their minds.

8-10 "Or suppose a woman has ten silver coins and she loses one of them. Surely she turns on the light, sweeps the house and searches carefully until she finds it? *9* And when she finds it, she calls her girlfriends and neighbors over and says, 'Celebrate with me, I've found that lost coin!' *10* In the same way, I tell you, there is celebrating in the presence of God's Messengers over one sinner who changes their minds."

11-16 Jesus said, "There was a guy who had two sons. *12* The younger son said to his father, 'Dad, give me my share of the estate.'

"So he divided up the property between them. *13* Not long after that, the younger son sold off everything he had, and went abroad to a distant country. He squandered his wealth extravagantly. *14* After he had spent everything, and there was a severe famine throughout the country, he started needing money. *15* So he went and hooked up to a citizen of that country, and he sent him out to his fields to feed the pigs. *16* He wished he could fill his stomach with the bean pods that the pigs were eating, but no one gave him anything.

17-24 "Finally he came to his senses and said, 'How many paid servants of my father's have more than enough food, and here I am starving to death! *18* I'll go and say to my father, "Father, I have sinned against heaven and against you! *19* I don't deserve to be called your son. Make me one of your paid servants!"'

20 "So he got up and went to his father. But when he was a long way off, his father saw him and was moved with compassion toward him. He ran to his son, threw his arms around him and kissed him. *21* The son said to him, 'Father, I have sinned against heaven and against you, and I don't deserve to be called your son!'

22 "But the father said to his slave servants, 'Quick! Bring the best coat we have, the finest,[1] and put it on him! Put a ring on his finger and sandals on his feet.[2] *23* Bring the fatted calf and kill it.[3] Let's have a party and celebrate! *24* This son of mine was a corpse and now he lives again - he was lost and now he's found!'"

24-32 "And the party began. *25* Meanwhile, the older son was out on the farm. As he approached the house, he heard music and dancing. *26* He called one of the servants over and asked him what was going on.

27 "The servant replied, 'Your brother has returned, and your father has killed the fattened calf because he has got him back all in one piece.'

28 "But the brother was so angry that he couldn't go into the house, so his father came out and pleaded with him. *29* But he answered his father, 'All these years I've been working for you and I never once disobeyed you. But you haven't even given me a young goat so I could give a dinner for my friends! *30* But when this precious son of yours[4] who has squandered your property with prostitutes comes, you kill the fatted calf for him!'

31 "His father answered, 'My child, you are always with me, and everything I have is yours. *32* But we had to have a party to celebrate, because your brother here was dead and lives - he was lost and now he is found.'"

Ch.16:1-6 Jesus told his disciples, "There was a certain rich person whose manager was accused of wasting money.[5] *2* So he summoned him and said,

---

[1] The στολή, *stole*, was a long and stately robe. Πρῶτος, *protos*, refers to the finest, the best in the house.

[2] The sandals were signs of a free person, as slave servants went barefoot.

[3] θύσατε, *thusate*, often means "sacrifice" but equally means "kill (for a meal)".

[4] ὁ υἱός σου οὗτος, *ho huios sou houtos*, contemptuous.

[5] Present participle: he was accused of habitually wasting money, not wasting money on a single occasion: he was accused of being a waster of money.

'What's this I hear about you? You'll have to give me an account of your management, because I'm about to give you the sack!'

3 "The manager said to himself, 'What I am I going to do now? The boss is about to give me the sack as the manager! I'm not strong enough to dig and I'm too ashamed to beg! *4* Oh, I know what I'll do! Then, when I lose my job as the manager here, people will welcome me into their houses!'

5 "So he summoned each and every one of his boss's debtors. He asked the first, 'How much do you owe the boss?'

6 "'100 barrels[1] of olive-oil,' the person replied.

"The manager said, 'Get your bill quickly - sit down and write on it 50.'

7-9 "Then he asked the second, 'How much do you owe?'

'100 bags of wheat,' the person replied.

He said, 'Take your bill and make it 80.'

8 "The boss praised the dishonest manager because of his good sense. This group of people has more practical wisdom in dealing with their own kind than do the people of the light. *9* And let me emphasize this, it's in your own interests to make friends of those people of the dishonest wealth,[2] so that when it fails, they will welcome you into their camps[3] for set periods of time.[4]

10-12 "The person who can be trusted with a small amount can also be trusted with a large amount, and the person who is dishonest with very little will be dishonest with a lot. *11* So if you haven't been trustworthy in handling dishonest wealth,[5] who will trust you with genuine riches? *12* And if you haven't been trustworthy with someone else's property, who will give you property of your own?

13 "No household servant can serve two masters. Either they will hate one and love the other, or alternatively they will be loyal to the one and despise the other. You are not able to serve both God and wealth."

14-16 The Pharisees, who were greedy,[6] were listening to this and turning up their noses at Jesus. *15* He said to them, "You are the ones who are making yourselves look good in the eyes of people, but God recognizes your hearts. What is good in people's estimation is an abomination in God's sight! *16* The Law and the prophets were up to the time of John: after then, the Good News about God's Realm has been announced, and many people get into it by illegal means.[7]

---

[1]   Literally a liquid measure, 10 gallons (45 litres). βάτος, *batos*, rare word, only here in the N.T. See *P.Oxy* 41.2982.9 (Oxyrhynchos, II-III).

[2]   μαμωνᾶς, *mamonas*. See note on Matt. 6:24.

[3]   σκηνή, *skene*, here in the plural, "camps" (metaphorical use), "abodes".

[4]   εἰς τὰς αἰωνιςους σκηνάς, *eis tas aionious skenas*. σκηναί, *skenai*, is used of temporary dwellings. αἰωνίους, *aionious*, means for set periods of time, for ages with a beginning and an end.

[5]   μαμωνᾶς, *mamonas*. See note on Matt. 6:24. Also in v. 13.

[6]   φιλάργυρος, *philarguros*, "stingy", "greedy". The adjective occurs only elsewhere in the N.T. in 2 Tim. 3:2. Greedy (φιλάργυρος, *philarguros*) doctors are criticized in *I.Eph.* IV.1386 (1ˢᵗ C.) MM gives a Hellenistic papyrological attestation. See discussion in *NDIEC* 4.140.

[7]   *Bia* is a technical legal term referring to the delict of hindering an owner or lawful possessor of their enjoyment of immovable property. The use of property without the lawful consent of the owner was considered to be a *bia*, and the suit prosecuted against the *bia* did not have to depend on actual force used by the accused. The point was that it was contrary to the legal owner's volition, and thus was considered to be a forcible act. ("Force" did not refer to physical violence, but to the rightful owner(s) being kept out.) Thus the point of the verse is not so much to complain that God's Realm is being illegally used, but that people who have legal right to it, such as for example, gay, lesbian, bi and transgender people, are being illegally kept from it. See note on Matthew 11:12.

17 "It is easier for the sky and earth to vanish than for the tiniest stroke of a letter to drop out of the Law.

18 "Anyone who divorces his wife and marries another commits adultery, and the man who marries a divorced woman commits adultery.[1]

19-31 "Now there was a certain rich person who dressed up in fine purple linen and lived in the lap of luxury every day. *20* A beggar named Lazarus lay ill at the rich person's gateway. *21* He was covered with sores, and he wished he could eat his fill of the scraps that fell from the rich person's table. Not only that, the dogs came and licked his ulcerated sores. *22* Well, it came to pass that the beggar died and was carried away by the Messengers to the place of honor, Abraham's side.[2] The rich person also died and was buried. *23* The rich person was being tormented[3] in Hades,[1] and looking up and seeing Abraham far away,

---

[1]   Luke has a most abbreviated statement about Jesus' teaching on divorce. A more in-depth account is provided in Matthew 19:3-14. This referred to people who had divorced by the "Any Matter" form of divorce, which Jesus rejected as illegal.

In Matthew 19:3, the Pharisees asked Jesus, "Is it legal for a person to divorce his wife on the grounds of 'Any Matter'?" The Rabbis were asking Jesus about his interpretation of Deuteronomy 24:1. The "Any Matter" is a technical term from Jewish divorce law, a form of divorce introduced by the Rabbi Hillel. The other type of divorce, on the ground of "General Sexual Immorality", was available to both men and women, both of whom were able to divorce the partner on the specific grounds based on Exodus 21:10-11. This traditional divorce was becoming rarer by the start of the first century, being replaced by the "Any Matter" divorce, which was for men only, and popular as no grounds had to be shown and there was no court case. For an "Any Matter" divorce, the man simply had to write out a certificate of divorce and give it to his wife. By Jesus' time, the "Any Matter" was the more popular form of divorce, but the rabbis were still arguing about the legalities of it. The disciples of Shammai were particularly opposed to it. See Josephus, *AJ* 4.253, "He who desires to be divorced from his wife who is living with him on the grounds of 'Any Matter'…must certify in writing…"; Philo, *Special Laws* 3.30, "…if a woman is parting from her husband on the grounds of 'Any Matter'"; see also the Rabbinic Commentary *Sifre Deuteronomy* 269. For modern scholarship, see D. Instone-Brewer, *op.cit.*

Jesus replied that a divorce on the grounds of "Any Matter" was not legal, that "whoever divorces his wife, unless it's on the grounds of 'General Sexual Immorality' and marries someone else, commits adultery". Jesus is simply saying that if someone divorces by a form other than the grounds of "General Sexual Immorality" form of divorce, they are not properly divorced and thus not free to remarry, and so are committing adultery if they do. He is continuing his statement that he disagrees with the "Any Matter" form of divorce.

It is most important to note the significance of the above. The way the passage has traditionally been translated implies that Jesus was asked the question, "Is it ever legal to divorce?" and he answered, "No, except on the grounds of sexual immorality." This is not the case. Jesus was asked if it was legal to divorce on the grounds of "Any Matter" and he answered, "No, only on the grounds of 'General Sexual Immorality'". In other words, he was disagreeing with the form of "Any Matter" form of divorce. He certainly was not saying that at that time, or in the time to come, people were never to divorce except for sexual immorality.

[2]   κόλπος, *kolpos*, the bosom, the place of honor at the feast, as noted by BDAG, *s.v.*

[3]   βάσανος, *basanos*, equally, "testing (by torture)". The word is literally the touchstone, on which gold, when rubbed on it, leaves a particular mark. Metaphorically it meant to test something to see if it was genuine, to question someone by torture. In Matthew 4:24 it occurs in its lesser meaning of "torment" of a tormenting disease. In N.T. only here and in verse 28.

with Lazarus next to him, *24* shouted out,, 'Father Abraham, have mercy on me! Please send Lazarus to dip the tip of his finger in some water and cool my tongue! I'm in agony in this fire!'

25 "But Abraham said, 'Remember, my child, all the good things that you fully received while you lived, and all the bad things that happened to Lazarus. But now this person is encouraged in this place and you're the one who is in distress. *26* And as if all this isn't enough, there's a great big gulf between us, in order that no one from either side is able cross over.'

27 "The rich person answered, 'Then I beg you, father, send Lazarus to my father's house, *28* because I've got five siblings. Tell him to give them a strong warning so they won't come here too, to this place of torment!'

29 "Abraham replied, 'They've got Moses and the Prophets - they can listen to them!'

30 "'No way, father Abraham!' the rich person said, 'It'd have to take someone from the dead going to see them - then they'd change their minds!'

31 "He said to him, 'If they don't listen to Moses and the Prophets, they're not going to be convinced by someone who rises from among the dead!'"[2]

Ch.17:1-4 Jesus said to his disciples, "Things that cause people to fall into a trap are going to come, but it's a sorry thing for that person who causes it! *2* They'd be better off hurled into the ocean with a large stone block tied around the neck than to cause one of my little ones to fall into a trap! *3* So watch yourselves! If your fellow believer sins, rebuke them,[3] and if they change their mind, forgive them. *4* Even if they sin against you seven times a day, and seven times come back and say, 'I'm sorry,' forgive them!"

5-6 The apostles said to the Lord, "Please increase our faith."

6 The Lord replied, "If you have faith like a mustard seed, you would say to this mulberry tree, 'Be uprooted and planted in the sea,' and it would listen to you and do as you say.

7-10 "Suppose one of you had a slave servant plowing or looking after the sheep. Would you say to the slave servant when they came in from the fields, 'Please come here now and sit down to lunch"?

8 "Surely you'd rather say, 'Get my lunch ready, then get yourself ready, and serve me while I eat and drink. After that you may eat and drink.'? *9* Will you favor the slave servant because they did what they were ordered to do? *10* In the same way you too, when you have done everything you were told to do, should say, 'We're unprofitable slave servants – we ought to do our duty.'"

11-19 When Jesus was on his way to Jerusalem, he went through the border between Samaria and Galilee. *12* As he was going into a village, ten lepers came out to meet him. They stood at a distance *13* and shouted out, "Jesus, Master, have pity on us!"

14 When he saw them, he said, "Go off and show yourselves to the priests."[4] And it turned out that as they slowly went off they were cleansed. *15* Then one of them, when he saw that he was instantly divinely healed, returned and praised God in a loud voice. *16* He threw himself at Jesus' feet and thanked him. And he was a Samaritan. *17* But weren't all ten of them cleansed?" Jesus asked. "So where are the other nine? *18* Why is it that no one else has come back and praised God except this foreigner?"*19* Then Jesus said, "Get up, off you go! Your faith has rescued and preserved you."

---

[1] Hades, the afterplace of the dead, a place separate from heaven, cf. for example, Acts 2:27, 31; Gen. 37:35, 44:29; Job 14:13, 17:13. Tartarus was a place of severe punishment, and the Greeks represented it as the furthermost place of Hades.

[2] ἐκ νεκρῶν, *ek nekron. See* note on Matt. 17:9.

[3] ἐπιτιμάω τινί, *epitimao tini.* There are two Greek words for "rebuke" used throughout the N.T. This is the one usually used for controlling hostile powers.

[4] Each person would go to the priest near the person's own home.

20-21 Once Jesus was asked by the Pharisees when God's Realm would come. Jesus said, "God's Realm won't come just because you're watching for it, *21* and neither can people say, 'Here it is!' or 'There it is', because God's Realm is actually within you!"

22-25 Then Jesus said to his disciples, "There will come a time when you will wish you could see one of the times of the Human Being and you will not see it. *23* And people will say to you, 'Over there! There he is!' or 'Look! Here he is!' Do not go running after them! *24* For the Human Being will be like the lightning that flashes and lights up one end of the sky to the other. *25* But first he must experience many things and be rejected by this people group.

26-37 "The Human Being's time will be the same as it was in Noah's time. *27* People were eating, drinking, marrying up to the very time that Noah went into the ark. Then the flood came and wiped them all out. *28* It was the same in the time of Lot. People were eating and drinking, buying and selling, planting and building. *29* But the very day that Lot left Sodom, fire and sulfur rained down on them from the sky and wiped them all out. *30* It will be the same on the Day when the Human Being will reveal himself. *31* On that day no one who is on the roof of the house should go down to get their possessions from inside the house. In the same way, no one out in the fields should go back for anything. *32* Remember Lot's wife!

33 "Whoever tries to keep their life will lose it, and whoever loses their life will preserve it. *34* On that night two people will be on one bed - one will be taken and the other one left. *35* Two women will be grinding grain together - one will be taken and the other one left."[1]

37 The disciples asked, "Where will this happen, Lord?"

He answered, "Where you find the body,[2] there you will find the eagles!

Ch.18:1-5 Then Jesus told them an example to demonstrate that it was necessary to pray always and not do it wrongly.[3] *2* He said, "There was a judge in a certain city who did not respect[4] God or respect people. *3* There was a widow in that city, and she was the one who came[5] and said to him, 'Get justice for me from my opponent at law!'

---

[1] Verse 36 is omitted as it was added by copyists.

[2] This verse is usually translated "Where the corpse is, there are the vultures gathered together." However, the word translated "corpse" is (the singular) τὸ σῶμα, *to soma*. This did mean "corpse" in the Ionian dialect, such as Homeric literature, but later came to mean either the living or dead body, dead body less frequently. The word νέκρος, *nekros*, is elsewhere used exclusively in the N.T. for dead body, so if there is an exception here, it would be noteworthy. Likewise, οἱ ἀετοι, *hoi aetoi*, means eagles rather than vultures. The Greek word for vulture is ὁ γύψ, cf. Euripides, *And.* 75. The Greeks were not careless in their identification of birds of prey, having two main words for hawk: ὁ ἱεϛραξ, *ho hierax*, and ὁ κίρκος, *ho kirkos*. The word for sea eagle is ὁ ἁλιαετος, *ho haliaetos*. Also, the use of the singular, "the body" is noteworthy.

[3] ἐγκακέω, *egkakeo*, to do something wrongly, to do something amiss. Used in the earlier writers for behaving badly or doing the wrong thing. It does not mean to "lose heart" or "to become discouraged". Furthermore, "to become discouraged" is in the passive voice whereas this verb is in the active voice. The verbs for losing heart and becoming discouraged are different verbs.

[4] φοβέομαι, *phobeomai*, "respect". See note On Luke 1:50.

[5] The Parable of the Aggressive Widow has been censored and turned into the Tale of the Persistent Widow. In verse 1, Matthew has also used the Greek word for "always" rather than the very common Greek word for "continually". Verse 5 does not contain the word "continually". Further, the verb "comes" in verse 3 is in the imperfect tense. Greek students are often taught that the imperfect tense refers to an action which continues in past

4 "And he didn't want to at the time, but afterwards he said to himself, 'I don't respect God or respect anyone, *5* but because this widow gives me trouble I'll give her what she wants alright, otherwise she might come and punch my lights out!'"[1]

6-8 The Lord says, "Pay attention to what the dishonest judge says. *7* God will certainly carry out justice for his chosen ones who call out to him night and day! He will certainly not delay over them! *8* He will see to it that they get justice, and quickly! But will the Human Being find faith on the earth when he comes?"

9-14 And Jesus told this example to some people who were confident that they were righteous and looked down on everyone else: *10* "Two people went up to the temple to pray – one was a Pharisee and the other one was a Tax Profiteer. *11* The Pharisee stood up and prayed to himself[2] as follows: 'God, I offer thanks to you that I'm not like other people – robbers,[3] evildoers, adulterers – or even like this Tax Profiteer! *12* I fast twice a week and I give a tenth of absolutely everything I get!'

13 "But the Tax Profiteer stood off at a distance. He dared not even look up at heaven but pounded his chest and said, 'God, please be merciful to me. I'm such a sinner!'

14 "I tell you, it was this person, not the other person, who went home pleasing God. All of you who have high opinions of yourselves will be put down, and all of you who humble yourselves will be honored."

15-17 People were also bringing young children to Jesus because they wanted him to touch them. When the disciples saw this, they rebuked them. *16* But Jesus called all the young children over and said, "Let the young children come to me - don't prevent them! God's Realm belongs to young children like these. *17* There is absolutely no way that someone who doesn't accept God's Realm like a little child will ever enter it."

18-25 A certain ruler asked Jesus, "Good teacher, what must I do to inherit eternal life?"

19 "Why do you call me good?" Jesus asked. "Only God is good – no one else is! *20* You know the commandments: 'Do not commit adultery, do not murder, do not steal, do not tell lies about others, honor your father and mother.'

21 "I've kept all these since I was a young man," he said.

---

time, rather than to a one-off completed action in past time. However, the Greek sometimes uses the imperfect tense in an idiom like the English "she was the one who did it." This idiom is found for example in Thucydides and Demosthenes. There are uses of the imperfect tense other than to express past continual action. Here we have the idiomatic use of imperfect tense, "she was the one who...", cf. idiomatic use of the imperfect "he was the one who ..."

[1] ὑπωπιάζω, *hupopiazo*, a technical wrestling term for giving someone a black eye or beating someone black and blue. See also 1 Cor. 9:27. Zerwick and Grosvenor, *op.cit.*, p. 253 translate, "give one a black eye, bruise, batter down." It occurs as "bruise" in *P.Lips* I. 39.13.

[2] "Prayed to himself": πρός ἑαυτόν, *pros heauton*.

[3] The term ἅρπαξ, *harpax*, was a technical legal term and means "plunderer" when used of immovable property, such as the illegal seizure of land. It is used with βιά, *bia*, and legally considered to be act of violence, but bear in mind that hindering someone from the use of their own property was prosecuted as a βιά, *bia*, whether or not actual physical force was involved. Here the Pharisea thanks God he is not a ἅρπαξ, *harpax*, like this τελώνης, *telones*, here. That can be seen as a nasty jab as the Tax Profiteers purchased one or more taxes, usually limited to a village, in a specific region at auction on a yearly basis. The Tax Profiteer made their profit by collecting more than the sum contracted to the state, thus the possible extortion reference.

22 When Jesus heard this, he said, "There's still one thing you need to do. Sell up everything you have and give it to the financially poor, and you will have a money bank stored up in the heavenly places. Then come on, follow me!" *23* When the ruler heard this, he became quite miserable, because he was extremely wealthy. *24* Jesus looked at him and said, "It's a really difficult thing for wealthy people to enter God's Realm! *25* In fact, pigs might fly before a rich person enters God's Realm!"[1]

26-30 The people who heard this exclaimed, "Then who can be saved?"

27 Jesus answered, "Things that are impossible for people are possible for God."

28 "But we left everything we had to follow you!" Peter protested.

29 Jesus replied, "Anyone who gives up their home, wife, brothers, parents or children for the sake of God's Realm *30* will get much more – and multiplied many times over - in this present life. They will also get eternal life in the age to come."

31-34 Jesus took the Twelve aside and said, "We're going up to Jerusalem now, and everything that was written by the prophets about the Human Being is about to happen. *32* He will be handed over to the non-Jews. They will poke fun at him, insult him, spit on him, *33* beat him with the Roman whip embedded with metal strips designed to rip off the flesh, and kill him. On the third day he will rise again."

34 The disciples didn't have a clue about what he was talking about. The concepts were hidden from them, and they didn't understand the meaning.

35-43 As Jesus approached Jericho, there was a blind person sitting by the side of the road begging. *36* When he heard the crowd passing, he asked what was happening. *37* They announced, "Jesus of Nazareth is going past."

38 He called out, "Jesus, David's descendant, have mercy on me!"

39 The people who were leading the way told him sharply to shut up, but this only made him shout even louder, "David's descendant, have mercy on me!"

40 Jesus stood still and ordered them to bring the person over. When he got close, Jesus asked him, *41* "What do you want me to do for you?"

"Lord, I want to see," he answered.

42 "Then see!" Jesus said. "Your faith has rescued and preserved you."

43 Straight away he could see, and he followed Jesus, praising God. The whole crowd saw it, and they praised God too.

Ch.19:1-10 Jesus entered Jericho and was passing through. *2* There was a man there whose name was Zacchaeus. He was a wealthy Tax Superintendent. *3* He wanted to see who Jesus was, but as he was short he wasn't able to see because of the crowd. *4* So he ran on ahead and climbed a fig-mulberry[2] tree which was right on Jesus' path, so he could see him. *5* When Jesus reached the spot, he looked up and said, "Zacchaeus, hurry up and come down. This very day I must stay at your house."

---

[1]   Greek idiom which needs to be expressed by English idiom. It was an hyperbolic expression to indicate the impossible by means of an absurdity. In non idiom it was word for word, "It's easier for a camel to pass through the eye of a needle..." Such sayings were common Rabbinic expressions. For example, the Talmud has two instances of a saying about an elephant passing through the eye of a needle to denote the impossible, as well as a camel dancing on a very small corn measure. There most certainly was no small gate in Jerusalem which a camel had to squeeze through or bend down to pass through. Nor is it correct that κάμιλος, *kamilos*, "cable", was accidentally substituted by scribal error for κάμηλος, *kamelos*, "camel".

[2]   συκομορέα, *sukomorea*, usually transliterated, "sycamore", but the translation is "fig-mulberry" (*ficus sycamoros*).

6 So Zacchaeus came down right away and welcomed Jesus happily. *7* All the people saw this and started complaining, "He's gone to stay at a sinner's house!"

8 Then Zacchaeus stood up and said, "Lord! I'm going to give half of what I own to the financially poor, and I'm going to pay back four times as much[1] to all the people I've ever cheated."

9 Jesus said to him, "Today salvation has come upon this house, because this person too is a descendant of Abraham. *10* The Human Being came to look for and save those who are lost."

11-15 While they were listening, Jesus told them another example. He did this because they were near Jerusalem and the people thought that God's Realm was about to appear at any moment. *12* He said, "A certain person of noble birth went to a distant country to have himself appointed king, and then return. *13* He called in ten of his own slave servants and gave them a large sum of money worth about two and half year's wages.[2] He instructed them, 'Carry on a business with this money while I'm away.'"

14 "His fellow citizens hated him and sent a delegation after him to say, 'We don't want this person to take up the kingship over us!' *15* At any rate, he was made king, and returned home. Then he sent for the slave servants to find out what profit they'd made on the money by doing business.

16-18 "The first one said, 'Sir, your sum of money worth 3 month's wages[3] has earned 10 times more!'

17 "'Good on you, you excellent servant!' his boss replied. 'Since you've been so trustworthy in a very small matter, I'm going to put you in charge of 10 cities!'

18 "The second one said, 'Sir, your sum of money worth 3 month's wages has earned 5 times more!'

19 "'I'm putting you in charge of 5 cities!' the boss replied.

20-21 "Then the other servant said, 'Sir, here is your sum of money worth 3 month's wages! I kept it stored away, wrapped in piece of cloth. *21* I was afraid of you, as I know you're a severe person! You can make money from practically nothing!"

---

[1] The *poena quadrupli* of Roman law required that an extortionist must pay back 4 times more than what was taken. Zacchaeus is offering to provide the standard restitution he would be required to make under Roman law. See *JEA* 40.107-11 (11/2/143 provenance unknown), a copy of the extract from the trial of a village scribe for wrongfully designating for public service a man from an official class granted immunity from such. The man fled and his possessions were sold. The sentence states, "Since you were to blame for his flight you were to blame for the sale of his possessions. You are subject to penalties. You will pay the fines at the treasury, but also you must pay this man four times as much as that for which his possessions were sold." For the fourfold restitution see J.D.M. Derrett, *Law in the New Testament*, (London: Darton, Longman & Todd, 1970, pp. 283-285; R. Taubenschlag, *The Law of Greco-Roman Egypt in the Light of the Papyri, 332BC-640AD*, (Warsaw: Panstwowe Wydawnictwo Naukowe, 1955), *repr*. Milan, 1972, pp. 552-553. An edict of Eudaimon provided a *poena sycophantiae* for Egypt, cf. *P.Oxy*. 2.237, (128 AD). Exodus 22:1 and 2 Samuel 12:6 mention the fourfold (or fivefold) restitution for an act of destructive robbery and Proverbs 6:31 mentions the sevenfold return. Exodus 22:4, 7 states that if the stolen property had not been consumed, double was to be paid. If the thief confessed and made voluntary restitution, the whole amount stolen was to be returned with one fifth added. However, Zacchaeus' offer to return fourfold is in keeping with current standard Roman law.
[2] Literally, 10 minas. Four minas were about a year's wage. One mina equaled 200 drachmae or denarii.
[3] Literally, 1 mina.

22-27 "His boss replied, 'You wicked[1] servant! I will judge you by your own words! So, you knew I was a severe person! You knew that I can make money from practically nothing! *23* Well then, you should have deposited my money with the public bankers, so when I came back I would have had the interest!'

24 "Then he said to the people who were standing around, 'Take away the sum of money worth 3 month's wages, and give it to the one who's got the large sum of money worth about two and half year's wages.' *25* But they said, 'Sir, that person already has the large sum of money worth about two and half year's wages!' *26* He replied, 'I tell you – to the person who has, more will be given, but to the person who doesn't have, what they do have will be taken away.' *27* Now as for those enemies of mine who didn't want me to be king over them – bring them here and execute them right here in front of me!"

28-31 After Jesus said this, he traveled on ahead and went up to Jerusalem. *29* As he approached Bethphage and Bethany at the hill called the 'Mount of Olives', he sent off two of his disciples *30* with the instructions, "Go into the village. Just as you enter it you'll find a colt that's never been ridden. It's tied up there. Untie it and bring it here. *31* If anyone asks you why you're untying it, tell them, 'The Lord needs it.'"[2]

32-35 The ones he sent ahead found it just as he'd described it to them. *33* As they were untying the young donkey, the owners said, "Why are you untying the young donkey?"

34 "The Lord needs it," they replied.

35 Then they led it to Jesus, threw their coats on it and mounted Jesus on it.

36-38 As he went along, people spread their coats out on the road. *37* By now he was approaching the descent from the Mount of Olives, and the whole crowd began to praise God joyfully in loud voices for all the powerful things they had seen him do: *38* "Happy is the one who is coming, the King, in the Name of the Lord!. Peace in heaven and honor in the Highest Realms!"

39-40 Some of the Pharisees called out to Jesus from the crowd, "Teacher, rebuke your disciples!"

40 But he answered, "If they keep quiet, the stones will yell out aloud!"

41-44 Then Jesus came closer and saw Jerusalem. He broke out crying over it *42* and said, "If only you had realized in these times just what would bring you peace – but now it's hidden from your sight. *43* The time will come when your enemies will throw up siege works to surround you and hem you from all sides. *44* They will smash you and your children to the ground, all of you inside your walls! They won't leave you one stone upon another, because you didn't recognize the time of God's visitation to you."

45-46 Then he went into the temple and started chasing out people who were selling things. *46* He said to them, "The Scriptures say, 'My house will be a house of prayer,' but you have made it a robber's hideout!"

47-48 He was teaching at the temple every day. But the chief priests, the Bible scholars and the leading citizens were looking for a way to kill him. *48* However, they weren't able to find a way to do it, because the whole crowd hung on his every word.

Ch.20:1-4 One day Jesus was teaching the people in the temple and announcing the Good News. The chief priests, the Bible scholars and the elders went over to him *2* and demanded, "Tell us – by what authority are you doing this? Who gave you the authority?"

3 "I myself will ask you a question too!" Jesus answered. *4* Tell me, by whose authority did John baptize? Was it heavenly or human?"

---

[1]   A strong adjective, πονηρός, *poneros*, "wicked", used to describe Adversary, cf. Eph. 6:16, "the evil one".

[2]   The official transport system allowed for a legitimate claimant to borrow a donkey, and return it afterwards. Donkeys were part of the public transport service, cf. J.M. Derrett, *NT* 13 (1971) 241-258.

5-8 They debated amongst themselves and said, "If we say 'By heavenly authority', he's going to say, 'So then why didn't you believe him?' *6* But if we say, 'By human authority', the whole crowd will stone us, because they're convinced that John was a prophet!"

7 So they answered, 'We don't know by whose authority it was."

8 "Well, I'm not going to tell you by what authority I'm doing these things!" Jesus retorted.

9-16 Jesus went on to tell the people this example: "There was a certain person who planted a vineyard, then rented it out to some farmers and went away from home for a long time. *10* At harvest time the owner sent a slave servant to the farmers to collect some of the vineyard's produce. But the farmers beat him up and sent him away empty-handed. *11* So he sent another servant, but they also beat him up and insulted him and sent him away empty-handed. *12* Then he sent a third servant, but they injured him and threw him out. *13* Then the owner of the vineyard said, 'What am I going to do? I'll send my own dear son, perhaps they will respect him!' *14* But when the farmers saw him, they discussed the matter. They said, 'This is the heir – let's kill him, then the inheritance will be ours!' *15* So they threw him out of the vineyard and killed him. So what do you think the owner of the vineyard will do to them? *16* He'll come and have the farmers put to death, and give the vineyard to others."

16-18 When the people heard this, they said, "Let's hope this never happens!"

17 Then Jesus looked straight at them and said, "So then what is the meaning of the Scripture: 'The stone which the builders rejected has become the cornerstone?'[1] *18* Everyone who falls on that stone will be smashed to pieces, and anyone on whom it falls will be crushed to powder!"

19-22 The Bible scholars and the chief priests searched for a way to arrest him at this very moment, because they knew that he had addressed this example to them. However, they were afraid of the crowd's reaction as the crowd favored Jesus so highly. *20* So they kept a close watch on Jesus, and sent spies who pretended to be for real. They were trying to catch Jesus out on something he said, so they could hand him over to the Governor's jurisdiction and authority. *21* So the spies put a question to him, "Teacher, we know what you speak and teach is correct, and that you don't take people on face value, but teach the truth about God's way. *22* So is it legal to pay taxes to Caesar, or not?"

23-26 Jesus saw through their cunning and said, *24* "Show me a silver coin.[2] Whose face and inscription are on it?"

"Caesar's!" they answered.

25 "Give back to Caesar what belongs to Caesar," Jesus said, "and give back to God what belongs to God!"

26 So they weren't able to catch him saying anything wrong in front of the crowd. They were amazed at his answer and kept quiet.

27-33 Some of the Sadducees who say there is no resurrection came up to Jesus and put the following question to him. *28* "Teacher, Moses wrote for us that if a man's brother dies and leaves a wife but no children, the man must marry the widow and have children for his brother. *29* Now, let's say there were seven brothers. The first one married a woman and died childless. *30* The second *31* and then the third married her. The seven of them all died in the same way, leaving no children. *32* Finally, the woman died too. *33* Now then, at the resurrection whose wife will she be, since the seven of them were all married to her?"

34-38 "The people of these times marry and are given in marriage," Jesus answered. *35* "But those who are considered worthy of taking part in the age to

---

[1] Psalm 118:22. There is no mention of "chief" in this scripture. The word "chief" is based on a mistranslation of κεφαλή, *kephale*, "source".

[2] A denarius.

come and in the resurrection of the dead will neither marry nor be given in marriage, *36* nor can they die anymore, as they're like Messengers. They are God's people, since they are associated with the resurrection. *37* But in the account of the bush, Moses clearly showed that the dead do rise, because he calls the Lord 'the God of Abraham, the God of Isaac and the God of Jacob.' *38* He is not the God of dead bodies, but the living. Everyone is alive as far as God is concerned."

39-40 Some of the Bible scholars said, "Well said, teacher!"

40 No one else dared to ask him any more questions.

41-44 Then Jesus asked them, "Why do they say that the Anointed One is David's descendant?" *42* David himself says in the Book of Psalms, 'The Lord said to my master, sit here in the place of honor at my right side, *43* until I put your enemies under your feet.' *44* "So then since David calls him 'master', how can he be David's descendant?"

45-47 In the hearing of the whole crowd, Jesus said to his disciples, *46* "Beware of the Bible scholars, who love to go around in long flowing robes and love to be greeted in the market places and have the most important seats in the synagogues, and the places of honor at dinners. *47* They gobble up widow's property and make a pretext of praying long prayers. These people are going to be liable to the most severe judgment!"

Ch.21:1-4 Jesus looked up and saw the rich people putting their gifts into the offering box. *2* He also saw a poor[1] widow put in two very small copper coins that together equaled a Roman cent. *3* He said, "This totally financially destitute widow has put in more than all the others, *4* because the others gave gifts out of what they had in abundance, but she gave everything she had out of her lack, and it was all she had to live on!"

5-9 Some of his disciples were commenting on the temple which was decorated with beautiful stones and with gifts dedicated to God.[2] *6* Jesus remarked, "As for these stones, the time will come when not one stone will be left on the other, and every single one of them will be pulled down."

7 "Teacher, when's this going to happen?" they asked. "What will be the sign that it's about to take place?"

8 "Be careful that you're not deceived," he answered. "Many will come claiming my authority, and claim, 'I am he!' and 'The time is near!' Don't follow them! *9* When you hear about wars and political disturbances, don't panic! These things have to happen first, but the end won't come at that point."

10-19 "Nation will rise against nation, and kingdom against kingdom," he continued. *11* "There will be massive earthquakes, famines and deadly infectious disorders, frightening terrors as well as mighty signs from the sky.[3] *12* But before all this happens, they will arrest you and persecute you. They will drag you to synagogues and prisons, and you will be put on trial before national authorities, all because of my Name. *13* But it will turn out to be an opportunity to be a witness to them. *14* But prepare in advance not to rehearse the way you will conduct your defense.[4] *15* I myself will give you

---

[1] πενιχρός, *penikhros*, "poor", not πτωχός, *ptokhos*, which is "financially destitute". The widow was described as πτωχός, *ptokhos*, after she put everything she had into the offering box. πενιχρός, *penikhros*, only here in N.T. The adjective occurs in *P.Oxy.* 3273 and tells of the confusion between two men of the same name and same village. One was mistakenly nominated for the other man's office, although he was ἄθετος καὶ πενιχρός, *athetos kai penikhros*, lacking the financial means to be appointed to the office. Horsley notes that this illustrates well the use of the adjective, cf. *NDIEC* 3.80.

[2] The columns of the portico were marble monoliths over forty feet high. Josephus, *B.J.* 5.5 gives a full account.

[3] Equally, "heaven".

[4] ἀπολογέομαι, *apologeomai*, "defend", a technical legal term.

wise words that your opponents will not be able to resist or contradict. *16* You will even be betrayed by parents, relatives and friends, and they'll be the cause of death of some of you. *17* You will be hated by everyone because of my Name. *18* But not a hair on your head will perish. *19* You will gain your lives by means of your endurance.

20-24 "When you see Jerusalem in the process of being surrounded[1] by armies, then realize that its destruction is near! *21* Then if you are in Judea, flee to the mountains! If you're in the city, get out! If you're in the country, don't go into the city! *22* Because this is the time of vengeance that must happen to fulfill what has been written. *23* How sad for the pregnant women and breastfeeding mothers in those times! For there will be severe constraints upon the earth, and anger at this people. *24* And they will fall by the blade of the sword and be taken as prisoners to all nations, and Jerusalem will be trampled on by the nations, until everything that needs to happen actually happens.

25-26 "There will be signs in the sun, moon and stars. On the earth, nations will be worried and at a loss at the sea's roar and the fury. *26* People will faint from fright, in anticipation of what is about to happen to the inhabited world, as the heavenly bodies will be shaken.

27-28 "And then they will see the Human Being coming in a cloud with great power and great splendor. *28* When these things begin to happen, straighten yourselves back up after cowering in fear and lift up your heads, because you are about to be set free – the ransom[2] has been paid for you!"

29-33 Jesus told them the following example. "Look at the fig tree and all the trees. *30* When they sprout leaves, you can see for yourselves that summer is already near. *31* In the same way too, when you see these things happening, you are to realize that God's Realm is near. *32* Truly, this people group[3] will not pass away until all these happen. *33* The sky and earth will pass away, but my words[4] will not pass away.

34-35 "Be careful that your minds are not weighed down with pigging out on food, drunkenness, and the preoccupied thoughts of everyday life – otherwise that day will come upon you suddenly and unexpectedly - just like the jaws of a trap snapping shut! *35* It will come upon everyone who lives on the face of the earth!

36 "Be alert on every occasion, while you are putting earnest requests to God, so that you will have the upper hand to escape everything that's going to happen,[5] and so that you will be able to stand firm in front of the Human Being.

37-38 Jesus taught at the temple by day, and during the nights he went out to the Mount of Olives to spend the night there. *38* The people were getting up early in the mornings, going eagerly to the temple to hear him speak.

Ch.22:1-6 The Feast of Unleavened Bread was approaching. *2* The chief priests and the Bible scholars were searching for a way to get rid of Jesus.

---

[1]   Important to note the tense of "being surrounded" – when the surrounding was completed, it would be too late. Plummer, *op.cit.*, p. 481 noted that no English version preserves this distinction.

[2]   ἀπολύτρωσις, *apolutrosis*, a strengthened form of λύτρωσις, *lutrosis*. ἐξαγοράζω, *exagorazo*, means "to buy up", and is a strengthened form of ἀγοράζω, *agorazo*, "to purchase". ἐξαγοράζω, *exagorazo*, stresses the price paid (the blood of Jesus). ἀπολύτρωσις, *apolutrosis*, stresses the actual deliverance.

[3]   γενεά, *genea*. Equally, "group of people", "tribe". The word can also mean "generation" and this is the way most of the other Bible versions have chosen to translate it. However, the word means "generation" as in a group of people, not with respect to a time frame.

[4]   λόγοι, *logoi*, not spoken words.

[5]   ἐκφεύγω, *ekpheugo*, with accusative, "escape (i.e. avoid) everything that's going to happen", not "escape from everything that's going to happen" which would be ἐκφεύγω, *ekpheugo*, with the genitive.

They had to find a way which would not turn the people against them, as they were afraid of them. *3* Then Adversary entered Judas Iscariot, one of the Twelve. *4* Judas went to the chief priests and the temple police and had a discussion with them about how he could betray Jesus. *5* They were overjoyed and made an agreement to pay him for it. *6* He fully agreed, and watched out for a good opportunity to hand Jesus over to them when the crowds weren't around.

7-13 Then the Feast of Unleavened Bread arrived – it was the one on which the Passover lamb had to be sacrificed. *8* Jesus sent Peter and John and said, "Go and get everything ready for us to eat the Passover Feast."

9 "Where would you like us to prepare it?" they asked.

10 "As you're going into the city, you will meet a person who's carrying a jar of water," Jesus answered. "Follow this person into the house *11* and say to the house's owner, 'The Teacher asks, "Where is the guest room? I want to eat the Passover Feast there with my disciples."' *12* The owner will show you a large furnished upstairs room. Make the preparations there." *13* They left and found everything exactly as Jesus had said, and made the preparations there.

14-16 When the time came, Jesus and his apostles sat down to eat. *15* He said to them, "I have eagerly wanted to eat this Passover Feast with you before I experience what's coming. *16* I won't eat it again until such time as God's Realm's comes."

17-23 After Jesus picked up the wine cup, he thanked God and said, "Take this and share it among yourselves. *18* From now on I will not drink again of the fruit of the vine until God's Realm comes." *19* He picked up some bread, thanked God and broke it. He gave it to them and said, "This is my body which is being given on your behalf. Do this continually to remember me." *20* In the same way, after the meal he picked up the wine cup and said, "This cup is the New Covenant in my Blood, which is poured out on your behalf.

21-23 "But the hand of the one who is betraying me is with me at the table! *22* The Human Being will go just as it's been appointed for him to go, but how terrible for the person who betrays him!"

23 They began discussing with each other as to which one of them could do such a thing!

24-30 Now it turned out that the disciples got into an argument over which of them was considered to be the most important. *25* Jesus said to them, "The kings of the non-Jews act like big shots over them, and the ones who wield authority over them call themselves 'Benefactors'. *26* But you are not to be like that! Instead, the most important one of you should be like the least important, and the one who has authority should be like someone who serves. *27* Which one is the more important – the person who sits down to eat, or the person who serves? Isn't it the person who sits down at the table? But I myself have come among you as a person who serves!

28 You are the ones who have stood by to support me throughout the times I was put though an ordeal[1] by Adversary. *29* I certainly leave you the Realm in my will, just as the Father left it to me. *30* You will eat and drink at my table in my Realm and sit on thrones, judging the twelve tribes of Israel.

31-34 "Simon, Simon, Adversary has demanded[2] you. He wants to shake the stuffing out of you! *32* But I made earnest request to God about you, and asked that your faith will never be lacking. And when you come to your senses, support your fellow believers!"

33 But Peter said, "Lord, I'm ready to go to prison with you and even go as far as dying for you!"

---

[1] περιασμός, *periasmos*. See note on Matt. 6:13.
[2] ἐξαιτέομαι, *exaiteomai*, "to demand", usually to demand the surrender of a person, especially a criminal, or to demand the surrender of a slave for torture.

34 "I'm telling you, Peter," Jesus said, "that on this very day, you will deny me three times before the rooster crows!"

35-38 Then Jesus said, "Now when I sent you out without a wallet, bag or shoes, was there anything that you lacked?"

"No, nothing!" they answered.

36 He said, "But on this occasion, if you have a wallet – take it! Also, take along a bag. If you haven't got a sword, sell your coat and buy one. *37* The Scriptures say: 'He was counted as one of the sinners,' and this must happen to me. Yes, what's been written about me is about to happen."

38 The disciples said, "Lord, here are two swords."

"Yes, that's enough," he said.

39-46 Jesus went out, as he usually did, to the Mount of Olives, followed by his disciples. *40* When they arrived at the place, Jesus said to them, "Pray that you don't have an ordeal.[1]"

41 He went about a stone's throw further on from them, knelt down and prayed, *42* "Father, if it's possible, let this suffering be taken away from me – but it's not what I want that counts, but what you want."[2] *45* He got up from his prayer and went back to the disciples and found them asleep, exhausted from their sorrow. *46* "Why were you asleep?" he exclaimed. "Get up and pray that you don't get put through an ordeal![3]"

47-51 While he was still speaking, a crowd led by Judas, one of the Twelve, arrived. He walked over to Jesus to kiss him, *48* but Jesus said to him, "So, Judas, you betray the Human Being with a kiss!"

49 When Jesus' followers saw what was going to happen, they exclaimed, "Lord, should we attack them with our swords?"

50 And one of them attacked the servant of the chief priest and cut off his right ear. *51* But Jesus said, "That's enough of that!" He touched the servant's ear and instantly divinely healed[4] him.

52-53 Then Jesus said to the chief priests, the temple police and the elders who had come to arrest him, "Do you think I'm leading a rebellion! You arrest me with swords and clubs! *53* I was with you day after day in the temple, and you didn't lay a hand on me! But this time belongs to you – and to the authority of darkness."

54-62 They arrested him and took him off to the Chief Priest's house. Peter was following at a distance. *55* They lit a fire in the courtyard and sat down together. Peter sat down with them. *56* A girl saw him sitting there in the firelight. She had a close look at him and said, "This person was with him too!"

57 "Lady,[5] I don't even know him!" Peter said.

58 A little later someone else saw him and said, "You're one of them, too!"

"I am not!" Peter denied.

59 About an hour later someone else insisted, "I'm sure this guy was with him, because he's from Galilee!"

60 "Listen to me," Peter insisted, "I don't know what you're talking about!" Immediately, the rooster crowed. *61* The Lord turned and looked straight at Peter. Then Peter remembered the words the Lord had spoken earlier, "Today you will deny you know me three times before the rooster crows." *62* He went outside and burst out crying bitterly.

---

[1]   περιασμός, *periasmos*. See note on Matt. 6:13.

[2]   Verses 43 and 44, although accepted as ancient, are not part of the original. For textual commentary see Metzger, *op.cit.*, p. 151. Here is the passage: *43* A Messenger appeared from heaven and strengthened him. *44* He was in dread and so prayed more earnestly. His sweat was like clots of blood falling on the ground.

[3]   περιασμός, *periasmos*. See note on Matt. 6:13.

[4]   ἰάομαι, *iaomai*. See note on Matt. 8:8.

[5]   γύναι, *gunai*, vocative, a polite address. See note on John 2:4.

63-65 The men who were in charge of Jesus started making fun of him and beating him up. *64* They blindfolded him and kept demanding, "Prophesy! Who was the one who hit you!" *65* They also said lots of other insulting things to him.

66-71 At daybreak the council of elders of the people, the chief priests as well as the Bible scholars met together and had Jesus brought to the council chamber *67* They said, "Tell us whether you're the Anointed One."

68 "If I tell you, you won't believe me!" Jesus said. "If I asked you anything, you wouldn't answer! *69* From now on, the Human Being will sit at the right side of the Power of God."[1]

70 They all said, "So are you then the Son of God?"

"You've said it right!" Jesus exclaimed.

71 Then they said, "Who needs any more evidence? We've heard it ourselves from his very own mouth!"

Ch.23:1-5 Then the whole assembly got up and took him off to Pilate. *2* They started accusing him: "We have found that this person is misleading our nation. He opposes paying taxes to Caesar, and claims to be an Anointed King."

3 "Are you the King of the Jews?" Pilate asked Jesus.

"You said it!" Jesus answered.

4 Then Pilate said to the chief priests and the crowd, "I can't find any basis for a charge against this person."

5 But they insisted, and said, "He stirs up all the people all through Judea with his teaching. He started off in Galilee and now he's come all the way here!"

6-12 When Pilate heard this, he asked if Jesus was from Galilee. *7* When he found out that Jesus was under Herod's jurisdiction, he sent him up to Herod who was in Jerusalem at that time.

8 When Herod saw Jesus, he was extremely pleased, because he had wanted to see Jesus for a long time. From what he'd heard about him, he was hoping he would perform some miraculous sign. *9* Herod questioned Jesus at some length, but Jesus didn't answer him at all. *10* The chief priests and Bible scholars were standing by, vigorously accusing him. *11* Then Herod and his soldiers made fun of him and mocked him. They dressed him in expensive clothes and sent him back to Pilate. *12* On that very day Herod and Pilate became friends, although previously they had been at odds with one other.

13-16 Pilate called together the chief priests, the rulers and the people, *14* and said "You've brought this person before me on the grounds that he was inciting the people to revolt. I've examined him in your presence and I can find no grounds for the charges against him. *15* And neither can Herod, because he sent him back to us. You can see that he hasn't done anything to deserve the death penalty. *16* So I will release him after I've had him punished[2]!"[3]

18-25 The whole crowd shouted in unison, "Away with him! Release Barabbas for us!"

19 Barabbas had been thrown into prison for starting a riot in the city, and for murder. *20* Pilate wanted to release Jesus, so he addressed them again, *21* but they kept shouting, "Crucify him! Crucify him!"

22 Then he spoke to them for the third time. "Why? What capital crime has he committed? I've found no grounds for the death penalty. So I will release him after I've had him punished!" *23* But they absolutely insisted

---

[1]   Luke adds "of God" for his non-Jewish audience. "The Power" was to avoid the Sacred Name.

[2]   παιδεύω, *paideuo*, the cognate verb of παιδεία, *paidea*. Here the meaning is "punish" although usually "educate", quite the same idiom as the English use in such a context. See note on Eph. 6:4. The method of punishing was whipping with the Roman whip embedded with metal spurs designed to rip off the flesh.

[3]   Verse 17 is omitted: it is not original and was added by copyists at a later date.

with loud shouts and demanded that he be crucified, and their shouts kept getting louder. *24* And Pilate decided that their request should be granted.[1] *25* He released the person they had asked for, the one who had been thrown in prison for starting a riot and for murder, and handed Jesus over to them for them to do as they wished.

26-31 As Jesus was being taken away, they grabbed Simon, a person from Cyrene. They put the cross on him and made him carry it behind Jesus. *27* A large crowd of people followed Jesus, including women who were mourning and crying. *28* Jesus turned and said to them, "Daughters of Jerusalem, don't cry over me, cry for yourselves and for your children, *29* because the time will come when you'll say, 'Happy are women who have never had children, wombs that were never pregnant, and breasts that never breastfed! *30* In those times they will say to the mountains, 'Fall on us!' and they will say to the hills, 'Cover us!' *31* If in fact people do these things when the wood is green, what will happen when it's dry?"

32-34 Two others, who were criminals, were taken with him to be executed. *33* When they arrived at the place called "Skull", they crucified Jesus there, along with the criminals – one on his right side, and one on his left.[2] *34* They divided up his clothes by gambling for them.

35-37 The crowd standing by looked on. They sneered at Jesus and even the rulers did too. "He saved others," they mocked, "let him save himself if he's really the Anointed Chosen One of God!"

36 The soldiers also poked fun at him. They offered him the soldiers' issue of wine vinegar[3] *37* and said, "If you're really King of the Jews, save yourself!"

38 There was a notice written above him, with the words, "This is the King of the Jews."

39-43 One of the two criminals who hung there hurled insults at him: "Aren't you the Anointed One! Save yourself, and us too!"

40 But the other criminal rebuked him. "Don't you respect God?" he asked. "You're under the same sentence yourself! *41* We're getting what's coming to us, and fair enough too, but this person hasn't done anything weird!" *42* He continued, "Jesus, remember me when you get into your Realm."

43 "Today you will be with me in Paradise[4]," Jesus replied.

---

[1] The reference in John 19:4-12 explains Pilate's motives. In verse 12, the Jews say to Pilate, "If you let this person go, you're no Friend of Caesar's! Anyone who claims to be a king opposes Caesar!" See note on Matt. 27:24.

[2] The first part of verse 34 is omitted as it is not original. It was added by copyists at an early date. Here is the first part of verse 33: "Jesus said, 'Forgive them, Father, because they don't know what they're doing.'"

[3] Spice with myrrh added in sufficient quantity to turn the wine into the drug. The intention was to ease the pain, and was in accordance with Jewish custom.

[4] παράδεισας, *paradeisis*, commonly transliterated as "paradise", a Persian loan word meaning a garden of fruit trees (or orchard) which first occurs in Greek in Xenophon's *Anabasis*, 1.2.7. It appears commonly in the papyri and inscriptions in the same meaning. See *I.Tyre* 1.108 (pl.47.1) (late Roman), "I solemnly request those who are going to acquire this orchard…"; *P.Petr.* i.16.2.7 (230 B.C.), "the produce of my orchards"; *P.Tebt* 1.5.53 (118 B.C.), "the tithes which they used to receive from the holdings and the orchards". *P.Lond* 933.12 (A.D. 211) notes a payment on account of an "olive orchard". See also the Rosetta Stone (OGIS 90.15, 196 B.C.). It occurs frequently in the LXX as a garden, sometimes as the abode of the blessed, see Cant. 5.13, Eccl. 2.5, and Neh. 2.8. The Midrash Haggadah (Midrash means a verse-by-verse interpretation of Scripture, and Haggadah is an interpretation and expansion of the non-legal portions of Scripture) describes Paradise in detail, as far as giving specific dimensions and furnishings of the chambers. The details are supposed

44-46 It was now about midday, and darkness came over the whole land and stayed that way for about three hours. *45* The sun stopped shining. The veil of the temple was ripped down the middle. *46* Jesus called out in a loud voice. He said, "Father, I commit my spirit into your hands." After he said this, he breathed his last.

47-49 When the Roman officer in charge of 100 men saw what happened he praised God and said, "This person certainly was right with God!"

48 When all the spectators saw what happened, they were very upset and went back home. *49* But all his close friends, including the women who had come with him from Galilee, stood off at a distance, watching.

50-56 There was a man named Joseph, a member of the High Council, an honest civic benefactor[1] *51* who had not agreed with their decisions and actions. He came from the Judean town of Arimathea, and he was waiting eagerly for God's Realm. *52* He went to Pilate and asked for Jesus' body. *53* Then he took it down from the cross, wrapped it in linen and placed it in a tomb cut into the rock. No one had ever been put into this tomb. *54* It was Preparation Day, and the Sabbath was about to begin. *55* The women who had come with Jesus from Galilee followed Joseph and looked at the tomb and how his body was laid in it. *56* Then they went back and prepared spices and perfumed oils.

56.Ch.24:1-8 And they rested on the Sabbath in accordance with the Law of Moses. But on the first day of the week, very early in the morning, the women took the spices they'd prepared and went into the tomb. *2* They found that the stone had been rolled away from the tomb, *3* but when they went inside, they did not find the body of the Lord Jesus! *4* While they were at a loss over this fact, two men in dazzling clothes as bright as a flash of lightning appeared and stood next to them!

5 The women, terrified, bowed down with their faces to the ground, but the men said to them, "Why are you searching for the living among the dead? *6* He's not here – he has risen! Remember how he told you when he was still with you in Galilee: *7* 'The Human Being must be handed over to sinful people, be crucified, and rise again on the third day.'" *8* Then they remembered what he'd said.

9-12 They returned from the tomb and reported all this to the Eleven and to all the others. *10* And it was Mary Magdalene, Joanna, Mary the mother of James, and their companions who told this to the apostles,[2] *11* but they didn't believe them, because they thought their words were a lot of nonsense. *12* However, Peter got up and ran to the tomb. He bent over to peep in and saw the strips of linen lying by themselves, and he went off wondering what on earth had happened.

13-24 The very same day two of them were going to a village called Emmaus, about seven miles from Jerusalem. *14* They were discussing everything that had happened with each other. *15* As they talked and

---

to have been supplied by individuals who visited Paradise while alive. It states that 9 mortals visited heaven while alive, and that one of these is Enoch. Enoch 20:7-8 states "Gabriel, one of the holy angels, who is over Paradise and the serpents and the Cherubim...", and supplies a description of Paradise in Chapters 23-38. Ezekiel's description of Paradise is similar: a great mountain in the middle of the earth which has streams of water flowing from under it. A palm tree grows in the middle of the center of the sacred enclosure. Similar descriptions are to be found in other apocalypses (e.g. Apoc. Baruch, 5; 2 Esd. 8.52). In Rabbinical literature the conception of paradise stands in contradistinction to hell. Paradise is occasionally referred to as "the world to come". Occurs elsewhere in N.T. only in 2 Cor. 12:4 and Rev. 2:7.

[1] ἀνὴρ ἀγαθός, *aner agathos*, "civic benefactor". Traditionally translated as "good man", but recent discoveries from the inscriptions have shown it is a common honorific term meaning a civic benefactor. See *I. Smyrna* II.1; *Chiron* 17=*SEG* 37.

[2] ἀπόστολος, *apostolos*. See note on Matt. 10:2.

discussed matters, Jesus himself came up and walked along with them, *16* but they were kept from recognizing him. *17* "What are you talking about as you're walking along?" he asked.

They stood still, their faces downcast. *18* One of them of them by the name of Cleopas exclaimed, "Are you the only person in Jerusalem who doesn't know what's been going on here lately?"

19 "What things?" he asked.

"About Jesus of Nazareth," they answered. "He was a prophet. Everything he said and did was powerful, in front of God and all the people. *20* The chief priests and our rulers arrested him and gave him the death sentence, and they crucified him, *21* but we'd hoped he was the one who was going to liberate Israel. And what's more, this is the third day after all this happened! *22* And what's even more, some of the women really shocked us. *23* They went to the tomb early this morning but couldn't find his body! So they came and told us that they'd seen a vision of Messengers who'd said he was alive. *24* Then some of our friends went to the tomb and found it just like the women said, but they didn't see Jesus!"

25-27 And Jesus said to them, "Hey! You're senseless! You're slow to believe everything that the prophets said! *26* Didn't you know that the Anointed One would have to experience all that so as to enter into his glorious state?"

27 He explained to them everything the Scriptures said about him, beginning at Moses and all the Prophets.

28-31 As they got close to the village where they were headed, Jesus indicated that he wanted to go on further. *29* But they pressured him, and said, "Please stay with us – it's nearly evening, the day's almost over." So he stayed with them.

30 When Jesus had reclined at the couch with them, he picked up some bread, blessed it, broke it into pieces and started handing it to them. *31* Their eyes were completely opened and they recognized him! Then he vanished right in front of them!

32-35 They asked each other, "Well, wasn't it like a fire burning in us when he was talking to us on the road and explaining the Scriptures to us?"

33 And they set out right there and then and returned to Jerusalem. They found the Eleven and their company there, assembled together. *34* They said, "It's true! The Lord has risen and he's appeared to Simon!" *35* Then the two told what had happened to them on the road, and how they recognized Jesus when he broke the bread into pieces.

36-43 As they were still talking about all this, Jesus himself appeared and stood right there in front of them! He said, "Hello! How are you!"

37 They were startled and absolutely terrified because they thought they were seeing a ghost! *38* "Why are you so scared?" he asked. "Why is there doubt in your minds? *39* Look at my hands and my feet! It's really me! Touch me – see for yourselves! A ghost doesn't have flesh and bones – but you can see I do!"

40 After he said this, he showed them his hands and feet. *41* While they still couldn't believe it because they were really happy and amazed, he asked them, "Do you have anything to eat?"

42 They gave him a piece of grilled fish. *43* He took it, and ate it right in front of them.

44-49 Jesus said to them, "This is the meaning of what I told you when I was still with you – everything that has been written about me in the Law of Moses, the Prophets and Psalms must happen."

45 Then he opened their minds so that they would understand the Scriptures. *46* He told them, "This is what the Scriptures say: The Anointed One will suffer and rise again from among the dead on the third day. *47* In his Name, the changing of minds for the cancellation of sins is to be proclaimed to all nations, starting at Jerusalem. *48* You are witnesses of these things. *49* I will certainly send my Father's Promise to you, but settle in the city until you are clothed with power from on high."

50-53 When he had led them out as far as Bethany, he raised his hands and blessed them. *51* While he was blessing them, he was separated from them and was taken up to heaven.[1] *52* Then they knelt down to worship him, and returned to Jerusalem, overjoyed! *53* And they were in the temple continually, praising God.

---

[1]   Equally, "the sky".

The Good News of John.

John, the son of Zebedee (and the brother of James), knew Jesus very well. He had been one of the Twelve disciples, and had gone with Peter and James to the Jews after the Jerusalem meeting c. 47 AD. John's Good News is clearly pre-war and written before 66 AD. John states that the pool has (not had) 5 porticoes, and describes the temple as still standing. Both were not standing after the catastrophic war of 66-70 AD between the Jews and the Romans in Palestine. In the war the temple was destroyed as were many parts of Jerusalem. The reference to Peter's prophesied manner of death in John 21:19 possibly suggests that John's Good News was written after 64 AD, the date of Peter's death in the Neronian persecution.

The old view that John was a poor fisherman in a small boat is just a myth. He was a partner in a fishing corporation (Luke 5:10) with Peter, James, and Andrew, and the business employed workers. His family employed servants (Luke 15:18, 22, 26). He was of the middle or upper class, as shown by the reference to Joanna, the wife of Herod's manager, Chuza. Further, the evidence suggests that John was the "other disciple" of John 18:15 who was a close friend of the chief priest. John's mother Salome was one of the women who financially provided for Jesus (Mark 15:41). In fact, Jesus entrusted the care of his mother to John. John was bilingual, with his first language being Aramaic and his second language being Greek. The majority of the middle and upper class citizens were bilingual, and in fact, some preferred their second language. John could speak and write Greek very well.

The authorship of John has been widely undisputed from the beginning of the 2nd c. The church fathers from Irenaeus onwards do not question John's authorship. As for the title, early papyri and 5th c. papyri have "The Good News According to John", while later manuscripts attest to the title, "The Sacred Good News According to John" Another title, "According to John" is also attested.

According to John.

Ch.1:1-5 In the beginning was the Word, and the Word stayed with God, and the Word was God. *2* In the beginning the Word stayed with God. *3* Everything came into being through him, and nothing came into being without him. *4* That which came into being, life, was by means of him, and the life was the light of humans. *5* And the light shines in the darkness, and the darkness did not suppress it.
6-8 A person appeared. He was sent out by God, and his name was John. *7* He came to testify about that light, so that everyone might believe because of him. *8* He himself was not the light - he appeared only as a witness to the light.
9-14 The genuine light that gives light to all humankind[1] was in the world. *10* And although the world was made through him, the world did not recognize him. *11* He came to his own people, but they did not accept him. *12* To everyone who accepted him, to everyone who believed his Name, he gave the right to become children of God – *13* children not from a woman[2] nor from the purposes of the natural realm nor from the purposes of a man, but born from God. *14* And the Word took human form and lived among us. We have seen his splendor, the splendor of the One and Only, who came from the Father, full of favor and truth.

---

[1]   Rabbinic expression for "all people who came into the world". Non gender specific.
[2]   Literally, "from streams of blood." The Greeks referred to the human embryo being made up of the seed of the father and the blood of the mother. John is saying that God's children were not born from a woman or a man, but from God. See Wisdom 7.2; 4 Macc. 13.20; Philo, *de opif. mund*, 45. Note the plural "streams of blood", cf. LSJ, *s.v.* who cite Aesch. Ag. 1293; Soph. Ant. 120; Eur. El. 1176.

15-18 John spoke words of truth about him and has shouted, "This is the One about whom I said, 'He comes after me, but was always more important than I am: he already existed before I was born!'" *16* We, all of us, have received one favor after another from the store of his abundant favor. *17* The Law was given through Moses - and favor and truth came about through Jesus the Anointed One. *18* No one has ever seen God at any time. The Only Son, the One who is closest to the Father's heart - he is the one who led the way to the place of honor at the Father's side!

19-23 And this is the evidence from John's life. This is what he said when certain Jews[1] sent priests and members of the tribe of Levi from Jerusalem to ask him who he was. *20* He agreed with what they said and didn't deny it. He said, "I'm not the one who's the Anointed!"

21 They asked him, "So what are you then! Are you the Prophet?"

"No!" he exclaimed.

22 "Well, who are you?" they demanded. "We have to give an answer to the people who sent us! What do you say about yourself?"

23 He said, "I am, 'The voice of one shouting in the desert, "Clear the road for the Lord!"' as the prophet Isaiah said!"

24-28 Now the people who were sent were members of the Pharisees. *25* They asked him, "If, as you say, you are not the Anointed One, nor Elijah, nor the Prophet, why then do you keep on baptizing?"

26 "I myself baptize with water," John answered, "but there is someone standing with you and you don't even know it! *27* He's the One who comes after me. I'm not even good enough to undo his sandal straps!" *28* All this happened in Bethany which is across the Jordan River, where John was baptizing.

29-31 The next day John saw Jesus coming up to him. "Look!" he indicated. "Here is the Lamb of God, who takes away the sin of the world! *30* He is the one I referred to when I said, 'The one who comes after me is far more important than I am, because he existed before I was born! *31* I myself didn't know him, but the reason I was baptizing with water was so that he would be revealed to Israel."

32-34 Then John gave this evidence – "I watched the Spirit come down from heaven[2] in the appearance of a dove and rest on him. *33* I sure did not know who he was, apart from the fact that the One who sent me to baptize with water told me, 'The person on whom you see the Spirit come down and rest is

---

[1] Ἰουδαῖοι, *Ioudaioi*. The sole Greek word has 2 different senses: Judean and Jewish, Judean referring to the geographical area of Judea, and Jewish to the people who used to be called Israelites, the descendants of Jacob, place of abode being irrelevant. One can only judge from the context. In the N.T. "Jewish" is more common than "Judean", and John also uses *Ioudaioi* to refer to those Jewish and Judean leaders who opposed Jesus. It is generally agreed that he is using metonymy (using a part to describe a whole), but the question is whether in his use of metonymy he is referring to Jews or Judeans. Some argue that he is using *Ioudaioi* in the meaning "Judean" stating that it is more probable for him as he was a Jew. Others argue that in John 7:1 and 11:8 the word *Ioudaioi* means: "Jewish leaders" / "Jewish authorities". It is not always easy to determine from the context when John is referring to certain Jewish leaders antagonistic to Jesus, leaders who happened to be concentrated in Jerusalem (which in turn, is in Judea), or when he is referring to Judeans or Jews in general.

The translation "certain Jews" considers John's use of metonymy. Many Bible versions translate "Jewish leaders" and it is clear in many instances from the context that the certain Jews in question were in fact leaders. Not all Pharisees opposed Jesus, nor did Jesus take exception to all Pharisees – it was certain Pharisees only. See note on Matt. 3:7.

[2] Equally, "the sky".

the One who will baptize with the Holy Spirit.' *34* And I for sure have spiritually seen and have testified, that this person is God's Son!"

35-39 The next day John was there again with two of his disciples. *36* When he looked at Jesus going past, he said, "Look over there! The Lamb of God!"

37 When the two disciples heard him say that, they followed Jesus. *38* Jesus turned around and saw them following. "What do you want?" he asked. They said, "Rabbi, (which means Teacher,) where are you staying?"

39 "Come and see!" Jesus said. So they went and saw where he was staying, and spent the rest of the day with him. It was about four o'clock in the afternoon.

40-42 Andrew, Simon Peter's brother, was one of the two who heard what John said, and who had followed Jesus. *41* The first thing Andrew did was find his brother Simon and tell him, "We have found the Messiah!" (which means the Anointed One). *42* He took him to Jesus. Jesus looked at him and said, "You are Simon the son of John. You are going to be called Cephas," (which translates as Peter).

43-51 The next day Jesus wanted to go away to Galilee. He found Philip and said to him, "Follow me!"

44 Philip, like Andrew and Peter, was from the city of Bethsaida. *45* Philip found Nathanael and told him, "We've found the One that Moses wrote about in the Law, and the One the prophets wrote about too – it's Jesus of Nazareth, the son of Joseph!"

46 "Nazareth!" Nathanael exclaimed, "Can anything good come out of that place!"[1]

"Come and see!" Philip said.

47 When Jesus saw Nathanael coming towards him, he said about him, "He is truly a real Israelite, and there's no deceit in him."

48 "How do you know me?" Nathanael asked.

Jesus answered, "Before Philip called you, I saw you while you were under the fig tree."

49 Nathanael said to him, "Rabbi, you are the Son of God, you are the King of Israel!"

50 "The reason you believe is because I told you I saw you under the fig tree," Jesus said. "You're going to see more impressive things than that!" *51* He added, "You will spiritually see heaven opened and God's Messengers ascending from and descending to the Human Being!"[2]

Ch.2:1-12 On the third day a wedding took place at Cana in Galilee. Jesus' mother was there. *2* Jesus and his disciples had been invited to the wedding too. *3* When the wine ran out, Jesus' mother said to him, "They don't have any wine!"

4 "My dear lady,[3] what does it have to do with me?" Jesus asked. "My time hasn't come yet!"

5 His mother said to the staff, "Do whatever he tells you to do!"

6 There were six stone water jars standing nearby, the kind used by the Jews for the ceremony of purification. Each one held from 16 to 27 gallons.[4] *7* Jesus said to the servants, "Fill the jars with water," and they filled them up to the brim. *8* Then he said, "Now take a bit out and give it to the head waiter."

---

[1] John 21:2 states that Nathanael is from Cana, and archaeologists have discovered that Cana is about 9 miles (15 km) from Nazareth.

[2] ὁ υἱὸς τοῦ ἀνθρώπου, *ho huios tou anthropou.* See note on Matt. 8:20.

[3] γύναι, *gunai,* vocative, common as a form of polite address in Greek, e.g. Aristophanes, *Acharnians,* 262 Dikaiopolos says, "Dear wife, you watch us from the roof. Let's go!" (Trans. J.Henderson.) Dawe also translates γυνή, *gune,* in Sophocles, O.T., 928, as "lady": R.D. Dawe, (ed.) *Sophocles: Oedipus Rex. Cambridge Greek and Latin Classics,* (Cambridge: C.U.P., 1982), p. 190.

[4] Each one held 2-3 measures, each being 8-9 gallons (39-40 litres).

And they did. *9* The head waiter tasted the water that had been turned into wine. He didn't know where it had come from, but the staff who had drawn out the water knew. He called the bridegroom over *10* and said to him, "Everyone serves the best wine first and then brings out the worse stuff when the guests have got drunk – but you've saved the best 'til now!"

11 This was the first of the miraculous signs that Jesus did. It was in Cana in Galilee. He demonstrated his splendor, and so his disciples believed him. *12* After this, he went up to Capernaum, with his mother, his brothers and his disciples, and stayed there for a few days.

13-17 When the Jewish Passover was approaching, Jesus went up to Jerusalem. *14* He found dealers in cattle, sheep and doves in the temple, as well as currency changers[1] sitting at other tables. *15* He made a whip out of cords, and chased them all from the temple area, including all the sheep and cattle. He tipped out the currency changers' coins and overturned their tables. *16* "Get them out of here!" he said to the dove dealers. "Stop turning my Father's house into a market!"

17 His disciples remembered that the Scripture said, "Passion for your house will consume me!"

18-22 Certain Jews asked him, "What miraculous sign can you show us to account for your actions?"

19 "Destroy this temple, and in three days I'll raise it up!" Jesus answered.

20 Certain Jews responded, "It has taken 46 years to build this temple – you're saying you're going to raise it up in three days?"

21 However, the temple Jesus had spoken about was his body. *22* After he was raised from among the dead, his disciples remembered what he had started to say. Then they believed the Scripture and the Word that Jesus had spoken.

23-25 Now while Jesus was in Jerusalem at the Passover Feast, many people saw the miraculous signs that he did and gave their allegiance to him. *24* But Jesus on his part did not entrust himself to them because he knew about everyone. *25* Jesus did not need anyone's evidence about humanity, as he already knew what humanity was like.

Ch.3:1-4 There was a certain person who was a member of the Pharisees – his name was Nikodemos and he was one of the rulers of the Jews. *2* This person came to Jesus at night and said, "Rabbi, we all know that you're a teacher who has come from God, as no one could perform the miraculous signs that you do, unless God were with them."

3 Jesus answered, "Let me emphasize this, that unless one is born from above,[2] one is not able to see God's Realm."

4 "How can a person be born again when they are already old?" Nikodemos asked. "Surely a person can't go back into their mother's womb a second time to be born again!"

5-8 Jesus answered, "Let me emphasize this, unless someone has been born from water and spirit, that person cannot enter God's Realm. *6* Living things of the natural realm can only give birth to other living things of the natural realm. It is the Spirit who gives birth to the spirit. *7* Don't be surprised at my statement, 'You must be born from above.' *8* Jesus continued, "The wind (the Spirit) blows wherever it (the Spirit) wants to, and you hear its (the Spirit's) sound, but you don't know where it (the Spirit) comes from or where it's (the Spirit's) going.[3] It is the same way with everyone who has been born from the Spirit."

9-16 "How is this possible?" Nikodemos exclaimed.

---

[1]   Money changers were those who changed Roman currency into Jewish currency to pay the temple tax.

[2]   ἄνωθεν, *anothen*, "from above" or "again". Ambiguity deliberate.

[3]   Here Jesus is playing on words, impossible to translate into English. The Greek word for "wind" and "spirit" is the same, both are meant here.

10 Jesus answered, "For a fact you are Israel's teacher and you don't understand these things! *11* Indeed, we are speaking about what we know, and we are speaking truthful words about what we have seen, and you people reject our evidence! *12* Since I have spoken to you people about earthly things and you people don't believe, how then will you believe when I speak about the things of the spirit realm? *13* And the only one who has gone up to heaven is the Human Being who came down from heaven. *14* Then the Human Being must be lifted up just as Moses lifted up the snake in the desert, *15* so that everyone who believes him has eternal life.[1]

16-21 "God loved the world so[2] he gave his one and only Son, so that everyone who believes him will not die but would at that point have eternal life. *17* God did not send his Son into the world in order to judge the world, but so that the world would be saved through his Son. *18* Whoever believes him is not judged; but whoever does not believe him has already been judged, because they have not believed the Name of God's only Son. *19* This is the judgment: the light has come into the world and people loved the darkness instead of the light, for their actions were evil. *20* Everyone who commits thoughtless acts hates the light and does not go towards the light, otherwise their actions would be exposed. *21* But the person who has the truth moves towards the light, so that it may be revealed that their actions have been carried out with God."

22-36 After this, Jesus and his disciples went out into the Judean countryside. He spent some time with them there, and he kept baptizing. *23* Now John was also baptizing at Aenon near Salim, because there was a lot of water. People were coming and being baptized. *24* (This was before John was thrown in prison.)

25 An argument developed on the part of John's disciples with a Jew over purification. *26* They went to John with the comments, "Rabbi, the man who was with you on the other side of the Jordan River – the one you testified about – well, he's baptizing, and everyone's going to him!"

27 John answered, "A person can't receive one single thing unless heaven has given it to them. *28* You yourselves can give evidence that I said, 'I'm not the Anointed One, that's for sure, but I'm certainly the one who's been sent ahead of him!' *29* The bridegroom is the one who has the bride, but the bridegroom's friend stands and listens to him, and is overjoyed when he hears the bridegroom's voice. So that joy is mine, and I have it now. *30* He must become more important, but I must become less important. *31* The one who comes from above is above everything. The one who is from the earth is from the earth and speaks in earthly ways. The one who comes from heaven is above everything. *32* And he gives evidence as to what he has seen and heard, but no one accepts his evidence. *33* The person who has accepted it has attested that God is truthful. *34* For the person God sends out speaks the words of God, for God gives the Spirit without limitation. *35* The Father loves the Son and has handed everything over to him. *36* The person who believes the Son has eternal life, but the person who is disobedient to the Son does not see life, but God's anger remains upon that person."

Ch.4:1-15 So the Pharisees heard that Jesus was gaining and baptizing more disciples than John – *2* although in fact it was not Jesus who baptized, but his disciples. *3* He left Judea and went back again to Galilee. *4* He had to go through Samaria. *5* So he went to a city in Samaria called Sychar,[3] which was

---

[1] The present tense for "has (eternal life)" signifies that from the second the person believes Jesus, from that time on they have eternal life.

[2] Not "loved the world so much that he gave…", a common mistranslation in many English translations. The term refers to the manner in which something is done.

[3] Today, over half a mile (almost one kilometre) north of the well mentioned in the note on verse 11, is a village called Askar, formerly known as Sychar.

near the field that Jacob had given to his son Joseph. *6* Jacob's well was there. Jesus was tired from traveling, and sat down next to the well. It was about midday. *7* A Samaritan woman came to draw water. Jesus said to her, "Could you give me a drink?" *8* (His disciples had gone off to town to buy food.)

9 So the Samaritan woman said to him, "Why would you, a Jew, ask me, a Samaritan woman, for a drink?" (The Jews don't have dealings with Samaritans.)

10 Jesus gave her the answer, "If you knew the gift of God and who it is who says to you, 'Could you give me a drink?' then you would have asked him for a drink, and he would have given you living water."

11 The woman said, "Sir, not only don't you have a bucket, but it's a deep well.[1] So where do you get that living water? *12* Surely you're not more important than our ancestor Jacob! He himself gave us the well and even drank from it himself, and so did his children and his livestock!"

13 "Everyone who drinks this water will be thirsty again," Jesus answered, *14* "but the person who drinks the water that I give them will never be thirsty again – this goes for all time! The water that I give a person will turn into a fountain of water in the person that bubbles up to eternal life."

15 The woman replied, "Sir, give me this water, so I won't get thirsty and have to keep coming here to draw water."

16-24 Jesus said, "Go and shout to your husband to come here!"

17 "I don't have a husband!" the woman said.

Jesus said to her, "You said it well when you said you didn't have a husband – *18* as you've had five husbands and the one you have right now[2] is not your husband – in that you've spoken truthfully!"

19 "Sir, I can tell that you're prophet!" the woman exclaimed. *20* "Our ancestors worshipped on this mountain,[3] but you Jews claim that the place we must worship is Jerusalem."

21 Jesus replied, "Believe me, my dear lady,[4] the time is coming when you will worship the Father – but not on this mountain or in Jerusalem! *22* You worship what you don't know – we worship what we do know, because the salvation comes from the Jews. *23* The time is coming when the true worshippers will be led by the Spirit to worship the Father truthfully. The Father is looking for people such as this to worship him. *24* God is Spirit, and those who worship him must be led by the Spirit to worship him truthfully."

---

[1]   The well referred to is the forty four yard (forty metre) deep well a few hundred yards from the traditional site of Joseph's tomb. From here the sacred mountain of the Samaritans, Mt Gerizim, can be seen.

[2]   The "now" is significant. The laws recognized several types of marriage. S.R. Llewelyn states that the different legal systems ran in parallel and each did exert influence on the other, cf. "Jewish and Christian Marriage," *NDIEC* 6.14. One type of marriage was *cohabite* (unwritten marriage), which meant that if a man and a woman were living together or even had sex they were considered to be legally married. This form of marriage was common among the lower classes. *ibid.*, p. 16; H.J. Wolff, *Written and Unwritten Marriages in Hellenistic and Postclassical Roman Law*, (Haverford, PA: American Philological Association, 1939), pp. 48ff; P.J. Sijpesteijn, "Marriage Contract in the Form of a Bank Diagraphe P. Mich. inv. 6551)". *ZPE* 34 (=*P.Mich.* XV 700) details the dowry of the woman as well as a prenuptial agreement. Greek marriage was usually written as an agreement between both the parties. S.R. Llewelyn, "Greek and Egyptian Matrimony," *NDIEC* 6.7. The Samaritan woman was not living with the sixth man, or he would legally be her husband. He may have been someone else's husband, or a casual relationship.

[3]   Located precisely as Mt Gerizim.

[4]   γύναι, *gunai*. See note on John 2:4.

25-26 The woman said, "I know that the Messiah is coming – he's called the Anointed One. When he comes, he'll explain everything to us."

26 Jesus said to her, "I am he, the One who's talking to you!"

27-30 At that point his disciples returned and were surprised to find him speaking with some woman. However, no one said, "What do you want?" or "Why are you speaking with her?"

28 So the woman then left her water jar, went off into the city and said to the people, *29* "Come and see a person who told me everything I ever did! Could this one be the Anointed One?" *30* They left the city and went to him.

31-38 Meanwhile, his disciples were urging him, "Rabbi, eat something!"

32 But he said to them, "I've got food to eat that you don't know about!"

33 So the disciples said to each other, "Surely no one's brought him anything to eat!"

34 Jesus said to them, "My food is to do the purpose of him who sent me, and to complete his work. *35* Don't you say, 'We can't harvest the crop for another four months'? Listen to me! Have a good look at the fields, and you will see that they are ripe, ready for harvest! *36* Even now the harvest worker is receiving wages, and gathering benefits for eternal life, so that both the one who sows and the one who harvests may celebrate together. *37* This is how the saying comes true, 'One sows and the other harvests.' *38* I have sent you to harvest that which you have not worked for – others have done all the work, and you have benefited from the results of their work."

39-42 Many of the Samaritans of that city believed him because of the woman's evidence: "He told me everything I had ever done."

40 So when the Samaritans went to see him, they asked him to stay with them, and he stayed there for two days. *41* Many more believed because of his Message. *42* They said to the lady, "We no longer believe just because of what you've said, but also because we've heard him for ourselves! We know that this one is truly the Savior of the world!"

43-45 Two days later Jesus left there and went to Galilee. *44* For Jesus himself testified that a prophet has no respect in his own native land. *45* So when he arrived in Galilee, the Galileans welcomed him. They had seen everything he had done in Jerusalem at the feast, as they had gone to the feast too.

46-54 So Jesus went again to Cana in Galilee, the place where he had turned the water into wine. And at Capernaum there was a certain royal official whose son was sick. *47* When he heard that Jesus had arrived in Galilee from Judea, he went to him and asked him to come down[1] and instantly divinely heal his son, as he was at death's door. *48* Jesus said to him, "You people will never believe unless you see miraculous signs and wonders!"

49 The royal official answered, "Sir, please come down before my son dies!"

50 Jesus said to him, "Off you go – your son lives!"

The person believed the statement that Jesus had spoken to him, and went away. *51* While he was going down, his servants met him and said, "Your son's doing nicely!"

52 So he asked them at what time his son began to improve. "It was yesterday afternoon at one o'clock that the fever left him," they answered.

53 So the father realized that it was the same time that Jesus said to him, "Your son lives!" And he himself believed, and so did his whole household. *54*

---

[1]   The words "come down" occur 3 times in this passage, in verses 46, 49, 51. καταβαίνω, *katabaino*, literally meant to go or come down in a literal, not metaphorical sense. Cana, mentioned in v. 46, is the modern Khirbet Qana, around 9 miles (15 kilometres) from Nazareth. The royal official's son lived at Capernaum. Between Cana and Capernaum the land falls many hundred yards, as Capernaum is well above sea level and Capernaum is 220 yards (200 metres) below sea level.

This again is the second miraculous sign that Jesus did when he went to Galilee from Judea.

Ch.5:1-3 After this, there was a Jewish feast, and Jesus went up to Jerusalem. *2* In Jerusalem there is a swimming pool next to the Sheep Gate. It's called "Bethsatha" in Hebrew and it has five covered colonnades.[1] *3* A large crowd of sick people – blind, crippled, withered - lay in the covered colonnades, and waited for the waters to move, *4* for the reason that a Messenger[2] went down at the right time to the pool, and stirred up the water. Whoever then next entered the waters after they were disturbed, was restored to their original undamaged state from whatever disease they had.[3]

5-9 There was a certain person there who had been sick for 38 years. *6* When Jesus saw him lying there and realized that he'd been lying there a long time, he said to him, "Do you want to be restored to your original undamaged state?"

7 The sick man answered, "Sir, I don't have a person to put me in the pool when the water's stirred up. While I'm on my way, someone else steps down in front of me!"

8 "Get up!" Jesus said. "Pick up your stretcher and walk!"

9 Immediately the person was restored to their original undamaged state! The person picked up their stretcher and walked around. This was the Sabbath day.

10-14 So the Jews said to the person who was healed,[4] "It is the Sabbath! It's not legal for you to carry your stretcher!"

11 He answered, "The person who restored me to my original undamaged state said to me, 'Pick up your stretcher and walk.'"

12 "Who's this person who said to you, 'Pick up your stretcher and walk?'" they asked.

13 But the person who was instantly divinely healed didn't know who it was, because Jesus had moved off due to the crowd in that place. *14* After this Jesus found him in the temple and said, "Hey, you're back to your original undamaged state now – you're not sick any more. Don't sin anymore, otherwise something worse might happen to you!"

15-18 The person left and told the Jews that it was Jesus who restored him to his original undamaged state. *16* This is why certain Jews started to persecute Jesus, because he did these things on the Sabbath. *17* Jesus' response was, "My Father is still at work and I myself am at work." *18* So because of this certain Jews tried even harder to kill him, not only because he broke the Sabbath, but also because he said that God was his Father, making himself equal with God.

19-23 Jesus said to them, "Let me emphasize this, the Son is not able to do anything independently. He can only do what he observes his Father doing. Whatever the Father does, the Son does in the same way. *20* The Father loves the Son and shows him everything he himself does. And to your amazement,

---

[1] Archaeologists have uncovered a double pool surrounded by four porticoes, with the fifth on a rock gangway between the two pools. The pool was approximately 35 yards (about 16 metres) deep. This is why the crippled person had to be helped into the water and supported in it. The pool is by the Sheep Gate in Jerusalem, and is the one described by John.

[2] The text does not say "a Messenger of the Lord", and καταβαίνω, *katabaino*, was used of pagan gods, and was used of one seeking an oracle, particularly chthonic cults. Aristophanes, *Clouds*, 508, used the typical term εἴσω καταναίνων, *eiso katabainon*: "Give me a honey cake first, for I'm as frightened at going down as if it were the cave of Trophonios." (Trophonios was a chthonic god.)

[3] Metzger omits verse 4 on the grounds that it is a gloss. However, it is clear that something needs to be inserted to make sense.

[4] θεραπεύω, *therapeuo*. See note on Matthew 4:23.

he will show him even greater things than these! *21* Just as the Father brings the dead back to life, in the same way too the Son gives life to whomever he wishes. *22* The Father does not judge anyone, but has handed over all issues to be decided to the Son, *23* so that everyone will honor the Son just as they honor the Father. The person who doesn't honor the Son doesn't honor the Father who sent him.

24-27 "Let me emphasize this, the person who hears my account and believes him who sent me has eternal life and does not come to judgment, but is transferred from death to life. *25* The time is coming and is now here when the dead will listen to the voice of the Son of God, and those who listen will live. *26* Just as the Father has life-giving power, in the same way too he has granted to the Son to have life-giving power. *27* And the Father has given the Son authority to decide issues, because he is a member of the human race.

28-30 "Don't be surprised at this, because the time is coming when all the people who are in their graves will hear his voice *29* and come out – those who have done good things will rise to live, and those who have done careless things will rise to be judged. *30* By myself I am not able to do anything! I judge just as I hear, and my judgment is just, because I don't try to please myself but I try to please the One who sent me.

31-36 "If I myself give evidence about myself, my testimony wouldn't be valid. *32* There is another who gives evidence about me, and I know that his testimony about me is valid. *33* You have sent people to John, and he has confirmed the truth. *34* I myself don't accept human testimony, but I mention it so that you may be saved. *35* John was a lamp that burned and gave out light, and for a while you chose to enjoy his light. *36* I myself have a more important testimony than John's. For those very deeds that the Father has given me to complete, and which I'm doing, is evidence that the Father has sent me.

37-40 "The Father who sent me has himself testified about me. You have never heard his voice nor have you seen what he looks like, *38* nor does his Word stay with you, because you don't believe the One he sent. *39* You study the Scriptures, because you think that by means of them you have eternal life. These are the Scriptures that give evidence about me, *40* and you refuse to come to me in order to have life!

41-47 "I do not look to people for a good reputation. *42* In fact I know you through and through, because I realize that you don't have God's love in you. *43* I certainly have come in my Father's Name, but you don't accept me – but if someone else comes in their own name, you will accept them! *44* How then can you believe, if you receive your good reputation from each other, and make no effort to aim for the good reputation that comes from the one and only God? *45* Don't suppose that I will accuse you to the Father! Your accuser is Moses, on whom your hopes rest. *46* If you believed Moses, you would believe me – as he wrote about me! *47* But since you don't believe his writings, how are you going to believe what I say?

Ch.6:1-4 After this Jesus crossed over to the far shore of the Sea of Galilee (which is the Tiberias Sea). *2* A large crowd followed him, because they watched the miraculous signs he performed on the sick. *3* Jesus went up a mountain and sat down there with his disciples. *4* The Jewish Passover Feast was soon.

5-9 When Jesus looked, and observed that a large crowd was coming towards him, he asked Philip, "Where are we going to buy bread for these people to eat?"

6 Jesus only asked him this to test him, because he already had in mind what he was going to do. *7* Philip answered, "Thousands of dollars' worth of bread isn't even enough for everyone to have a little bit!"

8 Another of his disciples, Andrew who was Simon Peter's brother, said *9* "Here's a person[1] with five small barley loaves and two small fish, but how far are they going to go among so many people!"

10-12 Jesus said, "Get the people to sit down." There was plenty of grass there, so they sat down. (There were about 5,000 men.) *11* Jesus picked up the bread and thanked God. He distributed the bread to those sitting down, and did the same with the fish. They could have as much as they wanted. *12* When they were full, Jesus said to his disciples, "Collect all the leftovers, so that nothing's wasted."

13-15 So they collected the leftovers and filled 12 wicker baskets with the pieces of the five barley loaves left over by those who had eaten. *14* When the people saw the miraculous sign that Jesus did, they said, "He really is the prophet who was to come into the world!" *15* When Jesus realized that they intended to come and grab him so they could make him king, he went away again by himself to the mountain.

16-21 When evening came, his disciples went down to the sea *17* and embarked on a boat. They set off across the sea to Capernaum. It was already dark and Jesus hadn't joined them yet. *18* A strong wind was coming in and the seas were rough. *19* When they had rowed about three miles,[2] they saw Jesus approaching the ship, walking on the water. They were terrified. *20* Jesus said to them, "It's me! Don't be afraid!" *21* So they intended to get him into the ship, but immediately the ship was at the shore where they were headed!

22-27 The next day the crowd was still on the opposite shore of the lake. The previous day they had noticed that only one boat had been there, and that Jesus hadn't got on board with his disciples, but that the disciples had gone off alone. *23* Then some boats from Tiberias landed near the place where the people had eaten the bread after the Lord had given thanks to God. *24* So when the crowd realized that Jesus wasn't there, nor were his disciples, they got into the boats and went to Capernaum to look for him. *25* When they found him on the other side of the lake, they asked, "Rabbi, when did you get here?"

26 "I want to make this quite clear," Jesus answered. "You're looking for me, not because you saw miraculous signs but because your hunger was satisfied by the bread you ate. *27* Do not work for perishable food, but for food that lasts, the food of eternal life, which the Human Being will give you. The Father has placed his seal of approval on him."

28-33 They asked him, "Then what do we have to do, in order to do the work God would have us do?"

29 "This is the work God would have you do – to believe the One he has sent!" Jesus answered.

30 They asked again, "What miraculous sign will you do, so we can see it and believe you? What are you going to do? *31* Our ancestors ate the manna in the desert, as the Scriptures say, 'He gave them bread from heaven[3] to eat.'"

32 Jesus replied, "Let me emphasize this, it isn't Moses who has given you the bread from heaven, but it is my Father who gives you the true bread from

---

[1] παιδάριον, *paidarion*, "slave", "young (free) man", "young (free) woman", "child", "girl", "manservant", "soldier", all meanings well attested. There is no evidence for the term "lad" or "boy", a tradition started by the KJV's "lad". Horsley, *NDIEC* 1.87, notes his surprise at the lack of interest shown in this word by the commentaries. Occurs frequently in the LXX with a wide range of meanings, but only here and in Matt. 11:16 in N.T.. At 2 Kings 13:22 and 14:21 it means "young (free) man", at Tob. 7:11 it describes a woman and means either "young woman" or "child" (as the speaker is her father). In 1 Kings 30:17 it is used to refer to soldiers.

[2] Literally about 25 or 30 *stadia*. A *stadion* was just over 600 feet, (just under 200 metres). They had rowed around three miles (5 kilometres).

[3] Equally, "the sky" (throughout the whole passage).

heaven. *33* God's bread is the One who comes down from heaven and gives life to the world."

34-40 "Sir, give us this bread all the time!" they exclaimed.

35 Jesus said to them, "I myself am the bread which gives life! The person who comes to me will never get hungry, and the person who believes me will never get thirsty. *36* But I've already told you, you have seen and still you don't believe! *37* Everyone the Father gives me will come to me, and I won't turn away anyone who comes to me. *38* I haven't come down from heaven to do what I want to do, but to do what him who sent me wants me to do. *39* This is what the One who sent me wants – that I won't lose any of the ones he has given me, but that I will raise them up on the Last Day. *40* This is my Father's purpose – that everyone who looks to the Son and believes him will have eternal life. I will certainly raise that person up on the Last Day.

41-46 So certain Jews started complaining about him, on the grounds that he had said, "I myself am the bread that came down from heaven."

42 They said, "Isn't this Jesus, the son of Joseph? We know his father and mother! How on earth can he say that he came down from heaven!'"

43 "Stop complaining among yourselves!" Jesus exclaimed. *44* No one can come to me unless the Father who sent me draws them to me, and I will certainly raise them up on the Last Day. *45* It has been written in the Prophets: 'They will all be taught by God.' Everyone who has listened to and learnt from the Father comes to me. *46* No one has seen the Father except the One who is from God – only he has seen the Father.

47-51 "Let me emphasize this, the person who believes has eternal life. *48* I certainly am the bread of life. *49* Your ancestors ate the manna in the desert and they died. *50* Here is the bread that comes down from heaven, bread that someone can eat and not die. *51* I am the living bread that came down from heaven. If anyone eats this bread, they will live forever. This bread is my flesh, which I will give so the world may live."

52 So certain Jews started fighting amongst themselves. They said, "How can this person give us his flesh to eat?"

53-59 Jesus said to them, "Let me make this quite clear, unless you eat the flesh of the Human Being and drink his blood, you'll have no life in you! *54* Whoever eats my flesh and drinks my blood has eternal life, and I will raise up that person on the Last Day. *55* My flesh is true food and my blood is true drink. *56* Whoever eats my flesh and drinks my blood remains with me, and I certainly remain with that person. *57* And as the Living Father sent me, and I live because of the Father, so the one who feeds on me will also live because of me. *58* This is the bread that came down from heaven. Your ancestors ate manna and died, but the person who eats this bread will live forever!" *59* Jesus said this when he was teaching in the synagogue in Capernaum.

60-65 When quite a few of his disciples heard this, they remarked, "This teaching is hard to take! Who can accept it?"

61 Jesus was aware that his disciples were complaining about this. He said to them, "Is this a problem for you? *62* What if you observe the Human Being go up to the place he was before? *63* It is the Spirit who gives life – the natural realm doesn't count for anything. The words I have spoken to you are spiritual and they have life. *64* But there are some of you who don't believe."

In fact Jesus knew from the beginning which of them didn't believe and just who would betray him. *65* He said, "This is why I told you that no one can come to me unless the Father has granted it to them."

66-71 After this happened, some of his disciples turned their backs on him and didn't follow him any more. *67* So Jesus said to the Twelve, "You don't want to leave too, do you?"

68 Simon Peter answered, "Lord, who is there to go to? Your words are the words of eternal life. *69* We have believed! We realize that you're the Holy One of God!"

70 "And haven't I chosen you Twelve!" Jesus exclaimed. "And one of you is a slanderer and liar!"[1] *71* (He meant Judas Iscariot – as this person, although one of the Twelve, would later betray Jesus.)

Ch.7:1-5 After this, Jesus traveled around Galilee, deliberately staying away from Judea because certain Jews[2] there were looking for a way to kill him. *2* But when the Jewish Feast of Tabernacles was near, *3* Jesus' brothers said to him, "You should leave here and go to Judea, so that your disciples can see the miraculous signs that you do. *4* No one who wants to be boldly out in the public view does things in secret! Since this is what you're doing, you need to show yourself to the world!" *5* (Even his own brothers didn't believe him.)

6-9 So Jesus told them, "It isn't the right time for me yet – but for you, any time is right! *7* The world can't hate you, but it hates me because I give evidence that what it does is evil. *8* You go up to the Feast! As for me, I won't go up to this Feast because it isn't the right time for me yet!" *9* Having said this, he stayed behind in Galilee.

10-13 However, after his brothers had gone up to the Feast, he went too, but in secret rather than in public. *11* So at the feast certain Jews were searching for him. They kept saying, "Where is he!"

12 People all through the crowds were complaining about him. Some said, "He's a good person," but others said, "No, he gets the people off the right track!"[3]

13 However, no one would speak freely and boldly about him in public because they were afraid of certain Jews.

14-19 Halfway through the Feast, Jesus went up to the temple courts and started teaching. *15* The Jews were amazed. "How did he get so learned without an education?" they asked.

16 "My teaching is not my own," Jesus answered. "It comes from him who sent me. *17* If someone wants to do God's purpose, they will find out whether my teaching originates from God or whether I speak on my own initiative! *18* People who want to bring honor on themselves speak for themselves, but people who want to honor the One who sent him are truthful, and are not dishonest in any way. *19* Hasn't Moses given you the Law? But none of you keep the Law! Why are you trying to kill me?"

20-24 The crowd answered, "You've got a demon! Who's trying to kill you?"

21 "I did one miraculous sign, and you're all shocked!" Jesus said *22* "Moses gave you circumcision (not that it originated from Moses, but from his ancestors), and so you circumcise a person on the Sabbath Day. *23* Since a person is circumcised on the Sabbath Day, so that the Law of Moses relating to circumcision won't be broken, why are you extremely enraged with me because I restored a person to their original undamaged state on the Sabbath Day? *24* Don't judge the surface of things, instead be just in your judgments!"

25-27 So some of the people who lived in Jerusalem said, "Isn't this the one they're trying to kill? *26* He's right here speaking out in public, and they're not saying a word to him! Have the authorities really come to the conclusion that he is the Anointed One? *27* We actually know where he really comes from, but when the Anointed One comes, no one will know where he comes from!"

28-31 Then Jesus, who was still teaching in the Temple, shouted out, "Yes, you know me and you know where I've come from. I haven't come on my own initiative, but the One who sent me is truthful! You don't know him! *29* But I know him for a fact, because I am from him, and he sent me!"

---

[1]   One word in the Greek, "slanderer-liar".

[2]   Or Judeans. This provides a contrast between Galileans, and Judeans (who are in Judea). Jews lived in both Judea and Galilee, whereas Judeans lived in Judea.

[3]   πλανάω, *planao*, "to wander off the path", the cognate noun being πλάνη, *plane*. See note on Rom. 1:27.

30 So they tried hard to arrest him, but no one laid a hand on him, because his time hadn't come. *31* Many of the crowd believed him and said, "When the Anointed One comes, could he possibly do more miraculous signs than this one has done!"

32-36 The Pharisees heard the crowd gossiping about all this, and so the Pharisees and the chief priests sent the Temple Police to arrest him. *33* So Jesus said, "I'll be with you a little while longer, and then I'll go to him who sent me. *34* You will look for me and not be able to find me, and where I am going, you can't come!"

35 "Where does he intend to go so that we won't be able to find him?" the Jews said among themselves. "Does he intend to go where our people live scattered among the Greeks, and teach the Greeks? *36* What did he mean by his statement: 'You will look for me and not be able to find me, and where I am going, you can't come'?"

37-39 On the last and most important day of the Feast, Jesus stood up and said in a loud voice, "If anyone's thirsty, let them come to me and drink. *38* Whoever believes me, as the Scripture has said, will have streams of living water flowing from within." *39* By this he meant the Spirit, whom those who believed Jesus would receive later on. Up to that time the Spirit hadn't yet been given, because at that point Jesus hadn't been given his full splendor.

40-49 When some of the crowd heard this, they said, "Surely he is the Prophet!" *41* Others said, "This one's the Anointed One!" Still others said, "Surely not! How can the Anointed One come from Galilee? *42* Doesn't the Scripture say that the Anointed One will come from David's descendants and from the village of Bethlehem where David was?"

43 So the crowd was divided over Jesus. *44* Some wanted to arrest him, but no one laid a hand on him. *45* So the Temple Police went to the chief priests and Pharisees, who said to them, "Why didn't you bring him in?"

46 The Temple Police answered, "No one has ever spoken like he did!"

47 "You're not deceived,[1] too, are you!" the Pharisees asked. *48* "Have any of the rulers or the Pharisees believed him? No! *49* Only this crowd that doesn't believe the Law – there's a strong curse on them!"

50-52 Nikodemos, who had gone to Jesus earlier, and was one of them, asked, *51* "Surely our Law doesn't judge anyone without hearing them first to find out what they're doing?"

52 "Surely you're not from Galilee too!" they said. "Look into it and you'll see that a prophet doesn't come out of Galilee!"

53.Ch.8:1-11[2] And they all went home. But Jesus went to the Mount of Olives. *2* At dawn he went again to the temple and the whole crowd gathered around him. He sat down and taught them. *3* The Bible scholars and the Pharisees brought in a woman caught in adultery and put her in the middle. *4* They said to him, "Teacher, here is a woman caught in the act of adultery. *5*

---

[1] πλανάω, *planao*, "to wander off the path", the cognate noun being πλάνη, *plane*. See note on Rom. 1:27.

[2] The passage (verses 7:53 to 8:12, often referred to as the "Pericope Adulterae"), is absent from significant early manuscripts, while appearing in many cursive manuscripts. Metzger (*op.cit.*, pp. 187-9) states that the passage is absent from the oldest form of the Syriac version, as well as from the Sahidic, the sub-Achmimic versions and the older Bohairic manuscripts. It is absent from the Gothic version and from several Old Latin manuscripts. No Greek Church Father earlier than the 12th c. mentions it. Furthermore, the style and the vocabulary differ markedly from any Johannine work. Metzger states that it is a piece of oral tradition which circulated in certain parts of the Western church. However, St Augustine refers to the passage and states that many excised the passage as they interpreted it as giving license for married women to commit adultery. Some witnesses place the passage after Luke 21:38, others after John 7:36, 7:52, or 21:24.

In the Law, Moses commands us to stone such women. So then, what do you have to say about it?"

6 They said this to trap Jesus, in order to have a reason to accuse him. But Jesus bent down and started writing on the ground with his finger. *7* When they kept asking him, he straightened up and said to them, "Let one of you who is sinless be the first to throw a stone at her." *8* And again he bent over and wrote on the ground. *9* But those who were listening started to leave, one at a time, the oldest ones first, until only Jesus was left, with the woman still standing there. *10* Jesus said to her, "Lady, where are they? Did anyone condemn you?"

11 "No one, sir," she answered.

"And I certainly do not condemn you!" Jesus said. "Off you go, don't sin any more."

12-18 When Jesus spoke to them again, he said, "I am the light of the world. Whoever follows me will never walk around in the dark, but will have light shining on their life."

13 The Pharisees said, "You're appearing as your own witness, so your testimony can't be true!"

14 Jesus answered, "Even if I do give evidence on my own behalf, my testimony is true. I know where I came from and I know where I'm going! But you don't have a clue where I've come from or where I'm going!" *15* He continued, "You judge in the way typical of the natural realm, but I certainly don't judge anyone! *16* And whenever I do judge, my judgment is correct, because I am not alone, but I am with the Father who sent me. *17* In your own law it has been written that the testimony of two people is valid. *18* I myself am the one who appears as my own witness, and my other witness is the Father, who sent me."

19-20 "So where's your Father then!" they demanded.

Jesus answered, "You don't know me or my Father! If you knew me, you would know my Father too!" *20* Jesus said all this while he was teaching in the Temple near the place where the offerings were put. And no one even laid a hand on him, because his time hadn't come.

21-26 Jesus spoke to them again, "I'm going away. You'll look for me, and you'll die while you still have your sins. You can't go where I'm going!"

22 So the Jews said, "Surely he's not going to kill himself! Is that why he says, 'You can't go where I'm going?'"

23 Jesus said to them, "You people are from below, but I am from above. You are from this world, but I'm not from this world. *24* I told you that you would die while you still have your sins. If you don't believe that I'm the One I claim to be, then you will die while you still have your sins, that's for sure!"

25 "Who are you?" they asked.

"Exactly what I've been claiming all along!" Jesus answered. *26* I have many things to say to you and to judge you for, but the One who sent me is truthful. What I've heard from him I'll tell the world."

27-30 They didn't understand a thing he was saying about his Father. *28* So Jesus said, "When you have lifted up the Human Being, then you'll know who I am. I don't do anything on my own initiative, but I say the things that my Father taught me. *29* The One who sent me is with me: he's never left me, because I always do things that please him." *30* While he was speaking, many people believed him.

31-38 Jesus said to the Jews who had believed him, "If you stick with my Word, then you certainly are my disciples. *32* And you will come to know the truth, and the truth will set you free."

33 They answered, "We are Abraham's descendants and we've never been anyone's slaves. So how can you say that we will be set free?"

34 "Let me emphasize this, everyone who sins is a slave to sin," Jesus replied. *35* "A slave doesn't have permanent standing in a family, but a son belongs to it forever. *36* So then if the Son sets you free, you will be free in reality. *37* Know that you are Abraham's children. Yet you are trying to kill me, because you haven't made room for my Word. *38* I am telling you what I have perceived from my Father – and you are doing what you heard from the Father!"

39-41 "Abraham is our father!" they cried.

Jesus said, "If you really were Abraham's children, then you would do the things that Abraham did! *40* But as it is you want to kill me, a person who has told you the truth that I heard from God. Abraham didn't do such things! *41* You are doing the deeds of your father!"

"We're not illegitimate and unfaithful to God!"[1] they exclaimed. "The only father we have is God!"

42-47 Jesus said to them, "If God were your Father, then you would love me! I have come from God and I'm here now. I haven't come on my own initiative – God sent me. *43* Why don't you understand what I'm saying to you? I'll tell you why – it's because you're not willing to listen to my message! *44* You belong to your father Slanderer-Liar and you want to carry out your father's desires. He was a murderer right from the start, and he doesn't rely on the truth because there's no truth in him. When he tells a lie, he's speaking in his native language, because he's a liar and the father of lies! *45* Because I'm telling you the truth, you don't believe me! *46* Which of you can expose me for sinning? Since I'm telling you the truth, why don't you believe me? *47* The person who belongs to God hears God's words. The reason you don't hear, is that you don't belong to God!"

48-53 Certain Jews exclaimed, "Aren't we right in saying that you're a Samaritan that has an evil spirit!"

49 "I certainly do not have an evil spirit," Jesus answered. "I honor my Father and you dishonor me! *50* I'm certainly not seeking my own honor – but there is One who is seeking and judging. *51* Let me emphasize this, anyone who holds on firmly to my Word will not experience death, ever!"

52 "Now we realize that you do have a demon!" certain Jews exclaimed. "Abraham is dead, so are the Prophets, yet you say, 'Anyone who holds on firmly to my Word will not experience death, ever!' *53* Are you more important than our ancestor Abraham, who is dead? And the Prophets are dead too! Who do you think you are!"

54-59 Jesus answered, "If I give myself honor, it wouldn't mean anything. It's my Father, the One you claim is your God, who gives me honor. *55* And you haven't come to know him, but I know him. If I said I didn't know him, I'd be a liar just like you lot. However, I do know him and I hold on firmly to his Word. *56* Your ancestor Abraham was thrilled to foresee my time – he saw it and he was happy!"

57 "You're not even fifty years old! How can you say you've seen Abraham!" certain Jews exclaimed.

58 Jesus answered, "Let me emphasize this, I have been in existence since before Abraham was born!" *59* So they picked up stones to throw at him, but Jesus hid and slipped out of the temple.

Ch.9:1-5 As Jesus was walking along, he saw a person who had been blind from birth. *2* His disciples asked him, "Rabbi, who was it who sinned – was it this guy or his parents, that caused him to be born blind?"

3 "It wasn't this person or his parents!" Jesus said. "However, his blindness resulted in the works of God being revealed through him. *4* While it is day, we must do the work of him who sent me. Night is coming, and then no one will be able to work. *5* As long as I am in the world, I am the light that lights up the world."

6-8 After Jesus said this, he spat on the ground and made some mud with the spit, and spread it on the person's eyes. *7* He told him, "Go and wash yourself in the Swimming Pool of Siloam." ("Siloam" means "Sent Out"). So he went off and washed himself, and came back seeing.

---

[1] The Greek word for "illegitimate" which encompassed an Old Testament metaphor for infidelity to God.

8 His neighbors and the people who had previously observed him begging asked, "Isn't this the same person who used to sit and beg?"

9-12 Some claimed that it was, but others said, "No way! It only looks like him!"

But the person himself insisted, "It's really me!"

10 "Well then, how were your eyes opened so you could see?" they asked.

11 He answered, "The person they call Jesus made some mud and spread it on my eyes. He told me to go to Siloam and wash myself. So I went there and washed myself, and then I could see!"

12 "Where is he?" they asked.

"I don't know!" he answered.

13-17 They took the person who used to be blind to the Pharisees. *14* Now the day on which Jesus had made the mud and restored the person's sight was a Sabbath Day. *15* So the Pharisees also asked him how he'd got his sight back. He responded, "He spread mud on my eyes, and I washed, and I came away able to see."

16 Some of the Pharisees said, "This person isn't from God, because he doesn't keep the Sabbath Day!"

Others said, "But how can a person who's a sinner do such miraculous signs?"

17 Then they turned back to the blind person and said, "So, what do you have to say about him, since it was your sight he restored?"

"He's a prophet!" the person exclaimed.

18-23 Certain Jews still didn't believe that the person had been blind and had received his sight until they sent for his parents. *19* They asked them, "Is this person your son? You reckon he was born blind? How is it that he can see now?"

20 The parents answered, "We know that he's our son, and that he was born blind, *21* but we haven't got a clue how he can see now, or who did it. Why don't you ask him! He's of age! He can speak for himself!"

22 His parents said this because they were scared of the certain Jews who had already decided that anyone who agreed that Jesus was the Anointed One would be put out of the synagogue. *23* This is why they said, "He's of age! He can speak for himself!"

24-29 So for the second time certain Jews summoned the person who had been blind. They said to him, "Give God the honor! We know that this guy is a sinner."

25 He answered, "I don't know whether he's a sinner or not! But there's one thing I do know – I used to be blind but now I can see!"

26 "What did he do to you? How did he restore your sight?" they asked.

27 He said, "I've already told you once but you didn't listen! Why do you want to hear it again? I don't suppose you want to become his disciples, too!"

28 So they hurled abuse at him. "You're this guy's disciple!" they exclaimed. "We're disciples of Moses! *29* We know that God spoke to Moses, but as for this guy, who knows where he comes from!"

30-33 "Well, what a surprise!" the person said. "You don't know where he comes from, yet he restored my sight! *31* We know that God doesn't listen to sinners, but listens to godly people who do his purpose. *32* No one's ever heard of giving sight to someone who was born blind! *33* If this person wasn't from God, he wouldn't be able to do anything!"

34 Certain Jews exclaimed, "You were born sinful, through and through! How dare you lecture us!" And they threw him out.

35-41 Jesus heard that they had thrown him out. When he found him, he asked him, "Do you believe the Human Being?

36 The person asked, "Who is he, sir? Tell me so I can place my faith in him."

37 "You've both seen and heard him!" Jesus answered. "It's me, the one who's speaking to you now!"

38 He said, "Lord, I believe!" and he worshipped him.

39 Jesus said, "I have come into this world to judge it, so that the blind will see and those who see will become blind."

40 So some of the Pharisees who were with him said, "Surely we're not blind, too?"

41 Jesus said to them, "If you were blind, you wouldn't have any sin, but the fact that you say, 'We see,' indicates your sin remains!

Ch.10:1-6 "I'll make this quite clear. The person who doesn't go into the sheep pen through the gateway, but climbs in some other way, is a thief and a robber. *2* The person who goes in through the gateway is the shepherd of the sheep. *3* The gatekeeper opens the gate for the shepherd, and the sheep hear their shepherd's voice. *4* The shepherd calls the sheep by name and leads them out. The sheep follow their shepherd, who leads them. The sheep follow the shepherd because they know their shepherd's voice. *5* They will never follow a stranger – in fact they'll run away from that person, because they don't recognize a stranger's voice." *4* This was the illustration[1] Jesus used, but they didn't understand what he was talking about.

7-13 So Jesus spoke to them again, "Let me make this clear. I am the gateway for the sheep. *8* All those who ever turned up before me were thieves and robbers, but the sheep didn't hear them. *9* I am the gateway. If anyone goes in through me, the gateway, that person will be saved, and will move about freely and will find grazing land. *10* The thief comes solely to rob and kill[2] and destroy. I come so that they will have life and have it excessively. *11* I myself am the good shepherd. The good shepherd lays down his life for the sheep. *12* The hired hand is not the shepherd who owns the sheep. *13* When the hired hand notices the wolf coming, the hired hand leaves the sheep and runs away – and the wolf grabs them and drags them off, and scatters them. The hired hand doesn't care about the sheep and thus runs away.

14-18 "I myself am the good shepherd and I recognize my sheep and my sheep recognize me. *15* In the same way too my Father recognizes me and I recognize the Father. And I lay down my life for the sheep. *16* I have other sheep that are not from this sheep pen. I must bring them, too. They too will listen to my voice, and there will be one flock and one shepherd. *17* The reason my Father loves me is that I lay down my life, in order to take it up again. *18* No one takes it from me, but I myself lay it down of my own free will. I have authority to lay it down and to take it up again. I have received this command from my Father."

19-21 The illustration caused another division among certain Jews. *20* Many of them said, "He's got an evil spirit and he's raving like a madman! Why do you listen to him?" *21* Others said, "These aren't the words of someone who has a bad spirit! Surely a demon can't restore sight to the blind!"

22-30 Now it was the Feast of Dedication at Jerusalem. It was winter, *23* and Jesus was walking in Solomon's Roofed Colonnade in the Temple. *24* Certain Jews surrounded him. "How long are you going to keep us in suspense?" they demanded. "If you really are the Anointed One, then tell us plainly!"

25 Jesus answered, "I did tell you, but you didn't believe me. The works that I do in my Father's Name speak for me! *26* But you don't believe, because you are not my sheep. *27* My sheep listen to my voice - I recognize them and they follow me. *28* I certainly give them eternal life and they will never perish – no one can snatch them out of my hand. *29* My Father, who has given them to me, is greater than all – no one is able to snatch them out of my Father's hand. *30* I and my Father are One."

---

[1]   John calls this παροιμία, *paroima*, "common saying", "proverb", whereas the other gospels use παραβολή, *parabole*, "example" (usually transliterated: "parable").
[2]   θύω, *thuo*, equally, "sacrifice". Usually signifying the sacrifice of victims. Not the usual word for "kill".

31-39 Yet again certain Jews picked up stones to stone him. *32* Jesus said, "I have shown you many wonderful deeds originating from the Father – which one of these do you want to stone me for?"

33 "We're not stoning you for any of these!" certain Jews answered. "We're stoning you for blasphemy, since you yourself, a mere human, claim that you're God!"

34 Jesus responded, "Hasn't it been written in your Law, 'I have said that you are gods.' *35* Note he called them 'gods'. Note that it was to them that God's Word came, and the Scripture can't be broken. *36* So why do you tell me, the One that the Father made sacred and sent into the world, that I'm blaspheming because I said I'm God's Son? *37* If I don't do my Father's work you don't have to believe me! *38* But if I do his work, although you don't believe me, you should believe the work! Then you would come to know me and realize that the Father is with me, and I am with him."

39 So they tried again to grab him, but he escaped from their clutches.

40-42 Jesus went back across the Jordan River to the place where John had been baptizing in the early days. He stayed there. *41* Many people came to him. They said, "John didn't perform any miraculous signs, but everything he said about this one was true!" *42* In that place many people believed him.

Ch.11:1-3 There was a certain person who was sick. His name was Lazarus and he was from the village of Mary and her sister Martha. *2* This Mary, whose brother Lazarus was now sick, was the same one who had poured perfumed lotion on the Lord and wiped his feet with her hair. *3* So the sisters sent word to Jesus: "Lord, your friend is sick."

4-8 When Jesus heard this, he said, "This sickness won't end in death. Rather, it will bring honor to God: God's Son will be honored through it." *5* Jesus loved Martha, her sister and Lazarus. *6* But when he heard that Lazarus was sick, he stayed where he was for two more days. *7* After that he said to his disciples, "Let's go back to Judea."

8 "Hang on, Rabbi," they exclaimed, "it was only a short time ago that certain Jews[1] wanted to stone you, and you want to go back there!"

9-16 Jesus answered, "Aren't there twelve hours of daylight? People who walk around in daylight won't fall over, because they can see due to this world's light. *10* It's when they walk at night that they fall over, because there's no light." *11* He continued, "Our friend Lazarus has fallen asleep, but I'm going there to wake him up."

12 The disciples said, "Lord, if he's just asleep, then he'll get better!"

13 Jesus had actually been speaking about Lazarus' death, but the disciples thought he meant natural sleep. *14* So then he told them plainly, "Lazarus died, *15* and I'm glad I wasn't there for your sake, because now you can believe. But let's go to him."

16 So then Thomas (who was called "Twin") remarked to the rest of his fellow disciples, "Yeah, right! Let's all go too so we can die with him!"[2]

17-27 So when Jesus arrived, he found that Lazarus had already been in the tomb for four days. *18* Bethany was about two miles[3] from Jerusalem. *19* Many Jews had come to comfort Martha and Mary over their brother. *20* So when Martha heard that Jesus was coming, she went out to meet him, but Mary stayed at home.

21 Martha said to Jesus, "Lord, if you'd been here, my brother wouldn't have died. *22* Anyway, even now I know that God will give you whatever you ask."

23 "Your brother will rise up!" Jesus told her.

---

[1]   Some argue the meaning here is "Judeans" as Galileans, who were Jews, were around Jesus at this time, and clearly they were not trying to kill him. However, it was not the population of Judea who sought to kill Jesus, but a small group of Jews.

[2]   Thomas is being highly sarcastic. Jesus and the disciples are going back to the place where the Jews are keen to kill Jesus.

[3]   Literally, "About 15 stadia". (Just over 3 kilometres.)

24 Martha said, "Yes, I know that he will rise up in the resurrection on the Last Day."

25 "I am the resurrection and the life," Jesus said. "The person who believes me will live, even if they die, *26* and everyone who lives and believes me will never die. Do you believe this?"

27 She said, "Yes, Lord. I firmly believe that you are the Anointed One, the Son of God, the One who was to come into the world."

28-37 And after she said this she went back, called her sister aside and said, "The teacher is here asking for you."

29 As soon as Mary heard this, she got up quickly and went to meet him. *30* Jesus hadn't reached the village yet, but was still at the place where Martha had met him. *31* When the Jews who had been with Mary in the house, comforting her, saw how fast she got up and ran out, they followed her, because they thought she was going to the tomb to cry. *32* When Mary reached the place where Jesus was and saw him, she fell down in front of him and said, "Lord, if you'd been here, my brother wouldn't have died!"

33 When Jesus saw her crying, and the Jews who'd come along with her crying too, he was deeply moved in his spirit and was overcome with intense emotion. *34* "Where have you put him?" he asked. *35* Jesus cried.

36 So the Jews said, "Look how much he liked him!"

37 But some of them said, "Surely this person who had the ability to restore sight to the blind person could have prevented this one's death."

38-44 So Jesus, once again deeply moved, came to the tomb. It was a cave with a stone laid across the entrance. *39* "Take the stone away," he said.

But Martha, the sister of the person who had died, said, "Lord, there's a bad smell by now – it's the fourth day!

40 Jesus said to her, "Didn't I tell you that if you believed, you would see God's splendor?"

41 So they took the stone away. Then Jesus looked upwards and said, "Father, thanks for listening to me. *42* I know for sure that you always listen to me, but I said this for the benefit of the people standing here, so that they will believe that you sent me." *43* After he said this, he shouted loudly, "Lazarus, come out here!"

44 The person who had been dead came out. His hands and feet were wrapped up with linen bandages, and there was a cloth around his face.

Jesus said to them, "Unwrap him! Set him free!"

45-48 Many of the Jews who had come to visit Mary and had seen what Jesus did, believed him. *46* But some of them went away to the Pharisees and told them what Jesus had done. *47* So the chief priests and the Pharisees called a meeting of the High Council. They said, "So what are we doing about the fact that this person is performing so many miraculous signs? *48* If we let him go on like this, then everyone will believe him, and then the Romans will come and take away not only the Temple but our nation as well!"

49-53 Then one of them by the name of Caiaphas, who was chief priest that year, spoke up. He said, "You lot don't know anything! *50* You're not taking into account that you're far better off if one person dies for the people, instead of the whole nation perishing!" *51* He didn't say this of his own accord, but being the chief priest that year he had prophesied that Jesus was destined to die for the Jewish nation, *52* and not only for the Jewish nation, but also for God's scattered children, in order to bring them together and to unite them. *53* So from that moment on they planned to kill Jesus.

54 So Jesus no longer moved around openly, boldly and freely[1] among the Jews. Instead he left there and went off to an area near the desert, to a city called Ephraim, and stayed there with the disciples.

---

[1] παρρησία, *parresia*. See background notes on *parresia* in Acts.

55-57 When it was almost time for the Jewish Passover, many people went up from the country to Jerusalem for their ceremonial cleansing before the Passover. *56* They kept looking out for Jesus. As they were standing in the Temple they kept asking each other, "What do you think? Do you think that he's not coming after all?"

57 But the chief priests and Pharisees had given orders that if anyone found out where Jesus was, they must report it so that Jesus could be arrested.

Ch.12:1-8 Six days before the Passover started, Jesus arrived at Bethany. This is where Lazarus lived – the one Jesus raised from the dead. *2* They gave a dinner for Jesus. Martha served, while Lazarus was one of the people sitting down to dinner with Jesus. *3* So Mary picked up perfumed ointment, three-quarters of a pound in weight,[1] and made from pure spikenard. She smeared Jesus' feet with it, and wiped his feet dry with her hair. The fragrance of the oil went right through the whole house. *4* But Judas Iscariot, Simon's son, - one of Jesus' disciples and the one who would later betray him - said, *5* "Why is it that this perfumed ointment wasn't sold for a year's wages[2] and given to the poor?"

6 He couldn't have cared less about the poor - this wasn't why he said it. He said it because he was a thief: as he was in charge of the money case, he used to help himself to the contents.

7 Jesus said, "Leave her alone! She's keeping it for the preparations for my burial! *8* You will always have the poor with you, but you won't always have me with you!"

9-11 Meanwhile the large crowd of Jews had realized that Jesus was there. They came, not just to see him, but also to see Lazarus whom he had raised from the dead. *10* Then the chief priests decided to kill Lazarus as well, *11* as because of him, many of the Jews were going over to Jesus and believing him.

12-15 The next day the large crowd that had come for the Feast heard that Jesus was on his way to Jerusalem. *13* They took palm branches and went out to meet him, shouting, "Hosanna! Happy is he who is coming in the Name of the Lord! The King of Israel!"

14 Jesus found a young donkey and sat on it, as it has been written: *15* "Do not be afraid, Daughter of Zion. Look, your King is coming, riding on a donkey's foal."

16-19 At first the disciples didn't understand any of this. It was only after Jesus was honored that they remembered that what had been done to Jesus had been recorded in Scripture. *17* The crowd, which had been with Jesus when he called Lazarus out of the tomb and raised him from the dead, kept telling people about him. *18* This is why the crowd went out to meet him – because he had performed this miraculous sign. *19* So the Pharisees said to each other, "See, we're not getting anywhere! On no, the whole world's going after him!"

20-28 There were some Greeks among those who went up to worship at the Feast. *21* They went to Philip, who was from Bethsaida in Galilee, and asked him, "Sir, may we see Jesus, please."

22 Philip went to tell Andrew, and then Andrew and Philip went to tell Jesus. *23* Jesus answered, "The time has come for the Human Being to be honored. *24* Let me make this clear. A grain of wheat will always be a single grain of wheat unless it falls to the ground and dies. If it dies, much fruit will grow from it. *25* The person who wants to preserve self will lose it, but whoever lets go of self in this world will keep it for eternal life. *26* The person that materially provides for[3] me must follow me. Where I am, my servant will be there too. My Father will honor the person who materially provides for me. *27* Now my soul has been distressed, and what am I going to say – 'Father,

---

1   Literally, a Roman pound. (1/3 kilogram.)
2   Literally, 300 denarii.
3   διακονέω τινί, *diakoneo tini*. See note on Matt. 27:55.

save me from this time'? No, it was for this very reason that I came to this time. *28* Father, give honor to your Name!"

28-34 Then a voice came from heaven: "I have given it honor, and I will also give it honor again."

29 The crowd standing listening said that there had been thunder, but others said that a Messenger had spoken to Jesus. *30* "This voice was for your benefit, not mine," Jesus remarked. *31* "Now is the turning point of this world, now the leader of this world will be thrown out! And I, *32* when I am lifted up from the earth,[1] will draw all people to me!" *33* He said this to indicate the sort of death by which he intended to die.

34 The crowd responded, "We heard from the Law that the Anointed One will remain forever. So why do you say, 'The Human Being must be lifted up'?[2] So who's this 'The Human Being'?"

35-36 Jesus answered, "You'll have the light among you just a little while longer. Walk around while you have the light, so that the darkness doesn't overshadow you – the person who walks around in the darkness doesn't know where they're going! *36* Believe the light while you have it, so that you will become people associated with light." After Jesus said this, he left there and hid from them.

37-41 They didn't believe Jesus despite the fact he had performed such great miraculous signs right in front of them. *38* This fulfilled the account by Isaiah the Prophet, who said, "Lord, who has believed our preaching? To whom has the Lord's power been revealed?" *39* This is the reason they couldn't believe, as Isaiah says elsewhere; *40* "He has blinded their eyes and hardened their hearts, so that they can't see with their eyes nor understand with their hearts nor be turned around, so that I could instantly divinely heal them." *41* Isaiah said these things because he saw Jesus' splendor and spoke about him.

42-43 However, many of the leaders did believe him, but because of the Pharisees they would not openly agree with it. If they did agree, they would be put out of the synagogue. *43* They loved praise from people more than they loved praise from God!

44-50 Then Jesus shouted, "When someone believes me, that person doesn't only believe me, that person also believes the One who sent me! *45* When that person looks at me, that person also looks at the One who sent me. *46* I certainly have come into the world as a light, so that no one who believes me will stay in the dark. *47* If a person listens to my words and doesn't put them into practice, I certainly won't judge that person, as I haven't come to judge the world, but to save the world. *48* The person who disregards me and doesn't receive my words already has their judge – the Word which I have spoken will judge that person on the Last Day. *49* I certainly didn't speak on my own initiative, but the Father who sent me commanded me as to what I am to say and what I am to speak. *50* And I know that his command is eternal life. So whatever I say is exactly what the Father has told me to say."

Ch.13:1-3 It was just before the Passover Feast. Jesus knew that the time had come for him to move on from this world and go to the Father. He had loved his own people who were in the world, and he loved them to the utmost extent. *2* It was time for the evening meal. Slanderer-Liar had already put it into the mind of Judas Iscariot, Simon's son, to betray Jesus. *3* Jesus knew that the Father had handed everything over to him, and that he came from God and was going back to God.

4-11 He got up from dinner and took off his coat, then wrapped a towel around his waist. *5* After that, he poured water into a basin and started washing the disciples' feet. He wiped them dry with the towel around his

---

[1]   ὑψωθῶ, *hupsotho*, aorist passive subjunctive of ὑψόω, *hupsoo*. This Greek term's semantic range included being crucified as well as being exalted.
[2]   That is, crucified.

waist. *6* Then he came to Simon Peter. "Lord, are you going to wash my feet!" Peter exclaimed.

7 Jesus answered, "You don't know what I'm doing now, but you'll realize afterwards."

8 "No way! You're never going to wash my feet!" Peter said.

"If I don't wash them, you and I are not sharing," Jesus answered.

9 Simon Peter said to him, "Lord, then don't just wash my feet but my hands and head as well!"

10 "A person who's had a bath only needs to wash their feet because the rest of them is clean," Jesus answered. "And you lot are clean, though not every one of you is." *11* Actually, Jesus knew who was going to betray him, so that was why he said that not all of them were clean.

12-17 When Jesus had finished washing their feet, he put his coat back on and went back to his place. "Do you realize what I've done for you?" he asked them. *13* "You call me 'Teacher' and 'Lord', and rightly so, because that's what I am. *14* So since I, your Lord and Teacher, have washed your feet, you also ought to wash each other's feet. *15* I have given you this example, so that you should do what I have done for you. *16* Let me make this quite clear, no slave servant is more important than their master, and no messenger is more important than the one who sent the messenger. *17* Now that you know this, you will be happy if you do it.

18-20 "Now I'm not talking about all of you - I certainly know the ones I picked out for myself. But the Scripture must be fulfilled: 'The one who eats my food has turned against me.' *19* I am telling you right now before it happens, so that when it does happen you'll believe that I am who I really am! *20* I will emphasize this, the person who welcomes the one I send, welcomes me, and the person who welcomes me, welcomes the One who sent me."

21-30 After Jesus said this, he was disturbed in his spirit, and solemnly declared, "Now listen carefully, one of you is going to betray me!"

22 The disciples looked at each other, wondering which one of them could do such a thing. *23* One of Jesus' disciples, the one he loved, was reclining for dinner close to him. *24* Simon Peter signaled to him to ask Jesus who he was talking about. *25* So he leant close to Jesus and whispered, "Lord, who is it?"

26 Jesus answered, "It's the one I'm about to give a piece of bread to after I've dipped it." So Jesus dipped the bread and gave it to Judas Iscariot, Simon's son. *27* When he did this, Adversary entered Judas.

Jesus said to him, "What you're about to do, do more quickly!" *28* No one at the table realized why Jesus had said this to him. *29* Some of them thought it was to do with Judas being in charge of the money: they thought that Jesus had meant, "Buy what we need for the feast," or that he should give some money to the poor. *30* But when Judas had taken the piece of bread, he immediately went out. It was night time.

31-35 When he had gone, Jesus said, "Now the Human Being is being given honor, and God is being given honor because of him. *32* Since God is given honor because of him, God will also bring honor to the Son. In fact, he will do this immediately. *33* My dear little members,[1] I'll be with you a little while longer. You will look for me, and what I told the Jews, I'm telling you now: where I'm going, you can't come. *34* I'm giving you a new command: love one another. You must love each other just like I have loved you. *35* Everyone will know by this, by the fact that you love one another, that you are my disciples."

36-38.Ch.14:1-4 Simon Peter asked, "Lord, where are you going?"

Jesus answered, "Where I'm going, you won't be able to follow now, but you will be able to later."

---

[1] τεκνίον, *teknion*, a diminutive of τέκνον, *teknon*, a term of endearment and not of immaturity. "Member" or "child".

37 "Lord, why can't I follow you now?" Peter asked. "I would give my life for you."

38 Jesus answered, "Would you really give your life for me? Listen carefully, before the rooster crows, you will disown me three times! *1* Don't be concerned. You believe God and you also believe me. *2* There are many rooms[1] in my Father's house[2] – if not, I would have told you, because I'm going there to prepare a place for you. *3* And since I'm going to prepare a place for you, I will come back and take you to be with me, so that you will be where I am too. *4* You know the way to the place I'm going."

5-7 Thomas asked, "Lord, we don't know where you're going, so how can we know the way?"

6 "I am the Way, the Truth and the Life," Jesus answered. "No one goes to the Father except through me. *7* If you had come to know me, then you would come to know the Father as well. From now on, you will come to know him; you have seen him."

8-14 Philip said to him, "Lord, show us the Father, and that'll be enough for us!"

9 Jesus replied, "I have been with you so long and you haven't come to know me, Philip! How can you say, 'Show us the Father'? *10* Don't you believe that I am in the Father and that the Father is in me? The words I say to you are not on my own initiative, but it is the Father who stays in me who does his work! *11* Believe me when I say that I am in my Father and the Father is in me: or at least believe because of the very deeds themselves! *12* In fact, whoever believes me will do the deeds that I do, and will actually do greater deeds than these, because I am going to the Father. *13* And the things you ask in my Name, I will do, so that honor is brought to the Father by means of the Son. *14* Whatever you ask me in my Name, I will certainly do."

15-21 "If you love me, then you will keep my commandments. *16* And for a fact I will ask the Father, and he will give you another One who is called to your side to help and encourage,[3] and that One will be with you forever. *17* This is the Spirit of truth, who the world doesn't accept, because it doesn't see him or recognize him. But you recognize him, because he is staying beside you and will be in you. *18* I will not leave you orphans: I will come to you. *19* In a short time, the world won't look at me anymore, but you will look at me. Because I will live, you will live too. *20* On that day, you will realize that I am in my Father, and you are in me, and I am in you. *21* The person who has my commandments and keeps them is the person who loves me. And the person who loves me will be loved by my Father, and I will love that person too and show myself to that person."

22-24 Then Judas (not Judas Iscariot) said, "Lord, why is it that you are going to show yourself to us, and not to the world?"

23 Jesus answered, "If anyone loves me, they will hold on firmly to my Word, and my Father will love them, and we will come to them and make our home[4] with them. *24* The person who doesn't love me will not hold on firmly to my teachings. And the Word which you hear is not mine: it is the Word of the Father who sent me."

25-31 "I have spoken all this while I'm still around with you. *26* But the One who is called to your side to help and encourage,[5] the Holy Spirit, whom the Father will send in my Name, will teach you everything and remind you of everything I've said to you. *27* I am leaving you peace – I am giving you peace –

---

1   Not "mansions". μονή, *mone*, is also used in John 14:23, "we will come to him and make our home with him." μονή, *mone*, can mean either "room" or "home".
2   Equally, "many homes in my Father's household".
3   παράκλητος, *parakletos*, is used only by John in the N.T., 4 times in the Gospel (14:16, 26; 15:26; 16:7) and 1 John 2:1. It literally refers to someone who is called to one's side, who acts as an advocate. The extended meaning is to comfort or support.
4   μονή, *mone*. This is the same word as in John 14:2.
5   παράκλητος, *parakletos*. See above note on John 14:16.

I am certainly giving it to you but not in the same way that the world gives it. Don't let your hearts be disturbed, and don't be cowardly.[1] *28* You certainly heard me say, 'I am going away and coming back to you. Since you love me, you should be happy because I'm going to the Father, as the Father is more important than I am. *29* I have told you about it before it happens! So when it actually does happen, you will believe it! *30* I won't be talking with you much longer, for the ruler of the world is coming, and he has nothing to do with me! *31* The world must realize that I love the Father, and that I must do what the Father ordered me to do. Come on, let's get out of here!

Ch.15:1-6 "I am the true vine, and my Father is the farmer. *2* He carries away every branch from me that doesn't have fruit, and prunes the ones that do have fruit so that they will grow even more fruit. *3* You are already pruned because of the Word I have spoken to you. *4* Stay with me, and I will stay with you. Just as the branch can't grow fruit unless it stays on the vine, neither will you, unless you stay with me. *5* I definitely am the vine, and you are the branches. The person who stays with me, and I with that person, produces a lot of fruit, because you can't do anything without me. *6* If anyone doesn't stay with me, that person will be thrown out like a branch and will wither. Those branches are picked up, thrown into the fire and burned.

7-8 "If you stay with me and my words stay within you, you will ask whatever you want, and it will happen for you. *8* You will produce a lot of fruit and will become my disciples. By this my Father is given honor.

9-17 "I love you the way the Father has loved me. Stay with my love for you! *10* If you hold on firmly to my commands, then you will stay with my love, just as I certainly have held on firmly to my Father's commands and stay with his love. *11* I have told you these things so that my happiness will stay with you and so that your happiness will be completely filled up!

12 "This is what I order you to do: to love each another just like I have loved you. *13* There is no greater love than for someone to lay down their life for their friends. *14* You are my friends if you do the things I have ordered you to do. *15* I don't call you slave servants anymore, because a slave servant is one who doesn't know what their master is doing. But I have called you friends, because the things I have heard from the Father I have made known to you. *16* You didn't choose me, but I chose you. And I appointed you to go and bear fruit, and at that, fruit that would last, so that the Father will give you the things that you ask for in my Name. *17* This is what I order you to do: to love one another.

18-25 "Since the world hates you, realize that it hated me even before it hated you! *19* If you belonged to the world, it would love you like it loves its own. The reason that the world hates you is because you don't belong to it, and because I selected you out of it for myself. *20* Remember the message that I spoke to you, 'A slave servant isn't more important than their master.' Since they persecuted me, they will persecute you. If they held on firmly to my message, they will hold on firmly to yours, too. *21* But they will do all these things to you because of my Name, because they don't know the One who sent me. *22* If I hadn't come and spoken to them, they wouldn't have had sin: but now they don't have any excuse for their sin. *23* The person who hates me, hates my Father too. *24* If I hadn't done among them the works that no one else did, they would have no sin: but now they have seen the works, and have hated both me and my Father. *25* But this happened to fulfill the Word that is written in their Law: 'They hated me for no reason.'

---

[1] μηδὲ δειλιάτω, *mede deiliato*: "Don't be cowardly" was the parting advice of Moses (Deut. 31:8), and the instruction of Joshua to his warriors (Josh. 10:25), as it was Yahweh's word to him (Josh. 1:9; 8:1). The N.T. states that God didn't give us a spirit of cowardice (2 Tim.1:7), and the book of Revelation ranks cowards with murderers and idol worshippers (Rev. 21:8). Note this is not "do not fear".

26-27 "When the One who is called to your side to help and encourage[1] comes, the One I will send from the Father, the Spirit of Truth who comes out from the Father, he will give evidence about me. *27* And you yourselves will give evidence, because you've been with me right from the beginning.

Ch.16:1-4 "I have told you these things so that you won't have a trap laid for you. *2* They will put you out of the synagogues. Not only that, but also the time will come when anyone who kills you will think they're actually doing God a religious service! *3* They will do these things because they didn't recognize the Father or me. *4* But I have told you this so that when the time comes you will remember that I told you.

4-11 "I didn't tell you this at first, because I was still with you, *5* but now I'm going to the One who sent me, and none of you ask me, 'Where are you going?' *6* However, your hearts are full of sadness because I've said these things. *7* But I'm telling you the truth: it is for your benefit that I'm going away. If I didn't go away, the One who is called to your side to help and encourage wouldn't come to you. Since I am going, I will send him to you. *8* And when he comes, he will convince the world of the truth about sin, and about being made right with God, and about judgment. *9* About sin, because they don't believe me, *10* and also about being made right with God, because I'm going to the Father where you'll no longer see me, *11* and also about judgment, because the ruler of this world now stands judged.

12-16 "I have a lot more to say to you, more than you can stand at the moment. *13* But when the Spirit of Truth comes, he will guide you into all truth. He won't speak on his own initiative, but he will speak only what he hears, and he will announce to you things that will happen in the future. *14* He will bring honor to me, because he will take the message from me and announce it to you. *15* Everything that belongs to the Father is mine – that's why I said he would take the message from me and announce it to you. *16* In a little while you won't see me anymore, and then a little while after that you will see me."

17-18 So some of the disciples said to each other, "What on earth does he mean by saying, 'In a little while you won't see me anymore, and then a little while after that you will see me,' and 'Because I'm going to the Father'?"

18 They kept asking, "What on earth does he mean by 'a little while'? We don't have a clue what he's talking about!"

19-28 Jesus realized that they wanted to ask him about it, so he said, "Are you asking each other what I meant when I said, 'In a little while you won't be looking at me anymore, and then a little while after that you will see me'?

20 "I'll make it quite clear. You will cry and mourn while the world is happy. You will be sad, but your sadness will turn into happiness. *21* A woman who is giving birth is in pain because she's in labor, but then she doesn't remember the affliction after that because she's happy that a person has been born into the world. *22* And so it is in your case – on the one hand you have pain, but on the other hand I will see you again and you will be happy, and no one will take away your happiness. *23* At that time you won't ask me for anything. But I can tell you for a fact, the Father will give you anything you ask him for in my Name. *24* Up until now you haven't asked for anything in my Name. Ask and you will receive, so that you will be completely happy! *25* I have been speaking to you metaphorically. The time is coming when I won't speak to you metaphorically any more, but will tell you about the Father openly, plainly, and freely. *26* At that time you will ask in my Name. Now, I'm not telling you that I myself will ask the Father for you. *27* In fact, the Father himself likes you, because you have liked me and have believed that I came from God. *28* I have come from the Father and entered the world: now I'm leaving the world and going back to the Father."

---

[1] παράκλητος, *parakletos*. See note on John 14:16.

29-30 "At last!" the disciples exclaimed. "Now you're speaking plainly and clearly and not metaphorically! *30* Now we can see that you know everything and there's no need for anyone to ask you anything! Because of this we believe that you really came from God!"

31-33 "Finally! You believe!" Jesus exclaimed. *32* "But a time is coming - and actually has already come – when you will be scattered, and each of you will go on your own way. You will leave me all alone. But I'm not really alone, because the Father is with me *33* I've told you all this, so that you will have peace because of me. In the world you will have oppression. But be brave! I have had the victory over the world!"

Ch.17:1-5 After Jesus said this, he looked up to heaven and said, "Father, the time has come. Give your Son honor, so that your Son may give you honor. *2* You gave him authority over all humankind, so that he would give eternal life to all those you have given him. *3* This is eternal life – that they would come to know you, the only true God, and Jesus the Anointed One whom you sent. *4* I have certainly brought you honor on the earth by completing the work that you gave me to do. *5* And now, Father, give me the honor I had in your own presence, the honor that I had with you before the world began.

6-12 "I have revealed your Name to the people you gave me from the world. They were yours: you gave them to me and now they have held on firmly to your Word. *7* Now they realize that everything you have given me comes from you, *8* because I gave them the spoken words that you gave to me. They received them, and realized that I truly came from you, and they believed that you sent me. *9* I ask about them. I am not asking about the world, but for those you have given to me, because they are yours. *10* And everything I have is yours, and everything you have is mine, and I have been given honor because of these things. *11* I'm not in the world anymore, but they are to stay in the world, and I am coming to you. Holy Father, keep a firm hold on them through the power of your Name which you have given me. *12* While I was with them, I kept a firm hold on them by the power of your Name which you gave me, and I guarded them. None of them has been lost except the one destined to be lost, so that the Scripture would be fulfilled.

13-19 "Now I am coming to you and I say these things aloud[1] while I am in the world so that they will carry the happiness I have brought them. *14* I have given them your Word and the world has hated them, because they are not of the world just as certainly as I am not of the world. *15* I am not asking you to take them out of the world but I am asking you to firmly hold them away from the Evil One. *16* They are not of the world just as certainly as I am not of the world. *17* Make them sacred by the truth: your Word is the truth. *18* I have sent them into the world just as you sent me into the world. *19* And I make myself sacred for their benefit, so that they will also be made sacred by the truth.

20-26 "I am not just asking about these ones alone, but also about all who believe me because of the Word. *21* I ask that all of them may be unified, Father, just as you are in me and I am in you, so that the world will believe that you sent me. *22* And I have given them the honor that you gave me, so that they may be unified in the same way that we are unified: *23* I with them, and you with me. May they be brought to complete unity, so that the world will realize that you have sent me and loved them in the same way that you loved me. *24* Father, I wish that those whom you have given me will be where I am - with me - so that they may observe my honor which you have given me – because you loved me before the laying down of the world. *25* "Righteous Father, the world didn't recognize you, but I recognized you, and these people have known that you sent me. *26* And I made your Name known to them, and I will make it known, so that your love for me may be in them, and I will be in them."

---

[1]   λαλῶ, *lalo*, implies speaking these things aloud.

Ch.18:1-3 After Jesus said this, he left with his disciples and crossed over to the other side of the Kidron Valley. There was a garden there, and he and his disciples went into it. *2* But Judas his betrayer knew about the place too, because Jesus often met there with his disciples. *3* So Judas went there. He had laid hold of an army detachment and some officers from the chief priests and Pharisees. They were carrying torches, lights and foot soldiers' weapons.

4-11 Jesus knew everything that was going to happen to him. He went out and asked them, "Who are you looking for?"

5 They answered, "Jesus of Nazareth."

"That's me!" Jesus replied. Judas, who betrayed him, was standing there with them. *6* When Jesus said, "That's me," they went backwards[1] and fell to the ground.

7 Jesus asked them again, "Who are you looking for?"

"Jesus of Nazareth," they said.

8 Jesus answered, "I've already told you that it's me! So, since I'm the one you're looking for, let these ones go home."

9 This was so that the scripture would be fulfilled, "None of them has been lost."

10 So Simon Peter, who had a sword, drew it and hit the chief priest's slave servant, and cut off his right ear. (The slave servant's name was Malchos.) *11* So Jesus said to Peter, "Put your sword back in its scabbard! Do you think there's any way I'm going to avoid the suffering that the Father has assigned me!"

12-14 Then the army detachment, captain, and officers of the Jews arrested Jesus and tied him up. *13* They took him off to Annas first, as he was the father-in-law of Caiaphas, who was the chief priest that year. *14* Caiaphas was the one who had advised the people that it was a good idea if one person died on behalf of the people.

15-18 Simon Peter and another disciple were following Jesus. Because this particular disciple was a close friend of the chief priest, he went with Jesus into the chief priest's courtyard, *16* but Peter had to wait outside at the door. The other disciple, the one who was a close friend of the chief priest, came back, spoke to the girl who guarded the door, and brought Peter in. *17* So the girl who guarded the door said to Peter, "You're not one of his disciples, are you?

"No, I'm not!" Peter said.

18 It was cold, so the servants and officials stood around a coal fire they had made to keep warm. Peter stood with them too, and warmed himself.

19-24 Meanwhile, the chief priest questioned Jesus about his disciples and his teaching. *20* Jesus answered him, "I have spoken with the right of freedom of speech, openly, plainly and freely to the world. I always taught in synagogues or at the temple, where all the Jews met. I didn't say anything in secret. *21* So why question me? Ask the ones who heard me. Surely they'll know what I said!"

22 When Jesus said this, one of the nearby officials slapped him across the face, and said, "Is this the way you answer the chief priest!"

23 Jesus responded, "If I said something wrong, produce evidence of it! But if I spoke the truth, then why did you belt me?"[2]

24 Then Annas sent him, tied up, to Caiaphas the chief priest.

25-27 Simon Peter was standing there getting warm. They asked him, "You're not one of his disciples, are you?

Peter denied it. "I am not!"

26 One of the chief priest's slave servants, who was a relative of the person whose ear Peter cut off, said, "Didn't I see you with him in the garden?"

27 Again Peter denied it, and immediately the rooster crowed.

---

[1] ἀπῆλθον εἰς τὰ ὀπίσω καὶ ἔπεσαν χαμαί, *apelthon eis ta opiso kai epesan khamai*, they went backwards and fell down backwards, not "drew back".

[2] δέρω, *dero*, to thrash, flog, flay, far stronger than "hit".

28-32 Then they took Jesus from Caiaphas to the Roman Governor's headquarters. By now it was early in the morning, so the Jews didn't go into the Governor's headquarters to avoid ceremonial uncleanness. This was so they could eat the Passover meal. *29* Pilate went to see them outside and said to them, "What is the charge that you have laid against this person?"

30 They answered, "If he wasn't a criminal, we wouldn't have handed him over to you!"

31 So then Pilate said to them, "Then you yourselves take him and judge him by your own law!"

But those Jews complained, "But we can't legally have someone put to death!"

32 This happened so that the Word of Jesus would be fulfilled, when he spoke about the type of death by which he would die.

33-38 Pilate went back inside the Roman Governor's headquarters, and called out to Jesus, "Are you the king of the Jews?"

34 Jesus answered, "Did you think of this all by yourself, or have others been speaking to you about me?"

35 Pilate answered, "Am I a Jew! It was your own people and the chief priests who handed you over to me. What was it that you did?"

36 "My realm is not from this world," Jesus answered. "If my realm were from this world, then my officers would have been fighting to the last[1] to prevent me from being handed over to certain Jews. But as a matter of fact my realm isn't from here!"

37 "So then you are a king?" Pilate asked.

"You're the one who says I am a king!" Jesus answered. "This is the reason I was born, this is the reason I have come into the world – to give evidence about the truth. Everyone who is not deaf to the truth hears my voice."

38 Pilate said, "What is truth!"

38-40 After Pilate said this he went back out to those Jews and said, "I can't find any grounds for a charge against him. *39* You have a custom that I should release someone for you at the Passover. So do you want me to release the King of the Jews for you?"

40 So they all shouted, "No! Not him, but Barabbas! Release Barabbas!" Barabbas was a robber.

Ch.19:1-3 So then Pilate took Jesus and had him beaten with a Roman whip of leather straps embedded with metal designed to rip off the flesh. *2* The soldiers plaited a crown of thorns and put it on his head. They put a purple coat on him *3* and they kept going up to him, saying, "Greetings, King of the Jews!" And they slapped him across the face.

4-7 Pilate went outside again and said to them, "I am bringing him out to you so that you will realize that I don't find any grounds for a charge against him!"

5 When Jesus came out, wearing the crown of thorns and the purple coat, Pilate said, "Here he is!"

6 So then when the chief priests and the officers saw him, they shouted, "Crucify him! Crucify him!"

But Pilate said to them, "You take him and crucify him! As for me, I can't find any fault with him!"

7 Certain Jews answered, "We have a law and according to our law he must die, because he claimed to be God's Son!"

8-12 So when Pilate heard this statement, he was even more afraid, *9* and he went back into the Roman governor's headquarters and said to Jesus, "Where do you come from?" Jesus wouldn't answer him.

10 Pilate said, "Are you refusing to speak to me? Don't you know that I have the authority either to free you or to crucify you?"

---

[1] ἀγωνίζομαι, *agonizomai*, to contend for the prize, to fight to the last, to fight against a charge, not merely "to fight".

11 Jesus answered him, "You would have no authority over me if it wasn't given to you from above: for this reason the one who handed me over to you is guilty of a greater sin."

12 From this time on Pilate kept trying to find a way to free Jesus, but certain Jews kept shouting, "If you let this person go, you're no 'Friend of Caesar's'! Anyone who claims to be a king opposes Caesar!"

13-16 So when Pilate heard this serious threat he brought Jesus outside and sat down on the judge's seat at a place called the Stone Pavement (which in Aramaic is "Gabbatha"). *14* It was about midday on the Preparation Day of the Passover. Pilate said to those Jews, "Here is your king!"

15 So they shouted, "Get rid of him! Get rid of him! Crucify him!"

"Am I to crucify your king?" Pilate asked.

The chief priests answered, "Caesar's our only king!"

16 Then Pilate handed Jesus over to be crucified.[1] So they took Jesus away.

17-22 Jesus went out to Skull Place (which is called "Golgotha" in Aramaic). He was carrying his own cross. *18* They crucified him in this place with two others – one on each side and Jesus in the middle.

19 Pilate had a notice inscribed and had it attached to the cross. The inscription was, "Jesus of Nazareth, the King of the Jews."

20 So many of the Jews read the notice, as the place where Jesus was crucified was near the city. The notice was written in Aramaic, Latin and Greek. *21* So the chief priests of the Jews said to Pilate, "Don't write, 'King of the Jews,' but write that he claimed he was King of the Jews."

22 Pilate retorted, "What I've written, I've written!"

23-24 So the soldiers, when they crucified Jesus, took his coat and divided it into four shares, one for each of them, as well as the shirt. The shirt was seamless, woven in one piece from top to bottom. *24* They said to each other, "Let's not rip it up, but let's draw lots to see who will get it."

This happened so that the Scripture would be fulfilled: "They divided my clothes among themselves. They cast lots for my clothes." So much for what the soldiers did.

25-27 Jesus' mother, his mother's sister, Mary the wife of Klopas, and Mary Magdalene were standing near his cross. *26* When Jesus saw his mother and the disciple he loved standing beside her, he said to his mother, "Dear lady,[2] this is your son", *27* and to the disciple, "This is your mother." From then on, the disciple took her into his own home.

28-30 After this, Jesus, knowing that everything had already happened in order for the Scripture to be fulfilled, said, "I'm thirsty."

29 There was a jar of the soldier's standard issue of wine vinegar[3] standing there, so they soaked a sponge with it and put the sponge on the stalk of a hyssop plant, and lifted it to Jesus' mouth. *30* When Jesus had taken the wine-vinegar, he said, "It has been finished," and gave up the Spirit.

31-34 Now it was the Day of Preparation, and the next day was an important Sabbath. The Jews didn't want the bodies left on the crosses on the Sabbath day, so they asked Pilate to have the legs broken and the bodies taken down. *32* So the soldiers came and broke the legs of the first person crucified with Jesus, and then those of the other, *33* but when they came to Jesus they found that he was already dead, so they didn't break his legs. *34* Instead, one of the soldiers stuck a spear in Jesus' side, and immediately blood and water poured out.

---

[1] Tacitus (*Annals* 15.44) states, "The originator of the title (Christians) was Christ who had been put to death in the reign of Tiberius through the agency of Pontius Pilate the procurator." (Trans. John Bishop.)

[2] γύναι, *gunai*. See note on John 2:4.

[3] Spice with myrrh added in sufficient quantity to turn the wine into the drug. The intention was to ease the pain, and was in accordance with Jewish custom.

35-37 And he who saw it has given evidence about it, and his evidence is correct. He knows that he tells the truth, and he tells it so that you will believe too. *36* These things happened so that the Scriptures would be fulfilled, "Not one of his bones will be broken," *37* and, as another Scripture says, "They will look at the One they have pierced."

38-42 After this Joseph of Arimathea asked Pilate for Jesus' body. Joseph was a disciple of Jesus, but he kept it secret because he was afraid of the Jews. Pilate gave him permission. *39* Nikodemos went with him: he was the man who had earlier visited Jesus at night. Nikodemos brought a mixture of myrrh and aloes, about 12 ounces in weight.[1] *40* They wrapped Jesus' body in strips of linen with the scented herbs and oils, in accordance with the Jewish burial customs. *41* In the place where Jesus was crucified there was a garden. In the garden was a new tomb, and no one had been buried in it yet. *42* Because it was the Jewish Day of Preparation, they put Jesus there.

Ch.20:1-2 On the first day of the week Mary Magdalene went to the tomb early in the morning, while it was still dark, and saw that the stone had been taken away from the entrance. *2* She went running to Simon Peter and the other disciple, the one Jesus loved, and said, "They've taken the Lord out of the tomb, and we don't know where they've put him!"

3-10 So Peter and the other disciple headed for the tomb. *4* They were running together, but the other disciple ran faster and overtook Peter, and reached the tomb first. *5* He bent down and looked inside and saw the strips of linen lying there, but he didn't go in. *6* Then Simon Peter, who was behind him, arrived and went into the tomb. He saw the strips of linen lying there, *7* as well as the burial cloth that had been around Jesus' head. It had been rolled up and put by itself, away from the strips of linen. *8* So then the other disciple, the one who had reached the tomb first, went inside too. He saw and he also believed. *9* (Until then they had not understood the Scripture that Jesus had to rise from among the dead.) *10* So the disciples went back to their own homes.

11-18 Mary stood outside the tomb crying. As she cried, she bent over to look inside the tomb, *12* and saw two Messengers in white, sitting where Jesus' body had been. One was at the head and the other at the foot.

13 The Messengers said to her, "Dear lady,[2] why are you crying?"

She said, "They have taken away my Lord, and I don't know where they've put him."

14 Upon saying this she turned around and saw Jesus standing there, but she didn't know that it was Jesus. *15* Jesus said to her, "Dear lady, why are you crying? Who are you looking for?"

Mary thought he was the gardener. She said, "Sir, if you've carried him away, please tell me where you've put him, and I'll go and get him."

16 Jesus said to her, "Mary!"

She turned towards him and said in Hebrew, "Rabboni!" (which means "Teacher.")

17 "Stop hanging on to me!" Jesus said. "I haven't returned to the Father yet! Go on - go to the fellow believers[3] and tell them, 'I am going back to my Father and your Father, to my God and your God.'"

18 Mary Magdalene went to the disciples and announced, "I've seen the Lord!" She told them what he had said to her.

19-23 Early evening on the same day, which was the first day of the week, the disciples had shut the doors because they were scared of certain Jews. Jesus turned up and stood in the middle of them. He said to them, "Hello, how are you!"[4]

---

[1] Literally, "about 100 Roman pounds". (About 1/3 kilogram.)

[2] γύναι, *gunai*. See note on John 2:4. Again in v. 15.

[3] ἀδελφοί, *adelphoi*. See note on Matt. 5:22.

[4] Word for word, "Peace be with you" which is the idiomatic equivalent of our English expression, "Hello, how are you!"

20 After he said this, he showed them his hands and side. The disciples were thrilled when they saw the Lord. *21* Jesus said to them again, "Hello, how are you! I am sending you, just as the Father has sent me." *22* And having said that, he breathed on them and said, "Receive the Holy Spirit. *23* If you acquit someone for their sins, their sins are discharged,[1] but if you don't acquit someone for their sins, their sins are not discharged."

24-29 But Thomas, one of the Twelve (known as "Twin") wasn't with the other disciples when Jesus turned up. *25* So the other disciples said to him, "We've seen the Lord!"

But Thomas said, "There's no way I'm going to believe that, unless I see the nail marks[2] in his hands and put my finger where the nails were, and stick my hand in his side!"[3]

26 A week later Jesus' disciples were in the house again, and Thomas was with them. Even though the doors were locked, Jesus turned up and stood in the middle of them. He said, "Hello! How are you!" *27* Then he said to Thomas, "Come on, reach your finger here – look at my hands! Reach your hand over here and put it in my side! Don't prove yourself to be an unbeliever! Be a believer!"

28 Thomas said in reply, "My Lord and my God!"

29 Jesus said to him, "You have believed because you have seen me: happy are those who believed without seeing me!"

30-31 Indeed, in the presence of his disciples Jesus did many other miraculous signs, which aren't written in this book. *31* But these ones are written so that you will go on believing that Jesus is the Anointed One, the Son of God and so that by believing him, you will have life by the power of his Name.

Ch.21:1-3 After this happened, Jesus showed himself again to the disciples at the Tiberius Sea. This is how it happened: *2* Simon Peter, Thomas (called "Twin"), Nathanael from Cana in Galilee, the sons of Zebedee, and two other disciples were together.

3 Simon Peter said to them, "I'm going fishing!"

"Yeah, we'll go too!" they said.

So they went out and got into the ship, but didn't catch anything that night.

4-14 Early the next morning, Jesus stood on the shore. However, the disciples didn't know that it was Jesus. *5* He shouted out to them, "Hey, guys, haven't you caught anything to eat?"

"No!" they answered.

6 So he said, "Throw your net over the starboard side of the boat and you'll find some!"

They cast it, and they weren't able to haul the net in because of the immense number of fish. *7* So the disciple that Jesus loved said, "It's the Lord!"

When Simon Peter heard him say, "It's the Lord!" he wrapped his item of clothing[4] around himself (as he was stripped for work) and jumped into the water. *8* The other disciples followed in the ship, towing the net full of fish, as they

---

1 ἀφίημι, *aphiemi*, dative of person and accusative of thing: to acquit in a legal sense, to acquit someone of a charge, cf. Hdt. 6.30; Dem. 540.11, Ar. *Clouds.*, 1426.

2 τύπος, *tupos*. Here "mark" referring to an exact replica. See note on Acts 7:43.

3 Thomas was an interesting character with a dry sense of humor who said what he thought. The Greek scholar J.H. Bernard said that he could imagine Thomas saying "I told you so!" when Jesus was crucified. *op.cit.*, p. 264.

4 ἐπενδύτης, *ependutes*. The identity of this item of clothing is unknown. Rare; and only here in N.T. Only 2 instances in documentary sources of the times. However, it is established that it was an outer garment, worn outside the house, and could be worn by women or men. See confession inscription by the woman Antonia, *TAM* 5.1.238.4 (Koulia in Lydia, I-II): "I went up to the chorus in a dirty *ependutes*", and *SB* 6.9026.12 9Egypt, II).

weren't far from the shore, only about 100 yards.[1] *9* So they disembarked on the shore and saw a fire made from coals there, with cooked fish laid on it, and some bread. *10* Jesus said, "Bring some of those fish you've just caught!"

11 Simon Peter jumped aboard and dragged the net ashore. It was full of large fish, 153 of them, but even with so many, the net wasn't torn. *12* Jesus said, "Come here and have some breakfast!"

None of the disciples were game to ask him, "Who are you?" as they knew it was the Lord. *13* Jesus came and picked up the bread and gave it to them, and did the same with the fish. *14* This was now the third time that Jesus appeared to his disciples, after he was raised from the dead.

15-19 After they had breakfast, Jesus said to Simon Peter, "Simon, John's son, do you love me more than these?"[2]

Peter answered, "Yes, Lord, you know that I like you."[3]

Jesus said to him, "Feed my lambs!"

16 Jesus said to him a second time, "Simon, son of John, do you love me?"

Peter answered, "Yes, Lord, you know that I like you."

"Shepherd my sheep!" Jesus said.

17 Jesus said to him a third time, "Simon, son of John, do you like me?"

Peter was hurt because Jesus asked him a third time, "Do you like me?" He said, "Lord, you know everything! You realize that I do like you."

Jesus said to him, "Feed my sheep! *18* Let me make this clear, when you were young you dressed yourself and went around wherever you wanted to go, but when you are old you will stretch out your hands, and someone else will dress you and lead you where you don't want to go." *19* Jesus said this to indicate by what sort of death Peter would bring honor to God. After he'd said this, he said to Peter, "Follow me!"

20-23 Peter turned around and saw that the disciple that Jesus loved was following them. (This was the disciple who had been sitting close to Jesus at the dinner and had said, "Lord, who is going to betray you?").

21 When Peter saw him, he said to the Lord, "What about him?"

22 Jesus answered, 'If I want him to stay alive until I return, what's it to you? You must follow me!" *23* So the rumor spread around the fellow believers[4] that this disciple would not die. But Jesus didn't actually say that he wouldn't die, he only said, "If I want him to stay alive until I return, what's it to you?"

24-25 I am the disciple who gives this evidence and who wrote them down. We know that my evidence is true. *25* Jesus did many other things as well. If every one of them were written down, I don't suppose the whole world would have enough room for all the books that could be written!

---

[1]   Literally, about 200 cubits. (Over 90 metres.)

[2]   Equally possible in the Greek, "Do you love me more than these disciples love me?" or "Do you love me more than you love these disciples?"

[3]   ἀγαπάω, *agapao*, translated as "love" and φιλέω, *phileo* as "like" in the above passage to distinguish between the words, but there is distinct overlap in their semantic ranges. ἀγαπάω, *agapao*, did not refer to a special God-like love. The mistaken belief that there is a divine meaning behind the word ἀγαπάω, *agapao*, is treated by D.A. Carson in his book, *Exegetical Fallacies*, (Grand Rapids, MI: Baker Book House, 1996). The literature of the time also demonstrates that ἀγαπάω, *agapao*, certainly was not used particularly for "good" love or "God-like" love.

[4]   ἀδελφοί, *adelphoi*. See note on Matt. 5:22.

Acts.

The Acts was written by Luke, who also wrote the Good News of Luke. It covers the period from AD 33-63. The title, "Acts" or "Deeds (Acts) of the Apostles" was added later. In antiquity, titles were often devised well after the book was in circulation. The book is actually about the activities of the Holy Spirit.

Luke displays the rhetorical and literary skills of a highly educated person. He has constructed his narrative in a way which entertains the reader, using dramatic episodes to avoid recourse to abstract expression in addressing certain issues, and using variety by employing direct discourse and letters. Luke was an eyewitness to some events (for example, the "we" passages, Acts 16:10-17; 20:5 – 21:18; 27:1 – 28:16). Only Paul could have known other events (such as what happened in Athens).

Acts provides us with information about Paul's three missionary journeys and his visit to Rome. At times he was on foot: (possibly) Jerusalem to Damascus (Acts 9); Troas to Assos (Acts 20), Caesarea to Jerusalem (Acts 20-21), while his return to Caesarea (Acts 23) appears to be on horseback. At times he traveled by boat: to Cyprus and Antalya, Antalya to Antakya, Troas to Samothrace and Neapolis, Kenchreai to Ephesos, Ephesos to Caesarea, Greece to Miletos, Caesarea to Rome.

Acts 18:2 tells us that Priscilla and Aquila, as Jews, were expelled from Italy by Claudius. History tells us that Claudius expelled the Jews in 49 AD. Acts 13:7 mentions Sergius Paulus, the Proconsul of Cyprus. Other historical figures are Felix, who succeeded Cumanus as procurator of Judea in 52 AD (Acts 23:23 – 24:27); Porcius Festus, the successor to Felix (Acts 24:27 – 27:1); Agrippa II and Bernice, the daughter of Agrippa I (Acts 25:24, 26; 26:2). Acts 18:12 has Paul in Corinth when Gallio was Proconsul of Achaia in 51-52 AD.

There has been academic debate as to the genre of Acts, whether it is biography, novelistic narrative or history. As Acts is chronologically arranged and in part topically arranged, and as there is focus on particular individuals as well as claims of autopsy (that is, the "we" passages), the evidence suggests that history is the appropriate classification. In considering historical narrative the following factors should be considered: the purpose of the writer; the degree of bias of writer; whether the writing was contemporaneous with the events being covered: that is, how much time has passed between events and their recording; the writer's sources (and their values, concerns and prejudices), critical approach to sources; whether literary criticism is used (such as, for example, where Herodotos reflects that Homer discarded the true story of Helen's presence in Egypt during the Trojan War because it was unsuited to epic poetry); agreement/disagreement with other sources; and the historical context in which it was composed.

Acts.

Ch.1:1-5 Theophilos,[1] in my previous book I wrote about everything that Jesus did as well as taught, **2** right from the very beginning until the day he was

---

[1] Nothing is known of the Theophilos mentioned by Luke. The name is frequently attested in papyri (from 3rd c. BC). 66 instances are known from Rome, 33 of which indicate the status of the person. Of these, only one of is senatorial standing, another is free born, and the rest are either freed or slaves. See, for example, *AAWW* III. 439-44 (Iulia Gordos, 75/6), "Theophilos son of Thynites is of very noble ancestral stock". Luke refers to Theophilos as

taken up to heaven, after he had given instructions to the apostles he had chosen: he gave the instructions through the Holy Spirit. *3* After the suffering he also presented himself as alive to these apostles by substantial and certain proof.[1] He was seen by them from time to time[2] during a period of forty days. In this time he spoke about things in connection with God's Realm. *4* After he had shared a meal with them he ordered them not to leave Jerusalem. Instead, they were to wait for the Father's promise. He said, "You've heard about the promise from me. *5* John baptized with water, but you will be baptized with the Holy Spirit in a few days from now."

6-8 Every time they got together they kept on asking him, "Lord, are you going to restore the kingdom to Israel right now?"

7 But he answered, "It's none of your business to be aware of the times or the seasons which the Father has prepared by his own private authority! *8* But you will seize power when the Holy Spirit comes upon you! And you will tell about me in Jerusalem, as well as in all Judea and Samaria and as far as the ends of the earth."

9-11 After he had said this, and while they were actually watching, he was taken up. A cloud took him from their sight! *10* They were looking intently towards the sky as he went up, and suddenly two men were standing beside them in white clothes! *11* They said, "You Galileans,[3] why are you standing there looking up at the sky? This Jesus who was taken away from you to the sky, is going to come down in the same way that you saw him go up!"

12-14 Then they went back to Jerusalem from the mountain called Olive Grove, which is close to Jerusalem, just over a mile away.[4] *13* After they arrived, they went up into the upper room[5] where they were remaining in prayer:[1] Peter,

---

κράτιστος, *kratistos*, "honorable", usually used of an official. See note on Luke 1:3.

[1] τεκμήριον, *tekmerion*, "proof", properly of an argumentative kind, and one which is such that all doubt is removed. See Aris. *Rhet.* i.2. The proofs included Jesus speaking, walking and eating with the disciples several times after his resurrection, and demonstrating the proofs of the nails in his hands and feet to Thomas and others. The verb τεκμαίρομαι, *tekmairomai*, does not occur in the N.T., but occurs in a similar sense in a 1st century inscription *IG* 2.255 (Thessalonike).

[2] The preposition διά, *dia*, indicates that Jesus appeared from time to time within the period of forty days.

[3] ἄνδρες Γαλιλαῖοι, *andres Galilaioi*, "Galileans" not "men of Galilee". The Greeks commonly put the word ἄνδρες, *andres*, with a place name to indicate the inhabitants of that place. It had nothing to do with the male gender, and the word ἄνδρες, *andres*, should not be translated in the expression.

[4] Literally, a Sabbath day's journey, the journey a Jew was allowed to take on the Sabbath, which was 2,000 yards (1800 metres). The Rabbis arrived at this measure by a calculation based on Exodus 16:29.

[5] Note the use of definite article "the" rather than just "an" upper room. This suggests that this was not just any upper room. J. Rawson Lumby notes that the use of the definite article points to the room having been used previously for the Last Supper (Mark 14:15; Luke 12:12) and that although the noun is different, the disciples, being strangers in Jerusalem and finding a suitable room, would hardly be likely to look for another, and that the Passover room would be sanctified by what had happened at the Last Supper. *The Acts of the Apostles*, (Cambridge: C.U.P., 1904), p. 86. He notes that the use of καταμένοντες, *katamenontes*, in the next clause adds weight to this (see next note).

James, John and Andrew, Philip and Thomas, Bartholomew and Matthew, James (Alphaeus's son) and Simon the Zealot, and Judas the son of James. *14* They all persisted stubbornly in united prayer[2] with some women and Mary (Jesus' mother) and his siblings.[3]

15-20 In those days Peter stood up among the fellow believers[4] and said – there were about 120 persons[5] in all – *16* "You people, fellow believers, this scripture had to be fulfilled: the Holy Spirit spoke about Judas through David's mouth. Now Judas guided the people who arrested Jesus. *17* He was counted as one of us and was voted into this ministry.[6] *18* So when Judas bought a piece of land with the payment for his wrongdoing, he fell right over headlong in it! He burst open in the middle and out poured all his guts! *19* Everyone who lived in Jerusalem got to hear about it, so they call that piece of land (in their own language), 'Akeldama'. This means 'Field of Blood', *20* because the Scriptures say in the Book of Psalms, 'His living quarters must be made wasteland! No one will live there!' and 'Let someone else get his office!'

21-22 "So then, we have to choose someone else to take his place. It must be one of the men who was with us the whole time that the Lord Jesus went in and out among us – *22* starting from the baptism of John until the day when Jesus was taken from us. One of these men will become a witness of his resurrection, along with us."

23-26 So they nominated two, Joseph who was also known as Barnabas - his surname was Justus[7] - and Matthias. *24* And they prayed, "Lord, you know everyone's heart. Please show clearly which of these two men you have chosen *25* to take part in this ministry mission,[8] the same ministry mission which Judas renounced[9] to depart this life." *26* They voted,[1] and Matthias was chosen. He was added to the eleven apostles.

---

[1] καταμένοντες, *katamenontes*, participle of καταμένω, *katameno*, "to remain fixed", "to continue in a state", which here is the state of prayer. Periphrastic imperfect, particularly common in Luke.

[2] The use of the definite article, "the (prayer)" suggests that they were not persisting obstinately in just any old kind of prayer: they were engaged in a particular type of prayer.

[3] Jesus' brothers are named in Matthew 13:55 and Mark 6:3 as James, Joses (or Joseph), Simon and Judas. They are mentioned here as not included in the Eleven, which suggests that James the son of Alphaeus, and James the Lord's brother were different people. Note that the brothers of Jesus have changed their minds since John 7:5, where we are told that they did not believe Jesus.

[4] ἀδελφοί, *adelphoi*. See note on Matt. 5:22.

[5] ὄνομα, *onoma*, "names" synecdoche for "persons". Initially considered by some to be a Semitism until it was discovered in inscriptions, some pagan, of the time. See *I.Eph.* II.555 (II), a verse graffito, "Greetings, Eulalios, a person (ὄνομα, *onoma*) revered by the gods." See also inscription from sarcophagus of Imperial period, *I.Tyre*, 1.29B, "the 20 corpses of the people ("names" τῶν ονμάτων, *ton onomaton*)".

[6] For διακονία, *diakonia*, see Thuc. 1.133, Plato, *Rep.* 371 C, Dem. 296.29, Polyb. 15. 25, 4. *Diakonia* is the act of the *diakonos*. See note on Rom. 16:1.

[7] Joseph τὸν καλούμενον, *ton kaloumenon*, Barsabbas. A double by-name. The second name was originally a patronymic, but has developed into a name in itself.

[8] ἀποστολή, *apostle*, mission (in the sense of being sent out), despatch. See *P.Tebt* 1.112; *P.Oxy* IV.736. Elsewhere in N.T. only in Rom. 1:5, 1 Cor. 9:2; Gal. 2:8.

[9] παραβαίνω, *parabaino*, to turn one's back, to deviate, to renounce, not simply "go". See *P.Oxy* III.526 (of breaking one's word). The word is

Ch.2:1-4 And when the Day of Pentecost[2] was fully reached,[3] they were all added together. *2* Suddenly from heaven[4] came a roaring noise like a violent wind rushing along[5] and it filled the whole house where they were sitting. *3* Tongues which were like fire appeared right in front of their eyes! These distributed themselves and one sat on each of them. *4* And they were all filled with the Holy Spirit and began to speak with other supernaturally given languages as the Spirit began to act on them to make them speak.[6]

5-11 There were Jews living in Jerusalem: godly ladies and gentlemen[7] from all over the place,[8] *6* and when this sound was heard, a crowd gathered. They were confused, because each person heard them speak in their own language. *7* They were all being driven out of their minds! They were wondering, "Aren't all these people who are speaking, Galileans? *8* So why is it that each of them hears them in their own native language? *9* Parthians and Medes and Elamites, those who live in Mesopotamia, Judea and Cappadocia, Pontius and Asia, *10* Phrygia and Pamphylia, Egypt and the parts of Libya adjoining Cyrene, visitors from Rome both Jews and people converted to Judaism, *11* Cretans and Arabs - we all hear them speaking about the mighty words of God in our own languages!"

12-13 They were all shocked and completely at a loss, and to each other, "What does it all mean?"

---

commonly found in wills in the meaning to renounce, to disobey the conditions of the will.

[1] Voting was a provision of the Law (Leviticus 16:8). After the Holy Spirit was poured out, there is no more mention of voting.

[2] Pentecost was the second of the main Jewish feasts, the first being the Passover and the last being the Feast of Tabernacles. The name is derived from πεντεκοστός, *pentekostos*, "fiftieth" as it was kept the fiftieth day after the Passover Sabbath. It is also called the Feast of Harvest (Ex. 13:16) and the Feast of Weeks (Ex. 24:22; Deut. 16:9-10) as it was 7 weeks after Passover. The offering at Pentecost was a thank offering: the first 2 loaves made from the first portion of the wheat harvest of the year.

[3] συμπλήρωσις, *sumplerosis*, here the infinitive for the noun, as in Luke 8:23. In Luke the word means a boat being swamped by water, here it is of time. The sense is usually one of completion. In *P.Mich.* 649.144 (Aphrodite, VI), the people have received an amount of money being payment in full: "in fulfilment of the price" εἰς συμπλήρωσιν τῆς τιμῆς, *eis sumplerosin tes times*. See also *P.Mich* 666.32 (Aphrodite, VI) where it is used in the same sense. The tenant agrees to make payments "for the completion of the rent": ὑπὲρ τῆς συμπληρώσεως τοῦ φόρου, *huper tes sumpleroseos tou phorou*. The noun is more frequent than the verb in the papyri.

[4] Equally, "from the sky".

[5] φερομένης, *pheromenes*, aorist passive participle of φέρω, *phero*. Literally: "rushing along", "sweeping", referring to the sweeping away of waves or the course of the wind. See 2 Pet. 1:17 for the verb in the aorist passive participle.

[6] That is the Holy Spirit gave them utterance. One of the meanings for ἀποφθέγγομαι *apotheggomai*, is "to ring out". It is used for the sound made by a tin when the tin is hit. The sense is that the tin could not make the noise unless something acted upon it. The other meaning is of "inspired" persons, such as a prophet or pagan oracle. The verb was used when a Greek god was said to speak through a pagan oracle (prophet). The verb always carries the idea that someone else is behind the speaker's words.

[7] ἄνδρες, *andres*, implying respect, "Ladies and gentlemen".

[8] "From every nation under the sky", Greek hyperbole meaning from quite a lot of places. The same as the English expression, "They came from everywhere" which does not literally mean everywhere.

13 Others poked fun and said, "They're drunk on sweet new wine!"

14-21 Peter stood up with the Eleven, raised his voice and uttered the divinely inspired words[1] to them, "Judeans and all who live in Jerusalem, know this! Pay attention to my words! *15* These people aren't drunk, like you think! It's only nine o'clock in the morning! *16* This is that which was spoken about through the prophet Joel, *17* 'And it will come to pass in the last days, says God, that I will pour out my Spirit on all flesh, and your sons and your daughters will prophesy, and your young men will see visions, and your old men will dream dreams. *18* And indeed on my male slave servants and my female slave servants in those days I will pour out my Spirit, and they will prophesy. *19* And I will give wonders in the sky above and miraculous signs upon the earth below, blood and fire and streams of smoke; *20* 'The sun will be turned into darkness and the moon into blood, before the coming of the mighty[2] appearance of the Day of the Lord. *21* And it will turn out that whoever calls on the Name of the Lord will be saved.'

22-23 Israelites,[3] hear these facts! God publicly demonstrated about the man Jesus of Nazareth by powers and wonders and miraculous signs. God did these through Jesus among you all, as you yourselves are also well aware! *23* You crucified and destroyed this person by making use of lawless people: this person who was handed over to you by God's prearranged definite plan.

24-28 "God raised him up, after he destroyed the bonds of death. It was not possible for Jesus to be held in death's power. *25* This is what David says about Jesus: 'I see the Lord in front of my face all the time, because he is at my right hand so that I won't be shaken. *26* So my heart was happy, and my speech was full of joy, and more than that, my body will pitch its tent in hope, *27* because you will not leave my soul in the lurch in Hades, nor will you allow your Sacred One to rot and decay. *28* You have made known to me the pathways of life, you will fill me full of joy in your presence.'

29-31 "Fellow believers, let me speak freely and openly to you: the patriarch David wasn't talking about himself here – he's dead and buried, and his tomb is among us until this very day! *30* So then as he was a prophet from the beginning, and he knew that God had promised him that he would set one of his descendants on the throne, *31* he foresaw this. He spoke about the resurrection of the Anointed One. He said that his soul would not be left in Hades, nor would his body rot and decay."

32-36 "This was Jesus. God has raised him up, and we're all witnesses to it. So then as *33* he is in the highest place at the right hand of God, the Father gave him what he had promised, the Holy Spirit, to pour out on us. And he began pouring out the Holy Spirit. The pouring out of the Holy Spirit is what you now see and hear. *34* So David wasn't the one who went up to the heavenly places. David himself says, 'The Lord said to my master, Sit at my right hand, *35* until I make your enemies a footstool for your feet.' *36* Therefore let the whole

---

[1] See note on verse 4, above. ἀποφθέγγομαι, *apophtheggomai*, again. The Holy Spirit acted upon Peter and gave him utterance.

[2] ἐπιφανής, *epiphany*, occurs only here in the N.T., and is a quotation from LXX of Joel 3:4. The term is used of Hellenistic monarchs. It is used of the Roman emperor in *P.Oxy.* 12.1425.2 (318); of Julius Caesar in *I.Eph.* II.251; of Augustus in *I.Eph.* II.252; of Nerva in *I.Eph.* II. 265; of the emperor Hadrian in *I.Eph.* II.267, VII, 1.3410; of the Tetrarchs in *I.Eph.* VII, 2.3603, 3604.

[3] υἱός, *huios*, with a noun refers to a member of a class of people, and should not be translated as "son/child of." With a place name, it indicates inhabitants of that place. The *Benai Israel*, translated in the KJV as "children/sons of Israel" actually means "members of the class of people called Israel" and should be translated as "Israelites". The expression is also Greek, and found as early as Homer.

house of Israel know for sure that God has made this Jesus, the one you crucified, both Lord and the Anointed One!"

37-40 When they heard this, they were cut to the heart. They said to Peter and the rest of the apostles, 'Fellow believers, what should we do?'

38 Peter said to them, "Change your minds! Each one of you must be baptized in the Name of Jesus the Anointed One to cancel your sins, and you will take hold of the gift of the Holy Spirit. *39* The promise is for you and your children and to all who are a long way off, every single one that the Lord our God invites."

40 With many, many more words he gave evidence, and encouraged them. He said, "Be rescued and preserved from this crooked group of people!"

41-43 So then those who accepted his account were baptized and on that day about three thousand people[1] were added to them. *42* They continued faithfully in the apostles' teaching and partnership,[2] in the breaking of bread and in prayers. *43* Fear came upon every person, and the apostles did lots of wonders as well as miraculous signs.

44-47 All who believed were together and had everything in common *45* and kept selling all their possessions and goods. They were distributing the proceeds to anyone among all the people who had need of it. *46* Daily they continued faithfully and in unity in the temple. They broke bread house by house. They shared their food most joyfully and with a generous heart. *47* They praised God and had favor with everyone. And each day the Lord added more people who had become saved to their number.

Speeches in Acts.

Luke used a literary device when dealing with speeches. As he did not reproduce the whole speech, he says the speaker "began to say" (as in Luke 4:16) or says that the speaker had a lot more to say (as in Acts 2:40). In some cases the speeches are interrupted. In this way Luke is able to avoid retelling the whole speech.

Direct speech comprises around 25% of Acts. In fact, there are ten lengthy speeches in Acts. Bear in mind that these are abridged by Luke.

2:14-40. Peter to the Jews at Pentecost. (Jerusalem)
3:12-26. Peter to the Jews after healing a crippled man. (Jerusalem)
7:2-53. Stephen on trial before the Sanhedrin.
10:34-43. Peter to the Roman Cornelius. (Caesarea)
13:16-41. Paul in the synagogue. (Antioch by Pisidia)
17:22-31. Paul to the council of the Areopagos. (Athens)
20:18-35. Paul Christian elders from Ephesos. (Miletos)
22:3-21. Paul speaking in Hebrew to a hostile crowd. (Jerusalem)
24:2-21. Tertullus putting the Jewish leaders' case against Paul to Felix. (Caesarea)

---

[1] ψυχαί, *psychai*, "souls", synecdoche for "people".

[2] κοινωνία, *koinonia*, "partnership", cf. Woodhouse, *op.cit.*, p. 315. (Note κοινωνός, *koinonos*, "partner".) Horsley states, "The families of Zebedee and Jonah help each other as the need arises, and to that extent may be considered μέτοχοι, *metokhoi* (Lk. 5.7); cf. κοινωνοί, *koinonoi*, in vs. 10." *NDIEC* 5.102. A text detailing a family feud has γαμοῦ κοινωνίαn *gamou koinonian*, "marriage partnership", cf. J.W.B. Barns, *Studia Patristica* 1. *Papers Presented to the Second International Conference on Patristic Studies held at Christ Assembly*, Oxford, 1955. Part 1, ed. K. Aland/F.L. Cross (*Texte und Unterschungen* 63; Berlin, 1957) 3-9, *l*.5. F. Hauck, *Koinos, TDNT* 3 (1965) 798, states that κοινωνός, *koinonos*, is a "technical term for a business partner or associate". See also *P.Oxy.* 3270.5, 8, in which Aurelius Lucius "and his partners" make an offer for the lease of a fishing area to Aurelius Sarapion "and his partners".

Luke does not use his own style and language in the direct speeches he quotes. The speeches of Paul, for example, are very much written in Paul's own style. Of course, this is more noticeable when reading the original Greek.

Ch.3:1-6 Peter and John were going up to the temple at the hour of prayer, 3 p.m. *2* And a certain man, crippled from birth, was being carried in. Now every day, they'd laid this person at the temple gate which they call "Beautiful Gate", to beg money from the people who were going into the temple. *3* When he saw Peter and John about to go into the temple, he asked them for money. *4* Peter, looking intently at him, with John, said, "Look at us!"

5 And he gave them his attention, because he expected to get something from them. *6* Peter said, "Silver and gold don't belong to me, but I will give you this - I'll give you what does belong to me! In the Name of Jesus the Anointed One of Nazareth get up and walk!"

7-10 And he pulled him up to his feet by his right hand. Immediately his feet and ankle bones were made firm, *8* and he jumped up! Then he stood up and walked and went into the temple with them, walking and leaping and praising God! *9* And the whole crowd saw him walking and praising God. *10* They realized that he was the one who had been sitting begging for money at the Gate Beautiful of the temple! They were full of shock and complete amazement at what had happened to him!

11-18 As he was clutching onto Peter and John, the whole crowd ran together up to them in the roofed colonnade which is called Solomon's, shocked beyond measure. *12* When Peter saw this, he said to the whole crowd, "Israelites, why are you so surprised at this? Why are you staring at us! It's not as if we made this person walk by our own power or holiness! *13* The God of Abraham and of Isaac and of Jacob honored his own Son Jesus. Yes, Jesus, who you handed over and denied to Pilate's face, after he had decided to release him! *14* You denied the Holy and Just One and begged for a murderer to be granted to you! *15* You killed the Originator of Life whom God raised from among the dead – and we're witnesses to this! *16* And by faith in his Name this person here – you know this person, you can see him right here! – faith in his Name has made him strong, by the faith which comes through him. He has given him this complete health[1] right in front of all of you! *17* And as it is, fellow believers, I know that you acted in ignorance, and so did your rulers. *18* The Anointed One in fact had to go through all these things. God had already foretold all this through all the prophets' mouths, and he has fulfilled it.

19-23 "So then change your minds and turn back to God so that your sins can be canceled, so that refreshing times will come from the Lord's presence, *20* and that God would send the Anointed One Jesus, who was already chosen for you. *21* Heaven must wait for the Anointed One Jesus until it's time for him to return. God has spoken about the time of the return by the mouths of all his sacred prophets since the beginning.

22 "Moses said, 'The Lord your God will raise up a prophet like me from among your fellow believers. You must listen to everything he says, no matter what he says to you. *23* And it will turn out that everyone who doesn't listen to the Prophet will be completely destroyed and cut off from the people.'

---

[1] ὁλοκληρία, *holoklepia*, "complete health in all its parts", only here in N.T. Several papyri examples are published. See *PSI* 7.831; also *I.Nikaia* II, 1.1131 (Calti/Sogut, III), a dedication to Zeus Soter by P. Postumius Philiskos "for the complete health in all its parts" of himself, his family and his patron.

24-26 "In fact every prophet who spoke, right from the time of Samuel onwards has also announced these days. *25* You are offspring of the prophets, and you are offspring of the covenant God made with your ancestors.[1] He said to Abraham, 'Because of your descendants, all the tribes of the earth will be in a state of happiness!' *26* When God raised up his Son Jesus, he first of all sent him to bless you, by turning each one of you away from your evil ways."

Ch.4:1-4 While Peter and John were speaking to the people, the priests, the captain of the temple, and the Sadducees opposed them. *2* They were very disturbed because Peter and John were teaching and preaching the resurrection of the dead by the authority of Jesus. *3* So they arrested them, and put them in custody until the next day, as it was already evening. *4* Many of the people who heard the Word believed, and the number of ladies and gentlemen[2] came to about 5,000.

5-7 It turned out that on the next day, the rulers, the elders and the record keepers collected together at Jerusalem. *6* Along with them were Annas the high priest, Caiaphas, John and Alexander, and every last person of the high priest's family. *7* They sat Peter and John down in front of them. Then they questioned them, "By whose power or authority have you done this?"

8-12 Then Peter, filled with the Holy Spirit, said to them, "Rulers of the people and elders! *9* Are we today being judged on the grounds that we did a good deed to a sick person, because of the way in which he was rescued and preserved? *10* Well then! Let it be known to you all and to all the people of Israel, that by the name of Jesus the Anointed One of Nazareth, who you crucified, who God raised from among the dead, by Jesus this person stands here in front of you restored to his original condition. *11* Jesus is 'the stone, which was treated with contempt by you builders, which has become the cornerstone.' *12* Salvation is by no one else but him! We must be saved by this Name, and by no other – there is no other name under heaven which has been given to people by which we can be saved!"

13-18 When they saw the confidence of Peter and John and grasped the fact that they were uneducated and untrained people,[3] they were amazed. They fully realized that they had been with Jesus. *14* And as they could see the person who had been healed standing with them, they couldn't contradict it. *15* But after they had ordered them to wait outside the council, they conferred with each other. *16* They said, "What are we going to do to these people? It's quite obvious to everyone who lives in Jerusalem that an obvious miraculous sign has been done through them. We can't deny it! *17* Let's threaten them severely so that it doesn't spread any further among the people, and from now on they won't speak to any other person about this Name."

---

[1] τοὺς πατέρας, *tous pateres*, accusative plural of οἱ πατέρες, *hoi pateres*, ancestors. Used in the papyri and inscriptions as "ancestors" of both genders. Homer uses it in the *Iliad* (for example, in D 405) for ancestors. Autenrieth's 1877 *Homeric Dictionary* (London: Duckworth, 1877) lists the meaning "ancestors" under the entry for *pater*. The Liddell-Scott lexicon also lists the meaning "ancestor" under its entry.

[2] τῶν ἀνδρῶν, *ton andron*, as a formal term of respect, "Ladies and gentlemen". This use is widespread through all Greek literature.

[3] This is the perception of the chief priests, Bible scholars and elders who were members of the intellectual elite. The words "uneducated and untrained" simply indicate that they were laypersons. The families of Peter and Andrew, and of John and James, were financially well off (thus suggesting literacy and education), as they owned boats and fishing equipment. The families were able to release 2 sons for a period of 3 years, yet the sons were able to have access to the boats during this time, and were easily able to return to fishing work immediately after Jesus' resurrection.

18-20 And they summoned them and ordered them not to utter a word about it or teach in the Name of Jesus. *19* But Peter and John answered them, "Whether it's right in the sight of God to listen to you more than we listen to God, decide what you like! *20* As for us, we're not able to avoid speaking about the things which we saw and heard!"

21-22 So after they had given them a further warning they let them go. They couldn't find any way to punish them, because the people were praising God for what had happened. *22* In fact, the person on whom this miraculous sign of healing had been performed was over 40 years old.

23-26 When Peter and John had been released, they went back to their own company and reported everything that the chief priests and elders had said to them. *24* So when they'd heard it, they raised their voices to God in unity and said, "Master, it was you who made the sky and earth and the sea and everything in them. *25* It was you who said by the Holy Spirit, through our ancestor,[1] your servant David: 'Why were the nations insolent? Why did the people plan futile schemes? *26* The kings of the earth took their stand and the rulers joined forces for the very same purpose against the Lord and his Anointed One.'

27-30 "It was true all right that both Herod[2] and Pontius Pilate[3] joined forces with the non-Jews and the people of Israel to plot against your holy Son Jesus, whom you anointed. *28* They did whatever your power and your plan decided beforehand. *29* And about what's happening now, Lord – look at their threats! And grant to your slave servants that they will speak out your Word with the right of freedom of speech, and boldly, openly in public. *30* Also that they will use your power to heal, and also that miraculous signs and wonders will be done through the Name of your holy child Jesus."

31 After they put earnest requests, the place where they were assembled was shaken strongly, and they were all filled with the Holy Spirit and kept speaking out the Word of God with the right of freedom of speech, speaking boldly and openly in public.[4]

Parresia.

Parresia was both the freedom to speak one's mind, and a privilege conferred on the first citizens of Athens. Speakers of *parresia* spoke the truth freely, boldly and openly precisely because they were good citizens, were well born, had a respectful relation to the city, to the law, and to truth. *Parresia* constitutes pure frankness in speaking, even to the extent of ignorant outspokenness. In the New

---

[1] τοῦ πατρός, *tou patros*, ancestor. See note on Acts 3:25.

[2] This Herod was Herod Antipas the son of Herod the Great and his wife Malthace, a Samaritan. He was tribal ruler of Galilee and Peraea. The Galatians were divided into 3 tribes, and each was divided up again into 4, making 12 sections, each ruled by a Tribal Ruler (a tetrarch). The government was in the hands of 12 tribal rulers, controlled by a senate of 300 men. After Herod the Great died in 4 BC, half his kingdom - Judea, Idumaea and Samaria - was given to Archelaus. The remainder was split in half. The territories of Galilee and Peraea were given to Herod Antipas, and the Trachonitis and Gaulanitis regions were given to Herod Phillip. Herod Antipas ruled Galilee until his exile in 39 AD. See Strabo, *Geography*, 12.3.37; Pliny the Elder, *Natural Histories*, 5.42.

[3] The sixth Roman procurator of Judea. A procurator was a personal agent of the Roman emperor, and such people governed smaller provinces (such as Judea).

[4] παρρησία, *parresia*. Usually rendered in Bible translations simply as "boldly", "plainly", openly" or "with confidence". Occurs in Mark 8:32; John 7:4, 13, 26; 10:24: 11:14, 54; 16:25, 29; 18:20; Acts 2:29; 4:13, 29, 31; 28:31; 2 Cor. 3:12; 7:4; Eph. 3:12; 6:19; Phil. 1:20; Col. 2:15; 1 Titus 3:13; Philem. 8; Heb. 3:6; 4:16; 10:19, 35; 1 John 2:28, 3:21; 4:17; 5:14.

Testament, *parresia* is used in its standard sense of speaking boldly, freely and openly, often in a public setting. It carries nuances which cannot be expressed easily in English translation.

Parresia expresses primarily a complete openness and freedom of speech. The person who uses *parresia* says everything on their mind: such a person does not hide anything, but opens their heart and mind completely to other people through their speech. The speaker gives a complete and exact account of what they have in mind. *Parresia* often encompasses a risk or potential danger for the speaker in telling the truth. For instance a teacher may tell the truth to the students, but this does not constitute *parresia*. However, when someone complains to a king about his rulership, then that person takes a risk (since the king may become angry, may punish them, may exile them or may kill them).The risk is not always a risk of life. When, for example, one sees a friend doing something wrong and risks incurring their anger by telling them they are wrong, the speaker is using *parresia*. In such a case, the speaker does not risk their life, but may hurt the other by their remarks and consequently the friendship may suffer for it. If a criminal is forced to confess their crime, this cannot be considered as *parresia*.

Parresia was an essential characteristic of Athenian democracy. It was a guideline for democracy as well as an ethical and personal attitude characteristic of the good citizen. Athenian democracy was defined as a constitution in which people enjoyed democracy, the equal right of speech, the equal participation of all citizens in the exercise of power and free speech. During the New Testament times the political meaning evolved, and became centred in the relationship between the sovereign and their advisers or members of the court.

32-35 The whole company of those who had become believers were united in heart and soul. Not one single person designated anything they owned as their own personal property. Anyone was able to use anything that the other person had. *33* And the apostles handed over testimony about the resurrection of the Lord Jesus in a very powerful way. They all had enormous favor. *34* Not one single person among them was needy, because everyone who was an owner of land or houses would sell them, and would bring the proceeds of the things that were sold *35* and put them at the apostles' feet. Then they would distribute them to each person according to that person's specific need.

36-37.Ch.5:1-2 Here's an example. There was a person from the tribe of Levi who came from the country of Cyprus. His name was Joseph, and the apostles also called him "Barnabas" (which, when translated, means Bringer of Encouragement). *37* Joseph had land and sold it, and he brought the sum of money and put it at the apostles' feet. *1* But there was a certain man named Ananias. *2* Along with his wife Sapphira, he sold a piece of property and kept back some of the proceeds. His wife was also in the know. He brought a part of it and put it at the apostles' feet.

3-7 But Peter said, "Ananias, why has Adversary filled your heart to lie to the Holy Spirit and keep back part of the price of land for yourself? *4* While you still had it, wasn't it your own? And after it was sold, wasn't it in your own control? Why have you plotted this thing in your heart? It's not people you've lied to – it's God!"

5 When he heard these words, Ananias fell down and dropped dead! Great fear came upon everyone who heard this! *6* And the young men stood up and wrapped him up, carried him out and buried him. *7* It turned out that about three hours later his wife came in. She didn't know what had happened.

8-11 Peter asked her, "Tell me, did you sell the land for such-and-such an amount?"

"Yes, that's right, for such-and-such an amount," she answered.

9 "Why is it that you have agreed between yourselves to harass[1] the Spirit of the Lord?" Peter said to her. "The feet of those who buried your husband are at the door, and they will carry you out!"

10 Immediately she fell down at his feet and dropped dead! The young men came in and found her dead. They carried her out and buried her next to her husband. *11* It turned out that great awe came upon the whole assembly and upon everyone who heard these things.

12-15 Many miraculous signs and wonders were done by the apostles among the people. They all used to meet in unity in the roofed colonnade of Solomon. *13* None of the rest dared join them, but the people spoke highly of them. *14* More believers than ever were added to the Lord, large numbers of both men and women. *15* In fact, they actually brought the sick out onto the main street and laid them on mattresses and stretchers so that at the very least, Peter's shadow might cast its shadow on some of them as they went past.

16-20 Also a crowd gathered from the cities round about Jerusalem. They brought sick people and those who were tormented by unclean spirits, and they were all healed. *17* The high priest and his friends – they were all Sadducees - were filled with jealousy! *18* They arrested the apostles and had them put in the state prison. *19* During the night a Messenger of the Lord opened the prison doors and brought them out. The Messenger said to them, *20* "On your way! Stand up in the temple and tell all the people these living words!"

21-23 When they heard that, they went into the temple about dawn and taught. But the high priest and his officials arrived and called a meeting of the High Council[2] together with all the elders of the Israelites. They sent to the prison to have them brought out. *22-23* But the assistants arrived and didn't find them in the prison! They came back and said, "We found the prison locked up very securely and the guards standing at the doors, but when we opened up we didn't find anyone inside!"

24-25 Now when they heard these facts, the temple general and the chief priest were at a complete loss and wondered where it was all going to end. *25* Someone arrived and said to them, "Hey! The men you put in prison are standing in the temple teaching the people!"

26-28 Then the general went out with the officers and brought them in. They did it without force because they were scared that the people would stone them otherwise. *27* When they'd brought them they stood them in front of the council. The high priest questioned them, *28* "Now didn't we expressly order you not to teach in this Name! And look, not only have you gone and filled Jerusalem with your doctrine but you are determined to hold us responsible for the blood of this person as well!"

29-32 But Peter and the apostles said, "We must obey God rather than people. *30* The God of our ancestors raised up Jesus whom you did away with by hanging him on a cross. *31* God has lifted him up to his own right side to be Prince and Savior, so that Israel can change their minds and have their sins canceled. *32* And we are witnesses to these matters and so is the Holy Spirit whom God has given to those who obey him."

33 When they heard this they were infuriated and wanted to murder them!

34-39 Then a certain person of the council stood up, a Pharisee by the name of Gamaliel. He was a respected expert in the Law, regarded with honor by all the people. He ordered them to send the apostles outside for a short time. *35* And he said to them, "Israelites, be careful what you intend to do to these people! *36* Now, some time ago Theudas rose up, claiming to be somebody. A number of men, about 4,000 of them, joined him. He was killed and all his

---

1   πειράζω, *peirazo*. See note on Matt. 4:1.
2   That is, the Sanhedrin.

followers were scattered and it all came to nothing. *37* After this person, Judas of Galilee rose up in the days of the census, and led a number of people in revolt after him. He was killed too, and all his followers were scattered. *38* And in this instance I am telling you to keep away from these people and let them go, because if this plan or this work is from people, it will break up, *39* but if it is from God, you won't be able to overthrow it! Otherwise you might find yourselves fighting against God!"

And so they were persuaded by him.

40-42 So when they had summoned the apostles, they beat them, and expressly ordered them not to speak in the Name of Jesus. *41* Then they let them go. Therefore they emerged from the presence of the High Council, rejoicing that they were considered worthy to be despised for the Name. *42* And they didn't stop teaching and announcing the Good News of Anointed One Jesus on a daily basis in the temple and in every house.

Ch.6:1-4 In those days when the disciples were increasing in numbers, the Greek speaking Jews started complaining against the Hebrew speaking Jews,[1] because their widows had been slighted in the daily distribution of food. *2* The Twelve summoned a full meeting of the disciples and said, "It's obviously not satisfactory that we should give up the Word of God to serve out meals! *3* Thus, fellow believers, choose from among you seven respected men, who are full of the Holy Spirit and wisdom. We will put them in charge of this matter, *4* but we'll devote ourselves to prayer and to the ministry of the Word."

5-7 This idea pleased the whole crowd and they chose Stephen, a man full of faith and the Holy Spirit, and Philip, Prochoros, Nicanor, Timon, Parmenas, and Nicolas, a convert to Judaism from Antioch. *6* They presented them to the apostles. After the apostles prayed, they laid hands on them. *7* And the Word of God spread, and the number of disciples multiplied hugely in Jerusalem, and many Jewish priests believed[2] the faith.

8-11 Stephen, who was full of favor and power, did great wonders and miraculous signs among the people. *9* Then one day certain people from those who belonged to a group called the "Synagogue of the Freedmen" (Cyrenians, Alexandrians, and those from Cilicia and Asia), started disputing with Stephen. *10* They weren't strong enough to stand against his wisdom, and against the Spirit by whom he spoke. *11* So they secretly put up some men to say, "We have heard him speaking blasphemous words against Moses and God."

12-15 This stirred up the people, as well as the elders and the Bible scholars. Then they suddenly jumped out at him, grabbed him, and took him to the High Council. *13* They set up false witnesses who said, "This person doesn't stop speaking words against this sacred place and the Law. *14* In fact, we have heard him say that Jesus of Nazareth will destroy the Temple and change the customs which Moses handed down to us."

15 At this point everyone sitting on the High Council stared hard at him, because his face became just like the face of a Messenger!

---

[1]   Often translated as "Hellenists". Horsley, *NDIEC* 5.22, notes of them, "The 'Hellenists' of Acts 6.1 are most plausibly seen as ethnically Jewish Christians whose primary language was Greek." Horsley (*loc.cit.*) also states, "After examination of the epigraphical and other archaeological evidence Meyers/Strange, *Archaeology, the Rabbis and Early Christianity*, conclude (90-91) that while Greek was first an urban language in Judea, '…it appears that sometime during the first century BCE Aramaic and Greek changed places as Greek spread into the countryside and as knowledge of Aramaic declined among the educated and among urban dwellers…Aramaic never died, though it suffered a strong decline in favor of Greek.'"

[2]   "Paid attention to". See note on Matt. 8:27.

Ch.7:1-3 Then the high priest said, "Is this the case?"

2 Stephen said, "Ladies and gentlemen,[1] fellow believers, ancestors, listen! The God of honor appeared to our ancestor Abraham when he was in Mesopotamia, before he settled in Haran. *3* God told him, 'Get out of your country, leave your relatives, come here to the land that I'll show you!'

4-7 "Then Abraham left the land of the Chaldeans and settled in Haran. He stayed there until his father died. After that, God moved him to this land you now live in. *5* But God didn't give him an inheritance in the land, not so much as to set his foot on it! But although Abraham didn't have a child, God promised that he would give the land to him and to his descendants. *6* "But God did say this, that his descendants would be strangers in a foreign land, where they would be enslaved and oppressed for 400 years. *7* 'And I will judge the nation that enslaves them,' God said, 'and after this they will come out and worship me in this place.'

8-10 "And God gave Abraham the covenant of circumcision. And so Isaac, Abraham's son, was circumcised on the eighth day. Isaac was the father of Jacob, and Jacob was the father of the twelve patriarchs. *9* As the patriarchs were jealous of Joseph, they sold him into Egypt. But God was with him *10* and rescued him from all his troubles. He gave him favor and wisdom in the eyes of Pharaoh, king of Egypt, so Pharaoh appointed him governor over Egypt and all his palace business.

11-16 "A severe troublesome famine came over the whole land of Egypt, and our ancestors couldn't find any provisions. *12* When Jacob heard that there was grain in Egypt, he sent out our ancestors the first time. *13* And the second time they went, Joseph's identity was revealed to his brothers, and Joseph's family was revealed to Pharaoh. *14* Joseph sent off an invitation to his father Jacob and all his relatives, seventy five people in all. *15* And Jacob went down to Egypt. He died there, and so did our ancestors. *16* Their remains were later removed to Shechem and laid in the tomb that Abraham bought for a sum of silver from the tribe of Hamor in Shechem.

17-22 "As the time drew near for God to fulfill his promise, the one he had covenanted with Abraham, the number of our people increased in Egypt. *18* But another king arose in Egypt, a person who did not know Joseph. *19* This person plotted to outwit our people, and oppressed our ancestors, to the point of abandoning their babies out in the open so that they would die. *20* At this time Moses was born, and he was charming in the highest degree. He was brought up in his parent's house for three months. *21* But when he was abandoned out in the open, Pharaoh's daughter adopted him and brought him up as her own son. *22* Moses was educated[2] in all the wisdom of the Egyptians, and his words and actions were powerful.

23-29 "Now when he was approaching the age of forty years, it arose in his heart to go up to visit his fellows, the Israelites. *24* When he saw one of them being ill treated, he defended and avenged the oppressed man by striking down the Egyptian. *25* He thought that his fellow countrypeople would have understood that God would rescue them by his power, but they didn't understand. *26* The next day he came upon two of them as they were fighting, and he tried to get them to come to terms. He said, 'Gentlemen, you are fellow countrypeople! Why are you harming each other?'

27 "But the person who was hurting his neighbor pushed him away, and said, 'Who made you the ruler and judge over us? *28* Surely you don't intend to kill me like you killed the Egyptian yesterday?' *29* "Because of this statement Moses fled and went to live in Midian, where his two sons were born.

---

[1] ἄνδρες, *andres*, a formal term of respect, "Ladies and gentlemen". This use is widespread through Greek literature.

[2] παιδεύω, *paideuo*, cognate verb of παιδεία, *paidea*. See note on Eph. 6:4.

30-34 "And forty years later, in the desert of Mount Sinai, a Messenger appeared to him in the flame of a burning bush. *31* When Moses saw it, he was shocked at the sight. When he went closer to see what it actually was, the voice of the Lord came to him, *32* 'I am the God of your ancestors, the God of Abraham and Isaac, and Jacob.' And Moses was shaking and didn't dare look. *33* "Then the Lord said to him, 'Untie your sandals from your feet! The place you are standing on is sacred ground! *34* I have definitely seen the ill treatment of my people in Egypt and I have heard their groaning. I have come down to rescue them! Come on now, I'm going to send you out to Egypt!'"

35-37 "This very Moses whom they rejected by saying, 'Who made you ruler and judge?' is the very one God sent to be a ruler and deliverer through the Messenger who appeared to him in the bush. *36* He led them out of Egypt, after he had done wonders and miraculous signs in the land of Egypt, and in the Red Sea, and in the desert for forty years. *37* This is that same Moses who said to the Israelites, 'God will raise a Prophet like me from among your countrypeople.'

38-39 "Moses is the one who, when they were assembled in the desert with our ancestors, spoke with the Messenger who spoke to him on Mount Sinai. Moses was the one who received the living utterances of God to give to us. *39* Our ancestors were not willing to listen to Moses and do as he said. They pushed him away and turned back to Egypt in their hearts.

40-41 "They said to Aaron, 'Make gods for us that will to go out ahead of us! As for Moses who brought us out of the land of Egypt, we don't have a clue what's happened to him!'

41 "So at that time they made a calf idol, and offered sacrifices to it! They had a party in honor of the thing that they'd made with their own hands!

42-43 "God turned away from them. He handed them over to serve the sky company with prayers and sacrifices, as it stands written in the book of the Prophets, 'Did you offer me slaughtered animals and sacrifices during the forty years in the wilderness, house of Israel? *43* You took up the tents of Molech and the star of your god Remphan, the replicas[1] which you made so that you worship them, and I will exile you a long way beyond Babylon.'"

44-47 "Our ancestors had the Ark of the Testimony in the desert. God instructed Moses to make it according to the pattern[2] that he had seen. *45* Our ancestors (who had received it in the next generation) brought it when they, with Joshua, took possession of the land of the nations, which God drove out in front of them. It was there until David's time. *46* David found favor with God and prayed to find a dwelling place for the God of Jacob. *47* Solomon built him a house.

48-50 "However, the Most High does not live in temples made with hands, as the prophet says, *49* 'Heaven is my throne and earth is my footstool. What kind of house will you build for me? says the Lord, Or what is the place of my rest? *50* Surely my hand made all these things!'

51-53 "You stubborn lot, your minds and hearing are uncircumcised! You always resist the Holy Spirit. This is what your ancestors did, and you are doing exactly the same thing! *52* Was there even one single prophet whom your ancestors didn't prosecute? And your ancestors killed the prophets who foretold the coming of the Just One – and now you have become his betrayers and murderers! *53* Yes, you, you who received the Law when the Messengers established it! And you haven't kept the Law!'"

---

[1]   τύπος, *tupos*. The replicas are idols of pagan gods. The term always refers to replication in some form or other, such as a seal impression, an image, an outline. Copies of letters described by this term were copied verbatim and were not an approximation. See *P.Coll.Youtie* 66. Occurs in the following verse as "patterns".

[2]   The same word as in verse 23, τύπος, *tupos*, which there is "replicas".

54-56 When they heard this they were absolutely infuriated, and ground their teeth in rage. *55* Stephen, as he was full of the Holy Spirit, looked intently into Heaven and saw God's glory, and Jesus standing at God's right side. *56* He said, "I see the heavenly places[1] opened and the Human Being standing at God's right side!"

57-60.Ch.8:1-2 They shouted out with loud voices, covered their ears, and rushed at him in unity. *58* They threw him out of the city and stoned him. The witnesses put their coats down at the feet of a young man[2] named Saul. *59* They stoned Stephen as he was calling upon the Lord, saying, "Lord Jesus, receive my spirit!"

60 He fell on his knees and shouted loudly, "Lord, don't charge them with this sin!" And when he had said this, he fell asleep. *1* Saul was in entire agreement with his killing. On that day a great persecution arose against the assembly in Jerusalem, and all of them except the apostles were scattered down through the territories of Judea and Samaria. *2* Godly men carried Stephen away for burial with loud weeping and mourning over him.

3 Saul began to destroy the assembly. He went house to house, and dragged off men and women and threw them in prison.

4-8 So then those who were scattered went everywhere announcing the Good News of the Word, *5* but Philip went down to the city of Samaria and proclaimed the Anointed One to them. *6* The crowds in unity listened eagerly to what Philip said, when they heard and saw the miraculous signs that he did. *7* There were many instances of unclean spirits coming out of people (people who'd had the unclean spirits in them) and crying out with a loud shout as they went. Also, many people who were paralyzed and crippled were healed. *8* There was a great deal of happiness in that city.

9-10 There was a certain man by the name of Simon, who had previously practiced the magic arts of the Official Spiritual Advisers[3] in the city and astonished the nation of Samaria. *10* The Samarians said he was quite an important person, and every last one of them, from the least important to the most important, thought he was awesome and took notice of what he said. They said, "This person is the divine power which is called the Mighty Power!"

11-13 And the reason they thought he was awesome and took notice of what he said was because he had astonished them with his magic arts[4] for a long time. *12* But when they believed Philip when he announced the Good News about God's Realm, and the name of Jesus the Anointed One, both men and women were baptized. *13* And even Simon himself believed, and when he was baptized he continued to stay beside Philip. He was beside himself with amazement, as he saw both the miraculous signs and also the great deeds of power that were done.

14-16 When the apostles who were at Jerusalem heard that Samaria had taken hold of God's Word, they sent out Peter and John to join them. *15* When Peter and John had come down, they prayed about the Samaritans, that they would take hold of the Holy Spirit. *16* For as yet the Holy Spirit had not fallen on any of

---

[1]   Equally, "I see the skies opened."

[2]   The Greeks applied the term "young man" to a man up to the age of forty-five. MM *s.v.* See also Josephus, *Ant*, 18, 6. 7.

[3]   Here Simon is described as a Magos, μάγος, *magos*, one who practises magic arts, usually an Official Spiritual Advisor. Most versions translate the same word as "wise men" when it refers to those who took the gifts of gold, frankincense and myrrh to the young Jesus. The translators of the LXX translate μάγος, *magos*, as "astrologer".

[4]   μαγεία, *mageia*, "magic arts", occurs only here in the N.T.

them, but they had only made a beginning,[1] having been baptized in the Name of the Lord Jesus.

17-19 Then they kept laying hands on them and they kept taking hold of the Holy Spirit. *18* When Simon saw that through the laying on of the apostles' hands the Holy Spirit was given, he offered them money. *19* He said, "Give me this authority so that anyone I lay hands on will receive the Holy Spirit."

20-23 Peter said to him, "May your money perish with you! You thought that God's free gift could be purchased with silver! *21* You have no share nor part in this Word, as your heart isn't right in God's sight! *22* So change your mind, turn away from your wickedness, and pray to the Lord! Pray that perhaps he will forgive you for your intentions! *23* I can see that you're poisoned by bitterness and bound by wrongdoing!"

24-25 Simon answered, "Please put earnest requests to the Lord on my behalf so that none of the things you mentioned will happen to me!" *25* So then after they had testified and spoken the Word of the Lord they returned to Jerusalem, announcing the Good News in many villages of the Samaritans.

26-28 A Messenger of the Lord said to Philip, "Get up and go out towards the south on the road which goes down from Jerusalem to Gaza." (It is a desert road.)

27 He got up and went on his way. And there was an Ethiopian, a High Court Official[2] who had great power under the Kandake (Queen) of Ethiopia. In fact, he was in charge of her whole treasury. He had come to Jerusalem to worship, *28* and he was on his way back. He was sitting in the chariot, reading Isaiah the prophet aloud.

29-31 Then the Spirit said to Philip, "Overtake this chariot and join him!"

30 Philip ran up to him and heard him reading the prophet Isaiah, and said, "Do you understand what you're reading?"

31 And he said, "Well how can I, unless someone guides me!" and he urged Philip to get up and sit with him.

32-33 The place in the Scripture which he read was this: "He was led as a sheep to the slaughter, and in the same way that a lamb before the shearer is silent, he did not open his mouth. *33* In his low state his justice was taken away; and who can tell the full story of his descendants? Because his life is taken from the earth."

34-36 The High Court Official answered Philip, "Please tell me, who is the prophet talking about: himself or someone else?"

35 Philip opened his mouth, and beginning at this Scripture, announced the Good News of Jesus to him. *36* As they traveled along the road, they came to some water, and the High Court Official said, "Look, here's water! What's to stop me being baptized?"[3]

38-40 So he commanded the chariot to stand still. Both Philip and the High Court Official went down into the water, and he baptized him. *39* When they came up out of the water, the Spirit of the Lord seized Philip and carried him away, and the High Court Official never saw him again! He went off on his way rejoicing.

40 Philip found himself at Azotus! He passed through there, and announced the Good News in all the cities until he reached Caesarea.

---

[1] ὑπάρχω, *huparkho*, "to make a beginning". Some state that it is the equivalent of the verb 'to be". Both are possible.

[2] εὐνοῦχος, *eunoukhos*, often translated as "eunuch" but was actually a high court official. *NDIEC* 3:41 notes "court chamberlain (Acts 8.27,34,36,38,39)." See also a late 1st c./early 2nd c. coffin inscription where the term is applied to a married woman, *Mnem.* 31.418-20.

[3] Verse 37 is omitted as it is not original. It is a Western addition, and the evidence suggests it was inserted to add a confession of faith to the original passage, for theological reasons.

Caesarea.

Caesarea, which had the official name "Caesarea-by-the-sea" (*Caesarea Maritima*), was a most prominent Roman city. Tacitus described it as "the chief city of the province". (*Histories* 2, 78.) It was the usual residence of the governor, and the greater part of the Roman garrison was stationed there.

Caesarea was a new town. It occupied an old trading post called Strato's Tower, which had been founded in the 4th c. B.C. Strato had been a ruler of Sidon. Around the end of the 1st c. B.C. the emperor Augustus allocated the position to Herod the Great, and Herod settled on the old Strato's Tower. No doubt the founding of a new city appealed to Herod's personality. As well as the harbor, he built a beautiful palace and public buildings.

Ch.9:1-2 Saul, still breathing threats and murder against the disciples of the Lord, went to the high priest *2* and petitioned him to give him letters to the synagogues of Damascus. This was so that if he found any who were of the Way, whether men or women, he could bring them as prisoners to Jerusalem.
3-6 As he traveled he came close to Damascus. Suddenly there was a flash all around him like lightning from the sky! *4* He fell to the ground and heard a voice saying to him, "Saul, Saul, why are you persecuting me?"

5 And he said, "Who are you, Lord?"

He said, "I am Jesus, the One you're persecuting! *6* Get up and go into the city, and you will be told what you must do!"
7-9 The men who were traveling with him stood there speechless, as they heard a voice but didn't see anyone! *8* But Saul got up from the ground, and when he opened his eyes he couldn't see anyone. They led him by the hand and brought him to Damascus. *9* For three days he couldn't see, and he didn't eat or drink.
10-12 Now there was a certain disciple at Damascus by the name of Ananias, and the Lord said to him in a vision, "Ananias!"

"Here I am, Lord!" he said.

11 The Lord said to him, "Get up! Go without delay to the street called Straight,[1] and ask at the house of Judas for the one called Saul of Tarsus. He is praying at this very moment! *12* In a vision he has seen a man named Ananias come in and lay his hands on him to restore his sight."
13-16 Ananias answered, "Lord, I've heard about this man from lots of people! I've heard how much harm he's done to your people devoted to God in Jerusalem! *14* And in fact he's here with the authority from the chief priests to imprison everyone who calls on your Name!"

15 But the Lord said to him, "Off you go! This person is a chosen instrument of mine to carry my Name in front of nations, kings, and the Israelites. *16* I will show him how many things he must experience on behalf of my Name."
17-22 And so Ananias went away and entered the house. He laid his hands on him and said, "Brother Saul, the Lord Jesus, who appeared to you on the road, has sent me so that you can regain your sight and be filled with the Holy Spirit."

18 And immediately something like scales fell from his eyes, and he regained his sight at once, and got up and was baptized. *19* He felt strengthened after eating food. After this happened he spent several days with the disciples in Damascus. *20* Immediately Saul announced the Good News that Jesus is the Son of God in the synagogues. *21* Everyone who heard this was completely beside themselves with amazement! They said, "Isn't he the one who

---

[1] This major road, the main east-west street in Damascus, can seen today. It is now known as the Suk Meihat Pasha.

devastated everyone who called on this Name in Jerusalem, and imprisoned them and took them to the chief priest?"

22 But Saul's power increased more and more, confounding the Jews who lived in Damascus, by demonstrating that Jesus is the Anointed One.

Damascus.

Damascus presently has a population of 12 million, and lays claim to being oldest continuously inhabited city in the world, vying only with Aleppo for the distinction. Damascus is in south western Syria. It is about 190 miles north east of Jerusalem and 60 miles east of the Mediterranean port of Sidon. As with most great cities, it owed its popularity to its position on a trade route. The water from the Barada River made settlement in Damascus possible. The Barada River is the "Abana" that Naaman, the Syrian general, told Elisha was so much better than the Jordan. Abraham's steward Eliezer came from Damascus. Egyptian records too mention the city. The records of Thutmosis III record "Damishqa" as a conquered city, and it appears later in the Armana letters of the 14th c. B.C.

Three centuries later Damascus was the capital of an Aramaen kingdom. In c. 732 BC it fell to the Assyrians, later fell to the Babylonians under Nebuchadnezzar, and even later fell to the Persians in 530 BC. After the death of Alexander the Great, Damascus was ruled by the dynasties of his generals. In 64 BC it fell to the Romans under Pompey. Damascus did very well under Roman rule, being subject to the building activities for which the Romans are renowned. In 636 AD it was captured yet again, following the success of Khalid Ibn Al-Wahid at the Battle of Yarmuk the previous year. In 1076 AD the Seljuk Turks took the city. The Crusaders were never able to conquer Damascus, although made a concerted attempt to do so in 1148 AD.

Three quarters of the old city of Damascus is still surrounded by Roman walls. The walls have been knocked down and rebuilt many times over the last 2,000 years. The most preserved section is that between the Gate of Safety (*Bab as-Salama*) and the Thomas Gate (*Bab Touma*). Only the East Gate (*Bab as-Sharqi*) dates to Paul's time. *The Street Called Straight* (Acts 9:11), the main east-west street, can be seen today under the name "Suk Meihat Pasha". In Paul's time it was one hundred feet wide and lined by colonnades, providing passage for pedestrians as well as riders and horse drawn vehicles.

23-25 A long time later, the Jews plotted together to kill Saul, and Saul found out about their plot. *24* They kept a close watch on the gates for him night and day so they could kill him. *25* But the disciples took him one night and lowered him through an opening in the wall in a large person-sized mat basket.

26-27 After Saul arrived in Jerusalem he tried to join the disciples, but they were afraid of him and didn't believe that he was a disciple. *27* But Barnabas got hold of him and brought him to the apostles. Saul described to them how he had seen the Lord on the road, and that he had spoken to him, and how he had spoken with the right of freedom of speech, boldly and openly in public at Damascus by the power of Jesus' Name.

28-30 Saul now stayed with them going in and out of Jerusalem, *29* speaking with the right of freedom of speech, and speaking boldly and openly in public in the Name of the Lord. He disputed against the Greek-speaking Jews, and they attempted to kill him. *30* When the fellow believers found out, they brought him down to Caesarea and sent him out to Tarsus.

Tarsus.

Tarsus was situated in the fertile Cilician Plain of south-central Turkey, about ten miles from the Mediterranean coast. It was a large, wealthy and ancient city, situated on the crossroads of the main south-north and east-west trade routes. It is identified with the ancient kingdom of Kizzuwatna which controlled the Cilician plain.

In 833 BC, Tarsus was captured by the Assyrian king Shalmaneser III (833 BC), but a century later after rebelling was subsequently destroyed in the reign of Sennacherib. It was rebuilt and remained under Persian control until it was conquered by Alexander the Great in 333 BC. In a short space of time Tarsus was under the control of the Seleucid dynasty (312-65 BC), under whom they rebelled. In 64 BC, Tarsus became part of the Roman Empire and was named capital of the Roman province of Cilicia. Cicero, the famous orator, governed the city in 50 BC. In 41 BC, Cleopatra and Mark Antony met for the first time in Tarsus.

In Paul's time, Tarsus was a flourishing city with around half a million inhabitants and was both an educational and commercial centre. It was a centre for philosophy, particularly Stoicism, and its economy was based on agriculture and linen. Tarsus was considered to be one of the leading cities of the Eastern Roman Empire. It was a sea port in Paul's day, but now has silted up and is 9 miles (15 kilometres) from the sea. The big modern port is Mersin, on the Mediterranean. Modern Tarsus is still a prosperous city, and still beautifully lush thanks to the Cydnus River. Not much remains to be seen from Paul's time. St Paul's Gate/Cleopatra's Gate is likely to date after Paul's time, but was built from rubble from his city. Remains of a theatre have become a school playground. Tourists are shown St Paul's Well, and assured he drank from it and that it has healing properties! The city of Tarsus erected a plaque to Paul there in 1980. Remains of a Roman pavement lie nearby.

31 Therefore the whole assembly throughout the whole of Judea, Galilee and Samaria was left in peace. They were encouraged, and marched on with respect for the Lord. With the help of the Holy Spirit their numbers increased.

32-35 Now it came about in the course of his travels throughout the area that Peter also came down to the people devoted to God who lived in Lydda. *33* There he found a certain person by the name of Aeneas, who had been bed-ridden for eight years and was paralyzed. *34* Peter said to him, "Aeneas, Jesus the Anointed One instantly divinely heals you! Get up and see to your bed yourself!"

35 He got up immediately. Everyone who lived in Lydda and Sharon saw him, and in fact they turned to the Lord.

36-39 In Joppa there was a certain disciple by the name of Tabitha, which is translated Dorcas. This woman was full of good works and charitable acts. *37* It turned out that in those days she got sick and died. When they had washed her, they laid her in an upper room. *38* Since Lydda was there near Joppa, since the disciples heard that Peter was there, they sent two men to him. They begged him, "Don't waste any time getting through to us!"

39 Peter got up and went with them. When he arrived, they brought him to the upper room. All the widows stood next him crying, showing him the tunics and coats which Dorcas had made while she was with them.

40-43 Peter threw them all outside[1] then he knelt down and prayed. Then he turned to the body and said, "Tabitha, stand up!"

She opened her eyes, and when she saw Peter she sat up. *41* He gave her his hand and lifted her up, and when he had addressed the people devoted to God and the widows, he presented her alive! *42* The news spread all through Joppa, and many believed the Lord. *43* So it turned out that he stayed for some time in Joppa in the house of Simon, a tanner.

Ch.10:1-3 There was a certain gentleman in Caesarea by the name of Cornelius, a Roman officer in charge of 100 men in what was called the Italian Army Division of 600 Men.[2] *2* He was a godly person. He revered God, and so did all his household. He gave generously to the poor and made earnest requests

---

[1] ἐκβάλλω, *ekballo*, "threw them out". Quite a strong word. Not "put them out" or "sent them out".

[2] A centurion was in command of a sixth of a cohort.

of God constantly. *3* About 3 in the afternoon, he clearly saw a Messenger of God in a vision. The Messenger came in and said to him, "Cornelius!"

4-6 He stared at him, and getting really scared, he said, "What is it, sir?"

The Messenger said to him, "Your prayers and your gifts to the poor have gone up on record in God's presence. *5* Send men to Joppa at once! Send for Simon who's also known as Peter! *6* He's staying with Simon the tanner, whose house is by the sea."

7-8 When the Messenger who spoke to him had left, Cornelius called two of his household servants and a godly soldier who was attached to his service. *8* He told them everything that had happened and sent them off to Joppa.

9-16 The next day, as they went on their way and were approaching the city, Peter went up on the roof to pray, about midday.[1] *10* He became hungry and wanted to eat. While they were preparing the meal, he went into a displaced state[2] *11* and saw the sky opened and an object like a large sheet tied up at the four corners coming down, being lowered to the earth. *12* In it were all kinds of four-legged animals, reptiles of the earth and birds of the air. *13* A voice came to him, "Get up, Peter, kill and eat!"

14 But Peter said, "No way, Lord, because I've never eaten anything forbidden or unclean!"

15 A voice spoke to him again the second time, "What God has made clean you must not call forbidden!"

16 This happened three times, then immediately the object was taken up to the sky.

17-20 While Peter was quite at a loss and his head was spinning about the meaning of the vision he had seen, the men who had been sent from Cornelius asked for him at Simon's house and were actually standing at the gate! *18* They inquired whether Simon, also known as Peter, was staying here. *19* While Peter was thinking over the vision, the Spirit said to him, "Three men are looking for you! *20* Now get up, go down and go off with them. Do not discriminate, because I myself have sent them!"

21-22 Peter went down to the men and said, "I'm the one you're looking for; what's your reason for coming?"

22 They said, "Cornelius the Roman officer in charge of 100 men, a just man who fears God, and who has a good reputation among the whole nation of the Jews, was divinely instructed by a sacred Messenger to summon you to his house and to hear what you had to say."

23-27 So he invited them in to be his guests. On the next day he went with them, and certain fellow believers from Joppa accompanied him. *24* The next day they entered Caesarea. Cornelius was waiting for them. He had collected his relatives and close friends. *25* As Peter was coming in, Cornelius went to meet him, and fell to his knees and worshipped him. *26* Peter lifted him up and said, "Stand up! I'm just a human myself!" *27* And as he talked with him, he went inside and found a large gathering.

28-33 He said to them, "You know how unlawful it is for a Jewish man to associate with or to visit someone of another race. But God has shown to me that I must not call any person forbidden or unclean. *29* In fact, I came here without argument when I was sent for. May I ask you why you sent for me?"

30 Cornelius replied, "Four days ago at this time, 3 o'clock in the afternoon, I was praying in my house, when suddenly a man stood in front of me in shining clothes. *31* He said, 'Cornelius, your prayer was heard and your gifts to the poor were put on record in God's presence. *32* So send to Joppa for Simon who's also known as Peter. He is staying with Simon the

---

[1] Note that Cornelius' vision took place the day before Peter's vision. The messengers had time to approach Caesarea by the time Peter was ready to accept what they were saying. Joppa and Caesarea were 30 Roman miles apart.

[2] ἔκστασις, *ekstasis*, a displaced state, appears in documentary sources as "frenzied state". For the word for displaced tax, see *BGU* III.94.6.

tanner whose house is by the sea. *33* So I sent for you at once, and you were kind enough to come. So then, now we're all here in God's presence, to hear what the Lord has commanded you to tell us."

34-38 Peter opened his mouth and said, "I now realize how true it is that God doesn't show favoritism, *35* but that he accepts whoever respects him and does what's right, no matter what race of people they're from! *36* The Word which God sent to the Israelites, announcing the Good News of peace through Jesus the Anointed One - this one is Lord of all - *37* you yourselves know what has happened, the spoken word throughout the whole of Judea, beginning from Galilee after the baptism which John proclaimed, *38* namely how God anointed Jesus of Nazareth with the Holy Spirit and with power - and he went around doing good and instantly divinely healing everyone who was overpowered by Slanderer-Liar, because God was with him.

39-43 "And we are witnesses to everything he did, both in the land of the Jews and in Jerusalem. And it's a fact that they killed him by hanging him on a cross. *40* But God raised him up on the third day and allowed him to appear, *41* not to all the people, but to us. We were witnesses chosen beforehand by God. We ate and drank with him after he was raised up from among the dead. *42* He commanded us to pass around the command to the people and to call solemnly to witness that he is the one appointed by God to judge the living and the dead. *43* He is the one all the prophets testified about. They said that by his Name, whoever believes in him will have their sins canceled."

44-48 While Peter was still saying this, the Holy Spirit fell on everyone who was listening. *45* The believers from among the circumcision[1] who had come with Peter were shocked, because the gift of the Holy Spirit was poured out on the non-Jews as well, *46* as they heard them speak in supernaturally-given languages, and greatly praise God. Then Peter said, *47* "Who could stop these people from being baptized in water! They have received the Holy Spirit just as we have!"

48 He commanded them to be baptized in the Name of Jesus the Anointed One. Then they asked him to stay a few more days.

Ch.11:1-3 The apostles and the fellow believers who were throughout Judea heard that the non-Jews had also received the Word of God. *2* So when Peter came up to Jerusalem, the believers from among the circumcision (the Jewish believers) disputed with him. *3* They said, "You went into the house of men with foreskins and ate with them!"

4-9 Peter explained it to them in the order that it happened. He said, *5* "Now I was in the city of Joppa praying. I was in a displaced state and I saw a vision of an object that looked like a large sheet being let down by four corners from the sky, and it got close to me. *6* I looked at it intently and took careful note of it, and I saw four-legged animals of the earth, and wild beasts, reptiles and birds of the air. *7* And I heard a voice saying to me, 'Get up, Peter, kill and eat!'

8 "But I said, 'No way, Lord, because I've never eaten anything forbidden or unclean.'

9 "The voice came out of the sky again and answered me, 'What God has made clean you must not call forbidden!'

10-14 "This happened three times, and everything was drawn up to the sky. *11* And suddenly, the three men who had been sent by Cornelius to me had come up to the house where I was. *12* Then the Spirit told me to go with them and not to discriminate. Furthermore these six fellow believers accompanied me, and we went into the man's house. *13* He announced to us how he had seen a Messenger standing in his house, who had said to him, 'Send off to Joppa for Simon who is also known as Peter! *14* He will tell you how you and your whole household will be saved.'

---

[1]   That is, the Jewish believers.

15-17 "And as I began to speak the Holy Spirit fell on them just as on us at the beginning. *16* Then I remembered the spoken words of the Lord, how he said, 'John baptized you with water, but I will baptize you with the Holy Spirit.'

17 "So then, if God gave them the same gift that he gave us when we believed the Lord Jesus the Anointed One, well - who was I to be able to stand in God's way!"

18 When they heard this they became silent, and they praised God. They said, "So then, God has also granted to the non-Jews that they change their minds, which leads to life!"

19-21 Now those who were scattered because of the persecution that arose over Stephen, traveled as far as Phoenicia, Cyprus and Antioch, speaking the Word to no one but the Jews. *20* However, some of them were men from Cyprus and Cyrene, who, when they had come to Antioch, spoke to the Greek-speaking Jews, and announced the Good News, the Lord Jesus. *21* The Lord's power was with them, and a great number believed and turned to the Lord.

22-26 The assembly in Jerusalem heard this news, and they sent out Barnabas to go as far as Antioch. *23* When he arrived and saw God's favor, he was happy about it. *24* He was a civic benefactor[1] full of the Holy Spirit and of faith, and so encouraged them to be determined to remain faithful to the Lord with all their hearts. And a large number of people were added to the Lord. *25* Then he went to Tarsus to look for Saul. *26* And when he found him, he brought him to Antioch. So it happened that for a whole year they met with the assembly and taught a large number of people. In fact, the disciples were called[2] "Christians" for the first time at Antioch.

Antioch in Syria.

Antioch in Roman Syria (also known as "Antioch on the Orontes", modern Antakya) was 300 miles north of Jerusalem, situated on a major trade route at the junction of the Lebanon Mountains and the Taurus Mountains. It was built partly on an island and partly on the banks of Mount Silpius, 15 miles inland from the Mediterranean Sea. It was founded c. 300 BC by Seleucus I Nicator, one of Alexander the Great's generals, and named after his father Antiochus. Its harbor was the mouth of the Orontes River, a river famous as the site of the Battle of Kadesh fought between the Hittites and the Egyptian Pharaoh Ramesses II centuries earlier, and famous as the scene of Cleopatra, with Antony in attendance, being rowed along dressed as Venus. In Paul's time, Antioch was the third largest city of the Roman empire, behind Rome itself and Alexandria. Its population has been estimated at half a million people. It was at Antioch that Alexander the Great almost drowned (one of two places he is said to have nearly drowned), and where he defeated Darius III in 333 BC.

27-30 In those days prophets came from Jerusalem to Antioch. *28* One of them, Agabus by name, stood up and revealed by the Spirit that there was about to be a bad famine throughout the whole land. This in fact happened in the time of Claudius Caesar. *29* Every one of the disciples, according to their amount of wealth, assigned a sum to send as relief to the fellow believers who were living in Jerusalem. *30* This is how they sent it: they sent it to the elders in the care of Barnabas and Saul.

---

[1] ἀνὴρ ἀγαθός, *aner agathos*. See note on Luke 23:50.
[2] χρηματισθέντες, *khrematisthentes*, aorist passive participle of χρεματίζω, *khrematizo*, usually "impart a revelation" or "impart a warning", with God as the source of the revelation or warning. See Matt. 2:12. The related noun occurs only in Rom. 11:4, and appears in *SGPI*, the collection of Ptolemaic inscriptions.; see also *OGIS* 56, *OGIS* 139, all in the simple meaning "report". It occurs in the meaning "divine utterance" in *I.Nikaia* II, 1.1071.

Ch.12:1-5 Now about this time Herod[1] the king used his power to harm some of the ones from the assembly. *2* He beheaded James the brother of John. *3* When he saw that this pleased the Jews, he went further and arrested Peter – it was at the time of the Unleavened Bread Feast. *4* After he arrested him, he put him in prison, handing him over to four squads each made up of four soldiers to guard him. He intended to bring him before the people after Passover. *5* So then on the one hand Peter was kept in prison, but on the other hand prayer was vehemently going on about him by the assembly to God.

6-9 The night before Herod was going to bring him out for punishment, Peter was asleep bound up with two chains between two soldiers, and the guards in front of the door were guarding the prison. *7* Suddenly a Messenger of the Lord came up to him, and a light shone in the place, and he struck Peter on the side and lifted him up! He said, "Get up quickly!" Peter's chains fell off his hands. *8* Then the Messenger said to him, "Get dressed and put on your sandals!"

He did this. And he said to him, "Throw on your coat and keep following me!"

9 Peter went out and followed him. But he did not know that what was happening was real - he thought he was seeing a vision.

10-11 When they were past the first and second guard posts, they came to the iron gate that leads to the city. It opened up for him all by itself, and they went out and down one lane. Immediately the Messenger left him. *11* When Peter had recovered his wits, he said, "Now I know for sure that the Lord has sent his Messenger, and he's rescued me from Herod's power and from everything that the Jews expected to happen!"

12-15 When this had dawned on him, he went to the house of Mary,[2] the mother of John (who was also called Mark), where enough people had gathered and were praying. *13* As he was knocking at the entrance door, a servant named Rhoda came to answer.[3] *14* When she recognized Peter's voice, she was so overjoyed that she didn't open the entrance, but ran back and announced that Peter was standing at the entrance!

15 They said to her, "You're mad!" But she kept insisting that was the case. They said, "It must be his Messenger!"

16-19 But Peter kept on knocking. When they opened up and saw him, they were shocked! *17* He signaled to them to be quiet, then he described how the Lord had brought him out of prison. He said, "Tell James and the fellow believers about it!" And he left and went off somewhere else. *18* When it was day, there was a large commotion among the soldiers because of Peter's disappearance. When Herod searched for him and couldn't find him, he interrogated the guards and then he ordered that they be executed.

19-23 Herod went down from Judea to Caesarea and spent some time there. *20* Now Herod had been extremely angry with the people of Tyre and Sidon, but now they joined forces. After they made friends with Blastus, the king's High Court Official, they asked for peace, due to the fact that their country was economically dependent on the royal country. *21* On a set day Herod, arrayed in royal robes, sat on his throne and gave an address to them. *22* The people were shouting, "This is the voice of a god and not a human!"

23 Immediately a Messenger of the Lord struck him, because he did not give honor to God. And he was eaten up by worms and died![4]

---

[1]   Herod Agrippa I, the son of Aristobolos and grandson of Herod the Great. Josephus (*Ant*. 19.7.3) says that Herod Agrippa I acted as a godly Jew.

[2]   Mary was Barnabas's sister. (See Col. 4:10).

[3]   ὑπακούω, *hupakouo*, the word usually translated elsewhere in most Bible versions as "submit" or "obey", when in fact it means "answer", "pay attention".

[4]   The historian Josephus, *Ant*, 17.6.5, gives a full account of Herod's bizarre death: "But now Herod's distemper greatly increased upon him after a severe manner, and this by God's judgment upon him for his sins; for a fire glowed in him slowly, which did not so much appear to the touch outwardly,

24-25 But God's Word grew and multiplied. *25* Barnabas and Saul returned to Jerusalem, after they had fulfilled their ministry, taking John (who was also known as Mark) along with them.

Ch.13:1-4 Now in the assembly that was here and there in Antioch were certain prophets and teachers: Barnabas, Simon (who was called "Black"), Lucius of Cyrene, Manaen who was like a brother to Herod the tribal ruler, and Saul. *2* As they ministered to the Lord and fasted, the Holy Spirit said, "Come now, set apart for me Barnabas and Saul for the work to which I have called them."

3 Then after they fasted and prayed, they laid hands on them and discharged them. *4* So then, as they were sent out by the Holy Spirit, they went down to Seleucia,[1] and from there they sailed away to Cyprus.

5-8 And when they arrived in Salamis, they declared the Word of God in the synagogues of the Jews. They also had John as their attendant. *6* When they had gone through the whole island to Paphos, they found a certain Official Spiritual Advisor,[2] a false prophet, a Jew by the name of Bar-Jesus, *7* who was with the Regional Governor, Sergius Paulus, an intelligent man. This person called for Barnabas and Saul and wanted to hear the Word of God. *8* But Elymas the Official Spiritual Advisor (as his name "Elymas" means "Official Spiritual Advisor") opposed them, making an attempt to turn the Regional Governor away from the faith.

Sergius Paulus.

Sergius Paulus, the "intelligent man" was the Regional Governor (proconsul) of Cyprus, which had been a Roman province from 58 BC and a Senatorial province from 27 BC. The family of Sergius Paulus, the Sergii Paulli, owned a large country estate near Antioch by Pisidia. Most cities in the rural province of Galatia (whose main products were cereals and wool) were small, and the cities were linked by the Roman roads.

In place of cities were substantial country estates owned by families. It has been suggested[3] that Paul decided to visit Antioch next due to Sergius' link

---

as it augmented his pains inwardly; for it brought upon him a vehement appetite to eating, which he could not avoid to supply with one sort of food or other. His entrails were also ex-ulcerated, and the chief violence of his pain lay on his colon; an aqueous and transparent liquor also had settled itself about his feet, and a like matter afflicted him at the bottom of his belly. Nay, further, his privy-member was putrefied, and produced worms; and when he sat upright, he had a difficulty of breathing, which was very loathsome, on account of the stench of his breath, and the quickness of its returns; he had also convulsions in all parts of his body, which increased his strength to an insufferable degree. It was said by those who pretended to divine, and who were endued with wisdom to foretell such things, that God inflicted this punishment on the king on account of his great impiety; yet was he still in hopes of recovering, though his afflictions seemed greater than any one could bear." (Trans. William Whiston.) (See also 17.6. 6-7.)

[1] Seleucia (modern Samandag) also known as Seleucia Pieria, to distinguish it from the other places named Seleucia, is the seaport of Antioch on the Mediterranean on the mouth of the Orontes River. Paul set sail on his first missionary journey from here. Today the port has silted up and is only accessed by small fishing boats. It was founded in Hellenistic times by Seleucis I Nicator, one of Alexander the Great's generals.

[2] μάγος, *magos*, the same word usually translated "wise man" by Bible versions, the Magoi were well known for giving the gifts of gold, frankincense and myrrh to the young Jesus. This same word is usually translated "astrologer" in the book of Daniel. See background notes on Magoi in Matt. 2.

[3] By Mitchell, *ANRW* II.7.2 (1980) 1053-1081, esp. 1074 n. 134.

with the city, no doubt provided with an entry from Sergius to the upper class there. An inscription on a boundary stone on the bank of the Tiber River names Sergius Paulus as "curator of the banks of the Tiber" (one of five curators), dated to early in the reign of Claudius. In fact, a monument found at Antioch by Pisidia in Galatia mentions a Sergius Paulus who may have been the Regional Governor's son.

Salamis and Paphos on Cyprus.

The mountainous island of Cyprus is the third largest in the Mediterranean, being 140 miles long and 60 miles wide. Cyprus had been a Roman province from 58 BC and a Senatorial province from 27 BC. It was the home of Barnabas. Salamis was on the east coast of Cyprus, and was its commercial center. Today Salamis is an amazing place to visit, with sites such as an amphitheater, agora, aqueduct, baths, forum, 44-seater set of latrines, gymnasium, villas as well as beautiful mosaics. Due to a series of earthquakes in the first century, much of what remains today is from the fourth century. Paphos has the more beautiful mosaics, revealed after the considerable excavations which have taken place. Today Salamis is Turkish and Paphos is Greek, and the two are divided after much bloodshed, but Paul was presented with no traveling complications. Paul had to pass the Temple of Apollo on his way from Salamis to Paphos, a temple whose remains can be seen today. The Rock of Romios, situated between Curium and Paphos, is in the bay which legend holds to be the birthplace of Aphrodite from sea foam.

9-12 Saul, who is also known as Paul, filled with the Holy Spirit, fixed his eyes on him! *10* He said, "You associate of Slanderer-Liar, full of every deceit and every fraud, you enemy of righteousness, will you never stop perverting the straight ways of the Lord! *11* And now suddenly the hand of the Lord is against you, and you will be struck blind, and you won't be able to see the sun the sun for a time!"

Immediately a dimness of vision and a darkness fell on him, and he went around trying to find someone to lead him by the hand. *12* When he saw what had happened, the Regional Governor believed, as he was completely awestruck by the teaching about the Lord.

13-15 Paul and his companions set sail to Paphos in Pamphylia. John left them and went back to Jerusalem. *14* When they had gone through Paphos they arrived at Antioch in Pisidia, and went into the synagogue on the Sabbath day[1] and sat down. *15* After the reading from the Law and the Prophets, the rulers of the synagogue[2] sent a message to them which said, "Gentlemen, fellow believers, if you have any message of encouragement for the people, speak!"

16-22 Paul stood up, and signaling with his hand, said, "Israelites[3] and you who respect God, listen! *17* The God of this people Israel chose our ancestors, and raised up the people when they lived as foreigners in Egypt. Then he powerfully brought them out of it. *18* He put up with their behavior for about forty years in the desert. *19* When he had destroyed seven nations in the land of Canaan, he gave the land to them as their inheritance for about 450 years. *20* After that he gave them judges, until the time of Samuel the prophet. *21* And after that they asked for a king, and God gave them Saul the son of Kish, a man of the tribe of Benjamin, for 40 years. *22* After he

---

[1]   See note on Luke 4:16.
[2]   ἀρχισυνάγωγος, *archisunagogos*. See Luke 8:49.
[3]   ἄνδρες Ἰσραηλῖται, *andres Israelitai*, "Israelites" not "men of Israel". The Greeks as a rule put the word ἄνδρες, *andres*, with a place name to indicate the inhabitants of that place. It had nothing to do with the male gender, and the word ἄνδρες, *andres*, should not be translated in the expression.

removed him, he raised up David as king for them. This is what he said about David: 'I have found David, the son of Jesse, a man after my own heart, who will carry out all my wishes!'

23-25 "From this person's descendants, in accordance with the promise, God brought Israel a Savior, Jesus. *24* Before Jesus came, John had first publicly proclaimed the baptism of changing minds to all the people of Israel. *25* As John was about to complete his race, he said, 'Who do you suppose I am? I am certainly not he! But someone will come after me, and I'm not even good enough to untie his sandals!'

26-35 "Ladies and gentlemen,[1] fellow believers, descendants of the race of Abraham, and those among you who respect God, to you indeed the Message of this salvation has been sent! *27* Because those who live in Jerusalem and their rulers did not recognize him, and by condemning him did no more than fulfill the voices of the prophets that are read every Sabbath. *28* And although they could find no grounds for the death sentence, they asked Pilate to execute him. *29* Now when they had fulfilled everything that was written about him, they took him down from the cross and laid him in a tomb. *30* But God raised him from among the dead. *31* He was seen for many days by those who accompanied him from Galilee to Jerusalem, those who are his witnesses to the people. *32* We truly announce the Good News to you of the promise made to our ancestors, *33* that God has completely fulfilled to us, their descendants, by raising up Jesus. This is also written in the second Psalm, 'You are my Son, today I have become your Father.' *34* And this is what he said because he raised him from among the dead, no more to return to decay: 'I will give you the trustworthy mercies of David.' *35* Because he also says in another Psalm, 'You will not allow your Holy One to see decay.''

36-41 "So then David, after he had served God's purpose for his own generation, fell asleep, and he was buried with his ancestors and decayed, *37* but the One God raised up did not decay. *38* So realize this, ladies and gentlemen,[2] fellow believers, it is through this person that the cancellation of sins is being preached to you. *39* Because of him, everyone who believes is made right with God from everything for which you could not be made right with God by the Law of Moses. *40* So then beware lest what has been spoken in the prophets happens to you: *41* 'See, you scornful, wonder and disappear! Because I will do something in your days, that you will never believe, even if someone told you!'"

Antioch by Pisidia often called "Pisidian Antioch" (modern Yalvac).

Antioch was in the Roman province of Galatia, and 300 miles north of Jerusalem, on the Pisidian border. It was a Seleucid colony, but a Roman colony known as *Colonia Caesarea* in 25 BC. Antioch is high in the Sultandag mountains and built on top of a cliff almost two miles in circumference. The city can only be approached from the west, as the other sides are very steep. The site is not built on a nice flat plateau, even the cliff top is hilly. At the time of Paul's trip inland to Antioch, there was a newly completed Roman road which was begun under Tiberius and finished under Gaius. It was by far the most likely route for Paul on his visit to Antioch. Antioch is still being excavated and is open for tourists. Remains from Paul's time are in poor condition, but include the colonnaded street, the stadium, the Augustus temple, the entrance gate and the walls. The arches of the Roman aqueduct are still quite striking. Tourists are also able to see the Western Gate (212 AD) and the Church of St Paul (IV) both of which post date Paul. In 16 AD, Antioch was the site of the first recorded workers' strike. Laborers working on the aqueduct went on strike against Tiberius.

---

[1] ἄνδρες, *andres*. See note on Acts 7:2.
[2] ἄνδρες, *andres*. See note on Acts 7:2.

42-43 As they were leaving the synagogue, the people asked them to come back on the next Sabbath day and speak to them again about it. *43* When the congregation had broken up, many of the Jews and godly converts to Judaism followed Paul and Barnabas, who spoke to them and persuaded them to continue having God's favor.

44-47 On the next Sabbath almost the whole city collected to hear the Word of the Lord. *45* When the Jews saw the crowds they were filled with envy. They hurled abuse and contradicted what Paul was saying. *46* Both Paul and Barnabas spoke out freely, boldly and openly in public. They said, "It was necessary for the Word of God to be spoken to you first, but since you reject it, and don't think you're worthy of everlasting life, see this! We're turning to the non-Jews! *47* This is what the Lord instructed us to do: 'I have sent you as a light to the non-Jews so that you will bring salvation to the ends of the earth.'"

48-52 When the non-Jews heard this they were happy and praised the Word of the Lord, and everyone who was stationed in battle order for eternal life believed. *49* The Word of the Lord was being spread around the whole country. *50* But the Jews incited the godly and influential women and the chief men of the city. They instigated persecution against Paul and Barnabas and threw them out of their territory. *51* But they shook the dust from their feet as an insult against them, and went to Iconium. *52* The disciples were filled the joy of the Holy Spirit.

Iconium (modern Konya).

Iconium was the third largest city of Galatia (after Ankyra and Antioch by Pisidia). Its population was ethnically mixed, and it was on the borders of Phrygia and Lycaonia. Iconium became Roman when Attalus III of Pergamon died without heirs and bequeathed it to Rome. In 1979, numismatic evidence revealed that there were two separate communities in Iconium, *Colonia Iulia Augusta Iconium* and *Claudeikonion*. It was a double community, the two separate communities having administrative and judicial independence from each other. It was both a *polis* and a Roman *colonia*, at least from the time of Claudius, but amalgamated under Hadrian. Note that Luke describes regions by their geographical names, and Paul by their Roman provincial names. For example, when Luke speaks of Galatia he refers to the northern geographical district of Asia Minor, and when Paul speaks of Galatia he refers to the Roman province of Galatia, which was to the south.

Ch.14:1-3 The same thing happened in Iconium when Paul and Barnabas went into the synagogue of the Jews. They spoke in such a way that a large crowd both of Jews and non-Jews believed. *2* But the unbelieving Jews stirred up the non-Jews and poisoned their minds against the fellow believers. *3* The fellow believers stayed there for a considerable time, and spoke out freely, boldly and openly in public. They did this by relying upon the Lord, who was proving the Message of his favor, by granting that they did miraculous signs and wonders.

4-7 But the population of the city was divided. Some sided with the Jews, and the others sided with the apostles. *5* Then the non-Jews and the Jews along with their rulers made their move. They intended to manhandle them and stone them. *6* However, they found out about it and escaped to the Lycaonian cities of Lystra and Derbe,[1] and to the surrounding countryside, *7* and kept announcing the Good News there.

8-10 Now in Lystra there was a certain man who didn't have any strength in his feet. He was crippled from birth. In fact, he had never walked. *9* This person heard Paul speaking. Paul fixed his eyes on him, and seeing he had the

---

[1]   The implication here is that Iconium was Phrygian, not Lycaonian. This is not surprising as it was on both borders.

faith to be rescued and preserved, *10* said in a loud voice, "Stand up straight on your feet!"

And he leapt up and walked!

11-13 The whole crowd saw what Paul had done and raised their voices, and called out in the Lycaonian language, "The gods have come down to us in human form!" *12* They called Barnabas "Zeus",[1] and they called Paul "Hermes" because he was the main speaker.[2] *13* The priest of Zeus, whose temple was in front of their city, brought bulls and wreaths to the gates intending to sacrifice with the crowds to Barnabas and Paul.[3]

14-18 But when the apostles Barnabas and Paul heard this, they tore their clothes and rushed out into the crowd, *15* calling out, "Ladies and gentlemen,[4] why are you doing this? We're humans just like you! In fact, the Good News that we announce to you says that you should turn from these useless things to the living God, who made the sky, the earth, the sea, and everything in them! *16* In past generations God let all nations do what they liked. *17* However, he did not leave you without evidence about himself. He has shown kindness, giving you rain from the sky and thus crops in their season, filling your appetites with food to make you happy!" *18* Even though they said this, they still had difficulty preventing the crowds from sacrificing to them.

19-22 Then Jews from Antioch[5] and Iconium arrived and won the crowd over. They stoned Paul and dragged him outside the city thinking he was dead. *20* When the disciples surrounded him he got up and went into the city. And the next day he left for Derbe with Barnabas. *21* After they announced the Good News in that city and won a large number of disciples, they returned to Lystra, Iconium, and Antioch. *22* They strengthened the lives of the disciples, encouraging them to continue in the faith. They said, "It's necessary for us to enter God's Realm, because there are many oppressions."[6]

23-28 They ordained elders in every assembly and prayed with fasting, and then they committed them to the Lord in whom they had believed. *24* And after they had passed through Pisidia, they came to Pamphylia. *25* Then when they had declared the Word in Perga, they went down to Attalia.[7] *26* From there they sailed back to Antioch. It was in Antioch that they had been handed over to God's powerful favor, for the work which they had now completed. *27* When they arrived, they collected the assembly together. Then they reported everything that God had done among them, and that he had opened the door of faith to the non-Jews. *28* They stayed there for a long time with the disciples.

---

[1] The Roman name for Zeus was Jupiter.

[2] Hermes was the messenger god. The Romans called him Mercury. Zeus and Hermes were associated with the area. A stone altar found near Lystra was dedicated to both Zeus and Hermes, as was an inscription at nearby Sedasa.

[3] Ovid's famous story (in *Metamorphoses*) tells of Philemon and Baucis, who took in two strangers (Zeus and Hermes) when the rest of the village refused them hospitality, and thus were saved from the destruction which came upon the rest of the village.

[4] ἄνδρες, *andres*. See note on Acts 7:2.

[5] This is Pisidian Antioch, which was situated on the northern border of Pisidia near Galatia. It is high in the Sultandag mountains. Ruins can be seen at the site today, but they are in poor condition. Pisidian Antioch (also known as Antioch-by-Pisidia) is not to be confused with the other Antioch (Antioch-on-the-Orontes, modern Antakya), Paul's missionary base and a most important city.

[6] That is, it is necessary to enter the realm to avoid, or to know what to do about, the oppressions.

[7] Attalia in Pamphylia (modern Antalya) is a magnificent harbor city founded by Attalus II, the king of Pergamon in the 2nd century BC.

Perga.

Perga (properly Perge) was a prosperous city at the time of Paul's visits. It was defended by an imposing wall equipped with gates and towers. Under Claudius, Perga was made part of the Roman Empire, and the wall was abandoned due to the ensuing stability of Roman rule. Prior to this, Perga had been much fought-over.

Several prominent Roman families settled in the area. By the time of Paul's visits, a number of spectacular buildings had been commenced, the most famous building being the Temple of Artemis. Strabo (14, 4, 2) states that it was on a hill near town, but the site has not as yet been found.

The remains of the city are in an excellent state of preservation. There is a theater which could seat 14,000, paved marble colonnaded streets, Hellenistic gate and towers, and Roman baths. The gate and towers and part of the palaestra, the gymnasium built by Gaius Julius Cornutus and dedicated to the emperor Claudius, as well as the Roman baths, were there when Paul visited. However, the main streets were not built by AD 80. Paul visited Perga in on the way to Antioch by Pisidia (Acts 13:13-14) and on the way home again (Acts 14:25). Perga was the city where John Mark left Paul and Barnabas.

Ch.15:1 Certain people came down from Judea and were teaching the fellow believers, "Unless you are circumcised in accordance with the custom of Moses, you cannot get saved!"

2-3 When Paul and Barnabas met with controversy and had a rather large dispute with them, it was arranged that Paul and Barnabas and certain others should go up to Jerusalem to the apostles and elders, about this matter in question. *3* So then, when they were sent on their way by the assembly, they passed through Phoenicia and Samaria, describing in detail the conversion of the non-Jews. This made the believers extremely happy.

4-5 When they arrived in Jerusalem, they were welcomed by the assembly, the apostles and the elders, and they reported everything that God had done among them. *5* But some of the sect of the Pharisees who had become believers stood up and said, "Circumcise them and command them to keep the Law of Moses!"

6-11 Both the apostles and the elders met together to discuss the matter. *7* When much controversy had come about, Peter said to them, "Ladies and gentlemen,[1] fellow believers, you are aware that from the early days God chose me from among you, that the non-Jews would hear the Word of the Good News from my mouth, and become believers. *8* And now God, who knows the heart, has given evidence in their favor by giving them the Holy Spirit, just as he did to us! *9* He made no distinction between us and them - he's purified their hearts by means of faith. *10* Now then, why on earth are you provoking God by putting a yoke on the neck of the disciples which neither we nor our ancestors were able to carry? *11* On the contrary, we believe that we were saved through the Lord Jesus showing us favor, in the same way as these people were."

12-18 Then the whole crowd became silent and they listened to Paul and Barnabas telling at length how many miraculous signs and wonders God had worked through them among the non-Jews. *13* After they had finished speaking, James answered, "Ladies and gentlemen,[2] fellow believers, listen to me! *14* Simon has told at length how God at first visited the non-Jews to take a people for himself. *15* The words of the prophets agree with this, just as the Scriptures say, *16* 'After this I will return and rebuild the tent of David which has fallen down and I will restore its ruins; *17* so that they will seek the Lord –

---

[1] ἄνδρες, *andres*. See note on Acts 7:2.
[2] ἄνδρες, *andres*. See note on Acts 7:2.

the rest of humanity and all the non-Jews who are called by my Name, says the Lord, who does these things *18* that were known from the beginning of time.'

19-21 "For this reason it is indeed my judgment that we should stop bothering those of the non-Jews who are turning to God. *20* However, we should write to them and tell them to abstain from things polluted by idols, from *porneia*,[1] from eating strangled animals, and from consuming blood. *21* For these laws of Moses have been proclaimed in each city. In fact for many generations they've been read in the synagogues every Sabbath day!"

22-29 Then the apostles and elders, along with the whole assembly, decided to send chosen men from their own company to Antioch with Paul and Barnabas: Judas (who was called Barsabbas), and Silas, who were leading men among the fellow believers. *23* They sent the following letter with them: "From: The apostles, the elders, the fellow believers, To: The fellow believers who are non-Jews in Antioch, Syria and Cilicia: Hello! *24* As we have found out that some went out from us without our authorization and have upset you by their words, unsettling your lives, *25* it seemed a good idea to us, after we agreed about it, to send chosen men to you with our much loved Barnabas and Paul, *26* people who have dedicated their lives to the name of Jesus the Anointed One. *27* So then we have sent Judas and Silas, who will also tell you the same things verbally. *28* It seemed good to the Holy Spirit, and to us, that no further burden should be imposed on you apart from these necessary things: *29* that you abstain from the flesh of pagan sacrificial victims, from consuming blood, from eating strangled animals, and from *porneia*.[2] If you keep yourselves free of these, you'll do well! Goodbye."

Letters in Acts.

There are two letters in Acts, the one above which was sent to the non-Jew believers in Syria and Cilicia by the Christian leaders in Jerusalem (15:23-29), and a letter between two Roman administrators concerning Paul (23:26-30). Luke prefaces the letter between the Romans by, "He wrote a letter as per the following copy (τύπος, *tupos*)." τύπος, *tupos* means an exact replication and does not mean "as follows". Here it should not be taken to imply a rhetorical approximation. For further reading on τύπος, *tupos*, see E.A. Judge, "A state schoolteacher makes a salary bid," NDIEC 1.72-78. E.A. Judge (p.78) notes also: "The letter of Lysias is highly individualistic and appropriate to its occasion, as is that of Philopater in 3 Macc. 3.12-29, where the τύπος (*tupos*) of it is also said to be given (30). Judge (p. 78) concludes that Luke meant his readers to take the letters as the direct citation of transcripts available to him.

30-35 So they were sent off, and came down to Antioch. When they had gathered the crowd together, they handed over the letter. *31* When they read it they were delighted with its encouragement. *32* Judas and Silas, who themselves were prophets too, encouraged and strengthened the fellow believers at some length. *33* After they had spent some time with them, they were sent back with greetings from the fellow believers to those who had sent them.[3] *35* Paul and Barnabas stayed in Antioch, and along with many others taught and announced the Good News, the Word of the Lord.

36-40 Now then after some days, Paul said to Barnabas, "Let's go and see how our fellow believers are getting on in every city where we've preached the Word of the Lord." *37* Barnabas wanted to take John (who was called Mark) along with them. *38* But Paul didn't think it fit and proper to take with them the one who had left Pamphylia and had not gone along with them to

---

[1] πορνεία, *porneia*. See note on Matt. 15:19.
[2] See note on Matt. 15:19.
[3] Verse 34 is omitted as it was inserted much later by copyists to explain the presence of Silas in Antioch in verse 40.

the work there. *39* It turned out that the disagreement between them was so sharp that they parted from one another. Barnabas took Mark and sailed from Cyprus, *40* but Paul chose Silas and left, after he was handed over by the fellow believers to the Lord's favor.

41.Ch.16:1-5 Paul went through Syria and Cilicia, strengthening the assemblies. *1* Paul continued on to Derbe and then on to Lystra. A certain disciple was there, named Timothy, the son of a Jewish woman believer. His father was Greek. *2* He was well regarded by the fellow believers at Lystra and Iconium.[1] *3* Paul wanted Timothy to go away with him, and he took him and circumcised him on account of the Jews who lived in that area, as they knew his father was Greek. *4* As Paul and Timothy traveled through the cities, they handed over the decisions that had been determined by the apostles and elders in Jerusalem. *5* So the assemblies had their faith strengthened, and they increased in number every day.

6-10 Paul and Timothy traveled through the region of Phrygian Galatia, after they were prevented by the Holy Spirit from declaring the Word in Asia. *7* After they arrived in Mysia, they had tried to go into Bithynia, but the Spirit of Jesus wouldn't allow them to. *8* So they passed by Mysia, and came down to Troas.[2] *9* And this vision appeared to Paul during the night: a certain Macedonian stood and begged, "Come over to Macedonia and help us!"

10 When he had seen the vision, we[3] immediately tried to go to Macedonia, concluding that God had appointed us to announce the Good News to them.

11-12 We set sail from Troas[4] and made a straight run to Samothrace. On the next day we came to Neapolis,[5] *12* and from there to Philippi, a Roman colony,[6] and the most important city in Macedon. We stayed in that city for some time.

---

[1] Iconium in Galatic Phrygia (modern Konya) is an ancient town. It fell into Roman hands in 133 BC, when Attalus II of Pergamum died without heirs and bequeathed his empire to Rome.

[2] Alexandria Troas was an important artificial harbor. It was 12 miles (20 km) southwest of the ancient site of Troy. It had become a Roman colony under Augustus. Alexandria was founded in the 4th c. BC by Antigonus I Monopthalmos, one of Alexander the Great's generals. He named it Antigonia after himself. The city was subsequently conquered by another of Alexander's generals, who renamed it.

[3] Luke now writes as an eye-witness. The "we" passages are 16:10-17; 20:5-12:18; 27:1-28:16.

[4] Troas, properly known as Alexandria Troas was an important artificial harbor and stood 12 miles (20 km) from the ancient site of Troy. Paul used the harbor to sail to Neapolis (ancient Kavala).

[5] Neapolis (modern Kavala) was in Macedonia. It was, and still is, a popular harbor for fishing vessels. Neapolis was a very wealthy city due its proximity to the rich gold mines in the nearby hills and its position on the Via Egnatia, the east-west main Roman road through Macedonia. The Via Egnatia was almost 500 miles long, and ran from Dyrrhachium on the Adriatic Sea, to Byzantium. Paul traveled west on the Via Egnatia from Neapolis to Philippi, then Thessalonica. In Paul's time Neapolis was the port city for Philippi, 10 miles to the north. It sat on a neck of land between two bays, each of which served as a harbor. Neapolis fell to Rome in 168 BC and served as a base for Julius Caesar's assassins, Brutus and Cassius, before their defeat at nearby Philippi.

[6] Philippi, in Macedonia Prima, was a Roman garrison town. The city was the scene of the famous battle between Octavius and Anthony, and Julius Caesar's assassins Brutus and Cassius, which ended the Roman Empire. The remains at the site today are mostly 2nd century Roman.

13-15 And on the Sabbath day we went outside the city gate to the riverside[1] where we thought there would be a synagogue.[2] After we sat down we spoke to the women who met there. *14* A certain woman by the name of Lydia heard us. She was a dealer in purple cloth from the city of Thyatira, and she was a "Convert to Judaism".[3] The Lord opened her mind to devote herself to the things that Paul said. *15* When she and her household were baptized, she urged us to stay with her. She said, "If you have judged that I'm a believer in the Lord, please come and stay at my house!" And she pressured us.

16-18 Once as we were going to the synagogue, a certain slave girl who had a spirit, a future predicting spirit,[4] met with us. She made a good business for

---

[1] Rivers were important to the Jews because of their many ceremonial washings.

[2] προσευχή, *proseuche*, often rendered in Bible translations as "place of prayer". However, the word is well attested as meaning "synagogue". See lengthy discussion in Martin Hengel, "Proseuche and Synagoge. Judische Gemeinde, Gotteshaus und Gottesdienst in der Diaspora und in Palastina," *Festschrift Karl George Kuhn. Tradition und Glaube* (ed. Gert Jeremias, Heinz-Wolfgang Kuhn and Hartmut Stegemann; Gottingen; 1971, 157-184 and B.J. Brooten, *Women Leaders in the Ancient Synagogue*, Brown Judaic Studies 36, (Atlanta: Scholars Press, 1982), pp. 139-141. The reason it was rendered "place of prayer" may well be that only women congregants were mentioned, and it was supposed that women could not attend the synagogue. However, Acts 17:4 and 18:26 speak of women attending the synagogue, and there is ample evidence for women as synagogue leaders. Rabbinic sources speak of women participating in synagogue services. Inscriptional evidence testifies that women were synagogue leaders as well as elders. For example, Sophia of Gortyn was an elder and synagogue leader (*CII* 731 c, "Sophia of Gortyn, elder and head of the synagogue of Kisamos (lies) here. The memory of the righteous one forever. Amen.") The woman Rufina was head of a synagogue (*CII* 741; *IGR* IV 1452) as were Theopempte (*CII* 756) and Peristeria (*CII* 696b). Women as Jewish elders are attested in inscriptional evidence: Rebeka (*CII* 692), Beronikene (*CII* 581; *CIL* IX 6226), Mannine (*CII* 590; *CIL* IX 6230), Faustina (*CII* 597; *CIL* IX 6209), Mazauzala (*SEG* 27.1201), Sara Ura (*CII* 400). Further, three Jewish inscriptions from the 1st c. B.C.E. to the 4th c. C.E. mention women priests: *CII* 1514 (*SEG* 1.574); *CII* 315; *CII* 1007.

[3] σεβουμένς τον Θεόν, *seboumene ton Theon*, cognate term for Θεοσεβείς, *Theosebeis*. The exact meaning of this term is uncertain, but it has been established that the word is a formal designation for a group enrolled in a synagogue, but a group distinct from proselytes and native Jews. A synagogue inscription from Aphrodisias in Karia lists several individuals as *Theosebeia*. The term has been variously rendered in N.T. translations as "godliness", "worship of God", "religion". It has recently been established, in light of recent evidence, that the word applied to a convert (male or female) to Judaism, to someone who was not prepared to be baptized or circumcised., cf. M. Wilcox, *JSNT* 13 (1981) 102-122. A synagogue inscription from Aphrodisias in Karia lists several individuals as *Theosebeis*, and the list confirmed that the term was a formal designation for a group separate from proselytes and native Jews, but still enrolled in the membership of a synagogue. See also J. Reynolds and R. Tannenbaum, *Jews and Godfearers at Aphrodisias*, Cambridge Philological Society Supp. Vol. 12, (Cambridge, 1987).

[4] Here the type of spirit is named. It is a Pythian (Delphian) spirit. This is an epithet of Apollo, the Greek god of prophecy. Apollo was also associated with music and archery, as well as medicine. Apollo's oracular shrines were famous, the most famous being Delphi. Apollo also spoke through shrines at Branchidae, Didyma, Claros, Boeotia, Torad and Lycia. The method was by possession: the oracle (person) was said to be filled with the spirit of Apollo or by his inspiration.

her masters by forecasting the future. *17* This girl followed Paul and us, and she kept calling out, "These people are the slave servants of the Most High God! They're telling us how to get saved!"

18 She did this for many days. Finally Paul came to the end of his tether, and turned around and said to the spirit, "I command you in the Name of Jesus the Anointed One to come out of her!" It came out at that very instant.

19-24 But when her masters saw that all hope of profit had gone out with it, they grabbed Paul and Silas and dragged them off to the authorities in the marketplace. *20* They took them to the chief magistrates, and said, "These people, who are Jews, have seriously disrupted our city! *21* They're teaching customs which are illegal for us, as we're Romans!"

22 So the whole crowd rose up together against them, and the chief magistrates ordered that they have their clothes ripped off and that they be beaten with rods. *23* When they had inflicted many wounds on them, they threw them in prison, and ordered the jailer to guard them securely. *24* In view of these orders, he put them in the inner cell and secured their feet in stocks.

25-26 But about midnight, Paul and Silas were praying, singing festive songs to God, and the other prisoners were listening to them. *26* Suddenly there was such a major earthquake, that the foundations of the prison were rendered unstable! Immediately all the doors were opened and everyone's chains became loose.[1]

27-34 The jailer upon waking up from his sleep, saw the prison doors opened and assumed that the prisoners had escaped. He drew his sword and was about to kill himself. *28* But Paul shouted out loudly, "Don't harm yourself – we're all here!"

29 He called for lights, rushed in, and fell down trembling in front of Paul and Silas. *30* Then he took them outside and said, "Sirs, what do I have do to get saved?"

31 They said, "Believe the Lord Jesus and you will be saved – this goes for you and also for anyone in your household who believes."[2]

32 And they spoke the Word of the Lord to him and all his household. *33* Even at that hour of the night he took them along with him and washed the blood from their wounds, then immediately he as well as all his household were baptized. *34* When he had brought them into his house he gave them a meal, and he rejoiced with the whole household, because he believed God.

35-40 At dawn, the chief magistrates sent the officers with the order to release them. *36* The jailer reported the words to Paul, and said, "The magistrates have ordered that you be released. You can leave. Go in peace."

37 But Paul said to them, "They beat us in public, uncondemned Romans, and have thrown us in prison, and now do they want to get rid of us secretly! Oh, no! Certainly not! Let them come themselves and get us out!"

38 The officers reported these words to the chief magistrates, and they were afraid when they heard the words, "They're Romans!"[3]

39 So they came and pleaded with them and escorted them out, and requested that they leave the city. *40* After they got out of prison they went to Lydia's house, where they met with the fellow believers and encouraged them. Then they left.

People would approach the oracle and ask questions, and once possessed, the oracle would answer. The Delphic oracle was known as the Pythia, and may originally have been a young virgin, but in later times was elderly.

[1]   The chains were fastened to the masonry wall.

[2]   The Greek in no way suggests that if the jailer is saved, his household (which includes slaves and servants) will be too, or that God is working in family units.

[3]   The magistrates had in fact broken two laws, the Lex Valeria and the Lex Porcia. There were severe penalties for breaking these laws.

Ch.17:1-3 When they had traveled through Amphipolis and Apollonia,[1] they came to Thessalonika, where there was a Jewish synagogue. *2* As was his custom, Paul attended their meetings, and for three Sabbaths held discussions with them from the Scriptures. *3* He explained and demonstrated that the Anointed One had to suffer and rise again from among the dead. He said, "This Jesus that I'm telling you about is the Anointed One!"

Amphipolis.

Amphipolis was on the Via Egnatia, about 32 miles west of Philippi and 3 miles from the Aegean Sea. The Strymon River encircled it. Amphipolis was colonized by Athens in 437 BC. In 424 BC it was captured by the famous Spartan Brasidas, who defeated the equally famous Cleon, known also for being on the receiving end of the playwright Aristophanes' cutting wit. Cleon tried to recapture Amphipolis two years later. Philip II of Macedonia occupied it in 357 BC, and it remained under Macedonian control until 168 BC, when Rome made it a free city. Amphipolis controlled the trade route from northern Greece to the Hellespont to the east, as well as the route to the timber, gold, silver and timber of Mount Pangaion in Thrace. The Arch of Augustus and the Roman Forum, both from Paul's time, are being excavated today.

Thessalonika.

Thessalonika was a port city about 100 miles west of Philippi and 190 miles northwest of Athens. It was originally a Hellenistic city, named after the sister of Alexander the Great. Mark Antony and Octavian visited it after their victory a Philippi and made it a free city, and Cicero was exiled here. In Paul's time it was the largest city in Macedonia.

4-9 Some of them were convinced, and a huge crowd of the godly Greeks and quite a few of the leading women joined Paul and Silas. *5* But the Jews, motivated by jealousy, rounded up some unsavory characters who hung out on the streets. They gathered up a mob, and set the whole city in a riot. They attacked Jason's house,[2] looking for Paul and Silas so they could bring them before the People's Assembly. *6* But when they couldn't find them, they dragged Jason and some fellow believers to the Politarchs,[3] and shouted, "These people who've turned the world upside down have come here too! *7* Jason has welcomed them into his house! They are acting contrary to Caesar's

---

[1] Apollonia was maritime city of Macedonia situated on the Via Egnatia, 38 miles east of Thessalonika.

[2] The sense is that they attacked Jason's house, perhaps knocking down the door, in their attempt to attack the occupants of the house.

[3] πολιτάρχης, *politarkhes*, "Politarch". The office was one of annual tenure, and could be held contemporaneously with other offices. The office was widespread in Macedonian cities, but is not found in Roman provinces such as Philippi in the province. The magistrates were usually from wealthy families. The earliest inscription which can be dated definitely comes from 119/8BC. However, there is an earlier law from Beroia (a Macedonian city) that twice refers to politarchs. Scholarship generally agrees on an earlier date for the law, but that date is uncertain. Apart from the Acts 17:6 reference, a literary attestation also occurs in Aeneas Tacitus 26.12. (The difference in the suffix, -αρχος / -αρχης, *-arkhos* / *-arkhes*, is merely one of dialect.) There have been three important studies of this term since the mid 20th c. C. Schuler, *CP* (1960) 90-100, provides a list of all inscriptions which refer to politarchs of Macedonia. See also E.A. Judge *RTR* 30 (1971) 1-7. Regarding this term, Horsley states, "Obsolete discussions dating back to the end of last century (19th c) have remained the reference points in some works for the biblical field" (*NDIEC* 2.34), and " The MM and BAGD entries both need a complete overhaul." (*NDIEC* 2.35).

decrees, saying that there is another king, one called Jesus!" *8* When they heard this, the crowd and the rulers of the city were provoked. *9* They made Jason and the others post bail, and then they let them go.

10-15 During the night the fellow believers immediately sent Paul and Silas away to Berea.[1] When they arrived, they went into the synagogue of the Jews. *11* These people were more fair-minded than those in Thessalonika, in that they received the Word very eagerly, and searched the Scriptures day by day to study whether these things were actually so. *12* So it turned out that many of them became believers, and quite a few of the influential Greek women as well, and Greek men.*13* But when the Jews from Thessalonika learned that the Word of God was preached by Paul in Berea, they went there too and stirred up the crowds. *14* Immediately the fellow believers sent Paul away to travel as far as the sea coast, but Silas and Timothy stayed behind. *15* The people who escorted Paul brought him to Athens, and then left with instructions for Silas and Timothy to come to him as quickly as possible.

16-18 While Paul was in Athens waiting for them, his spirit was spurred on[2] within him when he saw that the city was full of Epicurean and Stoic philosophical tenets.[3] *17* He held discussions in the synagogue with the Jews and with the worshippers, and in the marketplace each day with anyone who happened to turn up. *18* Now on the other hand a group of Epicurean and Stoic philosophers started having discussions with him. Some said, "Talk about an idle babbler! What on earth is he trying to say?"

---

[1]   Berea (modern Veria) belonged to the kingdom of Macedon and became a favored part of the Roman province of Macedonia in 168 BC. Today there are 37 Byzantine churches on the site.

[2]   παρωξύνετο, *paroksuneto*, imperfect passive of παροξύνω, *paroksuno*, to be spurred on, to be urged on, to be provoked to do something. The Greek does not say that Paul was angry: rather, it suggests that he saw a great opportunity to announce the Good News as the city was full of Epicurean and Stoics, the very ones who would be interested to hear what he had to say. Translators have assumed that Paul was angry because they have not understood the term, κατείδωλος, *kateidolos* (see below) thinking it referred to pagan idols. See Thucydides 1.84, "we are likely to give in shamefacedly to other people's views when they try to spur us on by their accusations." In 5.99 the term is used in the passive, "Athenians, we are not so much frightened of states on the continent. They have their freedom, and this means that it will be quite some time before they start taking precautions against us. We are more concerned about islanders like yourselves...or subjects who have already become spurred on/provoked by the constraint our empire imposes on them." Here the people were spurred on/provoked to war against the Athenians. As Paul knew the tenets of Epicurean and Stoic philosophy, he may have been overjoyed to find such people who, by the very nature of their beliefs, would be very open to hearing the Good News.

[3]   This is a very clever play on words which cannot be translated into English. The Epicureans maintained that "Idols" (εἴδωλα, *eidola*, plural of εἴδωλον, *eidolon*) are being cast off by every object continually. (Note that "Idols" is merely the way translators have transliterated εἴδωλα, *eidola*, and here the word may well have nothing to do with the idols of pagan gods.) The Idol of an object was said to be composed of a very fine layer of atoms. Here the term is κατείδωλος, *kateidolos*: full of εἴδωλα, *eidola*: "Idols" in the Epicurean sense but also meaning an image in the mind, an idea, a phantom of the mind, a fancy, especially of the Stoics. Paul's spirit is provoked when he sees that the city is full of Epicurean and Stoic philosophical tenets. The word has a wider semantic range than the context with philosophers. In, for example, *P.Leid.W* 26 it is used for the "nine constellations", and in *P.Ryl* II.63 it was used for astrological "images". It was also used for images of pagan gods, although this is a lesser meaning.

Others said, "He seems to be putting the case for foreign gods!" They said this because he was announcing the Good News, Jesus and the resurrection, to them. **19-21** Then they took him and brought him to a meeting of the Areopagos. They said to him, "Please tell us about this new doctrine that you're presenting! *20* You're bringing some ideas that sound strange to us, and we'd like to know what it's all about!" *21* You see, all the Athenians and the temporary residents who were there spent their leisure time doing nothing else but talking about or listening to the latest ideas.[1]

Areopagos.

In the Roman period, the council of the Areopagos was a body similar to a municipal or colonial senate, and was the governing body of the *polis*. It had several functions – judicial, financial, foreign relations, and determination of citizen status. The Areopagos had around 100 members.

Geagen, *The Athenian Constitution after Sulla* (Princeton: *Hesperia* Suppl. 12; 1967), 50, argues that the account of Paul's speech before the Areopagos indicates the body's surveillance over the introduction of foreign divinities.

Epicureanism.

The philosopher Epicurus was concerned with the question "How to live?" Prior to Epicureanism, Pyrrho the philosopher maintained that we cannot know: there is no evidence to lead us to trust the senses rather than reason or reason rather the senses. Epicurus declared that all true knowledge comes from the senses. The basis of Epicureanism is the infallibility of the senses.

Epicurus maintained that physical sight is caused by "Idols" (εἴδωλα, *eidola*, plural of εἴδωλον, *eidolon*, see Acts 17:16) which are being cast off by every object continually. ("Idols" is the way translators have traditionally rendered εἴδωλα, *eidola*.) The Idol of an object is composed of a very fine layer of atoms. One of the best known Epicureans, Lucretius, describes it as "when the grasshoppers lay aside their smooth coats in summer". (*De Rerum Natura*, IV.38.) Epicurus stated that the atoms of the Idol impinge upon the atoms of our eyes and so cause sight.

Lucretius describes Epicurus as "the man of Greece who first dared raise his mortal eyes to face the fiend Superstition, hovering with gruesome feature above prostrate humanity, and who, not deterred by myth or thunderbolt, first craved to burst the blockades of nature's gates." (I.72-4).

The main features of the Epicurean system are made clear in Lucretius' celebrated work, *De Rerum Natura*, "On the Nature of Things". The Epicurean sought after *ataraxia*, the ideal state. To achieve *ataraxia*, humanity must be taught that the soul dies with the body, being made of atoms as is the body, thus freeing people from fear of punishment after death. By teaching that the gods are disinterested and that the world is explained by natural causes, humanity is freed from the fear of the gods. The theme of *De Rerum Natura* is the removal of fear of the gods, for it is only when the obstacle of fear is removed that humanity can find its way to *ataraxia*.

Lucretius states that the gods are composed of physical atoms, and therefore are controlled by physical science. They have no concern with the affairs of the world. The fear of the gods is denounced as the cause of infinite evil to the world. If people are to cease to fear the gods, they must learn the laws of natural science. If they are to cease to fear punishment after death, they must learn the

---

[1]   These people were intellectual thinkers and the reference has nothing to do with gossips. Athens had long been the center of intellectual minds. They were open-minded and keen to hear what Paul had to say.

nature of the soul. Tales of torment in an afterlife are merely allegories of the miseries of the present life.

According to Lucretius, fear of death must logically subside with the last hope of indefinite life. Not only does Lucretius expose the fear of death as irrational, he demonstrates his belief that the acceptance of nature as the governor of the physical world is a dictate of reason. By giving the continued assurance of an orderly, atom-founded universe, and removing all interest of the gods in the fact of death and its aftermath, and by establishing the complete dissolution of the soul after death, Lucretius seeks to free humanity from the fear of the gods.

Epicureanism states that humanity must make its peace with mortality to achieve *ataraxia* as an involuntary reflex within the laws of the universe. It states that the light to dispel the terror of the mind, the fear of the gods, can only come through an understanding of the nature of things.

Stoics.

The Stoics considered fear to be part of the human condition. The main issue of Stoic philosophy is the control of such passions and the attainment of inner peace through conformity with nature. The Stoics believed that the passions must be crushed, and their objective was a state of *impatientia*. *Impatientia* was the equivalent to the Greek *apathia*, not quite the same as the Epicurean ideal of *ataraxia*, although both involve the removal of the obstacle of fear.

22-25 Paul stood up before them in the Areopagos and said, "Athenians! I see that you are very religious in every way, *23* as while I was passing through and looking carefully at your objects of worship, I even found an altar with this inscription: 'To the unknown god.' So, I'm going to tell you about the unknown One that you worship without even knowing it! *24* God, who made the world and everything in it, is the Lord of heaven and earth and does not live in temples made by people. *25* Nor is he provided for by people,[1] as if he needed anything! In fact, he's the one who gives life, breath and everything else to all people!

26-28 "From one human he made all races of people that live on the face of the earth, and he appointed the seasons for them and he set the boundaries, so that they would seek God, *27* and possibly would grope their way to him and find him. And in fact, he's not far from each one of us! *28* For because of him we live and move and have our very being! As certain ones of your own poets have said, 'For we are also his offspring.'[2]

29-31 "So then, since we are God's offspring, we ought not to think that the Divine Nature is like gold or silver or stone, something crafted by art and human design. *30* So then, on the one hand, in past times God overlooked such ignorance, but on the other hand, in the present he now commands all people everywhere to change their minds. *31* He has set up a Day on which he will judge the world justly by the Man whom he has ordained. He has provided all of us with assurance of this by raising him from among the dead."

---

[1]   ἀνθρώπικινος, *anthropikinos*, people, humanity, mortals. See papyrus letter from Anatolios to his brother Neilos, *BJRL* 51.164-83 (Hermopolis Magna, Thebald, IV).
[2]   This is a quotation from two the classical writers, Aratois, *Phainomena*, 5, and Keleanthes, *Hymn to Zeus*, 5. Paul quotes the Athenians' own literature back to them. Paul is relating to the listeners on a personal level.

32-34 When they heard about the resurrection from the dead some of them mocked,[1] but others said, "We'd like to hear from you again on this matter!"

33 At that, Paul left. **34** Certain of the ladies and gentlemen[2] to whom he was speaking believed, among whom especially were Dionysus a member of the Areopagos and the woman by the name of Damaris;[3] and others, together with them.

Ch.18:1-3 After this Paul left Athens and went away to Corinth. **2** And he found a certain Jew by the name of Aquila, who was born in Pontus. He had recently come from Italy with his wife Priscilla, because Claudius had ordered all the Jews to leave Rome.[4] Paul went to see them. **3** And because he was of the same craft - they were tentmakers by trade - he stayed with them and worked.

Corinth.

Corinth in Achaia was a huge and wealthy city, owing its prosperity to its position straddling the Isthmus of Corinth with its two ports, Kenchreai on the Aegean, and Lekheon on the Ionian Sea. Corinth had trade links all over the ancient world. It was 6 miles (10 km) from the celebrated biennial Isthmian Games. Note that Paul in 1 Corinthians 9:24-27 mentions the victor's perishable wreath of wild celery: this was the prize at the Isthmian Games.

The marble judgment seat of the court mentioned in Acts 18:12-17 has been located after excavations in the agora. Also excavated is an extensive business area. The meat market (mentioned in 1 Corinthians 10:25) has been identified, and is located next to temples where the animals were sacrificed. An inscription found near the theater names Erastus: "Erastus, in return for his election as city treasurer, laid the pavement at his own expense." This could well be the Erastus of Romans 16:23.

Corinth was sacked by the Romans in 146 BC for revolting, but was rebuilt by Julius Caesar in 44 BC and became a commercial center with trade links all over the ancient world. It was close to ports to the east and west, and a favorite place for sailors. The Temple of Aphrodite, which Strabo states held 1,000 sacred prostitutes, was on the Acrocorinth, the fortress dominating the city. The Acrocorinth also housed temples to Hermes, Apollo, Herakles, Poseidon and Asklepios.

4-6 He held discussions in the synagogue every Sabbath and tried to persuade both Jews and Greeks. **5** When Silas and Timothy came down from Macedonia, Paul devoted himself entirely to the Word, testifying to the Jews that Jesus was the Anointed One. **6** But when they opposed him and hurled abuse at him, he shook out his cloak in protest and said to them, "Your blood be on your own heads! I'm clear of responsibility! From now on I'm going to move on to the non-Jews!"

---

[1] χλευάζω, *khleuazo*, only here in N.T. (Some concordances state that it occurs also at Acts 2:13, but the word there is διαχλευάζω, *diakhleuazo*.) Only three late papyrus attestations occur for this verb. MM cites two papyrus attestations: *P.Cair.Masp.* I (Aphrodite, 553), "…and now I have been mocked by him", and *PSI* 5.481.9-10 (V/VI), "He… made himself a mockery…". See also *P.Laur.* 43 (V), "If you… mocked not me, but yourselves…"

[2] τινὲς δὲ ἄνδρες, *tines de andres*. ἀνήρ, *aner*, was commonly a term of formal respect referring to both genders.

[3] It was not unusual for women to be present at philosophical discussions, and indeed, the Hetairai are well known for their presence at symposiums..

[4] In Rome in AD 41 Claudius denied the Jews the right to hold meetings, presumably as the result of disturbances, and when these continued, in AD 49 expelled the Jews from Rome. Suetonius, *Claudius*, 25.4, states, "Because the Jews at Rome caused continuous disturbances at the instigation of Chrestus, he expelled them from the City." (Chrestus is Latin for "Christ", that is, the Anointed One.)

7-8 And he left there and went to the house of a certain person by the name of Titius Justus, a 'Convert to Judaism'.[1] His house was adjoining the synagogue. *8* Crispus, the synagogue ruler, and his whole household believed the Lord. Many of the Corinthians who heard him believed and were baptized.

9-11 One night the Lord spoke to Paul in a vision: "Don't be afraid, but continue to speak and do not be silent, *10* because I am with you, and no one will attack you and harm you, because I have many people in this city!" *11* He stayed there for a year and six months, teaching the Word of God among them.

12-17 When Gallio[2] was Regional Governor of Achaia, the Jews combined to rise up against Paul and bring him to court. *13* They said, "This person is inciting people to worship God in illegal ways!" *14* But when Paul was about to open his mouth, Gallio said to the Jews, "Now you Jews, if it were a question of violent crimes or fraud, it would be reasonable for me to give you a hearing. *15* But since the point at issue is one of doctrine, terminology and your own law, you must see to it yourselves - I don't want to be a judge of such matters!" *16* He dismissed them from the court. *17* Then they all grabbed Sosthenes[3] the synagogue ruler, and beat him up in front of the court. But none of these things were of any concern whatsoever to Gallio.

Ephesos.

Ephesos was arguably the most spectacular Greco-Roman site in the ancient world. It was a magnificent white marble city, with breathtaking ruins today, and to date only around 5% of it has been excavated. Paul would have seen the Temple of Artemis (one of the Seven Wonders of the Ancient World), the theater, two Agoras, the Processional Way, the East Gymnasium, the Koressian Gates, the Bouleuterion, the monument of Pollio, a large fountain supplied by aqueduct, the stadium, and shops and terrace houses. The Prytaneum housed the sacred flame of Hestia Bouleia, the goddess of the hearth, a flame which was not permitted to go out.

Ephesus was the capital city of the Roman province of Asia, and had approximately 100,000 inhabitants. It was about 47 miles south of Smyrna (modern Izmir) and about 3 miles inland from the Aegean Sea. Ephesos was an important communication center due to its strategic position. The city was linked to the harbor by a 10 yard wide marble-paved road, "The Arcadian Way", flanked by huge columns.

Ephesos was well known historically as a center for magical practices, spell casting and the conjuring of evil spirits, and was the cult center of the worship of the Ephesian goddess Artemis (not to be confused with the Greek Artemis), known as "the greatest" and "the supreme power". The city held the title of Temple Warden of the goddess. She was said to have authority over all the demons of the dead as well as the harmful spirits of nature. Artemis was known as a mother goddess, a fertility goddess and a nature

---

[1] σεβουμένου τὸν Θεόν, *seboumene ton Theon*. See note on Acts 16:14.

[2] Gallio was the brother of Seneca, Nero's tutor. Seneca in fact dedicated two of his works, *De Ira* and *De Vita Beata*, to Gallio. Gallio is featured in an inscription at Delphi. *De Ira* is an extended study in the observation of neurosis. These were nightmarish times. In *De Ira* III, xv, Seneca relates the story of the King of Persia setting a certain adviser's children before him at a banquet, and then ordering the children's heads to be brought in. Seneca was also aware that Nero had his brother and mother killed, and again in *De Ira* II, xxxiii, 4, tells of Caligula killing a man's son and then forcing him to drink a toast. Through his plays Seneca shows anger to be the most destructive of passions. The importance of philosophy and rhetoric in Seneca's tragedies has long been acknowledged, so much so that his plays are considered to be declamatory dramas. See Stoicism.

[3] A very common name.

goddess. Her followers believed that she had powers superior to those who controlled the fate of people.

Ephesos was also a center of emperor worship, having three official temples, and was one of the very few cities to hold the title of Temple Warden of the deified, dead emperor. It was a large pilgrimage center and as such had a major tourist trade.

18-21 Paul stayed on in Corinth for some time. Then he said goodbye to the fellow believers and sailed away to Syria, and with him were Priscilla and Aquila. He had his head shaven at Kenchreai,[1] as he had taken a vow.[2] *19* When he came down to Ephesos, he left them behind there, but he went on alone into the synagogue and held discussions with the Jews. *20* They asked him to spend more time with them, but he didn't say he would. *21* Instead, he said goodbye to them, and said, "I will return to you if it's in God's purpose for me to!" Then he set sail from Ephesos.

22-23 When he had come down to Caesarea, he went up and greeted the assembly. After that he went down to Antioch. *23* After he had spent some time there, he left and traveled through the region of Phrygian Galatia, very much strengthening the disciples.

Harbor of Augustus in Caesarea.

Herod had trouble finding a suitable port on the Mediterranean. Not only were natural ports scant, but some ports that were suitable were not under his control. Finally Herod settled on Caesarea, but the harbor needed to be rebuilt as an artificial port. Josephus speaks of the harbor: "(Herod) adorned it with... the greatest work of all which required most labor, a sheltered harbor as big as the Piraeus. ... Surrounding the harbor was an unbroken row of houses of polished stone, and in the middle was a hill on which stood a temple of the emperor, which could be seen at a distance from approaching ships, containing statues of Rome and Caesar." (*Ant.* 15, 331-41). Josephus details the construction of the harbor which involved sinking huge amounts of rock as foundations, as well as a complicated sewage system. This has been verified by archaeologists.

Shortly after Herod's death in AD 6, Caesarea became the Roman capital of the region and remained so for around 600 years.

---

[1]   Kenchreai was the eastern port of Corinth, and was one of the two important ports for Corinth.

[2]   εὐχή, *eukhe*, "claim", "vow", not "prayer". The noun occurs only 3 times in N.T., Acts 18:18; 21:23; James 5:15. The verb appears in Acts 26:29; 27:29; Rom. 9:3; 1 Cor. 13:7,9; James 5:16; 3 John 2:1. The noun appears in the sense "dedication" in *I. Kyme* 41, an inscription from Kyme in Asia Minor, first ed. by A. Salac, *BCH* 51 (1927) 378-383, reprinted by H. Engelmann as *I. Kyme* 41, pp. 97-108 (pl. 11). "Demetrios, son of Artemidoros, also called Thraseas, from Magnesia on the Maeander, made this claim to Isis. ... I am Isis, the ruler of every land. I was educated by Hermes and I invented with Hermes sacred and public writing in order that everything might not be written in the same script. I laid down laws for people and legislated what no one can alter. I am the eldest daughter of Chronos. I am the wife and sister of King Osiris. I am the one who discovered fruit for people. I am the mother of King Horos. I am the one who rises in the constellation of the Dog." This quoted section comprises about 14 lines of 50, all claims of Isis as to her attributes.

24-26 A certain Jew named Apollos, born at Alexandria,[1] who was an eloquent man and powerful in his knowledge of the Scriptures, came to Ephesos. *25* This person had been orally taught the way of the Lord. As he was spiritually passionate, he spoke and taught accurately about the things of Jesus, although he only knew about the baptism carried out by John. *26* So he began to speak out boldly in the synagogue.[2] When Priscilla and Aquila heard him, they took him aside and explained the way of God more accurately.

27-28 When Apollos wanted to cross over to Achaia, the fellow believers wrote and encouraged the disciples to welcome him. Once he arrived, he was a great help to those who had by God's favor become believers. *28* He vigorously and thoroughly refuted the Jews in public, and demonstrated from the Scriptures that Jesus is the Anointed One.

Ch.19:1-7 It turned out that while Apollos was at Corinth, that Paul came down to Ephesos after he had traveled through the upper districts. *2* Upon finding some disciples, he said to them, "Did you receive the Holy Spirit when you became believers?"

"But we haven't even so much as heard whether the Holy Spirit exists!" they answered.

3 "Then with what baptism were you baptized?" Paul asked.

"With the baptism that John carried out!" they said.

4 Paul said, "John baptized with a baptism which was about you changing your minds, and told the people that they should believe the One who was going to come after him, that is, on Jesus." *5* When they heard this they were baptized in the Name of the Lord Jesus. *6* And when Paul laid his hands upon them, the Holy Spirit came upon them, and they spoke in supernaturally given languages and prophesied. *7* There were about twelve men in all.

8-10 Then Paul went into the synagogue and spoke out freely, boldly and openly in public for three months. He discussed and persuaded concerning God's Realm. *9* But when some people were obstinate and disbelieved, and verbally abused the Way in front of the community, he withdrew from them and took the disciples away. Then he held discussions each day in the lecture hall of Tyrannos. *10* This continued for two years, so that all the inhabitants of the province of Asia heard the Word of the Lord, both Jews and Greeks.

11-16 God worked extraordinary powers at the hands of Paul, *12* so that even when handkerchiefs or cloths were carried away from his skin and laid upon the sick, the diseases were removed from them and also evil spirits marched out of them. *13* Then some of the Jewish exorcists who traveled around took it upon themselves to call the Name of the Lord Jesus over those who had evil spirits, saying, "I exorcise you by Jesus who Paul proclaims."

14 Seven sons of Sceva, a Jewish chief priest, did this, *15* but the evil spirit answered them, "Jesus I know, and Paul I know, but who are you!" *16* Then the person who had the evil spirit in him, pounced on them, overpowered them all and beat them up! They ran out of the house naked and bleeding!

17-20 Everyone who lived in Ephesos, both Jews and Greeks, heard about it. They were all awestruck, and the Name of the Lord Jesus was greatly praised. *18* Many people who had already become believers kept coming and made public announcements of what they had been up to. *19* Quite a few people who had practiced the gaining of supernatural knowledge collected their books and burnt them in front of everyone. They calculated the value of

---

[1]   Alexandria was in Egypt. The name Apollos is most rarely attested outside Egypt, but is a common name in Egypt. There are numerous texts attesting to this. See, for example, *SB* 10999.6 (early 1st c.), 11016.7 (private letter, 17/4/13); 11130.13 (private letter, III/IV).

[2]   As yet no synagogue has been found at Ephesos, but *archisynagogoi* and *presbyteroi* are mentioned in *I.Eph.* IV.1251. For the possible location of two synagogues, see A. Bammer, *Ephesos. Stadt am Fluss und Meer*, Graz, 1988, 154-55.

the books and found it was several million dollars worth![1] *20* Thus with great forceful power the Word of the Lord grew and became strong.

21-22 After all this had come about, Paul resolved by means of the Spirit to pass through Macedonia and Achaia, and then go on to Jerusalem. He said, "After I've been there I must see Rome as well!" *22* He sent two of his assistants who financially provided for him, Timothy and Erastus, to Macedonia while he stayed on a little longer in the province of Asia.

23-27 It happened that about that time a considerable disturbance about the Way arose. *24* There was a certain silversmith by the name of Demetrius, who made silver shrines of Artemis. These brought in considerable business for the craftspeople.[2] *25* He called them together, along with the workers in similar trades, and said, "Ladies and gentlemen,[3] you know that our high standard of living depends on this trade. *26* Furthermore you see and hear that not only at Ephesos, but also in practically the whole of Asia, this Paul has persuaded large crowds and led them astray by saying that gods made by people are not gods at all! *27* So not only is this trade of ours in danger of falling into disrepute, but also the temple of the great goddess Artemis will be considered of no account and she will end up by being robbed of her majesty - Artemis, who is worshipped by all Asia and the world!"[4]

28-29 When they heard this, they were infuriated and shouted out, "Great is Artemis of the Ephesians!"

29 The whole city was thrown into confusion.[5] The people grabbed and carried off Gaius and Aristarchos, Paul's traveling companions, and rushed into the theater[6] all together.

30-32 Paul wanted to appear before the People's Assembly, but the disciples wouldn't let him. *31* Also, some of his friends who were Roman officials called "Asiarchs"[7] sent messages to him pleading for him not to venture into

---

[1]   50,000 drachmas, a wage for 100 years.

[2]   This sentence shows the motive for the craftspeople was economic: they were protecting their jobs.

[3]   ἄνδρες, *andres*. See note on Acts 7:2.

[4]   This sentence is supported by Pausanias 4.31.8.

[5]   An inscription, a proconsular decree *I.Eph*. II.125, demonstrates the involvement of the guilds in causing urban strife: "with the result that it happens that sometimes the demos falls into confusion and uproar because of the assembling together and insolence of the bakers at the agora." W.H. Buckler in W.M. Calder (eds.), *Anatolian Studies Presented to W.M. Ramsay* (Manchester, 1923) 30-33, pl. 2. Tacitus states that the crowd had the greatest licence: *ubi plurima vulgi licentia*, able to influence imperial policy.

[6]   Chariton, a 1st c. novelist, speaks of meetings in theatres as commonplace. Chariton, 1.1.11; 3.4.17; 7.3.10. The huge Theater of Ephesos, built into the slope of Mt Pion in the Hellenistic period and enlarged under Claudius (AD 41-54), could seat over 24,000 people. The auditorium rose over 33 yards (around 30 metres) over the orchestra. The acoustics were wonderful. Today the theatre is in an excellent state of preservation.

[7]   An Asiarch was a Roman official elected annually. The Asiarch administered public worship and presided over provincial assemblies, and retained their office title after his term of office was over. The Asiarchs were high priests of the cult of the goddess Roma and of the Emperor cult. Well over 100 Asiarchs are recorded in inscriptions dating from the late 1st to the mid 3rd centuries, and the inscriptions have been found in more than 40 cities. One of the early inscriptions at Ephesos (*I.Eph*. Ia.27.220-46 pls. 35,36) is dated around 50 years after the reference to Asiarchs in Acts 19:31. Another group of office bearers, both men and women, is known as *archiereus* or *archiereia*. This title is thought to be synonymous with Asiarch, but the evidence is not conclusive. The woman Iulia Lydia Laterane had been a Chief Magistrate at Ephesos, and then became an

the theater. *32* The People's Assembly was in confusion. Some were shouting one thing and some another. Most of them didn't even know why they had assembled there!

33-34 Some of the Jews pushed Alexander out in front, and some of the crowd shouted instructions at him. He motioned for silence and wanted to make his defense[1] before the People's Assembly. *34* But when they realized that he was a Jew, they all shouted in unison for about two hours, "Great is Artemis of the Ephesians!"[2]

35-41 The city clerk calmed them down and said, "Ephesians! After all, every single person knows that the city of Ephesos is the custodian[3] of the great Temple of Artemis and of her image, fallen from Zeus![4] *36* Therefore, since these things can't be denied, you ought to keep calm and not do anything reckless! *37* You have brought these gentlemen here, and they're not temple robbers nor even blasphemers of our goddess![5] *38* So then, if Demetrios and his fellow craftspeople have a case against anyone, the courts are open and there are Regional Governors. Let them bring charges against one another! *39* But if you're looking for anything further to bring up, it must be settled in a legal assembly. *40* As it stands we are in danger of being charged with rioting for today's events, and there is no explanation we can give to account for this mob!" *41* After he had said this he dismissed the assembly.

Ch.20:1-6 After the uproar had ceased, Paul sent for the disciples, said goodbye to them, and set out to travel to Macedonia. *2* He went through that district and encouraged them on many occasions, and finally arrived in Greece, *3* where he stayed for three months. When the Jews plotted against him when he was about to sail for Syria, he decided to return through Macedonia. *4* Sopater, Pyrrhus's son from Berea, accompanied him to Asia, as did Aristarchos and Secundus from Thessalonika, Gaius from Derbe, Timothy also, and Tychikos and Trophimos of Asia. *5* These people went on ahead and waited for us in Troas. *6* But we sailed away from Philippi after

---

archiereia. (*I.Eph.* V.1601e; *I.Eph.* II.424a.) Another woman, Vedia Marcia, was both a Chief Magistrate at Ephesos and an *archiereia* of Asia. (*I. Eph.* IV.1017.)

[1]   ἀπολογέομαι, *apologeomai*, "defend", a technical legal term.

[2]   The silversmiths perceived the threat as coming from the Jews. At this time, it was too early for the Christians to be identified as a group separate from Jews by the silversmiths, non-Jews who had no close contact with Christians.

[3]   That is, Temple Warden.

[4]   That is to say, "fallen from heaven". The Ephesians saw themselves as ἡ τροφὸς τῆς ἰδίας θεοῦ τῆς Ἐφεσίας, *he trophos tes idias theou tes Ephesias*, "the nurturer of its own Ephesian goddess". The word *neokoros* (warden) came to express Ephesos' role as ἡ τροφός, *he trophos*, of Artemis. This was documented on a 1st c. coin, cf. *RE* Suppl. 12, col. 330. Other coins depict Ephesos as the personification of a female holding the cult statue of Artemis in the palm of her outstretched hand, cf. nos. 314, 346, 384, B.V. Head, *Catalogue of the Greek Coins in the British Museum: Ionia*, (London, 1892, repr. Bologna, 1964). *I.Eph.* Ia, 2, records that when an embassy, which was sent from Ephesos to the shrine of Artemis at Sardis, was insulted, the several dozen men who had committed the insults were to be punished by the death penalty. There were several solemn festival days in honor of Artemis. Both the civic and temple officials were involved in the celebration of Artemis' birthday, and texts of civic decisions were displayed in the Artemision, cf. *I.Eph.* VI, 2004. Ephesos was closely associated with Artemis in the time of Xenophon (4th c. BC), as he mentions "Megabyzos, son of Megabyzos, warden of Artemis in Ephesos." (*Anabasis* 5.3.6.) See also *I.Eph.* Ia, 27, *l.*259; *I.Eph.* V, 1522.

[5]   Note the above footnote, cf. *I.Eph.* Ia, 2 which records blasphemers of the goddess as being liable to the death penalty.

the Feast of the Unleavened Bread,[1] and five days later joined the others at Troas, where we stayed for seven days.

7-12 On the first day of the week we gathered together to break bread. Paul spoke to the people, and since he was intending to go away the next day, prolonged his talking until midnight. *8* There were many lamps in the upper room where we were meeting. *9* A certain young man named Eutuchos[2] was sitting in a window, and he was sinking into a deep sleep. He was overcome by sleep, and when Paul kept speaking at great length, he fell down from the third story to the ground and was picked up dead. *10* But Paul went down, threw himself upon him and took him in his arms. He said, "Stop making this fuss: he's alive!"

11 Then he went upstairs again, broke bread and ate. He talked for a long time, right until dawn, and then left. *12* And they brought the young man in alive and they were extremely relieved.

13-17 We went ahead to the ship and set sail to Assos,[3] intending to take Paul aboard there. He had made this arrangement because he was going there on foot. *14* When he met us at Assos, we took him on board and went to Mytilene.[4] *15* We sailed away from there, and the next day arrived off Chios.[5] The following day we arrived at Samos[6] and stayed at Trogyllium. On the day after that we arrived at Miletos. *16* Paul had decided to sail past Ephesos to avoid spending time in Asia, as he was in a hurry to reach Jerusalem, if at all possible, by the day of Pentecost. *17* From Miletos he sent to Ephesos and called for the elders of the assembly.

Miletos.

In Paul's time, two lions sat at the entrance of the harbor at Miletos. The entrance to the harbor was so narrow that it could be chained off. Today one lion remains, and the harbor has silted up due to the changing path of the River Maeander.

Many famous minds came from Miletos: Thales the philosopher, who predicated a solar eclipse in the 6th c. B.C., Hippodamos the town planner, Anaximander the philosopher, and Anaximenes the geographer. Miletos became one of the most important free cities in the Roman province of Asia. Paul would have seen the remains of Roman monuments, including the commemoration of Octavian and Agrippa's victory over Antony and Cleopatra. Today, the remains include a Greco-Roman stadium seating about 15,000, the Baths of Faustina (an enormous well preserved baths complex), a huge agora, a smaller agora, a Hellenistic gymnasium, a shrine to Apollo (the Delphinion), a Roman bath complex, and a Jewish synagogue (which exists only in traces), a Hellenistic bouleuterion, a type of theater seating 1,5000, and a Roman nymphaeum (fountain complex) with water brought over 3 ½ miles (6 k.m.) by an aqueduct.

18-23 When they arrived, he said to them, "You know how I lived the whole time I was with you, from the first day that I came into Asia. *19* I have served the Lord with great humility, with many tears and ordeals[7] which happened to me because of the Jews' plotting. *20* You know how I didn't hold back anything which was for your benefit. Instead, I reported it to you,

---

[1]   This may refer to the Passover of Thursday, April 7, 57 AD.

[2]   Interestingly, Eutuchos in the Greek means "Lucky"!

[3]   Assos was situated on the edges of a volcanic cone on the edge of the sea. The rich volcanic soil made it a wonderful wheat producing area.

[4]   Mytilene is on Lesbos, the third largest of the Greek islands, 9 miles from the Turkish coast.

[5]   Chios, said to be the birthplace of Homer, is an island in the Aegean between Samos and Lesbos, 5 miles from the Turkish coast. It features spectacular cliffs.

[6]   Samos is a mile from the Turkish coast, and is only 27 miles long.

[7]   περιασμός, *periasmos*. See note on Matt. 6:13.

and taught you publicly and from house to house. *21* I have told both Jews and Greeks about changing your minds, turning towards God, and faith in the Lord Jesus. *22* And now, you see, I am bound by the Spirit to travel to Jerusalem, and I don't know what will happen to me there, *23* except that the Holy Spirit testifies to me that imprisonment and oppressions are facing me!

24-27 "But as for myself, I regard my life in no sense precious to me, so long as I finish the race and complete the ministry the Lord Jesus has given me, which is the task of speaking truthfully about the Good News of God's favor. *25* And now, I know for certain that none of you to whom I've gone around reporting about God's Realm, will ever see my face again! *26* Because I tell you truthful words this day that I am clear of the responsibility of the blood of all people. *27* For I have not avoided proclaiming to you God's whole purpose.

28-32 "Take care for yourselves and for all the flock, of which the Holy Spirit has made you guardians. Be shepherds of God's assembly, which he bought with his own blood. *29* I myself know that after I leave, violent wolves will come in among you and they won't spare the flock. *30* Also from among yourselves men will arise, speaking distortions of the truth in order to draw away disciples after them. *31* So then keep your wits about you! Remember that for three years I never stopped tearfully warning every one of you day and night. *32* As for the present, fellow believers, I commit you to God and to the Message about his favor, which is able to build you up and give you an inheritance among all those who are made sacred.

33-35 "I have not coveted anyone's silver or gold or clothing. *34* You yourselves know that these hands of mine have supplied my own needs and the needs of my companions. *35* I have pointed out to you, by laboring like this, that in all respects we must assist the weak. We must remember the words of the Lord Jesus, that he said, 'It is more blessed to give than to receive!'"

36-38 When he had said these things he fell on his knees and prayed with all of them. *37* Everyone was crying a lot. They hugged him and kissed him. *38* They were the most distressed about him saying that he wouldn't see them any more. They escorted him to the ship.

Ch.21:1-4 And so it happened that after we were parted from them, we set sail and steered a straight course to Cos.[1] The next day we went to Rhodes[2] and from there to Patara.[3] *2* When we found a ship crossing over to Phoenicia, we went on board and set sail. *3* We sighted Cyprus and passed it on the port side, and then we sailed on to Syria. We put into port at Tyre, where our ship was to unload its cargo. *4* As we found disciples there, we stayed on there for seven days. Through the Spirit they told Paul not to go up to Jerusalem.

5-6 So it happened that when our time was finished we left and went on our way. They all accompanied us with their wives and children until we were outside the city. There, on the seashore, we knelt to pray. *6* When we had said goodbye to each other, we boarded the ship and they returned home.

7-9 When we finished our voyage from Tyre, we came down to Ptolemais,[4] where we greeted the fellow believers and stayed with them for one day. *8* On the next day we left and came to Caesarea. There we entered the house of

---

[1] Cos is in the Aegean Sea, 3 miles off the Turkish coast. It is the oldest site of the healing cult of Asklepios, and also known as the site where Hippocrates practiced.

[2] The Colossus of Rhodes on the island of Rhodes in Greece was one of the Seven Wonders of the Ancient World. Paul would have seen its remains.

[3] In Paul's time, Patara in Roman Lycia was a good all-weather port. The port has now disappeared, and due to extensive silting-up, Patara is no longer on the coast.

[4] At Ptolemais was the only natural harbor on the Mediterranean coast. Formerly known as Acre, it became a semi-independent state under Ptolemy II Philadelphus (238-246 BC), and was renamed Ptolemais.

Philip the Good News announcer, who was one of the Seven, and stayed with him. *9* He had four unmarried[1] daughters who prophesied.

10-14 After we had stayed there for several days, a certain prophet named Agabos came down from Judea. *11* He came over to us, took Paul's belt, tied his own hands and feet with it and said, "Thus says the Holy Spirit, 'In this way the Jews of Jerusalem will bind the man to whom this belt belongs, and will hand him over to the non-Jews!'"

12 When we heard this, both we and the local people pleaded with Paul not to go up to Jerusalem. *13* Then Paul answered, "What do you mean by crying and breaking my heart? I am ready not only to be bound, but also to die in Jerusalem for the name of the Lord Jesus!"

14 So when he couldn't be persuaded we gave up and said, "Let the Lord's purpose be done!"

15-19 After this, we packed up and went to Jerusalem. *16* Also, some of the disciples from Caesarea went with us and brought us to the home of a certain Mnason from Cyprus who had offered us hospitality. He had been a disciple for a long time. *17* When we arrived at Jerusalem, the fellow believers greeted us with delight. *18* The following day, Paul and the rest of us went to see James, and all the elders were present. *19* When he had greeted them, he related in detail what God had done among the non-Jews through his ministry.

20-25 When they heard this they praised God, and said to him, "You see, fellow believer, how many tens of thousands of Jews have believed, and all of them are zealous about the Law! *21* They have been informed that you teach all the Jews who live among the non-Jews to depart from Moses, saying that they ought not circumcise their children or to observe our customs. *22* What then is to be done? They will certainly hear that you have come, *23* so now, do what we tell you to do! We have taken four men who have taken a vow on themselves. *24* Take them and join in their purification ceremony and pay their expenses on their behalf, so that they can have their heads shaved. Then everyone will know that there is nothing in what they say about you, but that you yourself also keep the Law. *25* Now about the non-Jew believers, we have written to them our decision that they should avoid food sacrificed to idols, from consuming blood, from the eating of strangled animals, and from *porneia*."[2]

26-27 Then the next day Paul took the men and purified himself along with them. Then he went to the Temple to give notice of the date when the period of purification would be completed, at which time an offering would be made for each of them. *27* When the seven days were almost over, some Jews from Asia noticed Paul in the Temple. They stirred up the whole crowd and grabbed him.

28-32 They shouted, "Israelites, help! This is the person who teaches all people everywhere, attacking our people, the Law, and this place! And what's more, he also brought Greeks into the Temple[3] and has defiled this sacred place!"

29 (They had previously seen Trophimos the Ephesian in the city with him, and they assumed that Paul had brought him into the temple.) *30* The whole city

---

[1] παρθένος, *parthenos*. See note on Matt.1:23.

[2] πορνεία, *porneia*. See note on Matt. 15:19.

[3] Greeks certainly were not allowed in the Temple. Philo speaks of a four foot high balustrade, with warning notices in both Greek and Latin showing the area forbidden to foreigners. Josephus states that non-Jews (with the obvious exception of proselytes and the group designated as Theosebia) were not allowed past the outer court, and states that the Roman authorities would allow the execution of Roman citizens for doing so. One of the warnings, *OGIS* 598, reads, "No foreigner may enter within the barricade which surrounds the temple and enclosure. Anyone who is caught doing so will have themselves to thank for their ensuing death." For a similar warning see *SEG* 8.169.

was disturbed, and a crowd gathered. They grabbed Paul and dragged him out of the Temple, and immediately the gates were shut. *31* While they were attempting to kill him, news reached the commander of the company of 600 soldiers that the whole of Jerusalem was in turmoil. *32* At once he took soldiers and Roman officers in charge of 100 men, and rushed down to them. When they saw the commander and the soldiers, they stopped beating Paul.

33-36 Then the commander went over to Paul and arrested him. He ordered that he be bound with two chains, and asked him who he was and what he had done. *34* Some people in the crowd were shouting one thing, and some were shouting another. When he couldn't get at the facts because of the uproar, he commanded that Paul be taken back into the barracks. *35* When Paul arrived at the stairs, he had to be carried by the soldiers because the violence of the mob was so great. *36* The crowd of people followed and kept shouting out, "Kill him!"

37-39 As Paul was about to be led into the barracks, he asked the commander, "May I have a word with you?"

"So you speak Greek, do you!"[1] he replied. *38* "Aren't you the Egyptian who started a revolt and led 4,000 terrorists out of the desert some time ago?"

39 But Paul said, "I in fact am a Jew, from Tarsus in Cilicia, a citizen of a most distinguished city.[2] Please allow me to speak to the people!"

40.Ch.22:1-11 So he gave him permission, and Paul stood on the stairs and motioned for silence to the people. When everything was perfectly quiet, he spoke to them in the Hebrew language,[3] *1* "Ladies and gentlemen,[4] fellow believers,[5] parents,[6] now listen to my defense!"

2 When they heard him speak in the Hebrew language, they caused less fuss.[7] And he said, *3* "I am indeed a Jew, born in Tarsus of Cilicia, brought

---

[1] Primary bilingualism refers to a speaker who picked up the second language by force of circumstances (such as the work environment). Secondary bilingualism refers to the speaker who has learned the language by systematic instruction. Some people, such as the Punic philosopher Hasdrubal (also known as Kleitomachos) preferred his second language to his first. Further, there was a difference between receptive and productive bilingualism. Receptive bilingualism refers to the speaker who can understand and read the language, but not write it or speak it. Productive bilingualism refers to the person who can speak and write the second language as well. Paul was a productive bilingualist, and it is to this fact that the commander expresses his surprise. See discussion in *NDIEC* 5.18-26.

[2] οὐκ ἀσήμου πόλεως, *ouk asemou poleos*, word-for-word, "not undistinguished city": typical Greek litotes (an ironic understatement using a negative of its contrary): "not undistinguished city" which means in English "a most distinguished city". For litotes see also Romans 1:16; 10:11; 1 Pet. 2:6; Rev. 3:5.

[3] The speech Paul gave here was either in Hebrew or Aramaic.

[4] ἄνδρες, *andres*. See note on Acts 7:2.

[5] ἀδελφοί, *adelphoi*. See note on Matt. 5:22.

[6] πατέρες, *pateres*, occurs in the papyri and inscriptions as an honorific title. There is no English equivalent of its use as an honorific title. The word could mean "father" but also meant "female parent", or just "parent", non-gender specific. P.J. Sijpesteijn lists 2 examples in papyri of individual women called *pater*. P.J. Sijpesteijn, *Tyche* 2 (1987) 171-74. The papyri of New Testament times show that terms such as *adelphos, pater, huios*, in the singular and plural, were used to indicate social relationships in non related people and were used of both genders.

[7] ἡσυχίαν, *hesuchian*, to become quiet in behaviour. It does not refer to verbal quietness. Here it does not mean they became more verbally silent (which, of course, would be an absurd expression), but they became quieter in behavior, that is to say, they caused less fuss. See in Antiphon, *Second Tetralogy, First Speech for the Defence*, 11.1, where ἡσύχιος, *hesuchios*, is

up in this city under the instruction of Gamaliel. I was educated in accordance with the strictness of the Law of our ancestors, and was zealous about it, as you all are today. *4* I persecuted this Way to the death, arresting both men and women and throwing them in prison, *5* as also the chief priest and all the council of elders bears me witness. From them I even obtained letters to their fellows in Damascus, to bring those who were there to Jerusalem as prisoners to be punished. *7* It happened that as I went on my way and approached Damascus at about midday that a bright light from the sky suddenly flashed all around me! *7* I fell to the ground and heard a voice saying to me, 'Saul, Saul, why are you persecuting me?'

8 "So I answered, 'Who are you, Lord?' And he said to me, 'I am Jesus of Nazareth, whom you are persecuting.'

9 "My companions saw the light, but they didn't hear the voice of him who spoke with me. *10* So I said, 'What am I to do, Lord?'

"And the Lord said to me, 'Get up and go to Damascus, and you will be told everything that you have been assigned to do.' *11* And as I couldn't see because of the dazzling brightness of that light, my companions led me by the hand into Damascus.

12-16 "A certain man named Ananias came to see me. He was a godly observer of the Law and highly regarded by all the Jews living there. *13* He came up and stood next to me and said, 'Brother Saul, receive your sight!' At that very instant I looked up at him. *14* Then he said, 'The God of our ancestors[1] has already chosen you to know his purpose, and see the Just One, and hear what he has to say *15* because you will be his witness to every race of people about everything that you've seen and heard. *16* And now what are you waiting for? Get up and have yourself baptized and wash away your sins, calling on his Name.'"

17-21 "Now it happened that when I had come back to Jerusalem and was praying in the Temple, I went into a displaced state *18* and saw him speaking to me: 'Quick! Get out of Jerusalem in a hurry, as they won't accept your truthful words about me!'

19 "So I said, 'Lord, they themselves know that in every synagogue I imprisoned and beat those who believe you. *20* And when the blood of your martyr Stephen was shed, I too was standing by, giving my approval, and minding the clothes of those who were killing him!'

21 "Then he said to me, 'Get going! I will send you far away to the non-Jews.'"

22-29 They listened to him up to this point, then they raised their voices and shouted, "Rid the earth of him! A guy like this isn't fit to live!"

23 Then, as they were shouting and throwing off their clocks and throwing dust into the air, *24* the commander ordered Paul to be taken into the barracks. He said that he should be questioned under flogging so that he could find out the reason why the people were shouting at him like this. *25* As they were tying him up with straps, Paul said to the Roman officer in charge of 100 men who stood by, "Is it legal for you to flog a Roman citizen who hasn't been condemned?"[2]

---

translated by R.C. Jebb as "the man of peaceful disposition". *Selections from the Attic Orators*, Ed. R.C. Jebb, (London: Macmillan & Co, 1962), p. 203. The actual word in the speech is (τοὺς) ἡσύχιους, (*tous*) *hesuchious*, translated by K.J. Maidment, *Minor Attic Orators*, (Cambridge: Harvard University Press, 1953), p. 91, as "those who love peace".

[1] τῶν πατέρων, *ton pateron*, ancestors. Used in the papyri and inscriptions as "ancestors" of both genders.

[2] The penalties for pretending to be a Roman citizen were so severe that no one would dare lie about it.

26 When the Roman officer in charge of 100 men heard that, he reported to the commander. He said, "What do you intend to do? This person is a Roman citizen!"

27 Then the commander went to Paul and asked, "Tell me, are you a Roman citizen?"

"Yes!" he said.

28 The commander answered, "I myself had to pay a large sum of money for my citizenship!"

Paul said, "But I was born a citizen!"[1]

29 Then immediately the people who were about to question him withdrew from him. The commander was also afraid because he found out that Paul was a Roman citizen and he had actually imprisoned him.

30.Ch.23:1-3 The next day, because the commander wanted to know for certain why Paul was accused by the Jews, he released him and commanded the chief priests and all the High Council to assemble. He brought out Paul and made him stand before them. *1* Paul fixed his eyes on the High Council and said, "Ladies and gentlemen,[2] fellow believers, I myself have lived in good conscience before God to this day."

2 The high priest Ananias[3] commanded those who stood next to him to smack him across the mouth. *3* Then Paul said to him, "God will strike you, you whitewashed wall! For you sit to judge me according to the Law, and at the same time you command me to be struck which is against the Law!"

4-10 The people standing near Paul said, "How dare you insult the high priest!"

5 Paul said, "I didn't know, fellow believers, that he was the high priest, for the Scriptures say, 'Do not speak badly of a ruler of your people.'"

6 When Paul realized that some of them were Sadducees and others were Pharisees, he called out in the High Council, "Ladies and gentlemen,[4] fellow believers, I am a Pharisee, the son of a Pharisee. I stand on trial because of the expectation of the resurrection of the dead."

7 And when he had said this, a commotion broke out between the Pharisees and the Sadducees, and the High Council was divided. *8* (The Sadducees on the one hand say that there is no resurrection, nor Messengers nor spirits, but the Pharisees on the other hand acknowledge them all.) *9* Then a loud uproar broke out. The record keepers of the Pharisees' party stood up and joined issue with the others, saying, "We find no evil in this person! What if a spirit or a Messenger has spoken to him?"

10 The dispute became so violent that the commander was afraid that Paul would be torn to pieces by them. He commanded the troops to go down and seize him, carry him away from them by force and bring him to the barracks.

11-17 The following night the Lord came and stood next to Paul and said, "Keep up your courage! Just as you have given evidence about me in Jerusalem, so you must also give evidence in Rome!"

12 When day came, some of the Jews called a secret meeting and bound themselves under an oath, swearing that they wouldn't eat or drink until they had killed Paul. *13* Now there were more than forty men involved in this conspiracy. *14* They went to the chief priests and elders and said, "We've bound ourselves under a curse[5] to an oath that we will eat nothing until we've killed Paul! *15* Now then, you and the High Council convey to the commander that he bring him down before you on the pretext of wanting to investigate the facts about him more accurately. We are ready to kill him before he gets here!"

---

[1]   Paulus was an upper-class name and would have been part of his full Roman name.

[2]   ἄνδρες, *andres*. See note on Acts 7:2.

[3]   This is not the same Ananias of 5:1 and 9:10.

[4]   ἄνδρες, *andres*. See note on Acts 7:2.

[5]   ἀνάθεμα, *anathema*. See note on καταράομαι, *kataraomai*, in Luke 6:28.

16 The son of Paul's sister heard of this ambush, and went into the barracks and told Paul. *17* Then Paul summoned one of the Roman officers in charge of 100 men and said, "Take this young man to the commander - he has something to tell him."

18-21 So then he took him to the commander, and said, "Paul the prisoner summoned me and asked me to bring this young man to you. He has something to tell you."

19 So then the commander took the young man by the hand, drew him aside and asked him in private, "What do you want to tell me?"

20 He said, "The Jews have agreed to ask you to bring Paul before the High Council tomorrow on the pretext of wanting more accurate information about him. *21* So don't give in to them, because more than forty of them are waiting in ambush for him! They have taken an oath not to eat or drink until they have killed him. They're ready now, waiting for the word from you!"

22-24 So the commander sent the young man away with the order, "Don't tell anyone that you've told me this!" *23* He called for two Roman officers in charge of 100 men and said, "Get ready 200 soldiers, 70 horsemen, and 200 spearmen to go to Caesarea at nine o'clock tonight, *24* and provide mounts for Paul to ride so that he can be taken to Felix the governor in safety."

25-30 He wrote a letter as per the following copy:[1] *26* "From: Claudius Lysias, To: The honorable Governor[2] Felix: Hello! *27* This man was seized by the Jews and was about to be killed by them, but I came along with my troops and rescued him, as I had learnt that he is a Roman citizen. *28* When I wanted to know the reason why they accused him, I brought him before their High Council. *29* I found out that he was accused concerning questions of their Law, but that there was no charge[3] against him that in any way deserved death or imprisonment. *30* When I was informed about a plot which was about to take place against the man, I sent him to you at once. I also ordered his accusers to present to you their case against him."

31-35 So then the soldiers took Paul and brought him by night to Antipatris[4] in accordance with their orders. *32* But the next day they let the cavalry go on with him, and returned to the barracks. *33* When the cavalry arrived in Caesarea and had delivered the letter to the governor, they also presented Paul to him. *34* The governor read the letter and asked what province he was from. Learning that he was from Cilicia, *35* he said, "I will hear your case when your accusers arrive."

He ordered him to be guarded in Herod's official residence.

Ch.24:1-8 After five days Ananias the chief priest came down with the elders and a certain barrister named Tertullus. These ones gave evidence against Paul to the Governor. *2* When Paul was called upon, Tertullus began his accusation. He said, "We have enjoyed a long period of peace under you, and your foresight has brought about reform in this nation. *3* Everywhere and in every way, honorable Felix, we acknowledge this with all gratitude. *4* Furthermore, so as not to detain you any longer, I beg in your kindness to listen to us briefly. *5* We have found this man to be a pest! He's stirred up riots among the Jews all over the world, and he's a ringleader of the sect of

---

[1] τύπος, *tupos*. See note on Acts 7:43.

[2] Literally, "procurator". Procurators were either freedman of the imperial family (as was Felix), or, more commonly, *equites*. They were responsible for the government of minor provinces.

[3] ἔγκλημα, *egklema*, "charge", a technical legal term. Elsewhere in Acts 25:16.

[4] Antipatris was a Roman military relay station in the fertile Plain of Sharon, 10 miles northeast of Joppa and 25 miles south of Caesarea, marking the border between Judea and Samaria. It was rebuilt by Herod the Great who named it for his father Antipater.

the Nazarenes. *6* He even tried to desecrate the temple, so we arrested him.[1] *8* By questioning him yourself you may ascertain that all these charges we are bringing against him are true."

9 The Jews also joined in the accusation, alleging that these things were so.

10-21 Then Paul, after the governor had signaled to him to speak, said, "I know that for many years you have been a judge over this nation, so I state my defense in good spirits. *11* You are able to ascertain that it is no more than twelve days since I went up to Jerusalem to worship. *12* And no one found me disputing with anyone nor stirring up a crowd in the synagogues nor anywhere else in the city. *13* Nor can they prove to you the charges they are now making against me. *14* But this I will confess to you, that I worship the God of my ancestors as a follower of the Way, which they call a sect. I believe everything that agrees with the Law and is written in the Prophets, *15* and I have the same expectation in God which these people themselves also do, that there is destined to be a resurrection of both the just and the unjust. *16* In this expectation, I myself always strive to keep my conscience clear before God and people. *17* After several years I came to bring gifts to the poor and to present offerings to my nation. *18* Occupied in these sacrifices, they found me purified in the temple – and not with any crowd or uproar! But there are some Jews from Asia *19* who ought to be here before you and bring charges if they have anything against me. *20* Otherwise, these ones here should state what crime they found in me when I stood before the High Council, *21* unless it was because of this single expression I called out as I stood among them: 'I am indeed being judged by you today over the matter of the resurrection of the dead.'"

22-23 Felix,[2] being well informed about the subject of the Way, adjourned the proceedings and said, "When Lysias the commander comes, I will decide your case."

23 He ordered the Roman officer in charge of 100 men to keep Paul in custody, but to give him some privileges and to allow his friends to attend to his needs.

24-27 After a few days Felix arrived with his wife Drusilla, who was a Jew. He sent for Paul and listened to him as he spoke about faith in Jesus the Anointed One. *25* As Paul discoursed about righteousness, self control and the judgment to come, Felix was alarmed and said, "That's enough for the time being! You may go! I'll call for you when I get an opportunity."

26 At the same time he hoped that Paul would give him a bribe, so he sent for him all the more often and talked with him. *27* But after two years, Felix was succeeded by Porcius Festus,[3] and because Felix wanted to curry favor with the Jews, he left Paul imprisoned.

Ch.25:1-5 So three days after Festus arrived in the province, he went up from Caesarea to Jerusalem, *2* where the chief priests and the Jewish leaders appeared before him and brought up the case against Paul. *3* They requested that, as a favor to them, he have Paul transferred to Jerusalem. They were organizing an ambush on the way. *4* Festus answered that Paul should be kept at Caesarea, but that he himself was intending to march out of there without delay. *5* "Therefore," he said, "let those of you who are powerful come down with me and press charges against this man here, if he has done anything weird."

---

[1]   Verse 7, part of verses 6 and 8 are omitted. The passage is not original.

[2]   Felix succeeded Cumanus as procurator of Judea in 52 A.D. Josephus, *B J*. II. 13. 2 stated that territory over which Felix ruled included Samaria and the greater part of Galilee and Perea, and that Judea was added by Nero.

[3]   Felix was succeeded by Porcius Festus possibly between 59 and 61 A.D., although Eusebius, *Chron.,* puts the accession of Felix in the 11th year of Claudius (51 A.D.), and the accession of Festus in the 14th year (54 A.D.) Festus was involved in the controversy between Agrippa II (mentioned here in Acts) and the Jews. See Josephus, *Ant*, 20.8.9-10.

6-8 When Festus had spent no more than eight or ten days with them, he went down to Caesarea. The next day he took his seat in court and ordered that Paul be brought in. *7* When he arrived, the Jews who had come down from Jerusalem stood all around him, and laid many serious charges against him, which they were not able to prove. *8* In the course of his defense Paul said, "I have done nothing wrong to offend against the Law of the Jews, nor against the Temple, nor against Caesar."

9-12 But Festus wanted to curry favor with the Jews and said to Paul, "Are you willing to go up to Jerusalem and stand trial before me on these charges?"

10 Then Paul said, "I am now standing before Caesar's court, where I must stand trial. I have done nothing wrong to the Jews, as you yourself know very well. *11* Therefore if I have done anything wrong which deserves the death penalty, I do not seek to be excused from dying. But if there is anything in these charges brought against me by the Jews, no one can hand me over to them as a favor. I appeal to Caesar."

12 Then after Festus conferred with his council, he answered, "You have appealed to Caesar, to Caesar you will go!"

13-21 A few days later King Agrippa[1] and Bernice[2] arrived at Caesarea, greeting Festus on a complimentary visit. *14* When they had been there several days, Festus put Paul's case before the king and said, "There's a certain gentleman here who was left as a prisoner by Felix. *15* When I was in Jerusalem, the chief priests and the elders of the Jews laid charges against him and asked that he be condemned. *16* I answered that it isn't the custom of the Romans to hand over anyone before the accused meets the accusers face to face and has been afforded the opportunity to defend himself against the charges. *17* When they assembled here, without losing any time I convened the court the next day, and commanded that the man be brought in. *18* When they stood up around him, his accusers did not bring any of the charges which I had been supposing. *19* Their point at issue with him was about their own religion, and a certain dead person named Jesus who Paul claimed was alive. *20* Indeed, I was at a loss over such questions so I asked him if he would be willing to go to Jerusalem and stand trial there on these charges. *21* But when Paul appealed to be held over for the Emperor's decision, I ordered him to be held until I could send him up to Caesar."

22 Agrippa said to Festus, "I would like to hear this man myself."

He replied, "Tomorrow you will hear him!"

23-27 So the next day Agrippa and Bernice came with great ceremony and entered the audience hall with the high ranking officers and the prominent citizens. At the command of Festus, Paul was brought in. *24* And Festus said,

---

[1] Agrippa was appointed king of Chalcis. His subjects were mostly non-Jews, but Agrippa maintained close links with the Jews, and with his sister Bernice in 66 A.D. tried to prevent the Jewish Revolt. However, when his attempts failed, he supported the Roman government. He had the right as king to appoint the High Priests and to control the Temple treasury. Agrippa was not popular with the citizens of Caesarea. Upon his death the citizens hurled abuse at him and carried the statues of his daughters to the brothels where they set them on the rooftops. For a full account, see Josephus, *Ant.* 19.9.1. The account of Photius states that it was the women themselves rather than their statues, who suffered this treatment.

[2] Bernice, a Jew, was the daughter of Agrippa 1, and after the death of her husband (and uncle) Herod, king of Chalcis, lived with her brother Agrippa (mentioned in this verse). See Josephus, *The War of the Jews*, 2. 11.5. In 66 A.D. she (with Agrippa) tried to prevent the Jewish Revolt. Bernice, at great danger to herself, petitioned Florus to spare the Jews. She had taken a vow over the petition, and had offered sacrifices, abstained from wine, and shaved her head. Her petition was ignored. Josephus, *The War of the Jews*. 2.15.1.

"King Agrippa, all ladies and gentlemen present,[1] you see this man about whom the whole Jewish community interceded to me both in Jerusalem and also here in Caesarea, shouting that he shouldn't live any longer. *25* I for my part found that he hadn't done anything to deserve death, but I decided to send him to Rome as he himself had appealed to the Emperor. *26* But I have nothing definite to write to the Sovereign about him. Therefore, I have brought him before all of you, and especially before you, King Agrippa, so that after this questioning has taken place I may get hold of something to write. *27* It seems absurd to me to send a prisoner without specifying the charges against him!"

Ch.26:1-8 Then Agrippa said to Paul, "You have my permission to speak!"

Then Paul motioned for silence with his hand, and began his defense. *2* "King Agrippa, I consider myself blessed to stand before you today as I make my defense against all the accusations of the Jews, *3* and especially because you are an expert on all the Jewish customs and controversial issues. For this reason, I ask you to listen to me patiently. *4* All the Jews know the way I've led my life from my youth, from the very beginning of my life in my own country, and also in Jerusalem. *5* They have known me all along and they can testify, if they were willing to, that I lived as a Pharisee in accordance with the strictest sect of our religion. *6* And now it is because of my expectation of the promise that God has made to our ancestors that I am on trial today. *7* This is the promise that the twelve tribes of Israel are hoping to see fulfilled as they earnestly serve God day and night. *8* Why should any of you find it incredible that God raises the dead?

9-11 "Indeed I myself thought I must do many things to oppose the Name of Jesus of Nazareth. *10* And so I did in Jerusalem. In fact, I myself shut up many of the people devoted to God in prison, as I had authority to do so from the chief priests. When they were sentenced to death, it was I who cast my vote against them. *11* And I punished them often in every synagogue, and tried to force them to blaspheme. Boiling over with rage against them, I chased them even as far as foreign cities.

12-14 "In connection with this I was traveling to Damascus with the authority and commission of the chief priests. *13* At midday, Your Highness, as I was on the road, I saw a light from the sky even more intense than the brightness of the sun, shining around me and my companions. *14* After we fell to the ground, I heard a voice speaking to me and saying in the Hebrew language, 'Saul, Saul, why are you persecuting me? You're hurting yourself by resisting!'[2]

15-18 "I myself said, 'Who are you, Lord?'

"He said, 'I am Jesus, the one you are persecuting! *16* Get up and stand on your feet! This is the reason I have appeared to you: to pre-choose you as a laborer and a witness both of the things which you have seen, and of the things which I will reveal to you. *17* I will rescue you from your people and from the non-Jews, and it's to the non-Jews that I'll send you out, *18* to open their eyes, to turn them from darkness to light and from the authority of Adversary to God, so that, by faith in me, they will take hold of cancellation of sins as well as an inheritance among those who are made right with God!'"

---

[1] Ἄνδρες, *andres*, vocative, here formal term of address, "Ladies and gentlemen". Note the lady of high-standing, Bernice, is present.

[2] This is an idiomatic Greek expression, our English equivalent being, "You're flogging a dead horse!" It has the sense of doing something completely useless, or hurting oneself by resisting. κέντρον, *kentron*, "sting (of a horse whip)", here in its meaning "horse-whip", occurs elsewhere in the N.T. in 1 Cor. 15:55, 56; Rev. 9:10. It occurs in an epitaph for Theodorus, Pfuhl/Mobius I.172 (Byzantion, II) = Peek, *GVI* 1479, in its meaning "sting". For "horse-whip" see *Il.* 23.387. See also Soph., *O.T.* 809; Xen. *Cyr.* 7.1, 29.

19-23 "As this was the case, King Agrippa, I was not disobedient to the vision from heaven. *20* First to the people in Damascus, then to the people in Jerusalem and in the whole country of Judea, I brought the report that they should change their minds and turn to God, and prove that they had changed their minds by acting like it. *21* It was for these reasons that the Jews arrested me in the temple and tried to murder me. *22* But I have God's help right up to this very day, and so I stand here as witness to non-important people and important people alike. I am saying nothing apart from that which the prophets and Moses said is destined to happen: *23* that as the Anointed One would suffer and as he would be the first to rise from the dead, he would proclaim light to his own people and to the non-Jews."

24-27 As Paul was making his defense, Festus shouted loudly, "You're stark raving mad, Paul! Too much learning has driven you mad!"

25 But he said, "I'm not mad, honorable Festus: rather, I utter the words of truth and reason. *26* For the king, in whose presence I also speak freely, boldly and openly,[1] understands these things. I am sure that none of it escapes his notice, since this thing was not done in a corner. *27* King Agrippa, do you believe the prophets? I know that you do believe."

28-29 Then Agrippa said to Paul, "In a short time you persuade me to become a Christian!"

29 And Paul said, "Short or long - I claim[2] by God that not only you but everyone who hears me today will become just as I am - except for these bonds!"

30-32 When he had said these things, the king stood up, as did the governor and Bernice and the people who were sitting with them. *31* After they had withdrawn, they said to each other, "This person hasn't done anything that deserves death or imprisonment!"

32 Agrippa said to Festus, "This person could have been set free had he not appealed to Caesar!"

Ch.27:1-2 When it was decided that we should sail to Italy, they handed over Paul and some other prisoners to a certain person named Julius, a Roman officer in charge of 100 men who belonged to the Imperial regiment. *2* We boarded a ship from Adramuttium[3] and put to sea, intending to sail along the coasts of the province of Asia. Aristarchos, a Macedonian from Thessalonika, was with us.

3-8 The next day we put in at Sidon.[4] Julius treated Paul kindly, allowing him to visit his friends and enjoy their care. *4* From there, we put to sea again and passed over to the lee of Cyprus because the winds were against us. *5* When we had sailed over the open sea which is off Cilicia and Pamphylia, we put into port at Myra[5] in Lycia. *6* And there the Roman officer in charge of 100

---

[1] παρρησιαζόμαι, *parresiaszomai*. This refers to the citizen's right of free, open and bold speech, without the fear of retribution. The citizen was one of good standing.

[2] εὐχομαι, *eukhomai*, verb of εὐχή, *eukhe*, "claim" not "prayer". See note on Acts 18:18.

[3] Adramuttium was a seaport, southeast of Alexandria Troas and east of Assos, in the province of Mysia in Asia Minor.

[4] Sidon, like Tyre, was mentioned in both Old and New Testaments. Sidon was a port city like Tyre and prospered, like Tyre, through trade and the production of purple dye. And again like Tyre, Sidon had tried to hold at bay the Egyptians, Hittites, Babylonians, Persians and Assyrians. It was not always successful. In 351 BC, the Sidonians locked their gates and set fire to their city rather than to submit to the army of Artaxerxes III. More than 40,000 died. In 333 BC the city surrendered to Alexander the Great. It was a Phoenician city now in modern Lebanon.

[5] The harbor at Myra (modern Demre) in Lycia is today silted up. Myra was on good terms with Rome and was visited by Germanicus and Agrippina in AD 19.

men found an Alexandrian ship sailing to Italy, and he put us on board. *7* We made little headway for many days, and barely made it to Cnidos.[1] The wind didn't allow us to hold our course, so we sailed along the lee of Crete, opposite Salome.[2] *8* We sailed near the coast with difficulty and came to a place called Fair Havens,[3] near the city of Lasea.[4]

9-11 Much time had already been lost, and sailing was now precarious because by now it was after the Fast.[5] Paul warned them, *10* "Gentlemen, I speculate that this voyage will be disastrous and bring great loss not only to ship and cargo, but also to our own lives!" *11* But the Roman officer in charge of 100 men was more persuaded by the sailing master and the owner-charterer[6] than by anything that Paul said.

Tradition states that its wealth was due to myrrh, but there is no hard evidence. Myra is famous as the home of St Nicholas, known today as Santa Claus. St Nicholas anonymously distributed money to the poor.

[1]   The distance from Myra to Cnidos was about 170 miles. This section of the journey was against the northwesterly winds which prevail from June to September in the eastern section of the Mediterranean. Marcus Diaconus describes a similar journey from the same starting point as Paul, to Rhodes (*Vita Porphyrii Gazensis* 34), and his ship only traveled at 1.7 knots. The normal rate for ships working against the wind was from just under 2 knots to 2.5 knots. Ancient vessels averaged between 4 and 6 knots over open water, and less along islands or coasts. Luke states that they only reached Cnidos "with difficulty", so their voyage may have been even slower than Marcus Diaconus' 1.7 knots. Cnidos was on a narrow peninsula between the islands of Cos and Rhodes at the extreme south western part of Asia Minor.

[2]   Salome was on the east point of Crete on a promontory.

[3]   Fair Havens was on the south coast of Crete on a small sheltered bay.

[4]   In Paul's time, Lasea was one of the main harbours for Crete.

[5]   The Fast refers to the Day of Atonement (10th Tishri in the Jewish calendar) in late September or early October. The evidence suggests that in this particular year, the Fast occurred late, perhaps 5th October or 9th October. Navigation was considered safe from 27th May to 14th September, sailing was uncertain from 14th September to 10th November, and from 10th November to 10th March the season was closed. However, Pliny the Elder (*HN* 2.47) states that the sailing season began at the start of spring, 8th February.

[6]   The ship may have been carrying the Egyptian grain tribute as it was carrying grain (v.38) and was en-route from Alexandria to Italy (v.6). It is unknown whether the ναύκλερος, *naukleros*, owned or chartered the ship. Casson (*op.cit.*, p. 315, n. 67) states that the ναύκλερος, *naukleros*, was the person who had use of a ship, through ownership or charter. J. Velissaropoulos, *Les naucleres grecs. Recherches sur les institutions en Grece et dans l'Orient hellenise*, (Paris, 1980), extends the meaning to include an agent for the owner. The difficulty in translating the word is discussed by E.R. Bennett, *REG* 93, (1980) 543; and T. Drew-Bear, *CP* 78.345-346. However, it is certain that a ναύκλερος, *naukleros*, could be their own κυβερνήτης, *kubernetes*, cf. *P.Oxy.Hels.* 37; *P.Lond.* 3 (1907) 948.1-2, 236; *P.Cairo* inv.10580 + 10488.7, κυβερνήτης ἰδίου πλοίου αγωγῆς, *kubernetes idiou ploiou agoges*, and ναύκλερος κυβερνήτην [πλ]οίου ἰδιωτικοῦ, *naukleros kuberneten [pl]oiou idiotikou.*

Verses 9-12 have fuelled much academic debate (W.M. Ramsay, *St. Paul the Traveller and the Roman Citizen*, London, 1897, 323-26; E. Haenchen, *The Acts of the Apostles*, (Oxford: O.U.P.), repr. 1971, 699, n. 1; K.L. McKay, *below*) that the final responsibility as to whether or not to sail to Phoinix lay with the centurion. However, the text does not say this, it merely states that the centurion ignored Paul's warning and listened rather to the κυβερνήτης, *kubernetes*, and the ναύκλερος, *naukleros*, This suggests only that the centurion was not persuaded to leave ship, a view followed by K.L. McKay and reported in *NDIEC* 4.117.

12-20 As the harbor wasn't suitable to start wintering in, the majority decided that we should sail on, in the hope that perhaps they could reach Phoinix[1] and winter there. This was a harbor in Crete which faced both southwest and northwest. *13* When a light south wind sprang up, they thought they'd got what they intended. They weighed anchor and sailed close to Crete. *14* Not long after, a wind of hurricane force called the "Northeaster" tore down from the island. *15* The ship was caught by it and could not sail in the teeth of the wind, so we allowed ourselves to run before it. *16* We ran under the lee of a small island called Cauda,[2] and could hardly gain control of the small lifeboat. *17* When they had hoisted it abroad, they used cables to undergird the ship. Fearing that they would run aground on the sandbars of Syrtis,[3] they lowered the anchor,[4] and were driven along. *18* We were so violently battered by the storm that the next day they jettisoned the cargo. *19* On the third day, they threw the ship's tackle overboard with their very own hands. *20* Neither sun nor stars appeared for many days and the violent storm raged upon us, so we gave up any hope of being saved.

21-26 After they had been without food for a long time, and the lack of food started to be at a critical point, Paul stood up among them and said, "Gentlemen, you ought to have obeyed me[5] and not sailed from Crete, and then you would have spared yourselves this disaster and loss. *22* Now I'm urging you to keep up your courage, because not one of you will lose your lives – only the ship will be lost. *23* Last night a Messenger of God, to whom I belong and whom I serve, came and stood next to me *24* and said, 'Don't be afraid, Paul! You must stand trial before Caesar, and as a favor to you God has granted the lives of everyone who is sailing with you.' *25* So keep up your courage, gentlemen, as I believe God that it will happen just as he told me. *26* However, we must run aground on a certain island."

27-32 On the fourteenth night we were still being driven here and there across the Adriatic Sea, when about midnight the sailors sensed that land was approaching. *28* They took soundings and found it was 20 fathoms deep. After a short interval they took soundings again and it was 15 fathoms deep. *29* Fearing that we would be dashed against the rocks, they dropped four anchors from the stern and were claiming[6] that daylight was here. *30* In an attempt to abandon ship, the sailors let the lifeboat down into the sea on the pretext that they were going to lower some anchors from the bow. *31* Paul said to the Roman officer in charge of 100 men and the soldiers, "Unless these men stay on the ship, you can't be saved!" *32* At that moment the soldiers cut off the ropes that held the lifeboat and let it fall away.

33-38 Just before dawn Paul urged them all to eat and said, "Today is the fourteenth day you have waited in suspense and gone on without food and not eaten anything. *34* So then I urge you to take nourishment in the interests of preservation. Not a hair on your heads will be lost!" *35* After he said this, he picked up bread and thanked God in front of all of them. When he had broken it into pieces he started eating. *36* They all cheered themselves up and ate some food too. *37* In all there were 276 of us on board. *38* When they had eaten their fill, they lightened the ship by throwing grain into the sea.

---

[1]   Identified with modern Phineka. The voyage to *Phoinix* was only about 40 nautical miles by the most direct course. It should have only taken just over 12 hours with the favorable south wind.

[2]   Cauda is a small island 23 miles south of Phoinix. It is the southernmost border of Greece and Europe.

[3]   Syrtis is a long stretch of sandbanks along the northern coast of Africa.

[4]   Most probably the floating anchor which was used to reduce drift.

[5]   πειθαρχέω τινί, *peitharkheo tini*, "to obey one in authority".

[6]   εὔχομαι, *eukhomai*, the verb of εὐχή, *eukhe*, "claim", not "prayer". See note on Acts 18:18.

39-41 When daylight came, they could recognize not the land, but noticed a bay with a sandy beach, where they decided to run the ship ashore if they possibly could. *40* After they slipped the anchors, they left them in the sea, at the same time untying the ropes that held the rudders. They hoisted the foresail to the breeze and headed for the beach. *41* But when it came across a place which had the sea on both sides, the ship ran aground. The bow stuck fast and was jammed, but the stern was being smashed up by the pounding of the surf.

42-44 The soldiers planned to kill the prisoners to prevent any of them from swimming away and escaping, *43* but the Roman officer in charge of 100 men planned to bring Paul safely through and foiled their plan. *44* Of the rest, some were to get there on planks and others on parts of the ship. And thus it turned out that everyone reached land safely.

Ch.28:1-2 Now when we had come safely through, we found out that the island was called Melita. *2* The islanders were unusually kind to us. They built a fire and welcomed us all because it was cold and rainy.

3-6 Paul gathered a pile of brushwood, and as he put it in the fire, a snake, driven out by the heat, fastened itself onto his hand. *4* So when the islanders saw the wild beast hanging off his hand, they said to each other, "This guy must be a murderer for sure! He escaped from the sea, but Justice won't let him live!"

5 Paul shook the snake off into the fire and experienced no ill effects, *6* but the islanders expected him to swell up or suddenly drop dead. After they waited a long time and saw that nothing out of the ordinary happened to him, they changed their minds and said he was a god.

7-10 Now in the neighborhood of that place there was an estate belonging to the governor[1] of the island. His name was Publius. He welcomed us into his house and entertained us with considerable friendliness for three days. *8* His father was sick in bed. He had been gripped with fits of fever,[2] and dysentery. Paul went in to see him. After praying, Paul laid hands on him and instantly divinely healed him. *9* After this happened, the rest of the sick people on the island also kept coming and were healed. *10* They honored us in many ways, and when we were ready to set sail they gave us the supplies that we needed.

11-16 After three months we sailed in a ship that had wintered on the island. It was an Alexandrian ship with the figurehead of the twins Castor and Pollux. *12* We put in at Syracuse, and stayed for three days. *13* From there we circled round and reached Rhegium. The next day the south wind came up, and on the following day we reached Puteoli, *14* where we found fellow believers. They invited us to spend the week with them. And so we headed for Rome. *15* The fellow believers there heard that we were coming, and they traveled as far as the Forum of Appius and the Three Taverns to meet us. When Paul saw them, he thanked God and took heart. *16* When we arrived in Rome, Paul was allowed to live by himself with a soldier to guard him.

17-20 Three days later he called together the leaders of the Jews. When they had assembled, he said to them, "I for my part, ladies and gentlemen,[3] fellow believers, although I have done nothing against our people or against the customs of our ancestors, was handed over to the Romans as a prisoner from Jerusalem. *18* After questioning me, they were willing to release me, because I was not guilty of any crime which deserved the death penalty. *19* But when the Jews spoke against me, I was compelled to appeal to Caesar, not that I had any charge to bring against my own people. *20* So then this is the reason I have called for you, to see you and speak with you, because I am bound with this chain for the sake of the hope of Israel."

---

[1] ὁ πρῶτος, *ho protos*. Inscriptional evidence shows that this was the official title of the governor of Melita.

[2] πυρετός, *puretos*, here in the plural, which refers to fits of fever occurring at intervals. Not the singular "fever".

[3] ἄνδρες, *andres*. See note on Acts 7:2.

21-22 They said to him, "We haven't received any letters about you from Judea, nor have any of the fellow believers who have come reported or said anything against you. *22* But we want to know what your views are, as we know that people everywhere are talking against this sect."

23-24 They arranged to meet Paul on a certain day, and came in even larger numbers to the place where he was staying. From morning until evening he explained and testified to them about God's Realm and tried to convince them about Jesus from the Law of Moses and from the Prophets. *24* Some were convinced by what he said, but others refused to believe.

25-28 They broke up in disagreement and began to leave after Paul made this final statement: "The Holy Spirit spoke the truth to your ancestors when he said through Isaiah the prophet: *26* 'Go to this people and say, "Indeed you will always hear but never understand. Indeed you will always see but never perceive, *27* for the hearts of this people have become hardened. They hear with difficulty, and they refuse to see. Otherwise they might see with their eyes, hear with their ears, understand with their hearts, and turn back, and I would instantly divinely heal them."' *28* So then, let it be known to you that the salvation[1] of God has been sent to the non-Jews, and they will surely hear it!"[2]

30-31 For a period of two years Paul stayed there at his own expense and welcomed all who came to see him. *31* He proclaimed God's Realm and taught about Jesus the Anointed One freely, boldly and openly in public and without hindrance.

---

[1]   There are 2 closely related words for salvation in the N.T., ἡ σωτηρία, *he soteria*, and τὸ σωτήριον, *to soterion*. The latter, which occurs here, is the least common and only occurs in 3 other instances in the N.T.: Luke 2:20, 3:6; Eph. 6:17.

[2]   Verse 29 is omitted as it is an addition and not original. "After he had said these words, the Jews left and had great discussions among themselves."

Letter to the Romans.

The letter to the Romans[1] was written around 57 AD by Paul. Irenaeus, Ignatius, Polycarp, Justin Martyr and Marcion all assume Pauline authorship. 2 Cor. 8:10-11 shows that Paul was on his way from Ephesos to Corinth, and was directing the Corinthians in the matters of finances for the Jerusalem assembly. In Romans 15:26-28 Paul states that he has just completed the collection of finances for the believers in Jerusalem after visiting the believers in Macedonia and Achaia. This corresponds to Acts 20:1-3, thus pinpointing the time as the year after Paul left Ephesos on his third missionary journey.

Some have argued that Romans 16 was part of a letter originally sent to the Ephesians. Paul had ministered in Ephesos for three years and had not yet been to Rome, and the number of personal greetings is unusual for a place he had not visited. In 16:5, Paul greets Ephaenetos, "the first convert in Asia," which suggests perhaps that Ephaenetos was in Asia. Paul greets Priska and Aquila, who were in Ephesos shortly before Romans was written (1 Cor 16:19: "The assemblies of Asia greet you. Aquila and Priska greet you warmly, along with the assembly at their house") and in Ephesos when Paul wrote to Timothy (2 Tim 4:19: "Greet Priska and Aquila"). Verse 13, "Greet Rufus, who is chosen by the Lord, and his mother, who has been a mother to me, too," suggests a close familiarity with Rufus' mother, in keeping with a place Paul had spent some years, rather than a place he had not yet visited. The warning of verses 17-18 indicates Ephesos rather than Rome. Further, the doxology is at the end of chapter 15. The main contrary argument is that chapter 16 appears in all manuscripts, but Deissmann[2] argued that Romans 16 is a letter to the Ephesians found in Romans as it was first discovered from one of Paul's parchment notebooks. The matter remains contentious.

Paul gave the letter to Phoebe to take to Rome. He establishes her credentials as a leader in Romans 16:1-2 where he calls her a "deacon" and "presiding officer". Phoebe is coming to Rome on Paul's behalf for a specific project, and Paul asks the Romans to assist her. The question of Paul's whereabouts when he wrote the letter largely depends on whether chapter 16 is part of Romans. Chapter 16 appears to have been written from Corinth. Phoebe, who was to take the letter, was a deacon of the church in Kenchreai, the eastern port of Corinth. 1 Cor. 1:14 tells us that Gaius, Paul's host (16:23), was a prominent Christian leader at Corinth.

Letter to the Romans.

Ch.1:1-7 Paul, a slave servant of the Anointed One Jesus, called to be an apostle, appointed to the Good News of God – *2* the Good News God promised beforehand in the sacred Scriptures through his prophets. *3* The Good News is about his Son, who in the natural realm was born from David's family, *4* but by the Spirit of Holiness was marked out to be the powerful Son of God by the act of the resurrection from among the dead. I'm talking about Jesus the Anointed One our Lord. *5* Through him we have received the favor for our mission, so that we would go to the non-Jews, to lead them to pay attention to[3] what he says,

---

[1] Romans 1:7,15 identify this letter as being sent to the believers in Rome.

[2] A. Deissmann, *Light from the Ancient East* (Michigan: Hendrickson, *repr.* 1980), *passim*.

[3] ὑπακοή, *hupakoe*, pay attention, to listen and act on it. In the sense of listen, give ear to, pay attention, in Arist. *Wasps*. 273; 319; *Iliad* 8.4 "...Zeus...held an assembly of the gods on...Olumpos. He began to address them, and all the gods gave him their attention,"; *Odyssey* 14. 485. "He readily paid attention"; Euripides, *Alc.*, 400, "Listen, mother, listen to me, I beg of you. Mother, it is me who is calling you..." In the sense of listen and

and to have faith in his Name. *6* You too are among the ones invited by Jesus the Anointed One.

7 To: All of you in Rome who are dearly loved by God, all invited people devoted to God.

Hello! May you have peace from God our Father and from the Lord Jesus the Anointed One.

8-12 Firstly, I thank my God, through Jesus the Anointed One for you all, because the news about your faith is being preached throughout the whole world. I serve God spiritually by announcing the Good News about his Son. *9* God is my witness as to how I mention you without a break in my prayers at all times. *10* I earnestly request that now at last, the way will be smoothed and made prosperous[1] by means of God's purpose for me to come to you. *11* I long to see you, so that I may share some spiritual gift with you, so that you can get your footing on firm ground – *12* what I mean is that each of us may be encouraged by each other's faith.

13-17 Fellow believers,[2] I don't want you to be unaware that I often proposed to come to you - but was prevented until now - so that I would achieve some results among you just as I have with the rest of the non-Jews. *14* I am a debtor to Greeks as well as to non-Greeks, to the wise as well as to those who lack sense. *15* So, as for me, I am eager to announce the Good News to you people in Rome too. *16* I am thrilled about the Good News,[3] as it is the powerful way God brings about the salvation of everyone who believes – Jews firstly as well as Greeks. *17* In the Good News, God's justice is continually being revealed, beginning in faith and ending in faith, just as the Scriptures say, "The ones right with God will live by faith."

18-23 From heaven, God's anger is continually being revealed against every form of ungodliness and wrongdoing of people who suppress the truth by unjust means. *19* The reason for the revealing of God's anger is this: all that may be realized and known about God is evident to people - as God made it evident to them. *20* This knowledge is derived from the creation. The invisible things of God - his eternal power and divinity - are clearly seen in the world, in the creation.[4] Thus the mind sees the visible, the creation of the world, and understands the invisible, the things of God.[5] So these people don't have an

---

answer in *Odyssey* 4.283 "...we heard you calling and were both tempted to jump up and come out or give an instant answer from within"; *Odyssey* 10.83 "Herdsman calls to herdsman as one brings in his flocks and the other answers as he drives out his"; Theok. 13.59. In the sense "to answer", Andoc 15.13, to answer an enquiry; Plato, *Crito* 43A; to answer a knock at the door. In the sense of "yield, comply with" in Plato, *Rep.* 459 C "..and we commonly consider that a comparatively low-grade doctor can treat patients who are prepared to follow a diet and do not need medicine..."

[1] εὐοδωθήσομαι, *euodothesomai*, (future passive of εὐοδόω, *euodoo*), "to have a prosperous journey". It encompasses 1. removal of difficulties in the way, 2. material prosperity, 3. physical health. Emphasized most strongly in the Greek here.

[2] ἀδελφοί, *adelphoi*. See note on Matt. 5:22.

[3] Word for word from the Greek, "I am not ashamed," but the Greek language was fond of litotes: an ironic understatement using a negative of its contrary. For example, if a Greek person was very angry they would say "I am not a little angry," whereas the English equivalent is "I am very angry." If a Greek person wanted to say they were impressed with a city, they would say, "A not insignificant city" whereas English expression says, "A most impressive city." Paul speaks of Tarsus in this way in Acts 21:39. Here Paul is saying that he is thrilled with the Good News. Litotes in Rom. 10:11; Acts 21:30; 1 Pet. 2:6; Rev. 3:5.

[4] The mind sees the visible, the creation of the world, and by the act of seeing creation understands the invisible, the things of God.

[5] "Thus they are perceived through the things that are made."

excuse, **21** and this is why. Although they perceive God, they didn't praise him as God, or even thank him. Rather, their reasoning became useless and their stupid minds were darkened and obscured. **22** They alleged that they were wise, but they became fools! **23** They exchanged the splendor of the imperishable God for an image made like a perishable person – not to mention images of birds, and four-legged animals, and even reptiles!

24-25 So for this reason God handed them over[1] to ritual uncleanness, in their minds' wants and wishes, so that their bodies would be dishonored with each other. **25** They exchanged[2] God's truth for the lie,[3] the idol, and worshipped and served the creation other than[4] the Creator, who is blessed for the ages! Amen!

1.26+2"

26-32 Because of this, God handed them over to experiences of public stigma,[5] for the females exchanged natural sex for what is other than[6] nature.[7] **27** And the same goes for males too.[8] The males got rid of[9] natural sex with the female and burned[10] with their mutual[11] yearning[12] – males producing[13] indecency[14] with one another, and as a result got what was coming to them for their mistake.[15] **28** They didn't think it fit to acknowledge God, so he gave them

---

[1] παραδίδωμι, *paradidomai*, signifies to hand over to the power of another.

[2] μεταλλάσσω, *metallasso*, only found in the N.T. here and in verse 26. It signifies the giving up of one thing in exchange for another, and is a stronger form of ἀλλάσσω, *allasso*, in verse 23.

[3] Metonymy (the substitution of a word describing the nature or significance of an object instead of the object itself). Paul here equates the "lie" with the idol. Isaiah talks of an idol as a lie, cf. Isaiah 44:20.

[4] πάρα, *para*, with accusative, "other than" cf. Gal. 1:8, c.f. v. 9; Rom. 11:24. See Moule, *op.cit.*, p. 51. Also occurs in verse 26.

[5] ἀτιμία, *atimia* (not ἀτιμος, *atimos*, shameful, dishonored), public stigma. Herodotos 7.231 uses it for the public dishonor faced by Aristodemos when he returned to Lacedaemonia: no Spartan would speak to him. Can mean dishonor, insult, disgrace, but more in the sense of public stigma or infamy.

[6] πάρα, *para*, with accusative, "other than": see note above, on verse 25.

[7] In the whole context Paul is speaking of idolatry.

[8] Paul frequently starts a sentence with "And the same goes for" which signifies that the sense of the previous sentence is to be included in the sentence started with "And the same goes for", In this case there is a τε καὶ, *te kai*, "also".

[9] ἀφίημι, *aphiemi*, with accusative of thing, "get rid off". Here ἀφέντες, *aphentes*, aorist[2] participle of ἀφίημι, *aphiemi*.

[10] Aorist passive of ἐκκαίω, *ekkaio*, in passive, "to burn up".

[11] εἰς ἀλλήλους, *eis allelous*, "mutually". "For one another" is not strictly correct and follows the Latin *alter alterius*. For εἰς ἀλλήλους, *eis allelous*, πρὸς ἀλλήλους, *pros allelous*, see, for example, Aeschylus, *Prometheus Vinctus*, 491, "and what were their mutual hates, loves, and companionships" and 1086, "in a mutual fury" (although here in the sense "one against the other").

[12] ὄρεξις, *oreksis*, "yearning".

[13] κατεργάζομαι, *katergazomai*, "to get the job done".

[14] τὴν ἀσχημοσύνην, *ten askhemosune*, accusative of ἡ ἀσχημοσύνη, *he askhemosune*, "awkwardness", "indecency" not to be confused with τὸ ἀσχημόνημα, *to askhemonema*, "act of indecency".

[15] πλάνη, *plane*, "mistake", "error", "wandering off the path". Well attested in the papyri. It was formerly thought to mean "deceit", based on a single papyrus example where it was partially restored. However, this is now known not to be the case, cf. *NDIEC* 2.94 although it can be translated as "deceit" with the implication that one will be led off the right track by being deceived. See a petition by 3 brothers and their tax assessment based on an inaccurate calculation of their landholding. They state, "The village registrar, possibly through error, assessed us in the posted list of individual taxpayers." *P.Wiscon.*

an unfit mind,[1] to do things that are not appropriate. *29* They have been filled with every kind of wrongdoing, evil, greedy grasping behavior, malice - full to the utmost with jealousy, murder, quarrels, deceit, nasty dispositions. They are people who give out information, whether true or false, which is detrimental to the character or welfare of others.[2] *30* They are slanderers, God haters, insolent, arrogant, boastful, inventors of bad deeds. They are not obedient to parents,[3] *31* they don't have intelligence, they do not keep covenant,[4] they do not have natural affection,[5] they do not have mercy. *32* Although they are fully aware[6] of God's decree, which is that those who do such things deserve death, not only do they do these things, but also they are in agreement with those[7] who do them!

The Watchers, "other-than-nature".

In the whole context Paul is speaking of idolatry and people who did not acknowledge God. More specifically, he is speaking of women who went against nature, and men who went against nature due to their own burning passions. Apocryphal literature well documents the The Watchers as going "against nature" and "whoring after" humans.

Paul's words in this passage echo those of *2 Enoch* 10: "*1* And those two men led me up on to the Northern side, and showed me there a very terrible place, and there were all manner of tortures in that place: cruel darkness and unillumined gloom, and there is no light there, but murky fire constantly flaming aloft, and there is a fiery river coming forth, and that whole place is everywhere fire, and everywhere there is frost and ice, thirst and shivering, while the bonds are very cruel, and the angels fearful and merciless, bearing angry weapons, merciless torture, and I said: *2* Woe, woe, how very terrible is this place. *3* And those men said to me: This place, O Enoch, is prepared for those who dishonour God, who on earth practice sin against nature, which is child-corruption after the sodomitic fashion, magic-making, enchantments and devilish witchcrafts, and who boast of their wicked deeds, stealing, lies, calumnies, envy, rancour, fornication, murder, and who, accursed, steal the souls of men, who, seeing the poor take away their goods and themselves wax rich, injuring them for other men's goods; who being able to satisfy the empty, made the hungering to die; being able to clothe, stripped the naked; and who knew not their creator, and bowed to the soulless and lifeless gods, who cannot see nor hear, vain gods, who also built hewn images and bow

---

86.9-10 (Philadelphia, 244-246.) Also occurs in a document with details of payments. The scribe states that money was "not spent at that time by mistake but is now being spent." *Stud.Pal.* 20.85.

[1] Paul loves to play on words and here the wordplay cannot be brought out in the English. δοκιμάζω, *dokimazo*, means to scrutinize, to put to the test as gold is assayed. They put God to the test and decided not to acknowledge him. As a result, God put them to the test and they did not pass it, ἀδόκιμος, *adokimos*. Here the two words are rendered "fit" and "unfit", yet the wordplay needs to be read in the Greek to be appreciated.

[2] This sentence comprises the full meaning of ψιθυριστής, *psithuristes*. The translation "whisperers", while technically correct, does not bring out the full meaning of the Greek.

[3] ἀπειθής, *apeithes*, the first word in a list of 5, all beginning with a negative prefix.

[4] ἀσύνθετος, *asunhetos*, "covenant-breakers": here "they do not keep covenant" due to the negative prefix in previous verse. Cf. Dem. 383.6.

[5] ἄτοργος, *atorgos*, "without natural affection" occurs twice in N.T., here and in 2 Tim. 3:3. The meaning was consistent throughout Hellenistic times.

[6] ἐπιγιγνώσκω, *epigignosko*, "be fully aware", not merely "know".

[7] συνευδοκέω τινί, *suneudokeo tini*, "to be in agreement with someone", "to approve together", not simply "to approve".

down to unclean handiwork, for all these is prepared this place among these, for eternal inheritance." (*Trans*. Lawrence.)

Note also that the apocryphal *Testament of Naphtali* 3.3.4-5 states that the women of Sodom had sex with angels: "In like manner also the Watchers changed the order of their nature, whom also the Lord cursed at the flood, and for their sakes made desolate the earth, that it should be uninhabited and fruitless." (Note the term "changed the order of their nature.")

Both the *Book of Jubilees* and *1 Enoch* also speak of "the Watchers", stating that they were angels that came down to earth and had sex with human women and thus "became defiled". *2 Enoch*[1] states, "*1* They have rejected my commandments and my yoke, worthless seed has come up, not fearing God, and they would not bow down to me, but have begun to bow down to vain gods, and denied my unity, and have laden the whole earth with untruths, offences, abominable lecheries, namely one with another, and all manner of other unclean wickedness, which are disgusting to relate. *2* And therefore I will bring down a deluge upon the earth and will destroy all men, and the whole earth will crumble together into great darkness." (*Trans*. Lawrence.) *The Book of Jubilees* 7:20-2 states, "Noah... exhorted his sons... to avoid *porneia*, uncleanness, and injustice. For it was on account of these three things that the flood was on the earth, since it was due to *porneia* in which the Watchers against the ordinances of their authority had illicit intercourse and went a whoring after human women. When they married whomever they chose they committed the first acts of uncleanness. They fathered as sons the Nephilim."

• Jude 7 also speaks of going after "flesh of a different kind" in the context of angels. See Background Notes in Jude.

Ch.2:1-5 So then you, you who judge someone else, you have no excuse! Because when you judge someone else, you are condemning yourself, as you who are judging are doing the very same things! *2* And we know that God's judgment is rightly passed upon people who do such things. *3* And you, you who judge those people who do these things while you are actually doing the same thing, do you calculate[2] that you will completely escape God's judgment? *4* Or do you despise the wealth of his goodness, tolerance and patience? Aren't you aware that God's goodness is meant to lead you to a change of heart? *5* But because of your hardness of heart and your lack of changed heart, you are storing God's anger in a bank – but it will be withdrawn on the Day of God's Anger when his just judgment will be revealed.

6-12 God will give each person what's coming to them because of their actions! *7* On the one hand he will give eternal life to those who go after glory, honor and immortality, those who have endurance in doing good work. *8* But on the other hand there will be anger and rage for those who are self-seeking, those who do not obey the truth but who are persuaded by injustice. *9* There will be oppression and difficulties[3] for every human being who does bad things – first for the Jew and then for the Greek – *10* but praise, and honor and peace for everyone who does good things - first for the Jew and then for the Greek. *11* God certainly does not have favorites![4] *12* Everyone who has sinned[5]

---

[1] *2 Enoch* is also known as *The Book of the Secrets of Enoch*, or the *Slavonic Apocalypse of Enoch*.
[2] λογίζομαι, *logizomai*, is quite distinct from "think" and signifies a process of reasoning which is deliberate.
[3] στενοχωρία, *stenokhoria*, referring to difficulties or distress, or to narrowness of space or a confined space, a lack of room.
[4] That is, bias. προσωπολημψία, *prosopolempsia*.
[5] Paul is not speaking only of those who have sinned before the time of his letter. The aorist points back from the future time to sins committed during life on earth.

without law will also be utterly lost without law.[1] Everyone who has sinned under law will also be judged by law.

13-16 In fact it is not those who hear a law that are right in God's sight, but it is those who actually do the law that will be pronounced right with God. *14* For non-Jews who don't have a law, actually do the requirements of the Law naturally. Since they don't have a law, they are a law unto themselves. *15* This is because they show that the requirements of the Law are written on their minds. Their consciences also join in testifying to them. Their reasonings in their mind about other people either accuse them or defend them.[2] *16* This will happen on the day when God will judge the hidden things of people through Jesus the Anointed One, according to my Good News!

17-20 Now if you call yourself a Jew and depend on law, if you are proud of God, *18* then you recognize his purpose and examine the things that are different (as you have been orally instructed from the Law). *19* You are convinced that you are a guide for the blind, a light to those who are in darkness, *20* an instructor of the ignorant, a teacher of infants, for the reason that you have in the Law the outward shape of knowledge and truth.

21-24 So then, you who teach someone else – why it is that you don't teach yourself? You who proclaim not to steal, do you steal? *22* You who say, "Do not commit adultery", do you commit adultery? You who detest idols, do you commit sacrilege? *23* You who are proud of law, do you dishonor God by breaking the Law? *24* For "The Name of God is blasphemed among the non-Jews," just as the Scriptures say.

25-29 For on the one hand circumcision is of course a benefit if you do the Law, but if on the other hand you're a lawbreaker, then your circumcision turns into uncircumcision! *26* So then, if an uncircumcised man keeps the decrees of the Law, surely that fact doesn't count as him being circumcised when he is in fact uncircumcised! *27* The one who isn't physically circumcised and yet obeys the Law, will judge you, you who are a lawbreaker, even though you have the written code and circumcision! *28* You are not a Jew just because you're one on the outside! True circumcision doesn't show on the outside in the natural realm! *29* So you're a Jew if you're a Jew on the inside! Circumcision is of the mind and of the Spirit, not in the written law. Such a person receives their praise[3] from God and not from people.

Ch.3:1-8 So then what advantage is it to be a Jew, and what benefit is there to circumcision? *2* Much in every way! Mainly, indeed, because the Jews were entrusted with God's utterances. *3* So what if some of them were unfaithful? Did their faithlessness make the faithfulness of God inactive?[4]

4 Certainly not! Indeed, God must be true, and every person a liar! Just as the Scriptures say, "When you speak you will be shown to be right. And you will win the verdict when you go to law." *5* But if our lack of being right with God serves to show God's justice more clearly, what will we say? Will we say that God is unjust to unleash his anger on us, speaking in human terms?

6 Certainly not! If that were the case, how would God judge the world? *7* And if God's truth brings him greater honor because of my falsehood, then why am I also still judged as a sinner? *8* Why not say, "Let's do bad things, so that good things will come of it," as some are slanderously reporting about us and as some insist that we say! The judgment on them is fair!

---

[1] Not "the Law". No definite article in the instances of "law" in this sentence.
[2] Here Paul has used ἀπολογέομαι, *apologeomai*, in its legal terminology.
[3] Here is another of Paul's wordplays. Paul is playing on the words "Jew" and "praise". The word "Jew" is derived from the word "Judah" which means "praise". See Genesis 29:35; 49:8.
[4] καταργέω, *katargeo*, "to reduce to inactivity", not "abolish" or "nullify". The word implies a loss of activity rather than a loss of being.

9-12 So what is it? Are we Jews any better off? Of course not! In no way whatsoever! We have already laid the charge that both Jews and Greeks are subject to sin. *10* As the Scriptures say, "There is no one who is right with God, not even one. *11* There is no one who understands, no one who looks for God. *12* All have turned away, and at the same time have become useless. There is no one who does kind things, not even one."

13-18 "Their throats are open graves, their tongues deceive." "The poison of asps is on their lips." *14* "Their speech is loaded with curses[1] and bitterness." *15* "Their feet are swift to shed blood; *16* crushing and severe labor are in their paths, *17* and they do not know the path of peace." *18* "There is no respect[2] for God in their thoughts."

19-20 Now we know that whatever the Law says, it says to those who are within the jurisdiction of the law, so that no one will have anything to say in self-defense, and the whole world may be liable to be tried by God. *20* This is because no human can be made right in God's sight by deeds of law[3] - it is through law we become conscious of sin.

21-24 But now, quite apart from law, a rightness which comes from God has been revealed. The Law and the Prophets give evidence for this. *22* This rightness which comes from God is through faith in Jesus the Anointed One, and it is for everyone who believes. There is no difference! *23* Everyone has sinned and fallen short of God's glory, *24* and everyone is made right with God by his favor as a gift. This is shown by the fact that they are released by means of Jesus paying their ransom.

25-26 God put Jesus forward as a sacrifice for taking away sins – and this comes about through faith, by Jesus' own sacrificial death. God did this to demonstrate his justice, because he had overlooked[4] and dismissed[5] the sins which people had previously committed. *26* It was to show his justice at the right time, which is now: that he himself is just and that he would put right with him those people who are identified by their faith in Jesus.

27-31 So then, what ground is there for boasting? There isn't any: it was excluded! By what law was it excluded? Was it excluded by actions? No! It was excluded by the law of faith! *28* For we consider that a person is made right with God by faith, and this is a separate thing from the actions commanded by law.

29 Is God the God of the Jews only? Isn't he the God of the non-Jews too? Yes, of course he is! He is the God of the non-Jews too. *30* There is only one God, who will make the circumcised right with him by means of faith, and make the uncircumcised right with him by means of the same faith. *31* So then, do we render law inactive through this faith? Of course not! Rather, we make law stand!

---

[1] "Curses", not "cursing" in the sense of using foul language. The word, ἀρά, *ara*, means a prayer (to pagan gods) either for good, cf. Aesch. *Cho*. 138, or more commonly, for bad. Its primary meaning is "curse", and was the word used for the curse on Oedipus in Aeschylus, *Theb*. 70. It can also mean "ruin", and ἀρά, *ara*, is personified as the goddess of destruction and revenge. Found only here in N.T.

[2] φόβος, *phobos*, generally "fear", but the Greeks used it in the meaning "respect" when used in the case of gods or things sacred. See *P.Tebt* I.59, where someone writes to the priests of Tebtunis assuring them of his good will "because from old I revere and worship the temple". The use was the same from Classical times.

[3] Paul is speaking of "law" in generic terms rather than specifically of the Law, as "law", νόμος, *nomos*, in both instances in this sentence does not have the definite article. There is no definite article before "works", so the translation is "works of law" not "the works of the law".

[4] ἀνοχή, *anokhe*, a holding back, a stopping, usually used of a holding back or a stopping of hostilities. Also used of a truce.

[5] πάρεσις, paresis, dismissal in the sense of passing over, occurs only here in the N.T. Quite distinct from ἄφεσις, *aphesis*, which refers to remission of sins.

Ch.4:1-5 So then, what are we going to say that Abraham, our first founder of our family[1] by natural descent, has found? *2* Now if Abraham was made right with God by his actions, he'd have something to boast about! But he wouldn't have something to boast about to God. *3* What does the Scripture say? It says: "Abraham believed God, and thus he was considered to be made right with God."

4 The wages of a worker are calculated as what's due to them – they are not paid wages as a favor. *5* The person who doesn't do any work, but does believe God, who makes the ungodly right – this person's faith is counted as making that person right with God.

6-8 In the same way too, David describes the happiness of the person whom God considers to be right with him independent of their actions: *7* "Happy are those whose lawless deeds are forgiven, and whose sins are covered. *8* Happy is the person whose sins the Lord will not calculate against them."

9-12 So then, does this blessing only come upon the circumcised, or does it come upon the uncircumcised as well? Now we say, "Abraham's faith was counted as him being right with God." *10* Well how was it calculated? Was it when he was circumcised, or when he was uncircumcised? Actually, it wasn't when he was circumcised – it was when he was uncircumcised! *11* And he took hold of the sign of circumcision, a seal of being right with God which faith had given him. This was while he was still uncircumcised. This was with a view to being counted as the ancestor of all those believers who have not been circumcised – so that they also can be considered as being right with God. *12* Abraham is also the ancestor of the circumcised – those who don't rely just on their circumcision, but also walk in line with the footprints of the faith that our ancestor Abraham had while he was still uncircumcised.

13-15 The promise to Abraham and his descendants – that they would inherit the world – didn't come through law.[2] Rather, it came through the state of being right with God that came through faith. *14* Now if those who hold to the law are heirs, then faith has been made empty and the promise has been made useless. *15* For the law brings about retribution, but where there is no law there can be no breach of law!

16-17 This is why the promise is through faith, so that it is a matter of God's favor. This is so that the promise may be guaranteed as a valid purchase for all the descendants. This applies not only to those who are adherents of the Law, but also to those who are adherents of the faith of Abraham. Abraham is the ancestor of us all, *17* as the Scriptures say: "I will appoint you ancestor of many nations." The promise was valid in the sight of God whom he believed – that is, God, who makes the dead come to life and summons the things which do not exist, into existence.[3]

18 Abraham expected,[4] contrary to human expectation,[1] that he would become the ancestor of many nations, and this actually happened. This was what the words had said, namely, "Thus will your descendants be."

---

[1]   προπάτωρ, *propator*, "first founder of a family" (not "ancestor"), occurs only here in the N.T.

[2]   Again, no article, "law" is presented as a principle.

[3]   ὡς ὄντα, *hos onta*, "into existence": ὡς, *hos*, with participle. Here ὡς does not mean "as though (they were)", as ὡς, *hos*, can mean "as" with the indicative past tense, whereas here it is with the present participle. With the present participle, ὡς, *hos*, is used to denote cause, so it conveys the sense that the things which are not, are called on the ground that they are, or in other words, the things which do not exist, are called on the ground that they do exist.

[4]   Abraham believed on the basis of expectation, ἐπ ἐλπίδα, *ep' elpida*. The word "hope" can be substituted for "expectation" as the Greek word carries both meanings. However, the English word "hope" is not equivalent to the Greek word for "hope" as the Greek carried the meaning of expectation rather than mere wish or desire.

19-21 And Abraham's faith was not weakened when he carefully considered[2] his own body, which by now was as good as dead – he was about 100 years old in existing circumstances – and the state of deadness of Sarah's womb. *20* His faith did not weaken, nor was he undecided, but his faith was made strong, in view of God's promise. He honored God *21* and he was fully satisfied that what God had promised, he was also able to do.

22-25 This is why "he was considered to be made right with God". *23* The words, "he was considered" weren't written for his sake alone, *24* but also for ours. It is appointed for us to be considered right with God, we who believe that God raised Jesus our Lord from among the dead. *25* Jesus our Lord was delivered to death for our blunders and was raised up to make us right with God.

Ch.5:1-5 So then as we have been made right with God through faith, let us have peace with God through our Lord Jesus the Anointed One, *2* through whom we have gained access to God's favor. We take our stand on God's favor. And let us be proud about the expectation of God's splendor – God's splendor is to be ours. *3* And not only this, but let us also be proud of ordeals, as we know that ordeals produce endurance, *4* and endurance produces us getting through it, and us getting through it produces hope. *5* And hope does not disappoint, because the love of God has been poured out in our hearts by means of the Holy Spirit who was given to us.

6-9 For while we were still weak the Anointed One died at just the right time on behalf of ungodly people. *7* Now, it's rare that someone will die on behalf of a just person –possibly someone might dare to die on behalf of a civic benefactor![3] *8* But God offers his own love to us, because the Anointed One died for us, while we were still sinners. *9* All the more then, since we have now been made right with God by Jesus' blood, we will be saved from God's anger, through Jesus.

10-11 For, while we were still enemies with God, we were restored to friendship with God through the death of his Son. All the more then, now that we are restored to friendship with God, we will be saved by his Son's life. *11* And that's not all, but we also boast that we are friends with God through our Lord Jesus the Anointed One, as it is through him that we are now friends with God.

12-16 So it is that, just as sin entered the world through one person, and death entered the world through sin, thus death passed through to all people, seeing that all sinned. *13* Sin was in the world prior to law, but sin is not taken into account when there is no law. *14* But death established its reign from Adam until Moses, even over those who had not sinned in the same way as Adam. Adam is a pattern of him who was to come. *15* But God's favorable gift does not merely balance out the blunder, it far outweighs it. Many died because of the one person's blunder, yet its effect is vastly exceeded by God's favor and the gift given to so many people through one person, Jesus the Anointed One. *16* And again, the gift does not merely balance out the effects of sin through the one person. On the one hand the verdict which came from the one led to a verdict of condemnation, but on the other hand the gift following many blunders led to a verdict of acquittal.

17 For since death established its reign by one person's blunder, then so much more those who take hold of the excessive measure of God's favor, and his gift of being made right with him, will reign in life through the One, that is, Jesus the Anointed One.

---

[1]   That is, contrary to what one would normally expect.

[2]   κατανοέω, *katanoeo*, a strengthened form of νοέω, *noeo*: "to consider carefully". The Textus Receptus has "considered not his own body", the "not" having been added by later copyists. See Metzger, *op.cit.,* p. 451.
   Abraham did not ignore the natural circumstances, and the seemingly impossible circumstances did not weaken his faith.

[3]   ἀνὴρ ἀγαθός, *aner agathos*, "civic benefactor". See note on Luke 23:50.

18-19 To sum up: just as through one blunder the judgment came to all people and led to the verdict of condemnation, in the same way too through one act of justice, God's favor came to all people. This led to them being made right with God, and brought life. *19* Many were brought into the state of being sinners through one person failing to listen, and many were brought into the state of being made right with God by One paying attention.

20-21 But law was introduced, with the result that blunders increased. But this increase of sin only caused God's favor to multiply in a very large way! So then just as sin established its reign because of death, *21* in the same way also God's favor would establish its reign through being made right with God and lead to eternal life through Jesus the Anointed One our Lord.

Ch.6:1-5 So then, what are we going to say? Are we going to continue to sin so that God's favor can increase? *2* Certainly not! We who died to sin, how can we live in sin any longer? *3* Or are you unaware that all of us who were baptized into union with the Anointed One Jesus were baptized into union with his death? *4* So then we were buried in baptism - that meant we died with him. And since the Anointed One was raised from among the deadby the Father's splendor, in the same way too we should behave with a new quality of life. *5* For as we have become united with the likeness of his death, then certainly we are also united with the likeness of his resurrection!

6-11 We realize that our old person was crucified with him, so that the sinful body would be rendered inactive, so that we would not be a slave to sin[1] anymore. *7* For the person who died has had their sins canceled. *8* But since we died with the Anointed One, we believe that we will also live with him. *9* We know that the Anointed One was raised from among dead bodies and no longer dies – death has no mastery over him any longer. *10* In dying as he died, he died to sin once and for all. But in living as he lives, he lives only for God. *11* In the same way too, you count yourselves as dead to sin indeed, but living only for God through the Anointing of Jesus.

12-14 So then, do not let sin reign in your mortal body or you will end up listening to its wants and wishes![2] *13* And do not present your body parts to sin as weapons[3] to be used by injustice. Instead, present yourselves to God as living ones who were once dead ones, and present your body parts as weapons to be used by justice. *14* For sin will not have mastery over you – you are not subject to law, but subject to God's favor.

15-19 What then? Are we to commit sin, because we're not subject to law but subject to God's favor? Certainly not! *16* Don't you know that whenever you present yourselves as slaves to someone and intend to do as they say, then you are the slaves of the one you pay attention to,[4] whether you are a slave to sin which results in death, or whether you are a slave to paying attention to your master which results in being made right with God! *17* But it's thanks to God that, although you were once slaves of sin, you paid attention from the heart to that pattern of teaching to which you were handed over. *18* And being freed from sin, you became slaves of being made right with God. *19* I am speaking in human terms, because of your human limitations.[5] For just as you presented your body parts as enslaved to

---

[1]   Sin is personified as a ruler of a kingdom in verses 7, 12, 14, conscripting and paying its armies, verses 13, 23.

[2]   ἐπιθυμία, *epithumia*, "wants and wishes", "desire", not "lusts". The word itself does not have a negative connotation, and is used of good desire in Luke 22:15 and Phil. 1:3. The word simply refers to human wants, wishes, and desires. "Wants and wishes" is preferable to the translation "desires", as "desires" can be ambiguous in the English language.

[3]   Literally, the weapons of the foot-soldier.

[4]   ὑπακοη, *hupakoe*. See note on Rom. 1:5. Twice in this sentence.

[5]   "..because of your weakness in the natural realm."

uncleanness and illegal acts, which results in illegal acts, in the same way indeed you present your body parts as enslaved to the state of being right with God, which results in you being made sacred.

20-23 When you were slaves of sin, you were free with regard to being made right with God. *21* But what benefit did you get? Nothing, except what you're now ashamed of! The result of those things is death! *22* But now that you have been freed from sin and enslaved to God, you have your benefit – and this results in you being made sacred. And the result of this is eternal life. *23* Sin pays out death as its wages, but God pays out eternal life as his gift, due to the Anointed One Jesus our Lord.

Ch.7:1-3 Or are you unaware, fellow believers – for I'm speaking to those who understand law – that law has mastery over a person as long as they live? *2* That is to say,[1] a woman who is married is bound by law to her husband while he is alive. But if her husband dies, she has been discharged from the Law with regard to her husband. *3* So then, if she is with another man while her husband is still alive, she will be designated an adulterer. But if her husband dies, she is freed from that law, so that she is not an adulterer, even though she unites herself to another man.

4-6 This is my point: my fellow believers, you too have become dead to the Law through the body of the Anointed One, so that you may be united with the very One who was raised from among the dead. As a result, we can produce benefits for God. *5* When we were in a natural state, sinful matters were at work in our body parts through the Law. This produced benefits for death! *6* But in point of fact, we have been discharged from the Law, as we have died to that which was holding us down. This enables us to serve in newness of quality of spirit, and not in the obsolete code of the written law.

7-13[2] So then, what are we going to say to this? Is the Law sin? Certainly not! However, I only recognized sin through law, as I would not have known about longing for other people's things if the law had not said, "You are not to long for other people's things". *8* But sin, taking hold of a base of operations,[3] brought about in me all types of longing for other people's things through the commandment that prohibited it – for without law, sin is dead. *9* But I myself was alive formerly without law, but when the commandment came, sin lived anew.

But I myself died *10* and it proved to me that the commandment, which was supposed to bring life, this very commandment turned out instead to bring death. *11* For it was sin, taking hold of a base of operations through the commandment, which cheated[4] me and killed me through the commandment. *12* The result is that the Law indeed is sacred and the commandment is sacred and just and good. *13* So then, did that which is good bring me into the state of being of death? Certainly not! Rather, sin, so that it could be revealed as sin, was producing death in me by that which is good, so that sin would become sinful in the extreme through the commandment.

14-17 Now we know that the Law is of the spiritual realm but I am of the natural realm, sold and ruined under sin. *15* For that which I am achieving, I do not understand. And that which I don't want to do, that I practice. But what I hate

---

[1] Paul provides an illustration from the Law.

[2] Paul uses powerful rhetoric in 7:7-25.

[3] ἀφορμή, *aphorme*, used to denote a base of operations in war: "base of operations" as a military term (cf. Thuc. 1.90); "starting point"; "opportunity'; "occasion". See *P.Oxy* I.34; *P.Strass.* I.22; *BGU* II.615. Well attested.

[4] ἐξαπατάω, *exapatao*, to beguile, to cheat, to deceive thoroughly and utterly, with implications of foul play and often of supernatural means. A nearly complete papyrus sheet constituting an official circular forbidding magic and divination, cf. *P.Coll.Youtie* 1.30 "Since I have come across many people who consider themselves to be beguiled by means of divination…"

to do, that I do. *16* But those things I don't want to do – if I do them, I am agreeing with the Law that the Law is admirable. *17* But now it isn't any longer I myself that achieves it, but the sin which is living in me that achieves it.

18-20 For I know that in me, that is to say, in my natural self, no good thing lives – for my will is lying ready in wait in me, to achieve that which is not admirable. *19* The good I want to do, I do not do, but the bad I do not want to do, that I practice. *20* But if I do that which I do not want to do, then it isn't any longer I myself that achieves it, but the sin which is living in me that achieves it.

21-24 So it is then that I find the law:[1] that bad is ready at hand in me - me - the one who wishes to do good! *22* My inner person delights in God's Law, *23* but I observe another law at work in my body parts, carrying out a campaign against the law of my mind and bringing me into captivity under sin's law which is at work within my limbs. *24* What a miserable person I am! Who will deliver me out of this body doomed to death?

25.Ch.8:1-2 I thank God that deliverance comes through Jesus the Anointed One our Lord. So it is then that I myself serve the law of God with my mind, but I serve the law of sin with my nature. *1* So the case is that there is no condemnation to those who are united with the Anointing of Jesus. *2* For the law of the Spirit of life united with the Anointing of Jesus has set you free from the law of sin and death.

3-4 For what the Law has the inability to do because of the weakness of the natural realm, God did by sending his own Son. He sent him in the likeness of the sinful natural realm, and to be a sacrificial offering in place of sin. God passed judgment against sin in the natural realm. *4* He did this so that the commandment of the Law would be fulfilled in us, we who do not live out our lives in accordance with the natural realm,[2] but in accordance with the Spirit.

5-8 Those who live out their lives in accordance with the natural realm think on the level of the natural realm, but those who live out their lives in accordance with the Spirit think on the level of the spiritual realm. *6* For the outlook of the natural person is death, but the outlook of the spiritual person is life and peace. *7* In fact the thought processes of the natural realm are hostile to God, for they do not support the law of God nor do they have the ability to do so. *8* Those who are of the natural realm cannot please God.

9 But you are not of the natural realm; rather, you are of the spiritual realm, if indeed the Spirit of God lives in you. And if anyone does not have the Spirit of the Anointed One, this person does not belong to the Anointed One.

10-11 But if the Anointing is in you, on the one hand your body is a corpse because of sin, but on the other hand, your spirit is alive because you have been made right with God. *11* And since the Spirit of him who raised Jesus from among the dead lives in you, he who raised the Anointed One from among the dead will also bring your mortal bodies to life through his Spirit who lives in you.

12-13 Thus the case is, fellow believers, that we are debtors. But we are not debtors to the natural realm,[3] to live in accordance with the natural realm. *13* If you live in accordance with the natural realm, you are destined to die, but if you put the actions of the body to death by the Spirit,[4] you will live.

14-17 For all those people who are being led by the Spirit of God, these and none but these are the children of God. *15* You did not again take hold of a spirit of slavery to fear, but you did take hold of a spirit of adoption[5] by which we bawl out aloud, "Dad, Father." *16* The Spirit himself jointly gives witness with our spirit that we are God's children. *17* Since we are children, we are also heirs. On the one hand we are God's heirs, and on the other hand

---

[1] That is, the principle.
[2] The word "sinful" (or "sin") does not occur at all in the Greek here.
[3] The word "sinful" does not occur in verses 12-13 in the Greek.
[4] Equally, "by spiritual means".
[5] υιοθεσια, *huiothesia*, "adoption". See note on verse 23 below.

we are joint-heirs[1] with the Anointed One, since indeed we jointly experience things with him, so that we may also be jointly honored with him.
18-21 Now I calculate that our experiences in this present season of time are not worthy in comparison with the glory about to be revealed to us. *19* The creation looks forward with eager expectation to God's children being revealed. *20* Creation was joined to futility, not because it wanted to be, but because of him who made it so. Yet there was the hope *21* that creation itself also would be set free from slavery to decay,[2] and have the glorious freedom of God's children.
22-25 We know that all creation keeps sighing deeply together and is in birthing pains together up to the present time. *23* Not only that, but also we ourselves who have the Spirit given to us as the first offering, we also keep sighing deeply within ourselves looking forward to our adoption,[3] that is, the setting free of our body. *24* We were saved by hope: but hope that is looked at is not hope – for who hopes for what they look at? *25* But since we hope for what we do not look at, then we look forward to it with endurance.
26-30 In the same way also, the Spirit takes hold together with us in our weaknesses –we don't know how we are to pray so that our prayers will correspond to the need, but the Spirit super–intercedes[4] with deeply emotional heartfelt groanings. *27* And he who searches the hearts knows what the Spirit has in mind, that the Spirit intercedes on behalf of the people devoted to God, in line with God's plans. *28* We know that everything works in conjunction for good with those who love God, with those who are invited in accordance with his proposals. *29* Because the people that God foreknew, he also predestined to share the image of his Son, so that he would be the firstborn of many brothers and sisters.[5] *30* And those he predestined, he also invited; those he invited, he also made right with him; those he made right with him, he also gave his splendor.
31-32 So then, what are we going to say about these things? If God is for us, who can be against us? *32* He who certainly did not spare his own Son, but handed him over for us all, surely he will also give us all things as a favor, as well as giving us his Son!
33-39 Who can bring an accusation against God's chosen people? God is the One who brings the acquittal. *34* Who can pass sentence? It is the Anointed One Jesus who died, but rather, was raised up, who is at God's right side, and who also intercedes on our behalf. *35* What can separate us from the love of the Anointed One's love? Can oppression or difficulty or persecution, or hunger, or deprivation, or danger, or sword? *36* Just as the Scriptures say,

---

[1] συγκληρονόμος, *sugkleronomos*, "joint-heir". This word is very well attested in the papyri. The noun occurs also in Eph. 3:6; Heb. 11:9; 1 Pet. 3:7.
[2] φθορά, *phthora*, "decay", "destruction", "ruin", "death". The KJV translates "corruption" which in the early 1600s did indeed mean "decay", "destruction". Today "corruption" means fraud or vice and φθορά, *phthora*, cannot have this meaning. This has clearly influenced some modern translations in their mistranslation of this word, and their addition of the word "evil" to "desire(s)", when "evil" is not here in the Greek.
[3] υἱοθεσία, *huiothesia*, "adoption", non-gender specific language (see below), cf. Rom. 8:15, 23; 9.4; Eph. 1:5. This is a use of a technical adoption term from Greek law. F. Lyall, *JBL* 88 (1969) 458-66 argued that Paul's use of adoption terminology was a reference to Roman law, but this has later been shown to be a reference to Greek law. See discussion in *NDIEC* 3.17. υἱός, *huios*, is in reference to both males and females. The non-gender specific word τεκνοθεσία, *teknothesia*, occurs first in *P. Oxy.* 3271, referring to an adopted daughter.
[4] ὑπερεντυγχάνω, *huperentugkhano*. The Spirit super-intercedes, not merely "intercedes" or "makes intercession". The Spirit overly intercedes – the Spirit does more than intercede.
[5] Double meaning, "fellow believers".

"On account of you we are killed all the day long. We are calculated as sheep to be slaughtered." *37* But in all these situations we are super-abundantly victorious through him who loved us. *38* For I am convinced that neither death nor life, nor spirit messengers, nor rulers, nor things present, nor things to come, nor powers, *39* nor height, nor depth, nor any other created thing will have the ability to separate us from God's love, which comes by means of the Anointed One Jesus our Lord.

Intercede.

The word means to put a petition whether positive or negative (that is, against another) on behalf of another person rather than for oneself. A 1st c. inscription on a marble statue base, petition about the Ephesian mysteries, contains the word "intercede": "Sir, mysteries and sacrifices are performed every year at Ephesos, to Demeter, Karpophoros and Thesmosphoros and to the divine Augusti by initiates with much decorum and legal customs, together with the priestesses. The mysteries have been watched over for very many years by kings, emperors and the annual proconsuls, just as their attached letters say. So then, sir, since the mysteries will be soon upon us during your term of office, I intercede on behalf of those who are to perform the mysteries, so that you, in recognition of their rights..." *SIG*[3] 8.40 (Ephesos, 88/9).

Here is an example in the negative sense (to intercede against someone). A papyrus details a petition from a woman, Aurelia Tapammon, to two minor officials who were responsible for public order: "By inheritance from my parents I own with my sister Dioskouriaina a slave by the name of Sarmates, house-born from the female slave Thaesis. He has been providing us with income since the time of my parents' death. But now, from what motive I do not know, he is withdrawing from his work and is not willing to remain in our service or even pay what he owes, for reasons unknown to myself. So then, since I cannot out up with a slave's insolence, I am presenting this written document with the intention of interceding and requesting that through your attention the slave be forced to pay the income he owes and that he be ordered to remain in our service." *P.Oxy.Hels.* 26 (Oxyrhynchos, 13 June 296).

Ch.9:1-5 I speak the truth through the Anointing, and I do not lie. My conscience joins in testifying with me with the Holy Spirit, *2* that I have great sorrow and continual pain in my heart. *3* I could claim that I myself were accursedly[1] separated from the Anointed One, on behalf of my fellow believers, my fellow countrypersons in the natural realm, *4* who are Israelites. Theirs is the adoption,[2] and the splendor, and the covenants, and the legislation, and the worshipping of God, and the promises. *5* Theirs are the ancestors, and from them, with regard to his descent in the natural realm, came the Anointed One, who exists throughout time, God praised for the ages, amen!

6-13 Now of course it is not as if God's Word has failed! It is not all those who are descended from Israel who are Israel! *7* Nor are all the descendants of Abraham children, but, "Through Isaac your descendants will be invited." *8* That is to say, it is not the children born through the course of the natural realm who are God's children, but the children born through God's promise who are calculated to be Abraham's descendants. *9* Now this is the Word, the promise: "At the appointed time I will return, and Sarah will have a son." *10* Not only that, but Rebecca's children had one and the same father, our ancestor Isaac. *11* But before the children were born or had done anything good or worthless, it was said to Rebecca - so that the selection which God purposed would be preserved - this was not based on people's actions but based on God's

---

[1] ἀνάθεμα, *anathema*. See note on καταράομαι, *kataraomai*, in Luke 6:28.
[2] υἱοθεσία, *huiothesia*. See note on Romans 8:23.

invitation – *12* "The elder will serve the younger." *13* As the Scriptures say, "Jacob I loved, Esau I hated."

14-18 So then, what will we say to this? Is there injustice with God! Of course not! *15* For God said to Moses, "I will have mercy on those on whom I have mercy, and I will have compassion on those on whom I have compassion." *16* So then, it doesn't depend on someone who wants it, or even on someone who races for it, but it depends on God who has mercy. *17* For the Scripture said to Pharaoh, "I have raised you up for this very purpose, so that I may display my power because of you, and so that my Name will be sent as a message over the whole earth." *18* So then God has mercy on whomever he wants to, and makes stubborn whomever he wants to.

19-24 So then you will say to me, "Why does he still blame someone? Who can resist his wishes?"*20* Hey you, you person, who are you to answer God back! Will the thing that's molded say to the person who molded it, "Why did you make me like this?" *21* Come on now! Surely the potter has authority over the clay, and from the same lump of clay makes valuable vessels and worthless vessels!

22 But what if God wanted to show his anger and make his ability known, but instead very patiently put up with the objects of his anger, objects which had been prepared for destruction!¹ *23* What if he did this to make his splendid wealth known to the receptacles of his mercy, receptacles he had prepared beforehand for splendor – *24* that is us, whom he invited, not only from the Jews but also from the non-Jews!

25-26 As he also says in Hosea: "I will call them 'My people' who are not my people, and I will call her 'My loved one' who is not my loved one," *26* and, "It will happen in the very place where it was said to them, 'You are not my people', so that they will be called 'children of the Living God.'"

27-29 Isaiah calls out on behalf of Israel, "Although the number of the Israelites will be like the sand of the sea, only a small remaining number will be saved. *28* For the Lord will act, bringing his Word to pass, making a decisive end upon the earth." *29* And just as Isaiah has foretold, "Unless the Lord of Armies had left us a seed, we would have become like Sodom, and we would have made like Gomorrah."

30-33 So then, what will we say to this? That non-Jews, who did not chase after being made right with God, have seized it, and moreover, have seized the being made right with God that comes through faith. *31* But Israel, chasing after the law of being made right with God, has not chased after it. *32* Why not? Because they did not do it out of faith, but did it as if it could be seized by their actions. They tripped over the stone, the obstacle in their path. *33* As the Scriptures say, "I place a stone in Zion. It may be a stone to stumble over, a rock to trip over, but the person who trusts it will not be disappointed."

Ch.10:1-4 Fellow believers, my heart's desire and my earnest request to God on their behalf is for their salvation. *2* I testify to their Godly zeal, but not one which is directed by knowledge. *3* They are ignorant of God's rightness and seek to set up their own rightness. They are not supported by God's rightness. *4* For the Anointed One is the fulfillment² of law, and this leads to everyone who believes being made right with God.

5-10 Now Moses writes of the being made right with God which is based on the Law: "The person who does these things will live by them!" *6* Now the being made right with God which is based on faith speaks in this way: "Do not say in your heart, 'Who will go up into heaven?'" (that is, to bring the Anointed One down.) *7* Or, "Who will go down into the abyss?" (That is, to bring the Anointed One up from among the dead.) *8* But what does it say? "The spoken

---

¹ ἀπώλεια, *apoleia*, destruction of well-being.
² τέλος, *telos*, "fulfillment", not "end". τέλος, *telos*, refers to result, fulfillment or completion, not to cessation.

word is near you, in your mouth and in your heart." (That is, the spoken word of faith which we proclaim.) *9* Because if you agree with your mouth that Jesus is Lord, and believe in your heart that God raised him from among the dead, you will be saved. *10* For with the heart one believes, and this results in being made right with God, and with the mouth one agrees, and this results in salvation. **11-18** Now the scripture says, Everyone "who trusts in him will certainly not be disappointed."[1] *12* There is no distinction between Jew or Greek, for the same One is Lord over enough treasures to benefit of all who call on his Name for assistance. *13* Everyone who calls on the Lord's Name for assistance will be saved." *12* Yet how are they going to call for assistance on him in whom they haven't believed? And how are they going to believe him whom they haven't heard? *15* And how are they going to hear without someone to proclaim it? And how are they going to proclaim if they're not sent out? As the Scriptures say, "How beautiful are the feet of those who announce Good News about good things."

16 But they did not pay attention[2] to the Good News. For Isaiah says, "Lord, who has believed what they heard from us?" *17* So it is then, that faith comes from hearing the anointed spoken word. *18* But I say, didn't they hear? Certainly they did! "Their voice has gone out to the whole earth, and their spoken words to the limits of the inhabited world."

19-21 But I say, didn't Israel know? First Moses says, "I will make you jealous of those who are not a nation. I will make you angry about a nation which is void of understanding." *20* But Isaiah shows greater daring and says: "I was found by those who did not seek me, I showed myself to those who did not inquire after me." *21* But to Israel God says: "The whole day long I stretched out my hands, to a disobedient people who contradicted me."

Ch.11:1-3 So then I say, did God reject his people? Of course not! For I too am an Israelite, a descendant of Abraham, of the tribe of Benjamin. *2* God has not cast away his children whom he previously acknowledged. Utter rubbish![3] Don't you know what the Scripture says in the passage about Elijah, how he intercedes to God against Israel: *3* "Lord, they killed your prophets and tore down your altars! I alone am left and they're trying to kill me too!"

4-6 But what did the divine utterance[4] say to him? "I have left for myself 7,000 men, who have not worshipped Baal."[5] *5* So then, in the same way also there are some left in the present season of time, and they were chosen because of

---

[1] ὁ πιστεύων ἐπ' αὐτῷ οὐ καταισχυνθήσεται, *ho pisteuon ep' auto ou kataiskhunthesetai*, a quote from the last line of Isaiah 28:16. See also 1 Pet. 2:6 which is an expanded quote of Isaiah 28:16. This is litotes (an ironic understatement using a negative of its contrary). For litotes, see also Rom. 1:16, Acts 21:39; 1 Pet. 2:6 (mentioned above); Rev. 3:5. In this verse the quote is from the LXX which is slightly different: ὁ πιστεύων ἐπ' αὐτῷ οὐ καταισχυνθῇ, *ho pisteuon ep' auto ou me kataiskhunthe*. The Hebrew of Isaiah 28:16: "Thus says my Lord YHWH, See, I am laying in Zion a stone, a tested stone. A precious foundation corner is being founded. A firmness that will not give way." It is a pun. *Me'amin* means both one who believes, and also means a (foundation) pillar, something that holds up a building. The root *AMN* means "be firm", "let it be established", "held firm".

[2] ὑπακούω, *hupakouo*. See note on Matt. 8:27.

[3] Disjunctive particle.

[4] χρηματισμός, *khrematismos*, "divine utterance", noun, occurs only here in the N.T. It is well attested on inscriptions. It appears on the Rosetta Stone, *SGPI* 69 (time of Ptolemy V; =*OGIS* 90). It also occurs on the Kanopos decree, a Ptolemaic inscription, no. 38 (=*OGIS* 56), l.23; *I.Nikaia* II, 1.1071 (Golpazar, I or II).

[5] 1 Kings 19:18. Here the feminine article is used despite masculine article in the LXX, through the custom of reading aloud the deplorable name "Baal" as "Boseth" which is feminine grammatical gender.

God's favor. *6* But since it is by means of God's favor, then it can't be because of people's actions, otherwise favor ceases to be favor!

7-10 So what? That which Israel sought for, it did not attain. The chosen attained it, but the rest became hardened, *8* just as the Scriptures say: "God gave them a spirit of stupidity, so that their eyes could not see, and their ears could not hear, up to this very day." *9* And David says, "Let their dining table be made a snare, and a prey, and a trap and let them get what's coming to them. *10* Let their eyes be darkened so they do not see and let them bend over their backs all the time like people groping about in the dark."

11-12 So then, I say, did they trip over so that they would fall beyond recovery? Of course not! Rather, it was so that salvation would come to the non-Jews by means of the Israelites' blunder, and make the Israelites jealous. *12* Now if the Israelites' blunder means enrichment for the world and their loss means enrichment for the non-Jews, then how much greater enrichment for the world will their full number bring?

13-15 I have something to say to you non-Jews. I myself am an envoy[1] to the non-Jews, and thus I hereby honor my ministry,[2] *14* if by some way I may make my own people jealous and so save some of them. *15* For if their rejection means restoration of the world to friendship with God, then what does their acceptance mean? It means nothing less than being brought to life from the dead!

16-18 If the first offering of a lump of dough is sacred, so also is the whole lump. If the root is sacred, so are the branches. *17* Now if some of the branches were broken off, and you, a wild olive shoot, were grafted onto the others and now are a joint partner[3] in the sap of the olive tree, *18* don't boast about those branches! If you do, bear in mind that you don't support the root – the root supports you!

19-21 So then, you will say, "Branches were broken off so I could be grafted on."

20 Yes, that's true. that's true. But they were broken off by means of unbelief, but you stand by means of faith. Do not preoccupy yourself with thinking highly of yourself, but be afraid! *21* For if God hasn't spared the branches of nature,[4] it's not likely that he'll spare you!

22-24 Look at the kindness and harshness[5] of God: on the one hand harshness to those who fell, and on the other hand he is kind to you, provided that you continue to be kind! Otherwise you'll be cut off! *23* And they, if they do not continue with their unbelief, will be grafted on, for God is able to graft them on again. *24* If you were cut out of an olive tree that is a wild one in nature, and grafted into the cultivated olive tree – which is against nature- how much more easily will these, the natural branches, be grafted onto their own olive tree!

25-27 I do not want you to be ignorant, fellow believers, of this secret hidden truth, so that you won't be conceited: Israel has partly experienced a hardening until the full number of the non-Jews comes in, *26* and in this way all Israel will be saved, just as the Scriptures say: "The deliverer will come from Zion. He will turn ungodliness away from Jacob. *27* And this is my covenant with them, when I will take away their sins."

28-32 On the one hand, the Israelites are enemies so that the Good News can come to you, but on the other hand they are God's chosen people and God loves

---

[1]   Equally, "messenger", "apostle". ἀπόστολος, *apostolos*. See note on Matt. 10:2.

[2]   For διακονία, *diakonia*, see Thuc. 1.133, Plato, *Rep.* 371C, Dem. 296.29, Polyb. 15. 25, 4. *Diakonia* is the act of the *diakonos*. See note on Rom. 16:1.

[3]   συγκοινωνός, *sugkoinonos*, joint partner. Occurs, for example, in the letter by a state schoolteacher making a salary bid, *P.Coll.Youtie* 66. The schoolteacher is requesting an orchard, and states that his addressee can do this either in partnership with him or by himself. In N.T. also in 1 Cor. 9:23; Phil. 1:7; Rev. 1:9.

[4]   φύσις, *phusis*, "nature" as in the birds, the trees, the flowers, the grass, not the word Paul uses for the "natural realm".

[5]   ἀποτομία, *apotomia*. The noun occurs only here in the N.T. Paul is again playing on words. The word means "severity", but can also mean "cut off".

them because of their ancestors. *29* For God's gifts and his invitation cannot be altered or taken back. *30* Just as you were once disobedient to God, you have now obtained mercy through Israel's disobedience. *31* In the same way also Israel has now been disobedient, so that by the mercy shown to you they also may now obtain mercy. *32* God has enclosed everyone with disobedience, so that all may obtain mercy.

33 Oh the depth of the riches and wisdom and knowledge of God! How unsearchable are his decisions and his paths untraceable!

34-36 "For who has known the mind of the Lord? Or who has been his adviser?" *35* "Who has ever made a gift to God to receive a gift in return?"

36 He is the source of everything, everything exists because of him, and everything leads to him. To him be the honor for the ages, amen!

Ch.12:1-2 I encourage you, fellow believers, through God's compassion, to present your bodies a living sacrifice, sacred, pleasing to God, which is your rational worship. *2* And do not go along with the way of this present period of time,[1] but be transformed by the renewal of your minds, so that you will examine God's purpose which is good and pleasing and complete.

3-8 Through the favor that was given to me I say to each one of you – do not think more highly of yourselves than you should! Rather, think sensibly as God has portioned to each one a measure of faith.

4 Each of us has many parts of our body, and all the parts do not have the same function. *5* In the same way we are the many parts of the Anointed One's body, and individually we are parts of each other. *6* We have gifts that are different because of the favor that was given to us. Perhaps we have prophecy according to the proportion of our faith. *7* Perhaps we have the gift of ministry- then let us use it in ministry. Perhaps we have the gift of teaching - let us use it in instruction and training. *8* Perhaps we have the gift of encouraging - let us use it in encouraging. Let the person who gives a share, do it generously. Let the person who gives aid,[2] do it eagerly. Let the person who is merciful, do it cheerfully.

9-13 Your love must not be overly critical. Strongly detest evil! Cling to good! *10* Your love[3] for the fellow believers[4] is to be affectionate and warm.

---

[1] ὁ αἰὼν οὗτος, *ho aion houtos*, "this present period of dispensation", "this present age", "this present space of time". Not "world".

[2] προιστεμαι τινος, *proistemai tinos*, "care for", "give aid to". It carries the sense of presiding over activities in an official capacity. (Acknowledged by BGAD, *s.v.*) Also in 1 Tim. 3:4, 5; 5:17; Rom. 12:8; 1 Thess. 5:12; Titus 3:8, 14. Used in the papyri in the context of one who is a leader, patron, supervisor and director. The term was used for the pagan goddess Artemis of Ephesos in her capacity as patron of the city, cf. E.L. Hicks, *The Collection of Ancient Greek Inscriptions in the British Museum*, III.2 (Oxford, 1890) 482 (+addendum on p. 294), Ephesos, c. 162-64, *l.*16. See Horsley, "Holy Days in honor of Artemis" *NDEIC* 4.74-82. Artemis was described as savior, healer, protector, and was worshipped throughout the whole world, cf. Pausanias 4.31.8. In non-Biblical texts the term means, "be the leader of, rule, direct, be concerned about, care for, give aid." The word encompasses both care and concern and official rule and authority.

[3] φιλόστοργος, *philostorgos*, regard, affection, occurs only here in N.T. MM provide no documentary examples, although *IG, IGRR,* and *OGIS* were available in their time. Appears in *P.Oxy* 11.1380 (cf. *I.Kyme* 41) where Isis sees it as her role to promote φιλοστορία, *philostoria*, in families. See also *P.Tebt.* 2.408.5-10 (3 AD); *P.Oxy.* 495; *P.Grenf.* 2.71. To date no examples of the adjective have been found in the papyri. For the adjective, see also *P.Flor.* 3.338.10-12 (Arsinoite nome, III) where φιλόστοργος, *philostorgos*, forms an hendiadys with σπουδή, *spoude*.

[4] φιλαδελφία, *philadelphia*, love for fellow believers, love for fellow members of an association, love for siblings. This is the more common word for love of

Honor one another above yourselves. *11* Do not hesitate to be eager. Be spiritually boiling hot as a slave servant to the Lord!

12 Be joyful when you hope, have endurance when you are oppressed, persist obstinately when you pray! *13* Be in partnership with[1] the needs of the people devoted to God! Go after opportunities to be hospitable!

14-21 Bless[2] those who persecute you! Bless them and do not call down curses upon them! *15* Rejoice with those who rejoice, and cry with those who cry! *16* Think along the same lines as each other! Do not be high minded! Rather, associate with those of low social standing.[3] Do not become conceited. *17* Do not repay bad with bad. Have a concern beforehand about what is favorable in the sight of all people. *18* If possible on your part, live at peace with all people. *19* Do not take revenge, my dearly loved ones, but leave room for God's anger, as the Scriptures say: "Vengeance is mine, I indeed will repay," says the Lord.

20 On the contrary, "If your enemy is hungry, feed them! If they're thirsty, give them a drink! For by doing this, you will heap coals of fire on their head!"

21 Do not conquer by doing bad things, but conquer bad things by doing good things!

Ch.13:1-5 Every individual must be supportive[4] of the prominentauthorities, for there is no authority that isn't from God, but all those in existence have been posted[5] there by God. *2* As a result, someone

---

fellow believers in the N.T. The cognate term φιλάδελφος, *philadelphos*, occurs only in 1 Peter 3:8 in the N.T. φιλαδελφία, *philadelphia*, and φιλάδελφος, *philadelphos,* occur on Jewish inscriptions, for example, *CIJ* 1.125, 321, 263; *CIJ* 2.815, 1488, 1489. The cognate term φιλάδελφος, *philadelphos*, occurs, for example, in *SEG* 1157, "Here lies Philippus, lover of his fellow believers, who lived thirty-three years." See also *SEG* 1511. φιλάδελφος, *philadelphos*, also occurs in *CIJ* 2.1516, an epitaph for the 16 y.o. unmarried girl Sabbathin, μικρά φιλάδελφε, *mikra philadephe*. The word is found on an epitaph for a woman, *SEG* 20.534, and on an epitaph for a man, *SEG* 20.524.

[1] κοινωνέω τινί, *koinoneo tini*, "be in partnership with". F. Hauck, *Koinos*, *TDNT* 3 (1965) 798, states that the cognate noun is a "technical term for a business partner or associate". See *P.Oxy.* 3270.5, 8, in which Aurelius Lucius "and his partners" make an offer for the lease of a fishing area to Aurelius Sarapion "and his partners". See also note on Acts 2:42.

[2] εὐλογέω, *eulogeo*, "speak well of", "praise", "bless".

[3] ταπεινός, *tapeinos*, means those who are of a low level in society – they may be poor, brought down in some way, weak, downcast.

[4] ὑποτάσσω, *hupotasso*, in the passive means "to be attached to", "to be in support of"(cf. Luc. *Paras.* 49) and was used of attached/appended (supporting) documents in the postal system. See also Rom. 8:7, "For the thought processes of the natural realm are hostile to God, for they do not support (ὑποτάσσω, *hupotasso*) the law of God nor do they have the ability to do so." Horsley, *NDEIC* 1.3 states that a common non-N.T. use of ὑποτάσσω, *hupotasso*, is "append", "attach below" discussed by MM *s.v.* and is attested in a letter of 114 B.C. (*P.Tebt*, 1100). It was commonly used in the postal system with the meaning, "stick (to)", "attach". The English word "submit" is properly translated by ὑπείκω, *hupeiko*, with dative "submit to", cf. Heb. 13:17. See also Soph. *Aj.* 231, *O.T.* 625; Aesch. *Ag.* 1362; Eur. *I.A.* 139.

[5] Paul again plays on words. "Be posted with" is ὑποτάσσω, *hupotasso*, ὑπό, *hupo*, + τάσσω, *tasso*. "From (God)" is ὑπόν, *hupo*, and "has been posted (in the army) (by God)" is τάσσω, *tasso*. The theme is military. τάσσω, *tasso*, means to post, station (in the army), to draw up in battle order, to appoint as a ruler. ὑπό, *hupo*, with the genitive is "by" and is used to denote the agent of an act. τάσσω, *tasso*, is in the periphrastic perfect passive.

who ranges in battle[1] against the authority is ranging in battle against God's battle order posting, and will lay hold of judgment for themselves. *3* The rulers are only a terror to crime, not to good works. Do you want to be unafraid of authority? Then do what's good, and you will have their praise. *4* They are God's ministers working for your good. But if you do bad things, be afraid! They do not carry the sword without a reason! They are God's ministers, executors of justice to carry out his anger on wrongdoers.

5 So then, it is necessary that people support them, not only to avoid God's anger, but also to keep a clear conscience.

6-10 This is the reason that you also pay taxes – as they are God's public servants,[2] persisting obstinately in this very thing. *7* Give all people what you owe them. If you owe taxes, pay taxes; if you owe revenue, pay revenue; if you owe respect, pay respect; if you owe honor, pay honor. *8* Do not be a debtor to anyone, only owe love to one another. The person who loves their neighbor has fulfilled the law. *9* Note this: "You are not to commit adultery, you are not to commit murder, you are not to steal, you are not to long for other people's things," and if there is any other commandment, it is summed up in this Scripture: "You are to love your neighbor as yourself." *10* Love does no harm to its neighbor. Therefore love is the fulfillment of law.

11-14 And do this, knowing what season of time it is, because the hour is already here for you to wake up from your sleep! Our deliverance is nearer than when we first believed. *12* The night has progressed far, but the Day draws close. So then, we must rid ourselves of the works of darkness, and we must clothe ourselves with the weapons of light! *13* We must behave decently, as one behaves in daytime, not in orgies and drunkenness, not in sexual interludes[3] or vice, not in rivalries or jealousies.

14 Instead, clothe yourselves with the Lord Jesus the Anointed One, and do not have a regard for the wants and wishes of the natural realm.

Ch.14:1-3 Partner with one who is weak in the faith, but don't judge their thought processes. *2* One person's faith allows them to eat everything, but another person, whose faith is weak, eats vegetables. *3* Don't let the person that eats, look down on the person that doesn't eat. Don't let the person that doesn't eat, judge the person that eats, for God has taken them as a partner.

4-6 Who do you think you are to judge another person's servant! Whether they stand or fall is up to their own master. But they will stand, as the Lord has the ability to make them stand! *5* One person considers one day[4] more important than the other, but another person considers each day to be the same. Each person must be fully convinced in their own mind! *6* The person who considers that one day is special, does it to honor the Lord. The person that eats, does it to honor the Lord, for they offer thanks to the Lord. And the person that does not eat, does it to honor the Lord, and gives thanks to God.

7-13 No one lives for their own selves and no one dies for their own selves. *8* Rather, it is for the Lord that we must live, and it is for the Lord that we must die. Whether we live or die, we are the Lord's. *9* The reason that the Anointed One died and came to life was so that he would be Lord of both the living and the dead. *10* But you, why do you judge one of your fellow believers? Or how about you, why do you look down on one of your fellow believers? We are all going to stand before God's judgment seat! *11* For the

---

[1] ἀντιτάσσομαι, *antitassomai* (ἀντι– τάσσω, *anti - tasso*). More wordplay on the military theme. ἀντιτάσσομαι, *antitassomai*, means "to range in battle against". This word appears twice in this sentence.

[2] λειτουργός, *leitourgos*, public servant appointed for any work, whether civil or religious. Not the same word as in v. 4, διάκονος, *diakonos*, "minister", "deacon".

[3] κοίτη, *koite*, in plural, "sexual interludes".

[4] That is, considers certain days sacred. See note on Luke 4:16.

Scriptures say, "As I live, says the Lord, every knee will bow, and every tongue will fully agree."

12 Thus each one of us will give an account of ourselves to God. *13* So then let's not judge one another any more, but instead judge this: do not place an obstacle or a trap[1] in a fellow believer's way!

14-21 I know and I have been convinced by the Lord Jesus that there is nothing unclean[2] in itself, but it is actually unclean to someone who considers it to be unclean. *15* Now if your fellow believer is grieved because of what you eat, then you are not acting lovingly. Do not destroy the one the Anointed One died for, with your food! *16* So don't let what is a good thing for you be blasphemed. *17* God's Realm is not about eating and drinking, but is about justice, peace and joy by means of the Holy Spirit.

18 Someone who serves the Anointed One in this pleases God and finds approval with people. *19* So then, let's chase after things which constitute peace and things which constitute the building up of each another. *20* Do not dissolve God's work for the sake of food. Indeed all things are clean, but they are bad for the person whose eating causes a problem for someone else. *21* It's fine to abstain from eating meat or drinking wine or from doing something which causes your fellow believer to trip up.

22-23 Keep your own faith between you and God. The person who has a clear conscience about what they approve of is a happy person. *23* But the person who is undecided will stand condemned because their action does not spring from faith. Everything that does not arise from faith is sin.

Ch.15:1-6 We who are capable ought to embrace the weaknesses of those who are incapable and not just please ourselves. *2* Each of us should please our neighbor and consider what is good for them, for the purpose of building up the neighbor. *3* Even the Anointed One didn't please himself, but, as the Scriptures say, "The insults of those who insulted you fell on me." *4* Everything that was written beforehand was written to instruct and train us, so that through the endurance and encouragement of the Scriptures we would have hope. *5* And may God, who gives endurance and encouragement, give you the same mind as each other after the manner of the Anointed One Jesus, *6* so that you will praise the God and Father of our Lord Jesus the Anointed One with one mind and one voice.

7-13 So then, take each other as partners, in the same way also that the Anointed One took you as partners. *8* I mean that the Anointed One has become a minister to the Jews to maintain God's truth by guaranteeing the validity of the promises God made to their ancestors *9* and at the same time give the non-Jews reason to praise God for his mercy. As the Scriptures say, "For this reason I will fully agree with you among the non-Jews, and sing praises to your name." *10* And again he says, "Rejoice, you non-Jews, with his people!" *11* And again, "Praise the Lord, all you non-Jews! Let all the people praise him greatly!" *12* And again, Isaiah says, "There will be a root of Jesse, namely, he who will rise up to rule over the non-Jews. The non-Jews will put their hope in him!" *13* Now may God who is hope fill you with all happiness and peace by means of your faith in him, so that your hope may overflow by means of the Holy Spirit's power!

14-16 My fellow believers, I myself am certainly convinced that you yourselves are full to the utmost with goodness, filled with knowledge of every kind, and also able to give advice to one another. *15* Yet I have written to you rather boldly on some points, reminding you of them, *16* as God's favor has made me a public servant of the Anointed One Jesus to the non-Jews. My

---

[1] σκάνδαλον, *skandalon*, "trap" not "temptation".

[2] κοινός, *koinos*. A technical term for common things which were considered unclean for use in worship. cf. Jos. Ant. 13.i.1; 1 Macc. i. 47, 62.

ministry[1] is to teach the Good News of God, so that the offering of the non-Jews would be acceptable to God, an offering made sacred by the Holy Spirit.

17-21 Thus due to the Anointing of Jesus I am proud of my work for God. *18* I will not dare to speak of anything except that which the Anointing did through me which led to the non-Jews paying attention to the Good News. This was by means of speech and actions, *19* by means of powerful miraculous signs and wonders, by means of the power of the Spirit of God. As a result I have fully announced the Good News about the Anointed One from Jerusalem all the way around to Illyricum. *20* Thus my driving ambition is to announce the Good News where the Name of the Anointed One was absent, so that I would not be building on someone else's foundation. *21* Rather, as the Scriptures say, "Those who were not told about him will see, and those who have not heard will understand!"

22-24 This is why I have often been prevented from coming to you. *23* But now there is no more opportunity in these regions, and since I have had a desire[2] for many years to come and see you, *24* I plan to do so when I travel to Spain. For I hope to pass through and come and see you and have you send me on my way with money and supplies, after I've enjoyed your company for a while.[3]

25-29 But at the moment I'm off to Jerusalem to financially provide[4] for the people devoted to God. *26* For Macedonia and Achaia were most happy to bring about such and such an amount of partnership[5] for financially poor people among those devoted to God in Jerusalem. *27* They were very happy to do it and they owe it to them. For since the non-Jews have been in partnership with[6] the Jews in the spiritual realms, they also ought to render service to the Jews in the natural realms. *28* So then, when I have performed this act of worship[7] and have sealed these proceeds for them, I will go to Spain and visit you on the way. *29* Now I know that when I come to you, I will come with the Anointed One's full blessing.

30-33 Fellow believers, I encourage you, through our Lord Jesus the Anointed One and through the Spirit's love, to fight by my side in your prayers to God for me. *31* This is so that I would be drawn out of danger from those who are unbelievers in Judea. This is so that my contribution which I have for Jerusalem will be acceptable to the people devoted to God, *32* so that I will be able to come to you happily by means of God's purpose, and so that I will be refreshed with you. *33* May the God of peace be with you all! Amen.

Ch.16:1-2[8] I recommend[1] to you Phoebe our fellow believer, who is a deacon[2] of the assembly in Kenchreai,[3] *2* so that you will admit her into your

---

[1] ἱερουργέω, *hierourgeo*, only here in N.T. No equivalent English word. It was used of one who taught the rites and sacrifices and worship. In Classical Greek times, it referred to the presiding or initiating priest at Eleusis, and the priest of Demeter and Persephone in Sicily. The object of the verb here is the Good News of God.

[2] ἐπιθυμία, *epithumia*, "desire" (whether good or bad, simply a wish or want), the same word mistranslated in Bible versions as "evil lusts".

[3] Note that Paul becomes quite chatty and far less formal in tone when he leaves his teaching matters.

[4] διακονέω τινί, *diakoneo tini*. See note on Matt. 27:55.

[5] κοινωνία, *koinonia*, "partnership", cf. Woodhouse, *op.cit.*, p. 315. Here it refers to a certain sum of money. Zerwick and Grosvenor, *op.cit.*, p. 495, note that the partnership here amounted to a contribution. See note on Rom. 12:13.

[6] κοινωνέω τινί, *koinoneo tini*. See note on Rom. 12:13.

[7] ἐπιτελέω, *epiteleo*, "to perform an act of worship", "to sacrifice". Not τελέω, *teleo*, "to complete".

[8] Deissmann, *op.cit.*, argues that Romans 16 is a letter to the Ephesians, but always found in Romans as it was first discovered from one of Paul's parchment notebooks (cf. 2 Tim. 4:13). For discussion see also W. Bauer, *Orthodoxy and Heresy in Earliest Christianity* (Philadelphia: *ET*, 1971) p. 82; J.I.H. McDonald,

your company, the Lord's company,[4] in a manner worthy of the people devoted to God, and stand by her in whatever matters she needs you to help in. For indeed she became a presiding officer[5] over many, and over me also![6]
3-7 Greet Priska and Aquila[7] my coworkers of the Anointed One Jesus, *4* who risked their own necks for my life – I thank them for this! – not just them but also to the assemblies of the non-Jews, *5* and greet the assembly that is in their house.[8] Greet Ephaenetos, my dearly loved friend, who is Asia's first offering for the Anointed One. *6* Greet Mary, who worked hard for you. *7* Greet Andronicos and Junia,[9] my fellow people of my race[1] and

---

"Was Romans XVI a separate letter?" *NTS* 16 (1970) p. 370. The arguments are that the number of people greeted is unusual for a place Paul had not yet visited, the names of Ephaenetos, Priska and Aquila suggest the letter was written to the Ephesians, the familiarity shown to Rufus' mother suggests Ephesos as Paul has spent several years there, the warning of v. 17ff suits Ephesos and not Rome, and textual evidence such as the placement of the doxology at 15.33 in P^{46}.

[1]   συνίστημι, *sunistemi*, "recommend", carries connotations of praise more so than the English word "recommend".

[2]   διάκονος, *diakonos*, "deacon". Not "slave servant" which is δοῦλος, *doulos*. In the context of religion, the word meant an attendant or official. The word was taken over into Christianity as a church official, that is, a minister or deacon, as the terms were at first synonymous, "deacon" being the transliteration (putting Greek letters into English letters) of the Greek, and "minister" being the translation. There is ample evidence that women were deacons, in precisely the same role as male deacons, in the 1st and 2nd centuries. It is significant that Phoebe is the deacon of the church in Kenchreai, a large commercial city. (See below note.)

[3]   Kenchreai was the eastern port of Corinth, and was one of the two important ports for Corinth. Note that Corinth was Greece's commercial center. All trade from the north of Greece to Sparta and the Peloponnesus passed through Corinth, as did most of the east-west traffic. Ships from Asia Minor, Syria and Egypt docked at Kenchreai.

[4]   That is, the believers.

[5]   προστάτις, *prostatis*, "presiding officer", "leader and protector". B.J. Brooten, *Women Leaders in Ancient Synagogues*, Chico, 1982, p. 151; M. Boucher, "Women and Priestly Ministry: The New Testament Evidence," *CBQ* 41, 608-13. The προστάτις, *prostatis*, referred to a person of the front-rank, the chief of a body of people; in general, a ruler, someone who stands in front of people and protects them. The KJV and RSV incorrectly render προστάτις, *prostatis*, as "helper", the NIV as "(she has been) a great help", the NEV as "good friend". The word *prostatis* used here for a woman caused some discomfort as early as the 9th c., and it was altered in some inferior manuscripts to *parastasis*, "one who stands by / assistant", perhaps under the influence of the (Latin) *Vulgate* which incorrectly translated *prostatis* as the Latin *adstitit*, "one who stands by / assistant". Yet the word *prostatis* was used for women no less than it was for men. The term *prostatis* was status-laden and denoted position / office.

[6]   Paul is writing a formal recommendation, which necessitates giving Phoebe's title on the basis of her leadership. He establishes her credentials as his emissary to Rome.

[7]   "Priska and Aquila" refers to a woman (Priska) and her husband (Aquila). Their names are mentioned in 5 places, and in all but one (where Paul has first met them), Priska's name is first. The more senior person was always greeted first and this was a strict protocol of the times.

[8]   In early Christian times, churches met in the homes of the pastor.

[9]   The female name Junia occurs more than 250 times in inscriptions found in Rome alone, whereas the name "Junias", has not been found anywhere. Origin (185-253), the earliest commentator on Romans 16:7, referred to Junia as female. Jerome (c.340-420) and Chrysostom (4th c.) did likewise

fellow prisoners. They are famous among the apostles.[2] They were also followers of the Anointed One before I was.

8-16 Greet Amplias, my dear friend, a follower of the Lord. *9* Greet Urbanos, our coworker of the Anointed One, and Stachys, my dear friend. *10* Greet Apelles, who has found approval as a follower of the Anointed One. Greet the people of Aristobolos' household. *11* Greet Herodian, my relative. Greet those of the household of Narcissos who are the Lord's followers. *12* Greet Tryphena and Tryphosa,[3] who worked hard for the Lord. Greet my dear friend Persis, who worked hard for the Lord.

13 Greet Rufus, who is chosen by the Lord, and his mother, who has been a mother to me, too. *14* Greet Asyncritos, Phlegon, Hermes, Patrobas, Hermas, and the fellow believers with them. *15* Greet Philologos and Julia, Nereos and his sister, and Olympas and all the people devoted to God with them. *16* Greet one another with a sacred kiss. All the assemblies of the Anointed One send greetings.

17-19 I encourage you, fellow believers, to take careful note of those who are causing disputes and setting traps[4] which are contrary to the teaching you yourselves have learned from us. Turn away from them! *18* These people do not serve our Lord the Anointed One but rather their own appetites,[5] and by their smooth words and their praise, they beguile the minds of those who are ignorant of bad things.[6] *19* For everyone has heard that you pay attention and act on it.[7] This is why I am happy about you. Yet I want you to be wise about what's good, and innocent about evil.

20 The God of peace[8] will beat Adversary to a jelly[9] under your feet soon!

May the favor of our Lord Jesus the Anointed One be with you! Amen.

21-23 Timothy, my coworker, and Lucius, Jason, and Sosipater my fellow countrypeople greet you. *22* I, Tertius, who wrote this letter, greet you as a follower of the Lord.[10] *23* Gaius, my host and the host of the whole assembly, greets you. Erastus, the city treasurer,[11] greets you, as does our fellow believer Quartus.[12]

25-27 Now to him who is able to set your footing on firm ground, according to my Good News and the proclamation of Jesus the Anointed One, according to the revelation of the secret hidden truth, which has been kept secret, right from eternity, *26* but now it is revealed, and made known through the prophetic Scriptures too by the divine command of the eternal God, so that all the nations would listen to him by means of faith, *27* to God, who alone is wise, through Jesus the Anointed One, be the honor forever! Amen.

---

[1] Cf. Brooten, *op.cit.*, p. 233.

[2] A woman being noted among the apostles has caused problems for some theologians, with several trying to present cases that the clause means something else. ἀπόστολος, *apostolos*.

[3] Both are women, as is the Julia of verse 15.

[4] The use of the definite article demonstrates that the disputes and traps were known to the people to whom the letter was addressed, whether happening elsewhere, or personally to them.

[5] κοιλία, *koilia*, the bowels, the belly, the contents of the belly, the appetite.

[6] ἄκακος, *akakos*, one who is ignorant of bad things, one who is without malice.

[7] ὑπακοη, *hupakoe*. See note on Rom. 1:5.

[8] Equally possible in the Greek, "God of peace", or "God who is peace".

[9] συντρίβω, *suntribo*, "to beat one to a jelly" (used of persons, that is, not inanimate objects), cf. Eur. *Cycl.* 705.

[10] Paul dictated the letter to Tertius.

[11] οἰκονόμος τῆς πόλεως, *oikonomos tes poleos*, "city treasurer", "city manager". In 1929, archaeologists excavating in Corinth near the theater found an inscription dating to the second half of the 1st c. AD, reading: "Erastus, in return for his aedileship, laid the pavement at his own expense."

[12] Verse 24 is omitted by the best and earliest witnesses.

Letters to the Corinthians.

The letter we know as 1 Corinthians was written by Paul around 55 AD while he was in Ephesos on his third missionary journey. Paul wrote four letters to the Corinthians: the "previous" letter, 1 Corinthians, the "severe" letter (also written from Ephesos), and 2 Corinthians (written from Macedonia). Only the letters we know as 1 and 2 Corinthians have survived.

Paul had received reports about happenings in the church in Corinth. In response he wrote a letter (the "previous" letter of 1 Corinthians 5:9-11) which we do not have today. Chloe's congregation reported arguments in the church. The Corinthian church also sent a delegation with a list of questions in a letter to Paul. Paul's reaction was to send Timothy to Corinth. He then wrote a letter which we know now as 1 Corinthians, in an attempt to correct the problems. He answers the questions put to him by the Corinthians' letter, and also quotes the letter. 1 Corinthians 1:7 begins "now concerning the matters about which you wrote," indicating that Paul was also responding to issues set out in the letter brought by the delegation. περὶ δέ, *peri de*, "now concerning" is repeated in 7:1, 25; 8:1; 12:1; 15:1 (δέ, *de*), and 16:1. It is likely that the first six chapters address the issues raised by the people from Chloe's congregation as well as the misunderstandings from Paul's first letter, while chapters 7-16 address the questions raised in the Corinthians' letter.

It was in Corinth that Paul met Priscilla and Aquila who had been expelled from Rome in A.D. 49 at the time of Claudius. Paul remained 18 months and worked with Priscilla and Aquila as a tentmaker. During his stay he wrote the letters now known as First and Second Thessalonians. This was Paul's first visit. In 2 Corinthians 12:14, he speaks of his impending third visit: "For the third time I'm ready to visit you." During his third visit, Paul wrote his letter to the Romans.

Clement of Rome, writing in the 1st c., stated that 1 Corinthians is by Paul. Ignatius, Polycarp, Tertullian, Clement of Alexandria, Justin Martyr, Athenagoras, Irenaeus, Basilides, Marcion, Barnabas, and the Didache refer to 1 Corinthians.

Corinth was an ancient and wealthy city, in Paul's time the commercial center of Greece. Under Augustus, Corinth was made capital of Achaea and seat of its proconsul. Corinth had two ports, Kenchreai on the Aegean, and Lekhaion on the Ionian Sea, and had trade links all over the ancient world. Corinth stood on the southern end of the Greek peninsula, on the narrow isthmus connecting the Greek mainland with the Peloponnesus. It was about 40 miles west of Athens and was on a plain at the foot of the Acrocorinth, a rocky hill which rose almost 2,000 feet above sea level. Corinth was on a huge site, and was protected in part by a six mile wall which covered the sections the Acrocorinth did not. A feature of Corinth was the Temple of Aphrodite served by 1,000 female sacred prostitutes on the fortress which dominated the city. Strabo, the historian, said it was due to the sacred prostitutes that Corinth was "crowded with people and grew rich." Corinth, close to major ports, was home to large numbers of sailors, merchants, adventurers and retired soldiers. The lewd verb "to Corinthianize" was coined due to Corinth's reputation as a corrupt city, and "Corinthian girl" meant a prostitute.

Corinth was sacked by the Romans in 146 BC for revolting, but was rebuilt and refounded as a Roman colony in 44 BC by Julius Caesar. It was repopulated by Caesar with a predominance of freed slaves from Greece, Judea, Egypt and Syria. Corinth quickly regained its commercial prosperity and just as quickly rose to become one of the most important cities in the Roman Empire. All trade from the north of Greece to Sparta and the Peloponnesus had to pass through Corinth, as did most of the east-west traffic. There wasn't much choice – the alternative was to sail an extra 200 miles around Cape Malea (Cape Matapan) on the southernmost tip of Greece. The treachery of Cape Malea is revealed by two popular Greek sayings: "The person who sails round Malea can forget their home!" and, "The person who sails round Malea had better make their will first!" Ships from Asia Minor, Syria and Egypt docked at the eastern port of Kenchreai on the Saronic Gulf to the east, while those from Italy, Sicily and Spain docked at the northern port of Lekhaion on the Corinthian Gulf. After docking, small ships were placed on rollers and hauled the four miles across the isthmus to the other port on marble slip-way. The cargoes of larger ships were transported to ships waiting in the opposite port. This process was rendered unnecessary as late as 1893 by the completion of the Corinth Canal.

First Letter to the Corinthians.

Ch.1:1-3 From: Paul, called to be an apostle of the Anointed One Jesus through God's purpose, and from Sosthenes, our fellow believer.[1]

2 To: God's assembly at Corinth, to those who have been made sacred by the Anointing of Jesus, those invited to be people devoted to God, together with all those everywhere who call on the Name of our Lord Jesus the Anointed One, their Lord and ours!

3 Hello! May you have peace from God our Father and from the Lord Jesus the Anointed One.

4-9 I am always thanking my God for you. I thank him for his favor which was given to you by means of the Anointed One Jesus. *5* Because of him you were enriched in all ways. You were enriched with every kind of speech and knowledge. *6* The evidence for the Anointed One was confirmed in you. *7* Thus you are not lacking in any spiritual gift, and you are eagerly expecting the Lord Jesus the Anointed One to reveal himself. *8* He will keep you firm until the end, so that you are blameless on the Day of Our Lord Jesus the Anointed One. *9* God is trustworthy. He called you into partnership with his Son, Jesus the Anointed One our Lord.

10-11 Fellow believers, I encourage all of you through the Name of our Lord Jesus the Anointed One, to speak the same thing and that there be no divisions among you and that you will be completely equipped with the same mind and the same intention. *11* My fellow believers, it has been made clear to me about you, by Chloe's followers,[2] that there is rivalry among you.

12-17 What I mean is this: each of you is saying, "I follow Paul", "I follow Apollos", "I follow Cephas", "I follow the Anointed One." *13* Has the Anointed One been divided up? Was Paul crucified for you? Or were you baptized in the name of Paul? *14* I thank God that I didn't baptize any of you except Crispus and Gaius, *15* so that no one can say that I baptized in my own name! *16* I also baptized Stephanas' household.[3] Apart from that, I'm not aware that I baptized any one else!

17-19 In fact, the Anointed One did not send me out to baptize but to announce the Good News. He didn't send me out to speak wisely, otherwise the cross of the Anointed One would have been for nothing! *18* For the message of the cross is foolishness to those who are being undone, but it is God's power for those of us who have been saved. *19* The Scriptures say, "I

---

[1] ἀδελφοί, *adelphoi*. See note on Matt. 5:22.
[2] That is, Chloe's congregation. The expression is identical to that in the following verse, "I follow Paul" and so on. Certainly not "Chloe's household" or "Chloe's house".
[3] This does not mean Stephanas' immediate family although it does include them. It refers to all his household slaves and/or servants.

will utterly destroythe wisdom of the wise, and I will invalidate the intelligence of the intelligent."

20-25 Where is the wise person? Where is the Bible scholar? Where is the debater of the present age? Surely God has made the wisdom of this world foolish! *21* God in his wisdom was pleased to save those who believe through the foolishness of having the Good News proclaimed to them! The world did not recognize God by being wise! *22* The Jews demand a sign and the Greeks seek wisdom, *23* but we proclaim the Anointed One as having been crucified, which is a stumbling-block to the Jews, but foolishness to the non-Jews. *24* But to those who are invited, both Jews and Greeks, the Anointed One encompasses both God's power and God's wisdom. *25* God's foolishness is wiser than people's wisdom, and God's weakness is stronger than people's strength!

26-29 Fellow believers, consider what you were when you were invited! Not many of you were wise as far as the natural realm goes, not a lot of you were capable, not a lot of you were of noble birth. *27* But God picked out the foolish things of the world in order to put the wise to shame, and God selected the weak things of the world in order to put the strong to shame. *28* God selected the low-born things of the world and the things which have been looked down on, and the things which do not exist, in order to render inoperative those things which do exist, *29* so that the whole natural realm would have no grounds to boast in God's presence.

30-31 It is because of God that you have the Anointing of Jesus. Jesus became God's wisdom for us. It is because of him that we are made right with God, that we are sacred. He was the one who paid the ransom for our release. *31* The Scriptures say, "Let the person who is proud, be proud of the Lord!"

Ch.2:1-5 And I, fellow believers, when I came to you, did not come with superior speech or wisdom when I announced God's hidden secret truth to you! *2* In fact, while I was there I decided not to know anything except the Anointed One, and him crucified! *3* I came to you in a weak state, and I was earnest and very concerned. *4* And I did not speak and proclaim the Good News by means of persuasive wisdom but by means of the proof of spiritual power, *5* so that your faith would not be based on people's wisdom but on God's power!

6-9 We speak wisdom among those who are mature – I'm not talking about the wisdom of this age, nor about the governments of this age which are being rendered inoperative. *7* What I mean is that we speak God's wisdom which has been hidden in a secret hidden truth, which God arranged ahead of time before the ages to be used for our splendor. *8* If any of the governments of this age had known this, they would not have crucified the glorious Lord! *9* The Scriptures say, "Eye has not seen nor ear heard, nor has it occurred to a person, the things which God has prepared for those who love him."

10-11 God has uncovered them for us through the Spirit. For the Spirit searches after these things, yes indeed, the Spirit searches the depths of God! *11* What person can know things about a person except the person's spirit which is in the person? In the same way also no one perceives the things of God except the Spirit of God!

12-16 Now we have not taken hold of the world's spirit, but we have taken hold of the Spirit who is from God, so that we would know the things which were freely given to us by God. *13* We also speak about these things, not in words taught by human wisdom, but words taught by the Spirit. We compare and examine spiritual things by spiritual means.

14 A soulish person does not accept the things of the Spirit of God – for they are stupid in their eyes and they are not able to recognize them, because they can only be closely examined by spiritual means. *15* But the person who is spiritual closely examines all things, but no one is able to closely examine that person. *16* For, "Who has come to know the mind of the Lord so as to instruct him?"

But we have the mind of the Anointed One!

Ch.3:**1-4** Fellow believers, I wasn't able to speak to you as to spiritual people, but I had to speak to you as to natural people, as to babies in the Anointing. *2* I gave you milk to drink, not solid food - as you weren't able to eat it! But now you're still not able to eat it, *3* as you are still natural people! For in so far as there is jealousy and strife among you, aren't you natural people, behaving according to the manner of humanity? *4* For when someone says, "I surely am Paul's", and another says, "I am Apollos'", aren't you being human?

5-9 So then, who's Apollos? And who's Paul? We're ministers through whom you believed, as the Lord gave to each one! *6* I planted, Apollos watered, but God gave the growth. *7* So then the person who plants isn't anything, the person who waters isn't anything, but it is God who gives the growth. *8* Now the person who plants, as well as the person who waters, work as one. Each will receive their own reward according to their own labor. *9* We are God's fellow workers, and you are God's cultivated field, God's building.

10-11 Due to God's favor which was given to me, as a wise master builder I have laid the foundation and someone else builds on it. But let each one watch how they build on it! *11* No one can lay any foundation other than the one which has been laid – that is, Jesus the Anointed One.

12-15 Now if anyone builds on this foundation with gold, silver, jewels, wood, hay or straw, *13* then each one's work will become clear. For the Day will disclose it, because it will be revealed by fire, and the fire will test the quality of each person's work. *14* If the work which anyone has built on remains, they will receive a reward! *15* If anyone's work is burned, they will be punished. They themselves will be saved; nevertheless it will be like going through fire!

16-17 Don't you know that you are God's temple and the Spirit of God lives in you! *17* If anyone destroys the temple of God, God will destroy them. God's temple is sacred – and you are God's temple.

18-20 No one is to beguile themselves! If anyone among you seems to be wise by the standards of this age, let them become silly so that they can become wise! *19* The wisdom of this world is silliness next to God. The Scriptures say, "He traps the wise with their own cunning," *20* also "The Lord realizes that the thought processes of the wise are foolish."

21-23 So then, no one is to boast about people! For all things are yours, *22* whether Paul or Apollos or Cephas (Peter) or the world or life or death, or things present or things to come – all are yours! *23* And you are the Anointed One's, and the Anointed One is God's.

Ch.4:**1-5** Let a person calculate that we are attendants of the Anointed One and managers of the hidden secret truths of God! *2* In this connection, furthermore, what one looks for in managers[1] is that they are trustworthy. *3* But it doesn't matter in the least to me if I'm closely examined by you or some human court! In fact, I don't even closely examine myself! *4* I'm not aware of anything that's against me, but that doesn't mean that I stand acquitted by this. Rather, the one who closely examines me is the Lord. *5* Consequently, do not judge anything before the right moment, until the Lord comes. He will bring to light the hidden things of darkness and will make known the motives of the heart. And then each one's praise will come from God.

6-7 Fellow believers, I have changed the form of the metaphor and applied these things to myself and Apollos for your benefit, so that because of us you can learn not to think beyond what the Scriptures say, so that none of you may be bloated with pride, and favor someone at the expense of another. *7* Who makes you so different? What have you got that wasn't given to you? Even if in fact you did receive it as a gift, why do you take the credit for it?

8-13 You have already had your fill! You have already become rich! You have gained a kingdom without us! If only you really and truly had gained a kingdom, then we could reign together with you too! *9* For I suppose God has exhibited us,

---

[1]   οἰκονόμος, *oikonomos*, "manager", extensively attested. Also in following verse.

the apostles, last in the procession like people under a death sentence, because we've been made a public spectacle to the world, both to Messengers and also to people! *10* We are fools for the Anointed One's sake, but you are sensible because of the Anointed One. We are weak, but you are strong. You are famous, but we are dishonored.

11 Up to the present time we are hungry, thirsty, badly clothed, given a good physical thrashing, and always on the move. *12* And we labor, working with our own hands. We are verbally abused, and we bless. We are persecuted, and we last it out. *13* We have words of ill omen spoken about us, and we encourage. We've become like outcasts of the world, the scum scraped off everything up until now!

14-17 I'm not writing these things to shame you, but I'm warning you as my dearly loved children. *15* For although you might have 10,000 educators in the Anointed One, you don't have many fathers in the Anointed One! I surely became your father through the Good News by means of the Anointing of Jesus. *16* So then I encourage you to become imitators of me! *17* This is the reason I've sent Timothy to you. He is my dearly loved and trustworthy 'son' as a follower of the Lord. He will remind you of my ways in which I follow the Anointing, ways I teach everywhere in every assembly.

18-21.Ch.5:1-2 Some people are bloated with pride because they seem to think I am not going to visit you! *19* But I will visit you shortly, whenever the Lord wants me to, and I will realize who the ones bloated with pride are, not by their words but by their power. *20* God's Realm is not a realm of words, but of power!

21 So what do you want? Am I to come to you with a stick, or lovingly and with a gentle spirit? *1* It is actually reported that there is incest among you, and such that doesn't even occur among the non-Jews – that someone is with his stepmother![1] *2* Yet you are certainly remaining so smug! And no, instead, you don't even mourn about it and expel one who did it from your midst!

3-5 For I, absent in body but present in spirit, have certainly already judged (as though I were present) that the one who has done this deed - *4* in the Name of the Lord Jesus the Anointed One, when you are assembled, and me too in spirit, with the power of the Lord Jesus the Anointed One – *5* such a person should be handed over[2] to Adversary which will lead to destruction in the natural realm, so that person's spirit may be saved in the Day of the Lord.

6-8 Your boasting is not favorable! Don't you know that a small bit of yeast makes the whole lump of dough rise? *7* Get rid of the old yeast, so that you can be a new lump of dough, then you will be newly baked bread. Indeed the Anointed One, our Passover Lamb, was sacrificed for us. *8* As a result, let's keep the Festival, but let's do it without the old yeast, and without the yeast of malice and evil, but with the newly baked bread of genuineness and truth!

9-11 I told you in my letter not to associate with people who commit *porneia*.[3] *10* I certainly was not talking about the people of this world who commit *porneia*, or about the greedy, or the grasping, or the idol worshippers, since to avoid them you'd have to get off the planet! *11* But in point of fact I am writing[4] to tell you not to associate with anyone said to be one of the fellow believers, who commits *porneia*, or is greedy, or is an idol worshipper, or who uses abusive language, or is a drunkard, or cheats people in financial transactions - don't even eat with such people!

---

[1] This was forbidden by the Law, cf. Leviticus 18:8.

[2] παραδίδωμι, *paradidomi*, "to hand over to the power of another". The phrase here, "handed over to Satan" echoes that of 1 Tim. 1:20. In the LXX of Job 2:6, God tells Satan that he hands Job over to him, παραδίδωμί σοι αὐτόν. See epitaph warning, "Whoever performs any evil treachery against this tomb, I hand them over to the infernal gods", *I.Nikaia* 1.87 (Hisacik near Nikaia, Imperial period) 2-5.

[3] πορνεία, *porneia*. See note on Matt. 15:19.

[4] Epistolary aorist.

12-13 Now it's none of my business to judge those who are outside! Isn't it those who are inside that you judge! *13* It is God who judges those who are outside. "Expel the evil person out from among you."

Ch.6:1-3 Do any of you who have a lawsuit against another dare to take it to law court before people who are not right with God, and not before the people devoted to God! Utter rubbish!¹ *2* Don't you know that the people devoted to God will judge the world? And since the world will be judged by you, are you incompetent for even the most trifling standards of judgment?² *3* You know, don't you, that we will judge Messengers, let alone everyday matters!

4-8 If you have law courts dealing with everyday business, do you appoint judges from those who are despised in the assembly? *5* I'm saying this to put you to shame! Is it the case that there isn't even one wise person among you, not even one, who will be able to make a decision between one fellow believer and another? *6* But as it is, fellow believers are going to court against fellow believers, and to make it worse it's before unbelievers! *7* So then, it's already a complete failure for you, seeing that you're taking each other to court! Instead, why don't you put up with the wrongdoing? Instead, why don't you let yourselves be cheated? No! *8* You yourselves are dishonest and defrauders and you're fellow believers at that!

9-11 Don't you know that people who are not right with God won't obtain God's Realm as their inheritance? Make no mistake!³ People who engage in sexual acts against the Law of Moses, idol worshippers, adulterers, *cinaedi*,⁴ *arsenokoites*,⁵ *10* thieves, greedy people, drunkards, people who use abusive language, those who cheat people in financial transactions – will not obtain God's Realm as their inheritance! *11* And this is what some of you were. But you have had yourselves washed clean, but you were made sacred, you were made right with God by the Name of the Lord Jesus and by the Spirit of our God!

The Cinaedi.

μαλακός, *malakos*, "receptive male homosexual promiscuous cross dresser" or "coward", usually considered in this context to mean the former due to its proximity to the following word ἀρσενοκοίτης, *arsenokoites*. We have no equivalent English word. The Roman name was *cinaedus*. Romans (and it is worth noting that Corinth was a Roman colony) held the *cinaedi* in the utmost contempt, considering them to be deviants and detestable. Such men (and the *cinaedi* were mature men, not boys) were portrayed as effeminate cross dressers, many depicted with ringlets, women's jewelry, and cosmetics; with women's tastes in general. They were said to be highly promiscuous and voracious, and many were depicted as prostitutes. Martial (6.50) portrays some as exchanging sexual favors for material gain. See Apuleius, *Met.* 27.1; Juvenal 6.25; Pliny, *NH*, 12.84, Martial 7.58, 10.40. μαλακός, *malakos*, has a range of meanings, although its juxtaposition with the following word suggests its meaning here. It can also mean "coward", soft", and was used to describe wine in *PSI* 6.594.

---

1   Disjunctive particle.
2   κριτήριον, *kriterion*, in its primary sense "standards of judgment", cf. Horsley, *NDIEC* 4.157. The noun also carries the meaning "law-court" (as in verse 4 following) and "lawsuit, legal action". The only other instance of the noun is in James 2:6 in its primary meaning "standards of judgment".
3   πλανάω, *planao*, "to wander off the path", the cognate noun being πλάνη, *plane*. See Rom. 1:27.
4   μαλακός, *malakos*, "receptive male homosexual promiscuous cross dresser" or "coward". See Background Notes in this section.
5   ἀρσενοκοίτης, *arsenokoites*. See Background Notes in this section.

In Greek culture, sex was seen as active/passive rather than gender based. Accepted male-male relationships in Greece were those between an older male in pursuit of a younger male. Xenophon quotes Socrates as stating that a youth would not seek physical pleasure from his lover, rather, he was simply fulfilling his duty. The sources speak of transgression in those instances where both partners were of the same socio-economic status. A citizen male was not supposed to be the receptive partner, and receptive anal sex with its reported accompanying adoption of female characteristics was viewed as deviant in both Greek and Roman cultures. In Roman culture, the dominant man could have as a partner a man or a woman, and when a man showed a preference for either gender, this was noted as somewhat out of the ordinary. For example, Suetonius[1] notes that the Emperor Claudius was extremely passionate about women, but not at all interested in males.

For further reading, see A. Eichlin, "Not before Homosexuality: The Materiality of the *Cinaedus* and the Roman Law Against Love between Men", *Journal of the History of Sexuality*, 3.4 (1993); C. Williams, *Roman Homosexuality: Ideologies of Masculinity in Classical Antiquity*, (New York: O.U.P., 1999); "Penetrating the 'Man': The 'Butt' of Roman Sexual Humour", *Stele: Text, Artifact Context: The Interactions of Literature, Material Culture and Mentality in the Ancient World*, ed. P. Keegan, Vol. 5, 160-176, (Macquarie, 2001); Bruce W. Winter, "Roman Homosexual Activity and the Elite (1 Corinthians 6:9)" *After Paul Left Corinth: The Influence of Secular Ethics and Social Change*, (Michigan: W.B. Eerdmans, 2001), App. to Ch. 5.

ἀρσενοκοίτης, *arsenokoites*.

There is no English equivalent. The word does not mean "homosexual", but rather its semantic range includes one who anally penetrates another (female or male), rapist, murderer, or extortionist. When used in the meaning "anal penetrator", it does not apply exclusively to males as the receptors, as it was also used for women receptors, e.g. *Migne Patrologia Graeca* 82. See also Martial, 11.78. It occurs elsewhere in the N.T. only in 1 Tim. 1:10.

MM *s.v.* state that it was first found among the poets of the Imperial period, which puts it around the same time as this reference in the N.T. The word does not appear in any of the comedian Aristophanes' plays, which is noteworthy as Aristophanes used a wide range of words for men in sexual relationships with men[2] with comic effect: for example, καταπύγων, *katapugon*, an epithet, again no equivalent English word; noun διαβήτης, *diabetes*, a receptive homosexual. For other terms see (for example) *Clouds* 349 (where A.H. Sommerstein, *Clouds*, (Warminster: Aris & Phillips, 1982), says of a Greek word "This seems to have been a popular designation for promiscuous pederasts, cf. Aeschines 1.52"); *Knights* 77-78; *Wasps*, 688; *Lys.* 60; *Them.* 153; *Frogs* 148. See also Plato's *Symposium* for lengthy discourses on male-male love and male-male sex. ἀρσενοκοίτης, *arsenokoites*, is not mentioned there.

Leviticus 20:13 does not have ἀρσενοκοίτης, *arsenokoites*, but has the two words which make up the compound: "If a male has sex with a male as one lies with a woman, it is Abomination (*a technical term*)." (Note that other Abominations were wearing clothes with mixed textiles, eating raw meat, sowing a field with mixed seed, crossbreeding animals, having sex with a woman when she has her period.) Leviticus 18:22 also has both words in the same context as Leviticus 20:13. ἀρσενοκοίτης, *arsenokoites*, was used in this

---

[1]   Seutonius, *Claudius*, 33:2.

[2]   The word "homosexuality" first appeared in 14 April, 1851, in Leipzig, being then implemented by K.M. Benkert, Paragraph 143 of the Prussian penal code.

sense by Hippolytus in the 2nd c, by Polycarp, Origen, and Chrysostom, and by writers in later centuries. However, it must be emphasized that it is a grave error to assume Greek words can be be glossed as the sum of their parts. This is referred to as an "etymological fallacy". See D.A. Carson, *Exegetical Fallacies*, (Grand Rapids, MI: Baker Book House, 1996).

The verb appears in the *Sibylline Oracles* ii.73 μὴ ἀρσενοκοιτεῖν, μὴ συκοφαντεῖν, μήτε φονεύειν, *me arsenokoitein, me sukophantein, mete phoneuvein*, speaking of committing extortion and committing murder. Pseudo-Macarius Aegyptius, *Homiliae spirituales* IV 4.22, stated that the people of Sodom sinned greatly and did not repent, and "created the ultimate offense in their evil purpose against the angels, wishing to work *arsenokoitia* upon them". Both the above contexts suggest rape. Aristides said that the Greek gods commit murders and poisonings, adulteries, thefts and *arsenokoisias*. The 6th c. astrologer Rhetorius Aegyptius used the term as women with the receptors: "*arsenokoites* (of women) and rapists of women". For further reading, see also K.J. Dover, *Greek Homosexuality*, (Newburyport, MA:, Focus Publishing R Pullins Co, 1979); Bruce W. Winter, *op.cit.*

12-20 You quote me as saying, "I am free to do anything", but let me point out that not everything is useful for me! Yes, I am free to do anything, but I certainly will not let anything be free with me! *13* "Food is for the stomach and the stomach is for food", but God will put an end to both. On the other hand the body is not for *porneia*,[1] but for the Lord, and the Lord is for the body.

14 God not only raised up the Lord by his power but will raise us up too. *15* Don't you know that your bodies are body parts of the Anointed One? Will I take the body parts of the Anointed One and make them body parts of a prostitute? No way! Utter rubbish![2] *16* Don't you know that someone who is united with a prostitute is one body with her? For he says, "The two shall become a single body." *17* The person who is united[3] with the Lord is one spirit with him.

18 Flee from *porneia*![4] Every sin that someone does is outside the body, but the person who commits *porneia* sins against their own body! *19* Utter rubbish![5] Don't you know that your body is the temple of the Holy Spirit who is within you? That you have the Spirit from God, and you are not your own? *20* For you were bought with a price! So then, honor God with your body!

Ch.7:1-7 And now about those matters you wrote to me in your letter.

"It is good for a man not to have sex with a woman."[6]

2 Well then, my reply is that because of sexual immorality, each man should have his own woman and each woman should have her own man. *3* The man must give his woman what he owes her. And the same goes for women too – a woman must give her man what she owes him. *4* A woman does not have the authority over her own body, but the man does. And the same goes for men too - a man does not have the authority over his own body, but the woman does.[7] *5* Do not deprive each other – unless perhaps you both agree about it[1] so

---

[1]   See note on Matt. 15:19.

[2]   Disjunctive particle.

[3]   κολλάω, *kollao*, with the dative (as here) generally means to join fast together, to unite. With the prepositions περί, *peri*, or πρός, *pros* (which do not appear here) it means to glue or cement. With the accusative (which does not appear here) it means to join one metal to another, to weld it.

[4]   See note on Matt. 15:19.

[5]   Disjunctive particle.

[6]   Throughout 1 Cor. Paul quotes the letter he had received from the Corinthians.

[7]   In this passage, it is equally possible to substitute "husband and wife" for "man and woman".

that you can be free to devote yourselves to praying on a temporary basis – and come together again so that Adversary doesn't harass you because of your lack of self control. *6* Now I'm just saying that this is okay – it's not a divine command. *7* I wish that every person could be like me too[2] – but each person has their own gift from God, one has this, the other has that.

8-9 Now I do say this to the single people and to the widows – it's fine[3] if they stay that way, like me too. *9* Now if they can't control themselves, they must take a partner,[4] as it's better to take a partner than to burn with desire.[5]

10-11 I order those who are married[6] – I'm not the one doing the ordering, the Lord is – a woman is not to split up with her man. *11* But even if she[7] does split up with him, she must stay single or reconcile with her man. And a man is not to send his woman away.

12-16 But to people who are not both believers,[8] this is what I, not the Lord, say. If one of the fellow believers has a woman who is not a believer, and she wants to live with him, he doesn't have to send her away. *13* And if a woman has a man who's not a believer, if he wants to stay with her, she doesn't have to send him away. *14* For the unbelieving man is made sacred by the woman and the unbelieving woman is made sacred by the man. Otherwise your children would be unclean, but as it is, they're sacred![9]

15 But if the unbeliever wants to split up, let them split up! A female fellow believer or a male fellow believer is not under compulsion[10] in such

---

[1] The maintenance of sexual relations was an obligation under Jewish law and failure to do so was a ground for divorce. Abstention must result from an agreement between both parties. See discussion of the *kethubah* in S.R. Llewelyn, "Jewish and Christian Marriage," *NDIEC* 6.14-15. Note that Paul here refers to one of the three grounds of divorce from Exodus 21:10-11, neglecting to give a wife food, clothing, or sex.

[2] This implies that Paul was single at the time of writing. However, marriage was obligatory for all devout Jewish males on the basis of Genesis 1:28. We do not know what had happened to Paul's wife (if indeed he had one), but women commonly died in childbirth.

[3] "Fine", not "good". Paul is not saying that it is good to be unmarried or a widow, he is merely saying it is fine if they want to stay that way.

[4] "Take a partner" which in those times was the same as "marry". In Jewish law, sexual intercourse was a third method of marriage. This was paralleled by unwritten marriage in Greek law and marriage by cohabitation in Roman law. S.R. Llewelyn, "Jewish and Christian Marriage," *NDIEC* 6.12-18. Note also that Jewish marriage consisted of two stages, betrothal and nuptials. The term *qidesh* could refer to betrothal, or marriage in general. *ibid.*, p. 18.

[5] πυρόω, *puroo*, being consumed with a strong emotion. See *CIJ* 2.1522, where a mother is "burned up" with grief over the death of her daughter.

[6] Paul here is talking about a couple, both believers in a relationship, cf. 1 Cor. 5:10, 12, 13.

[7] In the letter we know as "1 Corinthians", Paul is answering specific questions put to him by the Corinthians. It is likely Paul here is speaking of a specific woman.

[8] "The others", that is, those who are not a couple of believers.

[9] For full discussion on the children being sanctified by believing parent(s), see D. Daube, "Pauline Contributions to a Pluralistic Culture," *Jesus and Man's Hope*, ed. D.G. Miller and D.Y. Hadidian, (Pittsburgh: Pickwick, 1971), pp. 223-45. As stated in above note 6, Jewish marriage consisted of two stages, betrothal and nuptials. The term *qidesh* could refer to betrothal, or marriage in general. *Qidesh* also meant "sanctify". S.R. Llewelyn, "Jewish and Christian Marriage," *NDIEC* 6.18.

[10] The perfect passive participle of δουλόω, *douloo*. The semantic range includes to be made subject, to be under compulsion, to be enslaved. In other words, they are free to remarry.

cases. God has called us into a state of peace![1] *16* You, lady, how do you know whether or not you will save your man? You, gentleman, how do you know whether or not you will save your woman?

17-24 But let a person live their life by the way the Lord has apportioned matters to each person, just as God has called each person! In fact set down[2] these arrangements in all the assemblies. *18* Was anyone called while circumcised?[3] Then stay circumcised! Was anyone called while uncircumcised? Then stay uncircumcised! *19* Circumcision is nothing and uncircumcision is nothing. Keeping the commands of God is what counts! *20* Let each person stay in the calling in which they were called. *21* Were you called while a slave? Don't be concerned about it. But if you're able to become free, certainly go for it all the more! *22* The person who is called while a slave is the Lord's free person. In the same way, the person who is called while free is the Lord's slave. *23* You were brought with a price – do not become slaves of people. *24* Fellow believers, each person is to stay in the spiritual[4] state that they were called, beside God.

25-28 Now about unmarried girls,[5] I don't have divine commands from the Lord. I'll give my opinion[6] as one who has been made trustworthy, thanks to the Lord's mercy. *26* So then I think it's a good idea for the person to stay as they are in this current time of stress. *27* Are you bound to a woman? Don't seek to be free! Have you been freed from a woman? Don't seek a woman! *28* But even if you do take a partner,[7] you have not sinned, and if an unmarried girl takes a partner, she has not sinned. These people will have oppressions in the natural realm,[8] and I indeed favor sparing you from those.

29-31 I will say this, fellow believers, the time is shortened! From now on, those who have women should act as if they don't,[9] *30* those who cry should be as those who don't cry, those who are rejoicing as though they were not rejoicing, those who buy as those who do not own, *31* and those who enjoy[10] this world as those who do not enjoy it to the full. For the character[11] of this world is changing.

---

[1] "For the sake of peace", a Rabbinic technical legal term used by courts upon giving a decision in a case where strict adherence to the law would have been unfair.

[2] Another Pauline play on words with a military metaphor. διατάσσω, *diatasso*, also means to draw up an army, to put in battle order.

[3] περιτέμνω, *peritemno*. See note on Luke 1:59.

[4] The word "spiritual" here to bring out the full meaning of the Greek, otherwise the passage would be ambiguous in the English.

[5] παρθένος, *parthenos*. See note on Matt. 1:23.

[6] "Opinion" not "judgment".

[7] In these times marriage could be a man and a woman who had a written marriage, or a man and a woman living together, or even a man and a woman having sex in an exclusive relationship.

[8] "In their earthly life". See Zerwick and Grosvenor, *op.cit.*, p.511. Dative of respect.

[9] Again, in these times marriage could be a man and a woman who had a written marriage, or a man and a woman living together.

[10] χράομαι, *kraomai*, with accusative, "enjoy (something)", a late and very rare construction. χράομαι, *kraomai*, with the dative means "use" but here it is with the accusative, not dative. The inscription *IG* XIV (1890) 1607 + 2171 (Imperial period) reads ἀλλ᾽ ἔθανον ἕνδεκα χρησαμένη μηνῶν φάος, *all' ethanon hendeka kresamene menon phaos*, "... but I died after enjoying the light of eleven months."

[11] σχῆμα, *skema*, "external appearance" cf. *I.Kyme* 47, an epitaph for Dionysios who "possessed to a large degree a righteous appearance among all people." Only occurs elsewhere in the N.T. in Phil. 2:8.

32-35 I do not want you to be preoccupied about anything. The person who is single is occupied with the things of the Lord – how they will please the Lord, *33* but the person who has a partner cares about the things of the world and is divided between how he will please the Lord and how he will please their woman.[1] *34* A single woman and an unmarried girl are occupied with the things of the Lord, and their body and spirit are sacred. But a woman who has a partner is occupied with the things of the world, how she will please her man. *35* I'm saying this for your benefit, not to throw a noose over your necks, but to point out what's proper, so that you will be devoted to the Lord without distraction.

Paul now answers three cases put to him by the Corinthian assembly, but we do not know any details of these queries.
The first case.
36-38 If someone thinks he is behaving dishonorably to the girl he is engaged to, if he is uncontrollably passionate and thus it must happen, let him do what he wishes, he hasn't sinned, let them get together. *37* The man who has his mind firmly made up, and is not under compulsion, but has control over his own will, and has judged for himself not to get together with his own engaged girl, does well. *38* Consequently also, he who gets together with her does well, but he who doesn't get together with her does better.
The second case.
39-40 A female believer is bound as long as her man is alive; but if her man passes away she is free and can marry the one she wants, only if he is a follower of the Lord.[2] *40* She will be happier if she stays that way, according to my opinion – and I suppose I have the Spirit of God!
The third case.
Ch.8:1-6 Now about meat that has been sacrificed to idols. We know that we all have knowledge. Knowledge makes you conceited, but love builds you up. *2* If someone thinks they have full knowledge, then they don't know anything that they ought to know! *3* But if someone loves God, then this person is fully known by God.

4 So then, about eating things offered to idols, we know that idols are nothing in the world and that there is no other God but one. *5* Granted that there are so-called gods, whether in the sky[3] or on earth - as indeed there are many gods and many lords – *6* but there is one God the Father, from whom all things come, and for whom we exist, and there is one Lord, Jesus the Anointed One, through whom all things exist, and through whom we live.

7-8 But not everyone is aware of this. There are some people who are so used to idol worshipping that they eat food with the sense of offering it to an idol, and their conscience, since it is weak, is polluted. *8* Now food does not recommend us to God: we're no better or worse off whether we eat or don't eat!

9-13 See to it that this authority of yours doesn't become an obstacle to those who are weak. *10* For if someone sees you who have knowledge sitting down to dinner in an idol's temple, won't the conscience of the weak person be encouraged to eat food which is offered to idols? *11* Should your knowledge be the cause of your weak fellow believer's ruin? The Anointed

---

[1]   Neglecting to provide food or clothing to a man's wife is one of the grounds of divorce in Exodus 21:10-11.
[2]   This freed childless widows from the obligation of Levirate marriage – that is, the obligation for a childless widow to marry her deceased husband's brother and produce children. Paul was giving the widow to same rights to remarry whomever she wished (as long as he was a follower of the Lord). The phrase "you may marry any Jewish man you wish" was standard in Jewish divorce certificates.
[3]   Equally, "in heaven".

One died for that person! *12* But when you sin in this way against the fellow believers, and strike their weak conscience, you're sinning against God! *13* That is why, if food is an obstacle to my fellow believer, there's no way I'll ever eat meat again, so that I don't set a trap for my fellow believer!

Paul answers an accusation voiced to him in the letter from the Corinthians.
Ch.9:1-2 Am I not free? Am I not an apostle? Have I not seen Jesus my Lord? Are you not my work as a follower of the Lord? *2* If I'm not an apostle to others, surely I am an apostle to you! For you are the signed and sealed certificate of my mission as a follower of[1] the Lord!

3-7 My defense to those who are interrogating me is as follows: *4* have we no right to eat and drink! *5* Have we no right to take around[2] a fellow believer wife[3] – as do the other apostles, the Lord's brothers, and Cephas (Peter)! *6* Utter rubbish![4] Is it only myself and Barnabas who have no right not to work! *7* Whoever serves as a soldier and pays their own salary![5] Whoever plants a vineyard and doesn't eat the plants? Whoever is a shepherd and doesn't drink the herd's milk!

8-11 Utter rubbish![6] Am I just saying this as a mere human? Utter rubbish![7] The Law says it too! *9* For it stands written in the Law of Moses, "You must not put a muzzle on an ox which threshes the grain." Is God really talking about oxen! *10* Utter rubbish![8] He's saying it for our sakes! It was written for our sakes, that the person who plows ought to plow in hope of sharing in the produce, and the person who threshes ought to thresh in hope of sharing in the produce. *11* Since we have sown spiritual things for you, is it a big deal if we harvest your material things?

12-18 Since you allow others to share in this authority, don't we have a stronger claim all the more? In any case we haven't used these rights, but we put up with everything so we don't interrupt the Good News of the Anointed One. *13* Don't you know that those who perform the Temple services eat the Temple offerings, and those who attend the altar jointly share in the sacrificial offerings?

---

[1] Not "in the Lord", a poor mistranslation which makes no sense in English, although has been learned as the Biblish dialect. (The English language only uses people being "in" for locations.) It actually means "as a follower of the Lord". The dative case with or without a preposition does not always mean "in" and certainly not in the case of persons!

[2] περιάγειν, *periagein*, to take someone with one, to have someone always with one. used in Herodotos 1.30 for Croesus entertaining Solon in his place, and then taking him around to see all his treasures.

[3] Note ἀδελφήν, *adelphen*, "(female) fellow believer". The addition of γυναῖκα, *gunaika*, suggests "wife" instead of woman, as ἀδελφήν, *adelphen*, by itself means "fellow believer woman". This is also suggested by the context. We know that the Corinthians objected to women, as Chloe's congregation had made complaints about the Corinthians (1 Cor. 1:11) and the letter Paul quotes in 1 Cor. 14:34-35 opposed women. As we know women were ministers, it makes sense here that the Corinthians are objecting to wives accompanying husbands. There is no doubt a specific background story to this, but sadly we only have Paul's response, minus the context. The context also suggests that the objection is on financial grounds. The Corinthians were possibly objecting to wives who did not do any ministry work, perhaps wishing to support financially solely the actual ones who did the ministry work.

[4] Disjunctive particle.

[5] ὀψώνιον, *opsonion*, "salary". Occurs elsewhere in N.T. in Luke 3:14; Rom. 6:23; 2 Cor. 9:7.

[6] Disjunctive particle.

[7] Disjunctive particle.

[8] Disjunctive particle.

14 In the same way too the Lord has commanded that those who preach the Good News should live from the Good News. *15* But I certainly have never used these rights. And I didn't write these things so that it would happen to me either! I'd rather die! Nor do I make an empty boast! *16* My boast is not that I preach, as the necessity has been laid upon me – woe to me if I don't announce the Good News! *17* For if I do this willingly, I have my pay, but if I do it against my will, I am simply discharging a trust. *18* So then what's my pay? In order that by my announcing the Good News, I may present the Good News free of charge, waiving my full rights to the Good News.

19-23 I am free from all people but I have made myself a slave to everyone, so that more people will be gained. *20* To the Jews I became like a Jew, to win Jews. To those who are under the Law, I became like those under the Law, to win those who are under the Law. *21* To those who are not under Law, I became like those who are not under Law, to win those who are not under Law. *22* To the weak I became like those who are weak, to win those who are weak. I have become all things to all people, so that in one way or another I would save some. *23* I do this for the sake of the Good News, so that I may be joint partners in it with you.

24-27 Don't you know that in a stadium running race, everyone who enters the race runs, but only one is awarded the contest prize?[1] Be like them, run to win it! *25* Everyone who is an athlete trains properly. They do it to obtain a winner's prize[2] that withers away,[3] but we do it for a winner's prize that lasts. *26* In point of fact, I certainly run to win, and I don't run in a way which lacks clear purpose! And I box,[4] in this way too, not like a boxer who punches the air![5] *27* Instead, I beat my body black and blue[6] and enslave it, so that, when I have proclaimed the Good News to others, I myself won't fail to pass muster!

Ch.10:1-5 Now, fellow believers, I don't want you to be unaware that all our ancestors[7] were under the pillar of cloud and all passed through the Red Sea. *2* All were baptized into the fellowship of Moses in the pillar of cloud and in the Red Sea. *3* All ate the same spiritual food. *4* All drank the same spiritual drink. They drank from the Rock that accompanied them, and that Rock was the Anointing. *5* But God was not well pleased with most of them, and so their corpses were scattered around in the desert.

6-10 Now these things became patterns[8] for us to follow, so that we would not want the bad things that they wanted. *7* And don't become idol worshippers like some of them were! As the Scriptures say, "The people sat down to eat and drink, and rose up to play around the idol."[9] *8* We must not

---

[1] βραβεῖον, *brabeion*, "awarded contest prize". *P.Oxy.* 7 (1910) 1050.11 (II/III), an expenditure account for public games at Oxyrhynchos. The title is well known in Lydian villages, cf. *BE* (1963) 221. The noun only here and in Phil. 3:14 in the N.T.

[2] στεᵔφανος, *stephanos*, often translated as "wreath" or "crown" but in general it was the winner's prize.

[3] The winner's prize at the biennial Isthmian Games, less than 6 miles (10 kilometres) from Corinth, was a wreath of wild celery. The athletic Games were held in the town of Isthmia, which lay east of Corinth.

[4] πυκτεύω, *pukteuo*, "box" not "fight", occurs only here in the N.T. This is a technical term used in texts relating to gladiators as well as boxers.

[5] A person who punches the air when boxing is either poorly trained and cannot hit the mark, or is so exhausted that they are flailing around wildly. Proper hard training and discipline prevent both these possibilities.

[6] ὑπωπιάζω, *hupopiazo*, is a technical wrestling term for giving someone a black eye or beating someone black and blue. See also Luke 18:5.

[7] οἱ πατέρες, *hoi pateres*. See note on Acts 3:25.

[8] τύπος, *tupos*. See note on Acts 7:43.

[9] That is, the idol of the golden calf. Exodus 32:6.

commit idolatry like some of them did! In one day 23,000 fell![1] *9* We must not provoke the Anointed One, like some of them provoked him and were killed by snakes. *10* We must not complain, like some of them complained, and were killed by the Destroyer!

11-13 These things happened to them as patterns, as they were written as a warning to us – the completion of the ages has arrived upon us! *12* Consequently, let the person who thinks they stand watch out in case they fall! *13* No ordeal has taken hold of you other than that which is common to humans. God is trustworthy – he will forbid an ordeal beyond your ability, but will make a way out which will carry you out of it.

14-22 So then, my dearly loved ones, flee from idol worshipping! *15* I'm speaking to you like I'd speak to sensible people. Judge for yourselves what I say! *16* The wine-cup of blessing which we bless, isn't it the partnership[2] with the Blood of the Anointed One! When we break the bread, isn't it the partnership with the body of the Anointed One! *17* Although there are a lot of us, we are one bread and one body, as we all share in that one bread.

18 Look at Israel in the natural realm! Aren't those who eat the sacrifices in partners in the altar? *19* What do I mean? Do I mean that food offered to an idol is something more than food, or an idol is something more than an idol?

20 Not at all! What I mean is that what the pagans offer as sacrifice, they offer as sacrifice to demons, and not to God! I do not want you to become partners with demons! *21* You cannot drink the wine-cup of the Lord and the wine-cup of demons – you cannot share in the Lord's dinner table and the dinner-table of demons. *22* Utter rubbish![3] Then we'd be making the Lord very angry! Are we stronger than he!

23-30 "We are free to do anything" you say, but not everything is good for you! Yes, "we are free to do anything" but not everything builds you up. *24* Each of you must consider other people's interests rather than your own. *25* You can eat everything sold in the meat market[4] without worrying about your conscience. *26* For "The earth and everything in it is the Lord's."

27 If an unbeliever invites you to dinner and you want to go, eat everything that's put in front of you without asking questions for the sake of your conscience. *28* But if someone says to you, "This food has been offered to idols", then you must not eat it, on account of that person and their conscience. *29* I'm talking about their conscience, not yours. Why should my freedom be judged by someone else's conscience? *30* If I participate freely, why should I be spoken about badly for eating food over which I have given thanks?

31-33.Ch.11:1 So then, whether you eat or drink, or whatever you do, do it all to honor God. *32* Become inoffensive to Jews and Greeks and God's assembly, *33* just as I too please everyone in everything I do. I'm not looking out for my own benefit, but for everyone's benefit, so that they will get saved. *1* Become imitators of me just like I too am an imitator of the Anointed One!

Paul addresses more complaints and questions from the Corinthian assembly.

---

[1]   Numbers 25:1-9, referring to the fall of thousands in a plague. Verse 3 says that the Lord was angry with the Israelites as Israel was joined to Baal of Peor because the Israelites bowed down to the pagan gods.

[2]   κοινωνία, *koinonia*. For the two examples of "partnership" in this verse, see note on 1 Corinthians 1:9.

[3]   Disjunctive particle.

[4]   The meat market in Corinth has been identified by archaeologists. It had 33 shops, and was in close proximity to temples where the animals were sacrificed.

2-3 I praise you for always keeping me in mind and for adhering to the teachings that I handed over to you. *3* [1]Now, I want you to know that the source[2] of every man is the Anointed One, the source of woman is man, and the source of the Anointed One is God.[3]

4-9 Every man who prays or prophesies with his head covered disgraces his head. *5* Every woman who prays or prophesies with her head uncovered[4]

---

[1]   The following passage becomes clear when the reader realizes that Paul is addressing both complaints about, and questions from, the Corinthian church. Paul had received disturbing reports about happenings in the church in Corinth. In response he wrote a letter which we do not have today. Chloe's followers reported arguments in the church, and Paul notes further complaints in 11:17. A letter also arrived asking questions.

[2]   κεφαλή, *kephale*, "source", has been mistranslated as "head (over)" by most Bible versions. A word in one language may have several meanings. Not all these meanings might apply in another language. That is why the Greek word "bowels" is translated as "compassion" or "heart" in 1 John 3:17 (as it can mean either in Greek), "But whoever has material possessions and observes their fellow believer in need, and shuts off their compassion from them, how can God's love stay with them?" If we did not understand semantic range, we would translate 1 John 3:17, "But whoever has material possessions and observes their fellow believer in need, and shuts off their bowels from them, how can God's love stay with them?" This is precisely same error as mistranslating κεφαλή, *kephale*, as "head (over someone)".

κεφαλή, *kephale*, has 5 meanings:
1) the literal head, with hair, eyes, etc
2) a wig or headdress
3) the source of something/someone, for example, the source of a river
4) the life, for example, to put one's head on the chopping block
5) metaphorically, the end point, sum, conclusion.

κεφαλή, *kephale*, cannot mean "head over someone". The English word "head" does mean this in English, but it cannot mean this in Greek. To translate it this way is exactly the same mistake as translating a Greek sentence which means "I have compassion for the poor" into English as "I have bowels for the poor."

The subject matter is clearly source, for Paul talks about men coming from women and women from men (verses 8, 9 and 12). Paul also makes a play on words (as he loves to do): κεφαλή, *kephale*, (as source) and κεφαλή, *kephale*, as the head which is covered. This wordplay cannot be brought out in the English language. κεφαλή, *kephale*, is first recorded as meaning "head (over someone)" centuries later in the Byzantine Empire.

For further reading, see S. Bedale, "The Meaning of *kephale* in the Pauline Epistles", *JTS* 5 (1951) 211-215; M. Boucher, "Some Unexplored Parallels to 1 Cor 11,11-12 and Gal 3:28: the NT on the Role of Women", *CBQ* 31 (1969) 50-58; C. Kroeger, "The Classical Concept of Head as 'Source'", in G. Gaebelein Hull, *Equal to Serve*, (Grand Rapids: Revell, 1987), 267-83; J.M. Holmes, *Text in a Whirlwind: A Critique of Four Exegetical Devices at 1 Timothy 2.9-15, Journal for the Study of the New Testament Supplement Series* 196, *Studies in New Testament Greek* 7, (Sheffield: Sheffield Academic Press, 1999), pp. 311-316.

[3]   Here we have "man", "woman", "Anointed One" in that order. Now it is clear that Paul cannot be talking about a hierarchy here, as the Anointed One is listed last. In fact, Paul is listing the three in their chronological order (which makes sense as the theme is "source"): Adam came first, woman (Eve) was next, followed by the Anointed One.

[4]   The Roman elegists used hair in connection with the erotic. The hair of Roman (and Greek) women has attracted much scholarship in the decade. See

disgraces her head – it would be one and the same if she'd had a shaved head. *6* If a woman doesn't cover her head, she might as well have her hair cut off, and since it is shameful for a woman to have her hair cut off or shaved off, she should cover her head.

    7 On the one hand, a man ought not to cover his head as the man is the portrait[1] of the beginning of God's splendor, and on the other hand the woman is the splendor of man. *8* Man is not from woman but the woman is from man, *9* for in fact man was not created by means of a woman, but the woman was created by means of a man.[2]

10-12 For this reason the woman ought to have her authority[3] upon her head[4] on account of the Messengers,[5] *11* except that, as far as the Lord is concerned, a woman isn't separate[6] from a man nor is a man separate from a woman. *12* It's a fact that just as the woman comes from the man, in the same way too the man comes through the woman! But all things are from God.

M. Myerowitz Levine, "The Gendered Grammar of Ancient Mediterranean Hair" in Eilberg-Schwartz and Doniger (edd.) *Off with Her Head! The Denial of Women's Identity in Myth, Religion, and Culture,* (Berkeley: University of California Press, 1995). Euripides' Electra (the person, in the play of the same name) cuts her hair, and states that this removes her from society (and makes her undesirable). Although Greek of several centuries earlier, this was typical for the Romans of the 1st century. The Roman elegists associated untidy hair with illicit sexual encounters as well as encounters with courtesans. A lifestyle outside the normal constraints was associated with natural, freely flowing hair (e.g. Ovid, Am. 1.1.20; 1.5.10; 1.7.10-12; 1.8; 3.14.33-34; AA 3.431-2; Tibullus 1.1.59-62; Propertius 1.2.7-12; 2.24.33-49; Martial 3.93.1-5).

[1] εἰκών, *eikon*, "portrait", cf. *ed.pr.* P. Herrmann, *AAWW* 111 (1974) 439-44 (pl. 2), A.D. 75/6 l. 19; *OGIS* 571.4-5 (Cadyanda in Lykia, Roman Imperial), noted by MM, *s.v.*

[2] διά, *dia*, here of agency. cf. Goodwin, *Greek Grammar, op.cit.,* 1206, p. 256. Not "on behalf of" which would require ὑπέρ, *huper*, with the genitive, or "for the sake of" which would require ἕνεκα, *heneka*, with the genitive.

[3] The possessive pronoun is omitted, thus the authority is the woman's own, according to normal rules of Greek grammar. J.M. Holmes states, "In the New Testament, *exousia* consistently appears in the active voice indicating the authority of the subject, so here is the woman's own." *op.cit.,* p. 314. This, of course, follows the usual rules for Greek syntax in the omission of a possessive pronoun. Note also that the word "submission" does not appear. Holmes, *ibid.*, p. 315, further states "Paul (v.10) agrees that woman, created because man needs her, has her own authority."

[4] For further reading see M. Hooker, "Authority on her head: An Examination of 1 Cor. xi, 10" *NTS* 10 (1963-4) 410-6.

[5] This is a word-for-word literal translation of the Greek. Some suggest that prayer and prophecy are mentioned because they bring the person into the presence of God and Messengers are in the presence of God. For this see G. Bilezikian, *Beyond Sex Roles*, 2nd ed., (Michigan: Baker Book House, 1995), pp. 141ff. There may be another explanation. In Rome at the time of Paul's writing, a woman who wore something on her head in public - a veil, a hood, any covering - was under the protection of Roman law. No man would dare approach such a woman under risk of grave penalties. The wearing of a sign of her authority on her head may indicate that the woman is under the protection of angels. In fact, this may be supported by verses 5 and 6. A Roman woman of the times who went into public with an uncovered head was not under the protection of Roman law, and an attacker was entitled to plead extenuating circumstances. Thus, in this light in 1 Cor. the woman would have the authority, the right, to be under the protection of angels.

[6] χωρίς, *khoris*, "separate from".

13-16 Judge for yourselves! Is it fitting for a woman to pray to God with her head uncovered? *14* Even nature itself teaches you that if a man has ornamentally arranged[1] hair it disgraces him, *15* but if a woman has ornamentally arranged hair it gives her splendor! Ornamentally arranged hair is given to her in place of a coat. *16* But if anyone is inclined to be obstinate about this, let me say that we have no such custom, nor do any of God's assemblies.[2]

17 Now in giving you these instructions I don't have any praise for you, because your meetings do more harm than good!

Paul now addresses a complaint made to him about the Corinthian assembly.

18-19 Primarily, I am told that when you meet as an assembly, divisions have begun among you, and I believe part of it. *19* (Yet divisions are necessary if only to show which of you have passed muster!)

20-22 So then, when you assemble altogether, it's impossible to eat the Lord's Supper. *21* One gobbles down their food before someone else can get to it, and one is hungry while the other one is drunk! *22* Don't you have homes to go to, to eat and drink in? What a lot of utter rubbish this is![3] You despise God's assembly and humiliate those who don't have anything! What is there to say to you? Am I likely to praise you? I don't think so!

23-26 I received what was handed over to me from the Lord, that which I also handed over to you: namely, that the Lord Jesus, on the night in which he was arrested, picked up some bread, *24* and after he had given thanks, he broke it into pieces and said, "This is my body which is for you: do this as a recollection of me."

25 In the same way also he picked up the wine-cup after dinner, and said, "This cup is the New Covenant in my Blood: do this, as often as you drink it, to recollect me." *26* For as often as you eat this bread and drink this cup, you proclaim the Lord's death until he comes.

27-32 Consequently, anyone who eats this bread or drinks this cup of the Lord in an unworthy manner will be liable to prosecution for the body and the blood!

28 But a person must examine themselves, and then eat the bread and drink the wine. *29* For the person who eats and drinks, eats and drinks the verdict to themselves if they do not exercise discernment about the Body. *30* This is the reason why many of you are sick and chronically ill! And aren't enough of you in the sleep of death! *31* Now if we exercise discernment about ourselves at the present time, we would not be judged in the present time. *32* When we are judged by the Lord we are educated,[4] so that we would not have sentence passed on us in company with the world.

33-34 Consequently, my fellow believers, when you assemble to eat, wait for each other! *34* If anyone is hungry, go home and eat! Then you won't have the guilty verdict passed on you when you meet together! I'll give directions about the remaining matters you asked about when I arrive.

---

[1] κομάω, *komao*, and κόμη, *kome*, have been commonly rendered in Bible versions as "grow the hair long" and "long hair" respectively. However, there is much evidence for the verb as "give oneself airs" and the noun as "a comet's tail", "the gill of a cuttlefish" and "the hair of the head". κόμη, *kome*, is used to translate *pe'er* (for example, in Ezek. 24:23), which can be a headdress, turban, an adornment, or a crown/wreath of beauty. Generically, the word refers to decoration. J.M. Holmes, *op.cit.*, p 314, suggests the translation "prettified hair", "dressed hair" and states, "κόμη, *kome*, should be translated along the lines of 'ornamentally arranged' hair".

[2] Bilezikian, *ibid.*, p. 144, sums the mistranslation of the whole passage well.

[3] Sentence to bring out full meaning of disjunctive particle: otherwise English translation would be clumsy.

[4] παιδεύω, *paideuo*, the cognate verb of παιδεία, *paidea*. See note on Eph. 6:4.

Ch.12:1-3 Now about spiritual matters,[1] fellow believers, I don't want you to be ignorant! *2* You know that when you were pagans, how you kept being irresistibly drawn away to silent idols. *3* This is why I make it known to you that no one speaking in supernaturally given languages by the Spirit of God calls Jesus cursed, and no one is able to say that Jesus is Lord, except by the Holy Spirit.

4-11 There are varieties of spiritual gifts, but the same Spirit. *5* There are varieties of ministries, but the same Lord. *6* There are varieties of activities, but it's the same God who activates all things in everyone. *7* The manifestation of the Spirit is given to each person for the benefit of everyone.

8 On the one hand, to one is given a message[2] of wisdom through the Spirit, on the other hand another is given a message of realization according to the same Spirit, *9* another is given faith by the same Spirit, another is given spiritual gifts of instant divine healings by the one Spirit. *10* On the other hand to another is given the working of powers, on the other hand to another prophecy, to another the discerning of spirits, to another speaking in supernaturally given languages of different races, to another interpretation of supernaturally given languages. *11* The one and the same Spirit activates all these things. The Spirit divides them up to each person just as the Spirit wishes.

12-24 Now the physical body is a single one and has many limbs, but all the limbs, quite a few of them, are part of that single body. The Anointed One is just like this. *13* Indeed we were all baptized into one single body by means of one Spirit – whether we're Jews or Greeks, or slaves or free people – and one single Spirit made us all grow. *14* The physical body is in fact many parts, not just one. *15* What if the foot said, "Because I'm not a hand, I'm not part of the body'. Isn't it still part of the body! *16* And if the ear said, "I'm not an eye, so I'm not part of the body," isn't it still part of the body! *17* If the whole body was made up of an eye, how could it hear? If the whole body was an ear, how could it smell? *18* But in point of fact God has set up all the parts of the body. *19* If the body consisted of just one part, it wouldn't be a body at all! *20* But as it is, on the one hand there are lots of parts, and on the other hand there's a single body. *21* The eye can't say to the hand, "I don't need you!" and the head can't say to the feet, "I don't need you!"

22 But rather, those particular parts of the body that seem to be the weaker ones are actually vital. *23* We treat those parts that we think are less honorable with even more honor, and we treat those parts which we don't present to the world with clothing. *24* Yet we don't need to do this with those parts that we do present to the world.

24-26 But God composed the body, and gave greater honor to those parts which lacked it, *25* so that there wouldn't be any division in the body, but that all the parts would look after each other in the same way. *26* And if something happens to one part, it happens to all the parts – or if one part is honored, all the parts are happy together.

27-31 You are the body of the Anointed One as well as individual parts! *28* God has set up the following in the assembly: first, apostles; second, prophets; third, teachers; then miracles; then spiritual gifts of instant divine healings; revealed knowledge; guidance;[3] supernaturally given languages of different races.

---

[1] πνευματικός, *pneumatikos*, either spiritual people or spiritual things.

[2] λόγος, *logos*, not ῥῆμα, *rhema*, "message", "account" rather than "utterance".

[3] κυβέρνησις, *kubernesis*, steering, guidance. The use of κυβέρνησις, *kubernesis*, (steering) here instead of κυβερνήτης, *kubernetes* (the one doing the steering), shows us that the last five mentioned here were the actual gifts, not the person with the gifts. Indeed, this is what the literal Greek says. Hauben, *ZPE* 28 (1978) 99-107, lists vessels from Ptolemaic Egypt with the names of their ναύκληροι, κυβερνήται (*naukleroi, kubernatai*) and owners. The ναύκληρος,

29 Everyone isn't an apostle!¹ Everyone isn't a prophet! Everyone isn't a teacher! Everyone doesn't do miracles! *30* Everyone doesn't have spiritual gifts of instant divine healings! Everyone doesn't speak in supernaturally given languages! Everyone doesn't interpret! Strive after the greater gifts!
31.Ch.13:1-3 Moreover, I am indeed showing you an excessively extreme pathway. *1* If I would speak with the supernaturally given languages of people and of Messengers, but not have love, I would be a bit of metal that makes a noise, or a clanging cymbal. *2* And if I have the gift of prophecy, and know all mysteries and all things that there are to know, and if I have all faith so that I can move mountains from one place to another, but don't have love, I am nothing! *3* And if I hand out all my possessions and hand over my body, so that I could boast about it, but don't have love, it wouldn't benefit me.
4-7 Love has perseverance, love is kind. Love does not envy. Love does not show off, love is not arrogant. *5* Love is not rude, is not self seeking, it is not hot tempered, it does not calculate wrong doings, *6* it is not happy over dishonesty, but is happy only with the truth; *7* it puts up with everything, it has endurance in all things.
8-13 Love never falls down. Prophecies will become inactive,² supernaturally given languages will cease, knowledge will become inactive.³ *9* For we have knowledge in part and we prophesy in part. *10* But when that which is complete⁴ comes, then that which is incomplete will become inactive.⁵ *11* When I was a baby, I spoke like a baby, I thought like a baby, I calculated like a baby. When I became a man, I did away with infantile things. *12* For now we look through a mirror in a riddle, but then we will look face to face – now we have knowledge in part, then we will have thorough knowledge just as we are thoroughly known. *13* But in point of fact all three of these will remain – faith, hope and love, and the greatest of these is love.
Ch.14:1-5 Chase after love, strive after spiritual gifts and strive especially to prophesy. *2* For the person who speaks in supernaturally given languages doesn't speak to people but to God – for no one understands: rather, they are speaking secret hidden truths spiritually. *3* But the person who prophesies speaks a building up, an encouragement, and a relief to people. *4* The person who speaks in a supernaturally given language builds themselves up, but the person who prophesies builds up the assembly. *5* I would like all of you to speak in supernaturally given languages, but I would prefer that you would prophesy. The person who prophesies is more important than the person who

---

naukleros, either owned the ship or chartered the ship. The earliest example of a ναύκληρος, *naukleros*, as one who charters a ship is in *P.Sorb.* inv. 2395, ed. J. Scherer in *BASP* 15 (1978) 95-101.This man had use of the ship. The κυβερνήτης, *kubernetes* was the captain, the one who steered the ship. Sometimes the ναύκληρος, *naukleros*, could be his own κυβερνήτης, *kubernetes* cf. *P.Oxy.Hels*. 37; Hauben, 240; Casson, 315-316; *P.Lond.* 3. 948. The evidence from *P.Oxy.Hels.* 37 suggests that the ναύκληρος, *naukleros*, had the final word in the handling of the ship.
¹   μή, *me*, used when the negation depends on the previous thought, whether expressed or implied, as opposed to οὐ, *ou*, which denies absolutely. The later writers did not differentiate, equating μή, *me*, with οὐ, *ou*. The KJV has followed the Vulgate in equating μή, *me*, with the Latin *num*, an interrogative expressing a negative answer, and has translated accordingly. Most modern versions have followed the KJV.
²   καταργέω, *katargeo*. See note on Rom. 3:3.
³   Same as earlier word, καταργέω, *katargeo*. See note on Rom. 3:3.
⁴   The definite article here is neuter, so this cannot be a reference to Jesus, as some have suggested.
⁵   Same word as in v. 8 (twice) and v. 11, καταργέω, *katargeo*. See note on Rom. 3:3.

speaks in supernaturally given languages unless that person interprets, so that the assembly can take advantage of the building up.

6-9 But as it is, fellow believers, if I come to you speaking in supernaturally given languages, what good will it do you unless I speak to you either by revelation, by knowledge, by prophesy or by teaching! *7* Even taking the example of inanimate objects that make sounds, like the flute or the harp – unless there's a distinct difference in the sounds, how can you tell which tune is being played? *8* Now then if the trumpet makes a vague sound, how are you going to make preparations for war? *9* So then you too, unless what comes out of your mouth has a clear meaning, how can anyone know what's been spoken? You will be speaking to the air!

10-15 Who knows how many voices there are in the world, and none of them is silent! *11* So then, if I don't know the meaning of a language, I will be a foreigner to the speaker, and the person who speaks will be a foreigner to me. *12* This goes for you too – since you strive after spiritual things, then let it be for the building up of the assembly that you seek to excel in. *13* So then the person who speaks in a supernaturally given language must pray that they would interpret. *14* For whenever I pray in a supernaturally given language, my spirit prays, but my understanding is useless. *15* So then, what's my point? I will pray in the Spirit, but I will also pray with the understanding. I will sing praise songs in the Spirit, but I will also sing praise songs with my understanding.

16-19 Since, if you are praising God by means of the Spirit, how is someone who is an outsider going to say "Amen!" to your giving of thanks, when they don't have a clue what you're saying! *17* Yes, indeed, you're giving thanks nicely, but the other person isn't being built up! *18* I thank God that I speak in supernaturally given languages more than all of you! *19* But in the assembly, I would rather speak five words that I can understand, so that I would verbally instruct others too, than 10,000 words in a supernaturally given language!

20-21 Fellow believers, don't be children in your outlook - as for wrongdoing, be babies, and as for your understanding, be adults. *21* In the Law the Scriptures say, "By those who speak other languages and by the lips of foreigners I will speak to this people, and yet, they won't listen to me," says the Lord.

22-25 Consequently, supernaturally given languages are a sign, not for believers, but for unbelievers. But prophesy is not for unbelievers, but for believers. *23* So then, whenever the whole assembly gets together, and everyone speaks in supernaturally given tongues, and someone comes along who's uninformed or an unbeliever, won't they say that you're stark raving mad! *24* But whenever everyone prophesies, and an unbeliever or an uninformed person comes along, that person is convinced by everyone, and is investigated by everyone. *25* The secrets of the heart come to light, and thus that person worships God, and reports that God is really, truly among you.

26-28 So then, fellow believers, why is it that when you get together, each one has a praise song, a teaching, a revelation, a supernaturally given language, an interpretation?[1] Everything must be done for building people up! *27* If anyone speaks in a supernaturally given language, let it be by twos and threes or so, each in turn,[2] and then let one person interpret. *28* But if there isn't any interpreter, then the person is to keep silent in the assembly, and they are to speak to themselves and to God.

---

[1] Paul is complaining about this behavior, not endorsing it!

[2] This has been mistranslated as: "If anyone speaks in a tongue, let there be two or at the most three, each in turn, and let one interpret." The Greek is actually a distributive, κατά... (*kata...*) "by twos and threes". It is an idiomatic expression equal to the English, "Let a few do it" or "Let a couple of you do it".

29-33 Let two or three or so[1] prophets speak, and let the other prophets discern.[2] *30* Whenever something is revealed to someone sitting nearby, let the first keep quiet. *31* For you can all prophesy one by one, so that all can learn and all can be encouraged. *32* And the spirits of the prophets are supported by the prophets. *33* God is not a God of disorder, but of peace.

Paul now quotes from the letter sent to him by the Corinthian assembly.[3]

34-38 "The women must be silent in the assemblies: for they are not allowed to speak, but to be supportive, just as indeed the law states. *35* And if they want to learn something, they are to ask their own husbands at home; for it is a disgrace for women to speak in the assembly."[4]

36 Utter rubbish![5] Did the Word of God come originally from you![6] Utter rubbish![7] Were you the only ones that it reached! *37* If anyone thinks they're a prophet or spiritual, they are to realize that what I'm writing to you is the Lord's commandment! *38* But if anyone is mistaken about this, then they are certainly mistaken!

39-40 Consequently, fellow believers, strive after prophesying, and don't prevent anyone from speaking in supernaturally given languages. *40* Everything is to be done decently[8] and in an orderly manner.

Ch.15:1-7 I remind you, fellow believers, of the Good News which I announced to you, which was also taken up by you, and on which you now take your stand *2* and by which means you are also saved. Do you hold on firmly to

---

[1] δύο ἤ τρεῖς, *duo e treis*, "two or three". Again, Greek idiom for "just a few", "just a couple". It does not mean literally 2 or 3 people, it means just a few.

[2] διακρίνω, *diakrino*.

[3] These words are a quotation from the letter sent to Paul by the church in Corinth. He quotes from this letter in 7:1, refers to it in 7:25, 36, 39; 8:1; 9:3. The language in the quotation resembles known Jewish oral law, cf. S. Aalen, "A Rabbinic Formula in 1 Cor. 14,34", in F. Cross (ed.) *Studia Evangelica*, II-III. *Papers*, Berlin, 1964, pp. 513-25; Holmes, *op.cit.*, p. 235.

[4] This passage has been terribly mistranslated. It has been put in as Paul's words, instead of a quote, and the following two instances of the disjunctive particle "Utter rubbish!" have been deleted. See the following for evidence that this passage is quoted by Paul, followed by his vehement disagreement with it: D.W. Odell-Scott, "Let the Women Speak in Church. An Egalitarian Interpretation of 1 Cor. 14:33b –36", *Biblical Theology Bulletin* Vol. XIII (1983), pp. 90-93; N.M. Flanagan and E.H. Snyder, "Did Paul Put Women Down in 1 Cor. 14:34-36?" *Biblical Theology Bulletin* Vol. XI, January 1981, pp.10-12; W.C. Kaiser, Jnr., "Paul, Women and the Church," *Worldwide Challenge*, September, 1976, pp. 9-12; J. Harper, *Women and the Gospel*, (G.B.: Pinner, 1974), pp. 14-15; J. Sidlow Baxter, *Explore the Book*, (Grand Rapids: Zondervan, 1987); J.A. Anderson, *Women's Warfare and Ministry: What Saith the Scriptures?* (Stonehaven: David Waldie, 1933), pp. 20-26; K.C. Bushnell, *God's Word to Women*, (Mossville, IL: God's Word to Women Publishers, n.d.): G. Bilezikian, *op.cit.*, pp. 144-153, 284-5. For a survey of current scholarship see J.M. Holmes, *op.cit.*, pp. 229-238. Holmes (*ibid.*, p. 237) (speaking of Paul) states, "He quotes the factional view (which he knows is not generally held), angrily rebukes its proponents, states his own authority, exhorts everyone to be eager to prophesy, and commands that no one forbid anyone to speak in tongues."

[5] Disjunctive particle.

[6] Masculine pronoun.

[7] Disjunctive particle.

[8] Cf. the decree for Athanadas of Rhegion (Delphi, c. 150/49), *Galates* no. 70. One of the grounds for honouring Athanadas of Rhegion is that during his stay in Delphi he "behaved well and decently". The adverb also in Rom. 13:13 and 1 Thess. 4:12.

that Word by which I announced the Good News to you? If not, you became believers without a purpose! *3* In the first place I handed over to that which I also took hold of – that the Anointed One died on behalf of our sins according to the Scriptures, *4* and that he was buried, and that he has been raised again on the third day according to the Scriptures, *5* and that he appeared to Cephas (Peter), and then to the Twelve. *6* After that he was seen by over 500 fellow believers at once. Most of them are still around, but some have passed away. *7* After that he was seen by James, and then all the apostles.

8-11 Then last of all he was seen by me too. You could say[1] this was an abortion![2] *9* I'm surely inferior to the other apostles, and I'm not worthy enough to be called an apostle, because I persecuted God's assembly! *10* But I am what I am because of God's favor! His favor to me was not in vain, but I worked exceedingly more than all of them – well, I myself didn't actually do it, it was God's favor which was with me. *11* Anyway, who cares – whether I did it or they did it - this is what we proclaim and you believed!

12-19 Now, since it has been proclaimed that the Anointed One has been raised from among the dead, why is it that some of you are saying that there's no resurrection of the dead? *13* If there's no resurrection of the dead, then the Anointed One hasn't been raised! *14* And if the Anointed One hasn't been raised, then there's no purpose to our preaching, and no purpose to your believing!

15 Then we'd be false witnesses of God, because then we would have given evidence against God that he raised up the Anointed One, when he wouldn't have raised him up at all – if in fact as you're saying, the dead don't rise up! *16* If the dead don't rise up, then the Anointed One didn't rise up! *17* And if the Anointed One hasn't risen, then your faith is pointless, and you still have your sins! *18* It would also mean that those who have passed away when followers of the Anointed One are utterly lost. *19* If it's only for this life that the Anointed One has given us hope, then we're more to be pitied than all people!

20-23 But in point of fact, the Anointed One has risen from among the dead and has become the first offering of those who have passed away. *21* For since death was due to a person, so also the raising from among the dead was due to a Person. *22* For just as everyone dies because of Adam, in the same way also everyone becomes alive because of the Anointed One, *23* each in their own military rank: the Anointed One being the first offering, and then those who belong to the Anointed One at his Coming.[3]

24-26 Next is the fulfillment, when he hands over the Realm to God the Father, after he renders inoperative every rule and every authority and power.[4] *25* It is necessary that he reigns until he has subdued every enemy. *26* The last enemy that will be rendered inoperative is death.

27-28 "He has attached all things to him in support of him, and subdued them." Now when it says that all things are attached to him, it cannot refer to God, as it is clear that God is the one who attached them. *28* When all things are attached to him, then the Son himself will be attached to God who attached everything to him, so that God will mean everything to everyone.

29-34 Then what will those who are baptized in connection putting the body to death do? If the dead do not rise, then what's the point of being baptized in connection with death? *30* And why too do we run risks all the time? *31* I swear by your reason to boast, that is, the Anointed One Jesus our Lord, that I die

---

[1] ὡσπερεί, *hosperei*, "you could say", a Greek colloquialism.

[2] ἔκτρωμα, *ektroma*. Equally, "miscarriage". Paul's metaphor signifies that he does not consider himself to be born, rather aborted/miscarried, as an apostle, because of his background. See discussion in *NDIEC* 2.81-2.

[3] παρουσία, *parousia*. See note on Matt. 243.

[4] Nothing suggests that all these rulers and principalities are demonic. The powers in Colossians 1:16 likewise are not referred to as evil in the Greek.

daily!¹ *32* If I fought with wild beasts at Ephesos just for human reasons, what was the point? If dead bodies are not raised, then "Let us eat and drink, for tomorrow we are to die!" *33* Don't be deceived! "Bad close company² destroys good habits!"³ *34* Come out of your sleep in the right way and do not sin! There are some who don't have any knowledge of God, and I say this to your shame!

35-49 But someone will say, "How are corpses raised up? What body will they have?" *36* You senseless person! What you sow doesn't come to life unless it dies first! *37* And what you actually sow isn't the form it will be in – you're merely sowing grain, perhaps wheat or some other sort. *38* But God gives it the body he purposes to give it, and gives each seed its own body. *39* All flesh is not the same, but there's one for people, and there's another for farm animals, and another for birds, and another for fish. *40* There are the bodies of heaven, and bodies of the earth: but the splendor of the bodies of heaven is different from the splendor of the bodies of the earth. *41* There is the splendor of the sun, another splendor of the moon, another splendor of the stars – and the splendor of one star is different to the splendor of another star. *42* It's the same too with the resurrection of dead bodies. The body is sown in perishability, and is raised in imperishability. *43* It is sown in dishonor, it is raised in splendor. It is sown in weakness, it is raised in power. *44* It is sown as a soulish body, it is raised as a spiritual body. There is a soulish body, and there is a spiritual body. *45* So too the Scriptures say, "The first human Adam became a living soul". The last Adam became a living spirit.

46 The spirit doesn't come first – the soul comes first, then the spirit comes. *47* The first person was from the dust, the second Person was from heaven. *48* All those of the dust are like the person who was from the dust – all those of heaven are like the Person who was from heaven. *49* And just as we have worn the likeness of the dust, so too will we wear the likeness of the Person from heaven.

50 Fellow believers, this is what I mean, that flesh and blood cannot inherit God's Realm, nor is the perishable able to inherit the imperishable.

51-58 Look, I'm telling you a hidden secret truth – everyone won't fall asleep, but everyone will be changed, *52* in a flash of time, in the blinking of an eye, at the last trumpet! For the trumpet will sound, and the corpses will be raised up as imperishable and we will be changed. *53* It is necessary for this perishable body to wear imperishability and this mortal body to wear immortality. *54* So when the perishable body wears imperishability and the mortal body wears immortality, then the Message of the Scriptures will come to pass: *55* "Death is swallowed up by victory!" "Death, where is your victory? Death, where is your sting?"

---

¹ This simple Greek sentence has been widely mistranslated, perhaps due to the fact that Paul used the common Greek expression for swearing (by a divinity) (νή, *ne*, with accusative) which perhaps some translators felt was improper for him to use and thus censored it. This Greek word has no other meaning. In Greek times, people frequently said, "I swear by Zeus!" and here Paul is saying, "I swear by your reason to boast!" and the Greek requires that the reason to boast, in the Greek, must have a divine implication. Paul used the word καύξησις, *kaukhesis*, "reason to boast", which cannot mean "pride" or "glory", and in no way is he suggesting here that he is proud of the Corinthians – quite the opposite. He is giving the Corinthians a severe roasting for their behaviour throughout 1 Corinthians. Paul is saying that his reason to boast is their reason to boast, and this reason to boast is Jesus.

² This word indicates very close company, and is also one of the words for sexual intercourse.

³ Here Paul is quoting the celebrated Menander, a comic poet of the New Comedy (342-291 B.C.) It is a word for word quote from Menander's play *Thais*.

56 The sting of death is sin. The power of sin is the Law. *57* I thank God, who gives us the victory through our Lord Jesus the Anointed One! *58* Consequently, my dearly loved fellow believers, be firm, immovable, having in abundance the Lord's possessions at all times, knowing that your labor for the Lord is not in vain.

Paul replies to the question about the collection, a question posed in the letter sent from the Corinthian assembly.

Ch.16:1-4 Now about the collection for the people devoted to God[1] - you must do just what I have set down as orders for the assemblies in Galatia – *2* On the first day of the week each one of you is to lay aside something from your store, according to how you prosper, so that the collection won't be going on when I come. *3* When I come on the scene, I will give letters of introduction to whomever you chose to take your gift to Jerusalem. *4* If it's worthwhile for me to go, then they will go with me.

5-9 Now I'm coming to you on my way through Macedonia (as my route is through Macedonia), *6* and possibly I'll stay, or even spend the winter with you. Then you yourselves can give me money and supplies for my journey, wherever I go. *7* My purpose isn't to see you now in passing, as I hope to stay on with you for some time, when the Lord would permit me to. *8* I'm going to stay on in Ephesos until Pentecost, *9* as a great, effective door has been opened to me, and there are many opponents.

10-11 When Timothy comes, see to it that he begins to feel at home with you – as he does the Lord's work, as I do too. *11* So then, don't let anyone slight him! Send him on his way peacefully, so that he can come to me –I'm waiting for him with the fellow believers.

The Corinthians have questioned Paul about Apollos.

12 Now, about our fellow believer Apollos. I strongly urged him to go to you with the fellow believers, but he really didn't want to go at that time. However, he will come when he has a more convenient time.

13-18 Keep your wits about you! Stand firm in the faith! Be courageous! Be mighty! *14* Let everything you do be done lovingly! *15* I urge you, fellow believers – you know that the people of Stephanas' household were the first converts in Achaia, and that they have devoted themselves to the ministry[2] for the people devoted to God – *16* so support them and all the fellow workers and laborers. *17* I'm glad to see that Stephanas, Fortunatos and Achaikos have arrived, as they made up for what was lacking on your part. *18* They have relieved my mind, and yours as well no doubt. So appreciate them!

19-24 The assemblies of Asia greet you. Aquila and Priska greet you warmly, along with the assembly at their house. *20* All the fellow believers greet you. Give greetings all around with a sacred kiss. *21* The greeting is written with my own hand – Paul's.

22 If anyone doesn't love the Lord, let them be cursed![3] Our Lord, come!
23 May the favor of our Lord Jesus be with you!
24 My love is with all of you followers of the Anointed One Jesus.

---

[1]   The Corinthians have questioned Paul about the financial collection for the people devoted to God.
[2]   Could also be "distribution" as the same word is used in Acts 6:1.
[3]   See note on καταράομαι, *kataraomai*, in Luke 6:28.

Second Letter to the Corinthians.

Paul arrived in Corinth and stayed there eighteen months (Acts 18:11), prior to sailing to Ephesos with Priscilla and Aquila. Paul returned to Antioch (Acts 18:18-22), leaving Priscilla and Aquila behind in Ephesos. While in Ephesos, Priscilla and Aquila taught Apollos, sending him back to Corinth to minister (Acts 18:24–19:1). A year later, Paul returned to Ephesos on his third missionary journey, and stayed there almost three years (Acts 20:31). During that time, Paul wrote his first letter to the Corinthians (cf. 1 Cor 5:9). He then wrote his second letter which we now refer to as 1 Corinthians, after learning of problems from both Chloe's congregation (1 Cor 1:11) and from the letter brought by the delegation of Corinthians. Paul then visited the Corinthians again. This was his "painful visit" (2 Cor 2:1). After the painful visit, Paul returned to Ephesos, and subsequently wrote the "severe letter" (2 Cor 2:3-4; 7:8), which apparently was carried by Titus (cf. 2 Cor 7:5-8). Paul left Ephesos for Macedonia, hoping to find Titus at Troas. He was unsuccessful, so sailed for Macedonia without him (2 Cor 2:12-13), hoping to meet him there. Paul did meet Titus in Macedonia, and discovered that the Corinthians are getting straightened out (2 Cor 7:6-16). Paul then wrote a fourth letter (our Second Corinthians) while in Macedonia (no later than 55 AD). Afterwards, Paul visited the Corinthians for the third time. (Acts 20:3; cf. 2 Cor 12:14). It was during this time that Paul wrote Romans.

Polycarp, Irenaeus, Clement of Alexandria, and Tertullian, Marcion and the Muratorian Canon all refer to 2 Corinthians.

Second Letter to the Corinthians.

Ch.1:1-2   From: Paul, an apostle of the Anointed One Jesus through God's purpose, and from Timothy, our fellow believer.[1]

2 To: God's assembly at Corinth, with all the people devoted to God who are in Achaia.

Hello! May you have peace from God our Father and the Lord Jesus the Anointed One!

3-5 Praise the God and Father of our Lord Jesus the Anointed One, the Father of compassion and the Father of all encouragement! *4* He encourages us throughout every oppression we experience, so that we in turn are able to encourage others who are oppressed, by sharing the encouragement God gives us. *5* And just as we have an abundant measure of the Anointed One's lessons of experience,[2] so we too have an abundant measure of encouragement by means of the Anointed One.

6-7 When we are oppressed, it is the price we pay for your encouragement and salvation. When we are encouraged, it is to help us encourage you. The encouragement continues throughout the enduring of the same lessons of experience which we also experience. *7* And our hope for you is shown to be valid, because we know that you are partners with our lessons of experience, just as you are partners with our encouragement.

8-11 Fellow believers, our purpose isn't for you to be ignorant about the oppressions that happened to us in the province of Asia – that we were excessively weighed down beyond our ability, and consequently we

---

[1]   *Adelphos,* singular of *adelphoi.* See note on Matt. 5:22.

[2]   πάθημα, *pathema,* "lessons of experience." The word "sufferings" does not occur in this verse. Cf. Hdt. 1.207; Aesch. Ag. 175; Ar. Thesm. 199; Plato, Symp. 222 B; "anything that happens to one", cf. Soph. Tr. 142; Hdt. 8.136; Soph. O.C. 361.

despaired of our very lives. *9* We had the sentence of death on ourselves, and as a result we did not trust ourselves but God who raises the dead. *10* God rescued us from so massive a death, and will rescue us – we trust that he will still rescue us. *11* You also cooperated with God by your earnest requests to him on our behalf. Many people need to be thanked on our behalf for the favor which many people gave us.

12-14 This is our reason for being proud: our conscience testifies that we conduct ourselves openly and sincerely in the world, and especially towards you. We have not done this by the wisdom of the natural realm but by the favor of God. *13* We are not writing anything to you other than what you know for a fact or fully understand. I hope that you will understand completely[1] - *14* just as your present full knowledge about us is partial – that we are have as much reason to be proud of you as you have to be proud of us, on the Day of our Lord Jesus.

15-16 As I was confident about this, I intended to visit you previously, so you would have the benefit of a double visit – *16* to visit you on my way to Macedonia, and to visit you on my way back again from Macedonia, and to be sent on my way with money and supplies by you on my way to Judea.

17-20 So then, when I was planning this, did I do it with that irresponsibility of which you accuse me?[2] Did I make my plans as someone of the natural realm would, with the result that I spoke in double-talk: "yes", "yes", and "no", "no" at the same time – not saying exactly what I meant? *18* As God is true,[3] our message to you was not "yes" and "no" - double-talk. *19* For the Son of God, Jesus the Anointed One, who was proclaimed among you by us - by me, Silvanos and Timothy - wasn't "yes" and "no", but was a lasting "yes". *20* All God's promises are "yes" because of Jesus the Anointed One – therefore when we honor God, it is through Jesus the Anointed One that we say "Amen!"

21-22 It is God who has guaranteed that we were purchased along with you, and it is God who has anointed us. *22* He also sealed us and gave us the Spirit in our hearts as a down payment[4] on what is to come.

23-24.Ch.2:1-2 I indeed call upon God as my witness and stake my life on it,[5] that it was to spare you that I haven't yet come to Corinth! *24* Not that we have mastery over your faith, but we as fellow workers work for your happiness. By faith you stand firm. *1* But I decided that I wouldn't come to you and make you feel bad. *2* Indeed if I make you feel bad, who is going to cheer me up, except you, whom I've upset?

3-4 This is the very point I made in my letter – I said that I didn't want to come and be saddened by the very people who should have cheered me up – and I was confident that if I am happy, it means that all of you will be happy! *4* The letter I sent you came out of much oppression and anguish of heart, and

---

[1] Paul plays on words: ἀναγινώσκω, *anaginosko*, and ἐπιγινώσκω, *epiginosko*. The "completely" contrasts with the μέρος, *meros*, "partial", in the next verse.

[2] The definite article implying "of which you accuse me", cf. Zerwick and Grosvenor, *op.cit.,* p. 536. Note also μήτι, *meti*, interrogative expecting the answer "No", and interrogative particle ἄρα, *ara*.

[3] Greek formula for swearing an oath, "As God is true".

[4] ἀρραβών, *arrabon*, "down payment". A standard business term dating from the 4th C. B.C. which speaks of the first installment of money, paid in advance, cf. *BGU* 2243.13 (1968), *SB* 10801.5 (III); F. Pringsheim, *The Greek Law of Sale*, (Weimar: Böhlaus, 1950), 333-429. Its metaphorical use is only attested to date in the New Testament. It occurs only elsewhere in 2 Cor, 5:5 and Eph. 1:14.

[5] ἐπὶ τὴν ἐμὴν ψυχήν, *epi ten emen psukhen*, idiom, "to stake one's life on it".

through many tears – my intention was not to upset you, but so that you'd know the abundant love which I have for you.

5-11 But if someone has caused sorrow – that person hasn't saddened me, but has in a way, not to exaggerate, caused all of you to be sad. *6* This penalty set down by the majority is enough for such a person! *7* Consequently, on the contrary, you should freely forgive and encourage the person; otherwise perhaps they will be overwhelmed with too much sorrow. *8* For this reason I encourage you to give the person a formal confirmation[1] of love. *9* To this end I'm also writing, so I would know whether you have stood up to the test, to see whether you are paying attention to everything I say. *10* Anyone who has your freely given forgiveness has mine too. That which I have forgiven – if indeed I have anything to forgive - I have done for your sake in the presence of the Anointed One, *11* so that we would not have Adversary claiming what isn't his due over us. We are not ignorant of his intentions!

12-13 When I arrived in Troas to preach the Good News of the Anointed One and where there was a door which had been opened for me by the Lord, *13* my spirit had no relief because I could not find Titus, my fellow believer. I said goodbye to them and went to Macedonia.

14-17 I thank God, who always leads us around as captives in the Anointed One's triumphal procession, and through us spreads the perfume of his knowledge in every place! *15* To God, we are the perfume of the Anointing, both for those who are on the way to salvation, and for those who are on the way to being ruined: *16* to one we are deadly perfume which leads to death, to the other living perfume which leads to life. And who can be adequate for such things? *17* For we are not, like so many, like so many, marketing God's word. Instead, we do it sincerely; we do it as we are from God, in the presence of God, and speaking with Anointed words.

Ch.3:1-3 Are we starting to recommend ourselves again? Utter rubbish![2] Do we need, like some do, letters of recommendation to you or from you? *2* Utter rubbish![3] You are our letter, which stands written on our hearts, realized and known for a fact by all people. *3* You are shown to be a letter of the Anointed One, provided by us, not written with ink but with the Spirit of the Living God, not on tablets of stone[4] but on tablets of natural hearts.

4-6 We make such claims in reliance on God through the Anointed One. *5* Not that we're adequate enough in ourselves to calculate that anything comes from us – rather, our adequacy comes from God. *6* He also made us adequate as ministers of a New Covenant – not of the written Law but of the Spirit, for the written Law puts to death, but the Spirit gives life.

---

[1] κυρόω, *kuroo*, "legally confirmed" also occurs in Gal.3:15. It appears at *I.Eph*. VI. 2054, "in accordance with the decree that was legally confirmed, (the city of Ephesos) honored the most illustrious city of the Knidians, their sister (city)". The compound verb, προκυπόω, *prokupoo*, "previously legally confirmed", occurs in Gal. 3:17: "And I tell you this – the Law, which came 430 years later, cannot annul the covenant that was previously legally confirmed in the presence of God by means of the Anointed One. This of course would make the promise invalid." The verb is found in an Ephesian decree concerning the distribution of water: "decrees which have been previously legally confirmed by the people". *I.Eph*. VI.2018 (4-14 A.D.). It also occurs twice in an inscription from Rhodes (II B.C.), which refers to matters laid down "in the previously legally confirmed decree". *SEG* 3 (1929) 674.28.

[2] Disjunctive particle.

[3] Disjunctive particle.

[4] A reference to the Law.

7-11 The ministry of death, written on stones, came with splendor, such splendor that the Israelites[1] could not keep their eyes on Moses because his face was so radiant. Although the splendor was destined to fade away, *8* how much more splendor has the ministry of the Spirit! *9* For since splendor accompanied the ministry of condemnation, far more excellent splendor accompanies the ministry of being right with God. *10* And in fact, what once had splendor no longer has any splendor at all, because of the splendor that has now outshone it. *11* If that which was destined to fade away had splendor, how much more splendor has that which remains!

12-16 So then, as we have such a hope as this, we use the right of freedom of speech and bold, open public speech, able to say what we like. *13* We're not like Moses, who used to put a veil over his face to keep the Israelites from gazing at that which was fading away until it was gone. *14* But their minds were callused. Until this very day the same veil is still there when the Old Covenant is read, because the Old Covenant is uncovered by means of the Anointed One. *15* Even to this day, whenever Moses is read, their minds are veiled. *16* But when someone turns to the Lord, the veil is removed.

17-18 Now the "Lord" mentioned here is the Spirit: where the Spirit of the Lord is, there is freedom. *18* All of us, as there is no veil over our face, reflect the Lord's splendor as in a mirror – we are being transformed into the same image, with more and more splendor, by the Spirit of the Lord.

Ch.4:1-2 On account of this - as we have this ministry and we've had mercy shown to us – we don't lose heart. *2* But we have renounced the things that people hide because they are ashamed of them, and we do not behave in a treacherous way, nor do we adulterate God's Word. Rather, it is by openly declaring the truth that we recommend ourselves to every person's conscience in the sight of God.

3-6 And if our Good News is veiled, it is veiled to those who are on the way to being undone, *4* whose minds the god of this present age has blinded, those who are unbelievers. He blinded them so that the light from the Good News about the splendor of the Anointed One, who is God's image, would not dawn on them. *5* It is not ourselves that we proclaim; rather we proclaim the Anointed One Jesus as Lord. We ourselves are your slave servants through Jesus. *6* In fact it is the same God who said, "Light will shine out of darkness!", who caused light to shine upon our minds, to give us the light of knowledge –knowledge about God's splendor in the presence of Jesus the Anointed One.

7-12 We are earthenware pots containing this treasure, and this shows that it comes from God and not from us. *8* We are oppressed in every way, but by no means at the end of our tether – we are at a loss, but by no means at our wits' end, *9* persecuted but not abandoned, rejected but not undone. *10* We always carry around the state of death of Jesus in our body - so that also the life Jesus lives would be clearly shown in our body. *11* For we who are living are always handed over to death on account of Jesus, so that the life Jesus lives may also be clearly shown in our natural mortal bodies. *12* Consequently death is at work in us, but living is at work in you.

13-15 As we have the same spirit of faith that the Scripture mentions, "I believed and therefore I spoke", we also believe, and therefore we also speak, *14* knowing that he who raised up the Lord Jesus will also raise us up with Jesus, and will bring you along with us to stand before him. *15* In fact everything is done for your sake, so that as God's favor is given out more and more, it may cause more people to give overflowing praise to God for his favor.

16-18 This is why we do not lose heart! Yes, our outer person is destroyed, yet the inward person is renewed on a daily basis. *17* Our oppressions are

---

[1]   υἱός, *huios*. See note on Luke 1:16.

lightweight and fleeting, but are conquering for us a most excessive degree of favor which lasts forever. *18* We do not keep our eyes on the things that are seen, but we keep our eyes on the things that are not seen – for the things that are seen are transient, but the things that are not seen are eternal.

Ch.5:1-5 We know that whenever our earthly house, which is this tent, is brought to an end, that we have a house from God, a house not made by hands, a house which lasts forever in the heavenly places. *2* And for a fact we groan for this, longing to put on our heavenly house, *3* so that once we've stripped off this body, we well and truly won't find ourselves in our underwear! *4* And in fact as we're in this tent we groan, as we're loaded down, because we don't want to strip off this body! Instead, we want to have on more clothes, so that our mortality can be encompassed by life. *5* It is God himself who has prepared us for this very thing, God who has given us the Spirit as down payment.

6-8 So then we can have confidence at all times, also knowing that while we're at home in the body we are away from home with the Lord. *7* We live[1] by faith and not by what we see. *8* We have confidence, and we would rather be away from home in the body, that is, at home at the Lord's.

9-10 For this reason too our driving ambition, whether away from home or at home, is to please the Lord. *10* We all must be seen for what we are before the Judgment Seat of the Anointed One. This is so that each one may receive what they deserve for their time spent in their body, in accordance with what they did, whether good or careless.

11-15 So then, as we know what it means to respect the Lord, we persuade people about him, and God knows us for what we are. And I hope that your consciences know you for what you are! *12* We are not recommending ourselves to you again, but we are giving you a base of operations to be proud about us, so that you would have an answer for those who are proud about someone's appearance and not about their mind. *13* For if we're out of our minds, it is for God that we're out of our minds - or if we are in the right mind, it is for you that we are in our right mind! *14* It is the Anointed One's love that holds us together! Indeed, we have reached the conclusion, that because One died for all of us, then all of us have died. *15* He died for everyone, so that those who live should no longer live for themselves, but should live for him who died and was raised up for them.

16-17 Consequently, from now on we don't estimate anyone on the basis of how they are in the natural realm. And although we did come to know the Anointed One on the basis of how he was in the natural realm, in point of fact we no longer know him on the basis of how he is in the natural realm. *17* And so, if someone is a follower of the Anointed One, they are a fresh creation: old things have passed away! Indeed, they have become new!

18-21 All things are from God, who has restored us to friendship with himself through the Anointed One. God has given us the ministry of restoring people to friendship with him. *19* That is to say, God restored the world to friendship with himself by means of the Anointed One, not holding people's blunders against them, and he entrusted us with the Message of restoration to friendship with him. *20* Therefore we are the Anointed One's ambassadors. It is as if God were encouraging you through us: on behalf of the Anointed One, we earnestly ask you to be restored to friendship with God! *21* God made the Anointed One who did not know sin become sin on our behalf, so that because of him we would become right with God!

Ch.6:1-2 We as God's fellow workers encourage you not to receive God's favor in vain. *2* He says, "In the acceptable time I listened to you, and in the

---

[1] περιπατέω, *peripateo*, to live, behave. The semantic range also includes the meanings to walk about (physically), to walk about while teaching and discoursing. "Walk by faith" is a mistranslation as it ignores semantic range.

day of salvation I helped you." Indeed, now is the acceptable time! Indeed, now is the day of salvation!

3-10 We in no way constitute an obstacle to you, and as a result our ministry will not be blamed! *4* But in all things we recommend ourselves as ministers of God – with much endurance, in oppressions, in necessities, in tight spots, *5* in physical blows, in prisons, in riots, in labors, in sleepless nights, in fasting, *6* with purity, with knowledge, with perseverance, with kindness, with the Holy Spirit, with uncritical love, *7* by means of the truthful Message, by means of God's power. We wield the foot soldiers' weapons[1] (the weapons being the state of being right with God) in our right hand as well as our left. *8* We do this whether we are being praised or dishonored, whether we have a bad reputation or a good reputation. We do this as those who wander off the right path[2] yet as those who are on the true path, *9* as unknown people yet fully known people, as dying people: yet take note! We live! We are educated[3] yet not put to death, *10* we are sad but always happy, we are poor but making many wealthy, we don't have anything yet we also possess everything.

11-13 Corinthians, we are completely open with you. We have opened our hearts to you. *12* Any constraint in our relationship is in your feelings, not ours. *13* So in return – I'm speaking to you as if you're children! – take your turn and you be open too!

14-18 Do not become yoked to unbelievers, like an animal that is yoked to an animal of another kind. Does justice have anything in common with illegal acts? Does light have any partnership with darkness? *15* Is the Anointed One in harmony with Belial? Does a believer have anything in common with an unbeliever? *16* Does the temple of God have any agreement with idols? Indeed we are the temple of the living God, as God said: "I will take up my home in them and walk among them. I will be their God, and they will be my people." *17* For this reason "Come out from among them and be separate", says the Lord, "And do not touch what is unclean, and I certainly will admit you. *18* And I will be a Father to you, and you shall be my sons and daughters", says the Lord Almighty.

Ch.7 So then as we have these promises, dearly loved friends, let us cleanse ourselves from all natural and spiritual pollution, thus performing an act of sacred worship out of respect for God.

2-4 Open up to us! We've wronged no one, we've ruined no one, we haven't claimed more than our share from anyone. *3* I'm really not saying this to accuse you – I have already said that you are in our hearts, in such a way that we are with you whether we die together or live together! *4* I am speaking frankly and freely to you! I have great reason to be proud of you. I am filled with encouragement. I am extremely happy throughout all our oppressions.

5-9 And in fact, when we arrived in Macedonia, we had no relief in the natural realm, but we were oppressed by everything – battles from the outside, fears on the inside! *6* But God, who encourages the downcast, encouraged us by the arrival of Titus, *7* and not just by his arrival, but also seeing how encouraged he was about you. He reported to us your longing, your grieving, your zeal for me, and that made me even happier.

8 Now if my letter made you unhappy, I don't regret it. I saw that the letter made you sad – although only for a while – *9* and now I'm happy, not because it made you sad, but because it was your sadness that led to you changing your

---

[1] The weapons of war carried by the foot soldier, not the weapons of Eph. 6:16.

[2] That is, those who are in error.

[3] παιδεύω, *paideuo*, the cognate verb of παιδεία, *paidea*. See note on Eph. 6:4.

minds. You were made sad, as God would have it, so that you would not sustain any loss because of us.

10-13 For Godly sadness brings about the changing of minds, which in turn leads to salvation – this sort of sadness is not regretted, unlike worldly sadness which produces death. *11* Now look at this very thing! You were sad with a godly sorrow and look how earnest it made you in dealing with the matter! What a speech in your defense you made! How severely irritated you were about the matter! What respect, longing and zeal you showed to me! What eagerness to see justice done you showed to the offender! You have shown yourselves to be free of blame in this matter! *12* So then, although I wrote to you, I didn't do it for the offender or for the victim, but I did it as I wanted you to realize, in God's sight, just how devoted you are to us. *13* That is why we have been encouraged.

13-16 In addition to our encouragement, we were even more delighted about Titus' own happiness, because you all have set his mind at rest. *14* My boasting about you to him has been justified –just as everything we said to you was true, even so our boasting about you to Titus was found to be true too. *15* And his heart goes out to you all the more as he remembers how compliant you all were, how you welcomed him earnestly and showed concern for him. *16* I am happy because I have every confidence in you.

Ch.8:1-7 Fellow believers, we must let you know about the gift God has given to the Macedonian assemblies. *2* They were oppressed, but came through the test with flying colors and they are extremely happy – although they were very poor, their wealth is now overflowing because they were generous to others.

3 Now I can testify that they did this voluntarily – they gave as much as they could afford, and in fact, they gave even more than they could afford. *4* They greatly urged us and earnestly requested us to accept the gift of partnership[1] they contributed to the people devoted to God. *5* Their giving was more than expected, as they gave their very selves to the Lord, and also to us, just as God wanted them to do. *6* This led us to encourage Titus, who began it all, to visit you and perform this act of worship among you with regard to this gift. *7* But just as you have abundance of everything – of faith and Word[2] and knowledge and all earnestness and of love for us – so too you have abundance because you have given this gift.

8-9 I'm not saying this as a divine command, but by telling you about the earnestness of others, I am seeing if your love passes the test as being for real. *9* I recognize our Lord Jesus the Anointed One's gift: he was wealthy yet he became financially poor for your sakes, so that because he became financially poor you could become wealthy.

10-15 And this is my advice in this matter and it's in your own interests: do this just as you did it in the first place last year. *11* You must perform this act of worship. Just as you eagerly intended to do it, so also you must actually perform this act of worship out of what you can afford. *12* Provided someone is eager to give, then God accepts the gift from what the person can afford – he doesn't ask for what the person cannot afford! *13* Now the purpose of this isn't so that others will have relief and you will have hardship – *14* at the present time your abundance meets their lack, so that one day their abundance will meet your lack, and the result will be equality. *15* Just as the Scriptures say: "The one who gathered much had nothing left over, and the one who gathered little had no lack."

16-19 I thank God that he has made Titus care as much about you as we do! *17* On the one hand Titus welcomed us urging him to visit you, and on the other hand he voluntarily visited you more eager than he was in the first place. *18* We have sent with him the fellow believer who is highly regarded

---

1   κοινωνία, *koinonia*. See note on Acts 2:42.
2   Equally, "speech".

for speaking about the Good News through all the assemblies. *19* Not only that, the assemblies appointed him to travel with us while we carry this gift which materially provides[1] for us while we eagerly honor the Lord himself.

20-22 We need to avoid any criticism over our financial handling of this generous gift. *21* We care about the right thing to do, not only in the sight of the Lord, but also in the sight of people. *22* With these people we have sent our fellow believer whom we have found to be most enthusiastic, and in point of fact he's even more enthusiastic because he is so confident about you.

23-24 If anyone wants to know about Titus, he is my partner[2] and fellow worker in dealings with you. If anyone wants to know about our fellow believers, they are delegates of our assemblies, and they have the glorious Anointing. *24* So then, demonstrate your love to them, and justify our pride about you through them to the assemblies.

Ch.9:1-2
Now about the contribution to the people devoted to God. It is superfluous for me to write to you about it, *2* as I know you are eager to contribute. In fact, I boast about this to the Macedonians, namely, that Achaia has been ready to contribute since last year, and your enthusiasm has stirred up most of them.

3-5 I sent the fellow believers so that our pride about you wouldn't prove to be in vain in this matter, so that, as I said, you would have the contribution ready. *4* Otherwise, if any Macedonians come with me and find you unprepared, we (and not to mention you!) would be disgraced over the confidence we have shown! *5* So then, I thought it necessary to encourage the fellow believers to go to you ahead of time to prearrange your generous gift that you promised beforehand. Then it will be ready as a blessing, rather than as something we claimed more than we should have.

6-9 But I will say this, that the person who sows sparingly will also harvest sparingly, and the person who sows liberally will also harvest liberally. *7* Each person is to give as they resolve in their hearts, with no sense of sadness or obligation - for God loves a cheerful giver. *8* God has the power to cause all kinds of gifts to overflow to you, so that you will be independently wealthy[3] in all things at all times, and will have much left over for every good work. *9* Just as the Scriptures say: "He dispersed his gifts around to the poor, his righteousness remains forever."

10 God who fully supplies every single expense, plus more,[4] to pay for the seed for the sower, and to pay for all the expenses[5] for bread to the eater, will

---

[1] διακονέω τινί, *diakoneo tini*. See note on Matt. 27:55.

[2] κοινωνός, *koinonos*. See note on Luke 5:7.

[3] αὐτάρκεια, *autarkeia*, "independently wealthy", cf. Arist. *Pol.* 1. 8, 14. αὐτάρκεια, *autarkeia*, was an important concept for the Greeks. Thucydides 1.37, 2.36, used it to describe Corcyra, a place which needed no help from others, supplied itself, needed no imports, needed no aid.

[4] ἐπιχορηγέω, *epikhoregeo*, ἐπί + χορηγέω, *epi* + *khoregeo*, fully supplies every expense, plus more. This term cannot be translated as "provides" or "supplies", two words which are a gross over-simplification of the actual meaning. The verb χορηγέω, *khoregeo*, (see following footnote) refers to the paying of all the expenses, every single one of them, and the ἐπί, *epi*, signifies that even additional expenses are paid.

[5] χορηγέω, *khoregeo*, "to pay for all the expenses", "to provide income", (see above note) is well attested in the papyri. See, for example, *P.Oxy.Hels.* 26.10, (13 June, 296) "...and since the death of my parents he has been providing us with income." Horsley states, "In *P.Oxy.Hels.* 26.10 the word χορηγέω, *khoregeo*, occurs with the same meaning as at 2 Cor. 9.10 and 1 Pet. 4.11; it is already well attested in MM." *NDIEC* 4.104. It occurs elsewhere in the N.T. only in 1 Pet. 4:11.

supply all the expenses to pay for, as well as multiply, the seed you sow, and make the crops of your righteousness grow!

11-15 You will be made rich in every way and you will be able to be generous. Such generosity will result in God being thanked, through our action. *12* This public service, that is, the giving of the contribution, doesn't only supply the shortages of God's people, it also results in abundant gratitude being given to God. *13* Through the evidence of this contribution, people praise God as they see your support of and agreement with the Good News of the Anointed One, that is, your generous partnership with them and with everyone. *14* They are praying earnestly for you and they look forward to seeing you, because of the exceedingly over-abundant favor God has given you. *15* Thank God for his indescribable free gift!

Ch.10:1-6 I myself, Paul, encourage you through the gentleness and kindness of the Anointed One – face to face I'm humble with you, but in my absence I'm confident among you! *2* But I earnestly ask that when I'm present with you, I won't have to use the confident self-assurance which I rely on for standing up to certain people, those people who treat us as if we were merely acting out our lives in the natural realm! *3* For although we do actually act out our lives in the natural realm we do not serve as a soldier (on active service) dictated to by the natural realm!

4 For the foot soldiers' weapons of our military campaign are not natural weapons. Indeed, our weapons are divinely powerful for the purpose of destroying strongholds, *5* destroying calculations and destroying the heights of enemy defenses that are raised up against people who are coming to know God. *6* These weapons take all your thoughts as prisoners of war so that you can pay attention to the Anointed One. In fact, we are in a state of readiness to take vengeance on every unwillingness to listen, once you have committed to paying attention.[1]

7 You were only seeing the things that are staring you right in the face! If anyone has convinced themselves that they are the Anointed One's, then let them go further and calculate this fact for themselves - that just as they are the Anointed One's, so we too are the Anointed One's!

8-11 In fact even if I should boast abundantly more about our authority, which the Lord gave for your building up and not for your destruction, I will not be put to shame! *9* Otherwise it seems, as it were, that I frighten you away by my letters! *10* Someone is saying, "His letters are heavy and strong, but in person he's unimpressive and as a speaker he doesn't amount to much!" *11* Let this individual calculate this – that when we arrive, we will be the very same people in action as we were in writing!

12-18 Now we don't dare put ourselves in the same class, or compare ourselves with those who recommend themselves! In measuring themselves by their own standards and comparing themselves with themselves, they're showing that they're not very bright! *13* We, however, do not intend to boast beyond what we should, but we will boast within the field which God allocated to us – a field which includes you. *14* In fact we are not overextending ourselves, as if we didn't reach as far as you – we were the first to come to you with the Good News about the Anointed One.

15 We're not boasting about things beyond what we should, that is to say, we are not boasting about other people's work. Rather, we hold the hope that as your faith grows, our proper allocation will be greatly magnified to a vast extent among you, *16* even to the point of us spreading the Good News to regions beyond you. Of course we wouldn't boast about work done in someone else's allocation of places where the Good News has already been announced. *17* "The person who boasts, let them boast about the Lord." *18* The person who

---

[1] ὑπακοή, *hupakoe*. See note on Rom. 1:5.

recommends themselves isn't approved, but the person whom the Lord recommends does!

Ch.11:1-2 Now if only you would put up with a little bit of foolishness from me – no, you must put up with it! *2* I am jealous about you and my jealousy is godly. I have promised you to a single husband, the Anointed One, so that I might present you as a pure unmarried girl to him.

3-6 I am afraid that, just as the snake beguiled Eve with his treachery, so might your minds be corrupted and turned away from the simplicity to be found in matters pertaining to the Anointed One. *4* Now if the snake comes and proclaims a Jesus other than the One we proclaimed, or if you take hold of a spirit other than the One you took hold of, or a different Good News from the one you welcomed – well, you manage to do that easily enough! *5* Now I calculate that I'm in no way inferior to these super-apostles! *6* If indeed I an amateur in speech, I am certainly not an amateur in knowledge! To the contrary, we have made that clear to you in every respect!

7-11 Did I commit a sin in lowering myself so that you would be exalted, announcing the Good News among you free of charge? *8* I "robbed" other assemblies, taking supplies and salary from them to minister to you. *9* And when I was present with you and needed things, I was a burden to no one – the fellow believers from Macedonia replenished what I needed, with extra. And in all ways I kept myself from being a burden to you, and I will continue to do so. *10* As surely as the truth of the Anointed One is in me, I will not be stifled from boasting in this matter throughout the territories of Achaia! *11* Why is this? Because I don't love you? God knows I do!

12-15 But what I am doing, I will keep on doing, to cut the ground from under the feet of those who want a base of operations. They do this in order to be found the same as us in the matters about which they are proud. *13* Such ones are fake apostles, workers of cunning deceit, changing their form[1] into apostles of the Anointed One. *14* And it's not surprising! Adversary himself changes his form into a Messenger of light! *15* So then it's no major thing for his ministers also to change their form into righteous ministers! They will get what they deserve for their actions!

16-21 I'm telling you again – let no one take me for a fool! If you really must, then welcome me as a fool so that I can do a little bit of boasting! *17* What I'm saying, I'm not saying as a follower of the Lord, but I'm speaking foolishly with the confidence that comes from boasting. *18* Since many boast about what they have done in the natural realm, I will too! *19* You happily put up with fools seeing that you're so wise![2] *20* You put up with it if someone reduces you to bondage, if someone preys on you, if someone gets you in their clutches, if someone is conceited, if someone belts you across the face! *21* And we were too weak to do that– what a dishonor, I say!

21-29 If someone is presumptuous, then I can indulge in it too! (I am speaking foolishly!) *22* Are they Hebrews? So am I! Are they descendants of Abraham? So am I! *23* Are they ministers of the Anointed One? So am I! I speak like a madman – I surpass them! More excessively hardworking, more excessively imprisoned, far more beaten up, many times faced with death!

24 5 times the Jews have given me 39 lashes. *25* 3 times I was beaten with rods, once I was stoned, 3 times I was shipwrecked, for 24 hours I was in the open sea. *26* I have been constantly on the road, I have been in danger from

---

[1] μετασχηματίζω, *metaskhematizo*, classical word. Occurs in Plato and Aristotle, also occurs in early Byzantine times. Used by Plato for the changing of the form of a metaphor in *Legg.* 906 C. *IGA* 5.587 = *SB* 5.3.8701 (Philai, VI), speaking of the changing of a temple of Isis into a church, states, "Theodorus, bishop, transformed this temple into the place of St. Stephen, for good, by the Anointed One's power."

[2] Paul is having a sarcastic dig at the Corinthians.

rivers, in danger from robbers, in danger from my own people, in danger from those who worship other gods, in dangers in the city, in dangers in deserted places, in dangers in the sea, in dangers among fake believers. *27* I have worked hard work and labored heavily, been sleepless often, been hungry and thirsty often, have fasted often, have been cold and lacked clothes. *28* Apart from everything else, my daily preoccupation is care for all the assemblies. *29* If anyone is weak, do I not share their weakness? If anyone is falls into a trap, do I not burn up with indignation about it?

30-33 If I must boast, I will boast about the things that show up my weakness![1] *31* The God and Father of our Lord Jesus knows – let him be praised forever! – that I am not lying. *32* In Damascus, the governor under Aretas the king was guarding the city of the Damascenes with a garrison so that he could arrest me, *33* but I was lowered in a basket through a window in a wall, and escaped from him.

Ch.12:1-5 It is necessary to boast – really there is no advantage in it, but on the other hand I will speak about visions and revelations given to me by the Lord. *2* I know a person, a follower of the Anointed One, who 14 years ago – whether in the body, I do not know, or out of the body, I do not know, God knows – this person was seized and carried off as far as a third heaven. *3* And I know how such a person – whether in the body or out of the body I do not know, God knows – *4* was seized and carried off to Paradise[2] and heard spoken words which were secret and forbidden to be spoken, spoken words which it is not permitted for a person to utter. *5* I will boast about such a person, but I will not boast about myself, unless I boast about my weaknesses.

6-10 Now although I would like to boast, it wouldn't be the boast of a fool – I will speak the truth. But I will restrain myself, as I would not like anyone to form an opinion of me beyond what they see or hear of me – and this applies too to the exceptional nature of my revelations. *7* For this reason, so that I wouldn't exalt myself, a prickle[3] was assigned to me in the natural realm, a Satanic Messenger, to give me a good thrashing, the result being that I didn't exalt myself. *8* Concerning the Satanic Messenger, I urged the Lord three times to make it keep away from me. *9* And he has said to me, "My favor keeps it away from you![4] Power[5] in the spirit comes to maturity by means of not being able in the natural!"

   10 For this reason I am well pleased with weaknesses, with acts of insolence, with constraints, with harassment, with tight spots, all on behalf of the Anointed One. For whenever I am not able (weak in the natural), then I am able (powerful in the spirit)![6]

11-13 I have become foolish! You drove me to it! Instead I should have been commended by you. In no way was I inferior even to the "super-apostles", though I myself am nothing. *12* Now it's a fact that I accomplished the miraculous signs of an apostle among you – work which called for endurance - miraculous signs as well as wonders and powers. *13* In what way

---

[1]   Paul is still being sarcastic.
[2]   παράδεισος, *paradeisos*. See note on Luke 23:43.
[3]   σκόλοπος, *skolopos*, prickle, splinter, thorn, anything pointed, a stake used for impaling.
[4]   ἀρκέω, *arkeo*, like Latin *arceo*, "to ward off", "to keep off", with dative of person, accusative of thing. Paul elsewhere frequently uses the word ἱκανός, *hikanos*, for "sufficient", "enough".
[5]   Not "My power" not "My strength".
[6]   "Not being able" in verses 8 and 9 is ἀσθενέω, *astheneo*, which also means "to be weak". Paul is playing on words again here, as the word for powerful, δύναμις, *dunamis*, also means to be able. Paul marks the contrast between being able and not being able rather than the contrast in being weak as opposed to powerful.

were you inferior to other assemblies, except that I myself wasn't a burden to you? How unfair of me! Please forgive me![1]

14-18 For the third time I'm ready to visit you,[2] and I won't be a burden to you. I'm not after what's yours, it is you I want! The children shouldn't make deposits into the bank for their parents, but the parents should for their children! *15* I will certainly gladly spend for you - and be spent for you! Yet if I love you excessively, am I to be loved less? *16* But be that as it may, I myself certainly did not burden you! Yet you say I made a start at being treacherous, and took you in by cunning deceit! *17* I certainly haven't taken advantage of you through any of the people I've sent to you, have I! *18* I urged Titus to go to you and I sent our fellow believer along with him. Surely Titus didn't take advantage of you, did he! Haven't our lives been guided by the same Spirit? Haven't we followed the same trail?

19-21 For ages you've been thinking that we have been addressing our defense to you! We speak in God's presence as followers of the Anointed One. All things, dearly loved ones, are to build you up.

20 I'm afraid that when I arrive, I won't find you as I want you to be, and you might find me different from what you wish. I fear I may find rivalry, jealousy, outbursts of anger, selfish ambition, acts of speaking the wrong things, gossiping, conceits, disturbances. *21* I'm afraid that when I come again, God will humble me in front of you, and I will mourn for many who continue in their former sins and have not changed their ways of their uncleanness, *porneia*,[3] and vice which they practiced.

Ch.13:1-4 This will be my third visit to you. "By the mouth of two or three witnesses, every spoken word will be confirmed." *2* I have told those of you who continue to sin as they did formerly, and all the rest of you when I was present on my second visit, and I repeat it now in my absence, that when I come again I will not be lenient, *3* since you seek evidence of the Anointed One speaking through me. The Anointed One is not weak with you, but makes his power known among you. *4* The Anointed One was weak when he was crucified, but he is alive by means of God's power. We who are weak in company with him - we will show you that we ourselves are very much alive in company with him by means of God's power.

5-6 Put yourselves to the test to see whether you are living the life of faith, examine yourselves! Or don't you fully understand that Jesus the Anointed One is among you? – unless, that is, in some way you are not up to what's called for! *6* I do hope that you will come to realize that we are up to what's called for!

7-9 We put our claim[4] to God that you won't do anything wrong - not so that we might be vindicated, but so that you would do what is right, even though we might seem to have been discredited. *8* We have no power to act against the truth, but only for it. *9* We are happy to be weak at any time, as long as you are strong. And we also put our claim to God that you will be completely equipped.

10 My purpose in writing this while I am absent is so that when I am present I won't need to deal with you severely with the authority the Lord gave me – authority for building up and not for pulling down.

11-13 Finally, fellow believers, be happy! Mend your ways! Encourage each other! Be of the same mind! Live at peace! May the God of love and peace be with you! *12* Greet each other with a sacred kiss. All the people devoted to God greet you. *13* May the favor of the Lord Jesus the Anointed One and the love of God and the partnership of the Holy Spirit be with you all!

---

[1] More sarcasm.

[2] During his third visit, Paul wrote his letter to the Romans.

[3] See note on Matthew 15:19.

[4] εὔχομαι, *eukhomai*, the verb of εὐχή, *eukhe*, "claim", not "prayer". See note on Acts 18:18. Accusative and infinitive construction, as in 3 John 2.

Letter to the Galatians.

The letter to the Galatians was written c. 48 AD by Paul. It is his first extant letter, written to the assemblies of southern Galatia soon after his return from the regions described in Acts 13-14. Paul and Barnabas traveled to the non Jews, to Galatia, where they established assemblies and declared that circumcision was not necessary for non Jewish believers. Some Jewish believers tried to overturn this, and Paul was also concerned that Peter and Barnabas had decided not to eat with non Jewish believers. His letter to the Galatians addresses these concerns. Paul is complaining that the Galatians have so quickly turned away from the Good News which was preached to them. It was only a matter of months after Paul's return to Antioch that the problems were reported.

Central to the dating of Paul's ministry is the reference in Acts 18:12-17 to his trial before Gallio in Corinth. Gallio's year as Proconsul was from July 1, 51 AD, to June 30, 52 AD.[1] Gallio was a Senate-appointed Proconsul in a civilian province, and these are the dates for the standard one year appointment. Paul's arrival in Corinth is dated to the latter part of 50 AD, and this is corroborated by the arrival of Priscilla and Aquila, who had been expelled along with other Jews from Italy by Claudius in 49 AD.[2] Acts 18:1-5 states, "After this Paul left Athens and went away to Corinth. And he found a certain Jew by the name of Aquila, who was born in Pontus. He had recently come from Italy with his wife Priscilla, because Claudius had ordered all the Jews to leave Rome. Paul went to see them. And because he was of the same craft - they were tentmakers by trade - he stayed with them and worked." Acts 18:11 states, "He stayed there for a year and six months, teaching God's Word among them." Paul's ministry is thus established at Corinth in 50-52 AD.

Galatians, as is clear from the context, was written prior to the council at Jerusalem of Acts 15. Paul makes no mention of the council's decision. Further, Galatians 2:1 says Paul visited Jerusalem "again", "fourteen years later" with Barnabas and Titus. This corresponds with Acts 11:30, the previous visit being Acts 9:26. Paul states that this was three years after his conversion. Paul's mention of years could be inclusive. Acts 19:8, 10 states that Paul's time in Ephesos was 2 years 3 months, yet Paul describes this period in Acts 20:31 as "three years". The above chronology places Paul's conversion at c. 34 AD; visits to Damascus, Arabia, Damascus at 34-36AD; first Jerusalem visit, 36AD; Syria, Cilicia, 36/37AD; Antioch-on-the-Orontes, 44AD; second visit to Jerusalem, 47AD; Cyprus, Galatia, 47-49AD; third visit to Jerusalem (the council decision), 49AD; Macedonia, Corinth, trial before Gallio (51-52AD), 49-52AD.

Galatia was a rural province whose main products were wool and cereals. The cities were isolated and small, but Galatia had numerous large country estates owned by families. The largest city was Ankyra, followed by Antioch by Pisidia and Iconium. The cities were linked by Roman roads. A Latin inscription discovered in the 1980s describes the system of the Roman roads linking the colonies of Pisidia with the cities on the Pamphylian coast. The Roman province of Galatia was formed under Augustus in 25 BC. Under Augustus, the governors were of praetorian or consular rank, but from Tiberius they were praetorians. Vespasian appointed consular legates with a praetorian assistant. Augustus was keen to promote the Imperial cult in Galatia, and commenced work on the Temple of Rome and Augustus at Ankyra (completed c. 19/20 AD).

---

[1]   As shown by inscription at Delphi.
[2]   Suetonius, *Claudius*, 25.

Letter to the Galatians.

Ch.1:1-2 From: Paul, an apostle (appointed not by people, not by their efforts, but by Jesus the Anointed One and God the Father who raised him from among the dead), *2* and from all the fellow believers[1] who are with me.

To: The assemblies in Galatia.

3-5 Favor and peace to you from God our Father and the Lord Jesus the Anointed One! *4* He offered himself in the place of our sins, just as our God and Father planned, so that he could carry us out of this present evil age! *5* May God be honored forever and ever, amen!

6-9 I am shocked that you are turning away so soon from God, who showed you favor by inviting you, and turning to a fake Good News! *7* There isn't another Good News, but instead some people are getting you all mixed up. They want to throw the Anointed One's Good News into disorder! *8* Now if ever we or a Messenger from heaven should preach[2] a so-called Good News other than the Good News which we have preached, they will be cursed![3] *9* As we have already said, we will now repeat: if anyone preaches a Good News to you other than the one you received, they will be cursed!

10 Am I trying to win over people or God? Do you imagine I am trying to please people? If I cared about what people think, I wouldn't be a slave servant of the Anointed One!

11-12 Now, fellow believers, I want you to realize that the Good News which I preached isn't a human one, *12* nor did I receive it by way of human instruction. I received it through revelation from Jesus the Anointed One.

13-17 You have heard about my way of life when I was a practicing Jew, how I went to the extreme in persecuting God's assembly and tried to destroy it. *14* And I progressed further in Judaism than many of my own people in my age group. In fact, right from the start I was most zealous about the traditional teachings of our ancestors. *15* But it seemed good to God (who, due to his favor upon me, selected me from my mother's womb and invited me) *16* to reveal his Son to me and through me, so that I would preach about him among the non-Jews. When this happened I did not consult with flesh and blood, *17* nor did I go up to Jerusalem to those who had been apostles before me. Instead, I immediately went to Arabia, and then I went back to Damascus.

18-24 Then three years later I went up to Jerusalem to see Cephas (Peter) and stayed with him for fifteen days. *19* But I didn't see any of the other apostles except James, the Lord's brother. *20* Now about these things I'm writing to you, let me tell you this: before God, I'm not lying! *21* Afterwards I went to the Syrian and Cilician territories. *22* My face was unknown to the Judean assemblies, followers of the Anointed One. *23* They knew me only by reputation: "The one who persecuted us now preaches the faith he once tried to destroy!" *24* And they kept praising God because of me.

Ch.2:1-3 Then fourteen years later I went up to Jerusalem again with Barnabas: I took Titus along too. *2* Now I went up as a result of revelation. And I imparted the Good News which I preach among the non-Jews in private to those who were held in high regard, so that my future efforts, as well as my past efforts, would not be in vain. *3* By the way, they did not even pressure Titus who was with me, and a Greek, to be circumcised!

---

[1] ἀδελφοί, *adelphoi*. See note on Matt. 5:22.

[2] εὐαγγελίζομαι, *euaggelizomai*, "preach". Philo (G. Friedrich, *TDNT* 2 (1964) 737) has 3 occurrences, 2 of which are noted by MM. The word is used by a scholiast to Sophocles, *Trachiniae*, which indicates it is not confined to Jewish writers.

[3] ἀνάθεμα, *anathema*. See note on καταράομαι, *kataraomai*, in Luke 6:28. "Cursed", not "outcast" or "eternally condemned".

4-6 I had to speak to them in private because of the undercover[1] fake fellow believers who were inserted[2] to spy[3] on the freedom that we have in Jesus' Anointing. Their intention was to reduce us to bondage. *5* We did not give them any support even for a moment, so that the truth of the Good News would hold its ground with you. *6* As for those who were held in high regard – and I couldn't care less, it makes no difference to me! God doesn't show personal favoritism to anyone! – they did not impose any conditions upon me.

7-10 On the contrary, they saw that I had been entrusted with the Good News for the uncircumcised (non-Jews), just as Peter had been entrusted with the Good News for the circumcised (Jews). *8* God had assisted Peter in his mission to the circumcised (Jews) just as he also assisted me with the non-Jews. *9* When James, Cephas (Peter) and John, who seemed to be the main supporters,[4] recognized the favor that had been given to me, they shook hands with me and Barnabas in token of our partnership. As a result, we were to go to the non-Jews and they to the circumcised (Jews). *10* All they said was that we must give funds to the people who were financially destitute, the very thing that I was most eager to do too.

11-13 Now when Cephas (Peter) arrived in Antioch,[5] I opposed him to his face as he was at fault. *12* Before the arrival of certain people sent by James, he would eat with the non-Jews, but when they arrived, he made a move to get away from them and keep away from them, as he was afraid of the group who were circumcised (Jews). *13* And the rest of the Jews joined in his legalistic type of behavior, to the point that even Barnabas was actually carried away with it too![6]

14-16 But when I saw that they weren't on the right road[7] to the truth about the Good News, I said to Peter in front of all of them, "Since you, a Jew, live like the non-Jews and not like the Jews, how can you put pressure on non-Jews to live like Jews?" *15* We are Jews by birth and not non-Jewish sinners! *16* We know that a person does not become right with God by acts of law but rather through faith in Jesus the Anointed One. And we know that we believed the Anointed One Jesus. This means that we are made right with God on the basis of faith in the Anointed One rather than on the basis of doing what the

---

[1] παρεισάκτος, *pareisaktos*, adjective, "undercover". Occurs only here in the N.T. Uncommon word. This was a nickname of Ptolemy XI. (Strabo, 17.1.8.) For the cognate verb, παρεισάγω, *pereisago*, see *P.Tor.* I. I. 8.4 where it occurs as "introduce" of persons to a public assembly without the sense of stealth. It occurs with the sense of stealth in Polybius 1.18.3; 2.7.8.

[2] παρεισῆλθον, *pareiselthon*, to be inserted. Uncommon word. Used by the medical writers. Occurs both with and without the idea of stealth. For the corresponding double compound παρεξέρχομαι, *parekserkhomai*, see *P.Lond.* 1075.17.

[3] κατασκοπέω, *kataskopeo*, to spy. See *P.Oxy* 7.1414; *BGU* 3.846. The form κατασκοπεύω, *kataskopeuo*, occurs in the LXX: for this form see *P.Tebt* 1.230.

[4] στῦλοι, *stuloi*, "pillars/columns (as supports)", metaphorically, "main supporters". The metaphorical use is common.

[5] That is, Peter arrived at Antioch in Syria (Antioch-on-the-Orontes, modern Antakya), not Antioch by Pisidia. Antioch in Roman Syria was 300 miles north of Jerusalem and situated on a major trade route at the junction of the Lebanon Mountains and Taurus Mountains. It was built partly on an island and partly on the banks of Mount Silpius, 15 miles inland from the Mediterranean Sea. Antioch in Syria was founded c. 300 BC by Seleucus I Nicator, one of Alexander the Great's generals, and named after his father Antiochus.

[6] There was alarm that Paul was preaching a circumcision-free Good News to the non-Jews. However these people were actually trying to convert non-Jewish Christians to the Jewish culture.

[7] ὀρθοποδέω, *orthopodeo*. See Zerwick and Grosvenor, *op.cit.,* 567, for recent evidence on this word. Until the two recent discoveries mentioned, ὀρθοποδέω, *orthopodeo*, had not been attested outside its use here.

Law says. Nothing of the natural realm will be made right with God on the basis of doing what the Law says.

17-21 But if we seek to be made right with God by the Anointed One, and thus are discovered to be sinners against the Law, would you say the Anointed One is a minister of sin? Certainly not! *18* For if I[1] reconstruct the legalism I have demolished, I show myself up as a sinner. *19* Through the Law I was led to have nothing more to do with legalism and instead to live for God. *20* I have been crucified with the Anointed One and died to legalism: that is to say, it is no longer I that live, but the Anointed One who lives in me. The life I now live in the natural realm, I live by means of faith in the Son of God who loved me and gave himself for me. *21* I do not invalidate God's favor. If being made right with God comes by way of legalism, then the Anointed One was crucified for nothing!

Ch.3:1-6 You senseless Galatians, who has cast a spell on you by using the evil eye![2] Before your very eyes[3] Jesus the Anointed One was publicly announced as crucified! *2* This is the only thing I want to learn from you: did you take hold of the Spirit by legalistic acts or by hearing and believing? *3* Why are you so senseless? You started with the spiritual; do you intend to finish with the natural? *4* Have you experienced so much for nothing? Was it really for nothing?

5 God fully supplies every single necessity, plus more, to supply the Spirit for you, and is active doing miracles and powerful things among you. Does this happen by legalistic acts or by hearing and believing? *6* In the same way, "Abraham believed God, and God calculated that by doing this Abraham was made right with God."

---

[1] Paul using 1st person for "anyone". He resumes the true 1st person in the next sentence, marked by ἐγώ, *ego.*

[2] βασκαίνω, *baskaino*, to use words to cast a spell on someone by means of the evil eye, causing illness, death, crop failure, delays, bad luck, any sort of trouble, or less commonly, allowing influence over the victim. (Frederick Thomas Elworthy's 1895 work, *The Evil Eye*, p.5, notes that Gal. 3:1 means that the evil eye has "overlooked" someone and worked on them a blighting influence.) Occurs only here in the N.T. yet does occur in the O.T. Proverbs 23:6-8 (in Hebrew) states, "Do not eat the food of a person who has the evil eye, do not crave their delicacies, for they are like someone calculating in their soul. You will vomit up the little bit you have eaten." (Most translations mistranslate "the evil eye" as "stingy".) The LXX of Prov. 23:6 has the same word as here in Galatians, βασκαίνω, *baskaino.*

Generally the evil eye was caused by jealousy, and the person responsible for putting the evil eye on someone could do so unaware, or deliberately. The ancient belief is continued today into many cultures, not all of which believe the evil eye can be cast deliberately. (Latin equivalent, *fascinare*, "to ward off the evil eye", "to cast a spell".) Some believed that the spell was broken by spitting three times, cf. Theokritos, VI, 35-40. A 3rd century A.D. stone inscription tells of the effects upon one who testifies to having the evil eye put on them, with the result that his wife and children were killed, *CIG* 9668. A funerary epigram for Apollodorus, Pfuhl/Mobius 1.1021, describes Hades as casting his evil eye upon honorable things. An amulet described by J. Russell, *JOB* 32 (1982) 539-548 has the wording "the seal of Solomon holds in check the evil eye." See also the early 1st c. inscription, *IG VII* 581.5 (Megara), which alludes to the pagan god Hades' jealousy of mortals who have higher thoughts; *I.Kret* 2.3.44 (Aptera, III AD), of a husband lamenting that the evil eye was put on him and thus his wife died; and *TAM* 3.1.810.8 (Termessos, II-III AD), an epitaph in which it states that fate cast her evil eye on the deceased.

[3] Paul makes a play on the word "eye/s", which he continues in the next chapter. Paul loves to play on words, a fact easily seen in the Greek, far less so in English.

7-9 You must realize that everyone who has faith is a child[1] of Abraham. *8* God was to make the non-Jews right with him through faith. The Scriptures made provision for this, with God announcing the news to Abraham beforehand: "All the non-Jews will be happy because of you!" *9* As a result, everyone who has faith is in a blessed state, in company with Abraham who had faith.

10-12 Everyone who is under bondage to acts of legalism is under a curse,[2] for the Scriptures say, "Everyone who does not practice everything written in the Book of the Law is doubly cursed." *11* It is clear that no one can be made right with God[3] by legalism. The Scriptures say, "Those who are right with God will live by means of faith." *12* On the contrary the law states, "The person who keeps the laws must live by these laws."

13-15 The Anointed One paid the price to remove us from the curse[4] of the Law. He became a curse[5] instead of us, as the Scriptures say, "Doubly cursed[6] is everyone who hangs on a cross." *14* He did this so Abraham's blessing would be extended, by means of the Anointed One Jesus, to the non-Jews. Consequently, through faith we are all able to have the promised Spirit. *15* Fellow believers, let me phrase it in the technical terms of human legal practice:

---

[1]   υἱός, *huios*, was used interchangeably with τέκνον, *teknon*. υἱός, *huios*, was traditionally translated in Bible versions as "sons". However, the Greek word *huios* means a child of either gender. τέκνον, *teknon*, is also used in the context of heirs in Mark 12:19; Luke 1:7, 15:31; Acts 7:5. Paul says in Romans 8:14-21: "For all those people who are being led by the Spirit of God, these and none but these are the *huioi* of God. For you did not again take hold of a spirit of slavery to fear, but you did take hold of a spirit of adoption (*huiothesia*) by which we bawl out aloud, "Dad, Father." The Spirit himself jointly gives witness with our spirit that we are God's *tekna*. Since we are *tekna*, we are also heirs. On the one hand we are God's heirs, and on the other hand we are joint-heirs with the Anointed One ...The creation looks forward with eager expectation to God's *huioi* being revealed. ...Yet there was the hope that creation itself also would be set free from slavery to decay, and have the glorious freedom of God's *tekna*."

[2]   κατάρα, *katara*, a compound of ἀρά, *ara*. κατάρα, *katara*, is literally to put a curse on one, not to be confused with "cursing" as in foul language. ἀρά (*ara*) or ἀραοῖς (*araois*) generally means "laden with a curse or curses", "cursed", "cursing". ἀρά, *ara*, is used of a prayer (to pagan gods either for good, cf. Aesch. Cho. 138, or more commonly, for bad). Its primary meaning is "curse", and was the word used for the curse on Oedipus in Aeschylus, *Theb.* 70. It can also mean "ruin", and ἀρά, *ara*, is personified as the goddess of destruction and revenge.

κατάράομαι, *kataraomai*, is the cognate verb of κατάρα, *katara*. It occurs, for example, in the LXX of Zech. 5.2-4, "He shall be answerable to the Most High God and may the curse's (τὸ ἀράς, *to aras*) sickle enter his house and leave no one behind." Another tomb warning, *MAMA* 6.335 states, "Such a person shall be doubly cursed (ἐπικατάρατος, *epikataratos*) and may whatever curses (ἀραί, *arai*) stand written in Deuteronomy come upon him and his children and his descendants and his entire family." The same word, ἐπικατάρατος, *epikataratos*, is used in Gal. 3:10, "Doubly cursed is everyone..." and 10:13, "Doubly cursed is everyone who hangs on a tree."

2 other words for "curse" are ἀνάθεμα and κατάθεμα (*anathema* and *katathema*) which occurs only once in the N.T. in Rev. 22:3. Both are used on a tomb warning in a 5th c. marble stele found in a church: *ed. pr.* M. Hatzidakis, *AD* 29 (1973/4 [1979]) *Chron.* 194. It is clear that ἀνάθεμα, *anathema*, was a curse, although a curse which differed in some way from κατάθεμα, *katathema*.

[3]   Also possible, "claims their rights".

[4]   κατάρα, *katara*. See note on Galatians 3:10.

[5]   κατάρα, *katara*. See note on Galatians 3:10.

[6]   ἐπικατάρατος, *epikataratos*, used in verse 10, above.

for all that, a Will and Testament Deed of Gift[1] has been legally confirmed, and no one can annul it or add a codicil to it.

16-18 Now it was to Abraham and his descendant that the promises were spoken. It did not say, "And to your descendants" as if it were referring to many descendants, but it spoke of a single descendant only, "And to your descendant," and that's the Anointed One! *17* And I tell you this: the Law, which came 430 years later, cannot annul the Covenant Deed of Gift that was previously legally confirmed[2] with Abraham in God's presence. This of course would break God's promise. *18* The inheritance cannot be based on both Law and promise. We know it is based on promise as God gave it to Abraham as a promise.

19-20 So then, what is the point of the Law? The breaking of laws necessitated the institution of the Law. It was meant to last until the arrival of the descendant, to whom the promise was made. And the Law was established through Messengers by means of a mediator.[3] *20* But a mediator is not needed for one party acting alone, and God is one.[4]

21-22 So then, is the Law against the promises of God? Certainly not! If the Law had been able to give life, then the Law would have resulted in people being made right with God. *22* But Scripture has enclosed everything by sin, so that faith in Jesus the Anointed One results in us being made right with God: the promise is given to those who believe.

---

[1]   This is a most significant and interesting statement. διαθήκη, *diatheke*, is usually translated "Testament" but is used in the New Testament as "Covenant". Paul uses the term here in this verse. In Greek and Roman law, a Will and Testament was not irrevocable: anyone could annul it or add a codicil to it. Note that Paul says he speaking here of a human διαθήκη, *diatheke*. In Greek speaking Jewish communities (it was possibly more widespread but there is as yet insufficient evidence) there was a transaction comparable to the *matenath bari* which was irrevocable, and denoted by the term διαθήκη, *diatheke*. The deed is also subject to public registration (and note Paul's use of the legal terms κεκυρωμένων, *kekuromenon*, ἀθετέω, *atheteo*, and ἐπιδιατάσσομαι, *epidiatassomai*, in this verse). Rabban Simon b. Gamaliel (*t. B. Bat.* 9.14) states, "He who writes *diethemen* in Greek, behold, this is a Gift." In fact, the Jewish Deed of Gift when written in Greek used "διαθήκη, *diatheke*". Greek speaking Jewish communities called the Will and Testament Deed of Gift a διαθήκη, *diatheke*: for example, *P. Yadin* 19, a Deed of Gift in Greek from Palestine (witnessed in Aramaic) by Judah, son of Elazar Khthousin, for his daughter Shelamzious. It has the terms used by Paul in Gal. 3:15: κεκυρωμένων, *kekuromenon*, ἀθετέω, *atheteo*, and ἐπιδιατάσσομαι, *epidiatassomai*, cf. *P.Yadin* 19 (AD 128) = N. Lewis, Y. Yadin and C. Greenfield, *The Documents from the Bar Kobba Period in the Cave of Letters* (Jerusalem, 1989).

The διαθήκη, *diatheke*, Deed of Gift, was a Jewish procedure from inheritance law which evolved in the Greek speaking communities of Palestine and the *diaspora*. The term to those used to Greek and Roman law could also mean Will and Testament, thus Paul's audience would not have a problem: at any rate, he does explain the term.

[2]   προκυπόω, *prokupoo*, "previously legally confirmed", only here in the N.T. προκυπόω, *prokupoo*, in this instance is in the aorist passive participle. It is not a "deponent". MM does not give an illustration of the verb. It is found in an Ephesian decree concerning the distribution of water: "decrees which have been previously legally confirmed by the people", *I.Eph.* VI.2018 (4-14 A.D.). It also occurs in an inscription from Rhodes (II B.C.), which refers to matters laid down "in the previously legally confirmed decree", *SEG* 3.674.28. The simple verb κυρόω, *kuroo*, "legally confirmed" occurs in 2 Cor. 2:8; Gal. 3:15.

[3]   That is, Moses.

[4]   That is, to make a promise one is enough.

23-25 Before faith came, we were being guarded by the law, being looked after while waiting for the faith which was destined to be revealed. *24* Consequently the Law was the guide who led us[1] to the Anointed One, so that we would be made right with God through faith. *25* Now that faith has arrived, we no longer need the guide.

26-29 For you all are legally adopted[2] by God on account of your faith in the Anointed One Jesus. *27* All of you who were baptized into the Anointed One have clothed yourselves[3] with the Anointing. *28* There is no such thing as Jew or Greek, slave or free, male or female: you are all one person in the Anointing of Jesus. *29* And since you belong to the Anointed One, then you are Abraham's "descendant", and heirs of the promises God gave to him.

Ch.4:1-7 This is what I mean: as long as the heir is under legal age, the heir is no different from a slave. The heir has a legal right to the whole inheritance, *2* but is under guardians and managers until the coming of age.[4] *3* In the same way we too, as under the legal age, were enslaved by the elemental spirits[5] of the world. *4* When the time set by God had reached its full term, God sent out his Son, born from a woman, born under law, *5* in order to buy out those who were under law, so that we would be legally adopted[6] by God. *6* You are adopted by God. God sent the spirit of adoption[1]

---

[1]   Often translated "tutor", this was not a tutor in our modern sense. It referred to the person who went with a boy from home to school and back again. It referred to someone who led the way (literally), but not in the sense of a teacher.

[2]   A technical term from Greek law. See notes following.

[3]   The figurative use of putting on clothes employed by Paul also in Rom. 13;14; Eph. 4;24; 6;11, 14 is paralleled in *AM* 36 (Nikaia, late Imperial period), "Putting on virginity you fled the world's wickedness."

[4]   προθεσμία, *prothesmia*, occurs only here in the N.T. but very frequent elsewhere. The coming of age, the time set by the father. It also means "the appointed time", cf. *P.Laur.* 35 (Arsinoite nome, 93-95) and occurs frequently in the documentary evidence.

[5]   στοιχεῖον, *stoikheion*, "elemental spirit". See also this meaning in verse 9; Col. 2:8, 20. The word appears also in Heb. 5:12 in the meaning "fundamental principles"; and 2 Pet. 3:10, 12 in the meaning "physical elements". For the meaning "elemental spirits", see also Aris. *Pol.* 1. 9, 12. The use of στοιχεῖον, *stoikheion*, is summed up by Joseph Blinzler, "Lexikalisches zu dem Terminus τὰ στοιχεῖα τοῦ κόσμου," *Studorium Paulinorum Congressus Internationalis Catholicus* II, Rome: Pontifical Biblical Institute, 1963, 429-43. Blinzler suggests the following semantic range: a. Letters, characters; b. The alphabet. (For this use see Clement of Alexandria, who commenting on Psalm 18:2 said, "…the sensible types are the alphabet, στοιχεῖα, *stoikheia*, we pronounce. Hence the Lord himself is called the Alpha and Omega, the beginning and the end'". [*Strom.* 6:141.6-7]); c. The foundation or principles of a science or institution. d. The rudiments or initial basis for something; e. The physical elements (such as earth, air, fire, water). (For this use see Philo, *Vit.Cont.* 3-4; *PGM* XVII 15.); f. Fundamentals; g. The planet and stars. (see 2 Enoch 12;1); h. Spirits of the physical elements, star-spirits (For this use see *2 Enoch* 16:7; *PGM* IV.1126-35; Vattius Valens 7.5); i. Demons, spirits. (Jews and pagans used στοιχεῖον, *stoikheion*, in this sense in the 1st c. AD.)

[6]   "To receive adoption" (from God), "to be legally adopted" (by God). ἀπολαμβάνω, *apolambano*, to take or receive from another, to receive that which is one's due. υἱοθεσία, *huiothesia*, "adoption", non-gender specific language (see note on Rom. 8:23), cf. Rom. 8:15, 23; 9.4; Eph. 1:5. This is a use of a technical adoption term from Greek law. F. Lyall, *JBL* 88 (1969) 458-66 (followed by F.F. Bruce, *NIGTC, Translator's Workplace*, SIL, on Galatians 4:5) argued that Paul's use of adoption terminology was a reference to Roman law, but

into your hearts, so that you would call out loudly, "Dad, Father!" *7* Consequently, you are no longer a slave but legally adopted, and since you are legally adopted, then by God's act you are an heir.

8-11 When you did not know God you were in bondage to nature beings who were not gods. *9* Now you have gained knowledge about God, why do you turn back to the weak and poor elemental spirits?[2] Do you wish to be in bondage all over again? *10* You observe Sabbaths,[3] the monthly celebrations,[4] the annual festivals and the sacred years. *11* I am afraid for you: I am afraid that perhaps I have worked in vain for you!

12-16 Fellow believers, I earnestly ask you to become like me, because I too was once like you! You did me no wrong. *13* You know that I preached the Good News to you the first time through weakness in the natural realm. *14* And you did not make light of[5] my ordeal[6] in the natural realm nor did you spit to break the effects of the evil eye spell.[7] Instead, you welcomed me as a messenger of God, just as you would have welcomed the Anointed One Jesus. *15* Where did that happiness go? I will say this for you: you would have done anything for me! If it had been possible, you would have even torn out your own eyes and given them to me![8] *16* So then have I become your enemy because I tell you the truth?

17-20 Those people are trying to win you over. Their motives are not good. They intend to shut you off from me so that you will side with them. *18* Now, providing you have good motives, it is fine to win someone over at all times and not just while I'm present with you. *19* My little children, I am in the pains of childbirth labor for you once more, until the Anointing is birthed in you. *20* If only I could be present with you now and change my tone, because I don't know what to make of you!

21-27 You who want to be under Law, tell me: why don't you pay attention to the Law? *22* The Scriptures say that Abraham had two sons, one with a female slave and one with a freewoman. *23* On the one hand, the son with the female slave was a child of the natural realm, but on the other hand, the son with the freewoman was a child of the promise. *24* These things are expressed in an allegory. The two women represent two covenants. Hagar is from Mount Sinai (in Arabia) and gives birth to bondage. *25* This represents the Jerusalem of today, currently in bondage with her children. *26* But the heavenly Jerusalem is free, and is this is our mother. *27* For the Scriptures

---

it was later shown to be a reference to Greek law. Note the papyrus sheet, *P.Oxy.* 3271, pp. 8-9 (pl.3), dated to 47-54 AD, a petition to a prefect by the adoptive daughter of Dionysios. The daughter was adopted under Greek, not Roman, law. See also note on Gal. 3:7. Paul is the only N.T. writer to use this noun.

[1] υἰοθεσία, *huiothesia*. See note on Rom. 8:23.

[2] στοιχεῖον, *stoikheion*, "elemental spirit". See verse 3.

[3] "Days". See note on Luke 4:16.

[4] "Months", "seasons', "years".

[5] No one as yet knows what this Greek word means. It has not been found elsewhere in all existing Greek literature. Similar words mean "make light of", but the word could well mean something else entirely.

[6] περιασμός, *periasmos*. See note on Matt. 6:13.

[7] "Spit", synecdoche for "spit to break the effects of the evil-eye spell", or equally possible, just "spit". It was a commonly held pagan belief that the effects of the spell (curse) brought about by using the evil eye could be broken by spitting three times, cf. Theokritos, VI, 35-40. This ties in with 2 Cor. 12:7-8. The words "bodily illness", "state of my poor body", and so on do not appear in the Greek. Some translations add "my illness / condition was a trial to you" which is not in the Greek.

[8] Paul is again playing on words, connecting "eyes" with the "spit against the evil eye" of the previous verse, just as he did in Galatians 3:1. This does not mean he had eye trouble: he is simply playing on words, as he loves to do.

say: "Be joyful, barren woman who does not give birth! Break through and shout, you who are not in labor! Because the solitary woman has many more children than she who has a husband!"

28-31 We, fellow believers, are children of the promise like Isaac. *29* But just as the child of the natural realm at that time persecuted the child of the Spirit, so is the case now. *30* What does the Scripture say? "Throw out the female slave and her son. The female slave's son will not be an heir with the freewoman's son." *31* For this reason, fellow believers, we are not children of the female slave but we are children of the freewoman.

Ch.5:1-4 The Anointed One set us free! As you are free, then stand firm! Do not get involved again in a burden of bondage! *2* I, Paul, am telling you this: if you get circumcised, the Anointed One won't give you any benefits for it! *3* Again, I solemnly declare to every person who gets circumcised that he will be under obligation to keep the whole Law! *4* You, you who want to be made right with God by Law, you have become cut off[1] from the Anointed One! Your favor has fallen off![2]

5-6 The Spirit makes us sure that we have been made right with God by our faith. *6* In the Anointing of Jesus, circumcision doesn't count for anything! Non circumcision doesn't count for anything! What does count is faith which is active and supported by love.

7-10 You were running well! Who cut in on you and blocked you from obeying the truth? *8* The obstinate behavior you display does not come from the One who invites you! *9* A little yeast goes through the whole lump of dough! *10* The Lord has given me confidence that you will get back on the track. As for the person who's getting you all mixed up: they will get what's coming to them, whoever it is!

11-12 And, fellow believers, if I am still advocating circumcision as some are saying, then why are the Jews persecuting me? If I advocate circumcision, then the snare of the cross is abolished! *12* If only those who are upsetting you would go that bit further and castrate themselves![3]

13-15 You, fellow believers, have been invited out to freedom. Don't let your freedom lead to a base of operations[4] in the natural realm. Instead, serve each other lovingly. *14* The whole Law is summed up in one scripture, which is, "Love your neighbor as you love yourself." *15* But if you bite at[5] and prey on each other, beware that you're not eaten up by each other![6]

16-21 This is what I mean: be led by the Spirit and then there is no way that you will perform the wants and wishes of the natural realm. *17* The natural realm wants things which are contrary to the Spirit, and the Spirit wants things which are contrary to the natural realm: they are in opposition to each other. So then don't just do whatever you please. *18* If you are led by the Spirit, then you are not under Law. *19* Actions of the natural realm are obvious:, *porneia*,[7] uncleanness, vice, *20* idol worshipping, sorcery, hostilities, rivalries, jealousies, fits of rage, political intrigues, disputes, heresies, *21* envies, drunken binges, wild parties and things like this, which I've warned you about. People who do such things will not inherit God's Realm.

---

[1]   Paul is again playing on words.

[2]   More of Paul's wit!

[3]   ἀποκόψονται, *apokopsontai*, "castrate". Zerwick and Grosvenor, *op.cit.*, p. 573 translate, "Would that they would go on and have themselves castrated!"

[4]   ἀφορμή, *aphorme*, "base of operations" as a military term (cf. Thucydides 1.90); "starting point"; "opportunity'; "occasion". See *P.Oxy* I.34; *P.Strass.* I.22; *BGU* II.615. Well attested.

[5]   δάκνω, *dakno*, metaphorical here, "annoyed", otherwise "bite".

[6]   ἀναλίσκω, *analisko*, to consume food, cf. Hipp. *Vet.Med.* 12. The play on words makes sense only in the Greek: "annoyed" in the Greek also means "bite".

[7]   πορνεία, *porneia*. See note on Matt. 15:19.

22-23 Listening to the leading of the Spirit will produce love, happiness, peace, tolerance towards others, kindness, goodness, faith, *23* gentleness,[1] self-control. There is no law against these!

24-26 Those who belong to the Anointed One Jesus have crucified the natural realm with its experiences and wants and wishes. *25* If we live in the Spirit, let us also follow the leading of the Spirit! *26* Let us not become conceited, challenging one another or envying one another!

Ch.6:1-5 Fellow believers, if a person makes a mistake, you who are spiritual should restore such a person to friendship, and do it with a gentle spirit. See to it that you too don't get harassed by the enemy! *2* Carry each other's burdens and thus fulfill the law of the Anointed One! *3* If someone thinks they're a big shot when they're really no one, they're deluding themselves! *4* Each person is to have a good hard look at their own actions, and then they will have a reason to boast about themselves alone, and not about someone else. *5* Each person is responsible for their own actions.

6-10 The person who is taught the Word is to be in partnership with the teacher in their wealth! *7* Make no mistake about it! God is not mocked! Whatever a person sows, this they will also reap! *8* The person who sows in the natural realm will harvest decay, but the person who sows in the spiritual realm will harvest eternal life from the Spirit. *9* Do not lose heart while doing such favorable things, as you will reap a harvest by your own measure provided you don't slacken off! *10* So then, as far as possible, let us provide funds to everyone, especially to those who are in the family of faith!

11-16 I am spelling this out to you in large letters[2] in my own handwriting![3] *12* It's the people who want to put on a good show who are trying to force circumcision on you! They want to avoid being persecuted because of the cross of the Anointed One! *13* They don't even obey the Law! They want you to be circumcised so they can boast that they forced you into it. *14* Far be it for me to boast! I will boast only about the cross of the Anointed One Jesus. Because of his crucifixion, I could not care less about the natural realm. *15* Circumcision doesn't mean a thing! Non-circumcision doesn't mean a thing! All that counts is a new creation! *16* Peace and mercy to everyone who does this! Peace and mercy to those referred to as "God's Israel"!

17 From now on, no one is to give me any trouble! On my very body I carry the scars of the Lord Jesus![4]

18 Fellow believers, may the favor of our Lord Jesus the Anointed One be with your spirit! Amen.

---

[1] πραΰτης, *prautes*, "gentleness", an important word for the Greeks. This was one of the attributes of a Greek hero. It had a wider meaning than our English word. πραΰτης, *prautes*, is mainly an attribute of people with authority. It is used in the LXX in quite another meaning, for the poor.

[2] That is, letters of the alphabet. Paul is trying to make a point.

[3] Epistolary aorist. The sense of this is hard to bring out in English, but Paul is trying to make his point - Hey, you! Look at this! Get the point! Read my lips!

[4] τὰ στίγματα, *ta stigmata*, marks (or brands) used to identify a slave, particularly those in temple service. Paul is implying he is Jesus' slave, and carries the scars of whipping on his body. See Herodotos 7.233: "Most of them were branded by Xerxes' command with the king's marks." Occurs only here in the N.T.

Letter to the Ephesians.

The letter to the Ephesians was written by Paul some time after the mid 50s AD. It was very well attested in the early Church and is found in the two earliest canons, Marcion's (which calls it "Laodiceans") and the Muratorian canon. Sections of Ephesians are quoted by Tertullian, Origen and Clement of Alexandria, and it is alluded to by Ignatius, Polycarp, Clement of Rome, Barnabas and Hermas.

Ephesos was well known historically as a center for magical practices, spell casting and the conjuring of evil spirits. Apollonius of Tyana (*Philostratus*, 4.10) tells of a plague demon which had been harassing the city. Apollonius discovers him in the form of a blind beggar. When he instructs the Ephesians to stone the beggar, it turns into a mad dog in front of them. The *Acts of Andrew* speaks of a large crowd of demons that lived on a rock next to a statue of Artemis. It was said to be impossible to travel past. Ephesos was the cult center of the worship of the Ephesian goddess Artemis (not to be confused with the Greek Artemis), known as "the greatest" and "the supreme power". The city held the title of Temple Warden of the goddess, who was said to have authority over all the demons of the dead as well as the harmful spirits of nature. Artemis was known as a mother goddess, a fertility goddess and a nature goddess. Her followers believed that she had powers superior to those who controlled the fate of people. In Acts 19:27, Demetrios states that Artemis is worshiped not only in Asia, but also in the whole world, and this is supported by Pausanias. Ephesos was also a center of emperor worship, having 3 official temples, and was one of the very few cities to hold the title of Temple Warden of the deified, dead emperor. It was a big pilgrimage center and as such had a major tourist trade.

Ephesos was the capital city of the province of Asia, and about the third largest in the Roman world. It had approximately 100,000 inhabitants. Josephus states that Ephesos had a large Jewish community, possibly as early as the mid 3rd c. BC. Ephesos was an important communication center due to its strategic position. The city was linked to the harbor by a 10 yard (11 metre) wide marble-paved road, "The Arcadian Way", flanked by huge columns.

Ephesos has been a rich source of inscriptions. From the 1980s, several thousand Greek and Latin inscriptions have been published, and others re-edited. Much work has been done on the city's coin issues.

Letter to the Ephesians.

Ch.1:1-2 From: Paul, an apostle of the Anointed One Jesus through God's plan.
To: The people devoted to God who are faithful to the Anointed One Jesus.
2 May you have favor and peace from God our Father and Lord Jesus the Anointed One!

3-6 Praise the God and Father of our Lord Jesus the Anointed One! Through the Anointed One, he gave us every spiritual blessing which he had in the heavenly places. *4* Because he loved us he chose us before the foundation of the world to be sacred and blameless in his sight. *5* He is the One who, before anything was created, set us apart to be adopted into his family through Jesus the Anointed One. He was well pleased with his plan. *6* He favored us by giving us Jesus whom he loved, and we richly praise God for his favor.

7-10 His favors to us are so abundant, that he bought us by paying the ransom for us with his Son's blood. This canceled our sins. *8* In fact, he showered us with so many favors that they overflowed, and he also gave us all types of wisdom as well as common sense. *9* He showed us the secret hidden truth of his plans. Actually, he was pleased to do this. He intended that the secret hidden truth would be revealed through the Anointed One. *10* God had a detailed plan for each period of time. The secret hidden truth of his plans was tied in to this: everything had to be just right to unite all things to the Anointed One: to unite things in the heavenly places to him and to unite things on the earth to him.

11-14 It was God's purpose to set us apart before anything was created. On account of what the Anointed One did, we were assigned an estate. God makes everything work according to his purpose and his plans. *12* This was so that we Jews, who had previously hoped for the Anointed One, would praise him greatly. *13* And after you heard the Message of truth, the Good News about our salvation, you non-Jews also believed the Anointed One and were stamped with the seal of the Holy Spirit. This guarantees us our covenant rights. *14* The Holy Spirit is the down payment of our inheritance. This is due to the fact that we own our freedom, as the ransom has been paid for it. And we greatly praise him for this!

15-23 On account of this, I too, after hearing of your faith in the Lord Jesus and your love for all the people devoted to God, *16* do not cease to give thanks for you when I mention you in my prayers! *17* I pray that God, the glorious Father of our Lord Jesus the Anointed One, will give you spiritual wisdom and that he will reveal his knowledge of the Anointed One to you. *18* I pray that the light dawns on your minds! Then you will know the hope to which he calls you, the wealth of his rich inheritance he has given to the people devoted to God. *19* I pray that you will know the vastness of his power available to us, we who trust him to work his powerful strength for us. *20* He works his powerful strength through the Anointed One. After all, he raised him from among the dead. The Anointed One took his seat at his right side in the heavenly places, *21* above every rule, authority, power, realm of power and everything that has a name, not only for this time, but for the time to come. *22* Everything draws its essence from him and God gave him, him alone, to the assembly as the source[1] of everything it needs. *23* The assembly is, in fact, his body, and every individual contributes to bringing his body to a state of completeness.

Ch.2:1-3 And you too, you were corpses due to your mistakes and sins. *2* You lived this way, just like anyone else in the world right now. You went along with the ruler of the authority of the air, the spirit that now works in disobedient people. *3* We used to be like this. We lived out our lives in the natural realm being dictated to by its wants and wishes. We did what the natural realm and our thoughts told us to do. We were just as much in danger of God's anger as the others. In fact, we were corpses due to our mistakes.

4-7 *4-5* But God was very merciful. When he brought the Anointed One to life from the dead he brought us, who were dead with our mistakes, to life too! He did this because he loved us so very much. It is by God's favor that you have been saved! *6* Because of what the Anointed One did, God raised us up and gave us seats with him in the heavenly places. *7* This was so he could demonstrate in the near future the way in which he favors us with his excessive wealth, his kindness to us because of what the Anointed One Jesus did.

8-10 Due to God's favor you have been saved through faith; and this is not due to anything you yourselves have done; rather, it is God's gift to you. *9* You weren't saved by your actions, and so no one can boast. *10* It is his workmanship that we are! We have been created by the Anointed One Jesus to do the good things God prepared beforehand for us to do, and to live how he wanted us to live.

---

[1]   Paul plays on words again but the meaning cannot be brought out in the English language. The Greek word "head" can mean either "source" or "(physical) head" but it cannot mean "head" in the sense of "ruler over", "authority", "leader" as it does in English. (Words in one language can have multiple meanings, but only one of these meanings may apply in another language.) Thus Jesus is represented as the (physical) head (source) and the church as the (physical) body.

11-12 So then remember this: you were once outsiders in the natural realm. You are called "The Uncircumcised Ones" (non-Jews) by the so-called "Circumcised Ones" (Jews), yet their circumcision is human-made, performed in the natural realm. *12* Remember that in that situation you were without the Anointed One, you were alienated from the society of Israel and you were strangers to the promised Covenants. You had no hope and you were in the world without God.

13-16 But in point of fact, because of the Anointed One Jesus, you who were once far away from God were brought close to God by the Anointed One's blood. *14* He himself has made peace: he has made both Jews and non-Jews one people. By dying as a sacrifice, he has destroyed the dividing wall between Jews and non-Jews, *15* and he has destroyed the hostility between them. He has annulled the Law of the commandments with its decrees, so as to create one new person from the two groups (Jews and non-Jews), thus making peace. *16* This was so that he could restore both of them, in one body, to friendship with God through the cross. It was with the cross that he put the hostility to death.

17-22 He announced the Good News: peace to you who were far away and peace to those who were near, *18* because through him we both have access by one Spirit to the Father. *19-20* So then you are no longer foreigners and strangers who don't have citizen rights. Instead, you are fellow citizens with the people devoted to God and members of God's house, which has been built on the foundation of the apostles and the prophets. *21* Jesus the Anointed One himself is the cornerstone of the whole building, which is being fitted together, growing into the Lord's sacred temple. *22* All of you are joined together and are being turned into a spiritual building of God.

Ch.3:1-4 For this reason I, Paul, am a prisoner for serving the Anointed One Jesus by preaching to you non-Jews. *2* No doubt you have heard of the detailed plan mapping out God's favor, the plan which was given to me for you, *3* the hidden secret truth given to me by means of revelation. I have previously written briefly on this matter. *4* As you read it, you will understand my insight into the secret hidden truth of the Anointed One.

5-7 In other generations this was not revealed to people. It has now been revealed by the Spirit to his sacred apostles and prophets. *6* As a result of the Good News, the non-Jews are joint-heirs, joint members of the same body, and joint sharers of the promised Anointed One. *7* I became a minister of the Good News due to God giving me favor and due to the continuous working of God's power in me.

8-12 And I am the most insignificant of all the people devoted to God! Yet this favor was given to me so that I could announce the Good News about the inexhaustible riches of the Anointed One to the non-Jews. *9* It was given to me so that I could enlighten everyone about the detailed plan of the hidden secret truth, which from the beginning of the ages has been hidden by God who created all things. *10* This is so that the many-faceted wisdom of God would now be made known through the assembly to all the rulers and authorities[1] in the heavenly places. *11* God's eternal plan culminated in the Anointed One Jesus our Lord. *12* Through Jesus we have the right of freedom of speech, able to say what we like, boldly in public. We have access to God with confidence through faith in Jesus.

13-19 This is why I beg you not to be discouraged at the oppression I am going through for you. Instead, you should be proud. *14-15* God is the Father

---

[1]   Nothing suggests that the rulers and principalities mentioned here are demonic. W. Carr, *Angels and Principalities* (*SNTSMS* 42, Cambridge, 1981, pp. 152, 176-7) demonstrates that the understanding of these powers as demonic is post-Pauline. See Col. 1:16, where the Greek does not state nor imply that the powers are demonic.

of all people groups[1] in heaven and on earth, and all derive their essence from him. I get on my knees and address him. *16* He favors you so richly, and I ask him to grant that your inner person will be powerfully strengthened by his Spirit. *17* I pray that the Anointing would inhabit your minds as you constantly use your faith, so that, as you have deep roots and loving firm foundations, *18* you may be in a strong enough position to grasp, along with all the people devoted to God, the width, length, height and depth *19* of the Anointed One's love, a love that goes far beyond knowledge. Then you will be filled to overflowing with everything God has for you.

20-21 To God who is able to do far and away beyond all that we ask or think by virtue of the power that constantly energizes in us, *21* to God be the praise by the assembly and by followers of the Anointed One Jesus from all people groups, throughout all the periods of time, amen!

Ch.4:1-3 I myself, a prisoner for serving the Lord, encourage you to behave in a way worthy of God's invitation to you, *2* with humility, gentleness, and tolerance towards others. Lovingly put up with each another, *3* and be eager to keep the unity of the Spirit by the bond of peace.

4-10 There is one body and one Spirit. You had one invitation. *5* There is one Lord, one faith, one baptism, *6* one God and Father of all, who is above everything, works through everything, and is in everything. *7* God measured out his favor to us and the Anointed One has given each one of us a gift. *8* This is why the Scriptures say, "When he ascended on high, he led along prisoners and gave gifts to people." *9* This "he ascended", what does it mean! It means that he also descended into the lower parts of the earth! *10* The one who descended is also the very one who ascended above all the heavenly places, in order to equip the universe.

11-13 He himself gave, as gifts, some people as apostles, others as prophets, others as evangelists, and others as shepherds[2] and teachers[3] *12* in order to equip God's people for the ministry[4] work. This was to build up the body of the Anointed One, *13* until we as a whole arrive at the unity of faith and knowledge of God's Son, growing into a complete man,[5] measuring up to the full maturity of the Anointed One.

14-16 This is so we would no longer be people who are under age. When winds of instruction and training blow this way and that, we would not be carried to and fro on the waves. We would not be tossed about at sea by the sleight of hand[6] and schemes of people, and we would not be driven off course by people's plots and schemes. *15* Instead, we should speak the truth in a loving way and grow up to maturity in every way, so that we will realize our closeness with our source[7] of growth, the Anointed One, and be more like him. *16* The whole body grows when individual parts of the body combine and are supplied by ligaments. The Anointed One is the source of the whole body, and love makes the body grow.

---

[1] πατριά, *patria*, a classical word, occurring in Herodotos as "tribe". In the LXX it occurs as "tribe", those descended from a common ancestor. Abbot, *op.cit.* p. 94, notes, "narrower than θυλή (*thule*) and wider than οἶκος (*oikos*)."

[2] ποιμήν, *poimen*, shepherd. The word occurs 18 times in the N.T., in most instances of literal shepherds shepherding animals. The word "pastor" is a modern word, which has been read back into translation in this verse in many Bible versions. See Heb. 13:20 and 1 Pet. 2:25.

[3] In the Greek, 4 not 5 groups appear to be mentioned, as shepherds and teachers appear to be put in the same group. The writer's meaning is unclear.

[4] For διακονία, *diakonia*, see Thuc. 1.133, Plato, Rep. 371 C, Dem. 296.29, Polyb. 15. 25, 4. *Diakonia* is the act of the *diakonos*. See note on Rom. 16:1.

[5] Unusual use of "man" here.

[6] κυβεία, *kubeia*, dice-playing.

[7] The Greek has the double meaning "head" as part of the body and "source".

17-24 The Lord would have me say this, and I urge you: please don't continue to behave the way the non-Jews behave, that is, mindlessly! *18* They can't think straight, they are alienated from God's family and away from the life God would have them lead. Their hard-heartedness makes them ignorant. *19* As they are apathetic, they have fallen prey to vice, and they push their involvement in every kind of perversion well past the limit. *20* You have not learned this from the Anointed One, *21* if indeed you have heard him and have been taught by him. The true teaching is that of Jesus. *22* This is - that you strip off the clothes of your former way of life, the old person[1] which is being destroyed by wants and wishes which deceive you. *23* Let your spirit be made new, and this will make your minds new. *24* Put on the clothes which are the new person, created in God's way, the right way, with truth and holiness.

25-27 For this reason take off the clothes of lying and throw them away! Each one of you is to speak the truth with your neighbor: remember, we are all parts of the same body. *26* If you lose your temper, do not sin. Do not hold onto your anger for too long. *27* Do not give Slanderer-Liar an opportunity!

28-32 The person who steals is not to steal any more. Instead, you are to work, doing good things with your own hands, so that you will have something to share with someone who is in need. *29* Do not let any foul language come out of your mouth. Only speak good things which will encourage someone. Let your words be a benefit to those who hear them. *30* Do not upset God's Holy Spirit. He was the one who marked you to be released when the ransom was paid. *31* Take off the clothes of bitterness, rage, anger, shouting and slander and throw them away! This goes for malice too. *32* Be kind and compassionate to each another. Forgive each other, just as God through the Anointed One forgave you.

Ch.5:1-5 You are dearly loved children of God. Imitate him, *2* and act in a loving way to others. The Anointed One loved us so much that he gave himself as a sacrifice for us. He offered himself as a fragrant smoking sacrifice to God. *3* But as for *porneia*,[2] and all types of dirty or greedy grasping behavior - you must keep so far away from it that it is not even suspected! This is fitting for people devoted to God. *4* Oh, I must add filth, foolish chatter, and double-entendre. These do not belong to God, but gratitude does. *5* You can be thoroughly assured of this, that no one who commits *porneia*,[3] any unclean person, or greedy grasping person, that is to say, an idol worshipper, has any inheritance to use now in the Realm of the Anointed One and God.

6-10 Do not be deceived by the shallow arguments that people put forward! God is angry with such disobedient people. *7* So don't be involved in it with them! *8* You were once out in the dark, but now you are in the Lord's light. Light shines: act like light and shine! *9* Goodness, justice and truth are all products of light. *10* Have a good close look at the things that please the Lord.

11-14 Do not become involved with unproductive dark works, but instead bring them to light. *12* Even the very mention of what they do in secret is shameful! *13* Everything that is brought to light is revealed by the light, for whatever makes something shown for what it is, is light. *14* This is why it is said, "Awake, you who sleep, and rise up from among the dead! And the Anointed One will shine upon you."[4]

15-20 So then see that you act carefully. Be wise people rather than fools, *16* and don't miss an opportunity because the days are evil. *17* This is why you need to understand the Lord's purpose and not be silly. *18* Do not get drunk on

---

1   The philosopher Pyrrho's aim was to "strip off human nature", ἐκδύναι τὸν ἄνθρωπον. *ekdunai ton anthropon*, Diogenes Laertes 9.66.

2   πορνεία, *porneia*. See note on Matt. 15:19.

3   πορνεία, *porneia*. See note on Matt. 15:19.

4   The quote is from an unknown source.

wine, which leads to desperation. Instead, be filled with the Spirit, *19* while you are chirping to yourselves in songs of praise, festive praise songs and spiritual songs, singing and playing the musical instruments to the Lord with all your heart. *20* Always offer thanks for everyone in the Name of our Lord Jesus the Anointed One to God the Father.

21-24 Be filled with the Spirit, while you are supporting[1] one another out of respect for the Anointed One, *22* wives, with your own husbands, as with the Lord.[2] *23* The man is the source of the woman just as the Anointed One is the source of the assembly. He himself is the protector of the body. *24* Just as the assembly is a support for the Anointed One, so also let the wives be a support for their husbands in everything.[3]

25-33 Husbands, love your wives, just as the Anointed One loved the assembly. He sacrificed himself *26* to make the assembly sacred and to cleanse it with baptism by the spoken word. *27* He did this so he would have a sacred and unblemished assembly, an assembly held in high honor, without stains or wrinkles or any flaws. *28* Husbands are obliged to love their own wives as their own bodies. He who loves his own wife loves himself. *29* No one hates his own body but provides for and cares for it, just as surely as the Lord provides for and cares for the assembly, *30* because we are the members of his body. *31* The Scriptures say, "For this reason a man will leave his father and mother and be joined to his wife and the two will be a single body." *32* This is an important hidden secret truth. But I am referring to the Anointed One and the assembly. *33* So to get back to the subject - each one of you is to love his own wife just as he loves himself, so that[4] the wife is able to respect her husband.

Ch.6:1-3 Children, pay attention[5] to your parents,[6] as this is the right thing to do. *2* "Honor your father and mother," is the first commandment and it contains a promise, *3* "so that everything will go well for you and you will have a long life."

---

[1] ὑποτάσσω, *hupotasso*, support. See below note.

[2] ὑποτάσσω, *hupotasso*, support. The oft-quoted verse, "Wives, submit to your husbands" does not occur in any known Greek text, yet has made its way into nearly every Bible version. The word, mistranslated as an imperative in verse 22 where no verb appears, is in fact a participle and is in verse 21: "supporting one another". Even if mistranslated "submitting", it would be "submitting to one another". The actual verb is "be filled" at the beginning of verse 21. For ὑποτάσσω, *hupotasso*, see note on Rom. 13:1.

[3] A play on words which cannot be brought out in English. The body (the church) supports, or holds up, the head (Anointed One). As mentioned previously, "head" in the Greek cannot mean "head over someone" as it does in English. Here it means "source". In the same way, the body (the wife) supports (holds up) the head (the husband), but bear in mind, the image is of a physical head and has nothing to do with authority, as the Greek word for "head" does not have the additional meaning "authority" as does the English word "head".

[4] ἵνα, *hina*, with subjunctive, final: "so that", "in order that". Some argue that it has lost its final sense in the Koine, but there are several N.T. examples.

[5] ὑπακούω, *hupakouo*. See note on Matt. 8:27.

[6] τοῖς γονεῦσιν, *tois goneusin*, parents, but properly, "begetters". (γονεύς, *goneus*, begetter, parent, uncommon in the singular.) The use of γονευς, *goneus*, instead of πατέρες, *pateres*, in verse 4 is interesting. γονεύς, *goneus*, occurs here where the attitude of children to parents is in focus. This is echoed in the papyri of the time and follows an old tradition. See also Matt. 10:21. The Eleusinian precept was that people were to honor their parents: γονεῖς τιμᾶν, *goneus timan*. A inscription (aretalogy of Iris) from the late 2nd or earliest 1st c. B.C. had the word γονεῖς, *goneis*, when describing children honoring their parents, and πατέρες, *pateres*, otherwise: "You made parents (γονεῖς, *goneis*) honored by their children, in that you cared for them not only as parents, (πατέρων, *pateron*) but also as gods." (Y. Grandjean, *Une nouvelle arétalogie*

4-9 Parents,[1] do not exasperate your children but provide them with education[2] and instruction about the Lord. *5* Slaves, pay attention to your masters in the natural realm. Show them earnestness and concern[3] with sincerity as if you were working for the Anointed One instead of people. *6* Don't do it with lip service like people-pleasers do, but do it as the Anointed One's slaves. Do God's purpose from your very soul. *7* Do it out of kindness, as if you were serving the Lord and not people. *8* Know this: whatever good anyone does, they will receive the same from the Lord, whether they are slaves or free people. *9* Masters, you must treat your slaves in the same way. Cease threatening them! Surely you are aware that the one who is their master and yours too is in heaven and he doesn't show any favoritism!

10-12 Finally, be empowered by the Lord and by the mighty forcefulness of the Lord's strength. *11* Put on the suit of armor of God so you can stand firm against the schemes of Slanderer-Liar; *12* because it is not flesh and blood that we wrestle to the ground and pin down.[4] Rather, it is governments,[5] authorities,[6] a powerful class of demon-gods[7] that inhabit this darkness,[8] and evil spirit entities[9] - these are in the heavenly places.

---

d'Isis à Maronée (Leiden: Brill, 1975), pls. 1-3.) Note that the use in the inscription parallels the use here in Ephesians. See also *I.Kyme* 41, pp. 97-108 (pl. 11) *ll.*21-22, for γονεῖς, *goneis*, used of the attitude from children to parents.

[1] πατέρες, *pateres*, "parents". Can mean "father" but also means "female parent", or just "parent", non-gender specific. P.J. Sijpesteijn (*Tyche* 2 (1987) 171-74) lists 2 examples in papyri of individual women called *pater*.

[2] παιδεία, *paidea*, education, instruction, training, teaching, rearing of a child, bringing up of a child, learning, accomplishments. Not "chastening" or "discipline". See *IG* XIV (1890) 1728, *ll.* 1-10. Also note, for example, the Just Argument's speech in Aristophanes, *Clouds*, 961-983, and in Thucydides 2.39; Plato, *Symposium*, 187D. The word is common in Greek literature. It occurs elsewhere in the N.T. in 2 Tim. 3:16; Heb. 12:5, 7, 8, 11.

[3] φόβου καὶ τρόμου, *phobou kai tromou*. See note on 1 Cor. 2:3.

[4] πάλη, *pale*, occurs only here in N.T. πάλη, *pale*, is a technical wrestling term for to throwing down an adversary and then keeping the adversary pinned to the ground, cf. Arist. *Rhet.* 1.5, 14. See also Plat. *Legg.* 796, Theok. 24. 109, Plut. 2.638 D.

[5] ἀρχή, *arkhe*, can mean "beginning". Greek magical texts, especially those of the Orphic religion, linked ἀρχή, *arkhe*, and τέλος, *telos*, beginning and end. ἀρχή, *arkhe*, refers to the first place/first power, sovereignty, dominion, empire, principality, supreme power. In the plural, as in verse 12, ἀρχαί, *arkhai*, means "the governments".

[6] ἐξουσία, *exousia*, a common Greek word which referred to "the authorities", any authorities in general. The corresponding verb was commonly used in someone having or granting authority over a property.

[7] κοσμοκράτωρ, *kosmokrator*, an uncommon Greek word, and occurs only here in the entire Bible. This category of powers is far more than a ruler. Supreme or very high-up pagan gods were often referred to as κοσμοκράτωρ, *kosmokrator*: for example, Zeus, Sarapis, Helios, and the Ephesian Artemis (not be confused with the Greek Artemis). One magical text names Sarapis as "Lord, glorious one, κοσμοκράτωρ, *kosmokrator*, of ten thousand names, greatest, nourisher, apportioner."(*PGM* XIII, 637ff.) κοσμοκράτωρ, *kosmokrator*, was also a title which could named in conjuring demons in the pagan magical texts.

[8] Note the 1st c. BC document *Testament of Solomon* 18:1-5: "Then I ordered another demon to appear before me. There came to me 36 *stoikheia*, their heads like formless dogs. Among them were those in human form, or bull form, or dragon form, with faces like birds, or wild animals, or the sphinx. When I, Solomon, saw these beings, I asked them, 'Who are you?' Together, answering with one voice, they said. 'We are the 36 *stoikheia*, the *kosmokrators* that inherit this darkness.'"

[9] Not "spirits". The Greek is either "Evil spiritual entities/forces" or "Spiritual entities/forces which constitute evil".

13-16 For this reason put on the suit of armor of God, so that you can make a stand in the evil day, and so that you can stand firm after you have overpowered them.[1] *14* So then stand firm, after you put a belt around your waist by means of truth,[2] and after you put on the breastplate[3] which represents the state of being made right with God,[4] *15* and after you put shoes on your feet in a state of preparation to share the Good News which brings peace. *16* In every case, stand firm after you have picked up the shield which represents faith. With this you can put out the Wicked One's weapons[5] which have been set on fire.

17-20 Accept[6] the helmet which is salvation[7] and the sword of the Spirit, which is the spoken Word of God. *18* Do this while you are praying with every type of prayer and earnest request, and while you are praying on every occasion with the leading of the Spirit – and make sure that you're doing this.[8] Be stubborn and persistent in your earnest requests about all the people who are devoted to God. *19* And for me - for the Word to be given to me when I open my mouth to speak, for me to speak with the right of freedom of speech, boldly, openly in public, to make known the hidden secret truths of the Good News. *20* It is because I preached the Good News that I am an ambassador in prison. Pray that in this state I will speak with freedom of speech, boldly and openly, just as I need to speak!

21-24 So that you'll also know how my affairs are, how I am doing, Tychikos, a beloved fellow believer and the Lord's faithful minister, will let you know everything. *22* He is the one I am sending to you for this very reason, so that you will know what's happening with us. He will be able to put your minds at rest.

23 May the fellow believers have peace! May God the Father and the Lord Jesus the Anointed One give them love and faith!

24 May favor and immortality be with all those who love our Lord Jesus the Anointed One!

---

[1] κατεργασάμενοι, *katergasamenoi*, aorist participle of κατεργασάμενοι, *katergazomai*, overpower, crush, subdue, conquer. It can also mean "to accomplish" or "to get the job done". Not "having done all".

[2] ἐν, *en*, instrumental: we put the belt around our waist by means of truth.

[3] θώραξ, *thorax*, breastplate, cf. *P.Petr.* 3.6a 26 (237 BC); *P.Giss* 1/47.6. It occurs also in 1 Thess. 5:8; Rev. 9:9, 17.

[4] Taking the genitives in this section as epexegetic.

[5] βέλος, *belos*, refers to anything thrown as a weapon, and even the sting of a scorpion. It was used by Homer for the ox's leg thrown at Odysseus by a suitor and for the rock thrown by the one-eyed monster Cyclops. Euripides, *Electra*, 115 used it of Clytemnestra's axe. Aristophanes, *Acharnians*, 345, used it humorously of a kitchen knife. It often referred to spears, but can mean any sort of weapon.

[6] Verse 17 is a break from the previous verses, marked by an imperative after a string of aorist participles. The verb changes to δέξασθε, *dexasthe*, "accept", not the ἀναλαμβάνω, *analambano*, "take up"/"put on" of verses 13 and 16. This is a command: "Accept!" There is emphasis on the "*which is* the spoken Word of God". We are to accept the helmet which is salvation, and the sword while we are praying.

[7] There are 2 closely related words for salvation in N.T., ἡ σωτηρία, *he soteria*, and τὸ σωτήριον, *to soterion*. The latter, which occurs here, is the least common and only in 3 other instances in the N.T.: Luke 2:20, 3:6; Acts 28:28.

[8] εἰς αὐτό, *kai eis auto,* in agreement in gender with πνεύματι, *pneumati*. Note the lack of agreement with gender in verse 17. The verb here is ἀγρυπνέω, *agrupneo*, which only occurs in 3 other places in the N.T.

Letter to the Philippians.

The letter to the Philippians was written by Paul when he was imprisoned in Rome. Festus, the Procurator of Judea, had sent Paul to Rome. Acts 25:1-6 states that Festus made this decision two weeks after his arrival and this is set c. 60 AD. Paul was imprisoned in Rome for two years, and the evidence suggests that he wrote the letter to the Philippians in this time. However, in recent years it has been suggested that Paul was imprisoned in Caesarea or Ephesos. Epaphroditos was with Paul when he wrote Ephesians, Colossians and Philemon, but Paul sent Epaphroditos to the Philippians with the letter. This indicates that Philippians was not written at the same time as the other letters.

Philippi was a Roman garrison town founded, as the name suggests, by Philip of Macedon. It was the scene of the famous battle between Octavius and Mark Antony and Caesar's assassins, Brutus and Cassius, the battle which ended the Roman Republic. Paul says, "We set sail from Troas and made a straight run to Samothrace. On the next day we came to Neapolis, and from there to Philippi, a Roman colony and the most important city in Macedon. We stayed in that city for some time." (Acts 16:11-12.) It was in Philippi that Paul was arrested, imprisoned and beaten, despite being a Roman citizen. It was here too that the Philippian jailer and his household became Christians. The Jewish synagogue[1] was by the river just outside the city gate, and Paul met Lydia, the purple seller, there.

Polycarp and Ignatius allude to the letter to Philippians, and Irenaeus quotes from it and attributes it to Paul.

Letter to the Philippians.

Ch.1:1-2 From: Paul and Timothy, slave servants of the Anointed One Jesus.

2 To: All the people devoted to God, followers of the Anointed One Jesus, who are in Philippi, with the guardians[2] and the deacons.[3]

Hello! May you have peace from God our Father and the Lord Jesus the Anointed One!

3-5 I thank God every time I remember you. *4* Every time I make my earnest requests on your behalf, I'm happy about it, *5* because of your partnership with the Good News from the first day until now.

6-7 I am convinced of precisely this, that he who began a good work in you will pay it back in full, right up to the Day of the Anointed One Jesus![1] *7* It's

---

[1] προσευχή, *proseuche*. See note on Acts 16:13.

[2] ἐπίσκοπος, *episkopos*, one who watches over, a guardian, a scout, a watcher. Homer used it to describe those who watched over the covenants made with gods, *Il*.22.225. It was also used as the term for the public officials sent by Athenians to their subject states. The word "Guardian" did not become "Bishop" after the time of Ignatius in the early 2nd century A.D. Prior to this, and at the time of Paul's writing, it meant one who watches over, an overseer, guardian. The Athenians used to send (secular) Guardians to their subject states. Note that 1 Timothy 3:1 says, "If any person aspires to be a Guardian, they are desiring a fine work".

[3] Phoebe of Rom. 16:1 is described as a "minister" or "deacon", the same word we have here. Prior to New Testament times, the Greek word *diakonos* in a non-religious context referred to a servant or messenger, but in a religious context always referred to an official. The word was adopted into Christian vocabulary. The terms "minister" and "deacon" were at first synonymous. "Deacon" is the transliteration (putting Greek letters into English letters) of the Greek, and "minister" is the translation.

only right that I have this understanding about you, on account of the fact that you are on my mind. You are all joint partners with me in receiving favor – whether I am imprisoned or whether I am making a speech in defense of the Good News, testifying to its validity.

8-11 God is my witness how much I miss you with the compassion of the Anointed One Jesus himself. *9* And this I pray, that your love will grow excessively, and your knowledge and perception about all things will grow. *10* In this way you would examine the things that make a difference, so that you would be sincere and not prove to be an obstacle right up to the day when Jesus returns! *11* I pray that you would be filled with the benefit of being made right with God which comes through Jesus the Anointed One, and leads to God being given splendid praise.

12-14 Fellow believers,[2] I want you to realize that my affairs have actually helped, rather than hindered, the progress of the Good News! *13* Consequently my imprisonment for speaking about the Anointed One has become well known to the whole palace guard, and everyone else knows about it, too. *14* Because of my imprisonment, the majority of the fellow believers, followers of the Lord, have become confident to speak the Word with excessive daring and fearlessness!

15-17 Now some people speak the Word out of jealousy and rivalry, but others proclaim the Anointed One because they're happy to do it. *16* These people proclaim him out of love, knowing that I am appointed to defend the Good News. *17* But the others announce the Anointed One out of self-seeking behavior, not with pure motives. They think they can add oppression to my imprisonment!

18-26 What does it matter? At least, in one way or another, the Anointed One is being announced, whether it's under pretense, or truthfully. I'm happy about this. Indeed I'll continue to be happy, *19* as I know my safe return will come about due to your earnest requests to God, and due to the more than full supply of everything supplied by the Spirit of Jesus the Anointed One. *20* I eagerly hope that I won't be disgraced in any way. Instead, with the right of freedom of speech and boldly, openly in public, now, as always, the greatness of the Anointed One will be shown by my bodily self, whether through my life or through my death. *21* For to me, life is the Anointed One, and I will profit by my death, *22* but if living on in the natural realm means that my work will produce benefits – in that case, I can't tell which to choose. *23* I'm caught between the two. I have a desire to depart[3] and be with the Anointed One, which is infinitely better! *24* But it's more necessary for me to stay on the natural realm for your sake. *25* And since I'm convinced of this, I know that I'll stay on and stay with all of you, so your faith will happily progress, *26* so that you will be excessively proud of the Anointing of Jesus when I'm with you again.

27-30 The single important thing is that your conduct as a citizen must be worthy of the Good News of the Anointed One, so that whether I come and see you, or whether I'm absent, I will hear the news that you are standing firm in one spirit, joining as one in the fight for the faith of the Good News *28* and not taking fright at your counterparts who oppose you! There's a legal

---

[1]   A set phrase referring to the Parousia, also known as the "coming", the "Advent". See Zerwick and Grosvenor, *op.cit.*, p. 592. Paul plays on words, as he loves to do, in this verse. ἐναρξαϛμενος, *enarxamenos,* can mean "make a beginning", or "perform an act of worship". ἐπιτελέω, *epiteleo,* can mean "pay back in full", or "complete". The second part of these component verbs is respectively ἀρχή, *arkhe,* "beginning", and τέλος, *telos,* "end".

[2]   ἀδελφοί, *adelphoi.* See note on Matt. 5:22.

[3]   ἀναλύω, *analuo,* "depart", euphemism for "die". An epitaph for a midwife states, "After a good life I departed home". *IGUR* 1240 (Rome, early Imperial). The verb occurs elsewhere in the N.T. only in Luke 12:36.

document against them! It's from God, and it's their loss, but your gain! *29* This is because it's been granted to you on the Anointed One's behalf, not only to believe on him but also to experience things on his behalf. *30* We're in this together: you have the same contest for the winner's prize which you saw me have – and now hear that I have!

Ch.2:1-4 So then if there is any encouragement by the Anointed One, if his love provides any relief, if there is any partnership with the Spirit, any compassion and pity, *2* then make my happiness complete by thinking along these same lines. Have the same love, have the same harmony of soul, be of the one mind. *3* Make sure nothing is done through self-seeking behavior or through conceit. Be humble minded to each other. Don't put yourself first – consider the other person. *4* Each one of you is to look out for your own interests, as well as the interests of others.

5-11 Have the same frame of mind as the Anointed One Jesus. *6* He was in the form of God from the beginning. He didn't think it was robbery to be equal with God! *7* Instead, he stripped himself of his reputation by becoming like a slave servant, and taking on the external appearance of a human. *8* He humbled himself, listening to God to the point of death, the death of the cross. *9* For this reason God exceedingly exalted him and gave him the Name which is beyond every name *10* so that at the Name of Jesus every knee would bow - this goes for those in heaven,[1] those on earth, and those down under the earth – *11* that every language would fully agree that Jesus the Anointed One is Lord, thus glorifying God the Father.

12-13 Consequently, my dearly loved ones, in the same way that you always paid attention[2] - not only just in my presence, but also now much more in my absence - accomplish your own deliverance with earnestness and concern! *13* For it is God who is at work in you, both in what you intend to do and what you actually do, and God considers that this is a good thing.

14-18 Do everything without complaining about it and getting into arguments over it, *15* so that you will become without reproach and uncorrupt, blameless little children of God in the middle of a twisted[3] family[4] which has been distorted.[5] You shine as stars in the world among them! *16* Hold onto the Word which gives life, as this will be my reason to be proud when Jesus returns, because I won't have run my race in vain or worked hard in vain. *17* But if indeed I am a drink offering[6] poured on the sacrifice, a public service which comes from your faith, I will be happy and rejoice together with all of you. *18* In the same way you too be happy and rejoice with me!

19-24 I expect by means of the Lord Jesus to send Timothy to you soon. I'll be very pleased to hear news about you! *20* I don't know of anyone else like him who genuinely cares about what's happening with you. *21* The others only care about what's happening with themselves, not about the things of Jesus the Anointed One! *22* But you've come to know what Timothy's really like – that he served with me for the Good News like a son would serve with his father. *23* So then on the one hand I expect to send him as soon as I see

---

[1] Equally, "the sky".

[2] ὑπακούω, *hupakouo*. See note on Matt. 8:27.

[3] σκολιός, *skolios*, twisted, tangled, bent, curved, winding, not straight, rarely used of people.

[4] γενεά, *genea*, clearly in its primary meaning of "family" here, in continuation of the metaphor of God's little children.

[5] διεστραμμένης, *diestrammenes*, perfect passive participle of διαστρέφω, *diastrepho*), to alter, to turn different ways, to dislocate, to twist about, and was used to refer to dislocated limbs.

[6] σπένδω, *spendo*, to pour a drink offering. In pagan terms some wine was poured on the altar before it was drunk.

what's going to happen with me, *24* but on the other hand the Lord has given me confidence that I myself will visit you soon, too.

25-30 Now I considered it necessary to send Epaphroditos[1] to you – he's my fellow believer, fellow worker and fellow soldier, and your envoy whom you sent to be a public servant to my needs. *26* He missed you all, and he was most dismayed because you'd all heard that he'd been sick at one point. *27* And in fact he did get so sick that he came close to death, but God had mercy on him, and not just on him but on me too – to spare me major sorrow! *28* So I sent him to you even more eagerly. You'll be happy when you see him, and I will be to a certain extent relieved. *29* So then welcome him as a follower of the Lord with a great deal of happiness, and hold people like him in honor. *30* It was through the Anointed One's work that he came close to death. He risked his life to render public service, making up for what all of you couldn't do for me.

Ch.3:1-3 Finally, my fellow believers, be happy about the Lord! Now I will repeat what I have written – it's no trouble for me and it's a safeguard for you! *2* Watch out for shameless, audacious people![2] Watch out for people who do bad things! Watch out for people who cut things off![3] *3* For we constitute the true circumcision, we who worship by the Spirit of God and are proud of the Anointing of Jesus and do not place our confidence in the natural realm.

4-7 Actually, you could say that I myself do have grounds to be confident about matters in the natural realm! In fact, if someone thinks they have confidence about matters in the natural realm, I for my part have even more! *5* I was circumcised on the eighth day, of the Israel race, of the tribe of Benjamin, a Hebrew of the Hebrews, with regard to the Law, a Pharisee. *6* As for being enthusiastic, I kept persecuting the church; as for being right with God in the sphere of the Law, I became blameless! *7* But whatever things I considered as gain, I now consider as a loss because of the Anointed One.

8-12 Yes, that's for sure! I consider all things as a loss on account of the surpassing excellence of the Anointed One Jesus my Lord, on account of whom I lost everything. To me they're just a pile of manure![4]

Their loss was so that I would gain the Anointed One, and to be made right with God by him. *9* I wasn't made right with God by the Law, but I was made right with God through faith in the Anointed One. This being made right with God is based on faith and comes from God. *10* This is so I would know him and know the power of his resurrection, and be in partnership with his experiences, being changed more and more because of his death. *11* If only I could come to the point of resurrection from the dead that Jesus experienced! *12* It's not that I have already taken hold of it or have already come to maturity. But I continue my pursuit of it, so that I will take possession of it, seeing that Jesus certainly already took possession of it for me.

13-16 Fellow believers, I don't calculate that I myself have taken possession of it: but one thing I do – I forget what's in the past, and instead forge eagerly ahead to what's ahead of me! *14* I chase after the goal to win the awarded contest prize, for which God, through the Anointing of Jesus, is inviting you to have from above. *15* So then, let all of us who are mature be like-minded! If there's anything you think differently about, God will reveal it to you. *16* Nevertheless, whatever stage we have reached, let's be consistent.

---

[1] An extremely common name, the 13th most commonly listed name at Rome, cf. Solin, *GPR* III.1439.
[2] The Greek word for "dogs", used metaphorically for a shameless or audacious person.
[3] Paul is making a joke and playing on words here: κατα-τομή, *kata-tome,* "cut-off," with περι- τομή, *peri-tome,* "circumcision," in the next sentence.
[4] σκύβαλον, *skubalon,* manure, but used here in its colloquial sense. It has been somewhat censored in Bible versions. There is no polite English equivalent.

17-19 Fellow believers, together be imitators of me! Keep an eye on those who behave in the same way as I do. We're a pattern for you to follow. *18* Now there are a lot of people who act – as I've often told you, and I'm crying about it as I tell you right now – as enemies of the cross of the Anointed One. *19* Their end will be loss. Their god is their belly, and its honor is in their disgrace. Their thinking is earthbound.

20-21.Ch.4:1 But our citizenship is in heaven and it's from heaven that we expect the Savior, Jesus the Anointed One. *21* He will change the form of our bodies from a humble state to a glorious body by working his power, and he supports all things by his power. *1* Consequently, my dearly loved and longed-for fellow believers, my happiness and my crown, stand firm with the help of the Lord, loved ones!

2-5 I encourage Euodia and I encourage Syntyche to think along the same lines along with the Lord. *3* Yes, and I ask you too, Synzugos, to assist[1] these women, seeing that they fought in the contest with me for the Good News, with Clement too, and the rest of my coworkers,[2] whose names are in the Book of Life.

4 Be happy about the Lord always! Again I say, be happy! *5* Let your fairness be known by all people. The Lord is approaching!

6-7 Do not be preoccupied about anything, but let the things you ask for be pointed out to God by means of prayer and earnest requests with gratitude. *7* And the peace of God, which conquers all processes of thinking, will keep watch over your minds and what you think about by means of the Anointed One Jesus.

8-9 Finally, fellow believers, analyze these things: things which are true,[3] things which are revered,[4] things which are just, things which are sacred, things which are kindly disposed[5] to another person or situation, things which cause one to abstain from speaking the wrong words,[6] things which are excellent and noble,[7] things which are praiseworthy. Analyze[1] these things, *9*

---

[1] συλλαμβάνομαι, *sullambanomai*, with dative, "assist" (in a significant, usually work matter). See *P.Oxy* 7.1064; *P.Giss* I.11. In Luke 5:7 it is used in the sense of business partners in the fishing industry calling for assistance. In *P.Oxy.Hels*. 47a it is used in a request to assist someone until they get the grain measured. See also Hdt. 6.125 and Jos. *Ant.* 12.240.

[2] Note that Paul asks Synzugos to assist the women Euodia and Syntyche. Paul calls these women his coworkers.

[3] "True" ("real", as opposed to "false").

[4] σεμνός, *semnos*, "revered", a term which was applied to pagan gods: revered, holy, stately, majestic, dignified. See inscription written on two sides of a coffin carriage, *SEG* 1536 (late 1st/early 2nd c. A.D).

[5] "To be kindly disposed", that is, to another person or to a situation. προσφιλής, *prophiles*, occurs only here in the N.T. The word appears on epitaphs. MM *s.v.* notes that the adjective is common on epitaphs but cites only one example. BDAG *s.v.* cites *OGIS* 331.9 which has an adverb rather than the adjective. προσφιλής, *prophiles*, also occurs in Pfuhl/Mobius 11, an epitaph for Dionysodoros which calls him πᾶσι προσφιλῆ, *pasi prosphile*, "kindly disposed to all", and *I.Eph*. III. 645. The formulaic use of the term occurs in funerary texts at Thasos. See *IG* XII 8.506, *CIL III* Add. 248.

[6] "To abstain from speaking the wrong words" was used in a pagan religious sense of abstaining from the wrong words in a religious sense or speaking words of good omen.

[7] ἀρετή, *arete*, a very important concept to the Greeks. It referred to someone or something which was good, noble, brave and had virtue, but virtue in the sense of active excellence and not virtue in today's moral sense. ἀρετή, *arete*, encompasses courage, temperance, liberality (specifically the giving and taking of wealth, especially in respect to giving), magnificence, a

the things I have passed on and you learnt from me, things you heard me say or saw me do. And the God of peace will be with you.

10-14 Now I greatly praised the Lord because at last you have revived your thoughts as to what you can do to benefit me. For that matter you surely did keep thinking of me, but you didn't have the opportunity to do anything practical about it. *11* Not that I'm speaking of any lack on my account, for I have certainly learned how to be independently wealthy[2] in the circumstances in which I find myself! *12* I also know how to be poorly off, and I also know how to have abundance! In each and every circumstance I have learned the revealed secret[3] of how to eat enough, and how to be hungry, how to have lack, and how to have abundance. *13* I prevail over everything through him who gives me power! *14* But still, you did well to be joint partners with me in spite of the fact you were going through oppression.

15-19 Now you Philippians know too, that in the beginning of the Good News, when I left Macedonia, no assembly went into partnership with me resulting in a bank account[4] of donations and income,[5] except you alone! *16* Because even when I was in Thessalonika you sent donations and income for my needs more than once or twice. *17* It's not that I'm looking for the gift, but I am looking for the profit that multiplies to excess on your bank account![6] *18* I have received payment in full for everything and have an over abundance! I have been fully supplied as I've welcomed from Epaphroditos the things you sent, the perfumed fragrance of a sacrifice which I received, and which pleased God. *19* My God will fully supply all your needs from his wealth, by means of the glorious Anointing of Jesus.

20 May our God and Father be praised for ever and ever! Amen!

21-23 Greet every person who is devoted to God and in fellowship with the Anointing of Jesus. The fellow believers who are with me greet you. *22* All the people devoted to God greet you, especially those from Caesar's household.

23 May the favor of the Lord Jesus the Anointed One be with your spirit!

---

good temperament, friendliness, truthfulness, a ready wit, justice, happiness and good manners.

1 λογίζεσθε, *logizesthe*, not "think on these things". The verb was used of numerical calculations: "calculate", "compute", "count".

2 αὐτάρκης, *autarkes*, was another very important concept to the Greeks. It referred to someone or something which was independently wealthy. For example, Thucydides used it to describe Corcyra, a place which needed no help from others, a place which supplied itself, needed no imports, needed no aid. αὐτάρκης, *autarkes*, certainly does not mean "content".

3 A technical term referring to initiation into the mysteries. Paul has had divine revelation on how to be wealthy. μεμύνμαι, *memunmai*, perfect passive of μυέω, *mueo*, "to initiate into the mysteries". It is a technical term. Paul has had divine revelation on how to be wealthy and how to be poor. For an example of this technical term in noun form see *I.Kyme* 41, an inscription from Kyme in Asia Minor, "I myself revealed initiations in the mysteries to people."

4 λόγος, *logos*, as "value", "money account", cf. Woodhouse, *op.cit.*, p. 7; Zerwick and Grosvenor, *op. cit.*, p. 602. For λόγοι, *logoi*, "financial accounts", "bank accounts", see turn of the era text, a soldier's concern about his debts, *BJRL* 51.151-154, "If Apollo's son comes to you about what remains, point out to him that it is coming with haste by Ptollas along with my back accounts."

5 λῆψις, *lepsis*, "income" cf. Ib. 343 D, Alc. 1. 123A.

6 λογος, *logos*, semantic range includes "value", "money account",

Letter to the Colossians.

The letter to the Colossian church was written by Paul around, possibly before, AD 60. The Colossians had heard the Good News from Epaphras. He had lived in Colosse for some time, but was now in jail with Paul in Rome. Many of the Colossians were non Jews. Aristarchos, Mark, and Epaphras were with Paul when he wrote Colossians, Ephesians and Philemon (cf. Col 4:10-14; Philemon 23-24). There have been recent arguments suggesting that Paul was imprisoned in Caesarea or Ephesos when he wrote both Colossians and Philemon. Luke is with Paul during his imprisonment (Col. 4:14; Philemon 24). Acts testifies to Luke being with Paul while he was in Rome, while there is no evidence to suggest Luke was with Paul in Ephesos.

In Colossians, Paul warns that certain people are coming in with pretended wisdom and useless cunning. The description of their practices, that is, that they take pleasure in humility and enter into Messengers' religious worship which they have seen, rashly becoming natural in their senses in the natural realm, and holding to things which promise wisdom because they offer self-imposed worship and humility and hard discipline of the body, suggests Merkabah Mysticism. The goal of Merkabah Mysticism was to enter a trance-like state by means of fasting, meditation, prayer and incantation, and thus ascend to God's heavenly throne room and experience God's Throne-Chariot (Hebrew: "Merkabah") as described in Ezekiel 1:15-25. Angels also feature prominently in the *Sefer Ha-Razim*, a collection of Jewish incantation texts. Origen and Clement both mention the *Kerygama Petrou*, which mentions the Jewish worship of angels. However, in the Jewish and pagan mystical texts, angels are invoked and commanded, usually for protective purposes, rather than worshipped.

Colosse was an important city about 100 miles (160 kilometres) east of Ephesos. It was on an important trade route, and was a defensible place with an abundant water supply. Colosse was agricultural and not known as a cultural center. When the main road was resited further west, it declined. It is now uninhabited.

Irenaeus, Clement of Alexandria, and Origen attribute the letter to the Colossians to Paul, while Justin Martyr, Ignatius, Polycarp and Barnabas allude to it. It is listed by Marcion's canon and the Muratorian canon.

Letter to the Colossians.

Ch.1:1-2   From: Paul, an apostle of the Anointed One Jesus through God's purpose, and from Timothy our fellow believer.
2 To: The people devoted to God and trustworthy fellow believers, followers of the Anointed One who are in Colosse.
Hello! May you be granted peace from God our Father!
3-5 We thank God, the Father of our Lord Jesus the Anointed One, for you every time we pray about you, *4* as we've heard about your faith in the Anointing of Jesus and your love for all the people devoted to God. *5* We pray that you will get what's stored away for you in the heavenly places. You've already heard about this in the true Message, which is the Good News.
6-8 The Good News is already present with you, just as it is with the whole world too. It is producing benefits and is growing, just as it is with you too, from the time you heard and fully realized the whole truth about God's favor. *7* You learned this from Epaphroditos, our dear fellow slave servant, who is a trustworthy minister of the Anointed One. He's standing in for you. *8* He's the one who told us of your spiritual love.

9 This is the reason that, from the day we heard it, we have not stopped praying and asking for you to be given complete knowledge about God's purpose and that you will do this by being very wise, by spiritually putting two and two together.

10-11 We don't stop praying and asking that you will behave in a way that's worthy of the Lord, that you will please him in everything, that every good thing that you do will be productive, and that your knowledge of God will grow until it's complete. *11* We don't stop praying and asking that you will be empowered with every type of power by means of God's forceful mighty power. This will lead to you having great endurance and perseverance.[1]

12-14 We thank the Father who made us qualified to receive a potion of our inheritance - we people devoted to God, who live in the light. *13* He rescued us from the authority of darkness and transferred us to the realm of his dear son. *14* Our sins are cancelled because his Son secured our release by paying the ransom price.

15-16 He is the portrait of the invisible God, the firstborn of the whole creation. *16* This is because all things were created by him – things that are in the heavenly places and things that are on the earth, things that are visible and invisible, things that are seats of power, realms of power or governments or authorities.[2] All these have been created by him and for him.

17-20 He came before everything, and everything has been brought into union with him. *18* He is the source[3] of the body, which is the assembly. He is the First Power, the firstborn from the dead, so that became the Holder of the First Place[4] in everything. *19* The full amount of God came to live in him, which God was pleased about. *20* Because of the First Power, God made peace with everything, as he had made peace through the Blood of the cross - this applies to things on the earth and things in the heavenly places.

21-23 He actually made peace with you, you who were once put out of the family, and were his enemies in your thought patterns because of the actions of the evil ones. He made this peace with you *22* through the death of Anointed One's natural body, to make you sacred, blameless and without reproach in his sight – *23* that is, if really and truly you continue to follow the faith. Your foundations must be laid in a stable way, and you can't shift around from the hope produced by the Good News which you've heard. The Good News was preached to the whole creation under heaven, and I, Paul, became a minister of it.

24 I am happy now about what I experienced on your behalf, and I contribute my share out of what belongs to me in the natural realm, to

---

[1] μακροθυμία, *makrothumia*, "perseverance". Can mean "tolerance towards others". Not "longsuffering" which gives the impression of someone suffering a long time. Not "patience".

[2] Nothing suggests that the rulers and principalities in every N.T. reference are demonic. W. Carr, *Angels and Principalities* (*SNTSMS* 42, Cambridge, 1981), pp. 152, 176-7 demonstrates that the understanding of these powers as demonic is post-Pauline. Here the Greek in no way suggests that these powers are demonic.

[3] κεφαλή, *kephale*. See note on 1 Corinthians 11:3.

[4] πρωτευω, *proteuo*, participle used as title. This word occurs only here in the N.T., although is not uncommon throughout Greek literature. It is a title, and although much about the title is as yet unknown, it means "The Holder of the First Place". (Note that "first" is used here in the sense of "superior".) MM, *s.v.*, cite three examples of this verb which denotes either political leadership in a city or an honorific title. Furthermore, its use occurs as a title of a count in the fragmentary document *P.Laur.* 27 (Arsinoe, 487-491). See discussion by Horsley in *NDIEC* 2.96 lamenting the fact that most commentators on Colossians ignore the fact that this word is a title.

balance out what is lacking due to the tight spots which happen to us as followers of the Anointed One. I do this on behalf of his body, which is the assembly.

25-29 I myself became a minister of the assembly in keeping with God's detailed plan. The detailed plan was given to me so that you could fulfill God's Word, *26* the hidden secret truth which has kept itself hidden from the ages and from races of people – but now is shown for what it is to those people who are devoted to God.

27 God made known the glorious wealth of this hidden secret truth to the people devoted to God among the nations. The hidden secret truth is the Anointing[1] in you, the glorious expectation *28* which we proclaim, and we warn and counsel every person, and teach wisdom to every person, so that we can produce every person as complete by the Anointing. *29* I work hard to this end too, fighting the contest for the prize with the Anointing's activity which is powerfully at work in me.

Ch.2:1-3 I want you to know the size of the contest I have on your behalf and on behalf of those in Laodicea, and on behalf of those who've never even seen me in the natural realm! *2* The goal is so that their hearts will be encouraged after they have been lovingly knit together. This also leads to the rich and absolute conviction that they've caught on to things, and this results in them having complete knowledge of God's hidden secret truth, that is, the Anointing. *3* All banks of wisdom and knowledge are kept hidden in the Anointing.

4-5 I'm telling you this so that no one will cheat you by giving reasons that sound probable, thus prompting you to draw false conclusions. *5* Although I'm absent in the natural realm, I'm actually with you in the spirit realm, and I'm happy to see your battle order[2] and war backbone produced by faith in the Anointed One.

6-7 So then, since you've received the Anointed One, the Lord Jesus, live your lives with him! *7* You have been planted and built up, the faith you were taught has been consolidated, and you have overflowing gratitude!

8-10 See to it that no one comes and robs you through their pretended wisdom and useless cunning! These actually line up with the traditional teachings of people, and line up with the world's elemental spirits.[3] These are against the Anointed One, *9* because the whole fullness of the divine nature lives in person in him, *10* and you have been made complete by him. He is the source of every ruler and authority.

11-13 You were also circumcised by him, not with the circumcision done by human hands, but by the stripping off[4] of the body of the natural realm – that is, the "circumcision" of the Anointed One. *12* You were jointly buried with

---

[1]   Equally, "the Anointed One", as in following verses.

[2]   τὴν τάξιν καὶ τὸ στερέωμα, *ten taxin kai to stereoma.* τάξις, *taxis*, technical battle term.

[3]   στοιχεῖον, *stoikheion*, "elemental spirit". See also this meaning in verse 20; Galatians 4:3, 9. The word appears also in Heb. 5:12 in the meaning "fundamental principles"; and 2 Pet. 3:10, 12 in the meaning "physical elements". See note on Gal. 4:3.

[4]   ἀπέκδυσις, *apekdusis*, "the stripping off". The corresponding verb is found in Col. 2:15 and Col. 3:9. No examples of the verb or noun earlier than the occurrences in Paul have been found, and both MM and Lightfoot accepted the two words as Pauline neologisms. However, the philosopher Pyrrho (*Diogenes Laertes* 9.66) (c. 360-272 B.C.) states that his aim is to ἐκδῦναι τὸν ἄνθρωπον, *ekdunai ton anthropon*, "strip off human nature". ἐκδύω, *ekduo*, is well attested from Homeric times as "to strip off", and ἔκδυσις, *ekdusis*, as "way out" "escape". The addition of the prefix ἀπό, *apo*, is emphatic.

him in baptism, and by this means you were jointly raised with him through having faith in what God does. It was God who raised him from among the dead. *13* And you who were dead because of your mistakes and foreskins of your natural nature, he jointly made you alive with him, and he granted you favor for all your mistakes.

14-15 He canceled the Legal Document of decrees which stood against us,[1] and he has once and for all removed it from our midst. He nailed it to the cross as a public display of cancellation. *15* After stripping off everything, weapons and all, from governments and powers, he made a public spectacle of them, and led them around as prisoners in a triumphal procession by means of the cross.

16-18 So then, don't let anyone judge you on the matter of food or drink, or on the subject of festivals, New Moons or Sabbath Days. *17* These are a shadow of things to come, but the actual body is the Anointed One. *18* Don't let someone disqualify you from your prize, by taking pleasure in being humble and entering into Messengers' religious worship which they have seen,[2] rashly becoming natural[3] in their senses in the natural realm.

---

[1]   The *Cheirographon* was a legal document or debt or receipt. It was written by the person who owed the debt, and was an acknowledgment of all debts owed. It was a simple document and did not have to be legally registered in the court, quite like an I.O.U. No witnesses were required and it could be written by the person or a local scribe. Such a debt document was not publicly displayed. However, decrees were publicly displayed and Paul has made it clear that this Cheirographon consisted of decrees (epexegetic genitive). Spoils of war were nailed for public display in temples and public buildings, cf. Diod. Sic. *Hist.*, 11.25.1, 12.70.5, 13.19.3.) Sometimes a person's name and lock of hair were nailed for public display. (Lucian, *Syr.D.* 60.12.) Paul is saying that the debt was publicly displayed as canceled. See discussion in S.R. Llewelyn, "'Having cancelled the bond which stood against us': Col.2.14 and the *Cheirographon*," *NDIEC* 6.105-111.

[2]   Here are two technical terms of initiation: θρησκεία, *threskia*, and ἐμβατεύων, *embateuo*, "to be initiated" (otherwise "entering into" with the sense of initiation). Paul is challenging a heresy, the name of which is not stated. Jewish mysticism dated from the 1st c. A.D. It was a variant of Hellenistic mysticism of the astral plane, in which the initiate is said to travel through and beyond seven astral planes. The Jewish initiate sought to be present in the throne room of God as per the description based on the first chapter of Ezekiel. Jewish mysticism traces to the Merkabah practices of the 1st c. AD. The goal of Merkabah Mysticism was to enter a trance-like state by means of fasting, meditation, prayer and incantation, and thus ascend to God's heavenly throne room and experience of God's Throne-Chariot (Hebrew: "Merkabah") as described in Ezekiel 1:15-25. The traveler must pass through 7 heavens, and once in the seventh heaven, the traveler must pass through seven concentric palaces. God's Throne-Chariot stands in the innermost of seven palaces, the gate to each place being barred by fierce guard angels. Once before God's throne, the traveler would worship God side by side with angels and thus observe the innermost secrets of all persons and things, otherwise unsolvable and invisible. The Talmud states of Merkabah Mysticism, "The subject of...the work of the chariot [may not be expounded]...unless one is a sage who has innate understanding of it. Whoever speculates on [the work of the chariot], it would have been better if they had not come into the world." (*Mishnah Hagigah* 2:1)

[3]   θυσιόω, *thusioo*, does not mean to become conceited, or puffed up with pride. To the contrary, it means in the passive, as here, to be made or become natural, cf. Arist. *Categ.* 8.3, Clem. *Al.* 859. In the active, it means "to dispose one naturally (to do a thing)".

19 Such a person does not take hold of the Source.[1] It's the Source that more than fully supplies the whole body, knits it together and makes it grow with growth from God through the ligaments and sinews.

20-21 Since you died with the Anointed One to the elemental spirits of the world, why do you subject yourself to decrees, as if you are living in the world? – *21* "Do not handle," "do not taste," "do not touch"!

22-23 All these things are destined to decay through misuse, as are the instructions and training of people. *23* These things hold the promise of wisdom because they offer self-imposed worship and humility and hard discipline of the body, but they don't have any value for getting what you need in the natural realm.

Ch.3:1-11 So then, since you were jointly raised with the Anointed One, seek the things that are above where the Anointed One is, sitting at God's right side. *2* Set your minds on the things above, not on things on the earth. *3* For you died, and your life has been hidden with the Anointed One in God. *4* When the Anointed One who is indeed our life, is shown for what he is, then you also will be shown for what you are with honor. *5* So then, make a corpse of your parts which are on the earth, pornography, uncleanness, bad desires - and greedy grasping behavior, which is idol worship. *6* Because of these things God's anger comes upon people who are disobedient. *7* This is how you once behaved, when you lived in this way. *8* But in point of fact you must get rid all these – anger, rage, bad ways, blasphemy, foul language. *9* Don't lie to each other!

You have stripped off clothing, the old person with its deeds. *10* You have put on a new person as your clothes. Your new person is constantly being renewed in the image of the One who created it, and as a result you have complete knowledge. *11* In the image of the Creator there is no Greek or Jew, circumcised or foreskin, foreigner, Skythian,[2] slave, free. Rather, the Anointing is in all of them, and the Creator is in all of them!

12-13 So then, as you are sacred chosen people of God, people he has always loved, you must put on clothes of compassion and kindness, and be humble-minded, even-tempered, tolerant towards others. *13* You must put up with each other. If you have a reason to blame someone, you must do them a favor. Just as the Anointed One did favors for you, you must do favors to others too.

14-15 The most important piece of clothing you must wear is love. Love is the thing that fastens everything together and makes all your clothes complete. *15* And let God's peace be the umpire of your minds. God's peace is the reason you were chosen to be members of one body – and be thankful for it!

16-17 The Word of the Anointed One must live in you richly and this will give you great wisdom. Teach, counsel and warn each other, with songs of praise, festive praise songs in honor of God, and favorable spiritual songs, singing to God with all your heart. *17* Whatever you do or say, do it in the Name of the Lord Jesus, while thanking God the Father through him.

18-25 Wives, be supportive of[3] your husbands, just as you are connected with[4] the Lord. *19* Husbands, love your wives, and don't be insensitive to

---

[1] κεφαλή, *kephale*, "source". Note the word play: "head" meaning natural head / source in the Greek. See note on 1 Corinthians 11:3.

[2] The Skythians typified barbarians.

[3] ὑποτάσσω, *hupotasso*. See note on Eph. 5:21.

[4] ἀνήκω, *aneko*, "be connected with", cf. Dem. 1390.17; Arist. *Eth. N.* 9.6, 2. Does not mean "is fitting". Note connection between ἀνήκω, *aneko*, and ὑποτάσσω, *hupotasso*, ἀνήκω, *aneko*, meaning "connect" and ὑποτάσσω, *hupotasso*, here "be supportive of" but its main meaning was "be attached to" and it was used for attached documents in the postal system. Paul is playing on words

them. *20* Children, pay attention[1] to your parents[2] about everything, as this pleases the Lord. *21* Fathers, don't aggravate your children – this is so that they don't become spiritless. *22* Slave servants, pay attention to your masters in everything. Don't make an outward show of it just to be people pleasers, but do it single-mindedly, out of respect[3] to the Lord. *23* And everything that you do, work at it with your whole heart as if you are doing it for the Lord and not for people, *24* knowing that you will be paid what is due to you. This is the inheritance from the Lord. You serve the Lord! *25* But the wrongdoer will get what's coming to them for what they have done, and the Lord won't show any favoritism.

Ch.4. Masters, supply your slave servants with what's fair and right, knowing that you also have a Master who is in heaven!

2-6 Persist obstinately when you pray, being stirred up about it, and thank God. *3* At the same time pray about us too. Pray that God will open a door for the Word for us, so that we can speak the hidden secret truth of the Anointed One. This was also the reason that I was imprisoned. *4* Pray that everything turns out all right so that I can speak very clearly. *5* Act wisely to outsiders, and make the most of every opportunity. *6* Your speech must always be favorable, and never insipid. You must know how to answer each individual person.

7-11 Tychikos, a much loved fellow believer, trustworthy minister and joint slave servant, a follower of the Lord, will tell you all the news about me. *8* I'm sending him to you for precisely this reason, so that you can find out all about us, and so that he can encourage you. *9* He's coming with Onesimos, a trustworthy and much loved fellow believer, who is one of you. They will fill you in on everything that's happening here. *10* Aristarchos my fellow prisoner greets you, as does Mark, Barnabas's cousin (you received instructions about him – if he comes to you, you must welcome him), *11* and Jesus who is called Justus. These are my only fellow workers for God's Realm who are of the circumcision (Jews) – and they have turned out to be a comfort to me.

12-15 Epaphras who is one of you, a slave servant of the Anointed One, says hello. He is always fighting for the winner's prize in the prayers for you. He prays that you will be absolutely convinced of all God's wishes, and then you will be in a state of completeness. *13* I can testify that he works extremely hard on your behalf, and for the people in Laodicea and in Heirapolis. *14* Luke the much loved doctor and Demas greet you. *15* Greet the fellow believers who are in Laodicea, and Nympha and the assembly that is in her house.[4]

16-18 When this letter is read in your presence, see that it's also read in the assembly of the Laodiceans, and that you also read the letter from Laodicea. *17* Also, say to Archippos, "See to it that you fulfill the ministry you have received which the Lord handed over to you."

18 This greeting is in my own handwriting – Paul's. Remember my imprisonment! May favor be with you!

---

again. This wordplay cannot be brought out in the English language. See also Eph. 5:4.

1   ὑπακούω, *hupakouo*. See note on Matt. 8:27.
2   πατέρες, *pateres*. See note on Eph. 6:4.
3   Often translated as "fear" but the correct translation in the connection of divinity is "respect". This is standard throughout Greek literature.
4   Both Tyndale's 1534 translation and KJV changed the female Nympha's name to a male termination and changed "in her house" to "in his house".

Letters to the Thessalonians.

The letters to the Thessalonians were written by Paul from Corinth around 50 AD, around 20 years after the death and resurrection of Jesus. Apart from Galatians, the letters are Paul's earliest surviving writings. 1 Thessalonians was written in Corinth soon after Paul's arrival there (1 Thess. 3:6; Acts 18:5). 1 Thessalonians was widely accepted, and was quoted by name by Irenaeus, Clement of Alexandria and Tertullian. It is included in Marcion's canon and the Muratorian canon.

Paul has been slandered by certain people, and he addresses this in his letter we now know as 1 Thessalonians. Someone claiming to be Paul has sent a letter to the Thessalonians saying that the Day of the Lord had already come. Paul sets the Thessalonians straight in 2 Thessalonians.

Thessalonika, the largest city of Macedonia and principal port of the region, was named after the half-sister of Alexander the Great (the daughter of Philip II). Mark Anthony and Octavian visited it after their victory at Philippi and made it a free city. It was at Thessalonika that the Roman orator, Cicero, was exiled. The famous Via Egnatia, which transversed Macedonia from east to west, passed through the city. It was the principal route of communication between Rome and its eastern provinces. Thessalonika was a wealthy commercial city. Today the Roman ruins under excavation at Thessalonika can be seen in front of today's modern city. The city was destroyed in the Second World War, and until then continued to have a very large Jewish community. Interestingly, the modern city preserves the street patterns of the ancient city.

First Letter to the Thessalonians.

Ch.1:1 From: Paul, Silvanos and Timothy.

To: The assembly of the Thessalonians who belong to God the Father and the Lord Jesus the Anointed One.

Hello! May you have peace!

2-7 We always thank God for you when we mention you in our prayers. *3* Without ceasing, in the presence of our God and Father, we remember your faithful work and your loving labor, your endurance which is based on the hope given to you by our Lord Jesus the Anointed One.

4 Dearly loved fellow believers,[1] we know you were chosen by God, *5* because our Good News did not come to you by means of word alone but also by means of power and the Holy Spirit, and with much absolute conviction. Likewise, you knew the kind of people we were when we were among you, and indeed, that we were like it for your sake. *6* And you became imitators of us and of the Lord, after you welcomed the Word, although it was accompanied by much oppression, with the joy given by the Holy Spirit. *7* Consequently you became patterns for all the believers in Macedonia and Achaia.

8-10 The Word of the Lord has been spoken out by you not only in Macedonia and Achaia, but also in every place! Your faith in God has proceeded out, and consequently we do not need to say anything. *9* These people themselves report the type of reception they had among you. They report how you turned from idols to God, to serve the living and true God, *10* and to wait for his Son from heaven, whom he raised from among the dead; Jesus, our rescuer from the anger which is coming.

---

[1] ἀδελφοί, *adelphoi*. See note on Matt. 5:22.

Ch.2:1-2 Fellow believers, you yourselves know that our visit to you was not useless. *2* But we had previously experienced insulting treatment in Philippi, just as you know, and we spoke the Good News to you with the right of freedom of speech, boldly, openly in public with God's help, in the midst of much arguing.

3-8 Now we didn't encourage you by means of error or mixed motives or uncleanness, or out of craftiness. *4* Rather, we have been approved by God to be entrusted with the Good News. Our words reflect this. We don't try to please people, but we try to please God who examines our hearts.

5 Not once did we use flattering words or a pretext for greedy grasping behavior – God is our witness! *6* Nor did we seek praise from people – either from you or from others – although we have the power to impose our weight as the Anointed One's apostles! *7* But we were kind when we were among you, just like a nurse would soothe her own little children. *8* Thus, as we cared about you, we were most pleased to impart to you not only the Good News of God but also our very lives, because you had become very dear to us.

9-16 You remember, fellow believers, the trouble and hard work that we went to. We worked night and day so that we would not be a burden to any one of you, while we proclaimed the Good News of God to you. *10* You are witnesses, as is God, of just how holy, honest and blameless we were among you believers. *11* You well know how we encouraged, cheered up and affirmed to each one of you like a parent[1] does their children, *12* to behave in a manner worthy of God who invites you into his own glorious Realm. *13* And on account of this too we thank God constantly, because you received God's Word which we handed over to you. In fact, you welcomed it not as the word of people but for what it really is, God's Word. God's Word is at work in you believers!

14 Fellow believers, you became imitators of the assemblies of God that are in Judea, followers of the Anointing of Jesus, because you also were treated in the same way by your fellow countrypeople as they were by the Jews. *15* Some of the Jews killed both the Lord Jesus and their own prophets, and they drove us out. They don't please God and they oppose everyone *16* by forbidding us to speak to the non-Jews in order to get them saved. By doing this, they've made up the full quota of their sins! No sooner did they do this than God's anger came upon them to the utmost!

17-18 But we, fellow believers, as we have been torn away from you for a short time, in presence, not in heart, we are even more excessively eager to see you face to face. In fact, we have a great desire to do so. *18* This is because we wanted to come to you a few times – I Paul am saying this – and Adversary threw obstacles in our way.

19-20 What is our expectation, our happiness, our crown of boasting? Isn't it indeed you, in the presence of our Lord Jesus at his Coming? *20* You are our glorious happiness!

Ch.3:1-5 For this reason, when we couldn't put up with it any more, we considered it a good thing to be left behind in Athens alone. *2* We sent Timothy, our fellow believer and our coworker of God for the Good News of the Anointed One, with the view to strengthening and encouraging you about your faith, *3* so that no one would be agitated by these oppressions. You yourselves know that we have been destined for this. *4* And in fact we foretold, when we were with you, that we would be oppressed, and it happened, as you know. *5* On account of this, when I really couldn't put up with it any longer, I sent to find out about your faith, in case somehow the

---

[1] πατήρ, *pater*. See note on Eph. 6:4.

Harasser[1] had harassed you, which would have meant the trouble we had gone to for you would have been for nothing.

6-8 But now Timothy has come back to us from you and announced to us the good news about your faith and love. He's told us that you always have good memories of us. We long to see you too, just as you long to see us. *7* On account of this we have been encouraged about you, because of your faith, fellow believers, as we go through this difficulty and oppression. *8* It's great that you are standing firm as followers of the Lord!

9-13 What gratitude can we possibly offer to God for you! We are so happy because of you! With this happiness we are in God's presence *10* day and night, over-excessively putting earnest requests to see you face to face and completely equip what is lacking in your faith. *11* Now may our God and Father himself, and our Lord Jesus, guide us and make us a path which is straight to you!

12 May the Lord make your love for each other and for everyone grow and overflow, just as our love for you overflows. *13* As a result, he will establish your hearts on firm ground, blameless and sacred in the presence of our God and Father when the Lord Jesus comes with all his people devoted to God. Amen!

Ch.4:1 Finally then, fellow believers, we ask and encourage you as followers of the Lord Jesus that you would receive what we've handed over to you, namely, how to behave in a way that pleases God, and that you would excel at it even more.

2-8 You know what instructions we gave you by the authority of the Lord Jesus. *3* This is God's purpose; that you are holy, and that you keep away from worshipping idols. *4* Each of you should know how to get control of your own living with holiness and honor, *5* not by carrying out your own wants and wishes like the people who worship other gods - these people don't know God. *6* This is so that you won't rip off your fellow believers in business dealings. Indeed the Lord is the avenger of all these people, as we have already told you and solemnly testified. *7* God didn't call us to dirty business, he called us to holiness. *8* Consequently, the person who rejects this isn't rejecting people, but is rejecting God, who gives his Holy Spirit to you!

9-12 Now about love for fellow-believers – there's need for me to write to you about this, as you yourselves are taught by God to love one another. *10* And indeed this is exactly how you act toward all the fellow believers who are in Macedonia. But we urge you, fellow believers, to excel at it even more, *11* so that your driving ambition will be to live in settled peace, and to carry out your own business affairs and to work at them actively, just as we instructed you. *12* This is so that you will behave decently to the outsiders and you won't need anything!

13-18 Now fellow believers, I don't want you to be ignorant about those who have passed away. Otherwise you might be sad like those other people who have no expectation. *14* Now since we believe that Jesus died and rose again, it's also a fact that when Jesus comes, God will also bring along those who have passed away.

15 Now we are saying this to you by the Word of the Lord, that we who are alive and left remaining at the Coming of the Lord definitely will not precede those who have passed away. *16* Indeed the Lord himself will come down from heaven with a summons, at the shout of the Chief Messenger and with the trumpet of God. And the corpses of those who were followers of the Anointed One will rise first. *17* Then we who are alive and left remaining will at the same time be caught up with them and carried off in the clouds to meet the

---

[1] "The Harasser" is another name for Adversary (the devil, Satan). See note on Matt. 4:1.

Lord in the air. And so we will be with the Lord at all times. *18* Consequently, encourage each other with these words.

Ch.5:1-3 Now, fellow believers, there's no need for me to write to you about the times and the specific occasions, *2* for you yourselves know perfectly well that the Day of the Lord will come like a thief in the night. *3* When they are saying, "Peace and stability," then suddenly destruction will come upon them by surprise just like the labor in a pregnant woman, and there is no escape.

4-8 But you, fellow believers, you are not in darkness that the Day would suddenly come upon you like a thief. *5* For you are all people associated with light and people associated with day. You are not people associated with night or people associated with darkness. *6* So then do not sleep as the rest of them do, but be awake and be clear-headed. *7* For those who sleep, sleep at night, and those who get drunk, get drunk at night. *8* But let us, as we belong to the day, be clear-headed. Let us put on the breastplate which is faith and love, and let us wear as a helmet, the fact that we expect to be delivered.

9-11 Indeed God did not prepare us for his anger, but he prepared us to be delivered through our Lord Jesus the Anointed One, *10* who died on our behalf. So then, whether we're awake or asleep, we will be alive together with him. *11* For this reason, encourage each other and build each other up, just as you're doing.

12-13 Now we ask you, brothers and sisters, to observe those among you who go to trouble for you, those you have chosen to care for you as the Lord's followers, those who warn you. *13* Have a regard for them which is beyond measure, and do so lovingly, on account of their work.

13-15 Live at peace with each other. *14* Fellow believers, we encourage you to warn those who are out of battle order! Cheer up those who are faint hearted! Stand your ground as a shield in front of those who are weak! Be tolerant with everyone! *15* See to it that no one repays wrongdoing with wrongdoing. Instead, at all times chase after good for one another and for everyone.

16-22 Always be happy!
17 Pray constantly!
18 Give thanks for everything! Indeed this is God's purpose for you as followers of the Anointed One Jesus.
19 Do not extinguish the Spirit!
20 Do not scorn prophecies!
21 Examine everything! Hold on tightly to what's favorable!
22 Keep away from every sort of evil!

23-24 Now may God himself, the God of peace, make your holiness quite complete, and may your whole self, that is, your spirit, soul and body, be guarded blameless at the Coming of our Lord Jesus the Anointed One.
24 He who invites you is trustworthy. He will bring it to pass!

25-27 Fellow believers, pray about us too!
26 Greet all the fellow believers with a sacred kiss.
27 I lay the duty on you by the Lord to read this letter to all the people devoted to God!

28 May the favor of our Lord Jesus the Anointed One be with you!

Second Letter to the Thessalonians.

2 Thessalonians did not enjoy the same widespread acceptance as 1 Thessalonians and is dated shortly after it. However, it is quoted by name by Irenaeus, and included in Marcion's canon and the Muratorian canon.

Second Letter to the Thessalonians.

Ch.1:1-2   From: Paul, Silvanos, and Timothy.
To: The assembly of the Thessalonians, followers of God our Father and the Lord Jesus the Anointed One.
2 Hello! May you be given peace by God our Father and the Lord Jesus the Anointed One!
3-6 We must thank God at all times for you, fellow believers, as is fitting, because your faith grows beyond measure, and the love you have for each other grows excessively. *4* Consequently, we ourselves take pride in you among the assemblies of God because of your endurance and your faith throughout all the harassment and oppressions which you put up with. *5* Harassment and oppressions will demonstrate the just judgment of God. They point out God's just decision which is determined to place you into God's Realm. This is the reason that you're experiencing these things. *6* But it's a fact that God's justice will give the oppressors what they deserve.
7-10 There will be relief for us as well as for those who are being oppressed, when the Lord Jesus is revealed from heaven with his powerful Messengers, *8* in a burning fire. He will inflict vengeance on those who do not know God and those who do not pay attention to the Good News of our Lord Jesus. *9* These individuals will pay the penalty of eternal loss away from the Lord's presence of and away from his glorious strength, when he comes on that Day. *10* His honor will be acknowledged among the people devoted to God and he will be wondered at by all those who became believers. You will be among them because you believed what we told you.
11-12 And so we also pray that you are always worthy of God's invitation. We pray that you will bring to completion every good work and that you will powerfully complete the work inspired by faith. *12* We pray that the Name of our Lord Jesus would be brought honor by you, and you would be brought honor by him. This will come about due to the favor of our God and Lord Jesus the Anointed One.
Ch.2:1-2 We ask you, fellow believers, concerning the Coming of our Lord Jesus the Anointed One and our gathering together to him, *2* not to let your thoughts be hastily disturbed or troubled, either by a prophesy, or by a report, or by a letter which was supposed to have come from us, saying that the Day of the Lord was at hand.
3-5 Don't let anyone beguile you in any way! That Day can't happen unless the Departure comes first, and the person associated with illegal acts is revealed in their true light! This is the person associated with destruction, *4* the opposing counterpart who exalts themselves above everything that is called a god or that is an object of worship, to the point of taking their seat in the temple of God, claiming that they are God. *5* Don't you remember when I was still with you I kept telling you these things?
6-8 And as it is, you know what is holding this one back, so that they will be revealed in their appointed time. *7* For the secret workings of lawlessness[1] are

---

[1]   Quoted by Jerome, *Ephesians*, 133.4. Note there he uses the Latin term *mulierculae*, a contemptuous colloquial expression referring to followers of heretics. Jerome here is attacking Pelagius and his female followers by reciting a satirical list of who had followed heretics from Nicholas of Antioch up to Priscillian. He added, "Both genders aiding one another, had

already at work, only that which is now restraining will do so until that one is separated from their midst. *8* And then the lawlessness in person will be revealed. The Lord will do away with that one by the breath of his mouth and render that one inoperative with the sudden appearance of his Coming.

9-10 His Coming is at the time of Adversary's activity, with all power, miraculous signs and deceptive wonders, *10* and every kind of dishonest deceit by means of foul play. The lawless one will use it on those who are on the road to destruction, because they did not welcome the love of truth which would have led to their deliverance.

11-12 And on account of this God will send them an active mistake. This will lead to them believing the falsehood, *12* so that everyone who did not believe the truth, but took pleasure in injustice, will be judged.

13-15 But we must thank God at all times for you, fellow believers very dear to the Lord! God chose you from the very beginning to be saved through the work of the Spirit that makes you sacred, and through faith in the truth. *14* He invited you to this by means of the Good News – this meant you took hold of the splendor of our Lord Jesus the Anointed One. *15* So then, fellow believers, stand firm, and take hold of the teachings which you were taught, whether by word or our letter.

16-17 Now may our Lord Jesus the Anointed One and God our Father who loved us and through his favor gave us encouragement for this age as well as good expectation, *17* encourage your minds and strengthen you for every good deed and word.

Ch.3:1-5 Finally, fellow believers, pray about us, for the Word of the Lord to move quickly and be honored just as it has been with you, *2* and for us to be delivered from weird and wicked people – for all do not have faith. *3* Now the Lord is trustworthy. He will establish your strength and guard you from the Evil One. *4* The Lord has given us confidence that you are doing and will do the things we instructed you to do. *5* May the Lord guide you on a straight path to God's love and to the endurance given by the Anointed One.

6-9 Fellow believers, I instruct you in the Name of the Lord Jesus to send for every fellow believer who behaves out of order and does not follow the traditional teachings which we have handed over to you. *7* For you yourselves know how you should copy us, because we weren't out of order when we were among you! *8* Nor did we eat anyone else's bread without paying for it, but we went to trouble and hard work, working night and day so that we wouldn't be a burden to any one of you. *9* This was not because we don't have authority! It was so that we would offer ourselves as a pattern for you to follow.

10-12 And in fact when we were with you, we gave you these instructions, that if someone does not want to work, they should not eat![1] *11* For we hear that there are some among you who behave out of order - they're not busy at all, but they are busybodies! *12* Now, by the authority of the Lord Jesus the Anointed One, we instruct these sorts of people that while they are idling their time away they are to eat their own bread!

13-18 As for you, fellow believers, do not lose heart while you are doing what's favorable! *14* But if someone doesn't pay attention to this letter, then take note of that person and don't associate with them, so that they will be turned about. *15* And don't consider them an enemy, but warn them as a fellow believer. *16* Now may the Lord of peace himself give you peace through all times in every way. May the Lord be with you! *17* The greeting is my own handwriting – Paul. This is a sign of authenticity in every letter - that's why I do it. *18* May the favor of Jesus the Anointed One be with you all!

---

contributed to 'the *musterion* of iniquity'." See 2 Tim. 3:6 for γυναικάριον, *gunaikarion*, the Greek for the Latin *mulierculae*.
[1]   The θέλει, *thelei*, "want to", has been left out of most Bible versions.

Letters to Timothy.

The authorship of the "pastoral epistles" (1 Timothy, 2 Timothy, and Titus) has been disputed since the 19th c. although attributed to Paul from the 2nd c. until that point. Irenaeus, Polycarp, Justin Martyr, and Herakleon cited the epistles as Pauline. The authorship of Paul is doubted on several grounds, citing as reasons the different vocabulary from the Pauline corpus and the absence of usual Pauline theological terms. It has been suggested that if Paul indeed was the author that he used an amanuensis. Those differences can be explained by the different subject matter. The vocabulary of 1 Timothy alludes to various magical practices of Ephesos and to the problem of Gnosticism. The date of 1 Timothy is generally placed after Paul's release from his first Roman imprisonment (c. 61 AD) and prior to Paul's final imprisonment and death in 64.

Timothy's mother was a Jew and his father was a Greek. His mother Eunice became a Christian. Timothy came from Lystra which had been a Roman colony from the time of Augustus. Paul spent some time in Lystra, being stoned there, and visiting the believers there on his second missionary journey. Today, there are at least two Lystras and the ancient site is in dispute. The Greek gods Zeus and Hermes (Roman names Jupiter and Mercury) were associated with Lystra.

Paul had left Timothy in Ephesos to care for the church there, and Timothy is in Ephesos at the time of the letter known as 1 Timothy. This is highly significant. Ephesos was the capital city of the Roman province of Asia, and had about one third of a million inhabitants. Ephesos was well known historically as a center for magical practices, spell casting and the conjuring of evil spirits. The New Testament links Ephesos with much demonic activity. Ephesos was the cult center of the worship of the Ephesian goddess Artemis (not to be confused with the Greek Artemis), known as "the greatest" and "the supreme power". The city held the title of Temple Warden of the goddess. She was said to have authority over all the demons of the dead as well as the harmful spirits of nature. Artemis was known as a mother goddess, a fertility goddess and a nature goddess. Pausanias tells us that the worship of Artemis was widespread. Ephesos was also associated with Gnosticism, and the focus of the pastoral epistles is the problem of false teaching.

Today, Ephesos provides a wealth of attractions for the tourist. The Temple of Domitian was the first place of worship in Ephesos to be dedicated to a Roman emperor. The Emperor Domitian (AD 81-96) referred to himself as "ruler and god" and employed tyrannical methods. The temple was built on the best site in Ephesos and cost the Ephesians a small fortune to build. Hadrian's temple (built c. A.D. 138) was the second place of worship in Ephesos to be dedicated to a Roman emperor. The temple is Corinthian. The podium originally held the statue of Emperor Hadrian, who was worshipped as a god. The Houses on the Slope can be seen today behind the ruins of the temple. These were inhabited by the most wealthy citizens and date to the time of Augustan. Most of the houses had three floors and were heavily ornamented. The walls were frescoed in mythological scenes, and the floors were decorated with high quality mosaics. One of the houses, a 1st c. residence, has been restored. It was a house of two floors and 990 square yards (c. 900 m).

Before the temple was partially demolished in 400 AD, it underwent restorations, and at this time four decorative reliefs were added. Three of the reliefs were taken from other Ephesian buildings and date to the 3rd c. AD. The fourth was made during the restorations. Strangely, it features King Theodosios, a professing Christian who was strongly opposed to paganism, standing with his wife and son and standing beside a figure of the Ephesian Artemis. At each end of the block of this particular relief appears a portrayal of Athena. Next to the figure of Theodosios is a portrayal of his father in a half-naked dead state.

The Fountain of Trajan (built A.D. 102-104) was consecrated to the Emperor Trajan. The temple is Corinthian. Many sculptures of Dionysus, Aphrodite and Satyr as well as members of the Imperial family once populated the fountain. The arch featured the bust of a goddess. A huge statue of the Emperor Trajan rose to the top of the two-storied building and stood in the middle section where the water flowed into a pool.

First Letter to Timothy.

Ch.1:1-2   From: Paul, an apostle of the Anointed One Jesus, by the divine command of God our Savior and the Anointed One Jesus our hope.

2 To: Timothy, a genuine member of those who follow the faith.

Hello! May you have mercy and peace from God the Father and the Anointed One Jesus our Lord!

3-4 Just as I encouraged you when I was traveling to Macedonia - stay on in Ephesos to instruct some people not to teach errors! *4* Nor should they devote themselves to fiction[1] and the countless making out of family trees.[2] This leads to speculation rather than to us following God's detailed plans[3] which are carried out by means of faith.

5-7 The aim of the instruction is to act lovingly with a clean heart, a good conscience and non-overly critical faith. *6* Now some people have stepped out of line and have turned aside from this. They've turned out to be full of hot air! *7* They want to be experts in the Law, although they don't understand what they're talking about or being so dogmatic about.

---

[1]   One of the lesser meanings of μῦθος, *muthos*, is "myth", but all the meanings encompass the sense "fiction". Note the pejorative use of μῦθοι, *muthoi*, in 1 Tim. 1:4; 4:7; 2 Tim. 4:4; Titus 1:14, 2 Pet. 1:16. The Egyptians called the Greek deities μυθολογία, *muthologia*, mythological, fictional and significantly, used this term to contrast the πράξεις ἐναργεῖς, *prakseis enargeis*, of Isis, suggesting that any so-called manifestation of a Greek god was fiction. An inscription on a statue base, E.L. Hicks, *The Collection of Greek Inscriptions in the British Museum*, III.2 (Oxford, 1890) 482 (+addendum on p. 294) (Ephesos c. 162-64), B *ll*.6-14 states, "Since the goddess Artemis, leader of our city, is honored not only her own homeland, which she has made the most illustrious of all cities through her own divine nature, but also among Greeks and also foreigners, the result is that everywhere her shrines and sanctuaries have been established, and temples have been funded for her, and altars dedicated to her because of the visible manifestations (ἐναργεῖς, *enargeis*) effected by her." *I.Eph.* 1a27.385 uses the epithet ἐπιφανεστάτη, *epiphanestate*, "most appearing", "most manifesting", for Artemis. There is much Gnostic fiction based on Genesis 1-3. See Elaine Pagels, "Adam, Eve and the Serpent in Genesis 1-3," in *Images of the Feminine in Gnosticism*, 412. See note on 1 Timothy 2:16.

[2]   The Old Testament shows that Jews have always carefully recorded their genealogies. After the return from the Exile, the need for family trees was of importance due to the determination to avoid mixed marriages, cf. Ezra and Nehemiah.

[3]   The KJV's mistranslation here, "edifying", was due to the fact that the translators misread οἰκονομία, *oikonomia*, mistaking it for οἰκοδμήν, *oikodmen*. This is noted by G.V. Wigram, *The Englishman's Greek Concordance of the New Testament*, Massachusetts 1998, p. 526. See note on Luke 16:2.

8-11 Now we know the Law is fine if someone uses it legally. *9* But know this, that law is not instituted for honest people, but for lawless and rebellious people, ungodly sinners, lawless godless people, murderers of fathers and murderers of mothers, people killers, *10* people who engage in *porneia*, *arsenokoites*,[1] kidnappers,[2] liars, perjurers, and anything else that is opposed to completely healthy instruction and training. *11* And I say this according to the Good News about God's glorious blessing which was entrusted to me.

12-14 I thank the Anointed One Jesus our Lord who empowered me and still empowers me. He considered that I was trustworthy to be appointed to the ministry, *13* although I used to be a blasphemer, a persecutor, and an arrogant person. But I was shown mercy because I did it ignorantly out of unbelief. *14* Our Lord greatly, and even excessively, favored me with the faith and love given by Jesus with the Anointing.

15-17 This is a trustworthy message, and worthy to be accepted fully, "The Anointed One Jesus came into the world to save sinners", of whom I am the foremost sinner! *16* But it was for this reason that I was shown mercy, so that I could be an example of one to whom the Anointed One could show great tolerance, a pattern sketched out for those who are going to believe on him and thus have everlasting life. *17* To the King of the ages, immortal, invisible, to the only God, be honor and praise forever and ever, amen!

18-20 This is the instruction I give you, Timothy my child: serve as a soldier in the fine war campaign by means of those prophecies which were foretold to you! *19* Do it with faith and a good conscience, on which some have turned their back, and have shipwrecked their faith. *20* Among these are Hymenaios and Alexander, whom I handed over to Adversary so that they would be educated not to blaspheme.

Ch.2:1-7 Therefore I encourage above all else that earnest requests, prayers, intercessions, and gratitude are to be made on behalf of all people, *2* on behalf of kings and all prominent people, so that we would lead an undisturbed life in a dignified and godly manner. *3* This is favorable and welcome in the sight of our Savior God, *4* who wants all people to be saved and to come to the full knowledge of truth. *5* For there is one God, and one mediator between God and people, the person the Anointed One Jesus. *6* He gave himself as the payment of everyone's ransom. This is the evidence that God gave at the proper time. *7* I was appointed a proclaimer and a messenger of this – I am speaking the truth and not lying – as a true and faithful teacher of the non-Jews.

8-10 [3]So then I would like the men everywhere to pray,[4] leading clean lives,[1] without anger or argument. *9* And the same goes for women too.[2] I

---

[1] ἀρσενοκοίτης, *arsenokoites*. There is no ready English translation for this Greek word. See note on 1 Cor. 6:9.

[2] ἀνδραποδίστης, *andrapodistes*. This is translated in the Vulgate by *plagiarius*. See Greek prefectural papyrus, a translation of a Latin text, a list of criminal charges including kidnapping: *ed.pr.* N. Lewis, *RD* 50 (1972) 5-12, Col. 2, *l.*5. Horsley (*NDIEC* 1.50) states, "BAGD suggests 'procurer' as the meaning here, but that is not necessary; 'kidnapper' fits quite satisfactorily into this NT vice list since by no means all the words given relate to sexual misdemeanors."

[3] The verses to the end of this chapter have been significantly and widely mistranslated. Classical scholar, J.M. Holmes, *Text in a Whirlwind: A Critique of Four Exegetical Devices at 1 Timothy 2.9-15, Journal for the Study of the New Testament Supplement Series* 196, *Studies in New Testament Greek* 7, Sheffield, 1999, p. 26, states, "There is substantial reason to conclude that some components of 1 Tim. 2.9-15 have been universally misunderstood."

[4] Equally, "on every occasion".

would like women to dress themselves with good taste[3] and in decent[4] clothes with modesty and good sense,[5] not with ornamentally arranged hair[6] or gold or pearls[7] or very expensive clothes,[8] *10* which is fitting for women while they are giving a 'Convert to Judaism'[9] instructions,[10] and which is fitting for women while they are doing good works.[1]

---

[1] ὁσίους χεῖρας, *hosious kheiras*. Greek idiom for leading clean lives. "Pure" in the sense "clean", "sinless" lives. Not "holy". The term "pure hands" is found in Aesch. *Cho.* 378, Soph. *O.C.* 470. The adjective rarely means "holy" and then only of gods.

[2] A frequent Pauline idiom.

[3] κόσμιος, *kosmios*, "with good taste", occurs only here (of woman's dress) and in 1. Tim. 3:2 of a Guardian's behavior in the NT. In both places the word is used in connection with σώφρων, *sophron*.

[4] In the sense of moderate.

[5] σωφροσύνη, *sophrosune*, reason, good sense. For the adjective σώφρων, *sophron,* see 1 Tim. 3:2.

[6] κομάω, *komao*, and κόμη, *kome*, have been commonly rendered in Bible versions as "grow the hair long" and "long hair" respectively. However, there is much evidence for the verb as "give oneself airs", and for the noun as a comet's tail, the gill of a cuttlefish, and the hair of the head. κόμη, *kome*, is used to translate *pe'er* (for example, in Ezek. 24:23), which can be a headdress, turban, an adornment, or a crown/wreath of beauty. Generically, the word refers to decoration. J.M. Holmes, *op.cit.*, p 314, suggests the translation "prettified hair", "dressed hair" and states, "κόμη, *kome*, should be translated along the lines of 'ornamentally arranged' hair".

[7] The women of the time often wore a *stola* held on at the shoulder by brooches. Paul does not mention the highly colorful and inexpensive embroidery and dyes or the many materials, both inexpensive and highly expensive, other than gold and pearls used in jewelry. It is clear Paul is not referring to all artificial adornment.

[8] J.M. Holmes, *op.cit.* p. 69 notes that the chief issue is that ostentation of conspicuous wealth should be avoided, the context being consistently concerned for attracting outsiders to salvation. ἱματισμός, *himatismos*, "clothes". See LXX Ps. 21:19, quoted in John 19:24. It occurs elsewhere in the NT in Luke 7:25; 9:29; Acts 20:33. See *P.Oxy* 1 (1898) 91.14 (187); fragmentary papyrus *CPR* 18 (Pesia).

[9] This is the key to this passage. θεοσέβεια, *theosebeia*. Before the meaning of this word was known, it was variously rendered in New Testament translations as "godliness", "worship of God", "religion". It has been established that the word is a formal designation for a group enrolled in a synagogue, but a group distinct from proselytes and native Jews, specifically a convert (male or female) to Judaism, to someone who was not prepared to be baptized or, in the case of a man, circumcised. J. Reynolds and R. Tannenbaum, *Jews and Godfearers at Aphrodisias,* Cambridge Philological Society Supp. Vol. 12, 1987, p. 50, state, "To be a God-fearer is something short of becoming a full Jew, but it does involve some kind of commitment to some aspects of Judaism." Lydia is described by the cognate term σεβουμένς τὸν Θεόν, *seboumene ton Theon*, in Acts 16:14. A synagogue inscription from Aphrodisias in Karia (published by J. Reynolds) lists several individuals as *Theosebeis*. *AJA* 81 (1977) 306. See inscription which speaks of a section of seating reserved for "Jews as well as *Theosebeis*", *CIJ* 748 (=*SEG* 4.441). M. Wilcox, *JSNT* 13 (1981) 102-22; *Numen* 28.113-26; *JJS* 33. 445-62. For women *Theosebeis* from Rome, Rhodes, Cos and Tralles, see *CIJ* 1.228; *IG* 12.1.593.

[10] ἐπαγγέλομαι, *epaggelomai*, with the accusative. With the dative it generally means "promise", but with the accusative means to give orders to

11-14 [2]A woman must learn[3] and she is to learn[4] without causing a fuss[1] and be supportive[2] in everything.[3] *12* [4]I most certainly do not grant authority to a

---

someone, or to proclaim (something) by authority. It was also a technical word for teaching any form of wisdom for pay. Colson and Whitaker, *edd*, in Philo, *Poster.* C. 501 n. 139. See also a prefect's circular forbidding magic, *P.Coll.Youtie* 1 30 (2nd c) where the verb with the accusative (as here) is translated as giving oneself out as an expert. Here is the verb in context: "Therefore neither through oracles, viz., written documents ostensibly emanating in the presence of the divinity, nor by means of the procession of images or similar trickery, let anyone lay claim to have knowledge of the supernatural, or give themselves out as an expert about the obscurity of future events."

Women are attested as synagogue leaders (and thus teachers). Synagogue leaders and elders were classified also as teachers, cf. Epiphanius of Salamis, *Panarion*, 30.18.2 (*PG* 41.436A); Justin Martyr, *Dialogue with Trypho*, 137. Other people in the synagogue could also be teachers of the Law. Synagogues were places of teaching, cf. *Donateurs* 79.2,2,3 (Jerusalem, I), "Theodotos, son of Vettenus, priest and synagogue leader, son of a synagogue leader, grandson of a synagogue leader, built the synagogue for the reading of the law and the teaching of the commandments".

Inscriptional evidence includes women as Jewish leaders, testifying that women were elders as well as synagogue leaders. For example, *CIJ* 2 741 = *IGRR* 4.1452 speaks of a female synagogue leader. Sophia of Gortyn was an elder and synagogue leader (*CII* 731c), Rufina was a synagogue leader (*CII* 741; *IGR* IV 1452; *I.Smyrna* 1.295.1), as was Theopempte (*CII* 756). Three Jewish inscriptions from the first century BC to the fourth century AD mention women priests (*CII* 1514 (*SEG* 1 [1923] no. 574); *CII* 315; *CII* 1007). Women as Jewish elders are attested in inscriptional evidence: Rebeka (*CII* 692), Beronikene (*CII* 581; *CIL* IX 6226), Mannine (*CII* 590; *CIL* IX 6230), Faustina (*CII* 597; *CIL* IX 6209), Mazauzala (*SEG* 27 (1977) no. 1201), Sara Ura (*CII* 400). See K. Mentzu-Meimare's list of titles for Jewish women elders in Greek inscriptions from the 4th to 5th centuries: *JOB* 32.2 (1982) 433-43. See also B.J. Brooten, *Women Leaders in the Ancient Synagogue*, Brown Judaic Studies, 36, Chico, 1982. The attestations are most significant as there is a dearth to date of Jewish literature from Asia Minor or Crete, or Graeco-Jewish literature of the period.

[1] διά, *dia*, with the genitive to express attendant circumstances. Cited as such for this verse by Moule, *op.cit.*, p. 57. The good works are in addition. The sense is "and which is fitting also for women doing good works."

[2] There would appear to be a change of subject here. The next part talks about learning women. The women in verse 10 are giving orders, but the learning women in the following verses are told they are not to do anything at this point. Why? The answer is that the women in verse 10 are a specific group of women, for they are instructing the Converts to Judaism. These women are now to learn about Christianity, and as students, must be quiet. They were teachers of the Law, but now as new Christians have to go back to square one and be students again: they cannot be teachers of Christianity just because they were teachers of the Law. First they must learn.

[3] The imperative (third person imperative) is that women must learn. A woman in a teaching position must first learn.

[4] Translated thus to bring out the imperative sense of the Greek and to distinguish between the imperative (here) and the (not here) impersonal construction with δεῖ, *dei*, "it is necessary for a woman to learn with inactivity..." This is not the sense here, and the emphasis is on the imperative (exhortation).

woman to teach that she is the originator[5] of a man[1] -rather, she is not to cause a fuss[2]- *13* for Adam was formed first, then Eve.[3] *14* And Adam was

---

[1] ἡσυχία, *hesukhia*, which appears here in verse 10 and in verse 11 is not "silence": rather, it is inactivity or lack of fuss. It means to become quiet in behavior. It can mean "quietness" as in a state of being inactive or at ease. It does not mean verbal silence, and while it could encompass that sense, it is not the meaning. "Silence (verbal quietness)" is ἡ σιγή, ἡ σιωπή, *he sige, he siope*. Acts 22:2 could not mean the crowd became more verbally silent (which, of course, would be an absurd expression), but means that they became quieter in behavior, that is to say, they caused less fuss. See in Antiphon, *Second Tetralogy, First Speech for the Defence*, 11. 1, where ἡσύχιος, *hesuchios*, is translated by R.C. Jebb as "the man of peaceful disposition". *Selections from the Attic Orators*, Ed. R.C. Jebb, London, 1962, p. 203. The actual word in the speech is (τούς) ἡσυχίους, (*tous*) *hesuchious*, translated by K.J. Maidment, *Minor Attic Orators*, Cambridge, 1953, p. 91, as "those who love peace". Holmes, *op.cit.*, p. 77 states that the meaning is "quietness" and not "silence". S.B. Clark, *Man and Woman in Christ*, Michigan, 1980, p. 195, states that ἡσυχία, *hesukhia*, requires abstention not from speech but from teaching/direction.

[2] τῇ ὑποταγῇ, *he hupotage*. See note on 2 Cor. 9:13.

[3] The object of the support is to what is learned. Holmes, *op.cit.*, pp. 75-6; S.H. Gritz, *Paul, Women Teachers, and the Mother Goddess at Ephesus*, Lantham, 1991, p. 130.

[4] The sentence is in the nominative and infinitive construction: "I most certainly do not permit a woman to teach herself to be (in English, "that she is") the originator of a man…". Nominative and infinitive constructions are indirect statements and thus take the negative οὐ, *ou*, rather than μή, *me*. Strong prohibitions generally take the infinitive. When a negative is followed by a compound negative (as here), the negation is strengthened. In an emphatic prohibition the compound negative is the second negative, as here. The double infinitive is usual, particularly after διδάσκειν, *didaskein*. An alternate rendering is "I do not turn over teaching or being the originator of a man to a woman: rather they are to be inactive" (i.e. not to cause a fuss). Either way, this is a slap at Gnosticism.

[5] Not "have authority over", αὐθεντέω τινος, *authenteo tinos*. αὐθεντέω, *authenteo*, is a rare word which occurs only here in the N.T. It occurs very rarely in the Classical Greek authors, where it appears in the meanings "murderer", "perpetrator, author". The verb and noun occur in the Classical authors as follows: in Herodotos once in the meaning murderer; in Thucydides once in the meaning murderer; in Aeschylus twice (*Eumenides* and *Agamemnon*) in the meaning murderer; in Apollonius of Rhodes (although he was a little later, 3rd century BC) in his *Argonautica* twice in the meaning murderer; 6 times in Antiphon in the meaning killer/ murderer (sometimes with reference to suicide) although does occur ambiguously in some of these as author, originator, perpetrator; and 8 times in Euripides' works, twice in *Herakles* in the meaning murderer; twice in *Andromache* in the meaning murderer; once in *The Trojan Women* in the meaning murderer; once in *Iphigenia in Aulis* in the meaning murder; once in *Rhesus* in the meaning murderer; and once in *Suppliants*, in the meaning originate. The word occurs over 20 times in the papyri in the meaning "original", "originator of". It does not take on the meaning "master", "mastery (over)" until later centuries. However, at Nag Hammadi, αὐθέντης, *authentes*, is used in II 96,2, αὐθεντία, *authentia*, in II 29,12, XI 4,29, BG 60,17, αὐθάδης, *authades*, in II 94,24. It is significant that these are Greek loan words in the Coptic. (αὐθεντέω, *authenteo*, does not occur in the Manichaean writings.) For the corresponding adjective αὐθεντίκος,

not deceived, but the woman made a mistake[4] as she was beguiled, *15* and she will be saved by means of the Birth of the Child[5] if they continue to be trustworthy, loving and holy and have good sense.[6]

---

authentikos, see Buresch, *Aus Lydien*, no. 46 (pp.89-106), an inscription recording parts of two rescripts from the proconsul Maximilianus to the Asiarch Dominus Rufus. The text reads, "I deposited a copy of the commands…the original (αὐθεντίκην, *authentike*,) command which was written…" (trans. G.H.R. Horsley, *NDEIC* 2.76). It also occurs in the Nag Hammadi writings in VI 35,23. The particular women to whom Paul (or the writer of 1Timothy) is referring are to learn decently and properly rather than trying to assert themselves as leaders before they were trained. They were still in the learning stages and had to act accordingly.

[1]   "A man", not "her husband".

[2]   Double meaning, to be inactive/not to cause a fuss. Verse 12 is talking about the learning woman, which is clear from the Greek. In 1 Tim. 1:6-7 Paul tells Timothy about people who want to become teachers of the Law without understanding what they are doing. The women are not to become teachers until they have completed their learning stage. Note that in 1 Timothy 1:7, Paul says of "some people" (v.6), "They want to be experts in the Law, although they don't understand what they're talking about or being so dogmatic about."

[3]   The Gnostics, however, stated that Eve was formed prior to Adam in *On the Origin of the World*. See note on verse 15.

[4]   παράβασις, *parabasis*, "made a mistake/blunder", not "fell into sin". The Bible clearly states that Adam was the one who sinned (and Paul clearly states this in Romans 5:14). Adam was disobedient, Eve was deceived. "Blunder" and "sin" are two quite separate words in the Greek.

The most influential background to the Pastorals is false teaching. For 1 Timothy's focus on this see Richard Clark Kroeger and Catherine Clark Kroeger, *Rethinking 1 Timothy 2:11-15 in Light of Ancient Evidence: I Suffer Not a Woman*, Michigan, 1993, *passim*; Holmes, *op.cit.*, pp. 107f. See the below note for relevance of Paul's mention of Eve to the false teaching of Gnosticism. Even apart from Gnosticism, Paul calls on an Old Testament example to illustrate his point. Adam was first, Eve was second. In the Ephesian church, certain Ephesian women have only just become teachers of Christianity and many are in the learning process. Eve made a blunder as she was less informed. God told Adam not to eat of the Tree of Knowledge of Good and Evil – Eve had not been created at this stage. Eve only heard it second hand. Eve was second on the scene, and needed to get her facts straight. The blunder happened because she did not get her facts straight before she made a decision, and this is how Adversary took the advantage. She was deceived. Adam was deliberately disobedient. At no point did God rebuke Eve. He said, "What's this that you've done?" She stated the fact, "The serpent deceived me, and I ate."

[5]   A refutation of Gnostic belief. Eve was beguiled (the Greek word suggesting by cunning or supernatural means): Adam was disobedient and sinned. The result was the fall. The human race was saved through the birth of Jesus, pointing back to Genesis 3:15, where God said that Eve's offspring would be the downfall of Adversary. Note that the "she" at the beginning of this verse refers to Eve, and the "they" at the second part of the verse represents Adam and Eve.

[6]   Certain women are new converts. The men have been converts for some time. The women are learning so they cannot assume the authority of teachers or cause a fuss, but must be inactive while learning. Learners will get people into trouble if they assume authority while they are still in the learning process. In the pastorals, Paul's primary concern is false teaching. For

Ch.3:1-7 This is a faithful saying. If any person[1] aspires to be a Guardian,[2] they are desiring a fine work. *2* So then it is necessary that they are blameless and faithful to their partner,[3] not a drunkard, sensible,[1] well behaved,[2]

---

discussion, see Richard Clark Kroeger and Catherine Clark Kroeger, *Rethinking 1 Timothy 2:11-15 in Light of Ancient Evidence: I Suffer Not a Woman*, Michigan, 1993. Eve was venerated by the Gnostics as the revealer of knowledge. In 1945 the Nag Hammadi Library, a collection of thirteen ancient codices containing over fifty Gnostic texts, was discovered in upper Egypt. Nag Hammadi texts which include the Genesis creation accounts are: *On the Origin of the World, Gospel of Philip, Exegesis on the Soul, Hypostasis of the Archon, Thunder: Perfect Mind, Apocryphon of John, Apocalypse of Adam,* and *Testimony of Truth.* The account in *On the Origin of the World* is as follows: "After the day of rest Sophia sent her daughter Zoe, being called Eve, as an instructor in order that she might make Adam, who had no soul, arise so that those whom he should engender might become containers of light. When Eve saw her male counterpart prostrate she had pity upon him, and she said, 'Adam! Become alive! Arise upon the earth!' Immediately her word became accomplished fact. For Adam, having arisen, suddenly opened his eyes. When he saw her he said, 'You shall be called "Mother of the Living". For it is you who have given me life.'" (*On the Origin of the World* 115:31-35, 116:1-7, The Nag Hammadi Library, ed. James Robinson, rev. ed. San Francisco: Harper, 1988). Eve is also a central figure in *The Hypostasis of the Archons,* and *The Apocalypse of Adam.* Verses 2:13-15 make sense in the light of the threat of Gnosticism.

[1]   Non gender-specific in the Greek.
[2]   ἐπίσκοπος, *episkopos.* See note on Phil. 1:2.
[3]   μιᾶ γυναικὸς ἄνδρα, *mias gunaikos andra,* "faithful to one's partner". See also 1 Tim. 5:9, ἑνὸς ἀνδρὸς γυνή, *henos andros gune.* For references to where this term, or its Latin equivalent, was used on epitaphs to describe a woman faithful to her husband, see C. Keever, *And Marries Another,* Hendrickson, 1991, pp. 91-2. Dr Instone Brewer states, "In New Testament times those phrases meant "a one-woman man" or a "one-man woman", i.e. someone who was faithful. Timothy was being told to make sure his deacons were not sexually immoral, which was very difficult in a society where you were allowed to sleep with your slaves and where a host was expected to provide prostitutes after a banquet." *Divorce and Remarriage in the Church: Biblical Solutions for Pastoral Realities,* Great Britain, 2003, p. 177.

Bear in mind that it was common for men to be unfaithful, but not for wives. Historically, it was socially accepted in Roman society for men to be unfaithful. At the time of Paul's preaching, 5-10% of pregnancies ended in the death of the mother. Augustus had made changes to family law in 18 and 17 B.C. and in A.D. 9. He as good as forced upper-class couples to reproduce by restricting inheritance rights if they failed to reproduce. The law prohibited unmarried men between the ages of 20 and 60, and unmarried, widowed and divorced women between 18 and 50 from receiving inheritances. Women were expected to have one child by the age of 20, men by the age of 25, while widows were expected to remarry within a year, and a divorced woman within 6 months. Roman law under Augustus enabled a woman to be released from guardianship if she produced children: three in the case of a freeborn woman, and four in the case of a freed slave. The quota of three was usually fulfilled by the time a woman was 20. Augustan laws encouraged Roman parents to keep the first three children, but further children, whether girls or boys, were usually exposed (left out to die). Girls as well as boys counted in Augustus' requirement of three. The taking in and subsequent adoption of an exposed child was forbidden by law.

hospitable, skilled in teaching, *3* not a drunk nor someone who gets into fist fights, but they must be fair, peaceful and free from greed.

4 They must provide for their own household, and have their little children in support, and to do so in a most dignified manner. *5* (For if someone doesn't know how to provide for their own household, how will they manage God's house!)

6 They can't be a novice, or they might get wrapped in clouds of conceit and silliness which would lead to them falling prey to Slanderer-Liar's law court. *7* They must also have a fine reputation with the outsiders, so that they don't fall into disgrace, as this is a trick set up by Slanderer-Liar.[3]

Women often became pregnant again soon after giving birth. Multiple pregnancies were responsible for high mortality rates. Women often turned to abortion after the requisite three children, but some drugs taken for this purpose resulted in death. Physicians commonly refused to perform an abortion by instrument on the grounds that abortion could be a means of concealing adultery, and a physician who performed such an abortion was liable to the same penalties as the adulterers. The law did not penalize abortion, but did penalize the death of the mother. Note that adultery was opposed purely on the grounds of protecting rights of inheritance, not on moral grounds. Wives usually stopped having sex with the husband after the third child, partly to avoid having to expose the child, and partly because of the high likelihood of the wife's death with multiple pregnancies. Childbirth commonly was fatal. By setting the law at three children, upper-class women were protected from the risks of birth. Women who were celibate (and thus preserved their lives) were greatly admired. This was not the case with men. Yet a man who produced more than three children with his wife was labeled with the insulting term *uxorious*. Men were encouraged to have sex with concubines, freed women, or female slaves, thus again protecting the wife from the danger of death through childbirth. Roman code imposed duties on concubines and compelled them to remain faithful to their master. Some wives chose a concubine for their husbands. The upper-class women were thus spared the threat of death by multiple births. This was the case in Roman, Greek and Jewish society: all three regulated sexual reproduction in order to keep upper-class women alive.

Polygamy was still practiced among Palestinian Jews, although was not supposed to occur in Graeco-Roman society. Legal Jewish marriages allowed for polygamy. For example, *P.Yadin* 10 (Palestine, 126 AD) is a marriage contract between Judah and his second wife Babatha. That is to say, Judah had another wife, and upon his marriage to Babatha, was married to two women at once. *P.Yadin* 10 is an Aramaic contract. Judah chose a Greek marriage contract for his daughter's marriage two years later (*P.Yadin* 18) but for his polygamous marriage, had to choose an Aramaic contract.

[1] σώφρων, *sophron*, sensible. This word is used of the emperor Theodosios' father at *I.Eph.* IV.1311. A winner at the festival of Artemis is praised as σώφρονος, *sophronos*, *I.Eph.* V.1606.10 (Imperial period). It is used of males also in *Pfuhl/Mobius* II.1699 (Odessos II) pl.248; *IGM* 2 (Phigalia, IV – III BC); *IGB* 395 (Athens 6 BC).

[2] κόσμιος, *kosmios*, "with good taste", occurs only here (of a Guardian's behavior) and in 2:9 of women's dress.

[3] Subjective genitive, genitive of author. The trick is παγίς, *pagis*, not the σκάνδαλον, *skandalon*, of, for example, Rom. 14:13; 16:17; 1 Cor. 8:13; 2 Cor. 11:29; Gal. 5:11. παγίς, *pagis*, was used to refer to the wooden horse of Troy, and otherwise refers to a trick in the form of a trap which will hold one fast.

8-13 In the same way also[1] deacons must be dignified, not two-faced, not addicted to wine, not greedy for dishonest profit. *9* They must possess the hidden secret truth of the faith with a clean conscience. *10* And after they have first been examined,[2] and found to be without reproach, then let them serve as deacons. *11* In the same way also,[3] female deacons[4] must be dignified, not slanderers or drunks, but trustworthy in everything.

12 Deacons must be faithful to their partner,[5] and provide for their children and their household well.[6] *13* For those who have served as deacons obtain for themselves an advanced standing. They also have much right to speak freely, boldly and openly, by means of the faith that comes from the Anointing of Jesus.

14-16 *14-15* I expect to visit you soon, but if I'm delayed, I'm writing these things so that you'll know how you are to behave in God's household, which is the assembly of the living God, the pillar and firm base of the truth. *16* Most certainly, the revealed secret truth of godliness is great: He was made evident in the natural realm, made right in the spiritual realm, seen by Messengers, proclaimed among the non-Jews, believed by the world, taken back again with honor.

Ch.4:1-5 The Spirit says publicly, "In the last days some will depart from the faith, devoting themselves to spirits of error and to instruction and training by demons, *2* telling lies by means of being pedantic and hair splitting. Their consciences don't bother them. *3* They forbid people to get married and command people to abstain from eating certain foods which God created to be taken with gratitude by those who are faithful and have a full understanding of the truth. *4* Indeed every thing that God created is favorable and nothing is to be refused if it is taken with gratitude, *5* because it is made sacred by means of God's Word and by the act of intercession."

6-11 By instructing the fellow believers about these things you will be a fine minister of the Anointed One Jesus, as you have been nourished by accounts of the faith and by the fine instruction and training which you continue to follow closely. *7* But decline godless old wives' tales![7]

---

[1] Frequent Pauline idiom.

[2] That is, scrutinized.

[3] Frequent Pauline idiom. Note verse 8.

[4] Around 180 AD, Clement of Alexandria wrote, "For we know that the honorable Paul in one of his letters to Timothy prescribed regarding women deacons." In the 3rd century, John Chrysostom, commenting on this verse, stated, "Some have thought that this is said of women generally, but it is not so, for why should he [Paul] introduce anything about women to interfere with his subject? He is speaking of those who hold the rank of deaconesses." Some prefer the translation "wives of deacons" despite the omission of the definite article, which would be required for proper grammar. Nevertheless, there is an abundance of evidence for women deacons at the time of, and subsequent to, the New Testament, and Phoebe is called a "deacon" in Romans 16:1. See also the note on verse 12 following. A 6th c. inscription takes the reference here to be to women deacons.

[5] μιᾶ γυναικὸς ἄνδρα, *mias gunaikos andra*. See note on 1 Tim. 3:2.

[6] See 6th c. inscription, g. Jacobi, *R.Ist.d'Arch.e Storia dell'Arte* (1937) 33-36, figs 135-37 (Archelais, Capodocia, VI) which contains a reference to this verse: "Here lies Maria the deacon, of pious and blessed memory, who in accordance with the statement of the apostle reared children, practised hospitality, washed the feet of the saints, distributed her bread to the afflicted. Remember her, Lord, when you come into your kingdom." (Trans. Horsley, *NDIEC* 2.194.)

[7] Hendiadys. Again, an allusion to the "fiction" of 1 Timothy 1:4. Note also that 1 Timothy 5:13 speaks of women περιεγρία, *periergia*, which also

Engage in athletic training for doing your sacred duty to God. *8* For athletic training for the body is profitable for a short time, but athletic training for doing your sacred duty to God is profitable for all time as it has the promise both for the life that is now and the life that is to come.

9 This is a faithful saying and worthy to be fully accepted. *10* It's for this reason that we go to all this trouble and contend for the winner's prize, because we have set our expectation on the living God, who is the Savior of all people, especially believers. *11* Instruct and teach these things.

12-16 Do not let anyone scorn your youth, but let your speech, the way you live your life, your love, faith and holiness be a pattern for the believers. *13* Until I can get there, you must continue to devote yourself to reading, to encouraging, and to instruction and training. *14* Never neglect the spiritual gift that is in you, which was given to you by means of prophecy with the laying on of hands by the body of elders.

15 Cultivate these things, immerse yourself in them, so that your progress will be clear to everyone. *16* Be attentive to yourself and to your instruction and training. Continue doing it. This will keep both yourself and those who hear you safe.

Ch.5:1-8 Do not verbally attack an older man, but encourage him as a father, and younger men as a brothers, *2* older women as mothers, and younger women as sisters, with a great deal of holiness.

3 Honor[1] widows[2] who are really and truly widows with practical help and financial support. *4* But if any widow has children or grandchildren at home, let them first learn to do their duty to their own household and to pay back what is due to their parents and grandparents. This is pleasing in God's sight. *5* Now she who is a widow and who is in need of financial assistance, and has no dowry,[3] has put her expectation upon God and stays in prayer and

---

means to have the ability to write documents by means of spirit(s), to have knowledge of the supernatural, and to have the knowledge of future events.

[1] τιμάω, *timao*, encompasses the meaning of honoring one with practical help and financial support, like the 5th commandment. The Greco-Roman society was honor-driven by nature.

[2] Augustus passed laws prohibiting widows between the ages of 18 and 50 from receiving inheritances. Widows were expected to remarry within a year.

[3] A widow who is left alone: technically, one who has no dowry and is in need of financial assistance. Widows without dowries were left to depend on food distributions and on the weekly distributions made by synagogues to travelers and the poor. In the upper classes, the bride's father or mother provided the dowry, usually money or real estate, to the husband's household. Technically, it was provided to the bride who brought it into the marriage, although this later changed. It provided for her maintenance and for the succession of property through the female line. The money was held in trust for the wife by the husband, who usually invested the money as soon as he got his hands on it! Upon divorce, he had to return the dowry (minus the interest) immediately. The dowry was separate to the property of the wife, and consisted of such items as jewelry, clothing, land and slaves. There was an increasing acknowledgement of the wife's property rights independent of her husband.

When the divorced wife left her husband's household she received back her dowry. At this point, the husband no longer had responsibility for the wife's maintenance. The issue of the receipt for the returned dowry indicated the termination of the marriage.

Jewish marriage was somewhat different, although was evolving during the New Testament period, perhaps under the influence of Greek law. In the Old Testament, the father gave his daughter in betrothal. By New Testament times, betrothal had become an agreement between the couple. A girl was

earnest requests night and day. *6* But she who lives a life of self-indulgence[1] has been dying. *7* Give all these instructions, so that they would not be put in the position of being blamed. *8* Now if anyone doesn't provide for their own relatives, especially for their own household, they have declined the faith and are worse than an unbeliever.

9-10 Don't let a widow be enrolled as a widow if she's under sixty years of age and has a man as well as her husband.[2] *10* She must have a good reputation: for rearing children, for showing hospitality, for washing the feet of the people devoted to God, for paying for the expenses of people who are oppressed, from devoting herself to every good work.

11-16 Decline younger widows as whenever they run riot against the Anointed One, they're just looking for sex,[3] *12* and the verdict is that they invalidate their first faith. *13* At the same time too they learn to be idle, going around from house to house, gossiping and gaining knowledge by supernatural means,[4] speaking about things which they should not speak!

14 So then I would like the younger widows to marry, have children, have mastery over the household, and give the Opposing Counterpart[5] no base of operations for ranting and raving. *15* For already some have turned aside, back to Adversary.

16 If any female believer[6] has widows in her family, she must pay their expenses[7] and not let the assembly be burdened, so that the assembly can pay the expenses of those who are really and truly widows.

---

emancipated at the age of twelve and half years plus one day, and could marry at will. Levirate and polygamous marriage was declining. The bride price, *mohar*, paid by the bridegroom to the bride's father was replaced by the *kethubah*, the bill obliging the sum's payment, on divorce or death, to the wife, and was secured by a pledge over the husband's property. The minimum amount was set by Jewish law. However, unlike Greek and Roman dowry return, the wife stood behind the other creditors of the estate.

[1] σπαταλάω, *spatalao*, to live a life of self indulgence (luxurious not licentious). So Zerwick and Grosvenor, *op.cit.*, p. 633; Holmes, *op.cit.*, p. 152. σπαταλάω, *spatalao*, is used in the LXX of Ezekiel 16:49 for an idle and luxurious life, and the compound κατασπαταλάω, *kataspatalao*, at Prov. 29:21 and Amos 6:4 in the same meaning. σπαταλάω, *spatalao*, is used in Sir. 21:15 for abandonment to pleasure and comfort. Occurs elsewhere in N.T. only in James 5:5.

[2] The concern here is for finances. If the woman had a partner apart from her deceased husband, he was to support her financially. One could remarry without getting a divorce, as did Herod's wife Herodias, who was still married to her first husband Philip. See also note on 1 Timothy 3:2.

[3] A Gnostic belief was that one could gain Knowledge (γνῶσις, *gnosis*) from having sex with someone.

[4] περίεργος, *periergos*. The semantic range includes "being interfering busybodies". This word is interesting. It can mean to be a busybody, or to gain knowledge by supernatural means (as in its only other NT occurrence, Acts 19:19). The same term is found in the papyrus circular forbidding magic, *P.Coll.Youtie* 1 30. In the papyri, the term referred to the writing of documents by means of spirit(s), to those having knowledge of the supernatural, and to those having the knowledge of future events.

[5] ἀντικείμαι, *antikeimai*. "Opposing Counterpart", "Opponent", one who sets themselves against one, to be opposite or opposed. See *P.Par.* 45.6. Used by the rhetoricians in the meaning "antithetical".

[6] The KJV and Tyndale's translation both added "or man" here.

[7] Believing women are asked to care for widows, and this was not the social norm. Widows who were not in control of their own finances were maintained by the male who inherited the management of the widow's

dowry. Evidence from Plutarch indicates that mothers favor sons because they will give them financial aid.

By the end of the 1st c. B.C., marriages where the wife was subject to the authority of the husband or his father had come to an end. Even during this time, a woman who had married under the old way had the right to force the man who held authority over her to give her liberty. Augustus ended the agnatic (brother or paternal uncle) control over women who had three children – which changed from three live children to three full term pregnancies (four for women who were freed slaves). Such Roman women had power to administer their own property and to enter into legal transactions. There were women who owned ships, ran shipping companies, and women who were merchants. In fact, the term "manager of an estate" is found in reference to women no less than men. Furthermore, some "estate managers" are listed whose employers are women. Claudius ended agnatic guardianship for freeborn women.

Paul is using conventional reciprocity terminology in his discussion on church and kinship responsibilities towards widows. He endorses traditional social expectations concerning reciprocity to benefactors: εὐσεβεῖν, *eusebein*, προνεῖν, *pronein*, τιμᾶν, *timan*, ἀμοιναs ἀποδιδόναι, *amoinas apodidonai*. The terms occur in, for example, the honorific inscription *SEG* XI 948 (1st c. AD). Throughout the passage Paul uses the traditional language of benefaction and reciprocity, easily recognized by his Graeco-Roman audience, but not recognized by the reader of today. See good discussion in S.R. Llewelyn, "Benefaction Ideology and Christian Responsibility for Widows", *NDIEC* 8.106-116. A significant benefaction word is the verb *pronoeo* which appears in verse 8 - and elsewhere in the New Testament in Romans 12:17, 2 Corinthians 8:21. (The noun, *pronoia*, occurs in Acts 24:2, Romans 13:14.) This is an important word, and refers to the provision that benefactors bestowed on their communities. It is a public virtue. Those credited with exhibiting *pronoia* had usually demonstrated magnificence in civic administration as well as military or judicial expertise. Some examples of acts classed as *pronoia* are the lowering of taxes by considerable sums, the restoration of a synagogue, the meeting of a city's needs from one's own expenses, revisions of a city's oppressive financial policies. The term is also used to refer to concern over the constitution, and to the return of honor to benefactors. Philo refers to Jacob's storing up of food for the time of famine as an act of *pronoia*. To the Greeks, *pronoia* was the preserve of the socially powerful. So too, the Romans used the equivalent Latin term *providentia* to describe the acts taken by rulers to alleviate the living conditions of their subjects. Paul has taken the term from its elitist context and planted it firmly into the realm of family relationships. An important reciprocity word is *timao*, the "honor" of verse 3. As mentioned above, the word encompasses financial payment or material assistance, with social recognition. Yet the meaning does not end there: the concern is for reciprocity, and this was a cultural norm. In verse 4, Paul urges children and grandchildren to make the return by paying back what is due to their forebears. A philosopher of the time summed up the cultural attitude using the same language: "But we must begin with the assumption that the only measure of our gratitude to them is constant and unyielding eagerness to pay back what is due for their beneficence, since, even if we were to do a great deal for them, that would be far too inadequate." Hierokles, "How to Conduct Oneself Toward One's Parents", *Stob.* 3.52.

For typical example of a document where provision for widows by the church is laid out, see R. Rémondon, *Cr.c'Eg.* 47 (1972) 254-77 at p.266 (Oxyrhynchos, 21/1/480): "The holy church to Peter, administrator of Kosmas. Provide for Sophia, widow, from the coats you have, one coat for

17-18 Let the elders who give practical help be considered worthy of double honor, especially those who go to trouble instructing and training about the Word. *18* For the Scripture says, "You must not muzzle an ox which threshes grain," and "The worker is worthy of their wages."

19-21 Do not accept a charge against an elder except on the basis of two or three witnesses. *20* In front of everyone, rebuke those who are sinning, so that the rest will also be afraid. *21* I solemnly require, in the presence of God and the Anointed One Jesus and the chosen Messengers, that you watch over these things without any bias. Don't do anything with even an inclination to be biased!

22 Don't lay hands on anyone hastily anymore, and don't be in partnership with the sins of another person: keep yourself sacred!

23 Don't drink the water any more – you must use some wine instead – on account of the fact that the water is causing you the ailment of bladder frequency.[1]

24-25 Some people's sins are obvious. In fact, their sins stand out! On the other hand the sins of some others aren't as obvious, and follow along behind them. This will lead to them being judged. *25* In the same way too, the favorable actions of some people are obvious and stand out. But actions that aren't favorable can't be hidden indefinitely!

Ch.6:1-2 All slave servants who are in slavery are to consider their masters worthy of full respect, so that God's Name and our instruction and training won't be blasphemed. *2* Now, those of you who have masters who are believers, don't look down on them, because they are fellow believers! Instead serve them all the more, because the people who end up benefiting are believers and their loved fellow believers.

2-8 This is what you are to teach and encourage. *3* If someone teaches something different and doesn't cling to the completely healthy words of our Lord Jesus the Anointed One and to godly instruction and training, *4* then they are wrapped in clouds of conceit and silliness, and not skilled. Instead, they are diseased with investigations and wars about words, from which come jealousy, strife, blasphemies, evil intrigues,[2] *5* and mutual friction between people who have lost their wits and are defrauded of the truth. They think godliness is a way of gaining financially.[3] *6* This is great financial gain: godliness accompanied by independent wealth.[4] *7* For we brought nothing

---

fine use, total: 1 coat only. Fare well. In the year 156+125, Mecheir 1 of the third indiction."

[1] διά, *dia*, with accusative, "on account of". Hendiadys. The frequency of urination referred to is caused by drinking the water at Ephesos. τὸν στόμαχον καὶ τὰς πυκνάς σου ἀθενείας, *ton stomakhon kai tas puknas sou atheneias*, frequency of urination, cf. Hipp., *Aer.* 286. ("Stomach" is γαστήρ, *gaster*.)

[2] ὑπόνοια, *huponoia*, a stirring up by secret arts, stratagems or intrigues. The word can also mean "suspicions", but it is unlikely here, as the very strong word πονηρός, *poneros*, evil, is the adjective. πονηρός, *poneros*, is rarely used, and its use here rather than κακός, *kakos*, bad, is noteworthy. Occurs only here in the NT.

[3] πορισμός, *porismos*, "financial gain", occurs in the N.T. only here and in following verse. MM and BGAD do not provide any documentary examples. However, one of the inscriptions of Ephesos provides an illustration: "For whenever more joyful news comes from Rome, they misuse it for their own financial gain, and using the appearance of the divine building as a cover, they sell priesthoods as though at auction, and they summon people from every family to purchase them." *I.Eph.* Ia.18. So too LSJ *s.v.*

[4] αὐτάρκεια, *autarkeia*, was a very important concept to the Greeks, from the time of the Pythagoreans. It referred to someone or something which was

into this world, and consequently we can take nothing out, *8* but having sustenance and support, and clothing, we will have enough!

9-10 People who want to be rich fall prey to ordeals and tricks which are lying in wait for them, and fall prey to many senseless and disadvantageous wants and wishes. These sink people into destruction and ruin. *10* For being greedy with money[1] is a root of all kinds of bad things. Some people, aspiring to it, have wandered away[2] from the faith and have roasted themselves on a spit with much grief.

11-16 But you, you person of God, decline these things! Chase after being right, after godliness, after faith, love, endurance, gentleness. *12* Contend for the winner's prize in faith's contest, lay claim to eternal life, to which you were invited and agreed the fine agreement in the presence of many witnesses.

13 I instruct you in the presence of God who keeps all things alive, and in the presence of the Anointed One Jesus, who himself was in agreement with this in his testimony to Pontius Pilate, that you firmly keep this mandate. *14* I instruct that you are to be unblemished and blameless until the sudden appearance of our Lord Jesus the Anointed One, *15* which he will bring to light at his own proper time. He is the blessed and only Sovereign, the King of Kings and Lord of Lords. *16* He alone has immortality. He lives in unapproachable light, which no person has seen or is able to see. To him be the honor and mighty sovereignty forever, amen!

17-19 Instruct those who are wealthy in this present age not to be haughty or to set their expectation upon uncertain wealth, but upon God. God richly supplies us with everything which leads to our enjoyment, *18* for doing good, for being wealthy, for doing good deeds generously, for being partners with him. *19* It also leads to them storing up riches, a fine foundation for the future, so that they can lay claim to a way of life which is well and truly living!

20-21 Timothy, guard the deposit entrusted to you, and turn aside from polluted, useless speaking and from the opposing theoretical, technical arguments of falsely named knowledge.[3] *21* By making a profession of

---

independently wealthy. For example, Thucydides 1.37 used it to describe Corcyra, a place which needed no help from others, which supplied itself, needed no imports, needed no aid.

[1] φιλαργυρία, *philarguria*. Not "the love of money". Theokritos 10.54, tells of the Steward who is stingy with his drink and his food (lentils). Greedy doctors (φιλάργυροι ιατροί, *philarguroi iatroi*) are criticized in *I.Eph.* IV.1386 (probably 1st c). φιλαργυρία, *philarguria*, can mean "stingy" or "stingily covetous".

[2] αποπλανάω, *apoplanao*, occurs only here and in Mark 13:22. No parallel has been found for the meaning "lead astray" which appears in some translations, cf. John AL Lee & GHR Horsley, "A Lexicon of the NT with Documentary Parallels: Some Interim Entries, 2" *FilNT* 10 (1997) p. 65. The same authors also cite *SB* 4.7464.6 (Arsinoite nome, 248 AD): "A female piglet of my daughter's wandered off in the village."

[3] ψευδώνυμος γνῶσις, *pseudonmos gnosis*. *R.Ph.* 53.29-43. an imperial appeal for reconciliation (Athens 174/5) has γνῶσις, *gnosis*, as "result (of an investigation)" at *l.*25 and as "decision" at *ll.*56, 73. Clearly another attack on Gnosticism. The name "Gnostic" was taken from this Greek word. Professor Magella Franzmann says of Gnosticism: "For the Gnostics, all things made of matter are evil or at best fatally flawed. They belong to the realm of darkness. What is good is the spirit trapped within human flesh. Gnostics know of this spirit through an experience of awakening or insight (*gnosis*), by which they become aware of their spiritual origin from the world of light. In Gnostic Christian writings, Jesus the Saviour does not come to the world to exorcise evil or forgive sins, or to die for the sin of the world, but to awaken the elect to insight, prepare the way, and bring them home to the heavenly world of

falsely named knowledge some have failed with regard to faith. Favor be with you!

---

light." Professor Franzmann, School of Classics, History and Religion, University of New England, public lecture in Armidale, Australia, Thursday, October 11, 2001.

Second Letter to Timothy.

2 Timothy is dated shortly before Paul's death (cf. 1:16; 2:9; 4:13) which was around 64 AD. In 4:16, Paul notes, "At my first speech in defense no one was at hand to support me, but everyone left me in the lurch: may it not be held against them!" and in 4:6 states, "For I myself am surely poured out like a drink offering, and the time of my departure has come."

Second Letter to Timothy.

Ch.1:1-2 From: Paul, an apostle of the Anointed One Jesus, as purposed by God whose promise of life is found in the Anointed One Jesus.

2 To: Timothy, a most loved dear member.

Hello! May you have mercy and peace from God the Father and the Anointed One Jesus our Lord!

3-7 I thank God, whom I worship with a clean conscience (just as my ancestors did), when I constantly mention you in my earnest requests night and day. *4* I long to see you (and I remember your tears) so that I may be filled with joy. *5* I recollect the non-overly critical faith that is in you, which first inhabited your grandmother Lois and your mother Eunice, and I am convinced it's in you too. *6* This is the reason I remind you to rekindle God's spiritual gift that is in you because of me laying hands on you. *7* For God did not give us a spirit of cowardice,[1] but of power, love, and a sound mind.

8-10 So then, don't be ashamed of the testimony about our Lord, or of me a prisoner, but through God's power be a joint sharer with me in bad experiences, as this will benefit the Good News.

9 God saved us and invited us with a sacred invitation, not because of our actions, but because of his own purposes and his favor. His favor, to be found in the Anointing of Jesus, was given to us before the time of the ages began. *10* And thereafter it will be shown for what it is at the sudden appearance of our Savior, the Anointed One Jesus, who on the one hand rendered death inoperative and on the other hand brought life and immortality to light by means of the Good News.

11-14 It was to this that I was appointed as a proclaimer, messenger and teacher, *12* which is the reason I experience these things. But I'm not ashamed, as I know the One I have believed on, and I'm convinced that he has the power to guard the deposit entrusted to me until that Day. *13* Hold on to the pattern of completely sound words which you've heard from me, and do so with faith and love which are found in the Anointing of Jesus. *14* Guard that favorable deposit entrusted to you by means of the Holy Spirit who lives in you.

15 You're aware of this, that all those in the province of Asia have turned away from me. This includes Phygelos and Hermogenes.

16-18 May the Lord show mercy to Onesiphorus' household – he was often a breath of fresh air to me, and was not ashamed that I was a prisoner. *17* On the contrary, when he arrived in Rome he went to a lot of trouble to find me. *18* May the Lord grant that he will find mercy from the Lord on that Day.

---

[1] δειλία, *deilia*, "cowardice", not φόβος, *phobos*, "fear". "Cowardice" in classical Greek times was evading military service, deserting the ranks, and throwing away one's shield. Lysias 14.7 uses the legal term "cowardice" for a man who served in the cavalry when enrolled to serve in the (more dangerous) infantry. If a man was convicted of "cowardice", he lost his civil rights, cf. De. 15.32; Andoc. 1.74.

You're also very well aware of the many ways in which he ministered at Ephesos.

Ch.2:1-2 So then, my little child, you must be empowered by the favor which is found in the Anointing of Jesus. *2* Quote the things you heard from me through many witnesses as evidence to faithful teachers who are suitable to teach others too.

3-7 Be a joint sharer in putting up with bad experiences as a fine soldier of the Anointed One Jesus. *4* No one who is on active military service is involved in the general affairs of this world's way of life, so that they will please the one who enlisted them as a soldier. *5* And too, if someone competes in athletics, they don't win the prize unless they compete according to the rules. *6* The hardworking farmer must be the first to have a share of the crops. *7* Think about what I say, for the Lord will see to it that you catch on to everything.

8-13 Remember that Jesus the Anointed One, one of the descendants of David, was raised up from among the dead, according to my Good News! *9* It's for this reason that I put up with bad things even to the point of being imprisoned as a criminal – but God's Word is not imprisoned! *10* On account of this I endure everything for the sake of the chosen ones, so that they too obtain the salvation of the Anointed One Jesus and be given eternal honor. *11* Here is a faithful saying: "If we jointly died with him, we will also jointly live with him; *12* If we endure, we will also jointly reign with him; If we turn our back on him, he will also turn his back on us; *13* If we are faithless, he stays faithful, for he is not able to turn his back on himself."

14-18 Remind them of these things, and solemnly require in God's presence that they do not war about words, which is a useless thing to do, and results in the sudden end of the hearers. *15* Be eager to produce yourself to be proven to God as a laborer who has nothing to be ashamed of, and cut a direct path for the truthful Word. *16* Avoid polluted useless speakers, as that sort of thing progresses to more ungodliness *17* and their word will spread like gangrene. These ones include Hymenaios and Philetos. *18* They've missed the mark as far as truth goes! They say that the resurrection has already happened, and they're turning the faith of some people upside down.

19-21 However, the foundation of God is solid, and has this seal: "The Lord recognizes those who are his own," and, "Everyone who uses the Name of the Anointed One must withdraw from dishonesty."

20 In every large household there's not only gold and silver equipment, but there's also wooden and pottery equipment, some are valuable, but some are worthless.[1] *21* So then if someone cleanses themselves of these things, they will be equipment for special occasions, dedicated to God, useful to the Master, prepared for every good work.

22-26 Flee from revolutionary[2] wants and wishes, and chase after godliness, faith, love, and peace. Call upon the Lord out of a clean mind. *23* Turn your back on foolish, ignorant investigations, knowing that they cause fights. *24* A

---

[1] ἀτιμία, *atimia*, a common word, is sometimes mistranslated in Bible versions as vessels "for refuse", but ἀτιμία, *atimia*, commonly means worthless, cheap, without price or value. The semantic range of ἀτιμία, *atimia*, includes "dishonored" of people, and of things (as here), "worthless", "cheap". The semantic range does not include "for refuse". The cognate verb means to put to shame, not be assessed, not capable of being valued. See also Rom. 9:21. τιμή, *time*, a common word, of things means "valuable".

[2] νεωτερικός, *neoterikos*, "innovative", "revolutionary", especially to attempt political changes. Josephus, B.J. Prooem. 2, refers to the νεωτέριζον, *neoterizon*, "the revolutionary party". Not νεανικός, *neanikos*, "youthful". Most Bible versions add the words "evil", "lusts", or "passions", none of which are in the Greek.

slave servant of the Lord must not fight but must be kind to everyone, skilled in teaching, able to put up with bad things. *25* A slave servant of the Lord must gently educate those who offer resistance, in case God wants to grant that they change their minds and fully know the truth, *26* and in case they come to their senses out of the trick that Slanderer-Liar set for them to fall into, after he had captured them to carry out his purposes.

Ch.3:1-4 But be aware of this, that in the last days difficult times will be at hand. *2* For people will be selfish, stingy, imposters; they will be contemptuous, they will be blasphemers, disobedient to parents, ungrateful, unholy, *3* and without natural affection. They won't call a truce. They're slanderers, powerless, savage. They're not interested in doing good. *4* They're traitors. They're reckless and wrapped in clouds of conceit and silliness. They take delight in pleasure rather than taking delight in God.

5-9 They have the outward appearance of being godly, but they refuse the power of it. Turn away from such people! *6* This type of person makes their way into households and makes prisoners of war out of heretic followers[1] who have accumulated sins. They are led by all kinds of wants and wishes[2] *7* and are always learning but are never able to come to the full knowledge of truth. *8* In the same way that Jannes and Jambres took a stand against Moses, these ones too take a stand against the truth. They're people whose minds have been put into a sorry state. They don't pass muster concerning the faith. *9* But they won't progress any further, as they've lost their senses and this will become plain to everyone just as it did with Jannes and Jambres.

10-13 You have closely followed my instruction and training, my method, my proposals, my faith, my perseverance, my love, my endurance, *11* my ordeals, my experiences, such as happened to me in Antioch, Iconium and Lystra.

The ordeals I put up with! And the Lord rescued me out of all of them!

12 Yes, all those who want to live godly lives as followers of the Anointed One Jesus will be harassed. *13* Evil[3] people and sorcerers[4] will progress from bad to worse, leading people off the path and being led off the path themselves.

---

[1] γυναικάριον, *gunaikarion*. A very rare word. A contemptuous colloquial expression referring to followers of heretics. (Appears in form as the diminutive of γυνη, *gune*, and so has often been mistranslated as "little women".) Note that Jerome attacked Pelagius and his female followers by reciting a satirical list of *mulierculae* (the Latin for "γυναικάριον, *gunaikarion*") who had followed heretics from Nicholas of Antioch up to Priscillian. He added, "Both genders aiding one another, had contributed to 'the *musterion* of iniquity'. " Jerome, *Ephesians*, 133.4 (quoting 2 Thess. 2:7).

[2] Again, the word "evil" does not occur in the Greek.

[3] πονηρός, *poneros*, "evil". A strong word, not simply "bad".

[4] γόης, *goes*, "sorcerer", "enchanter", "spellbinder", "form-changer". Cf. Eur. *Hipp.* 1038, *Bacch.* 234; Hdt. 4.105., 7.191. It does not mean "seducer", "imposter" or "charlatan". It does not refer to a magician or witch, but refers to a specific sort of spellcaster. Herodotos uses it to refer to the spellcasting by which a person can turn into a wolf for a few days and then turn back again. (By the way, Herodotos states that he does not believe the story.) Herodotos also uses the term to refer to the type of spellcasting claimed by the Persians to bring an end to a three-day storm. (The spell was addressed to the wind.) Herodotos also uses the term to describe an enchanter who changes form, cf. 4.105. Note that in Euripides' *Bacchae*, Pentheus accuses Dionysos of being a γόης, *goes*. Dionysos appears in the form of a snake, bull and lion, cf. *Bacchae* 539, 1174, 1185, 855, 917. γόης, *goes*, occurs only here in the N.T.

14-17 You must continue with the things that you learnt and put your faith in, for you know the people you learnt them from. *15* And you know that you have learnt the sacred Scriptures from infancy. This has empowered you to be wise and has led to your salvation through faith in Jesus the Anointed One. *16* All Scripture is made alive by God and is also profitable for instruction and training, for evidence, for improvement, and for education in how to be made godly, *17* so that the person who follows God may be fully equipped for every good work.

Ch.4:1-5 I solemnly require in the presence of God and the Anointed One Jesus, who will judge the living and the dead, and in view of his sudden appearance and his realm that you: *2* Proclaim the Word! Take up your post at convenient times and at inconvenient times! Refute! Encourage! Be tolerant towards others and in your teaching. *3* For the time will come when they won't put up with completely sound instruction and training, but they will accumulate for themselves teachers who tickle their fancy and who line up with their own wants and wishes. *4* They will turn away from hearing the truth, and turn instead to fiction.[1]

5 Now you must be clear headed in everything! Put up with bad things! Do the work of an announcer of the Good News! Be absolutely convinced of your ministry!

6-8 For I myself am surely being poured out like a drink offering, and the time of my departure has come. *7* I have contended for the prize in the fine contest, I have completed my race, I have firmly kept the faith. *8* Finally, my winners' prize of righteousness has been stored away for me. The Lord, the righteous judge, will award it to me on that Day, and not only to me but to everyone who has loved his sudden appearance.

9-13 Be keen to visit me soon, *10* as Demas loved this present age and has left me in the lurch and gone off to Thessalonika! Crescens has gone to Galatia, and Titus has gone to Dalmatia.

11 Luke is the only one with me. Get hold of Mark and bring him with you, as he's useful to me in the ministry. *12* I've sent Tychikos off to Ephesos. *13* When you come, would you bring that coat I left behind in Troas with Carpos, and the scrolls, especially the parchment notebooks.

14-15 Alexander the coppersmith caused me considerable harm. The Lord will give him what's coming to him. *15* You must be on your guard about him too, as he very, very much took a stand against our words.

16-18 At my first speech in defense no one was at hand to support me, but everyone left me in the lurch: may it not be held against them! *17* The Lord was at hand to support me and he empowered me, so that because of me the proclamation would be fully believed, and so that all the non-Jews would hear it. I was rescued from the mouth of the lion! *18* The Lord will rescue me from every evil work and deliver me into his realm, the heavenly realm. May he be honored forever and ever, amen!

19-22 Greet Priska and Aquila, and the household of Onesiphorus.

20 Erastos stayed in Corinth, but I've left Trophimos behind in Miletos as he's weak.[2]

21 Be keen to get here before winter. Euboulos greets you, and so do Pudens, Linus, Claudia and all the fellow believers.

22 The Lord is with your spirit. May favor be with you!

---

[1] μῦθος, *muthos*. See note on 1 Tim. 1:4.
[2] In the Greek, either spiritually or physically.

Letter to Titus.

The letter to Titus was written by Paul around 63. Titus was a Greek and a coworker of Paul. After Paul's first Roman imprisonment, Paul left Titus in Crete to direct the new assemblies. Paul continued on to Macedonia, and on the way left Timothy in Ephesos. At a later point, before his final imprisonment, Paul wrote the letter we know as Titus. Titus 1:5 sets out the purpose for the letter. Paul says, "This was the reason I left you behind in Crete – that you would set straight what needs to be done and appoint elders in each city, just as I left in my instructions for you."

Letter to Titus.

Ch.1:1-4 From: Paul, a slave servant of God, an apostle of Jesus the Anointed One, sent out to further the faith of God's chosen ones and the full knowledge of the godly truth *2* and the expectation of eternal life. God, who is without lie and deceit, promised this before the ages began. *3* God showed his Word for what it is at his own proper time through its preaching, and this was entrusted to me by the divine command of God our Savior.

4 To: Titus, my genuine member[1] of our common faith.

Hello! May you have peace from God the Father and the Anointed One Jesus our Savior!

5-9 This was the reason I left you behind in Crete – that you would set straight what needs to be done and appoint elders in each city, just as I left in my instructions for you. *6* Such a person[2] must be without reproach, being faithful to their partner,[3] whose children are believers, and must not be charged with being undisciplined or unruly. *7* It's necessary that a Guardian be without reproach as God's manager, not stubborn, not irritable, not a drunk, not someone who gets into fist fights, not greedy for dishonest profit. *8* Instead, they must be hospitable, love goodness, be sensible, just, holy, self-controlled, *9* and stand their ground when teaching the faithful Word. This is so that they are able both to encourage by completely sound instruction and training, as well as to refute those people who contradict it.

10-14 There are many unruly people – they're full of hot air and have deluded minds, especially those of the circumcision (the Jews). *11* It is necessary to rein them in. They turn whole households upside down, teaching things that they must not, for the sake of dishonest profit. *12* One of them, actually one of their own[4] prophets, said, "Cretans are always liars, nasty beasts, lazy bellies!"[5] *13* This testimony is in fact true! This is the reason that you need to refute them severely, so that their faith will be completely sound *14* and they will not devote themselves to Jewish fiction[6] and commands of people, which turn them away from the truth.

15-16 Everything is clean to those who are clean, but nothing is clean to those who have been polluted and are unbelieving. But in their case, even their minds and their consciences have been polluted. *16* They agree that they know God, but they refuse him by their actions. They are disgusting, disobedient, and are shown to be unfit for doing any good work.

---

[1]   τέκνον, *teknon*, member. See also 1 Tim. 1:2; 2 John 1.
[2]   Non-gender specific.
[3]   μιᾶ γυναικὸς ἄνδρα, *mias gunaikos andra*. See note on 1 Tim. 3:2.
[4]   "Their own" is emphasized here, by the (τις ἐξ) αὐτῶν, *auton*, as well as the ἴδιος αὐτῶν, *idios auton*.
[5]   This verse, in dactylic hexameter, was said by Epimenides, a Cretan poet of the 6th century B.C.
[6]   μῦθος, *muthos*. See note on 1 Tim. 1:4.

Ch.2:1-8 But as for you, what you say must be appropriate for completely sound instruction and training. *2* Male elders are to be clear headed, well respected, sensible. Their faith, love and endurance must be completely sound. *3* The same goes for female elders too. They are to be suitably holy as is fitting for their appointment, not slanderers, not enslaved by wine, teachers who provide instruction in what is right. *4* Then they can bring the new[1] women to their senses to love their husbands, to love their children, *5* to be clear headed, holy, the mistress of the house, supportive[2] of their own husbands, so that the Word of God won't be blasphemed. *6* The same goes for newer men too. Encourage them to be clear headed. *7* In every aspect, set yourself as a pattern for all favorable matters, for instruction and training, for being uncorrupt, for being dignified. *8* Do this by means of a completely sound message that cannot be condemned, so that those who are hostile to you will be put to shame and won't have anything worth saying.

9-10 Encourage slave servants to be supportive of their masters in everything, to please them well, and not to contradict them *10* or steal things from them. Instead, they are to be completely trustworthy, so that in every way they make the instruction about God our Savior attractive.

11-15 God's favor suddenly appeared bringing salvation for all people, *12* educating us that we should turn our backs on ungodliness and worldly wants and wishes, and live in a clear headed way, righteous and dutiful to God in this present age. *13* It educated us that we are to wait for the expected blessed, sudden appearance of our glorious mighty God and Savior Jesus the Anointed One. *14* He gave himself for us, so that he would pay our ransom for every lawless act, and cleanse his own special people for himself, people who are extremely enthusiastic to do all sorts of fine deeds. *15* Speak about these things, encourage, refute, and speak with divine command. Don't let anyone look down on you.

Ch.3:1-7 Remind them to support and obey the ruling authorities, and to be ready to do good deeds. *2* Remind them not to blaspheme anyone, to be peaceful, fair, and to be gentle to all people. *3* Indeed we ourselves were once senseless too – we were disobedient, misled, in bondage to our own wants and wishes and various pleasures. We were passing our lives in bad ways. We were envious, and hated each other. *4* But when the kindness and liking for people of God our Savior suddenly appeared, *5* he saved us due to his mercy – and it wasn't because of anything right that we did. He saved us by the washing of rebirth and by the new birth by the Holy Spirit. *6* He richly poured the Holy Spirit on us through Jesus the Anointed One our Savior, *7* so that after we were made right with God because of his favor, we would become heirs with the expectation of eternal life.

8-11 This is a faithful saying: I also want you to be dogmatic about this: that those who believe in God must take thought for taking the lead in favorable deeds. This is favorable and useful for everyone. *9* Avoid foolish speculations. Avoid making out family trees.[3] Avoid strife. Avoid fighting about things related to the Law. These things are useless and pointless. *10* Excuse yourself from an heretical person after one or two warnings, *11* knowing that such a person is completely altered, is sinning, and has sentenced themselves.

12-15 After I send Artemas or Tychikos to you, make sure you visit me at Nicopolis, as I've decided to spend the winter there. *13* Make sure you send Zenas the lawyer and Apollos on their way with money and supplies, so that they don't lack anything. *14* Our own people must also learn to take the lead in favorable deeds in order to meet necessities, so that they won't be unproductive. *15* Everyone who is with me says hello. Say hello to everyone who is our friend and who shares our faith. Goodbye to all of you!

---

[1] Paul playing on words, contrasting "elders" with νέος, *neos*, "new" (youth).

[2] ὑποτάσσω, *hupotasso*. See note on Eph. 5:22.

[3] See note on family trees in 1 Tim. 1:4.

Letter to Philemon.

The letter to Philemon, a member of the assembly at Colosse and the master of the slave Onesimos, was written by Paul while he was in prison in Rome, 59-61 AD. Unlike Philippians, Paul does not indicate that his imprisonment is about to be terminated. Verse 19 suggests that Philemon became a Christian through Paul's ministry. Onesimos, one of his slaves, had fled to Rome. As with the other two letters which were written at the same time, Colossians and Ephesians, Paul's place of writing has been disputed, some suggesting Caesarea, others suggesting Ephesos. The letter to the Philippians is found in Marcion's canon and the Muratorian canon.

Letter to Philemon.

1-3 From: Paul, a prisoner because of the Anointed One Jesus, and Timothy our fellow believer.[1]

3 To: Philemon our dear friend and coworker, *2* and to Apphia our fellow believer,[2] and to Archippos our fellow soldier, and to the assembly which meets in your house.

3 Hello! May you have peace from God our Father and Lord Jesus the Anointed One!

4-11 I always thank my God at all times as I mention you in my prayers, *5* because I hear about the love and faith you have towards the Lord Jesus and towards all the people devoted to God. *6* As a result of this, the partnership of your faith will be activated when you fully understand every good thing which the Anointed One brings us. *7* Indeed we were greatly happy and encouraged by your love, because the hearts of the people devoted to God have been refreshed through you, my fellow believer! *8* So it is that – although by means of the Anointed One I should have the right of freedom of speech, speaking boldly and openly, to order you to do what you should do – *9* I prefer to appeal to you on the basis of love. I then, as Paul, an elder and now also a prisoner because of the Anointed One Jesus, *10* appeal to you on behalf of my son, Onesimos, whom I have fathered while in my imprisonment. *11* Once he was useless to you, but now he is really useful[3] to you and me!

12-17 I am sending him back to you in person – him, whom I consider part of myself! *13* I would have liked to have kept him with me to stand in for you,, to materially provide for me while I am imprisoned because of the Good News. *14* But I didn't want to do anything without your consent, so that your good deed wouldn't be under compulsion, but of your own free will. *15* For perhaps this is why he went away[4] from you for a while, so that you might have him back forever – *16* no longer as a slave, but more than a slave, as a dear fellow believer - exceptionally so to me and how much more to you, both in the natural realm and also as a follower of the Lord! *17* Therefore since you have me as a partner, take him as a partner like me.

18-22 But if he has wronged you or owes anything, put it on my account. *19* I, Paul, am spelling this out to you in my own handwriting![5] I myself will pay you back! Not to mention that you owe me your very self! *20* Yes, my fellow believer, do me this favor as a follower of the Lord! Cheer me up as a

---

[1] ἀδελφός, *adelphos*. See note on Matt.5:22.

[2] τῇ ἀδελφῇ, *te adelphe*. See note on ἀδελφός, *adelphos*, on Matt.5:22.

[3] Paul loves to play on words. The name Onesimos means "useful". Paul is saying that Onesimos is now really useful, useful not only in name.

[4] χωρίζω, *khorizo*, aorist passive, euphemism for "ran away".

[5] Paul is saying this to emphasize his point.

follower of the Anointed One! *21* I write to you with confidence that you will pay attention to what I say.[1] I know that you will do even more than what I say. *22* But at the same time get a guest room ready for me – as I expect that through your prayers my release will be granted to you.[2]

23-25 Epaphras, my fellow prisoner because of the Anointed One Jesus greets you, *24* and so do Mark, Aristarchos, Demas and Luke, my fellow workers. *24* May the favor of Lord Jesus the Anointed One be with your spirit!

---

[1] ὑπακοή, *hupakoe*. See note on Rom. 1:5.
[2] That is, freed from prison.

Letter to the Hebrews.

Hebrews was written between 49 and 70 AD, most likely between 64 and 70 AD. It is (clearly) prior to its citation by Clement of Rome c. 95 AD, and so is prior to the destruction of the Temple in Jerusalem. Another clue to the date is that the Levitical system was still in place when Hebrews was written. Further, Hebrews 13:23 is the only mention in the whole New Testament of Timothy being imprisoned, which has led some to conclude that Hebrews must be after Paul's death. In all his frequent mentions in the Pauline letters Timothy is shown to be a free man, and is in Ephesos at the time of Paul's final imprisonment.

Hebrews shows the most sophisticated Greek of all writers of the New Testament. The identity of the writer has not been established, nor has the identity of the readers. Origen stated, "Whoever wrote the epistle, God only knows for sure." Hebrews 2:3 does reveal that the author had not heard Jesus. Luther suggested the author was Apollos, and modern scholarship has suggested Apollos' teacher Priscilla. A scholar and a Jew who had been associated with Paul in his teaching ministry, Priscilla was well qualified to write Hebrews, to address the relation of the old and new covenants. Hebrews is unique among New Testament writings for the conspiracy of anonymity which surrounded its author. The scholarly evidence suggests a definite blackout of authorship. This would be explained by a Priscillan authorship, as anonymity would have been necessary for a woman writing to certain anti-female biased congregations. Adolf von Harnack, "Probabilia uber die Adresse und den Verfasser des Hebraerbriefes" *ZNW* 1 (1900) 16-41 first put forward Priscilla's name as the author of Hebrews. He argued that the lack of attribution, indeed, the conspiracy of silence over the authorship, did indicate a woman writer. Priscilla as author has been argued for by Ruth Hoppin, *Priscilla: Author of the Epistle to the Hebrews, and Other Essays* (New York: Exposition, 1969). Some object to a Priscillan authorship on the basis of the masculine participle at 11:32, but this is baseless as it could be the authorial masculine. Another suggestion has been Priscilla and Aquila as joint authors. Two authors would explain the interchange between the first person singular and plural ("I" and "we") throughout the book. Timothy is mentioned in Hebrews 13:23. Priscilla and Aquila knew Timothy as the three of them worked with Paul in Corinth and Ephesus.

Tertullian, *De Pudicitia* 20, ascribes the book to Barnabas and asserts that this was the common belief of the time. Barnabas had worked closely with Paul (Acts 9:27; 11;30; 13:1-14:28). Other supporters of a Barnabas authorship note that he was a Levite (Acts 4:36) and a major theme in Hebrews is the Levitical law and priesthood. Clement of Alexandria argued that it had been written in Aramaic and translated into Greek by Luke. Origen states that some ascribed it to Clement of Rome, and others to Luke. The Pauline authorship was seriously disputed in the Reformation by Luther, Erasmus, and Calvin. Luther argued for Apollos as author and Calvin argued for Luke.

Letter to the Hebrews.

Ch.1:1-3 In ancient times, God spoke to our ancestors through the prophets bit by bit, and in versatile ways. *2* But in these last days he has spoken to us by his Son, whom he has appointed to be heir of everything. Through his Son, he made all the periods of time which exist.[1] *3* The Son is the radiance

---

[1]   οἱ αἰῶνες, *hoi aiones*, "the complete period of all existence", cf. Arist. *Coel.* 1. 9. 15. Not "universe" or "worlds".

of God's splendor and the exact likeness[1] of his real nature.[2] He produces everything by the power of his spoken word. After he had provided for the cleansing of sins, he sat down at the right side of the Majesty on high.

4-9 He became as much superior to the Messengers as the Name he has inherited is more distinguished than theirs. *5* Now did God ever say this to a Messenger - "You are my Son, and today I have become your Father"? Or again, "I will be his Father, and he will be my Son?" *6* And again, when God will bring his first-born into the world, he says of this, "All God's Messengers must worship him!" *7* Speaking to the Messengers he says, "He makes his Messengers spirits, and his otherworldly ministers[3] fiery flames." *8* But to the Son he says, "God, your throne is forever and ever, and a scepter of uprightness is the scepter of your Kingdom. *9* You have loved justice and hated lawlessness! For this reason God, your God, has anointed you with the oil of great happiness rather than those who are in partnership with you."

10-12 And, "Lord, in the beginning you laid the foundations of the earth and the skies are the work of your hands; *11* they will perish, but you will continue, and they will all wear out like a coat, *12* And you will roll them up like a cloak, and they will be changed; but you are the same, and your years will never end."

13-14 And did God say to any of the Messengers, "Sit at my right side, until I turn your enemies into a footstool for your feet!"? *14* Aren't all Messengers ministering spirits sent out to minister to those who are to inherit salvation!

Ch.2:1-4 For this reason we must increasingly pay attention to the things we have heard, so that we don't drift away. *2* For as the message spoken through Messengers was valid, and every overstepping of the mark and disobedience got what it deserved,[4] *3* then how can we escape if we neglect such a great salvation! This salvation, which was first proclaimed by the Lord, was guaranteed as valid to us by those who heard him. *4* God also testified to it by miraculous signs and wonders and different types of powers, and distributions by the Holy Spirit as he wished.

5-8 God did not cause the inhabited world, about which we're speaking, to come in order to support Messengers. *6* Someone testified somewhere and said, "What is humanity that you remember it, or the Human Being[5] that you visit him? *7* You made him lower than Messengers for a short time, and crowned him with glory and honor, *8* for he caused all things under his feet to support him." Everything has been caused to support him and there is nothing that has not been caused to support him. But at the moment we don't yet see everything that has been caused to support him.

9-13 But we see Jesus, who was made lower than the Messengers for a short time, now crowned with glorious honor on account of the fact that he paid the penalty through death. This was so that he would experience death on behalf of everyone, because of God's favor to everyone. *10* It was fitting that God, on account of whom and through whom everything exists, would lead many children to glorious state and would bring the leader of their salvation to a complete state through his experiences. *11* For both he who makes sacred and those who are being made sacred are all from one family. For this reason Jesus is not ashamed to call them brothers and sisters. *12* He says, "I will announce your name to my brothers and sisters, I will sing

---

[1] χαρακτήρ, *kharakter*, "exact likeness". Occurs only here in the N.T. For inscriptional evidence see *I.Eph.* Ia.25.8-10, an imperial decision which mentions the exact likenesses of the emperors in statue form.

[2] ὑπόστασις, *hupostasis*, "underlying and supporting its outward form and properties", cf. LSJ *s.v.*

[3] λειτουργός, *leitourgos*, "minister", "priest", not "servant", although does mean "public servant".

[4] μισθαποδοσία, *misthapodosia*. No documentary attestation is yet known.

[5] ὁ υἱὸς τοῦ ἀνθρώπου, *ho huios tou anthropou*. See note on Matt. 8:20.

festive praise songs to you in the midst of the assembly." *13* And again, "I will put my trust in him." And again he says, "Indeed, here I am, and the children that God has given to me."

14-15 So since the children went into partnership with flesh and blood, he also pretty much shared in their flesh and blood. This was so that through his death he would abolish the effects of him who holds the power over death, that is to say, Slanderer-Liar, *15* and release the ones from death, those in fear, who all their lives were liable to the penalty of slavery.

16-18 Obviously, I hardly need to say that he doesn't do the work for Messengers, but he does do the work for Abraham's descendants. *17* This being the case, he had to become like his brothers and sisters in every aspect, in order that he would become a merciful and trustworthy high priest in the things pertaining to God, so that he could take away the sins of the people. *18* For as he himself has experienced ordeals, he is able to help those who are going through ordeals.

Ch.3:1-6 As this is the case, sacred fellow believers, who are partners in the invitation from heaven, think very carefully about Jesus, the apostle and high priest with whom is our legally binding agreement. *2* He is faithful to the One who appointed him, Moses also was faithful in the whole of God's household. *3* Jesus has been considered worthy of greater honor than Moses, just as the builder of a house has greater honor than the house itself. *4* Every house is built by someone, but God is the builder of everything. *5* Indeed Moses was faithful as a companion in arms in all God's household, as evidence of words to be said in the future. *6* But the Anointed One is faithful as a Son for the extent of God's household. And we are in his household, if we hold firmly to the boldness, freedom and openness of speech and to the expectation about which we are confident.

7-11 Therefore, as the Holy Spirit says, "Today, if you hear his voice, *8* Do not harden your hearts as you did in the rebellion, during the time of ordeals[1] in the desert, *9* when your ancestors put me to the test, and put me under scrutiny to see if I measured up,[2] and for forty years saw what I did. *10* That is why I was burdened by that race of people, and I said, 'Their hearts are always wandering off, and they have not come to know my ways.' *11* So I swore my oath in anger: 'There's no way they will enter my rest.'"

12-14 Take care, fellow believers, that none of you has an evil unbelieving heart that avoids the living God. *13* Rather, encourage each other day by day, as long as it is called "Today", so that none of you will be hardened by sin's deceit - *14* for we have come to be in business partnership[3] with the Anointed One if we hold on firmly and securely to our original ground of expectation until the end. *15*As has just been said, "Today, if you hear his voice, do not harden your hearts as you did in the rebellion."

16-18 And who were the ones who heard and rebelled? Surely they were all the ones that Moses led out of Egypt! *17* By whom was he burdened for forty years? Surely it was by those who sinned, whose bodies lay where they fell in the desert! *18* Who were the ones that God swore to that they'd never enter his rest? Surely it was the ones who disobeyed!

19.Ch.4:1-2 And now we observe that they were not able to enter in because of their unbelief. *1* Therefore, while the promise of entering his rest remains open, let's be careful that none of you are found to have missed it! *2*

---

[1] περιασμός, *periasmos*. See note on Matt. 6:13.

[2] δοκιμασία, *dokimasia*, a word used of magistrates after their election, referring to the process of determining whether they fulfilled the legal requirements of legitimacy and full citizenship.

[3] μέτοχοι, *metokhoi*. See note on Luke 5:7. Horsley states, "At Heb. 3.14 the relationship between Christ and the addressees of the letter is conceived of in the binding terms of a business partnership." *NDIEC* 1.85.

For we too have had the Good News announced to us, just as they did - but the message they heard wasn't any good to them, because the people that heard it didn't combine it with faith.

3-11 Indeed, those of us who have believed do enter into the rest, as he has said - "I swore my oath in anger: 'There's no way they will enter into my rest.'" - although God's works have been completed since the foundation of the world. *4* Somewhere he has spoken about the seventh day in this way, "And on the seventh day God ceased from all his work." *5* And in this context again, "There's no way they will enter my rest." *6* Therefore the fact remains that some will enter that rest, and that those who previously had the Good News announced to them didn't enter, because of their disobedience. *7* So God again fixed a certain day and called it "Today", when a long time later he spoke through David, as was said before, "Today, if you hear his voice, do not harden your hearts."

8 For if Joshua had given them rest, God would not have spoken about another day after that. *9* Therefore there remains an observance of the Sabbath Day for God's people. *10* For anyone who enters into God's rest also ceases from their own work, just as God did from his. *11* So then let us be extremely eager to enter into that rest, so that no one will follow an example of disobedience, and fall.

12-13 For God's Word is living and active and is sharper than every double-edged sword, piercing to the extent of dividing soul and spirit, joints and marrow. It is able to discern the reasonings and thoughts of the heart. *13* And there is no creation that is unseen in his presence, but everything is naked and laid open to scrutiny in his eyes, and in his view, the Word is our responsibility.

14-16 Therefore, as we have a high priest who has passed through the heavenly places, Jesus the Son of God, we must hold fast to our agreement. *15* For we do not have a high priest who is not able to sympathize with our weaknesses, but we have one who has been harasses by the enemy in all respects like we are, and was without sin.[1] *16* Therefore we must come to the throne of God who grants favor with the right of free and bold, open and frank speech, able to say what we like, in order to take hold of mercy and find favor which leads to help in time of need.

Ch.5:1-6 For every high priest is taken from among people and is appointed on behalf of people in the things pertaining to God, to offer gifts and sacrifices on behalf of sins. *2* They are able to deal gently with those who are ignorant and are wandering off, since they themselves have also been clothed in weakness. *3* And this is why they have to offer sacrifices on behalf of their sins, as well as on behalf of the sins of the people. *4* And no one takes this honor upon themselves - they must be invited by God, just as Aaron was. *5* So too the Anointed One did not do himself the honor of becoming a high priest. But God said to him, "You are my Son, today I have conceived you." *6* And he says in another place, "You are a priest forever, in the succession of Melchizedek."

7-10 During the days when Jesus was of the earthly life, with loud shouts and tears he offered up earnest requests as well as prayers claiming the right of help and protection[2] to him who was able to save him from death. His

---

[1]   No "but (was without sin)" in the Greek – no contrast of thought is stated.

[2]   ἡ ἱκετηρία, *he iketeria*, literally, an olive branch which the suppliant held their hand as a symbol of their condition and as a claim for help and protection, cf. Aesch. Supp. 192, Hdt. 5.51., 7.141, Ar. Pl. 393, Andoc. 15.2, Dem. 262.16. Jesus offered up earnest requests as well as prayers claiming the right of help and protection. These prayers were called here in the N.T ἱκετηρία, *hiketeria*. In pagan terms it was always honored. If all else failed, the ἱκετηρία, *hiketeria*, could be offered. See for example Aeschylus, *The Suppliant Maidens*, 192. The daughters of Danaus are fleeing from Egypt. When they see armed crowds coming as well as horses and chariots, their father advises the ἱκετηρία,

precaution[1] was listened to. *8* Although he was a Son, he learnt to pay attention from the things that happened to him. *9* And when he had been brought to maturity, he became the cause of salvation to all who pay attention to him. *10* This was after he had been proclaimed as high priest by God "in the succession of Melchizedek."

11-14 We have much to say to you and it is difficult to explain in words, since your hearing has become dull and sluggish. *12* For although you ought to have become teachers by this time, once again you need someone to teach you the fundamental principles of the very foundation of the Words[2] of God. You have become people who need milk and not solid food. *13* Everyone who participates in milk is without experience in the just Word, and is childish, not speaking, still unfit to bear weapons.[3] *14* Solid food is for mature people, those who are skilled as the result of practice and have trained their perceptions to decide what is favorable and what is bad.

Ch.6:1-3 So then, we will leave the basic teachings about the Anointed One, and move on to maturity – we won't go back to laying down the basics of turning away from dead acts, laying down the foundations of faith in God, *2* teaching about cleansing rites, about laying on of hands, about the resurrection of the dead, and about eternal judgment. *3* And we will do this, if, that is, God entrusts it to us.

4-6 Those who have fallen away after experiencing the heavenly gift, after being in partnership with the Holy Spirit, *5* after experiencing the favor brought by God's spoken Word and the power of the coming age, *6* these people are impossible to renew – it is impossible to crucify the Son of God a second time for them to change their own minds! This makes a mockery of him!

7-8 Ground which soaks up rain that often falls on it, produces a crop useful to those for whom it is cultivated, and receives in exchange[4] a blessing from God. *8* But if it produces thorn bushes and thistles, it fails the test and comes near to being cursed – its end result is to be burned.

9-12 But, dear friends, we are sure of better things in your case – things that cling closely to salvation – even though we're speaking like this! *10* God is not unjust: he will not overlook your work and the love you have displayed

---

hiketeria, to be on the safe side. See also Herodotos 7.141: the Athenians sent their envoys to Delphi to consult the oracle. The priestess foretold a terrible fate. They were about to give up in dismay, when someone suggested they should approach the oracle the second time as suppliants, holding the olive branch. The priestess then gave a more favorable prophecy. The Greek in these examples is the same as in verse 7. See also Soph. *OT*, 911-923.

[1] εὐλάβεια, *eulabeia*, means "precaution", not "reverent submission". The word for "submission" does not appear here in the Greek, nor does "godly fear" or "fear". This noun is not to be confused with the noun εὐλαβής, *eulabes*, which can mean "reverent", "pious" or "religious", particularly hundreds of years after the N.T. was written. For the cognate verb of εὐλάβεια, *eulabeia*, see for example, *P.Oxy.Hels*. 23 (Oxyrhynchos, April 23, 212.) A man called Theon is taking legal action to restrain his former employee from carrying out unspecified threats against him. He writes, "Therefore, I am presenting this petition by way of safe-guarding myself, taking the precaution lest what he threatened should actually come about." Only here and in Heb. 12:28 in N.T.

[2] Not spoken words.

[3] νήπιος, *nepios*. The writer of Hebrews here takes advantage of wordplay, the meaning of which cannot be brought out by a simple word or two in an English translation. The word literally means "childish", "not speaking", and also refers to someone who is still unfit to bear arms, usually up to the age of 15 years, cf. Il. 2.136, 9.440, Eur. Ion. 1399, Andr. 755, Id. Heracl. 956, Polyb. 4.20, 8, Diod. 1.74.

[4] μεταλαμβάνω, *metalambano*, with accusative, "to take in exchange", "to take a share of". ("To share in" is μεταλαμβάνω, *metalambano*, with genitive.)

for his Name, by financially providing for the people devoted to God and continuing to financially provide for them. *11* We long for every one of you to display the same eagerness, until you receive in full what you hope for, *12* so that you do not become lazy, but instead imitate those who are inheriting the promises through faith and perseverance.

13-20 Indeed when God promised Abraham, since he couldn't make an oath by anyone greater, he made an oath by himself. *14* He said, "In all truth, I will abundantly bless you and I will abundantly multiply you." *15* And so, after he had persevered, Abraham hit the mark and got the promise. *16* For people make an oath by the one who is more important, and the oath confirms what is said and puts an end to any dispute. *17* God intervened with an oath because he wanted to demonstrate even more forcibly the unchangeable position of his purpose to the heirs of the promise. *18* This was so that through two unchangeable things, in which it is impossible for God to say what is untrue, we who have taken refuge in him would have strong encouragement to seize firm hold of the hope that has already been settled beforehand. *19* We have this hope as an anchor of the soul, unfailing and trustworthy. It enters the inner sanctuary behind the veil, *20* where Jesus, our forerunner, has entered on our behalf. He has become a high priest from the line of succession of Melchizedek.

Ch.7:1-3 This Melchizedek was the king of Salem and a priest of the Most High God. He went out to meet Abraham, who was returning from the slaughter of the kings, and blessed him. *2* Abraham gave him a tenth of everything. Firstly, his name means "king of righteousness", and secondly, "king of Salem" means "king of peace". He remains a priest continually forever, like the Son of God. *3* There is no record of his father or recorded mother, he has no genealogy. There is no record of his beginning of days or end of life.

4-6 Now think about what a great person he was – even the patriarch Abraham gave him a tenth of the best plunder of war. *5* Now on the one hand the law requires the descendants of Levi who hold the office of priest to receive the one-tenth from the people –that is to say, their fellow believers – even though their fellow believers are descended from Abraham. *6* But on the other hand, this person has not traced his descent to Levi, but he has collected the one-tenth from Abraham and has blessed the one (Abraham) who had the promises.

7-10 Without any dispute whatsoever, the lesser is blessed by the more important. *8* In the one case, the one-tenth keeps being collected by people who die, but in the other case, it keeps being collected by him who is witnessed as being alive. *9* It could even be said that Levi, who is the receiver of the one-tenths, paid the one-tenths through Abraham, *10* for he was still in the body of his father when Melchizedek went out to meet him.

11-17 Therefore, if then there had been completion through the Levitical priesthood (for under the Law it was given to the people), why was there still a need for a different priest to come – one from the line of succession of Melchizedek, not from the line of succession of Aaron? *12* For when there's a change of priesthood, it's necessary that there be a change of the law. *13* The One about whom these things are said participated in a different tribe, and no one from that tribe has ever devoted themselves to sacrificial duties. *14* For it is clear that our Lord descended from Judah, and Moses didn't speak anything about that tribe with regard to the priesthood. *15* And it is even more obvious if another priest like Melchizedek arises, one who has become a priest *16* not on the basis of the Law's command about selection due to ancestry, but on the basis of power of indissoluble life. *17* For it is testified, "You are a priest forever, from the line of succession of Melchizedek."

18-22 For on the one hand there is an annulment of the previous command because of its weakness and uselessness – *19* as the Law did not bring anything to completion – but on the other hand there is the introduction of a superior hope, through which we draw near to God. *20* And it was not without an oath being sworn! *21* Indeed others became priests without any oath being sworn, but he became a priest with an oath being sworn through God saying to him, "The Lord has sworn and will not change his mind. 'You are a priest forever.'" *22* So to the same degree, Jesus has become the pledge of a superior covenant.

23-25 Now there have been numerous priests, because death prevented them from staying in office, *24* but because Jesus lives forever, he has a permanent priesthood. *25* And so he is completely able to rescue and preserve those who come to God through him, because he is always alive to intercede on their behalf.

26-28 Such a high priest is suitable for us – one who is godly, without malice and is unpolluted, one who has been separated from sinners, one who has become higher than the heavenly places. *27* Unlike the former high priests, he does not need to offer sacrifices day after day, first for his own sins, and then for the sins of the people. He sacrificed for their sins once and for all when he offered himself. *28* Indeed the Law appoints people who have weaknesses as high priests, but the Word sworn on oath, which came after the Law, ordained the Son, who has been made complete forever.

Ch.8:1-2 Now this is the main point of what we are saying: we do have such a High Priest, who sat down at the right side of the Majesty in heaven, *2* and who ministers in the sanctuary, the true tabernacle erected by the Lord, not by people.

3-6 Every high priest is ordained to offer both gifts and sacrifices. This being the case, it is necessary for this High Priest to have something to offer. *4* So if he were on the earth, he would not be a priest, since there are already people who keep offering the gifts prescribed by the Law. *5* They minister at a sanctuary that is a pattern and a shadow of the heavenly places. This is why Moses received the divine revelation when he was about to build the tabernacle: "See to it that you make everything according to the plan that was sketched out to you on the mountain." *6* In fact, the ministry that has fallen to Jesus is as superior to theirs, as the covenant of which he is mediator is superior to the old one, seeing that it has been legislated on the basis of better promises.

7-13 For if that first covenant had been blameless, there would have been no need for a second. *8* Because he found fault with the Israelites, he said, "Indeed! The days are coming," says the Lord, "when I will finish off a new covenant with the house of Israel and the house of Judah. *9* It will not be like the covenant I made with their ancestors when I took them by the hand and led them out of Egypt, because they did not remain in my covenant, and I neglected them," says the Lord. *10* "Because this is the covenant I will draw up with the house of Israel after those days, says the Lord. I will put my laws in their understanding and write them on their hearts. I will be their God, and they will be my people. *11* No longer will someone teach their neighbor, or will someone teach their sibling, saying, 'Come to know the Lord,' because they all will know me, from the least of them to the greatest. *12* For I will be merciful to their offenses, and I won't remember their sins any more." *13* By calling this covenant "new" he has made the first one obsolete. What is obsolete and aged is close to ceasing to exist.

Ch.9:1-5 Now the first covenant had regulations for worship and a sanctuary which was earthly. *2* A tabernacle was constructed. In its first[1] room were the lamp stand, the table and the setting out of the sacred bread[2] – this was called the Holy Place. *3* Behind the second veil[3] was a room called the Holiest of Holies *4* which had the golden incense altar and the gold-covered Ark of the Covenant. This ark contained the gold jar of manna,

---

[1]   That is, the outer room.
[2]   This describes the 12 freshly baked loaves of bread placed every Sabbath in 2 rows on a table before God in the tabernacle and later eaten by the priests. (Lev. 34.5-9)
[3]   The first veil (curtain) hung at the entrance to the Holy Place, and the second separated the Holiest of Holies.

Aaron's staff that had budded, and the stone tablets of the covenant. *5* Above the ark were the cherubim of the Splendor, overshadowing the mercy seat.[1] But we can't discuss these things in detail right now.

6-10 After these things had been constructed like this, the priests kept going into the outer room to carry out their acts of worship. *7* But only the high priest could go into the inner room, and he could only do that once a year. He could never go into the inner room without blood, which he offered for himself and for those sins that the people had committed without knowing that they were sins. *8* The Holy Spirit revealed this – that the way into the Holiest of Holies was not yet made known while the first tabernacle was still standing. *9* This is a symbol for the present time, indicating that the gifts and sacrifices being offered were not able to clear the conscience of the worshipper. *10* The gifts and sacrifices were only on the level of eating and drinking and cleansing rites – regulations for things of the natural realm to stay in effect until the time a new way was laid down.

11-15 But when the Anointed One came, he was a high priest of the good things that are already here. He went through the greater and more complete tabernacle that is not made by humans - that is to say, not a part of this creation. *12* He did not enter it by means of the blood of goats and calves, but he entered the Holiest of Holies once and for all by his own blood, as he had paid the ransom forever. *13* The blood of goats and bulls and ashes of a heifer sprinkled on those who are ceremonially unclean makes them holy as far as the cleansing of the natural realm goes. *14* So how much more then will the blood of the Anointed One, who through the eternal Spirit offered himself up as an unblemished sacrifice to God, cleanse our consciences from things done when we were corpses, so that we may worship the living God! *15* And on account of this the Anointed One is the mediator of the New Covenant between God and people, so that those who have been invited may take hold of the promise, namely, the inheritance which lasts forever. It was his death that led to their offenses being released when he paid the ransom for them during the time of the first covenant.

16-17 For where there is a will and testament, it is necessary for the person who made the will and testament to die. *17* For the will and testament is guaranteed as valid only after people are dead, since it cannot go into effect while the person who made it is alive.

18-22 Hence not even the first covenant has been dedicated without blood. *19* For when Moses had spoken each command to all the people according to the Law, he took the blood of calves, as well as water, crimson wool and hyssop, and sprinkled the book itself and all the people. *20* He said, "This is the blood of the covenant which God made with you." *21* And in the same way he sprinkled the tabernacle as well as all the vessels of service used in the worship with the blood. *22* And according to the Law nearly everything must be cleansed with blood, and without the shedding of blood there is no cancellation.

23-26 Therefore it is necessary for the patterns of the things in the heavenly places to be cleansed by these means, but for the things of the heavenly places themselves be cleansed with better sacrifices than these. *24* For the Anointed One did not enter a sanctuary made by humans, an echoing of the real things, but into heaven itself, as the case now stands to appear in the presence of God on our behalf. *25* Not that he offers himself up often, just as the high priest enters the Holiest of Holies year by year with blood that is not his own – *26* as in that case he would have had to experience it often, right

---

[1]   The 2 cherubim stood facing each other on top of the ark of the covenant. Their wings were stretched over the mercy seat. This was the throne signifying the divine presence. The mercy seat was sprinkled by the high priest on the Day of Atonement with the blood of sacrifices for the expiation of sins.

from the foundation of the world. But as it is, he has been revealed once at the completion of the ages to annul sin by sacrificing himself.

27-28 And just as it is in store for people to die once, and after that is the court trial, *28* so too the Anointed One offered himself once to take the sins of many on himself. He will be seen a second time, yet this time not in relation to sin, but rather to those who are expecting him, for the purpose of deliverance.

Ch.10:1-4 For the Law was a shadow of the good things in store for us. The Law is not itself an exact image of these things. Indeed, for the same reason it can never make those who draw near to God in worship complete by means of these same sacrifices which they offer up continually again and again, year after year. *2* If it could do this, then they would have stopped offering up these sacrifices! In that case the worshippers would have been cleansed once and for all, and they would no longer have any conscience about sins. *3* But those sacrifices cause sins to be remembered year after year. *4* For it is not possible for blood of bulls and goats to carry away sins.

5-7 And this is why he said this when he came into the world: "You did not want sacrifice and offering, but you fully equipped a body for me. *6* You were not content with burnt offerings and sin offerings. *7* Then I said, 'Indeed! I have come - in the scroll of the book it stands written about me - to do your purpose, God.'"

8-10 In the above Scriptures he said, "You did not want sacrifices, offerings, burnt sacrifices or sin offerings - nor were you content with them," - namely those which are offered up according to the Law. *9* Then he has said, "Indeed! I have come to do your purpose." He takes away the first in order to set up the second. *10* By God's purpose we have been made sacred once and for all through the offering up of the body of Jesus the Anointed One.

11-14 Now on the one hand, day after day every priest stands and offers worship. Again and again they offer up the same sacrifices, which are never able to strip off sins. *12* But on the other hand this One, after he had offered one sacrifice on behalf of sins forever, sat down at God's right side. *13* From then on he waits until his enemies are turned into his footstool. *14* By one offering he has made those who are being made sacred, complete for all time.

15-18 But the Holy Spirit also testifies to us about this. After previously saying this: *16* "This is the covenant I will draw up with the house of Israel after those days," says the Lord. "I will put my laws in their understanding and write them on their hearts." *17* Then he adds, "I will definitely not remember their sins and lawless acts any more." *18* And where these have been canceled, there is no longer any offering on behalf of sin.

19-23 Therefore, fellow believers, as you have the freedom, boldness and openness of speech for entering the Holiest of Holies by means of the blood of Jesus, *20* by a recent and living pathway which he set down for us, through the veil – the pathway was his body – *21* and as we have a High Priest in God's house, *22* then with a sincere heart and the certainty which faith gives us, let us draw near to God. Our hearts have been sprinkled with his blood to cleanse us from an evil conscience and our bodies have been washed with pure water. *23* Let us hold on firmly to the agreement about what we hope for without being moved, for he who promised is to be trusted!

24-25 Let us consider how we can spur each other on to do loving and favorable acts. *25* Don't give up gathering together – as some have got into the habit of doing – but encourage each other – and all the more so eagerly expecting the Day as it draws near.

26-31 If we deliberately keep on sinning continually after we have taken hold of the knowledge of the truth, there is no sacrifice for sin left for us. *27* Instead, there is a certain terrifying expectation of judgment and a raging fire ready to eat up those who are in opposition. *28* Anyone who disregards Moses' Law dies without pity on the evidence of two or three witnesses. *29* How much more do you suppose a person deserves to be punished who has trampled the Son of God under their feet, and who has regarded the blood of the Covenant which made them sacred as a common thing, and who has mocked the Spirit who gives us favors? *30* For we know him who said, "Revenge is mine, I will repay it!" and again, "The Lord will judge his people." *31* It is a terrifying thing to fall into the hands of the living God!

32-35 But remember the earlier times after you had been enlightened, when you stood your ground in a major athletic combat with the things that were happening to you![1] *33* On some occasions you were made a public spectacle and were shamefully treated as well as oppressed, while on other occasions you became partners with those who were living like this. *34* For you sympathized with those in prison and happily accepted the confiscation of your possessions, because you realized that you yourselves had superior and lasting possessions. *35* So then, do not throw away your boldness, freedom and openness of speech, as it brings you great payment; that is to say, that you will get what you deserve.

36-39 There is a need for you to have endurance, so that after you do what God wants you to, you will receive the promise in full: *37* "For still a very little while, he who is to come will come and will not delay. *38* But my righteous person will live from faith and if they cower with fear, my soul is not content with them." *39* But we certainly are not those who cower with fear and who are destroyed: we are those who have faith and who secure life.

Ch.11:1-3 Now faith is the real nature, the foundation of things we hope for, the evidence of actions which we don't see. *2* This is what the elders had a reputation for. *3* By faith we understand that the ages were completely equipped by God's spoken words in such a way that things which are seen came into being from things which were not made to appear.

4-5 By faith Abel offered a better sacrifice to God than Cain did. By faith he got a reputation for being a righteous person, as God approved of his offerings. And by faith he still speaks, even though he is dead.

5 By faith Enoch was transferred from one place to another so that he didn't experience death, and could not be found, because God had taken him away – since before he was transferred from one place to another he had the reputation that he had pleased God.

6 Now it is impossible to please God without faith, as the person who comes forward to speak to God must believe that God exists, and that people who seek him out will receive their payment for it.

7 By faith Noah, when he received the divine revelation about things not yet seen, paid attention and fully equipped an ark for the safekeeping of his household. By doing this he was giving judgment against the world, and he became an inheritor of the rightness with God which comes because of faith.

8-10 By faith Abraham succeeded, when called to go to a place which was intended for him to take as his inheritance - and he went, even though he wasn't capable of going. *9* By faith he came from home to live in the promised land like someone who was living in someone else's tent. Isaac and Jacob lived with him in tents too – they were joint-heirs of the same promise as Abraham. *10* For Abraham was receiving the city with foundations, whose artist and craftsperson[2] is God.

---

[1] πάθημα, *pathema*, "anything that befalls one", "the lessons of experience", cf. Soph. *Tr.* 142 mostly in the plural (as here), Hdt. 1.207, 8.136; Aesch. *Ag.* 175, Ar. *Them.* 199, Plat., *Symp.* 222B.

[2] τεχνίτης καὶ δημιουργός, *tekhnites kai demiourgos*. Both words mean "artist", "craftsman", not "builder and maker".

11 By faith Sarah herself – although she was sterile - also laid hold of power for the depositing[1] of offspring although she was well past it in age, since she considered that the promise was believable.

12-16 And so from one person, and moreover no better than a corpse as well, came as many descendants as multitudes of stars in the sky and as countless as sand on the seashore. *13* All these people were still living by faith when they died. They had not laid hold of the promises, but after seeing them from far away, they clung to them and verbally agreed that they were foreigners and people living in a foreign place on the earth. *14* For people who say such a thing are clearly showing that they're searching for their homeland. *15* And indeed if they kept remembering what[2] they had come out of, they would have had an opportunity to return. *16* But on the other hand they were reaching out for what was superior – in other words, the heavenly places. And for this reason God was not ashamed to be nicknamed 'Their God" - for he has a city ready for them.

17-19 By faith Abraham attempted[3] to offer up Isaac. Abraham who had received the promises was trying to offer up his only son, *18* even though it had been said to him, "Offspring will be summoned in Isaac for you." *19* Abraham figured that God was able to raise up corpses, and symbolically, he did get Isaac back.

20-31 By faith Isaac blessed Jacob and Esau and spoke of things that were to happen.

21 By faith Jacob, when he was dying, blessed each of Joseph's sons, and bowed down in worship while he was leaning on the top of his staff.

22 By faith Joseph, when he was coming to an end, remembered the exodus of the Israelites from Egypt, and gave instructions about what to do with his bones.

23 By faith Moses, after he was born, was hidden for three months by his parents[4] because they saw he was a clever little child, and they weren't afraid of the king's decree. *24* By faith Moses, when he grew up, refused to be called the son of Pharaoh's daughter. *25* Instead, he chose to put up with hardship with God's people rather than enjoy the short-lived pleasures of sins. *26* He considered the insults attached to being Anointed was a greater wealth than the treasures in Egypt, for he was giving his attention to the payment of what was owed him.[5] *27* By faith he abandoned Egypt, not being

---

[1] καταβολή, *katabole*, in the sense of paying a deposit by installments rather than in the sense of merely "having" offspring. This verse which shows that Sarah laid hold of power to have offspring, has caused a huge problem for translations and commentaries. Tyndale's 1534 translation translates correctly. However, some Bible versions add the word "Abraham" and "enabled to become a father", none of which appear in the Greek text, and has Abraham as the one who considered that the promise was believable. σπέρμα, *sperma*, regularly means "offspring".

[2] There is no mention of "place", "country", "land".

[3] See Heb. 11:29: in that instance the noun is used as "attempt" for the Egyptians attempting to cross the Red Sea. πειράζω, *peirazo*, "to make an attempt", "to attempt", cf. Polyb. Fr. Hist. 60; Luc. Amor. 26, 36. Not to be put to the test with hostile intent (usually rendered in Bible versions as "fall into temptation"). πειράζω, *peirazo*, is never used of being put to the test by God (see prohibition in James 1:13) – the verb so used is δοκιμάζω, *dokimazo*.

[4] Moses was hidden ὑπὸ τῶν πατέρων αὐτοῦ, *hupo ton pateron autou*, "by his parents". πατέρες, *pateres*, can mean "fathers" but also meant "female parents", or just "parents", non-gender specific. P.J. Sijpesteijn lists 2 examples in papyri of individual women called *pater. ed. pr.* P.J. Sijpesteijn, *Tyche* 2 (1987) 171-74. Here clearly, Moses' mother is included in the term, as is normal Greek practice.

[5] μισθαποδοσία, *misthapodosia*. Meaning unknown. As yet no documentary evidence for this word is known earlier than the 4th c. AD. The verb occurs only in

afraid of the king's rage, as he was patient for the invisible just as if he were able to see it. *28* By faith he kept the Passover and the pouring of blood, so that the Destroyer who destroyed the firstborn of people and animals[1] wouldn't touch them. *29* By faith they crossed the Red Sea on dry land, whereas when the Egyptians attempted it, they were swallowed up by the sea.

30 By faith the walls of Jericho fell down after they had been surrounded for seven days.

31 By faith Rahab the prostitute did not die with the unbelievers because she peacefully welcomed the spies.

32-35 And what more can I say! I don't have enough time to tell you about Gideon, Barak, Samson, Jephthah, David, as well as Samuel and the prophets! *33* Because through faith they conquered kingdoms, worked justice, hit the mark with regard to promises, blocked lions' mouths, *34* put out the power of fire, escaped the edge of the sword, were empowered out of a state of weakness, became strong in warfare, and wheeled ranks drawn up in battle-order, ranks which belonged to others. *35* Women received corpses raised back to life.

35-40 Others were beaten to death, refusing to accept release, so that they would gain a better resurrection. *36* Still others had fun poked at them and were beaten with the Roman whip of leather straps embedded with metal designed to rip of the flesh, and were even put in chains and thrown into prison. *37* They were stoned, they were sawn up, they were murdered by the sword. They went around in sheepskins and goatskins, and were destitute, oppressed and ill treated. *38* The world wasn't worthy of them! They wandered around in deserts and mountains, and in caves and crevices in the ground. *40* And all of these, although they were well spoken of because of their faith, did not obtain the promise. *40* God planned something better for us, so that they couldn't reach the finish without us.

Ch.12:1-3 Consequently, we also, since we're surrounded by such a big cloud of witnesses, must get rid of every arrow tip in us and the sin which easily stands around us. We must run the race that surrounds us by using endurance. *2* We must fix our eyes on Jesus, the originator and completer of faith. Instead of the happiness set in front of him, he chose to undergo the cross, thinking nothing of the shame. He has taken his seat at the right side of God's throne. *3* So think about Jesus who underwent such opposition from sinners so that you won't become worn down and fall apart in your lives.

4-6 You haven't come to the point of bloodshed yet in opposing sin, fighting against it. *5* And have you completely forgotten the encouragement which addresses you as his children: "My child, don't make light of the Lord's education.[2] Don't fall apart when you are put under scrutiny by him. *6* Because the Lord educates the ones he loves, and he uses the rod on everyone he welcomes as a child."

Heb. 2:2; 10:35 (and here) in the N.T. and has not been found elsewhere in any Greek literature. The noun μισθοδότης, *misthodotes*, likewise has no documentary attestation. It occurs in Heb. 11:6 (and in a sole reference which draws from this verse in Hebrews). Related words refer to the paying of wages. μισθαποδοσία, *misthapodosia*, means "payment of wages"; μισθοδότης, *misthodotes*, means "one who pays wages", "a paymaster", and μισθοδοτέω, *mistheodoteo*, means "to pay wages". Taking ἀπό, *apo*, in the middle of the word μισθαποδοσία, *misthapodosia*, in its causal meaning ("in consequence of"), thus μισθαποδοσία, *misthapodosia*, as "a payment of what's owed". It clearly has this sense in Heb. 2:2.

[1] Neuter plural, "the first-born of people and animals".

[2] παιδεία, *paidea*. See note on Eph. 6:4. Also note, for example, the Just Argument's speech in Aristophanes, *Clouds*, 961-983, and in Thucydides 2.39; Plato, *Symposium*, 187D. The word is common in Greek literature. Occurs in the N.T. in Eph. 6:4; 2 Tim. 3:16, and elsewhere in this chapter in verses 7, 8, 11.

7-11 Because you undergo education, God treats you like his children – what child is there that a parent[1] doesn't educate? *8* But if you go without education – which everyone is a business partner[2] with! – then you're illegitimate and you're not children! *9* Then again we have human parents who educate us and we listen to them. Surely we should follow the Father of our spirits and live! *10* For on the one hand our parents educated us for a short time in the best way they could, but on the other hand he educates us for our benefit, so that we can share in his holiness. *11* Now on the one hand education doesn't seem like much fun at the time, as it's painful! However, later on it produces a harvest of peace and righteousness by those who have been trained in it!

12-13 So then, strengthen your arms which hang limply at your sides and your weak knees, *13* and make straight paths for your feet, so that any part of you that's crippled won't be put out of joint, but instead will be instantly divinely healed!

14-17 Strive to be at peace with everyone and to be holy, without such no one will see the Lord. *15* See to it that no one misses out on God's favor and that no bitter root grows up to cause trouble. This causes many people to be tainted. *16* See to it that no one is an idol worshipper or godless like Esau, who, for one bowl of food, sold the inheritance rights due to him as the oldest son. *17* For we know that later on, when he wanted to inherit the blessings, he was rejected. He couldn't get Isaac to change his mind, although he tried to with many tears.

18-21 Now you haven't drawn close to a tangible burning fire, and to a darkness and a gloom and a whirlwind, *19* and the ringing sound of a trumpet and the sound of the voice of spoken words, so that those who heard it begged that the Word would not be spoken to them any more. *20* They couldn't bear what was being commanded, "If even a wild animal touches the mountain, it must be stoned." *21* It was such a terrifying sight that Moses said, "I'm shaking with fear!"

22-24 But you have drawn close to Mount Zion and to the city of the Living God, the Jerusalem in heaven, and countless numbers of Messengers, *23* in a festival and assembly of the firstborn entered in the list in heaven. And you have drawn close to God, the judge of all, and to the spirits of righteous people who have been made complete, *24* and to Jesus the mediator of the New Covenant, and to the blood of sprinkling that speaks better things than the blood of Abel.

25-29 See to it that you don't turn your back on The Speaker. For as they didn't escape when they turned their back on him who gave divine revelations[3] on the earth, how much more won't we escape if we turn away from him who gives divine revelations from heaven! *26* At that time his voice rocked the earth, but now he has promised this: "Just one more time I will shake not only the earth, but the sky[4] as well." *27* Now the words, "Just one more time" point to the transference of what can be rocked, like things which have been created, so that the things which cannot be rocked will remain. *28* So, since we're receiving our succession rights to a kingdom that cannot be rocked, we must be thankful. And for this reason we must worship God in a way which pleases him, with reverence and awe, *29* for our God is a consuming fire!

Ch.13:1-4 You must continue to love the fellow believers.[5] *2* Do not neglect to give hospitality to strangers, as in this way some people have entertained Messengers as guests without being aware that they were Messengers. *3* Take

---

[1] πατήρ, *pater*, "parent". Can mean "father" but also meant just "parent", non-gender specific. P.J. Sijpesteijn lists two examples in papyri of individual women called *pater*. P.J. Sijpesteijn, *Tyche* 2 (1987) 171-74.

[2] μέτοχοι, *metokhoi*. See note on Luke 5:7.

[3] The same verb χρηματίζω, *khrematizo*, twice in this sentence (see also Heb. 8:5), to give a divine revelation, or to transact business. It is used in the middle voice for transacting business, especially in money matters, or to make money.

[4] Equally possible, "heaven".

[5] φιλαδελφία, *philadelphia*. See note on Rom. 12:10.

thought for the people in prison, as if you were prisoners with them. Take thought for those who have been badly treated as if it were happening to you in person. *4* Marriage is honorable and so is everything in it and the bed is undefiled. God will judge those who commit *porneia*[1] and are adulterers.

5-8 Your way of life must be free from greed for money. Be satisfied with what is there, for he himself has said, "I certainly will not leave you alone or fail you." *6* So we can say with confidence, "The Lord is my helper, I won't fear. What can any person do to me!" *7* Remember your leaders, who spoke God's Word to you! Have a close look at the outcome of the way they behave, and imitate their faith! *8* Jesus the Anointed One is the same yesterday, today, and forever.

9-15 Do not get carried away with different types of doctrines or strange doctrines. It is a good thing for our minds to be strengthened by God's favor, not by ceremonial foods that haven't been of any benefit to those who follow that way of life. *10* We have an altar and those who minister at the tabernacle have no right to eat from it. *11* The high priest carries the blood of animals into the Holiest of Holies as a sin offering, but the bodies are burned outside the camp. *12* And Jesus, so that he would make the people sacred through his own blood, experienced what he did outside the gate. *13* So then, we must go out to him outside the camp, carrying insults with him. *14* For we do not have a city that remains but we are searching for a city that is intended. *15* For this reason we must continually offer up to God a praise sacrifice through Jesus - that is to say, the product of speech that acknowledges his Name.

16-17 Don't forget good deeds and partnerships – God is pleased with such offerings! *17* Obey[2] your leaders and submit[3] to them, for they are being watchful for your lives, since they will have to give an account for it. Let them do this – and be agreeable about it and don't complain – for that wouldn't do you any good!

18-19 Pray for us! We believe that we have a good conscience, and that we want to behave well in every way. *19* I particularly urge you to do this – to pray that I will return to you sooner.

20-21 May the God of peace, who, through the blood of the age-long[4] Covenant, brought our Lord Jesus the Anointed One back from among the dead – that great Shepherd of the Sheep – *21* completely equip you with every good thing so that you can do what he wants you to do.

May he work in us that which pleases him, by means of Jesus the Anointed One, to whom be the honor for ever and ever, amen!

22-25 Fellow believers, I urge you to put up with my word of encouragement, for in fact I've written you just a short letter.

23 I want you to know that our fellow believer Timothy has been released. If he arrives soon, I'll come with him to see you.

24 Greet all your leaders and all the people devoted to God. Everyone here sends you greetings from Italy.[5] *25* May favor be with you all!

---

[1] πορνεία, *porneia*. See note on Matt. 15:19.
[2] πείθω, *peitho*, with dative, "obey", "have confidence in", "trust", "be persuaded by".
[3] ὑπείκω, *hupeiko*, with dative, "submit to".
[4] Not "everlasting", but "lasting for an age".
[5] Equally possible, "The Italians here send you greetings."

James.

James' letter was written before 50 AD. Galatians 2:7-9 speaks of the Jerusalem meeting which we know was c. 47 AD. There is no hint of this meeting in this letter. Josephus states that James was martyred in 62 AD. James was Jesus' brother and was not originally a disciple. He is not to be confused with the James who was one of the Twelve, the son of Zebedee and the brother of John. The author identifies himself as James in 1:1 and it was James who made an impact on the believers in Jerusalem (Acts 15 and 21). Galatians 1:19 tells us that Paul met James ("the Lord's brother") in Jerusalem. Acts 21 tells us that Paul agreed with James's request to take the men who had taken a vow, join in their purification ceremony, and pay their expenses so that they could have their heads shaved.

James.

Ch.1:1 From: James, a slave servant of God and of the Lord Jesus the Anointed One.

To: The twelve tribes which are scattered around.

Hello!

2-4 My fellow believers, be very happy when you fall into various types of ordeals, *3* realizing that when your faith passes muster, the result is endurance. *4* Now let endurance have its complete action, so that you will be complete and entire, not lacking anything.

5-8 If any of you lack wisdom, they should ask God, who gives to everyone generously and without demeaning them, and it will be given to them. *6* But they must ask with faith and not be undecided, for someone who is undecided is like surf being moved and tossed around by the wind. *7* That person must not think that they will receive anything from the Lord, *8* as they are a double-minded person, unstable in all their ways.

9-11 Let the lowly believer boast[1] of their high position, *10* and let the rich believer boast of their low position, because this person will pass away like a wildflower. *11* Indeed, the sun rises with a scorching heat and withers the wildflowers - they fall off and their beauty is destroyed. In the same way, the rich person will wilt away while they go on their journey.

12-15 Happy is the person who holds up under ordeals, because when they have successfully been through the ordeals, they will seize the crown of life which God has promised to those who love him. *13* When someone is being put through an ordeal, they are not to say, "I'm being put through an ordeal by God," as God cannot be put through an ordeal, and God indeed puts no one through a ordeal! *14* Rather, each person goes through ordeals by being dragged along and hooked on a bait by their own wants and wishes.[2] *15* Then wants and wishes conceive and give birth to sin, and sin when it grows up produces death.

16-21 Make no mistake, my dearly loved fellow believers! *17* Every good legacy[3] and every complete gift is from above, and comes down from the Father of the celestial lights, in whom there is no variation or shadow of change. *18* He deliberately brought us into being by means of the truthful Word to be some of the first offerings of his creations. *19* You may be certain of that, my dearly loved fellow believers! A person is to be quick to listen and slow to speak! Be slow to anger, *20* for a person's anger does not make them right with God *21* So you must get rid of all sordidness and bad excesses in a gentle way, and you must accept the Word planted in you that is able to save your souls.

---

[1] καυχάομαι, *kaukhaomai,* censored in most translations as "glory in", "take pride in". It actually means "to boast" or "to be loud-mouthed".

[2] The Greek does not mention the word "evil".

[3] δόσις, *dosis,* bequest or legacy.

22-25 Be doers of the Word and not just hearers of it, deceiving yourselves. *23* Because if someone is a hearer of the Word and not a doer of it, they are like a person studying the face they were born with in a mirror: *24* the person studies themselves and then goes away, and immediately they forget what they're like. *25* But the person who peers more closely into the complete law which gives freedom and continues to do so – not forgetting what they hear but doing it - will be happy in what they do.

26-27 If someone thinks they are religious but doesn't guide[1] their tongue, they are deceiving themselves and their religion is useless. *27* And this is God's view of pure and unpolluted religion: firstly to visit orphans and widows in order to help them out in their troubles, and secondly to keep themselves unstained from the world.

Ch.2:1-4 My fellow believers, as believers of our glorious Lord, Jesus the Anointed One, don't show favoritism! *2* Suppose a gentleman comes into your worship meeting wearing gold rings and expensive clothes, and a poor person in dirty clothes comes in too. *3* What if you give special attention to the gentleman in expensive clothes and say, "Here's a good seat for you!" but say to the poor person, "You can stand over there!" or, "Sit on the floor near my feet!" *4* Then you've discriminated among yourselves and used evil standards of judgment!

5-7 Listen, my dear fellow believers! Hasn't God chosen those who are financially poor in the eyes of the world to be rich in faith and to be inheritors of the Realm that he promised to those who love him? *6* But you have insulted the financially poor person! Isn't it the wealthy who are exploiting you? Aren't they the ones who are dragging you into the law court? *7* Aren't they the ones who are blaspheming the fine Name that has been given to you?

8-13 If you really fulfill the royal law according to the Scripture, "Love your neighbor as you love yourself," you're doing well; *9* but if you show favoritism, then you're committing a sin, and you're convicted by the law as law breakers. *10* For whoever holds firmly to the whole law and fails on one point of it, is guilty of breaking the whole lot. *11* For he who said, "Do not commit adultery," also said, "Do not murder." If you don't commit adultery but you do commit murder, you have become a law breaker. *12* So speak as well as act like those who are going to be judged by the law that gives freedom. *13* For the judicial sentence shows no mercy to the one who has shown no mercy.

14-18 My fellow believers, what good does it do you if someone says they have faith but does not have action? Is faith able to save them? *15* Suppose a fellow believer needs clothes and daily food. *16* If one of you says to them, "Off you go, I wish you well. Warm yourself! Eat as much as you like!" but you don't actually give them what they physically need, what good does it do them? *17* It's exactly the same way with faith too – faith by itself, that does not involve actions, is a dead corpse. *18* But someone might say, "You have faith and I have actions." Well then, you show me your faith without actions, and I will show you my faith by my actions!

19-23 You believe that there is one God. Big deal! Even the demons believe that – and they quake in their boots! *20* You empty-headed person, do you need convincing that faith without actions is useless? *21* Wasn't Abraham our ancestor considered right with God[2] by means of his actions when he offered Isaac his son on the altar? *22* You can take note that his faith was cooperating with his actions, and that his faith was completed by his actions! *23* And the Scripture was fulfilled that says, "Abraham believed God, so it was calculated that he was made right with God." And he was called God's friend.

24-26 You can see that a person is made right with God by actions and not just by faith alone. *25* In the same way too, Rahab the prostitute claimed her rights when she looked after the messengers and sent them off in a different direction.

---

1 χαλιναγωγέω, *khalinagogeo*, "to guide as with a bridle".
2 δικαιόω, *dikaioo*, also "to claim one's rights" cf. Thuc. 1:140, 5.105, Hdt. 9.93.

26 For just like the body without the spirit is a dead corpse, so also faith without actions is a dead corpse.

Ch.3:1-4 My fellow believers, not many of you should become teachers, because you know that we who teach will be judged more so. *2* For we all make mistakes in lots of things. If someone doesn't make a mistake in speech, they are a complete person able to guide their whole body as if with a bridle.[1] *3* For sure, we put bits in horses' mouths so that they will obey us, and we move their whole bodies from one place to another, changing their course. *4* Look at ships too – although they are so big and are driven by rough winds, they are guided from one place to another by a very small rudder, at the impulse of the person at the helm.

5-12 In the same way also, the tongue is a small body part and confidently says major things. Look how small the tongue is and how great a forest it sets on fire! *6* And the tongue is a fire - the tongue is the world of wrongdoing set among our body parts, staining the whole body. It sets aflame the cycle of human life and is set aflame by the Garbage Pit Gehenna. *7* For every kind of wild animal, bird, reptile, marine life can be tamed and has been tamed by humankind, *8* but the tongue is not able to be tamed by people. It is a fickle evil, full of death-bearing poison. *9* With the tongue we praise our Lord and Father and with the same tongue we put curses[2] on people, who have been made in God's likeness. *10* Out of the same tongue proceed blessings and curses.[3] My fellow believers, this shouldn't be! *11* Can fresh water and water that's unfit to drink flow from the same spring? *12* My fellow believers, can a fig tree bear olives, or a grape-vine bear figs? Neither can a salt spring produce fresh water!

13-18 Who is wise and knowledgeable among you? Let them show by their fine behavior that their actions are done gently, with wisdom. *14* Now if you have bitter jealousy and selfish ambition in your hearts, do not boast against and lie against the truth. *15* This type of "wisdom" doesn't come down from above, but is earthly, of the natural realm, and demon-like.[4] *16* For where you have jealousy and selfish ambition, there you have a state of disorder and all worthless matters.[5] *17* But the wisdom which comes from above is primarily holy, then peaceful, considerate, reasonable, full of mercy, unprejudiced, and without pretense. *18* Peacemakers who sow in peace reap a harvest of righteousness.

Ch.4:1-8 Where do battles and fights among you come from? Don't they come from your desires that war within you? *2* You desire something but you don't get it. You murder and strive after things, but you can't hit the mark. You fight and battle, but you don't have what you want because you don't ask for it. *3* You ask and you don't receive because you ask wrongly, so that you can spend it on your pleasures. *4* Adulteresses![6] Don't you know that friendship with the world is hostility to God! Therefore whoever wants to be a friend of the world appoints themselves as an enemy of God! *5* Or do you suppose that the Scripture doesn't have a good reason for saying, "The Spirit whom God causes to live within us longs for us jealously." *6* But he gives more favor. Therefore the scripture says, "God opposes the arrogant, but gives favor to those of low rank." *7* So then be attached to God. Take a stand in battle against Slanderer-Liar and he will flee from you.[7] *8* Draw near to God and he will draw near to you.

8-10 You sinners, cleanse your lives! You double-minded people, purify your minds! *9* Be miserable and mourn and weep! Turn your mourning into

---

1 χαλιναγωγέω, *khalinagogeo*, "to guide as with a bridle", not "restrain".

2 καταράομαι, *kataraomai*. See note on Luke 6:28.

3 καταρα, *katara*. See note on Gal. 3:10.

4 δαιμονιώδης, *daimoniodes*, adjective, "like a demon", cf. Schol. Ar. Ran. 295. Not "of the devil".

5 φαῦλον, *phaulon*, "worthless", "sorry", "bad", "mean"; not "evil".

6 μοιχαλίς, *moikhalis*. In the O.T. this word is used of Israel as the unfaithful spouse of God, cf. Ps. 73:27; Is. 54.5; Jer. 3:20; Ez. 16:15ff; Hos. 9:1.

7 Warfare metaphors: those of low rank, take up your posts, take a stand.

laughter and your gloom into happiness! *10* Bring yourself to a low station in the eyes of the Lord, and he will lift you up high.

11-12 My fellow believers, don't speak against[1] each other. The person who speaks against one of the fellow believers, and judges that person, is actually speaking against the law and judging the law. If you judge the law, you're not a doer of the law, but a judge of it! *12* There is one Lawgiver and one Judge – he who is able to save and to destroy. So who do you think you are – to judge your neighbor!

13-17 Come on now, you who say, "Today or tomorrow we're going to go to such-and-such a city, spend the year there, carry on business and make stacks of money"! *14* You don't know what's going to happen tomorrow! What's your life? You're just a vapor that appears for a little while then vanishes. *15* Instead of saying, "Whatever the Lord purposes", and, "We will live life to the fullest and do this or that", *16* in point of fact you are boasting and arrogant! All this type of boasting is evil! *17* So then, someone who knows the right things to do and doesn't do them, is sinning.

Ch.5:1-8 Come on now, you rich people, cry and howl because of the misery that is coming upon you! *2* Your wealth has rotted and your clothes are moth eaten. *3* Your gold and silver have corroded away. Their corrosion will testify against you and eat your flesh like fire! You have stored up treasure for the last days. *4* Indeed! You have robbed the workers who cut the harvest in your fields, and their wages are shouting out against you! The shouts of the harvesters have reached the ears of the Lord of Armies! *5* You have lived in luxury and self-indulgence on the earth. You have fattened yourselves for the day of your slaughter. *6* You have condemned and murdered the righteous who weren't taking the stand in the battle against you. *7* So be patient, fellow believers, until the Coming of the Lord! For example, look how the farmer waits for the valuable crop of the ground, waiting patiently for it until it receives the early and late rains. *8* And you be patient too! Get your footing on firm ground, because the Coming of the Lord has drawn near!

9-12 Fellow believers, don't blame each other, or you will be judged! Indeed! The judge is standing at the doors! *10* Fellow believers, take the example of the suffering and patience of the prophets who spoke with the authority of the Lord's Name. *11* We certainly call the ones who stand firm "happy". You've heard about Job's endurance and the outcome which the Lord brought about, because the Lord is full of compassion and he's merciful! *12* Above all, my fellow believers, do not swear an oath by heaven or by earth or by any other oath - rather, let your "yes" be "yes" and your "no" be "no" - otherwise, you'll fall under the sentence of judgment.

13-18 Are any of you suffering? You must pray! Is anyone happy? Then sing praise songs! *14* Are any of you sick? Then call for the elders of the assembly and have them pray over them, anointing them with oil in the Lord's Name. *15* And the claim[2] of faith will rescue and preserve the person who is getting the worst of it and the Lord will raise that person up. And if that person has committed sins that person will be forgiven for them. *16* So then fully confess your sins to each other, and claim on behalf of each other so that you will be instantly divinely healed. The earnest request of a righteous person is very strong and effective. *17* Elijah was a person with a similar nature to ours, and he prayed that it would not rain – and it didn't rain on the land for three years and six months. *18* And then he prayed again, and the sky gave rain, and the land produced its harvest.

19-20 My fellow believers, if one of you wanders from the truth and someone brings them back, *20* realize that the person who turns a sinner from wandering from the truth will save the sinner's soul from death and will cover a large number of sins!

---

[1] καταλαλέω τινός, *katalaleo tinos*, to gossip, babble or blab about someone, to wear someone down by talking, or to talk a person down.

[2] εὐχή, *eukhe*. See note on Acts 18:18.

Peter's Letters.

Peter was the first person to take the Good News to the people of Jerusalem, after which he took it to Judea, Samaria and Galilee. Peter knew Jesus very well and had been one of the Twelve disciples. Peter had been a fishing partner of John in Capernaum (Luke 5:10). Galatians 2:7-9 speaks of the Jerusalem meeting (which we know was c. 47 AD). Paul and Barnabas were to go to the non-Jews, and James, Peter and John were to go to the Jews.

Peter was a Galilean, originating from Bethsaida, east of the Jordan near the Sea of Galilee, in the territory of Gaulanitis, a Hellenized region. He was bilingual. Aramaic was his first language and he was competent in the Greek language. His original name "Simon" was Greek. Silas/Silvanus is mentioned in this letter. He was a Jew, a Roman citizen, and a prophet from the church in Jerusalem. He prepared a letter to churches in Antioch, Syria, Cilicia, and Galatia, which he helped to deliver. He accompanied Paul in his missionary journey of southern Galatia to Troas, to Macedonia and to Achaia. It has been suggested that Peter used an amanuensis for 1 Peter, yet wrote 2 Peter himself. It has also been suggested that Luke helped Peter write the letter, as 2 Tim. 4:11 states that Luke alone was with Paul at the end of his last imprisonment. Silas/Silvanus, mentioned in 1 Pet. 5:12, was not with Paul at the time.

Eusebius (*HE* 2.14.6) states that Peter visited Rome in the time of Claudius (41-54 AD). Peter was martyred in Rome during Nero's persecution after the Great Fire of AD 64. It is supposed that 1 Peter 1:6-7; 4:12, 14-16 refer to actual persecution in the provinces, which poses a difficulty as the Nero persecution was local. However, there is nothing in 1 Peter to suggest that the persecution was official Roman persecution. Irenaeus quotes from the letter, and attributes it to Peter. It is cited by Clement of Alexandria, Tertullian, and Theophilus of Antioch, and is quoted by Polycarp.

First Letter of Peter.

Ch.1:1-2 From: Peter, an apostle of Jesus the Anointed One.
To: God's chosen, scattered people in Pontus, Galatia, Cappadocia, Asia and Bithynia, *2* who have been chosen by the advance knowledge of God the Father, through the work of the Spirit which makes you sacred. This leads to you paying attention to Jesus the Anointed One and to you being sprinkled by his blood.
May your favor and peace be increased!
3-4 Praise the God and Father of our Lord Jesus the Anointed One! Due to his abundant mercy he has caused us to be born again and thus given us a hope that lives on. He did this by the resurrection of Jesus the Anointed One from among the dead. *4* He has also caused us to be born again and he has given us an inheritance. This inheritance does not perish, it is unpolluted and it does not fade away. It is being guarded in heaven for you.
5-7 Because of your faith, you are guarded with an army garrison by God's power, until the deliverance that is now ready to be revealed in the last season of time. *6* You can be very happy about this, even if you've had to put up with distress from different types of ordeals lately. *7* This means that your faith which has proven to have brought you through this – far more valuable than gold which perishes, even though it is proven through fire – will result in glorious praise and honor when Jesus the Anointed One is revealed.
8-9 You love him although you haven't seen him. Even though you don't see him, you believe him. You are filled with a happiness that can't be expressed, a full and glorious happiness, *9* as you are receiving what is promised to you – what is owed to you because of your faith – the deliverance of your lives.
10-13 The prophets, who studied the favor that was destined for you, researched this deliverance with the greatest care, *11* trying to find out the time and the circumstances the Spirit of the Anointed One in them was declaring, when he

predicted the experiences which lead to the Anointed One and the honors that would follow. *12* It was revealed to them that they were not providing for themselves, but for you. These things have now been told to you by the preachers of the Good News by means of the Holy Spirit sent from heaven. Messengers have a yearning to peep into these things. *13* So then, get your minds ready for action! Be self-controlled, and completely fix your hope on the favor that will be brought to you when Jesus the Anointed One is revealed.

14-16 Just like attentive children, don't follow the pattern of your former ignorant desires.[1] *15* But just like the One who called you is holy, you be holy too in the way you live your lives, *16* because the Scriptures say, "Be holy, because I indeed am holy!"

17-22 The Father judges everyone according to their actions and he isn't biased. Since you call upon him as your Father, see to it that throughout the time you're living here as foreigners on the earth, you conduct yourselves with respect. *18* You do know that it was not with perishable things such as silver or gold that your ransom was paid to buy you out of your useless traditional way of life. *19* Rather, your ransom was paid for with the precious blood of the Anointed One, a lamb without blemish and without defect. *20* On the one hand, he was chosen before the creation of the world, but on the other hand he was revealed in these last times for your sake. *21* And it is on account of him that you trust God, who raised him from the dead and granted him honor. Consequently, your faith and hope rest upon God. *22* By paying attention to the truth, you have purified yourselves to the point of feeling sincere love for your fellow believers. So then, love each other wholeheartedly.

23-26 You have been born again from a parentage that doesn't perish, not from a parentage that perishes, born through God's Word that is living and remains. *24* For "The whole natural realm is like grass, and all its splendor is like the flowers of the field. The grass withers and the flowers fall off, *25* but the Lord's spoken word remains forever." This is the spoken word that was preached to you.

Ch.2:1-3 Therefore, rid yourselves of every form of wickedness, and all deceit, overly critical behavior in examining matters, envy, and back-biting. *2* Be like newborn babies and crave spiritual unadulterated milk so that you will grow up in safety. *3* You have experienced that the Lord is kind.

4-5 As you come to him, the Living Stone – who has been rejected by people but chosen and valuable in the eyes of God – *5* you too, like living stones, are being built into a spiritual house. You are being built into a sacred priesthood, offering spiritual sacrifices acceptable to God through Jesus the Anointed One.

6-8 So the Scripture says: "Indeed, I place in Zion a stone, a chosen and valuable cornerstone, and the person who trusts him will certainly not be disappointed." *7* So to you who believe, the stone is valuable, but to those who don't believe, "The stone that the builders rejected, has become the cornerstone," *8* and, "A stone that trips you up, a rock that is a trap." They trip over by disobeying the Word. This is what they were appointed to do!

9-10 But you are a chosen generation, a royal priesthood, a sacred race, a people acquired by God to proclaim the wonders of him who called you out of darkness into his amazing light. *10* Once you weren't God's people, but now you are. Once you didn't have mercy shown to you, but now you receive mercy.

11-12 Dearly loved friends, I urge you, as temporary residents and strangers in the world, to keep away from the wants and wishes of the natural realm which serve in the army against your lives. *12* Live honorably amongst those who worship other gods, so that although they accuse you of doing wrong, they will

---

[1]   Some translations have "evil desires", yet the word "evil" is not in the Greek.

be eye witnesses[1] to your honorable actions, and praise God on the day of the inspection of the troops.

13-17 So then, support every human institution for the Lord's sake, whether the king as a prominent human institution, *14* or governors, who are sent by the Lord to punish wrongdoers and to praise the ones who do good. *15* This is God's purpose. By doing what's right you will muzzle the silly talk of ignorant people. *16* You are free, but don't use your freedom as a cover-up for doing bad things – live as servants of God! *17* Honor everyone! Love the fellow believers! Respect God! Honor the king!

18-20 Household slaves, respectfully support your masters, not only the good and considerate ones but also the nasty ones. *19* It is certainly a credit to you that your conscience leads you to endure being sad when you are treated unjustly. *20* In fact, there's no honor due to you if you do wrong and put up with a beating for it! But when you do good and get treated this way and put up with it patiently, this is a credit to you in God's sight.

21-25 You were called to do this, as the Anointed One suffered on your behalf. Thus he has left you an example and you should follow in his footsteps. *22* "He didn't commit any sin, nor did any deceit come out of his mouth." *23* When they abused him, he didn't abuse them back: when he suffered, he didn't threaten them, but he handed himself over to the One who judges justly. *24* He took our sins upon himself in his own body on the cross, so that we would stop living in a sinful way, but instead would live in a way which is right with God. By his wound[2] you were instantly divinely healed! *25* You used to be like sheep who had wandered away, but now you have returned to the Shepherd, the One who watches over your lives.

Ch.3:1-2 The same goes for[3] you wives. Support[4] your own husbands, so that the ones who disobey the Word, may be gained without the Word *2* when they are eyewitnesses[5] to the way of life of their wives, wives filled with the sacred awe[6] of God.[1]

---

[1] ἐποπτεύω, *epopteuo*. Technical term from mystery cult. It carries the implication that the eyewitness will in some way be much better off in a spiritual sense from being an eyewitness to something spiritually excellent. This is one of 2 examples of ἐποπτεύω, *epopteuo*, in N.T., the other being 1 Pet. 3:2. Occurs in *IG* XII.8.205.3 = *SIG*³ 1053 (Samothrace, post 90 B.C.); *IG* I2.6.49-53 = *SIG*³ 42 (Athens, pre-460 BC), a law concerning the Eleusinian Mysteries), and Plut. *Alk.* 22.3. The academic consensus of opinion is that the terminology of the mystery cult is being drawn on in the N.T. examples, cf. *NDIEC* 2.87.

[2] μώλωψ, *molops*, "wound", "mauling", the wound left by the flogging with the Roman scourge, a leather whip embedded with iron tusks designed to rip the skin off someone's back. Here the noun is in the singular as welts were usually hard to distinguish in the person who had suffered the flogging, as often there was no skin whatsoever left on the back. Thus in relation to Jesus there was clearly one huge wound rather than a series of welts. Many people could not be recognized after a flogging with the scourge. Only here in N.T.

[3] ὁμοίως, *homoios*, frequent Pauline idiom.

[4] ὑποτάσσω, *hupostasso*. See note on Eph. 5:21.

[5] ἐποπτεύω, *epopteuo*. The same word as in verse 12 above, a technical term from mystery cult. It demonstrates that the eye-witness, here the husband disobedient to the Word, will in some way be much better off in a spiritual sense from something spiritual that he has witnessed, viz. the wife is filled with the sacred awe of God.

[6] φόβος, *phobos*, usually means to fear, but the Greeks used it in the meaning "respect", "reverence", when used in the case of gods, or things sacred. See, for example, *P.Tebt* I.59, where someone writes to the priests of Tebtunis assuring them of his good will "because from old I revere and worship the temple". The use was the same from Classical times.

3-7 Don't just concern yourselves with making yourselves look nice on the outside, such as plaiting your hair,[2] wearing gold jewelry and dressing in fancy clothes. *4* Instead, let the part that you make look fancy be the inner self, the imperishability of a calm and tranquil spirit which is not angry or prone to temper. This is very expensive in God's eyes. *5* In this way too, once upon a time, the holy women who fixed their hopes on God adorned themselves. They supported[3] their own husbands, *6* in the way that Sarah paid attention to[4] Abraham, calling him "sir". You are her children if you do the right thing and you're not afraid of intimidation. *7* Husbands, the above goes for you too.[5] Live with your wives in the realization that the wife has the weaker[6] livelihood.[7] Show her honor. She is a joint-heir[8] with you in the spiritual favor in life. If you don't, your prayers will be blocked!

8-12 Finally, all of you be united in your thinking. Be sympathetic, have affection for your fellow believers,[9] be compassionate and humble-minded. *9* Don't repay evil with evil or insults with insults. On the contrary, repay it with blessings. This is what you were called to do so that you will inherit a blessing. *10* For, "Whoever would love life and see good times, must prevent their tongue from speaking evil and their lips from speaking deceit. *11* They must turn away from evil and do good, they must look for peace and chase after it, *12* because the eyes of the Lord are on those who do right, and his ears listen to their requests, but the Lord sets his face against evildoers."

13-14 Who is going to hurt you if you're enthusiastic about becoming good? *14* But if you did suffer because you were doing right, you would be blessed. "And don't be afraid of or be disturbed by their threats."

15-17 Treat the Anointed One, that is, the Lord, as sacred in your thoughts. Always be ready to give an answer to everyone who asks you to give them a

---

1 φόβος, *phobos*, with ἁγνός, *agnos*. ἁγνός, *agnos,* is to be filled with holy or religious awe. It is well attested from Homer to Hellenistic times.

2 ἐμπλοκή, *emploke*, plaiting hair. See note on κομάω, *komao*, and κόμη, *kome* on 1 Tim. 2:9.

3 ὑποτάσσω, *hupotasso*. See note on Eph. 5:21.

4 ὑπακούω, *hupakouo,* See note on Matt. 8:27.

5 ὁμοίως, *homoios*, frequent Pauline idiom.

6 ἀσθενής, *asthenes*, in the comparative, "weaker". The word can mean: a. of body, sickly, weak; b. of mind, weak, feeble; c. in power, lacking, weak d. in property, poor. For "weaker" financially see *P.Theas* 20.1. Herodotos (2.47; 8.51) uses it with βίου, *biou*, (life) for "poverty". e. of things, insignificant (small streams). With σκεῦος, *skeuos*, following, it means to be in a disadvantaged position for getting a living. See below note.

7 σκεῦος, *skeuos*. For the Greek idiom, σκεῦος κτᾶσθαι, *skeuos ktasthai*, to gain control of one's living, see 1 Thess. 4:4. σκεῦος, *skeuos*, is a common word with a variety of meanings. It means an implement, equipment, a living (as in one's financial state), furniture, goods, ship's tackle. With ἀσθενής, *asthenes*, it means to be in a disadvantaged position for getting a living.

8 συγκληρονόμος, *sugkleronomos*, "joint-heir". See note on Rom. 8:17. Eph 3:6; Heb. 11:9.

9 φιλάδελφος, *philadelphos*. Only here in N.T., the more common word for love of fellow believers in N.T. being φιλαδελφία, *philadelphia*. The term φιλάδελφος, *philadelphos*, occurred in Classical times, and in Hellenistic times was a title for Ptolemy II. The term was taken over by Jews and Christians, and used by Josephus and Philo. See *SEG* 1157; *SEG* 1511; *CIJ* 1.125, 321, 263; *CIJ* 2.815, 1488, 1489. φιλάδελφος, *philadelphus*, also occurs in *CIJ* 2.1516, an epitaph for the 16 y.o. unmarried girl Sabbathin, μικρὰ φιλάδελφε, *mikra philadephe*. The word is found on an epitaph for a woman, *SEG* 20.534, and on an epitaph for a man, *SEG* 20.524. It was a common term in Egypt, but quite uncommon in Asia Minor.

rational explanation for the hope that you have. Do this gently and with a respectful attitude, *16* and keep a clear conscience. Then those who are saying bad things about your good behavior as followers of the Anointed One will be put to shame because of their slander. *17* It is better to suffer because you are doing good things, if they are in God's purpose, than to suffer for doing the wrong thing.

18-19 This is because the Anointed One died once for sins, the Just on behalf of the unjust, in order to bring you to God. On the one hand, he was put to death in the natural realm, but on the other hand he was brought to life in the spiritual realm, *19* in which he also traveled and preached to the spirits in prison.

20-22 Long ago the spirits were disobedient when God was waiting patiently in the time of Noah while the ark was being built. In the ark only a few people were brought safely through the water - eight in all. *21* This symbolizes the baptism that now saves you too – not getting rid of dirt from the body but the pledge of a good conscience toward God. It saves you through the resurrection of Jesus the Anointed One. *22* He has gone to heaven and is at the right side of God. Messengers and authorities and powers support him.

Ch.4:1-6 Therefore as the Anointed One put up with things in the natural realm, arm yourselves with the same frame of mind. The person who has put up with things in the natural realm has broken free from sin. *2* As a result, they do not live out the rest of their lives in the natural realm following their human wants and wishes,[1] but instead for God's purpose. *3* For you've spent enough time in the past doing what people who worship other gods do - living in debaucheries, wants and wishes, drunkenness, orgies, drinking bouts and messing around with summoned spirits, which is forbidden by the natural law of reason and conscience. *4* They think it's strange that you don't rush into the same out-pouring of desperation, and they slander you. *5* They will give an account to him who is ready to judge the living and the dead. *6* This is why the Good News was announced to the dead, so that on the one hand they could be judged like humans in the natural realm, but on the other hand live in the spiritual realm like God does.

7-11 But the end of everything is near. So be sensible and clear-headed in your prayers. *8* Above all, love each other earnestly, because "love covers a multitude of sins." *9* Be hospitable to each other without complaining about it. *10* Just as each one of you has received a spiritual gift, use it in financially providing for one another, as suitable managers of God's various favors. *11* The person who speaks, should utter words inspired by God. The person who financially provides, should do it in the strength for which God pays all the expenses. This is so that God will be praised through Jesus the Anointed One, to whom belongs the honor and the mighty sovereignty for ever and ever, amen!

12-14 Dearly loved friends, don't think it's strange that you are being harassed by a fiery ordeal, as if it was a foreign thing that's happening to you! *13* Instead, be happy in so far as you are partners with the experiences of the Anointed One, so that when his splendor is revealed, you too will be completely thrilled. *14* If you're insulted for the Name of Jesus, be happy, because the glorious Spirit, the Spirit of God, rests upon you!

15-19 If someone suffers, it should not be as the result of being a murderer, a thief, an evil-doer, or an interfering busy-body! *16* If you suffer as a Christian, don't be ashamed, but praise God that you bear the Anointed One's Name. *17* This is because the time has come for judgment to begin at God's household: if it begins with us first, what's going to become of those who disobey the Good News of God? *18* Also, "If the person who is made right with God is barely saved, what will become of the godless sinner?" *19* Consequently, those who are suffering within God's purpose should entrust themselves to their faithful Creator and keep doing what's good.

---

[1]   There is no mention of "evil" desires in the Greek.

Ch.5:1-4 So to the elders among you - I appeal to you as a fellow-elder and a witness of what happened to the Anointed One, as well as someone who is in partnership with the splendor that is to be revealed – *2* be shepherds of God's flock that's in your care, as you are the ones who watch over them. Don't do it because you have to, but because you want to, which is how God wants it. See to it that you do it eagerly and that you are not greedy for profits. *3* Don't lord it over the ones entrusted to you, but be examples to the flock. *4* And when the Chief Shepherd appears, you will receive a crown of glory that never fades away.

5-7 In the same way, you younger people, support those who are older, but all of you must wrap yourselves in clothes of humble minds, because "God opposes the arrogant and gives favor to the humble-minded." *6* So be humble-minded in the presence of the forceful, mighty power of God, so that he will lift you up at the proper time. *7* Dump all your concerns onto him, because he cares about you.

8-11 Be clear headed! Keep your wits about you! Your defendant opposition,[1] Slanderer-Liar, walks around like a roaring lion searching for someone to gulp down. *9* Take up your stand in opposition against him! Be stubborn with your faith knowing that your fellow believers in the world are suffering the same type of thing happening to them! *10* But the God of every type of favor, who has invited you to his eternal splendor by Jesus the Anointed One, will completely equip you after you have suffered briefly – he will stabilize you, strengthen you and establish you. *11* To him be the mighty sovereignty forever, amen!

12-14 I have written these few words to you through Silas,[2] whom I consider to be my faithful fellow believer. I have encouraged you and testified that this is the true favor of God. Take your stand on it![3] *13* The lady in Babylon,[4] who was chosen with you, sends her greetings to you. So does my son Mark. *14* Greet each other with a loving kiss. May all of you who are followers of the Anointed One have peace!

---

[1] ἀντίδικος, *antidikos*, a technical legal term used for lawsuits of the opponent, usually always the defendant. It does not mean "adversary". διάβολος, *diabolos*, means "slanderer", which suits the legal metaphor.
[2] This does not necessarily indicate that Silas was an amanuensis, for the expression is likely to refer to the deliverer of the letter. The same expression occurs in Eusebius, *H.E.* 4.23.11, in which Eusebius mentions the letter from Dionysius of Corinth written to the church at Rome, a letter in which Dionysius refers to *1 Clement* as a letter "written through Clement." As *1 Clement* was written by Clement, the idiom there does not refer to an amanuensis. In the *Martyrdom of Polycarp* 20, the church in Smyrna writes to the church in Philomelium "through our brother Marcianus." The fact that the writer of the letter is stated to be Euarestus, this does not rule out the possibility that 1 Peter was written with an amanuensis.
[3] The evidence suggests that Peter himself wrote verses 12-14. Note εἰς, *eis*, for ἐν, *en*, not found anywhere else in the epistles of Peter.
[4] There are only 3 possibilities: Mesopotamian Babylon, Egyptian Babylon, and Rome. Egyptian Babylon was tiny. Peter was never associated with it nor was he with Mesopotamian Babylon which was sparsely populated. Rome is the likely possibility. Peter was martyred in Rome during Nero's persecution after the Great Fire of 64 AD. Note also the use of "Babylon" for Rome in late Jewish writings.

Second Letter of Peter.

If Peter was the author, this letter is dated just before Peter's death in 64 AD. The authorship of the letter is the most disputed of all New Testament works. Scholarship is divided as to whether the Apostolic Fathers mentioned 2 Peter. Origen states that there are doubts about its authenticity. It has often been suggested that the Greek in 2 Peter is far inferior to that of 1 Peter. It has also been pointed out that there seems to be reference to Gnosticism, which poses problems for those who place Gnosticism in the 2nd c. as well as cite Peter as the author. It has also been argued that Peter's education was minimal as he was a fisherman, but this disregards the high status of fishermen at the time.

Second Letter of Peter.

Ch.1:1-3   From: Simon Peter, a slave servant and apostle of Jesus the Anointed One.

To: Those people who have an equal privilege with us, who received their share of faith, given to us by Jesus the Anointed One, our God and Savior, who makes us right with God.

2 May your favor and peace increase as you come to know about God and Jesus our Lord!

3-7 He invited us, and through his own splendor and excellence, his divine power has given us everything we need for life and godliness through us coming to know him. Through his own splendor and excellence *4* he has given us his valuable and greatest promises, so that because of these you can be partners with the divine nature, as you have escaped from the decay caused by desire for the world. *5* And for this very reason, eagerly supplement your faith with excellence, and supplement excellence with knowledge. *6* Eagerly add self-control to knowledge, and to it add endurance, *7* add godliness, add affection for the fellow believers, and add love.

8-11 For if these things are increasingly yours, your knowledge about our Lord Jesus the Anointed One won't be useless and unproductive. *9* The person who lacks these things is blind and short-sighted, and they have forgotten that they were cleansed from their past sins. *10* So then, fellow believers, do as much as you can to make your invitation and choosing by God valid. If you do this you won't trip up. *11* You will be fully supplied with an entrance into the eternal kingdom of our Lord and Savior Jesus the Anointed One!

12-15 So then it is always my intention to remind you about these things, even though you know them, and are well grounded in the truth that has reached you. *13* I think it's right that I stir you up, as long as I live in this tent of a body. *14* This is because I know that I'll soon be rid of my tent, just as our Lord Jesus the Anointed One explained to me. *15* But I'm very keen to see that you'll always have a reminder of these things after my departure as well.

16-18 For we didn't follow cleverly concocted fiction when we told you about the power of our Lord Jesus the Anointed One and his Coming, but we had been made eye-witnesses of his majesty. *17* He received honor and praise from the Father when a shout was swept along to him from the Majestic Glory, saying, "This is my dearly loved Son and I am very pleased with him." *18* We heard this voice – it came from heaven when we were with him on the sacred mountain.

19-21.Ch.2:1-3 And so we have the prophetic word with all the more validity. It's a good idea for you to pay attention to it like a light that shines in a dark place, until the day dawns and the morning star rises in your hearts. *20* Above all else, realize that no prophecy of Scripture happened by the prophet's own interpretation. *21* For prophecy never had its origin in human will. Rather, people of God spoke as they were swept along by the Holy Spirit. *1* But there were also false prophets among the people, as there will also be false teachers amongst you. They will introduce destructive ways of thinking, even disowning the Master who bought them. They will bring swift destruction down on themselves. *2* And many will follow their destructive ways. The truthful way will be brought to disrespect because of them. *3* Through their greedy grasping behavior, they will exploit you with fabrications. Their judgment has been a long time coming, and their destruction isn't sleeping!

4-8 [1]God didn't spare the Messengers who sinned but handed them over to Tartarus[2] in ropes[3] in the underworld's gloom where they are firmly held for judgment.[4] *5* God did not spare the ancient world, but guarded Noah, a preacher of justice, and seven others,[5] when he brought the flood upon those who committed sacrilege. *6* God condemned the cities of Sodom and Gomorrah, reducing them to ashes and a sudden end,[6] as an example of what's in store[7] for those who commit sacrilege. *7* God rescued righteous Lot who was oppressed by the debauched conduct of the unprincipled. *8* That righteous person lived among them day after day and his righteous soul was tortured by the illegal deeds he saw and heard!

9-11 The Lord knows how to rescue the godly from ordeals[8] and keep the unjust under punishment until the Day of Judgment. *10* This especially

---

[1]   This passage is about the Messengers (angels, the "Watchers") who came down to earth and rebelled against God's ordinances by "whoring after" human women (including those of Sodom and Gomorrah, cf. *Testament of Naphtali* 3.3.4-5). *1 Enoch* 6-10 states that 200 angels (The Watchers) came to earth, lusted after human women causing "defilement" and producing progeny. As a consequence God sent down angels with specific instructions to punish The Watchers. The *Book of Jubilees* 5 sets out the punishment by God upon The Watchers and says that the flood was due to the Watcher's taking human wives but that God saved Noah from it. There is a parallel account to 2 Peter 2:4-8 in Jude. Jude states that Messengers did not uphold their own office, are held with ropes in darkness, that Sodom and Gomorrah went after strange flesh (angels having sex with human women). (*See Background Notes on Romans 1, and Jude.*)

[2]   Both places "Tartarus" and "Gehenna" are rendered simply under the one term "Hell" in most Bible versions. Tartarus was the depths of the underworld, far below Hades. In fact, the Greeks believed Hades was midway between heaven and Tartarus. See Aesch. *Prom.* 152-6: "Would that he had hurled me underneath the earth and underneath the House of Hades, host to the dead – yes, down to limitless Tartarus, yes, though he bound me cruelly in chains breakable." (Trans. David Grene.)

[3]   σειρά, *seira*, a rope, cord, lasso. Used by the Sagartians and Sarmatians to entangle and drag away their enemies, cf. Hdt. 7.85, Paus. 1.21.5.

[4]   The Greeks had an interesting concept that justice made darkness into light, and revealed the truth through a fog of claim and counterclaim. Euripides, *Fr.* 555, speaks of justice making dark into light, and speaks of the light of justice, *Supp.* 564; *Trag. Adesp. Fr.* 500. Aesch. *Ag.* 773 speaks of justice being a light in dark places. Aristophanes, *Acharnians*, speaks of the "gloom of justice" when an innocent man is condemned.

[5]   Lit. "Noah, preacher of righteousness, as the eighth," classical idiom for "Noah and seven others."

[6]   It is uncertain from the textual evidence whether these words were original or added by scribes. See Metzger, *op.cit.*, p. 632.

[7]   That is, a warning.

[8]   περιασμός, *periasmos*. See note on Matt. 6:13.

applies to those who follow along after the foul, polluted[1] desire of the natural realm, and scorn powerful realms.[2] They are insolent and arrogant, and don't worry about slandering reputations,[3] *11* whereas Messengers, who have greater strength and power, don't pronounce abusive judgments on them on the Lord's behalf.

12-16 But these, like senseless animals born to be captured and destroyed, speak abusively of things they don't understand, and they will be destroyed. *13* They will be paid back with wrongdoing for doing wrong. Their idea of fun is to be insolent in broad daylight. They are stains and disgraces, reveling in their treachery while they party with you. *14* They have eyes for nothing but adultery and their sins are unceasing![4] They hook unstable souls on a bait. Their minds are trained in greedy grasping behavior – they're an accursed[5] lot! *15* They have abandoned the straight road and have wandered off[6] to follow the road of Balaam the son of Beor, who loved his reward for wrongdoing. *16* But he was rebuked for his lawlessness by a beast of burden that couldn't speak. It uttered divinely inspired words[7] in a human voice and prevented the prophet's insanity.

17-22 These people are springs without water and mists driven by wind storms. The ropes of the gloomy underworld have been kept for them. *18* They are made to utter[8] inflated, foolish words, and by means of the desires of the natural realm, that is, vices, they hook on a bait people who are barely escaping from wandering off the path, wandering backwards and forwards.[9] *19* They promise them freedom, whereas they themselves are slaves of destruction – for whatever a person is defeated by, to that they have been enslaved. *20* If they have escaped the foul pollutions of the world by knowing about our Lord and Savior Jesus the Anointed One, then get entangled in it again and defeated, they're worse off than they were to start with! *21* They would have been better off if they had never come to know the righteous road, than to come to know it, and then turn their backs on the sacred command that was handed over to them. *22* What the proverbs say about them is true, "A dog turns back to its own vomit!" and, "After a sow washes herself she goes back to wallowing in the mud!"

---

[1] Two adjectives to bring out the full force of μιασμός, *miasmos*.

[2] κυριότης, *kuristes*, in the plural, "dominions".

[3] αἱ δόξαι, *hai doxai*, "reputations".

[4] ἀκατάπαυστος, *akatapaustos*, "unceasing". This word was commonly found on love charms, magical spells which summoned the power and authority of pagan gods. See, for example, *ZPE* 24.89-90.

[5] κατάρα, *katara*. See note on Galatians 3:10. Here *huios* is used with the noun to express a similarity to the noun. See also Luke 11:11.

[6] πλανάω, *planao*, "to wander off the path", the cognate noun being πλάνη, *plane*. See Rom. 1:27.

[7] φθέγγαομαι, *phtheggaomai*, "rang out", not "spoke". It means to utter a word by means of a supernatural or divine agency. It was used of Peter on the Day of Pentecost when the Holy Spirit gave him utterance. ἀποφθέγγαομαι, *apotheggomai*, is used for the sound made by a tin when the tin is hit. The sense is that the tin could not make the noise unless something acted upon it. The other meaning is of "inspired" persons, such as a prophet or pagan oracle. The verb was used when a Greek god was said to speak through a pagan oracle (prophet). The verb always carries the idea that someone else is behind the speaker's words.

[8] Again, "ring out" not "speak". It means to ring out as acted upon by an agency – here, by Adversary or his kingdom. The people are not merely speaking foolish, inflated words by their own volition: they are uttering them as prompted by the kingdom of darkness.

[9] That is, in spiritual matters. ἀναστρεφομένους, *anastrephomenous*, means "to go here and there", "to go backwards and forwards".

Ch.3:1-2 Dearly loved friends, this is now my second letter to you. I've written both of them as reminders to stimulate your minds to unmixed[1] thinking. *2* Remember the words spoken in the past by the sacred prophets, and the command given by our Lord and Savior through your apostles.

3-4 First of all, you must realize that in the last days tricksters will come, deceiving and traveling after their own private wants and wishes. *4* They will say, "So, where is this promise of his Coming? From the time that our ancestors fell asleep, everything remains firmly like it has been since the beginning of creation!"

5-7 They deliberately ignore the fact that, long ago, the skies existed and the earth was put together from and through water, by God's Word. *6* Through these waters the world of that time was flooded and destroyed, *7* but now the skies and the earth, which are now preserved by the same Word, are reserved for fire, being kept for the Day of Judgment, for the ruin of people who commit sacrilege.

8-9 But you must not ignore this one thing, dearly loved friends – one day from the Lord is as 1,000 years, and 1,000 years as one day. *9* The Lord hasn't delayed in keeping his promise, as some understand delay, but is showing patience toward you. He doesn't want anyone to be destroyed, but he wants everyone to change their minds.

10-13 It will come, the Day of the Lord, like a thief! The skies will pass by with a loud rushing noise, the physical elements[2] will be burned and then dissolved and the earth as well as everything in it will be found no more! *11* Since all these things will be dissolved, what kind of people should you be! Your way of living must be holy and godly, *12* while you are expecting and hurrying up the Coming of God's Day in which the skies will be set on fire and the physical elements will melt in the heat. *13* But we are expecting fresh skies and a fresh earth, in which righteousness will live, according to his promise.

14-17 Therefore, my dearly loved friends, since you are expecting these things, be eager to avoid disgrace, and to be above reproach, and to be found to be at peace with him. *15* Keep in mind that the Lord's patience with us is our deliverance, just as our dear fellow believer Paul wrote to you with the wisdom that God gave him. *16* He writes the same way in all his letters,[3] speaking about these matters in them. His letters contain some things which are hard to understand, which ill-mannered[4] and unstable people distort, like they do to the remaining Scriptures, to their own destruction.

17 Therefore, my dearly loved friends, since you know all this beforehand, be on your guard so that you won't be led away by lawless people wandering off the path, and thus lose your own stability.

18 May your favor from, and your knowledge of, our Lord and Savior Jesus the Anointed One increase! May he be honored both now and on the Day when eternity begins! Amen!

---

[1] εἰλικρινής, *eilikrines*, "genuine", "unmixed", "pure (intellect)", "distinct". The word has nothing to do with wholesome thinking or pure, cleansed thoughts. Plato uses the two words in this verse for "pure intellect" (*Phaed.* 66A). It means something which is tested and found to be genuine by the light of day.

[2] στοιχεῖον, *stoikheion*, "physical element". Occurs in this meaning only in the N.T. The word appears also in Gal. 4:3, 9; Col. 2:8, 20 in the meaning "elemental spirits"; and Hebrews in the meaning "fundamental principles". See note on Gal. 4:3.

[3] Polycarp and Ignatius also allude to the Pauline letters as a corporate entity.

[4] ἀμαθής, *amathes*, "ignorant" in the sense of "ill-mannered", "boorish", occurs only here in the N.T. See *P.Mert* 2.82.11 (Egypt, II), "Was I so rude as not to write to you?" See also *P.Haun* 2.15.16 (Egypt, II). It is a rare word.

The Letters of John.

Although the letters are anonymous, there is academic agreement that all three were written by the apostle John. The letters are dated to the end of the 1st c., c. 85 - 95 AD. Irenaeus cites 1 and 2 John, and quotes 2 John. Irenaeus states that 1 John was written by the disciple John who was also the author of the Gospel of John. Origen, Clement of Alexandria and Tertullian all frequently quote 1 John, and refer to the author as "John the Apostle". Eusebius noted that Dionysios of Alexandria considered 1 John and the Gospel of John to be written by the same author, and Revelation to be written by a different author. The Muratorian Canon states that John wrote the Gospel of John and refers to his "letters".

Apart from 1 John, Hebrews is the only other book of the NT which does not name its author. However, 1 John 1:1-4 reveals that the author was an eyewitness to Jesus' life and ministry. It is clear that the author is well known to the readership (cf. the term "my dear members", 2:1, 12, 28; 3:7, 18; 4:4; 5:21) and thus a statement of identity would be unnecessary. 1 John contains bare clues as to the readership of the letter: we know they are Christians who are well known to John. Certain people have left the assembly. I John 2:19 states, "They went out from us, but they did not belong to us". 1 John 3:7 warns the people not to be misled, and 1 John 5:21 warns the people to guard themselves from idols.

John spent his latter years at Ephesos, and tradition has it that the Basilica of St John (very close to Ephesos) is built over his burial site. In fact, in AD 4 the first Christian basilica was built with a wooden covering on the site. The ruins of the Basilica we see today date to the reign of Justinian in the 6th c. The Basilica has an interesting history. Between the 7th and 9th centuries, the threat of Arab invasions prompted the building of a surrounding wall which connected the Basilica to the Castle. Excavations reveal that a chapel was built in the 10th c., with frescoes depicting Jesus, John and the disciples. In medieval times the Basilica became a destination for pilgrims. At the time there was widespread belief that the site had healing properties. In the 14th c. the Basilica became a mosque, but at the end of the century a devastating earthquake reduced the building to ruins. In the 1920s, restoration work began.

The First Letter of John.

Ch.1:1-4 The One who was from the beginning, the One whom we have heard, the One whom we have seen with our eyes, the One whom we looked at and our hands touched - I am referring to the Word of Life. *2* The Life appeared! We have seen him and testify to it, and we proclaim the Life to you, the Life who was beside the Father and appeared to us. *3* We are telling you what we have seen and heard, so that you may be in partnership with us too. Our partnership is with the Father and with his Son, Jesus the Anointed One. *4* We are writing these things to make us truly happy.

5-10 And this is the message which we heard from him and are reporting to you - God is light, there is no darkness in him at all. *6* If we say we are in partnership with him but are living our lives in darkness, we are lying and we are not acting in the way that truth demands. *7* But if we live in the light just as he lives in the light, then we have partnership with each other, and the blood of Jesus, his Son, cleanses us from all sin. *8* If we say we don't have any sin, we're fooling ourselves and the truth isn't in us. *9* If we agree that we have sin, he is to be trusted and he shows justice in canceling our sins and cleansing us from all dishonesty. *10* If we say we haven't sinned, then we're making out he is a liar, and his word has no place with us.

Ch.2:1-6 My dear members,[1] I am writing these things to you so that you won't sin. And if anyone ever does commit a sin, we have One who is called to our side to help and encourage us. He speaks with the Father in our defense. I'm talking about Jesus the Anointed One, the Just One. *2* And he himself is the means for taking away our sins, and not just our sins, but also the sins of the whole world. *3* For this reason - namely that, if we keep his commandments - we continually have the experience of realizing that we have come to know him. *4* Anyone who says, "I have come to know him" and doesn't keep his commandments, is a liar and the truth isn't in them. *5* But truly God's love has come to maturity in anyone who observes his Word. This is how we know that we are his followers: *6* whoever claims to remain God's follower ought to behave like Jesus behaved.

7-11 My dearly loved ones,[2] I am not writing a new commandment to you, but an old commandment which you have had from the beginning. The old commandment is the Word you have heard. *8* It is at the same time a new commandment. This is verified by him and by you, because the darkness is passing away and the genuine light is already shining. *9* Anyone who claims to be in the light and hates their fellow believer is still in the darkness. *10* Anyone who loves their fellow believer stays in the light, and there is no trap laid for them. *11* But anyone who hates their fellow believer is in the darkness, their behaviour is in darkness, and they do not know where they are going, because the darkness has blinded their eyes.

12-14 My dear members, I am writing to you, because your sins have been canceled because of his Name. *13* Parents,[3] I am writing to you because you have come to know him who was from the beginning. Young men, I write to you, because you have had the victory over Evil One. Youngsters, I write to you, because you have come to know the Father. *14* Parents, I have written to you, because you have come to know him who was from the beginning. Young men, I have written to you, because you are strong and you observe God's Word, and you have had the victory over Evil One.

15-17 Do not love the world or the things in the world. If anyone loves the world, they do not have the love which the Father has. *16* Everything in the world, the wants and wishes of the natural realm, and the wants and wishes that we see, and the material things of life, are not from the Father but from the world. *17* And the world and its wants and wishes are passing away, but the person who does God's purpose lasts forever.

18-20 Youngsters, this is the last hour. You have heard that an anti-anointing[4] was coming, but in fact many anti-anointings have come about. By this we recognize that this is the last hour. *19* They went out from us, but they did not belong to us. If they had belonged to us, they would have stayed with us - the fact that they left makes it clear that none of them belong to us. *20* And you have an anointing from the Holy One, and you all know it.

21-25 I am not writing to you because you do not know the truth, but because you do know it, and because no lie can come from the truth. *22* Who is the liar?[5] The one who denies that Jesus is the Anointed One! Such a

---

1   τεκνίον, *teknion*, a diminutive of τέκνον, *teknon*, a term of endearment and not of immaturity. "Member" or "child".
2   ἀγαπητοι, *agapetoi*, "dearly loved ones", "beloved", "loved friends", "dear friends"; certainly not "brethren".
3   πατέρες, *pateres*. See note on Eph. 6:4.
4   ἀντίχριστος, *antichristos*. The term "anti-anointing" ("Antichrist") is used only by John in the N.T., in this letter and the next letter. It does not appear in Revelation.
5   The use of the definite article does not indicate a specific person, but merely indicates the change from the abstract in verse 21 to the concrete in verse 22.

person is the anti-anointing – they deny the Father and the Son. *23* No one who denies the Son has the Father, and whoever acknowledges the Son, has the Father also. *24* As for you,[1] see to it that what you heard from the beginning stays with you. And if that which you heard from the beginning stays with you, then you will also stay with the Son, and with the Father. *25* And this is the promise he has promised us - eternal life!

Antichrists. (Anti-anointings.)
Not an individual!

There is much speculation among some Christian groups as to who the "Antichrist" will be in the end times. However, the Antichrist as an actual sole person is just a myth - the term is not mentioned at all in Revelation, and in fact is mentioned only in this letter and in 2 John (just once). John uses the term in the plural - he says that anyone who denies that Jesus is the Anointed One is an antichrist (anti-anointing) and says that many antichrists (anti-anointings) have come into the world. At no point does John refer to an "Antichrist" (Anti-anointing) as an individual. There appears to be some confusion among many contemporary Christians who appear to have confused the "Beast" of Revelation with the term "Antichrist".

Again, the term "Antichrist" is never used to refer to an individual, and the term appears only here and in 2 John and does not appear in Revelation.

26-28 I am writingthese things to you about those who would try to mislead you. *27* And as for you, the anointing you received from him stays with you, and there is no need for anyone to teach you. His anointing teaches you about everything, and is true and is not a lie. Stay with him, just as the anointing has taught you. *28* And now, my dear members, stay with him, so that, if he appears, we will have complete confidence and not be ashamed in front of him at his Coming.

29.Ch.3:1-3 If you know that he is made right with God, then you realize that everyone who is made right with God has been born as his child. *1* Look how great is the love that the Father has given us, that we would be called the children of God! And we are! *2* My dearly loved ones, we are God's children now, and what we will be has not yet been revealed to us. We do know that when he appears, we will be like him, for we will see him just as he is. *3* And everyone who sets their hope on him purifies themselves, just as he is pure.

4-6 Everyone who sins does a lawless act, and sin is a lawless act. *5* And you know that he was revealed in order to take away our sins. There is no sin in him. *6* No one who stays with him keeps on sinning. No one who keeps on sinning has either seen him or come to know him.

7-11 My dear members, don't let anyone mislead you! The person who keeps doing what is right is righteous, just as he is righteous. *8* The person that keeps doing sin belongs to Slanderer-Liar, because Slanderer-Liar has kept sinning from the beginning. The reason that the Son of God was revealed was so that he would destroy the works of Slanderer-Liar. *9* Whoever has become a child of God does not keep sinning, because God's seed stays in them. They cannot keep on sinning, because they have become a child of God.

10 This is why it is clear who the children of God are and who the children of the Slanderer-Liar are: anyone who does not do right is not of God, that is, anyone who does not love their fellow believer. *11* For the message you heard from the beginning is this: we should love each other.

12 Do not be like Cain, who belonged to Evil One, and violently murdered his brother. And just why did he murder him? Because the things he did were evil and the things his brother did were just.

---

[1] "You" being the youngsters John is addressing in verse 18.

13-15 Do not be surprised, fellow believers, if the world hates you. *14* We ourselves know that we have passed out of death into life, because we love the fellow believers. Anyone who does not love, stays in the realm of death. *15* Anyone who hates their fellow believer is a killer,[1] and you know that eternal life does not stay with any killer!

16-20 This is how we know what love is, that he laid down his life for our sakes. And we indeed ought to lay down our lives for our fellow believers. *17* But whoever has material possessions and observes their fellow believer in need, and shuts off their compassion from them, how can God's love stay with them? *18* My dear members, don't let us act in a loving way with lip service only, but with our actions and in a truthful way, *19* and that is how we know that we belong to the truth. In his presence we will reassure our minds, *20* if ever our mind condemns us. Indeed God is more important than our minds, and he knows everything.

21-24 My dearly loved ones, if our mind does not condemn us, then we have the right of freedom of speech, able to speak boldly and openly to God. *22* And we receive whatever we ask him for, because we obey his commands and do what pleases him. *23* And this is his command: to keep believing the Name of his Son, Jesus the Anointed One, and to keep loving one another as he commanded us. *24* Those who keep his commands stay with him and he stays with them. And this is how we realize that he stays with us - we know it by the Spirit he gave us.

Ch.4:1-3 My dearly loved ones, do not believe every spirit but examine the spirits to see whether they are of God, because many false prophets have gone off into the world. *2* This is how you can recognize the Spirit of God - every spirit that agrees that Jesus the Anointed One has come in human form is from God, *3* and every spirit that does not acknowledge Jesus, is not from God. This is the spirit of the anti-anointing, which you have heard is coming and even now is already in the world.

4-6 You, my dear members, are certainly from God's family and have had the victory over them, because the One who is in you is greater than the one who is in the world. *5* They are of the world, and for this reason they speak from the world, and the world hears them. *6* You indeed are from God's family The person who has come to know God hears us, and the person who is not from God's family does not hear us. This is how we perceive the spirit of truth and the spirit of error.

7-11 Dearly loved ones, let us love one another, because love is from God, and everyone that loves has been born as God's child, and knows God. *8* The person who does not love did not know God, because God is love. *9* This is how God's love was made clear to us - God has sent his only born Son into the world so that we would come to life on account of him. *10* This is what love is, not that we loved God, but that he loved us, and sent his Son to be the means of taking away our sins. *11* Dearly loved ones, since God loved us like this, we also ought to love one another.

12-14 No one has ever watched God at any time. If we love one another, God remains with us and his love has been completed in us. *13* This is how we realize that we stay with him, and he stays with us - because he has given his Spirit to us. *14* And we ourselves have watched and testify that the Father has sent the Son to be the Savior of the world.

15 If someone agrees that Jesus is the Son of God, then God stays with them and they stay with God.

16-21 And we ourselves have come to know and have believed the love which God has for us. God is love, and the person who keeps acting in a loving way stays with God, and God stays with them. *17* This is how love has been

---

[1] ἀνθρωποκτόνος, *anthropoktonos*, "person-slayer", occurs only twice in the N.T: here and in John 8:14 where it refers to Slanderer-Liar.

made complete in us – that we may have the right of freedom of speech, able to speak boldly and openly in the Day of Judgment, because we are like him in this world. *18* There is no fear in love: rather, complete love throws out fear, because fear implies punishment, and the person who keeps being afraid has not been made complete in the way they love. *19* We ourselves love, because he himself first loved us. *20* If someone says, "I love God," and hates their fellow believer, they are a liar! For the person who doesn't love their fellow believer whom they have seen, cannot love God whom they are not able to see! *21* And this is the command we have from him - that those who love God must love their fellow believers too.

Ch.5:1-5 Everyone who believes that Jesus is the Anointed One has been born as God's child. Everyone who loves the Father, loves his Son as well. *2* This is how we realize that we love God's children - by loving God and carrying out his orders. *3* For this is what it means to love God - that we keep his commands, and his commands are not oppressive. *4* Everyone who has been born as God's child is victorious over the world, and this is the victory that was victorious over the world - our faith! *5* The person who is victorious over the world is the person who believes that Jesus is the Son of God.

6-8 This is the One who came by means of water and blood - Jesus the Anointed One. He did not come by water alone, but by water and by blood. And it is the Spirit who testifies to this, because the Spirit is truth. *7* For there are three that testify,[1] *8* the Spirit and the water and the blood, and these three are in the One.

9-13 Now we do accept the testimony of people, but the testimony of God is greater, because the testimony of God is this - he has testified and is testifying about his Son. *10* The person who believes the Son of God has the testimony inside themselves. The one who does not keep believing God is making him out to be a liar, because they have not believed the testimony that God has confirmed about his Son. *11* And this is the testimony - that God has given us eternal life, and this life is in his Son. *12* The person who has the Son has life. The person who does not have the Son does not have life. *13* I am writing these things to you who believe the Name of the Son of God, so that you will know that you have eternal life.

14-15 And this is the right of freedom of speech, able to say whatever we like, boldly and openly, that we have toward him - that if we request anything that is in his purpose, we know that he hears us. *15* And since we know that he hears us, we know we have the things that we have asked of him – whatever we ask!

16-17 If anyone sees their fellow believer commit a sin, not a sin which leads to death, they will ask, and he will grant them (the person[2] who is committing a sin which does not lead to death) life. There is sin which leads to death. I'm not saying they should ask about that. *17* All injustice is sin, and there is sin which does not lead to death.

18-21 We know that everyone who has been born as God's child does not sin, but the One who was born from God guards them, and Evil One won't lay a hand on them. *19* We know that we are from God and the whole world is assigned to Evil One. *20* We know that the Son of God has come and has given the faculty of thought so that we would recognize him who is genuine - and we are with the genuine, that is, with his Son Jesus the Anointed One. This is the genuine God and eternal life. *21* My dear members, guard yourselves from idols!

---

[1]   End of v. 7 and the beginning of v. 8 is absent from all but 8 extant Greek manuscripts, and the eight contain the passage in what is evidently a translation from a late recension of the Latin Vulgate. See Metzger, *op.cit.,* pp. 648f.

[2]   That is, the person putting the request to God. In v. 16, the phrase "and he will grant him", the "him" refers to the person putting the request to God.

Second Letter of John.

It is generally considered that 2 John and 1 John were written around the same time, c. 85 - 95 AD. Polycarp and Irenaeus allude to it, but it is disputed by Origen and Eusebius. It is considered authentic by Jerome, Augustine, Cyril of Jerusalem, Marcion's canon and the Muratorian Canon.

The letter was sent to a church leader, an unnamed woman, and the members of her assembly. Holding to a circular argument, it has been held that there was no woman church leader, that this instead was a church. It is often translated "chosen lady" but this ignores the word κυρία, *kuria*, "authority", the feminine of "Lord" or "Master".

Second Letter of John.

1 From: The Elder.

To: The chosen Lady Authority[1] and her members,[2] whom I certainly love, and that's the truth! - and I myself am not the only one who does, but also all those who have come to know the truth – *2* because of the truth, which stays with us, and will be with us forever.

3 May favor, mercy, and peace from God the Father and Jesus the Anointed One be with us truthfully and lovingly!

4 I was extremely happy that I have found some of your dearly loved members living in a truthful manner, just as we were ordered to by the Father. *5* And now I ask you, Lady Authority - by the way, I'm not writing a new commandment to you, but an old commandment which you have had from the beginning - that we love one another. *6* And this is what love is - that we live according to his commands. This is the command - and you've heard it from the beginning - that you should live in this way. *7* This is because many who wander off the path have emerged in the world, and they don't agree that Jesus the Anointed One has come in human form. This is one who wanders off the path, this is one who is an anti-anointing. *8* Watch out for yourselves, that you don't lose what you have worked for, but that you will receive your full reward. *9* Anyone who goes ahead and doesn't continue with the teaching of the Anointed One doesn't have God. Whoever continues with the teaching, has both the Father and the Son. *10* If anyone comes to you and doesn't bring this teaching, do not receive them into your house and do not welcome them, *11* as the one who welcomes them is in partnership with their evil deeds!

12 Although I have much to write to you, I don't want to use paper and ink. Instead I hope to visit you and talk with you face to face, so that we will be totally happy.

13 The members of your chosen lady fellow believer[3] send their greetings.

---

[1] κυρία, *kuria*, a (female) authority, feminine for "Lord" or "Master". *P.Oxy* VI. 9395, 9: a servant writes, "by the recovery of my mistress from the sickness that overtook her"; also *P.Tebt* II 413.1,6,90. A courteous form of address in ordinary correspondence, cf. *P.Oxy* IV.744 (1 BC); *P.Oxy* I.112 1,3,7 (3/4 AD). Interestingly, Louw & Nida *s.v.* disregard the evidence from the papyri, and have for κυριος, *kurios*, "Lord, owner, ruler, sir", but for κυρία, *kuria*, have "lady".

[2] τέκνον, *teknon*, member. See 1 Tim. 1:2; Titus 1:4.

[3] τῇ ἀδελφῇ, *te adelphe*, "fellow believer". See note on Matt. 5:22.

The Third Letter of John.

3 John is similar in style to 1 and 2 John. There is not much evidence to attest to its authenticity prior to the 3rd c., but this could be due to its brevity and subject matter. The author identifies himself as "The Elder" as in 2 John. The date is uncertain: if written around the same time as 1 and 2 John, it would be the end of the 1st c.

The Third Letter of John.

1 From: The Elder.
To: My dear friend Gaius, whom I truthfully love!
2 My dear friend, I claim[1] that you have a prosperous path with regard to all things and are completely healthy with regard to all things,[2] just as your life[3] has a prosperous path. *3* You made me very happy when fellow believers arrived and testified about your truthfulness, that you keep living in a truthful way. *4* I have no greater[4] happiness than to know that my dear members are living in a truthful way.
5 My dear friend, you are doing a faithful work for the fellow believers, who are strangers to you. *6* They've told about your love in front of the assembly. You will do well to send them on their way in a manner worthy of God.[5] *7* For when they left for the sake of the Name, they didn't take any help from the people who worship other gods. *8* So then we owe it to them to support such people as these, so that we would work together for the truth.
9 I wrote to the church, but Diotrephes, who likes to dominate them, doesn't accept us. *10* For this reason when I come, I will bring up his actions, namely, that he is gossiping about us maliciously. And not only is he not satisfied with that, he even refuses to welcome the fellow believers! He also prevents those who want to welcome the fellow believers and throws them out of the assembly!
11 My dear friend, don't imitate bad things but only imitate good things. Anyone who does good things is from God. Anyone who has done bad things hasn't seen God.
12 Demetrios is spoken of in a favorable light by everyone - and even by the truth itself. We speak well of him too, and you know our testimony is true.
13 There's so much I have to write to you, but I don't want to write to you with pen and ink.
14 I hope to see you very, very soon, and we will speak face to face. May you have peace! Our friends send their greetings. Give my friends there my greetings individually.

---

[1] εὔχομαι, *eukhomai*, the verb of εὐχή, *eukhe*, "claim", not "prayer". See note on Acts 18:18.
[2] εὐδόομαι, *eudoomai*, literally, "to have a smooth and prosperous journey". It encompasses 1. the removal of difficulties in the way, 2. material prosperity, 3. physical health. This verse is very similar to the LXX of Joshua 1:8.
[3] Metonymy. Greeks used the word "soul" as the equivalent of English "life".
[4] μειζότερος, *meizoteros*, Koine form for μείζων, *meizon*. Occurs only here in N.T.
[5] προπέμψας, *propempsas*. That is, supply them with finances and supplies. See also Zerwick and Grosvenor, *op.cit.*, p. 736.

Jude.

The author identifies himself in verse 1 as "Jude, a slave servant of Jesus the Anointed One and brother of James". As Jude was the younger brother of Jesus, it is likely that he died around or prior to 70 - 80 AD. The 3 main dates proposed for Jude are sometime during the apostolic age (c. 50s-60s), the latter part of the 1st c, and the first 2 decades of the 2nd c.

Jude was widely accepted in patristic literature, but doubts came about later mostly due to its use of the pseudegraphical 1 Enoch, a point commented upon by Tertullian who considered that 1 Enoch should be included in the canon.

Jude speaks of angels who came to earth and went after different flesh, that is, had sex with human women. There is a parallel account in 2 Peter 2:4-8. See also Genesis 6:1-4, "When humankind began to increase on the face of the earth, and daughters were born to them, those associated with God[1] saw that the human women were beautiful and so they took wives for themselves from any they chose. ... The Nephilim were on the earth in those times, and also afterwards, when those associated with God were having sexual relations with the human women, who gave birth to their children. They were the mighty heroes of ancient times, the famous ones." The *Septuagint*, Philo of Alexandria, Josephus, Justin Martyr, Irenaeus, Athenagoras, Clement of Alexandria, Tertullian, Lactantius, Eusebius, Ambrose of Milan, Jerome, Sulpicius Severus, and Augustine of Hippo all identified the "Sons of God" of Genesis 6:1-4 with the angels who came to earth and had sex with human women.

Jude.

1-2 From: Jude, a slave servant of Jesus the Anointed One and brother of James.

To: Those who are loved and invited by God the Father, those who have been held firmly by Jesus the Anointed One.

2 May mercy, peace and love be increased for you!

3-4 Dearly loved friends, while I was eagerly writing to you about the salvation we share, a necessity came upon me to write to you and to urge you to contend for the faith that was once and for all handed over to the people devoted to God. *4* For certain people have crept in unnoticed, people whose judgment was written down beforehand a long time ago. They commit sacrilege, and they use God's favor as a license to commit vice. They disown our only Master and Lord, Jesus the Anointed One.

5-7 Although you already know all about this, I want to remind you that the Lord saved his people out of Egypt, but the next time destroyed the ones who didn't believe. *6* And as for the Messengers who did not uphold their own office but deserted their own places, he has held them firmly in eternal ropes down in the gloom, waiting for the Judgment of the Great Day.[2] *7* Just like these, Sodom and Gomorrah as well as the surrounding cities, which in a similar way committed *porneia* and went after different flesh, serve as an example of those who undergo punishment in the eternal fire.[3]

---

[1]   Often translated as "sons of God" (but the word sons/children with a noun indicates an association with the noun and should be translated thus), this occurs only elsewhere in Job 1:6; 2:1; 38:7, where it is clear these are angels.

[2]   *1 Enoch* 10 says the main angel who was responsible was bound hand and foot and cast into in darkness where he would remain until the Great Day of Judgement.

[3]   Parallel account in 2 Peter 2:4-8 about the Messengers (angels, the Watchers) who came to earth and had sex with human women, including

8-9 In the same way, however, while these dreamers[1] on the one hand foully pollute the natural realm, on the other hand they reject realms of power, and on the other hand they slander visions. *9* [2]But Michael the Chief Messenger, when he was deciding the dispute, discoursing with Slanderer-Liar about Moses' body, did not dare to impose an abusive sentence on him, but said, "May the Lord impose the penalty on you!"

10-13 But on the one hand, these people are abusive about whatever they don't know about! And on the other hand, the things they do know about by instinct, like wild animals, these are the very things that cause their ruin! *11* Alas for them, because they have traveled on the road of Cain - they were spread out as they wandered off the path like Balaam did for a reward[3] and they were destroyed in Korah's rebellion.[4] *12* These are stains in your fellowship meals. They are the stains who feast along with you, with no scruples, looking out for themselves. They are clouds without water, late autumn trees without fruit, twice dead, pulled up by the roots, *13* raging waves of the sea, foaming up their own disfavor. They are stars wandering about for whom the gloomy underworld of darkness is reserved forever.

σαρκὸς ἑτέρας, *sarkos heteras*, different flesh, flesh of another kind.

This is nothing to do with homosexuality, but rather, the sexual union of angels ("The Watchers") with humans. Jude states that Messengers (angels) did not uphold their own office, are held with ropes in darkness, and just like these, Sodom and Gomorrah went after strange flesh (angels having sex with human women). The *Testament of Naphtali* 3.3.4-5 states that the women of Sodom had sex with angels. The passage here in Jude goes on to speak of "these dreamers" (see below note) and then Balaam who used sorcery. In the same verse, he speaks of Korah who rebelled against God. Significantly, Jude states in verse 9 that Michael, the Chief Messenger (angel) did not dare impose a sentence upon Slanderer-Liar (Satan). All Jude's statements are related. The context is the Watchers (angels) (*see Background Notes on Romans 1*) who came down to earth and rebelled against God's ordinances by "whoring after" human women, and as a consequence God sent down angels with specific instructions to punish The Watchers. The *Book of Jubilees* 5 sets out the punishment by God upon The Watchers. Magic is also associated with The Watchers. *2 Enoch* states that the people of Sodom committed abominable acts, child-corruption, magic-making, enchantments and devillish witchcraft. The Church Father Irenaeus stated, "And wickedness very long-continued and widespread pervaded all the races of men, until very little seed of justice

---

those of Sodom: "God didn't spare the Messengers who sinned but handed them over to Tartarus in ropes in the underworld's gloom where they are firmly held for judgment. God did not spare the ancient world, but guarded Noah, a preacher of justice, and seven others, when he brought the flood upon those who committed sacrilege. God condemned the cities of Sodom and Gomorrah, reducing them to ashes and a sudden end, as an example of what's in store for those who commit sacrilege."

[1] ἐνυπνιαζομενοι, *enupniazomenoi*. This refers to the "certain people who have crept in", literally "dreamers" in some sort of a spiritual sense, not in our English sense of daydreamers or people in the process of using their imagination.

[2] Jude quotes from the pseudegraphical *The Assumption of Moses*.

[3] Balaam was offered money to curse Israel. Although he was a prophet, he used sorcery. See Numbers 22-24.

[4] Korah and his brothers led a rebellion against Moses and Aaron, and then were swallowed up by the earth. See Numbers 16:1-24.

was in them. For unlawful unions came about on earth, as angels linked themselves with offspring of the daughters of men, who bore to them sons, who on account of their exceeding great were called Giants. The angels, then, brought to their wives as gifts teachings of evil, for they taught them the virtues of roots and herbs, and dyeing and cosmetics and discoveries of precious materials, love-philtes, hatreds, amours, passions, constraints of love, the bonds of witchcraft, every sorcery and idolatry, hateful to God; and when this was come into the world, the affairs of wickedness were propagated to overflowing, and those of justice dwindled to very little."[1]

The 2nd c. theologian Tatian, *2 Apology* 5, stated, "God committed the care of people and of everything under heaven to angels whom he appointed over them. But the angels disobeyed this appointment, and were captivated by the love of women, and produced children who are those who are called demons; and not only that, they later subdued the human race for themselves, partly by magical writings, and partly by fears and the punishments they induced, and partly by teaching them to offer sacrifices, incense, and libations, as it was these things they stood in need after they were enslaved by lustful passions. And among humanity they sowed murders, wars, adulteries, immoderate deeds, and all wickedness."

Clement of Alexandria, *Miscellanies* 5.1.10 stated, "To this also we shall add, that the angels who had obtained the superior rank, having sunk into pleasures, told the women the secrets which had come to their knowledge."

Jude mentions the three elements that are linked in accounts of The Watchers, sorcery, going after a different flesh, and punishment of angels. Furthermore, it is accepted that Jude was heavily influenced by *1 Enoch*, a fact commented upon by Tertullian in the 2nd c. AD. Jude quotes *1 Enoch 1:9* in verses 14-15. *1 Enoch* 6-10 states that 200 angels (The Watchers) came to earth, lusted after human women causing "defilement" and producing progeny. *1 Enoch* states that the Watchers taught to humans, among other things, sorceries, enhantments, and the binding of enchantments. Tertullian, *Women*, 1.2 stated that angels fell through lust for women and referred to their progeny as a "more wicked demon-brood".

The *Testament of Naphtali* 3.3.4-5 states that the women of Sodom had sex with angels. It states, "In like manner also the Watchers changed the order of their nature, whom also the Lord cursed at the flood, and for their sakes made desolate the earth, that it should be uninhabited and fruitless." Note the term "changed the order of their nature" which is similar to Jude's term, "went after different flesh" and to Paul's statement, "for the females exchanged natural sex for what is other than nature. And the same goes for males too," in Romans 1:26.

14-16 Now Enoch, the seventh from Adam, prophesied to these people too. He said, "The Lord comes with tens of thousands of his devoted people, *15* to carry out judgments on everyone, to cross-examine every soul among them who has committed sacrilege, about their sacrilegious acts, and about all the harsh things that sacrilegious sinners have said about him."[2] *16* These people are complaining grumblers going the way of their own wants and wishes. They boast excessively about themselves, and flatter other people for their own benefit.

17-21 But you, dearly loved friends, remember what the apostles of our Lord Jesus the Anointed One foretold. *18* They said to you, "In the last age there will be scoffers who will follow their own sacrilegious desires."

19 These people cause divisions, and are soulish, as they don't have the Spirit. *20* But you, dearly loved friends, build up your most sacred faith,

---

[1] Irenaeus, *Demonstration*, 18. *Trans*. Joseph P. Smith.
[2] 1 Enoch 1:9.

praying by the leading of the Holy Spirit. *21* Keep yourselves within the sphere of God's love, and receive the mercy of our Lord Jesus the Anointed One which gives eternal life.

22-25 On the one hand be merciful to those who are undecided – *23* on the other hand save others by snatching them from the fire - and on the other hand be merciful to others while being extremely careful, hating even the coating which has been foully polluted by the natural realm! *24* Now to him who is able to guard you from harm and to stand you in the presence of his splendor without stain but with great happiness, *25* the only God, our Savior through Jesus the Anointed One our Lord, be the splendor, majesty, forceful power and authority as it was before the ages, as well as now and forever! Amen!

Revelation.

The title "Revelation" is from the Latin *revelatio*, the title given in the Vulgate. General opinion holds that Revelation was written in 95/6 AD by John, who also wrote the *Good News of John* and the *Letters of John*, and that John wrote Revelation on the island of Patmos[1] in the Mediterranean Sea offshore from Roman Asia. Irenaeus, Origin, Justin Martyr, Clement of Alexandria, and Hippolytus all hold that John is the author. The earliest clear reference to Revelation is in Justin Martyr. As we know he was martyred c. 165 AD the terminus *ante quem* is thus established.

Eusebius (*H.E.* 7.25.7-11) states that Dionysius of Alexandria (who died 265 AD) said that 1 John was written by the same author as the Gospel of John, but that Revelation was written by someone else. Eusebius stated that Revelation was written by a non-apostolic author. The reason for this is generally attributed to Eusebius' anti-millennialist viewpoint.

The author of Revelation names himself as "John" (Rev. 1:4, 9; 22:8), but the genre known as "Apocalypse" was by nature pseudographical (as it was written in times of danger), and thus authors other than John have been suggested, most notably Polycarp. Polycarp was born c. 69 AD.[2] Irenaeus wrote, in 180 AD, of information he had received from Polycarp whom he had known from his youth,[3] stating that he could "speak of the place in which the blessed Polycarp sat and disputed... how he reported his discourse with John and with others who had seen the Lord, how he remembered their words, and reported the things about the Lord that he had heard from them."[4] Irenaeus, *Martyrdom of Polycarp* 9.3, states that John remained permanently in the church of Ephesos until the reign of Trajan, which was in 98 AD. Ignatius' letter to Polycarp reveals that Polycarp was appointed bishop of Smyrna by apostles in Asia around that time. If Polycarp wrote the letter, it could well be dated to c. 135 AD.[5] G. Mussies, *The Morphology of Koine Greek as used in the Apocalypse of St. John, NovT Suppl.* 27; Leiden, 1971, 352, concludes that Revelation was not written by the author of John's gospel. He notes that the combination of the nouns κύριος, *kurios*, and θεός, *theos*, is not found in any or the epistles or John's gospel. However, in Revelation it occurs in 11 of the 21 places where κύριος, *kurios*, is used, mostly in addresses. In Rev. 11;17; 15:3; 16:7; 19:6; 21:22 παντοκράτωρ, *pantokrator*, is added. This is paralleled by the edict *SB* 11236 (Oxyrhynchos or Fayum, 120 AD).

Revelation, due to its symbolic nature, has been the source of much controversy. Some believe the book addresses only contemporary concerns, others believe it is entirely forecasting future events, while still others believe it applies both to current events and to the future.

Revelation.

Ch.1:1-3 The revelation[6] from Jesus the Anointed One, which God gave him in order to show his slave servants the things which will happen shortly.[7] He made it known by sending his Messenger to his servant John, *2* who bore

---

[1] Patmos is 37 miles (about 70 kilometres) off the western coast of Asia Minor. The island is 10 miles (16 kilometres) long and 6 miles (10 kilometres) wide and is in the Aegean Sea.

[2] Polycarp, when being martyred in 156 AD, stated that he had served his king (the Lord) for 86 years. *Martyrdom of Polycarp,* 9.3.

[3] Irenaeus, *Against Heresies*, 3.3.4.

[4] Quoted by Eusebius, *HE* 5.20.

[5] G. F. Somsel suggests Polycarp as author of Revelation, *per litt.*

[6] ἀποκάλυψις, *apokalupsis*, uncovering, revealing, unveiling.

[7] ἐν τάχει, *en taxei*, shortly. Could equally mean "quickly".

witnessto the Word of God and the martyrdom[1] of Jesus the Anointed One, as much as he saw. *3* Happy is the person who reads aloud,[2] and those who hear,[3] the words of this prophecy and observe the things which are written in it, as the time is near.

4-6 From: John.

To: The seven assemblies in the province of Asia.

Hello! May you have peace from him who was, and is, and is to come, and from the seven spirits in front of his throne, *5* and from Jesus the Anointed One, the witness, the faithful one, the firstborn from among the dead, the ruler of the kings of the earth.

To him who loves us and has freed us from our sins by his Blood, *6* and has made us a kingdom realm, priests to his God and Father, to him be the glorious mighty strength forever and ever. Amen.

7-8 He is coming in the clouds, and every eye will see him, even those who pierced him. And all the people groups of the earth will be grief-stricken because of him. Yes, amen!

8 "I indeed am the Alpha and Omega," says the Lord God, "who is, who was, and is to come, the Almighty."

9-11 I, John, your fellow believer and joint partner in the oppressions, kingdom realm, and endurance with Jesus, was on the island of Patmos, because of the Word of God and the testimony of Jesus. *10* On the Lord's day[4] I was in the Spirit, and behind me I heard a loud voice that sounded like a trumpet, *11* and it said, "Write down in a book what you see, and send it to the seven assemblies: to Ephesos, Smyrna, Pergamon, Thyatira, Sardis, Philadelphia and Laodicea."

12-16 I turned around to see who was speaking to me. When I turned around I saw seven golden lamp stands, *13* and I saw someone who looked like a Human Being[5] standing among them. He was dressed in a cloak that reached down to his feet, with a golden sash wrapped around his chest. *14* His head and hair were like wool, as white as snow, and his eyes were like flames of fire. *15* His feet were like bronze that has been glowing in a furnace, and his voice sounded like the roar of rushing water. *16* In his right hand he held seven stars, and a sharp, double-edged, large broadsword[6] came out of his mouth. His face was shining like the whole force of the sun.

17-20 When I saw him, I fell down at his feet like a corpse. Then he put his right hand on me and said, "Don't be afraid! I am indeed the First and the

---

[1] Equally, "testimony". See *AAWW* 111.439-44.

[2] ἀναγινώσκω, *anaginosko*. See inscription on marble stele, *AAWW* III.439-44 (Iulia Gordos, 75/6), "In the same way also it is resolved that Theophilos be escorted to his tomb and that this decree be read aloud so that all may know that people who live their lives on behalf of their country meet with such a testimony." For this word, Horsley, *NDEIC* 2.59, suggests "read aloud (published?)". Common in N.T.

[3] Some suggest here "..who reads aloud, and the congregation".

[4] The use of the noun ἡμέρα, *hemera*, to refer to sacred days is paralleled in an inscription from Ephesos, c. 162-164, "...the honorable proconsuls before me regarded the days of the festival of Artemisia as holy and have made this clear by edict." *ed.pr.* E.L. Hicks, *The Collection of Ancient Greek Inscriptions in the British Museum*, III.2 (Oxford, 1890) *l.* 7.

[5] υἱὸν ἀνθρώπου, *huion anthropou*, "child + of person" a set expression to indicate the likeness of a human being, or an association with a human being, or a human being. ("Son of Man" is a bad mistranslations.)

[6] ῥομφαία, *romphaia*. Not the general word for sword used throughout the N.T. This was a large broadsword used in Greek times by the Thracians.

Last. *18* I am the Living One. I was dead, and look! Now I am alive forever and ever! And I hold the keys of Death and Hades.[1]

19 So then, write what you have seen, what is happening now and what is to happen after. *20* The hidden truth of the seven stars that you saw in my right hand, and of the seven golden lamp stands is this: the seven stars are the Messengers of the seven assemblies, and the seven lamp stands are the seven assemblies.

Ch.2:1-6 Write this to the Messenger of the assembly in Ephesos:
The One who holds on firmly to the seven stars in his right hand, the One who walks around in the middle of the seven golden lamp stands says this: *2* I know your activities, your hard work and your endurance. I know that you can't put up with bad people, that you have put to the test those who say they are envoys but really are not, and have found them to be false. *3* You have endurance and have put up with hardships on account of my Name, and have not grown weary. *4* But I hold this against you - you have let go the fellowship meals that you first had. *5* Remember where you have fallen from! Change your minds, and do the activities you did in the first place. If you don't change your minds, I will come to you and move your lamp stand from its place. *6* But you have this in your favor - you hate the actions of the Nicolaitans,[2] which I hate too.

7 Hear, you who have ears! Hear what the Spirit says to the assemblies! To the person who is victorious, I will give the right to eat from the Tree of Life, which is in God's Paradise.[3]

8-10 Write this to the Messenger of the assembly in Smyrna:[4] These are the words of him who is the First and the Last, who became a corpse and became alive: *9* I know your oppression and your complete lack of finances, but you are financially wealthy! And I know the slanders of those who say they are Jews and are not, but are a Satanic synagogue.[5] *10* Do not be afraid of what you are about to experience. Indeed, Slanderer-Liar is about to throw some of

---

[1] The notion of Anoubis as the custodian of the keys of Hades was a standard element in magic spells. Many of these spells involved the conjuring of demons and people who had died.

[2] There is no certainty about the Nicolaitans. Irenaeus (*Adv. Haer.*, I, xxvi, 3; III, xi, 1) states that "they lead lives of unrestrained indulgence": "The Nicolaitans are the followers of that Nicolas who was one of the seven first ordained to the diaconate by the apostles. They lead lives of unrestrained indulgence. The character of these people is very plainly pointed out in the Apocalypse of John, [when they are represented] as teaching that it is a matter of indifference to practice adultery, and to eat things sacrificed to idols. See also: 'But this you have, that you hate the Nicolaitans' actions, which I also hate'" (*Adv. Haer.*, I, xxvi, 3), and, "John, the disciple of the Lord, preaches this faith, and seeks, by the proclamation of the Gospel, to remove that error which by Cerinthus had been circulated among people, and a long time prior to that by those termed Nicolaitans, who are an offset of that so-called "knowledge." (*Adv. Haer.*, 3; III, xi, 1) Tertullian refers to them, but adds no information (*De Praescrip.* xxxiii; *Adv. Marc.*, I, xxix; *De Pud.*, xvii). Hippolytus based his narrative on Irenaeus, but states that the deacon Nicholas was the author of the heresy and the sect (*Philosph.*, VII, xxvi). Clement of Alexandria (*Strom.*, III, iv) defends the deacon Nicholas, stating that the doctrine of promiscuity was falsely attributed to him. Eusebius (*H.E.*, III, xxix) states that the sect was short-lived.

[3] παράδεισας, *paradeisis*. See note on Luke 23:43.

[4] Smyrna was a wealthy port city which claimed to be the birthplace of Homer and built a shrine in his honor. An inscription, *CIJ* 2.742, from Smyrna records a woman ruler of a synagogue who was also the head of a household. Smyrna held a noted rivalry with Ephesos and Pergamon.

[5] A synagogue of Adversary.

you into prison so that he can harass you, and you will be oppressed for ten days. Be faithful right up to the point of death, and I will give you the winner's crown which is life!

11 Hear, you who have ears! Hear what the Spirit says to the assemblies! The person who is victorious will certainly not be harmed by the second death.

12-16 And to the Messenger of the assembly of Pergamon[1] write: he who has the sharp, double edged sword says this: *13* I know where you live, that's where Adversary has his throne. I know that you take hold of my Name, and that you did not renounce your faith in me even in the time of Antipas, my faithful martyr, who was executed in your city, which Adversary inhabits. *14* But I have a few things against you - you have some people there who hold to the teaching of Balaam, who taught Balak to entice the Israelites to sin by eating food sacrificed to idols, committing idolatry. *15* You also have some people who are hanging on to the teaching of the Nicolaitans! *16* So change your minds! Otherwise, I will come to you quickly, and will make war against them with the large broadsword of my mouth!

17 Those of you with ears, listen to what the Spirit says to the assemblies! To the person who is victorious, I will give some of the hidden manna.[2] I will also give them a white stone[3] (favorable vote) with a new name written on it. Only the person who is given the stone will know the name.

18 Write this to the Messenger of the assembly in Thyatira:[4] These are the words of the Son of God, whose eyes are like flames of fire and whose feet are like bronze that has been glowing in a furnace.

19-22 I know your actions, love and faith, your ministry and endurance, and that you are now doing more than you did at first. *20* But I certainly have this against you - that you tolerate the woman Jezebel, who calls herself a prophet. By her teaching she leads my servants into idolatry and the eating of food sacrificed to idols. *21* I have given her time to change her mind, but she is not willing to change her mind from her idolatries. *22* Indeed I will make her take to her bed, and I will make those who commit adultery with her be pressured greatly, unless they change their minds from her idol worshipping.[5]

---

[1] The Romans used Pergamon as an administrative center for the province of Asia. Pergamon was the cult center of the pagan healing god Asklepios. Although Asklepios was associated with three other major cites, Epidauros, Kos and Athens, it was at Pergamon that Asklepios was addressed as "savior", said to have "all powers", and praised for his protection at sea, power over the waves and calming of the winds. Inscriptions describe how Asklepios "stretched out his hand to heal", raised people from the dead and did miraculous healings. He was described as the "great miracle worker who does everything for the salvation of people" and Aristides said of him that he was the gentlest and most people-loving of the gods. The podium where the Altar of Zeus stood can be seen today. The podium is still on its original site in Pergamon, but the actual altar is now in the Pergamon Museum in Berlin.

[2] There was a pot of manna in the ark of the testimony (Exodus 16:4, 31-34). Later Jewish teaching states that Jeremiah rescued the ark when the temple was destroyed by the Babylonians. He hid it in a cave, where it was to stay until God came to rescue his children.

[3] The ψῆφος, *psephos*, was the stone used in voting: a black stone for voting against, and a white stone for voting in favor. It may equally be translated "favorable vote".

[4] Thyatira was situated at a cross section of commercial routes in a fertile valley. It too suffered earthquake damage during the reign of Augustus and was rebuilt with Roman help.

[5] The term "idolatry", "idol worshipping" in this paragraph is a technical term which also refers to sexual acts against the Law of Moses.

23-25 And I will strike her offspring well and truly dead! And everyone will realize that I am he who searches hearts and minds, and I will give each of you what's coming to you for your actions. *24* I say to the rest of you in Thyatira, who don't adhere to her teaching, who have not realized the so called deep things of Adversary, that I will not put any other burden on you, *25* except that you must take hold of what you have until I come.

26-28 And to the one who conquers and does my work until the end, I will give authority over the nations – *27* "He will shepherd them with an iron rod. They will be smashed to pieces like pottery" - the same authority that I have received from my Father. *28* I will also give this person the morning star.

29 Those of you with ears, listen to what the Spirit says to the assemblies!

Ch.3:1-3 Write this to the Messenger in the assembly in Sardis:[1] These are the words of him who has the seven spirits of God and the seven stars. I know your actions - you have the reputation of being alive but you are dead! *2* Keep your wits about you! Put your footing on firm ground for what remains yet is on the point of death! I have not found your actions complete in God's sight! *3* So remember what you have received and heard - hold on firmly to it and change your minds! But if you do not keep your wits about you, I will come like a thief, and you will not recognize the point of time that I will come upon you!

4-5 But you have a few people in Sardis who have not soiled their clothes. They will walk around with me, dressed in white, because they are worthy. *5* The one who conquers will be dressed in white like them. I will never blot out this one's name from the Book of Life, but will acknowledge their name in front of my Father and his Messengers.

6 Those of you with ears, listen to what the Spirit says to the assemblies!

7 Write this to the Messenger of the assembly in Philadelphia:[2] These are the words of him who is holy and true, who holds the key of David. What he opens, no one can shut, and what he shuts, no one can open.

8-10 I know your actions. Indeed I have placed an opened door, that no one can shut, in front of you! I know that you have a small amount of power and that you held on firmly to my Word and have not denied my Name. *9* Indeed I will place those of the Satanic synagogue[3] who claim they are Jews, but are not - they're liars - I will certainly make them come and prostrate themselves at your feet in worship and admit that I loved you. *10* Because you held on firmly to my Word and had endurance, I also will keep you firmly from the season of tribulation that is to come upon the whole inhabited earth to put the inhabitants of the earth through an ordeal.

11-12 I am coming soon. Hold on firmly to what you have, so that no one will take your winner's prize. *12* I will make the one who has the victory a pillar in the temple of my God, and they will certainly never go outside it any more. I will write the name of my God and the name of the city of my God, the new Jerusalem, which is coming down from heaven from my God. I will also write a new name on them.

13 Those of you with ears, listen to what the Spirit says to the assemblies!

---

[1]   Sardis has been excavated and studied intensively in recent times. Gold refineries have been discovered north of the city. The wealth of Sardis and its last king Croesus is legendary. The synagogue found at Sardis was the largest and most opulent of the time. Pliny, *NH* 7.56.195 states that the Lydians invented the purple-dying of wool at Sardis.

[2]   Philadelphia was on an important trade route between Pergamon in the north and Laodicea. It was devastated by an earthquake in A.D. 17, and rebuilt with financial support from Tiberius.

[3]   "Synagogue of Adversary."

14 Write this to the Messenger of the assembly in Laodicea:[1] these are the words of the Amen, the faithful and true witness, the ultimate source of God's creation.

15-16 I know your actions - that you are neither hot nor cold. I wish you were either hot or cold! *16* So, because you are lukewarm and not hot or cold,[2] I will vomit you out of my mouth!

17-18 You say, "I am rich - I have become wealthy and I don't need anything! But you don't know that it is you who are the wretched one! You are to be pitied! You are totally financially poor, naked and blind! *18* I advise you to buy from me gold refined by fire, so that you can become rich, and white clothes[3] to hide your shameful nakedness, and eye salve so that you can see!

19-21 I indeed rebuke and educate those I love. So be eager and change your minds! *20* Indeed, I stand at the door and knock. If anyone hears my voice and opens the door, I will come in and we will have dinner together. *21* To the one who has the victory, I will give the right to sit with me on my throne, just as I had the victory and sat down with my Father on his throne.

22 Those of you with ears, listen to what the Spirit says to the assemblies!

Ch.4 After this, I looked. There was a door which had been standing open in heaven! And the voice I had first heard that sounded like a trumpet speaking with me said, "Come up here! I will show you things which must happen after these things!"

2-4 Immediately I was in the Spirit! Right in front of me was a throne in heaven and there was someone sitting on it! *3* The One who sat on it had the appearance of jasper and carnelian. A rainbow, resembling an emerald, encircled the throne. *4* And encircling the throne were 24 other thrones, and there were 24 elders sitting on them. They were dressed in white cloaks and had gold crowns on their heads.

5-8 Flashes of lightning, rumblings and claps of thunder issued out of the throne. There were seven flaming torches burning in front of the throne. These are the seven spirits of God. *6* Also in front of the throne there was something that looked like a sea of glass, as clear as a crystal. In a circle, around the throne, were four living creatures. They were covered with eyes, front and back. *7* The first living creature was like a lion, the second was like a calf, the third had a face like a human, and the fourth was like a flying eagle. *8* Each of the four living creatures had six wings and was covered with eyes all over, even under their wings. All day and all night they never stop saying, "Holy, holy, holy, Lord God Almighty, Who was, and is, and is to come!"

9-11 Whenever the living creatures give glory, honor and thanks to him who sits on the throne and who lives forever and ever, *10* the 24 elders fall down before him who sits on the throne, and worship him who lives forever and ever. They throw their crowns in front of the throne and say, *11* "You are worthy, our Lord and God, to seize glory, honor and power, for you created all things, and by reason of your purpose they exist, and were created."

Ch.5:1-5 And I saw in the right hand of him who sat on the throne a book with writing on both sides. It was sealed with seven seals. *2* And I saw a

---

[1] Laodicea was a prosperous banking center.

[2] Laodicea lacked a natural water supply. Water was brought in by aqueduct from hot springs 6 miles away at Heirapolis (modern Pamukkale), and would have been lukewarm by the time it arrived in Laodicea. Nearby Colosse had cold springs. The Laodiceans used hot water for bathing and cold water for drinking. Lukewarm water had no use. Laodicea was destroyed by earthquake in 60 A.D., and Tacitus, *Annals*, 14:27 records that the Laodiceans refused aid from the Romans, preferring to rebuild it from their own resources. It stood on the junction of several major trade routes.

[3] The area around Laodicea was renowned for its black sheep.

powerful Messenger proclaiming in a loud voice, "Who is worthy to break the seals and open the book?" *3* But no one in heaven or in earth or under the earth could open the book or even look inside it. *4* I cried and cried because no one could be found who was worthy to open the book or look inside it. *5* Then one of the elders said to me, "Don't cry! The Lion of the Tribe of Judah, the Root of David, conquered, in order to open the book and its seven seals!"

6-10 And I saw a Lamb, looking as if it had been slain, standing in the middle of the throne, encircled by the four living creatures and the elders. He had seven horns and seven eyes, which are the seven spirits of God sent out to all the earth. *7* He came and took the book from the right hand of him who sat on the throne. *8* When he took the scroll, the four living creatures and the 24 elders fell down in front of the Lamb. Each one had a harp and they were holding golden bowls full of incense, which are the prayers of the people devoted to God. *9* And they sang a new song: "You are worthy to take the scroll and to open the seals, because you were slain, and have bought us for God by your Blood, from every tribe, language, people and nation. *10* You have made them a kingdom realm and priests[1] to our God, and they will reign upon the earth."

11-14 And I looked, and I heard the voice of many Messengers, numbering ten thousands of ten thousands, and thousands of thousands. They encircled the throne, the living creatures and the elders. *12* They sang in a loud voice: "Worthy is the Lamb who was slain to take power, wealth, wisdom and strength honor, glory and praise!" *13* Then I heard every created thing in the sky[2] and upon earth and under the earth and upon the sea, and all that is in them, saying, "To him who sits upon the throne and to the Lamb, be praise, honor, glory and mighty sovereignty, forever and ever!" *14* The   4   living creatures said, "Amen," and the elders fell down and worshipped.

Ch.6:1-2 And I saw the Lamb open the first of the seven seals. And I heard one of the four living creatures say in a voice like thunder, "Come!" *2* I looked. There was a white horse! Its rider held a bow and a crown was given to the rider. The rider rode out conquering, and was intent on conquering.

3-4 When the Lamb opened the second seal, I heard the second living creature say, "Come!" *4* And another horse came out, a chestnut one. Its rider was given permission to take peace from the earth and to make people slaughter each other. A large sword was given to the rider.

5-6 And when the Lamb opened the third seal, I heard the third living creature say, "Come!" I looked. And there was a black horse right in front of me! Its rider was holding a pair of scales in their hand. *6* And I heard what sounded like a voice from among the four living creatures, saying, "A measure[3] of wheat for a day's wages, and three measures of barley for a day's wages, and do not damage the oil and the wine!"

7-8 And when the Lamb opened the fourth seal, I heard the voice of the fourth living creature say, "Come!" *8* I looked. And there right in front of me was a pale[4] horse! Its rider was named Death, and Hades was following close

---

[1]   Note, not "kings and priests".

[2]   Equally possible, "heaven".

[3]   χοῖνιξ, *khoinix*. The measure was about a quart (a little over a litre). This was about a day's ration of grain.

[4]   χλωρός, *khloros*. This word is not one of the colors normally used to describe a horse in Greek literature. The word can mean "green", "yellow" (like honey) or "pale". Occurs 3 other times in the N.T: to describe grass in Mark 6:39 and Rev. 8:7 and to describe any green thing (herbage) in Rev. 9:4. The same word was an epithet for fear: *Iliad* 7.479; *Odyssey* 11:43; Also used in Aeschylus, *The Suppliant Maidens*, 566, to describe the fear of people who saw Io: "And people who lived there at her strangeness trembled, With pale fear at heart, beheld a creature vexed, half-breed, In part a cow and woman in turn, a monster marveled at." (*Trans.* S.G. Benardete.)

behind. They were given authority over a quarter of the earth, to kill with the sword, with famine, with death, and with the creatures of the earth.

9-11 And when the Lamb opened the fifth seal, I saw under the altar the souls of those who had been slain because of the Word of God and because of the testimony they held. *10* They shouted out loudly, "How long, Holy and True Master, until you judge the inhabitants of the earth and avenge our blood?" *11* And each of them was given a white robe, and they were told to wait a little longer, until the number of their fellow slave-servants and fellow believers who were going to be killed was complete.

12-14 And I saw the Lamb open the sixth seal. There was a severe earthquake. The sun turned as black as sackcloth made of goat hair. The whole moon turned blood red. *13* The stars of the sky fell to earth, just like late figs drop off a fig tree when they are shaken by a strong wind. *14* The sky receded like a scroll rolling up. Every mountain and island was shifted out of its place.

15-17 And the kings of the earth, the great people, the high ranking officers, the wealthy and the strong, and every slave and every free person hid in caves and among the rocks in the mountains. *16* And they said to the mountains and the rocks, "Fall on us and hide us from the face of him who sits on the throne and from the Lamb's anger! *17* Because the mighty day of their anger has come, and who can withstand it!"

Ch.7 After this I saw four Messengers standing at the four corners of the earth, holding back the four winds of the earth to prevent the wind from blowing on the land, or on the sea or on any tree.

2-8 And I saw another Messenger coming up from the east. He had the seal of the living God. He shouted out in a loud voice to the four Messengers who had been given permission to harm the land and the sea: *3* "Do not harm the land or the sea or the trees until we put a seal on the foreheads of the servants of our God."

4 And I heard the number of those who had been sealed: 144,000 from all the tribes of Israel. *5* 12,000 from the tribe of Judah had been sealed, 12,000 from the tribe of Reuben, 12,000 from the tribe of Gad, *6* 12,000 from the tribe of Asher, 12,000 from the tribe of Naphtali, 12,000 from the tribe of Manasseh, *7* 12,000 from the tribe of Simeon, 12,000 from the tribe of Levi, 12,000 from the tribe of Issachar, *8* 12,000 from the tribe of Zebulun, 12,000 from the tribe of Joseph, 12,000 from the tribe of Benjamin.

9-10 After this I looked and right in front of me was a huge crowd that no one could count. They were from every nation, tribe, people and language, and were standing in front of the throne and in front of the Lamb. They were wearing long white robes and holding palm branches in their hands. *10* And they shouted out in loud voices, "Salvation is attributed to our God, who sits on the throne, and to the Lamb."

11-12 And all the Messengers were standing in a circle around the throne and around the elders and the four living creatures. They fell down on their faces and worshipped God, *12* saying, "Amen! Praise, glory, wisdom and thanks, honor and power be to our God for ever and ever. Amen!"

13-17 And one of the elders asked me, "Who are these people in the white robes? Where did they come from?"

14 And I answered him, "My lord, you must know!"

And he said to me, "These people are the ones who came out of the major oppression. They have washed their robes and made them white by the blood of the Lamb. *15* That is why they are in front of the throne of God and worship[1] him day and night in his temple. And the presence of him who sits on the throne will encamp over them. *16* They will never again go hungry or thirsty. The sun will not beat down on them, nor will any heat, *17* because the

---

[1] λατρεύω, *latreuo*. This is not the same "worship" as in the previous chapters where the elders fell down to worship God.

Lamb in the middle of the throne will be their shepherd. He will lead them to springs of living water. And God will wipe away every tear from their eyes."

Ch.8:1-5 And after he opened the seventh seal, there was silence in heaven for about half an hour. *2* I saw the seven Messengers who stand in front of God. Seven trumpets were given to them. *3* Another Messenger, who had a gold container for frankincense,[1] came and stood at the altar. He was given a lot of incense, so that he could offer it with the prayers of the people devoted to God on the golden altar which was in front of the throne. *4* And the smoke of the incense, along with the prayers of the people devoted to God, went up in God's presence out of the Messenger's hand. *5* Then the Messenger took the incense container and filled it with fire out of the altar, and hurled it to the earth, and then there arose claps of thunder, rumblings, flashes of lightning and an earthquake.

6-7 And the seven Messengers who had the seven trumpets got ready to blow them. *7* The first Messenger blew the trumpet. Then came hail and fire mixed with blood, and it was hurled down onto the earth. A third of the earth was burnt up, a third of the trees were burnt up, and all the green grass was burnt up.

8-9 The second Messenger blew the trumpet. Then something like a huge mountain, completely on fire, was hurled into the sea. A third of the sea turned to blood, *9* a third of the sea creatures died, and a third of the ships were destroyed.

10-12 The third Messenger blew the trumpet. Then a huge star, blazing like a torch, fell out of the sky on a third of the rivers and on the springs of water. *11* The name of the star is "Wormwood. (Bitterness.)"[2] A third of the waters turned bitter, and many people died as a result of the bitter water.

12 The fourth Messenger blew the trumpet. A third of the sun was struck, a third of the moon, a third of the stars, so that a third of them turned dark. A third of the day was without light, and so was a third of the night.

13 And I looked, and I heard an eagle that was flying high overhead shout out loudly, "Woe! Woe! Woe to the inhabitants of the earth, because of the trumpet blasts about to be sounded by the remaining three Messengers!"

Ch.9:1-6 And the fifth Messenger blew the trumpet. I saw a star that had fallen from the sky to the earth. The star was given the key to the shaft of the Abyss. *2* When he opened the abyss, smoke poured out of it like the smoke from a huge furnace. The smoke from the abyss darkened the sun and the sky. *3* And out of the smoke, locusts came down onto the earth. They were given authority like that of scorpions on the earth. *4* They were told not to harm the green of the earth, nor any plant or tree, only those people who did not have God's seal on their foreheads. *5* They were not allowed to kill them, only to torture them for five months. The torture they suffered was like the torture of a scorpion when it stings someone. *6* During that time people will look for death, but won't find it. They will really want to die, but death will escape them.

7-11 The locusts resembled horses ready for war. On their heads they wore what looked like gold crowns, and their faces looked like human faces. *8* They had hair like women's, and teeth like lions'. *9* They had iron breastplates, and their wings made a sound like the thundering of many horses and chariots rushing into battle. *10* They had tails and stings like scorpions, and in their tails was the authority to inflict harm on people for five months. *11* The king over

---

[1] λιβανωτός, *libanotos*, actually frankincense. It occurs only in the N.T. here and in v. 5 following, where the context requires the meaning censer / container. MM *s.v.* note that the word λιβανωτίς, *libanotis*, which usually means "censer", is used for the meaning "frankincense" in *SIG²* 588.156 (c. 180 BC) and suggest there may have been confusion of frankincense and its container. Another word for frankincense, λίβανος, *libanos*, occurs in Matt. 2:11 and Rev. 18:13.

[2] Wormwood is a bitter herb.

them was the Messenger of the Abyss, whose name in Hebrew is Abaddon, and in Greek, Apollyon (Destroyer).[1]

12-16 The first ghastly thing has happened. There are two more ghastly things to come. *13* And the sixth Messenger blew the trumpet. I heard a voice coming out of the four horns of the gold altar that is in God's presence. *14* It said to the sixth Messenger who had the trumpet, "Release the four Messengers who have been bound at[2] the great river Euphrates."*15* And the four Messengers who had been kept ready for this very hour and day and month and year were released to kill a third of all people. *16* The number of the cavalry was two hundred million. (I heard the number.)

17-19 The horses and riders that I saw in my vision looked like this: Their breastplates were fiery red, dark blue, and as yellow as sulfur. The horses' heads looked like lions, and fire, smoke and sulfur came out of their mouths. *18* A third of all people were killed by the three plagues of fire, smoke and sulfur that came out of their mouths. *19* The power of the horses was in their mouths and their tails. Their tails were like snakes, and the snakes had heads that inflicted injury.

20-21 The remainder of the people that were not killed by these plagues still did not change their minds from what they had done. They did not stop worshipping demons, and idols of gold, silver, bronze, stone and wood - idols that can't see, hear or walk. *21* They also did not change their minds about their murders, their sorcery, their idolatry[3] or their thefts.

Ch.10:1-4 And I saw another mighty Messenger coming down from heaven. He was clothed in a cloud and there was a rainbow above his head. His face was like the sun, and his legs were like columns of fire. *2* He was holding a little book, and it lay open in his hand. He placed his right leg on the sea and his left leg on the land, *3* and he gave a loud shout that sounded like a lion's roar. When he shouted, the voices of the seven thunders spoke. *4* When the seven thunders spoke, I was about to write it down, but I heard a voice from heaven say, "Seal up what the seven thunders have said and don't write it down."

5-7 And the Messenger I had seen standing on the sea and the earth raised his right hand to heaven. *6* He swore by him who lives forever and ever, who created the heavenly places and everything in them, the earth and everything in it, the sea and everything in it. And he said, "There will be no more delay! *7* But at the time of the sounding of the seventh Messenger's call, when he comes to blow his trumpet, the hidden secret purpose of God will be brought to fruition, just as he announced to his own slave servants, the prophets."

8 And the voice I heard from heaven spoke to me once more: "Go, take the book that lies open in the hand of the Messenger who is standing on the sea and the land."

9-11 And I went up to the Messenger and asked him to give me the little book. He said to me, "Take it and eat it. It will turn your stomach sour, but in your mouth it will taste as sweet as honey."

10 I took the little book from the Messenger's hand and ate it. It tasted as sweet as honey in my mouth, but when I'd eaten it, my stomach turned sour. *11* And they said to me, "It is necessary that you prophesy again about many peoples, nations, languages, and kings."

Ch.11:1-3 And I was given a stick like a measuring rod and was told, "Go and measure the temple of God and the altar, and count the worshippers there. *2* Exclude the outer court - don't measure it, because it's been given to the non-Jews. They will trample on the sacred city for 42 months. *3* And I will give permission to my two witnesses, so that they will prophesy for 1,260 days, clothed in sackcloth."

---

[1]   Abaddon and Apollyon mean "Destroyer".
[2]   Could also mean "assigned to the great river Euphrates."
[3]   πορνεία, *porneia*. See note on Matt. 15:19.

4-6 These are the two olive trees and the two lamp stands that stand in the presence of the Lord of the earth. *5* If anyone tries to hurt them, fire comes out of their mouths and eats up their enemies. This is the way anyone who intends to harm them must die. *6* These have the authority to shut up the sky so that it won't rain during the time they are prophesying, and they have authority to turn the waters into blood and to strike the earth with every kind of plague as often as they wish.

7-10 When they have finished their testimony, the beast that comes up from the abyss will attack them, conquer them and kill them. *8* Their corpses will lie in the street of the great city, which is spiritually called Sodom and Egypt,[1] where their Lord was also crucified. *9* And for three and a half days, those from every people, tribe, language and nation will look at their corpses and will not allow their corpses to be buried. *10* The inhabitants of the earth will gloat over them and will celebrate by sending each other presents, because these two prophets tormented them.

11-12 After three and a half days, a spirit[2] of life from God entered them, and they stood right up on their feet. Great terror struck everyone who saw them. *12* Then they heard a mighty voice from heaven saying to them, "Come up here!" And while their enemies were watching, they went up to heaven in a cloud.

13-14 At that very moment there was a severe earthquake and a tenth of the city collapsed. 7,000 people were killed in the earthquake. The survivors were terrified and praised the God of heaven.

14 The second ghastly thing has happened. The third is coming soon!

15 And the seventh Messenger blew the trumpet, and there were loud voices in heaven, which said, "The kingdom realm of the world has become the kingdom realm of our Lord and his Anointed One, and he will reign for ever and ever."

16-18 And the 24 elders, who were sitting on their thrones in God's presence, fell on their faces and worshipped God, *17* saying, "We thank you, Lord God Almighty, who is and who was, because you have taken your great power and have assumed kingship. *18* The non-Jews were angry, and you have become angry. The time has come for the dead to be judged, and for rewarding your servants the prophets as well as your people devoted to God and those who respect your Name - both insignificant and mighty - and for destroying those who destroy the earth."

19 And the temple of God in heaven was opened, and inside the temple the Ark of the Covenant was seen. And there were flashes of lightning, rumblings, thunder claps, an earthquake and a severe hailstorm.

Ch.12:1-2 And a mighty sign appeared in heaven. It was a woman clothed with the sun, with the moon under her feet and a crown of twelve stars on her head. *2* She was pregnant, and cried out in torture as she was in labor and about to give birth.

3-6 And I saw another sign in heaven. It was a huge red dragon with seven heads, ten horns, and seven diadems on the heads! *4* Its tail dragged a third of the stars out of the sky and hurled them to the earth. The dragon stood in front of the woman who was about to give birth, so that he could eat her child the moment it was born. *5* She gave birth to a son, who is destined to rule all the nations with an iron rod. Her child was snatched away and carried up to God and to his throne. *6* The woman escaped into the desert to a place that God had prepared for her, so that she would be taken care of for 1,260 days.

7-9 War broke out in heaven. Michael and his Messengers waged war against the dragon, and the dragon and his messengers fought back. *8* But the dragon wasn't strong enough, and thus they no longer had a place in heaven. *9* The mighty dragon was thrown down - that ancient snake called

---

1   Note also the use of "Babylon" for actual Rome.
2   Equally in the Greek, "breath".

"Slanderer-Liar", and also called "Adversary", who leads the whole earth astray. He and his Messengers were hurled to the earth.

10-12 Then I heard a loud voice in heaven saying: "Just now have come salvation and power and the kingdom realm of our God, and the authority of his Anointed One. Because the accuser of our fellow believers, who accuses them in front of our God day and night has been hurled down. *11* And they conquered him by the Blood of the Lamb and by the Message of their testimony. They were willing to give up their lives. *12* For this reason rejoice, you heavenly places and those who encamp in them. But alas for the earth and the sea, because Slanderer-Liar has gone down to you! He is in a major rage, because he knows the time is short!"

13-18 And when the dragon realized that it had been hurled to the earth, it chased the woman who had given birth to the male child. *14* The woman was given the two wings of a huge eagle, so that she could fly to the place prepared for her in the desert. In that place she would be taken care of for a time, times, and half a time. *15* And the snake spat out water like a river from its mouth, in order to overtake the woman and sweep her away in the current. *16* The earth helped the woman by swallowing the river that the dragon had spat out of its mouth. *17* The dragon was furious with the woman and went off to make war against the rest of her offspring - those who obey God's commandments and hold onto to Jesus' testimony. *18*   And   the   dragon stood on the seashore.

Ch.13:1-6 And I saw a creature[1] coming out of the sea. He had ten horns and seven heads. There were ten diadems on his horns, and a blasphemous name was on each head. *2* The creature I saw resembled a leopard, but had feet like a bear and a mouth like a lion. The dragon gave him his power and his throne and great authority. *3* And one of the heads of the creature appeared to have had a deadly wound, but the deadly wound was healed. After this the whole earth was amazed at the creature *4* and they worshipped the dragon because he had given the creature authority. They also worshipped the creature and said, "Who is like the creature? Who can make war against him?"

5 The creature was given a mouth to speak and he talked big and he spoke blasphemies. He was given authority to act for 42 months. *6* He opened his mouth to blaspheme God, and to blaspheme his Name and the place where he lives, and everyone who lives in heaven.

7-8 He was given permission to make war against the people devoted to God and to conquer them. He was also given authority over every tribe, people, language and nation. *8* All the inhabitants of the earth will worship the creature - all those whose names have not been written in the Lamb's Book of Life - the Lamb that was slain from the foundation of the world.

9   Anyone who has ears had better listen!

10 If anyone is to go into captivity, they will go into captivity. If anyone is to be killed by the sword, they will be killed by the sword. Such is the endurance and faith of the people devoted to God.

11-12 And I saw another creature coming up out of the earth. He had two horns like a lamb, but he was speaking like a dragon. *12* And he wields all the authority of the first creature on his behalf. He makes the earth and those who live on it worship the first creature, whose deadly wound was healed.

13-14 And he performs great miraculous signs so that he even makes fire come down from the sky to earth right in front of the people. *14* He misleads

---

[1]   θηρίον, *therion*, any living creature except human beings, or a human being who is either wicked (a brute, a beast,) or pathetic. Aristophanes, *Clouds*, 184, uses the word to describe a sorry group of people, comparing them to a group of thin prisoners who had been imprisoned for two years, ill fed, and without fresh air. Plato, *Phaedrus*, 240b uses the word for a horrible person, "a flatterer is a horrid creature who does great harm".

those who live on the earth by the miraculous signs he was able to do in the creature's presence. He tells those who live on the earth to make an image of the creature who was wounded by the sword and revived.

15-17 He was given the ability to give spirit[1] to the image of the first creature, so that it could speak and have everyone who refused to worship the image put to death. *16* And he made everyone, insignificant and mighty, wealthy and poor, free and slave, receive an inscription on their right hand or forehead, *17* so that no one could buy or sell unless they had the inscription. The inscription is the name of the creature or the number of his name.

18 The wisdom goes like this: if you have sense, count[2] the number of the creature, for it is the number of a person.[3] And their number is 666.

Ch.14:1-5 And I looked. I saw the Lamb standing on Mount Zion. With him were the 144,000 who had his Name and his Father's name written on their foreheads. *2* And I heard a sound from heaven like the roar of the ocean and a loud clap of thunder. The sound I heard sounded like harpists playing their harps. *3* They sang what seemed to be a new song in front of the throne and in front of the four living creatures and the elders. The 144,000 who had been bought from the earth were the only ones who were able to learn the song. *4* These were the ones who did not pollute themselves with women, for they were virgins. They follow the Lamb wherever he goes. They were bought from among people and were offered as the primal offering to God and the Lamb. *5* Lies never come out of their mouths, and they are blameless.

6-7 And I saw another Messenger flying high overhead, and he had the eternal Good News to announce to those living on the earth - to every nation, tribe, language and people. *7* He said with a loud voice, "Fear God and honor him, because the time of his judgment has come! Worship him who made heaven[4] and the earth and sea and springs of water!"

8 And a second Messenger followed. He said, "Fallen! Babylon the Great[5] has fallen! It made all the nations drink the raging wine of its idolatry!"

9-12 And a third Messenger followed them. He said in a loud voice, "If anyone worships the creature and his image, and receives the inscription on their forehead or on their hand, *10* then they themselves will drink the wine of God's rage, added undiluted to the cup of his anger. They will be tortured with burning sulfur in front of the sacred Messengers and in front of the Lamb. *11* And the smoke of their torture rises forever and ever. There is no relief day or night for those who worship the creature or his image, or for anyone who receives the inscription of his name. *12* Such is the endurance of the people devoted to God, who pay attention to God's commandments and have faith in Jesus.

13 And I heard a voice from heaven saying, "Write this! Happy are the corpses who die as followers of the Lord from now on!"

"Yes!" says the Spirit, "Let them rest from their labors, for their actions follow them!"

14-16 And I looked. And there was a white cloud! Sitting on the cloud was one who looked like a human being. He had a gold crown on his head and a

---

[1]   Equally in the Greek, "breath".

[2]   ψηφίσατω, *psephisto*, "count". Interesting choice of word here. Not the word used throughout the N.T. for "calculate". ψηφίσατω, *psephisto*, 3rd person aorist imperative, originating from ψῆφος, *psephos*, "pebble".

[3]   ἀριθμὸς γὰρ ἀνθρώπου ἐστίν, *arithmos gar anthropou estin*, "for it is the number of a person / human". It has also been suggested that this sentence means "for it is the number of humanity", although οἱ ἄνθρωποι, *hoi anthropoi*, is usually "humanity". This is a grammatical possibility.

[4]   Equally, "the sky".

[5]   "Babylon" for Rome, as in 1 Pet. 5:13, and in Rev. 16:9; 17:5; 18:10, 21. Late Jewish writings use "Babylon" for Rome. (BDAG provides a list of references.) For figurative name for city, note also Rev. 11:8.

sharp sickle in his hand. *15* And another Messenger came out of the temple and shouted out loudly to the one who was sitting on the cloud, "Send out your sickle and harvest, because the time to harvest has come, as the harvest of the earth has become withered!" *16* So the one who was sitting on the cloud threw his sickle upon the earth and the earth was harvested.

17-20 And another Messenger came out of the temple in heaven. He also had a sharp sickle. *18* And another Messenger came out of the altar. He had authority over the fire. He called out in a loud voice to the one who had the sharp sickle, "Send out your sharp sickle and gather the bunches of grapes from the vineyard of the earth, because the grapes are ripe."

19 And the Messenger threw his sickle to the earth and gathered the harvest of the earth. He threw them into the mighty winepress of God's rage. *20* They were trampled in the winepress outside the city. Blood flowed out of the winepress, and rose as high as the horses' bridles for a distance of 184 miles.[1]

Ch.15 And I saw another mighty and amazing sign in heaven - seven Messengers with the last seven plagues. They are "last" because with them, God's rage is completed.

2-4 And I saw what looked like a sea of glass mixed with fire, and, standing next to the sea were those who had been victorious over the creature and his image, and over the number of his name. They held harps that had been given to them by God, *3* and they sang the Song of Moses, the servant of God and of the Lamb: "Great and amazing are your deeds, Lord God Almighty. Just and true are your ways, King of the nations. *4* Who would not respect[2] you, Lord, and praise your Name? For you alone are sacred, all nations will come and fall down in worship in front of you, because your acts of justice have been made clear."

5-8 And after this I looked, and in heaven the temple of the Tabernacle of the Testimony was opened. *6* And the seven Messengers with the seven plagues came out of the temple. They were dressed in clean, gleaming white clothes and wore gold sashes around their chests. *7* And one of the four living creatures gave the seven Messengers seven gold bowls filled with the rage of God who lives forever and ever. *8* And the temple was filled with the smoke of God's splendor and his power, and no one could enter the temple until the seven plagues of the seven Messengers were completed.

Ch.16:1-2 And I heard a loud shout from the temple saying to the seven Messengers, "Go! Pour out the seven bowls of God's fury on the earth." *2* And the first Messenger went out and poured out his bowl on the land, and severe painful ulcers broke out on the people who had the inscription of the creature and worshipped his image.

3-6 And the second Messenger poured out his bowl on the sea, and it turned into blood like that of a corpse. Every living thing in the sea died. *4* And the third Messenger poured out his bowl on the rivers and springs of water and they turned into blood. And I heard the Messenger of the waters say, "You have pronounced these judgments justly, you who are, and were, the Holy One, *6* because they have shed the blood of your people devoted to God and prophets, and you have given them blood to drink just as they deserve!"

7 And I heard the altar say, "Yes, Lord God Almighty, true and just are your judgments."

8-12 The fourth Messenger poured out his bowl on the sun, and the sun was given permission to scorch people with fire. *9* They were scorched by the searing heat and they blasphemed the Name of God who had the authority over these plagues, but they refused to change their minds and praise him. *10* And the fifth Messenger poured out his bowl on the throne of the creature, and his kingdom realm was plunged into darkness. People bit their tongues because of the agony. *11* They blasphemed the God of heaven because of their miseries and their ulcers,

---

[1] Lit: 1600 *stadia*. (about 300 km).

[2] φόβος, *phobos*, used of gods in the Greek means to respect, not to fear.

but they refused to repent of what they had done. *12* And the sixth Messenger poured out his bowl on the mighty river Euphrates, and its water was dried up in order to make way for the kings from the East.

13-15 And I saw three unclean spirits that looked like frogs. They came out of the mouth of the dragon, out of the mouth of the creature, and out of the mouth of the false prophet. *14* They are spirits of demon-gods[1] performing miraculous signs. They go out to the kings of the whole world to gather them for battle on the mighty Day of God Almighty. *15* "I come like a thief! Happy are you who keep your wits about you and keep your clothes with you, so that you won't walk around naked, and they will all see your indecency!"

16 And they gathered them together to the place called in Hebrew, "Armageddon."[2]

17-21 And the seventh Messenger poured out his bowl into the air, and a loud voice came out of the temple and said, "It has happened!" *18* And there were flashes of lightning, rumblings, claps of thunder, and a severe earthquake. The earthquake was so massive, that there had never been one like it ever before, not since people have been on the earth. *19* And the mighty city was split into three parts, and the cities of the nations fell. God remembered Babylon the Great and gave her the cup filled with the wine of the fury of his anger. *20* Every island fled away and the mountains were no more. *21* Huge hailstones weighing about a hundred pounds each[3] fell out of the sky on people. The people blasphemed God because of the plague of hail, as the plague was so extremely severe.

Ch.17:1-5 And one of the seven Messengers who had the seven bowls came and said to me, "Come here, I'll show you the judgment on the mighty prostitute, who has taken her seat on many waters! *2* Every king of the earth has committed idolatry with her, and the inhabitants of the earth got drunk with the wine of her idol worshipping."

3 And he carried me away in the Spirit to the desert. And I saw a woman sitting on a scarlet creature that was covered with blasphemous names and had seven heads and ten horns. *4* And the woman was dressed in purple and scarlet, and decked out with gold, gemstones and pearls. She had a gold cup in her hand full of abominable things and the filth of her idolatries. *5* And this name had been written on her forehead, "Hidden Secret, Babylon the Great, the Mother of Idolatries and of the disgusting things of the Earth."

6-8 And I saw that the woman was drunk with the blood of the people devoted to God and with the blood of the martyrs of Jesus. I was utterly shocked at the sight of her. *7* And the Messenger said to me, "Why are you surprised? Indeed, I will explain to you the hidden secret of the woman and the creature that carries her, which has seven heads and ten horns! *8* The creature that you saw, once was, and now is not, and will come up out of the Abyss and go to his destruction. The inhabitants of the earth whose names have not been written in the Book of Life from the creation of the world will be shocked when they see the creature, because he once was, and now is not, and yet will come.

9-11 "This calls for a mind that has wisdom. The seven heads are in fact seven hills on which the woman sits. *10* And there are seven kings. Five have fallen, one is, and the other has not yet come. When he does come, he must stay for a short time. *11* The creature who once was, and now is not, is an eighth king, and at the same time, one of the seven. He is going to his destruction.

12-14 "The ten horns you saw are ten kings who have not yet taken a kingdom realm, but will take authority for one hour as kings along with the creature. *13* They are of one mind and will give their power and authority to the creature. *14* They will make war against the Lamb, but the Lamb will conquer them, because

---

[1] πνεύματα δαιμονίων, *pneumata daimonon*, "spirits of demon-gods". "Demon-god", not to be confused with "demon" or "unclean spirit." Uncommon in N.T.

[2] Armageddon: literally, "Mount Megiddo".

[3] About 50 kilos.

he is Lord of Lords and King of Kings. With him will be his called, chosen and faithful followers."

15-18 And the Messenger said to me, "The waters that you saw, where the prostitute sits, are peoples, crowds, nations and languages. *16* The creature and the ten horns you saw will hate the prostitute. They will make her deserted and leave her naked. They will eat her flesh and burn her up with fire. *17* For God has put it into their hearts, in order to carry out his purpose, to act in unison and to give their kingdom realm to the creature, until the words of God come to pass. *18* And the woman that you saw is the great city which has sovereignty over the kings of the earth."

Ch.18 After this I saw another Messenger coming down from heaven. He had great authority, and the earth was brightly lit up by his splendor.

2-3 He shouted in a strong voice, "Fallen! Mighty Babylon has fallen! She has become a home for demons and a prison for every unclean spirit and a prison for every unclean and detestable bird and a prison for every unclean creature. *3* Because all the nations have drunk the wine of the rage of her idolatry and the kings of the earth committed idolatry with her, and the merchants of the earth became rich from the power of her reveling."

4-8 And I heard another voice from heaven say, "Come away from her, my people, so that you will not share in her sins, so that you will not share in her plagues, *5* because her sins are piled up to heaven, and God has remembered her crimes. *6* Treat her as she has treated others, pay her back double for what she has done. Mix her a double portion from her own cup. *7* Give her as much torture and misery as the honor and reveling she gave herself. She says in her heart, 'I sit enthroned as a queen: I am not a widow and I most certainly will never see misery.' *8* For this reason her plagues will arrive in a single day - death, misery and famine. She will be burnt up by fire, because the Lord God who judged her is strong."

9-10 "When the kings of the earth who committed idolatry with her and shared her reveling see the smoke of her burning, they will cry and mourn over her. *10* They will stand far away from her because they are afraid of her torture and say, 'Woe! Woe! The mighty city, the strong city of Babylon, because in a single hour your judgment has come!'

11-17 "The merchants of the earth will cry and mourn over her because no one buys their cargoes any more – *12* cargoes of gold, silver, gemstones and pearls, fine linen, purple, silk and scarlet cloth; every type of citrus wood, and objects of every kind made from ivory, expensive wood, bronze, iron and marble, *13* cargoes of cinnamon and spice, of incense, perfumed ointment and frankincense, of wine and olive oil, of fine wheat flour and grain; pack animals and sheep; horses and carriages; and bodies and souls of people. *14* Babylon, the fruit that your soul longed for has gone from you! All your excesses and magnificent things have been lost from you and they are no more to be found! *15* The merchants who sold these things and gained their wealth from her will stand far away from her because of their fear at her torture. *16* They will cry and mourn and say, 'Woe! Woe! The mighty city, dressed in fine linen, purple and scarlet, and decked out in gold and gemstones and pearls! *17* In a single hour such great wealth was destroyed!'

17-20 "Every sea captain, everyone who travels by ship to this or that place, sailors, and all who do business by sea, stood far away from her. *18* They called out when they saw the smoke of her burning, 'Have you ever seen such a great city?'

19 They will throw dust on their heads and call out with crying and misery, 'Woe! Woe! The mighty city, where everyone who had ships on the sea became rich through her high prices! In a single hour she is destroyed! *20* Rejoice over her, heaven! Rejoice, people devoted to God, apostles and prophets! By pronouncing judgment on her, God has vindicated your cause!"

21-24 And a strong Messenger picked up a boulder the size of a huge millstone and threw it into the sea. He said, 'With a sudden onslaught

Babylon the great city will be thrown down, no longer to be found. *22* The music of harpists, musicians, flute players and trumpeters will no longer be heard in you! No craftspeople of any trade will be found in you any longer! The sound of a millstone will never be heard in you again! *23* The light of a lamp will never shine in you again! The voice of a bridegroom and bride will never be heard in you again! Your merchants were the world's magnates. By your sorcery all the nations were led astray. *24* In Babylon was found the blood of the prophets and the people devoted to God and all who have been killed on the earth."

Ch.19:1-3 After this I heard what sounded like the roar of a huge crowd in heaven shouting, "Hallelujah! Salvation, honor and power belong to our God, *2* because his judgments are true and just. He has judged the mighty prostitute, who corrupted the earth with her idolatries. He has taken vengeance on her for the blood of his servants - which was her fault."*3* And again they shouted, "Hallelujah! The smoke rises up from her for ever and ever!"

4 And the 24 elders and the four living creatures fell down and worshipped God, who was sitting on the throne. They said, "Amen! Hallelujah!"

5 And a voice came from the throne, saying, "Praise our God all his servants and you who respect him, both insignificant and important people."

6-8 And I heard what sounded like a large crowd, like the roar of rushing water and booming claps of thunder, saying, "Hallelujah! Because the Lord our God the Almighty has established his reign! *7* Let us rejoice and be exceedingly happy and praise him, because the marriage of the Lamb has come, and his Bride has made herself ready. *8* It was granted to her to wear fine linen, gleaming white and clean."

9-10 And the Messenger said to me, "Write this down! Happy are those who have been invited to the Lamb's marriage feast." And he said to me, "These are God's true words."

10 And I fell down at his feet to worship him. And he said to me, "Don't do that! I myself am your fellow slave servant and the fellow slave servant of your fellow believers who maintain their testimony about Jesus. Worship God! For the testimony about Jesus is the spirit of prophecy."[1]

11-16 And I saw heaven opened up! There was a white horse. And its rider was called Faithful and True. He judges and acts with justice. *12* His eyes are like flames of fire, and there are many crowns on his head. He has a name written on his head and he is the only one who knows it. *13* He is dressed in a robe dipped in blood, and he has been given the name "The Word of God".

14 The armies of heaven were following him, riding on white horses and dressed in fine linen, gleaming white and clean. *15* Out of his mouth comes out a sharp large broadsword so that he can strike the nations with it. He will shepherd them with a rod of iron. He treads the winepress of the fury of the anger of God Almighty. *16* On his robe and on his thigh this name has been written, "King of Kings and Lord of Lords."

17-18 And I saw a Messenger standing in the sun, and he called out in a loud voice to all the birds who were flying high overhead: "Come on, gather together for the great feast of God! *18* You can eat the flesh of kings, military tribunes, powerful people, horses and their riders, and the flesh of all people, free and slave, insignificant and important."

19-21 And I saw the creature and the kings of the earth and their armies gathered together to make war against the Rider on his horse and against his army. *20* And the creature was captured, and so was the false prophet who had performed the miraculous signs in his presence. With these miraculous signs he had misled those who had taken the inscription of the creature and worshipped his image. Both of them were thrown alive into the fiery lake of burning sulfur. *21* The rest of them were killed with the large broadsword

---

[1] Equally, "For the Spirit which is prophecy is the testimony of Jesus."

that came out of the mouth of the rider on the horse, and all the birds gorged themselves on their flesh.

Ch.20:1-3 And I saw a Messenger coming down out of heaven. He had the key to the Abyss and he held a very large chain in his hand. *2* He firmly seized the dragon, that ancient snake, who is Slanderer-Liar, also known as Adversary, and he bound him for 1,000 years. *3* And the Messenger threw him into the Abyss and shut it up and put a seal over it, to prevent him from tricking the nations any more until the 1,000 years had ended. After that, he must be set free for a short time.

4-6 And I saw thrones. Sitting on them were those who had been given permission to judge. And I saw the souls of those who had been beheaded because of their testimony about Jesus and because of the Word of God, all who had not worshipped the creature or taken his inscription on their foreheads or hands. They came to life and reigned with the Anointed One for 1,000 years. *5* (The rest of the dead did not come to life until the 1,000 years had finished.) This is the first resurrection. *6* Happy and sacred are those who take part in the first resurrection. The second death has no authority over them, but they will be priests of God and of the Anointed One and reign with him for 1,000 years.

7-10 And when the 1,000 years are over, Adversary will be released from his prison *8* and will go out to mislead the nations in the four corners of the earth - Gog and Magog - to collect them for war. Their numbers are like the sand on the shore. *9* And they went up across the breadth of the earth and surrounded the armed forces of the people devoted to God and the beloved city. Fire came down from heaven[1] and burnt them all up. *10* And Slanderer-Liar who led them astray was thrown into the fiery lake where the creature and the false prophet are. They will be tortured day and night forever and ever.

11-15 And I saw a large white throne and the One who was sitting on it. The earth and the sky fled from his presence and there was no place for them to go. *12* And I saw the dead, both insignificant and important, standing in front of the throne, and books were opened. And another book was opened - it was the Book of Life. The dead were judged from what had been written in the books, according to their actions. *13* And the sea gave up the dead that were in it, and Death and Hades gave up the dead that were in them. They were each judged according to their actions. *14* And Death and Hades were thrown into the fiery lake. This is the second death, the fiery lake. *15* If anyone was not found written in the Book of Life, they were thrown into the fiery lake.

Ch.21:1-4 And I saw a new[2] sky[3] and a new earth. For the first sky and the first earth had passed away, and there was no longer any sea. *2* And I saw the sacred city, the new Jerusalem, coming down out of the sky from God prepared as a bride decked out to meet her husband. *3* And I heard a loud voice from the throne saying, "The tabernacle of God is with humans, and he will live with them and they will be his people. God himself will be with them and be their God. *4* And he will wipe away all tears from their eyes. There will be no more death, misery, crying aloud or pain, because the former things have passed away."

5 He who was sitting on the throne said, "I am making everything new." He said, "Write this down, because these words are trustworthy and true!"

6-8 He said to me, "It has come to pass. And I myself am the Alpha and Omega, the Beginning and the End. To whomever is thirsty I will give a drink for free from the spring of the water of life. *7* The person who has the victory will inherit all this, and I will be their God and they will be my child. *8* But the cowardly, the faithless, the disgusting, murderers, pornographers, sorcerers, idol worshippers, liars, will have their share in the fiery lake of burning sulfur. This is the second death."

---

[1]   Equally, "the sky".

[2]   καινός, *kainos*, "new" ("fresh") of quality rather than time.

[3]   Equally possible: "heaven", here and in next two instances.

9-14 And one of the seven Messengers who had the seven bowls full of the seven last plagues came and said to me, "Come here! I will show you the bride, the Bride of the Lamb." *10* And he carried me away in the spirit to a high, mighty mountain, and showed me the sacred city Jerusalem coming down from heaven from God. *11* It shone with God's splendor, and its brilliance was like a most precious gemstone, like a jasper, as clear as crystal. *12* It had a high, mighty wall with twelve gates, and there were twelve Messengers at the gates. The names of the twelve tribes of Israel were written on the gates. *13* There were three gates on the east, three on the north, three on the south and three on the west. *14* The city wall had twelve foundation stones, and the names of the twelve apostles of the Lamb were written on them.

15-21 And the Messenger who talked with me had a measuring stick of gold to measure the city and its gates and walls. *16* The city was laid out like a square, as long as it was wide. He measured the city with the stick and found it to be 12,000 stadia[1] in length, and equally as high and as long. *17* He measured the wall and it was 144 cubits[2] thick, going by the measures that people use - which the Messenger was using. *18* The wall was made out of jasper, and the city was made out of pure gold, as clear as glass. *19* The foundation stones of the city walls were decorated with every kind of gemstone. The first foundation stone was jasper, the second sapphire, the third chalcedony, the fourth emerald, *20* the fifth carnelian, the sixth sardis, the seventh chrysolite, the eighth beryl, the ninth topaz, the tenth chrysoprase, the eleventh jacinth and the twelfth amethyst. *21* The twelve gates were twelve pearls. Each one of the gates was made of a single pearl. The wide main street of the city was made of pure gold, like transparent glass.

22-23 And I didn't see a temple, because the Lord God Almighty and the Lamb are its temple. *23* The city doesn't need the sun or the moon to shine on it, because God's splendor gives it light, and the Lamb is its lamp.

24-27 And the nations will walk around in its light, and the kings of the earth will bring their splendor into it. *25* And the gates will never be shut by day - and there is no night there. *26* The splendor and honor of the nations will be brought into it. *27* And nothing unclean will ever enter it, nor will anyone who does anything unclean or anything which is an abomination or false. The only ones who will enter it are those whose names have been written in the Lamb's Book of Life.

Ch.22:1-5 And the Messenger showed me the river of the water of life, as clear as crystal, flowing from the throne of God and of the Lamb, *2* down the middle of the wide main street of the city. The tree of life stood on each side of the river, bearing twelve crops of fruit. It grows its fruit each month. The leaves of the tree are for healing the nations. *3* And there will be no more curse.[3] The throne of God and of the Lamb will be in the city, and his servants will serve him. *4* They will see his face, and his Name will be on their foreheads. *5* There will be no more night. They won't need lamplight or sunlight, because the Lord God will give them light. And they will reign forever and ever.

6-7 And the Messenger said to me, "These words are trustworthy and true." The Lord God of the spirits of the prophets sent his Messenger to show his servants the things that must soon take place. *7* "I am coming soon! Happy is anyone who pays attention to the words of the prophecy of this book!"

8-11 And I myself, John, heard and saw these things. And when I had heard and seen them, I fell down in worship at the feet of the Messenger who had been showing them to me. *9* And he said to me, "I myself am your fellow slave servant, and the fellow slave servant of all your fellow believers the prophets and of all who pay attention to the words of this book. Worship God!"

---

[1]   1200 stadia = about 1,380 miles (2,400 km).
[2]   About 200 feet (65 metres).
[3]   κατάθεμα, *katathema*. Only here in N.T. There are several Greek words for curse. See note on καταράομαι, *kataraomai*, in Luke 6:28.

10 And he said to me, "Do not seal up the words of the prophecy of this book, because the time is near! *11* Let the person who is unjust continue to be unjust, let the person who is filthy continue to be fouled up; let the person who is honest continue to be honest, and let the person who is holy continue to be holy!"

12-16 "I am coming soon! My reward is with me, and I will give everyone what they deserve. *13* I am the Alpha and the Omega, the First and the Last, the Beginning and the End.[1] *14* Happy are those who wash their clothes so that they may have the right to the tree of life and may go through the gates into the city. *15* Outside the city are the shameless,[2] sorcerers, pornographers, murderers, idol worshippers and all those who love and practice deceit. *16* I myself, Jesus, have sent my Messenger to give you this testimony about the assemblies. I am the Root and the Family of David, the Bright and Morning Star."

17-19 And the Spirit and the Bride say, "Come!" And let the person who hears say, "Come!" Let the one who is thirsty, come. Let whoever wishes, take the water of life without paying for it. *18* And I indeed testify to everyone who hears the words of the prophecy of this book - if anyone adds anything to them, God will add to them the plagues that have been written in this book! *19* And if anyone takes words away from the words of the prophecy of this book, God will take away that person's share in the tree of life and the sacred city, which are described in this book!

20-21 He who testifies to these things says, "Yes! I am coming soon!"

Amen! Come, Lord Jesus!

21 May the favor of the Lord Jesus be with you all. Amen!

---

[1] "The beginning and the end" occurs in Greek magical texts and Greek poetic texts, and occurs in texts linked with the Orphic religion. See *PGM* IV.2786ff, magical hymn to Selene; the Orphic Hymns to Ouranos. See also *ZPE* 4.19-21. The second of the phrases in the verse is a quote from Isaiah 44:6 (= 48:12). Clement of Alexandria, commenting on Psalm 18:2, said, "Hence the Lord himself is called the Alpha and Omega, the beginning and the end'". (*Strom.* 6:141.6-7)

[2] κυνός, *kunos*. "Dog", also used metaphorically as a reproach for the shameless or audacious but did not always have a pejorative sense. In the LXX, dogs are often associated with the wicked (Psalm 22:16) with pigs (for example, 3 Kgdms 22:38) and prostitutes, or the term is used as one of denigration (1 Kgdms 17:43; 24:15). The dog appears as a pet in Tobit, AB 5:17 and on Pfuhl/Mobius 11.2196. For other pet dogs or affectionate attitudes to dogs, see Pfuhl/Mobius 11.2197-2201 (Aegean, coastal Asia Minor, II-III); *IG* XIV *Suppl.* 2566 (Bonn, n.d.); *IGM* 52 (provenance unknown, III); *IGM* 51 (Thessaly, V); *IGUR* 1230 (Antonine period).

Abbreviations of Bible Versions

CEV	Contemporary English Version
ESV	English Standard Version
JB	Jerusalem Bible
HCSB	Holman Christian Standard Version
KJV	King James Version ("Authorized Version")
NASV	New American Standard Bible
NEB	New English Version
NET	New English Translation
NIV	New International Version
NKJ	New King James
NLT	New Living Translation
PME	Philips Modern English
RSV	Revised Standard Version
TEV	Today's English Version
TM	The Message
TNIV	Today's New International Version

Abbreviations.

BAGD   Bauer / Arndt / Gingrich / Danker, *A Greek-English Lexicon of the New Testament and Other Early Literature,* Chicago, University of Chicago, 1979.

BE   J. and L. Robert, *Bulletin épigraphique* in *Revue des études grecques* 89 (1976) 415-595.

BDF   Blass / Debrunner / Funk, *A Greek Grammar of the New Testament and other Early Christian Literature*, Chicago, 1961.

BDR   Blass / Debrunner / Rehkopf, *Grammatik des neutestamentlichen Griechisch*, Gottingen, 1979.

BGU   *Agyptische Urkunden aus den staatlichen Museen ze Berlin-Griechische Urkunden* XIII. *Greek Papyri from Roman Egypt*, ed. W.M. Brashear, Berlin, 1976.

CIJ   J.P. Frey, *Corpus Inscriptionum Judaicarum*, 2 vols, Rome, 1936, 1952.

CMRDM   *Corpus Monumentarorum Religionis Dei Menis* (*CMRDM*), by E.N. Lane (4 vols., EPRO 19; Leiden 1971-1978).

I. Assos   *Inschriften griechischer Stadte aus Kleinasien* IV, *Die Inschriften von Assos*, ed. R. Merkelbach (Bonn, 1976).

I. Ephesos *Inschriften griechischer Stadte aus Kleinasien* XI-XVII, *Die Inschriften von Ephesos*, ed I-VIII, edd. H. Wankel / C. Borker, R. Merkelbach et al. (Bonn, 1979-1984).

IG IV^2.1   *Inscriptiones Graecae* IV^2, *Inscriptiones Argolidis* I. *Inscriptiones Epidauri*, ed. F. Hiller von Gaertringen (Berlin, 1929; repr. Chicago, 1977).

IG XIV *Suppl. Inscriptiones Graecae Galliae Hispaniae Britanniae Germaniae,* ed. G. Kaibel / A. Lebegue, with supplement by A.N. Oikonomides (Berlin, 1890; repr. with suppl. Chicago, 1978).

IGUR   *Inscriptiones Graecae Urbis Romae* III, ed. L. Moretti (Rome, 1979).

I.Kyme   *Inschriften griechischer Stadte aus Kleinasien* V, *Die Inschriften Kyme,* ed. H. Englemann (Bonn, 1976).

I.Lampsakos   *Inschriften griechischer Stadte aus Kleinasien* VI, *Die Inschriften Lampsakos*, ed. P. Frisch (Bonn, 1976).

I.Nikaia   *Inschriften griechischer Stadte aus Kleinasien* IX-X.2. *Katalog der antiken Inschriften des Museums von Iznik* (Nikaia) I-II.2, ed. S. Sahin (3 vols; Bonn, 1979-1982).

ISE   *Iscrizioni storiche ellenistiche* II, ed. L. Moretti, Florence, 1976.

MM   Moulton and Milligan, *The Vocabulary of the Greek Testament*, London, 1930, repr.

P.Col. Columbia Papyri VII. *Fourth Century Documents from Karanis*, transcribed R.S. Bagnall / N. Lewis, edited with translation and commentary by R.S. Bagnall (*American Studies in Papyrology*, 20; Missoula, 1979).

P.Col.Youtie Collectanae Papyrologica. *Texts published in Honor of H.C.Youtie*, ed. A.E. Hanson (2 voils.: Boinn, 1976).

P.Laur.Dai papyri della Biblioteca Medicea Laurenziana, ed. R.Pintaudi: 1 (Florence, 1976); II (Florence, 1977); III (*Papyrologica Florentina* 5; Florence, 1979).

P.Mich. The Aphrodite Papyri in the University of Michigan Papyrus Collection (*P.Mich. XIII*), ed. P.J. Sijpesteijn (Zutphen, 1977)

P.Oxy. The Oxyrhnchus Papyri, XLIV, edd. A.K. Bowman et al. (London, 1976); XLV, edd. A.K. Bowman et. al. (London, 1977); XLVI, ed. J.R. Rea (London, 1978).

P.Oxy.Hels. The Oxyrhnchus Papyri, edd. H. Zilliacus / J. Frosen / P. Hohti / J. Kaimio / M. Kaimio (*Commentationes Humanarum Litterum* 63; Helsinki, 1979).

P.Sakaon The Archive of Aurelis Sakaon. *Papers of an Egyptian Farmer in the Last Century of Theadelphia*, re-ed. G.M. Parassoglou (*Papyrologische Texte und Abhandlungen* 23; Bonn, 1978).

P.Tebt. The Tebtunis Papyri IV, edd. J.G. Keenan / J.C. Shelton (London, 1976).

P.Tebt.Tait Papyri from Tebtunis in Egyptian and in Greek, ed. W.J. Tait (London, 1977).

[*P.Theon*] The Family of the Tiberii Iulii Theoines, ed. P.J. Sijpesteijn (Amsterdam, 1976).

P.Wiscon. The Wisconsin Papyri II, ed. P.J. Sijpesteijn (Zutphen, 1977).

Pfuhl / Moblius*Die ostgriechischen Grabreliefs*, edd. E. Pfuhl / H. Mobius (2 vols, and 2 vols of plates; Mainz am Rhein 1977-1979).

SEG Supplementum Epigraphicum Graecum, 26 (1976/77 [1979]; 27 (1977 [1980]; 28 (1978 [1982]); 29 (1929 [1982]).

Spicq, NLNT I/III C. Spicq, *Notes de lexicographe néo-testamentaire* (2 vols, plus Suppl. vol; *Orbis Biblicus et Orientalis* 22.1-3; Gottingen, 1978-1982.

Tibiletti, *Lettere* La lettere private nei papyri greci dei III e IV secolo d. C. Tra paganesimo e cristianesimo, by G. Tibiletti (*Publicazioni della Universita Cattolica di Milano, Science filogiche e letteratura* 15; Milan, 1979).

Bibliography.

See also Abbreviations.

Primary.

Aelius Aristides
1973   *Aristides*, trans. C.A. Behr, Loeb 1, London.
Aland, B. Aland, K., Karavidopoulos, J, Martini, C.M., Metzger, B.M.
1993   *The Greek New Testament*, Stuttgart, Deutsche Bibelgesellschaft United Bible Societies.
Aeschylus
1957   *Aeschylus: Agamemnon*, Oxford, Clarendon, edd. J.D. Denniston and D. Page.
1982   *Matthew: A New Translation with Introduction and Commentary*, New York, Doubleday.
Apollonius Rhodius
1960   *Apollonius Rhodius: The Argonautica*, Loeb Edition, London, William Heinemann Ltd.
Aristophanes
1901   *Aristophanes: The Frogs*, Oxford, Clarendon, 5th ed. W.W. Merry.
1963   *Aristophanes: The Frogs*, Houndmills, Macmillan Education, ed. W.B. Standford.
Aristotle
1950   *Aristotle: Politics*, London, William Heinemann Ltd, ed. H. Rackham.
1977   *Politics*, Trans. H. Rackman, Loeb 21, London.
Euripides

1939   *Euripides: Electra, Orestes, Iphigenia in Taurica, Andromache, Cyclops,* in 4 vols, London, Heinemann, ed. A.S. Way.

Eusebius
1973   *The Ecclesiastical History*, Trans. J.E.L. Oulton, Loeb 2, London.

Galen
1979   *Galen: On the natural faculties.* Trans. A.J. Brock, Loeb, London.

Hippocrates
1988   *Hippocrates V: Affections, Diseases I, II.* Trans. P. Potter, Loeb 5, London.

Homer
1911   *OMHROU ILIAS*, Vols I and II, London, Macmillan and Co. Ltd, edd. W. Leaf, M.A. Bayfield,
1961   *The Iliad of Homer.* Trans. R. Lattimore, Chicago.
1965   *OMHROU ODUSSEIA*, Vols I and II, London, Macmillan and Co. Ltd, edd. W.B. Standford.
1977   *The Odyssey of Homer*, Vol. 2 (ed. W.B. Stanford) 2nd ed., London.

Horsley, G.H.R.
1982-1989 *New Documents Illustrating Early Christianity*, Vols 1-5, North Ryde, N.S.W., Macquarie University Ancient History Documentary Research Centre.

Inscriptions:
1892   *Inscriptiones Graecae* VII, *Inscriptiones Megaridis et Boeotiae*, Berlin.
1913   *Inscriptiones Graecae* II/III^2 1, *Inscriptiones Atticae Euclidis anno posteriores,* Berlin.
1929   *Inscriptiones Graecae* IV^2 1, *Inscriptiones Epidauri,* Berlin.
1935   *Inscriptiones Graecae* II/III^2 3, *Inscriptiones Atticae Euclidis anno posteriores,* Berlin.
1956   *Supplementum Epigraphicum Graecum*, Vol. 13, Leiden.
1957   *Supplementum Epigraphicum Graecum,* Vol. 14, Leiden.
1958   *Supplementum Epigraphicum Graecum*, Vol. 15, Leiden.
1962   *Supplementum Epigraphicum Graecum*, Vol. 18, Leiden.
1971   *Supplementum Epigraphicum Graecum*, Vol. 24, Leiden.

Josephus
1978   *Josephus VI: Jewish Antiquities*, 5-8, trans. R. Marcus, Loeb 6, London.

Page, T.E., Capps. E. Rouse, W.H.D. (eds)
1934   *Select Papyri* II, Loeb, London.

Philo
1967   *Philo*, trans. F.H. Colson, Loeb 9, London.

Plato
1888   *The Republic of Plato Books 1-V with Introduction and Notes*, London, Macmillan and Co., by T. Herbert Warren.
1890   *The Works of Plato, Vol 1: The Apology of Socrates, Gorgias, Thaeatetus, Crito, Protagoras, Euthyphron, Phaedo, Phaedrus, Lysis*, London, George Bell & Sons, H. Cary.
1953   *Platonis Protagoras*, Cambridge, University Press, edd. J. Adam and A.M. Adam.
1984   *Plato's Phaedo*, Oxford, Clarendon, ed. J. Burnet.

Sophocles
1963   *Sophocles: Ajax*, London, Macmillan & Co. Ltd, ed. W.B. Standford.

Spicq, C.
1978-1982. *Notes de lexicographe nevo-testamentaire* (2 vols, plus Suppl. vol; *Orbis Biblicus et Orientalis* 22.1-3; Gottingen,.

Llewelyn, S.R.
1992-2003 *New Documents Illustrating Early Christianity*, Vols 6-9, North Ryde, N.S.W., Macquarie University Ancient History Documentary Research Centre, William B. Eerdmans Publishing Company, Grand Rapids, Michigan.

Moulton, J.H.
1960   *An Introduction to the Study of New Testament Greek*, London, Epworth, 5th ed. revised by H.G. Meecham.

Moulton, J.H. and Milligan, G.

1930   *The Vocabulary of the Greek Testament*, London, 1 Vol. Edition, London, Hodder & Stoughton.

Oden, T.A.

1989   *First and Second Timothy and Titus*, Louisville, John Knox Press.

Pickering, S.R.

1991   "Recently Published New Testament Papyri P89 – P95" *Papyrology and Historical Perspectives*, Number 2, 1991, The Ancient History Documentary Research Centre, Macquarie University, Sydney.

Rahlfs, A. (ed.)

1979   *Septuaginta*, Stuttgart, Deutsche Bibelgesellschaft.

Rawlinson, A.E.J.

1949   *The Gospel According to St. Mark*, 7th ed., London, J.M. Dent & Sons.

Rawson Lumby, J.

1904   *The Acts of the Apostles*, Cambridge, Cambridge University Press.

Sommerstein, A.H.

1980   *The Comedies of Aristophanes, Vol. 1. Acharnians,* edited with translation and notes by Alan H. Sommerstein, London, Tudor.

Tyndale, W.

1989   Tyndale's New Testament, trans. William Tyndale in 1534, Introduction by David Daneill, Yale University, Y.U.P.

Vine, W.E.

1934   *The First Epistle of John*, London, Pickering and Inglis.

1935   *The Epistle to the Romans*, London, Pickering and Inglis.

Thucydides

n.d.   *Thucydides: Historiae*, Oxford, Clarendon, ed. Henricus Stuart Jones.

1902   *The Fourth Book of Thucydides*, New York, Macmillan and Co., ed. C.E. Graves.

1937   *Thucydides Book II*, London, Macmillan and Co, Ltd., ed. E.C. Marchant.

1949   *Thucydides: Histories, Book IV*, Oxford, Clarendon, ed. T.R. Mills.

1958   *The Fifth Book of Thucydides*, New York, Macmillan and Co. Ltd, ed. C.E. Graves.

Westcott, B.F.

1950   *St. Paul's Epistle to the Ephesians: The Greek Text with Notes and Addenda,* Michigan, W.M. B. Eerdmans.

Xenophon

1851   *The Anabasis of Xenophon based upon the text of Borneman*, London, George Bell, Whittaker and Co., ed. Rev. J.F. Macmichael.

1930   *Xenophon's Anabasis* Book II, London, Macmillan and Co., Ltd., ed. A.S. Walpole.

Secondary.

Aalen, S.

1964   "A Rabbinic Formula in 1 Cor. 14,34", in F. Cross (ed.), *Studia Evangelica*, II-III. *Papers*, Berlin, Akademic Verlag, 513-25.

Abbott, T.K.

1900   *The Epistles to the Ephesians and to the Colossians: the International Critical Commentary*, Edinburgh, T. & T. Clark.

Aldwinckle, R.

1972   *Death in the Secular City*, London, George Allen & Unwin.

Allison, R.W.

1988   "Let Women be Silent in the Churches (1 Cor. 14:33b-36): What Did Paul Really Say, and What Did it Mean?", *JSNT* 32, 27-60.

Anderson, J.A.

1933   *Women's Warfare and Ministry: What Saith the Scriptures?* Stonehaven.

Arnold, C.E.

1992   *Ephesians, Power and Magic: The Concept of Power in Ephesians in Light of Its Historical Setting*, Grand Rapids, Baker Book House.

1996   *The Colossian Syncretism: The Interface between Christianity and Folk Belief at Colosse*, Grand Rapids, Baker Book House.

Atkinson, B.F.C.

1944   *The Theology of Prepositions*, London, Methuen & Co. Ltd.

Autenrieth, G.

1877   *Homeric Dictionary*, London, Gerald Duckworth & C. Ltd.

Baldwin, H.S.

1995   "A Difficult Word: aujqentevw in 1 Timothy 2:12", in Kostenberger, Schreiner and Baldwin (eds), *Women in the Church: A Fresh Analysis of 1 Timothy 2:9-15*, Grand Rapids, Baker Book House, 1995.

Barclay, W.

1987   "To Judge the Quick and the Dead", *The Plain Man Looks at the Apostles' Creed*, London, *George Allen and Unwin*, 199-239.

Barnett, P.

1989   *Is the New Testament History?* Sydney, Hodder and Stoughton.

1999   *Jesus and the Rise of Early Christianity: A History of New Testament Times*, Illinois, InterVarsity Press.

Barthelemy, D.

1963   *Les devanciers d'Aquila*, Leiden, E.J. Brill.

Bauer, W: Bauer / Arndt / Gingrich / Danker.

1979   *A Greek-English Lexicon of the New Testament and other Early Christian Literature*, 2nd ed., revised and augmented by F. Wilbur Gingrich and F.W. Danker from Walter Bauer's 5th Edition, Chicago, University of Chicago Press.

Bauer, W: Bauer / Danker /Arndt / Gingrich.

2000   *A Greek-English Lexicon of the New Testament and other Early Christian Literature*, 3rd ed., revised and augmented by F. Wilbur Gingrich and F.W. Danker from Walter Bauer's 5th Edition, Chicago, University of Chicago Press.

Bedale, S.

1954   "The Meaning of kepahle/ in the Pauline Epistles," JTS 5, 211-15.

Belkin, S.

1940   *Philo and the Oral Law*, Cambridge, MA, Harvard University Press.

Bernard, J.H.

1899   *The Pastoral Epistles*, Cambridge, Cambridge University Press.

1928   *A Critical and Exegetical Commentary on the Gospel According to St. John: The International Critical Commentary*, Vols. 1 and 2, Edinburgh, T. & T. Clark.

Bilezikian, G.

1985   *Beyond Sex Roles: What the Bible Says About a Woman's Place in Church and Family*, Grand Rapids, Michigan, Baker Book House.

Boucher, M.

1969   "Some Unexplored Parallels to 1 Cor 11,11-12 and Gal 3,28: the NT on the Role of Women", *CBQ* 31, 50-58.

1979   "Women and Priestly Ministry: The New Testament Evidence," *CBQ* 41, 608-13.

Bradley. D.G.

1953   "The *Topos* as a Form in the Pauline Paraenesis," *JBL* 72, 238-46.

Brooten, B.J.

1982   *Women Leaders in Ancient Synagogues*, Chico, CA, Scholars Press.

Buck, C.D.

1928   *The Greek Dialects*, Chicago, University of Chicago Press.

Buckland Green, G.

1951   *Notes on Greek and Latin Syntax*, 5th ed., London, Methuen & Co. Ltd.

W.H. Buckler in W.M. Calder (eds.),

1923   *Anatolian Studies Presented to W.M. Ramsay*, Manchester.

Bushnell, K.C.

1923   *God's Word to Women*, repr. n.d. Illinois, God's Word to Women Publishers.

Busenitz, L.A.

1986   "Woman's Desire for Man: Genesis 3:16 reconsidered," *GTJ* 7.2, 203-12.

Casson, L.
1971   *Ships and Seamanship in the Ancient World*, Princeton.
Clark, S.B.
1980   *Man and Woman in Christ*, Michigan, Ann Arbor.
Cohen, A.
1949   *Everyman's Talmud*, London, J.M. Dent & Sons, 1932.
Dalman G.
1902   *The Works of Jesus*, Eng. trans. by D.M. Kay, Edinburgh.
Daube, D.
1971   "Pauline Contributions to a Pluralistic Culture," *Jesus and Man's Hope*, ed.
D.G. Miller and D.Y. Hadidian, Pittsburg.
1972/3   "Responsibilities of Masters and Disciples in the Gospels," *NTS* 19,15.
Deissman, G.A.
1898   *Die sprachliche Erforschung der grieschischen Bibel, ihr gegenwartiger Stand
und ihre Aufgaben*, Giessen, 1898.
1908   *The Philology of the Greek Bible*, London, 1908.
1929   *The NT in the Light of Modern Research, The Haskell Lectures*, London.
Denniston, J.D.
1987   *The Greek Particles,* Oxford, Clarendon Press.
Derrett, J.D.M.
1970   *Law in the New Testament*, London, 1970.
Dodds, E.R.
1973   *The Ancient Concept of Progress and other essays on Greek Literature and
Belief*, Oxford
Ellicott, C.J.
1864   *The Pastoral Epistles of St. Paul*, London, Longman.
Fanning, B.M.
1990   *Verbal Aspect in New Testament Greek*, Oxford, Clarendon Press.
Finkelstein, L.
1941   "The Transmission of the Early Rabbinic Traditions", *HUCA* 16, 115-35.
Flanagan, N.M. and Snyder, E.H.
1981, January   "Did Paul Put Women Down in 1 Cor. 14:34-36?" *Biblical Theology
Bulletin* Vol. XI.
Foucault, M.
1983   "Discourse and truth: the problematization of parrhesia", Six lectures given at
the University of California at Berkeley, Oct-Nov. 1983, ed. by Joseph Pearson in 1985.
Funk, R.W.
1961   *A Greek Grammar of the New Testament and Other Early Christian Literature
by F. Blass and A. Debrunner: A translation and Revision of the ninth-tenth German edition
incorporating supplementary notes of A. Debrunner*, Chicago, University of Chicago Press.
Gardner, J.F.
1986   *Women in Roman Law and Society*, Beckenham.
Goodwin, W.W.
1879   *A Greek Grammar* (repr. 1974; London, Macmillan).
1889   *Syntax of the Moods and Tenses of the Greek Verb* (repr. 1965; London,
Macmillan).
Gould, J.
1955   *The Development of Plato's Ethics*, Cambridge, Cambridge University Press.
Gritz, S.H.
1991   *Paul, Women Teachers, and the Mother Goddess at Ephesus*, Lantham,
University Press of America.
Grosvenor, M.
1993   *A Grammatical Analysis of the New Testament*, Editrice Pontificio Instituto
Biblico, Rome.
Gould, J.
1955   The Development of Plato's Ethics, Cambridge, University Press.
Gulzow,

1969   *Christentum und Sklaverei in den ersten drei Jahrhunderten*, Bonn.

Haenchen, E.
Repr. 1971   *The Acts of the Apostles*, Oxford, Oxford University Press.

Hackforth, R.
1933   *The Composition of Plato's Apology*, Cambridge, University Press.

Hage, G.
1968   *Eheguterrechtliche Verhaltnisse in den griechischen Papyri Agyptens bis Diokletian*, Koln-Graz, 1968

Hardie, W.F.R.
1968   *Aristotle's Ethical Theory*, Oxford, Clarendon.

Harper, J.
1974   *Women and the Gospel*, Pinner, Great Britain.

Hemer, C.J.
1982   "Towards a new Moulton and Milligan", *Novum Testamentum* 24, 97-123.

Herrenbruck, F.
1981   "Wer wren die >Zollner<?", *ZNTW* 72,178-194.

Hick, J.
1976   *Death and Eternal Life*, G.B., William Collins.

Hicks, E.L.
1890   *The Collection of Ancient Greek Inscriptions in the British Museum*, III.2, Oxford, Oxford University Press.

Hobart, W. K.
1982.   *The Medical Language of St. Luke*, Dublin, 1882

Holmes, J.M.
2000   *Text in a Whirlwind: A Critique of Four Exegetical Devices at 1 Timothy 2.9-15, Journal for the Study of the New Testament Supplement Series* 196, *Studies in New Testament Greek* 7, Sheffield, Sheffield Academic Press.

Hooker, M.
1963-4   "Authority on her head: An Examination of 1 Cor.xi, 10" *NTS* 10, 410-6.

Horsley, G.H.R.
1994   *Four Early Biblical Codex Fragments in Australia: Putting the Pieces Together,* Piers Crocker and Geoffery Jenkins (eds) B*uried History: Occasional Papers* No 1, Melbourne, The Australian Institute of Archaeology.
1999   "Some literary features of Acts." Public lecture delivered at the University of New England, Armidale, Australia, March 20, 1999.

Horsley G.H.R. and Lee, J.A.L.
1997   "A Lexicon of the New Testament with Documentary Parallels: Some Interim Entries, 1" *Etlologia Neotestamenataria*, Vol X Mavo Novembre 1997, 55-84.
1997   "A Lexicon of the New Testament with Documentary Parallels: Some Interim Entries, 2" *FilNT* 10: 79

Horsley, G.H.R., Dolan, M., Franzmann, M.A., Stanton, G.R., Wilcox, M.
1999   *The Acts of the Apostles: History and Literature. Proceedings of Armidale Seminar in Mediterranean Antiquity*, 1. Armidale, University of New England.

Hull, G.G.
1987   *Equal to Serve*, Old Tappan, N.J. Revell.

Judge, E.A.
1978   *The Conversion of Rome*, Sydney, Publication of the Macquarie Ancient History Association.

Kaiser, Jnr, W.C.
1976, September "Paul, Women and the Church," *Worldwide Challenge* 3: 9-12.

Kee, H.C.
1968   "The Terminology of Mark's Exorcism Stories" *NTS* 14, 232-246.

Knight, G.W.
1992   *The Pastoral Epistles*, Grand Rapids, Eerdmans.

Kroeger, C.C.
1979, Oct   "Ancient Heresies and a Strange Greek Verb", *RefJ*, 14-18

1987   "The Classical Concept of Head as 'Source'" in G.G. Hull, *Equal to Serve*, Old Tappan, N.J. Revell.

Kroeger, R.C. and Kroeger, C.C.

1992   *Rethinking 1 Timothy 2;11-15 in light of Ancient Evidence, I Suffer Not a Woman*, Grand Rapids, Baker Book House.

Kvanvig, J.

1993   *The Problem of Hell*, Oxford, Oxford University Press.

Lagrange, M.

1929   *E/vangile selon Saint Marc*, 5th ed., Paris.

Lampe

1961   *A Patristic Greek Lexicon*, Oxford, Oxford University Press, repr.

Liddell, H.G. and Scott, R.

1869   *A Greek-English Lexicon*, Sixth ed., Clarendon Press, Oxford.

Liddon, H.P.

1897   *Explanatory Analysis of St. Paul's First Epistle to Timothy*, London, Longmans.

Lightfoot, D.

1975   *Natural Logic and the Greek Moods: The Nature of the Subjunctive and Optative in Classical Greek*, The Hague, Mouton.

McKay, K.L.

1965   "The Use of the Ancient Greek Perfect down to the Second Century A.D.", *Institute of Classical Studies Bulletin* 12, 1-21.

1974   "Further remarks on the 'Historical' Present and Other Phenomena", *Foundations of Language* 11, 247-51.

1981   "On the Perfect and Other Aspects in New Testament Greek", *NovT* 23.4, 289-329.

1994   *A New Syntax of the Verb in New Testament Greek*, New York, Peter Lang.

Mandilaras, B.G.

1973   *The Verb in the Greek Non-Literary Papyri*, Athens, Hellenic Ministry of Culture and Sciences.

Maurer, C.

1972   "parati/qhmi", in *TDNT*, VIII, 162-4.

Massingberd Ford, J.

1968   " 'The Son of Man' – A Euphemism?" *JBL* 87, 257-67

Metzger, B.M.

1975   *A Textual Commentary on the Greek New Testament*, London, United Bible Societies.

Mickelsen, B. and Mickelsen, A.

1979, Oct 5 "Does Male Dominance Tarnish Our Translations?" *ChrT*, 23-29.

Mitchell, S.

1995   *Cremna in Pisidia: An Ancient City in Peace and War*, London, Gerald Duckworth & Co. Ltd.

Modrzejewski, J.

1981   "La structure juridique du mariage grec," *Scritti in onore di Orsolina Montevechhi*, Bologna.

Moffatt, J.

1918   *Introduction to the Literature of the New Testament*, Edinburgh, 3rd ed. T. & T. Clark.

Morpeth, N.A.

1982   "Aristotle, Plato and self-sufficiency: ancient and modern controversy in economic history and theory," *Ancient Society*, XVII, 1 (1982) 34-46.

Moule, C.D.F.

1968   *An Idiom Book of New Testament Greek*, Cambridge, Cambridge University Press.

Moulton, J.H.

1908   *A Grammar of New Testament Greek*, 1 (repr. 1985; Edinburgh, T. & T. Clark, 3rd ed.) T. & T. Clark.

Moulton, J.H. and Howard, W.F.
1908   *A Grammar of New Testament Greek, Prolegomena*, 3rd ed., Edinburgh, Vol. ii.
Munroe, A.L.
1995   "Money, Mammon and Wealth", Paper presented at the Faith-Learning Institute, Cedarville College, Cedarville, OH.
Norwood, G.
1931   *Greek Comedy*, London, Methuen.
1964   *Greek Tragedy*, London, Methuen.
Nyland, A.
2003   "Papyri, Women, and Word Meaning in the New Testament", *Priscilla Papers*, Vol. 17, no. 4., Fall, 2003, pp. 3-9.
2003   "Against Grudem: *Aner* and Masculinist Misprisions of New Testament Meaning", *Sea Changes: Journal of Women Scholars of Religion and Theology*, Vol. 3 (2003).
Odell-Scott, D.W.
1983   "Let the Women Speak in Church. An Egalitarian Interpretation of 1 Cor. 14:33b –36", *Biblical Theology Bulletin* Vol. XIII, pp. 90-93
Oster, R.
1988   "When Men Wore Veils to Worship: The Historical Context of 1 Corinthians 11.4", *NTS* 34, 481-505.
Pickering, S.R.
1991   *Recently Published New Testament Papyri: P89 –P95*, The Ancient History Documentary Research Centre, Macquarie University, Sydney.
Pickering, S.R. and Cook, R.R.E.
1989   *Has a Fragment of the Gospel of Mark Been Found at Qumran? Papyrology and Historical Perspectives* No. 1, The Ancient History Documentary Research Centre, Macquarie University, Sydney.
Plummer, A.
1910   *A Critical and Exegetical Commentary on the Gospel According to S. Luke: The International Critical Commentary on the Holy Scriptures of the Old and New Testaments*, 4th edition.
Porter, S.E.
1992   *Idioms of the Greek New Testament*, Sheffield, Sheffield Academic Press.
Pringsheim, F.
1950   *The Greek Law of Sale*, Weimar.
Ramsay, W.M.
1897   *St. Paul the Traveller and the Roman Citizen*, London, Hodder & Stoughton.
Raven, D.S.
1962   *Greek Metre*, London, Faber and Faber.
Rees, B.B.
1974   "Some Thoughts on Translation," *Greece and Rome*, Second Series, Oxford, Oxford University Press, October 1974, 1-127.
Reynolds, J., Tannenbaum, R.
1987   *Jews and Godfearers at Aphrodisias*, Cambridge Philological Society, Supp. Vol. 12, Cambridge, Cambridge Philological Society.
Roberts, M.D.
1983   "Woman Shall Be Saved; A Closer Look at 1 Timothy 2:15", *RefJ* 33, 18-22.
Rostovtzeff, M.
1904   *Geschichte der Staatspacht in der romischen Kaiserzeit*, in *Philologus*, Supplementband 9, 338
Sanday, W. and Headlam, A.C.
1896   *A Critical and Exegetical Commentary on the Epistle to the Romans*, 2nd ed., Edinburgh, T. & T. Clark.
Segal, A.F.
1981   "Hellenistic Magic: Some Questions of Definition," *Studies in Gnosticism and Hellenistic Religions*, EPRO 91, Leiden.
Silva, M.
1975/6   "Semantic borrowing in the NT", *NTS* 22, 104-10.

1978   "New lexical Semitisms?", *ZNW* 69 (1978) 253-57.
1980   "Bilingualism and the character of Palestinian Greek", *Biblica* 61 (1980) 198-219.
Simpson, G.M.
1976   *A Semantic Study of Words for Young Person, Servant and Child in the Septuagint and other early Koine Greek*, Sydney.
Smith, J.
1880   *The Voyage and Shipwreck of St. Paul*, London, John Murray.
Spencer, A.D.B.
1985   "Eve at Ephesus", *JETS* 17, 1974.
Taylor, V.
1952   *The Gospel According to St. Mark: The Greek text with Introduction, Notes and Indexes*. London, Macmillan.
Taubenschlag, R.
1972   *The Law of Greco-Roman Egypt in the Light of the Papyri, 332BC-640AD*, Warsaw, 1952, *repr.* Milan, 1972
Thorley, J.
1988   "Subjunctive Aktionsart in New Testament Greek: A Reassessment," *NovT* 30, 193-211.
1989   "Aktionsart in New Testament Greek: Infinitive and Imperative", *NovT* 31, 290-315.
Turner, N.
1963   *A Grammar of NT Greek*, III. *Syntax*, Edinburgh.
Walsh, C.
1996   "The Problem of Hell", unpublished Honors Philosophy Thesis, University of Adelaide.
Webster, T.B.L.
1971   *Greek Tragedy, Greece and Rome: Surveys in the Classics* No. 5, Oxford, Clarendon Press.
Wells, L.
1998   *The Greek Language of Healing from Homer to New Testament Times*, Berlin, Walter de Gruyter.
Wigram, G.V.
1998   *The Englishman's Greek Concordance of the New Testament,* Hendrickson, Massachusetts, Hendrickson Publishers.
Wilcox, M.
1965   *The Semitisms of Acts*, Oxford, Oxford University Press.
1984   "Semitisms in the NT", *ANRW* 11.25.2, Berlin, 978-1029.
1999   "Jews and non-Jews in Acts: the limits of assimilation". Public lecture delivered at the University of New England, Armidale, Australia, March 20, 1999.
2000   "The Dead Sea Scrolls: the present State of our Knowledge". Public lecture delivered at the University of New England, Armidale, Australia, November 2, 2000.
Williams, D.
1977   *The Apostle Paul and Women in the Church*, California, Regal.
Wolff, H.J.
1939   *Written and Unwritten Marriages in Hellenistic and Postclassical Roman Law*, Haverford.
Woodhouse, S.C.
1932   *English-Greek Dictionary*, George Routledge & Sons Ltd, London.
Wuellner, W.H.
1967   *The Meaning of 'Fishers of men'*, Philadelphia, Westminster, 26-63.
Youtie, H.C.
1967   "Publicans and Sinners", *ZPE* 1, 475-574.
Zerwick, Max S.J. and Grosvenor, M.
1993   *A Grammatical Analysis of the New Testament*, 4th Revised Ed., Editrice Pontifico Istituto Biblico, Roma.